Montana 1911

WILHELMINA MARIA UHLENBECK-MELCHIOR'S DIARY
and C. C. UHLENBECK'S ORIGINAL BLACKFOOT TEXTS
and A NEW SERIES OF BLACKFOOT TEXTS

Montana 1911

A PROFESSOR AND HIS WIFE AMONG THE BLACKFEET

Edited by Mary Eggermont-Molenaar
with contributions by Alice Kehoe, Inge Genee, and Klaas van Berkel
Translation from Dutch by Mary Eggermont-Molenaar

UNIVERSITY OF NEBRASKA–LINCOLN

UNIVERSITY OF
CALGARY
PRESS

© 2005 Mary Eggermont-Molenaar
Published by the University of Calgary Press
2500 University Drive NW, Calgary, Alberta, Canada T2N 1N4
www.uofcpress.com

Library and Archives Canada Cataloguing in Publication

Uhlenbeck-Melchior, Wilhelmina Maria
  Montana 1911 : a professor and his wife among the Blackfeet :
Wilhelmina Maria Uhlenbeck-Melchior's diary and C. C. Uhlenbeck's original Blackfoot
texts and a new series of Blackfoot texts / edited by Mary Eggermont-Molenaar ;
translation from Dutch by Mary Eggermont-Molenaar.

Includes bibliographical references.
ISBN 1-55238-114-5 (University of Calgary Press).—ISBN 0-8032-1828-1
(University of Nebraska Press)

  1. Uhlenbeck-Melchior, Wilhelmina Maria—Diaries. 2. Piegan Indians—Montana.
3. Siksika Indians. 4. Uhlenbeck, C. C. (Christianus Cornelius), 1866-1951. 5.
Blackfoot language—Texts. 6. Anthropologists' spouses—Montana—Diaries. 7.
Anthropologists—Montana—Biography. 8. Linguists—Montana—Biography. I.
Uhlenbeck, C. C. (Christianus Cornelius), 1866-1951. II. Eggermont-Molenaar, Mary,
1945- III. Title.

E99.S54U343 2005   978.6004'97352   C2005-904114-5

We acknowledge the financial support of the Government of Canada through the Book
Publishing Industry Development Program (BPIDP), the Alberta Foundation for the Arts
for our publishing activities. We acknowledge the support of the Canada Council for the
Arts for our publishing program. We acknowledge the support of the Alberta Lottery Fund
– Community Initiatives Program.

Printed and bound in Canada by Houghton Boston
∞This book is printed on 70 lb. Rolland opaque paper
Cover design, page design and typesetting by Mieka West.
Drawings by Colin McDonald
Production by Danny Miller

To Annie Tatsey and to all those who cook and who care

Contents

(left and centre)Christianus Cornelius Uhlenbeck (18 October 1866 – 12 August 1951). Courtesy of KNAW.
(far right) J.P.B. de Josselin de Jong (13 March 1886 – 15 November 1964)

PREFACE AND ACKNOWLEDGMENTS

Mary Eggermont-Molenaar

June 2002. After most of the material for this manuscript had been collected and recorded, a new friend with a weird name asked me how this project started. In the fall of 1998, I told her, I attended a reception at the Museum of the Regiments in Calgary, Canada, and met with a certain Mr. Charles Fidler, then Head of the Plains Indians Cultural Survival School, also in Calgary. We chatted and he asked whether I had ever heard of his great-great-great-grandfather, Peter Fidler, explorer and factor with the Hudson's Bay Company. I hadn't and asked him if I could interview him about Peter Fidler for *Yumtzilob, Tijdschrift* [Journal] *over de Americas*. Charles consented.

At the end of the interview Fidler lent me one of his many great-great-great-grandfather's diaries. Reading Peter Fidler's 1792–93 diary and realizing that more people would like to read it led to me to publish an abbreviated version of it in *Yumtzilob* (Eggermont-Molenaar 2000). One particular entry in the Fidler diary led to the birth of the present project: the publication of the diary of Wilhelmina Maria Uhlenbeck-Melchior, the wife of Dutch professor C. C. Uhlenbeck. She kept this diary over a period of three months while accompanying her husband

during his fieldwork in 1911 on the Blackfeet Reservation in Montana.[1] The text of her diary is reproduced here in full and is embellished by a sixfold introduction, footnotes, and a collage of texts recorded by her husband and a few others. The entry in Peter Fidler's diary for December 31, 1792, reads as follows:

> A place here called *Naw peu ooch eta cots* from whence this river Derives its name.
>
> On my inquiring concerning the origin of this spot, the Indians gave me a surprising & ridiculous account. They said that a White man (what they universally call Europeans) came from the South many ages ago, & built this for the Indians to Play at.[2]

While trying to find out about this "white man," I came across a paragraph in J.P.B. de Josselin de Jong's *Blackfoot Texts* (1914, 113), in which a white man appears as well. De Josselin de Jong, accompanied by his professor, C. C. Uhlenbeck, a Dutch linguist and, at that time, professor at the University of Leiden, collected these texts in the summer of

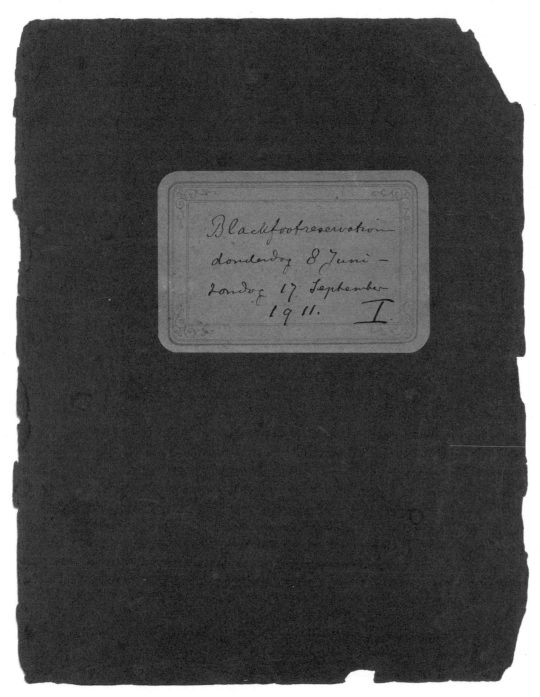

1910 on the Blackfeet Reservation in Montana.[3] Not long after the interview with Charles Fidler I had a conversation about encounters between white men and Blackfeet with Donald B. Smith, professor of Native history at the University of Calgary, who mentioned that one year later, in 1911, Uhlenbeck returned to Montana, this time not with his doctoral student but with his wife, and that she had kept a diary during their stay.

This information took me to the Glenbow Archives to investigate the diary – and possibly to discover more about a white man whom I suspected might have been spreading Olympic Games ideas among the Blackfoot. In his diary, Fidler went on:

> On my inquiring concerning the origin of this spot, the Indians gave me a surprising & ridiculous account. They said that a White man (what they universally call Europeans) came from the South many ages ago, & built this for the Indians to Play at, that is different nations whom he wished to meet here annually & bury all anamosities [*sic*] betwixt the different Tribes, by assembling here & playing together. They also say that this same person made Buffalo, on purpose for the Indians. They describe him as a very old white headed man & several more things very ridiculous (Fidler, 45).

I wondered about this man. *Naw peu* must be Napi, the primordial (creator/trickster) Blackfoot man, but tangible remains of the "Playground" in the form of small rocks in a semicircle can still be traced, in what is now southern Alberta.

The Glenbow Archives indeed possessed the diary of "Mrs. W. Uhlenbeck." After reading it – nothing about an Olympian in it, apart from Annie Tatsey – I became convinced that the diary has considerable value on its own. Not only does it contain a remarkable, intimate description of the way of life and ceremonies of the Blackfeet in 1911; the diary also gives vivid insight into the character and work habits of both Mrs. Uhlenbeck and her husband, C. C. Uhlenbeck (1866–1951).[4]

As *Yumtzilob* had published an abbreviated version of the Fidler diary, I thought that Mrs. Uhlenbeck's diary should also be published; but where? As I expected, C. C. Uhlenbeck had been a member of the Royal Academy of Sciences (KAW), based in Amsterdam. This Academy still exists (since 1937, known as the Royal Netherlands Academy of Arts and Sciences, KNAW) and publishes a *Jaarrapport* (Annual Report) in which is listed a Commission for Writing the History of the KNAW and its members. As in my opinion, Mrs. Uhlenbeck deserves posthumously to be made an honorary member, I decided to contact this Commission.

Dick de Boer, Professor of Medieval History in Groningen, who happened to be in Calgary, connected me with his colleague Klaas van Berkel, a member of the KNAW Commission. I informed Van Berkel about the diary and he agreed that publication would be of interest to his Commission; a report by Han Vermeulen, historical anthropologist at the University of Leiden, confirmed our opinion.

Van Berkel and I agreed that an introduction to the Uhlenbecks was necessary and decided to write one together. The University of Calgary Press was interested in sharing in the publication as the diary would also be of interest to the descendants of all the people Mrs. Uhlenbeck mentions in her diary and numerous others. During my conversation with Frits Pannekoek of the University of Calgary, he suggested that the material that Uhlenbeck collected in 1910 (*Original Blackfoot Texts*,

1911) and in 1911 (*A New Series of Blackfoot Texts*, 1912) should also be republished. "Why not," I ventured, "present a collage from Uhlenbeck's recordings – put the texts chronologically with Mrs. Uhlenbeck's remarks about who told her husband which story – and publish it simultaneously." Pannekoek agreed.

Not much later, I met with Inge Genee, a Dutch linguist at the University of Lethbridge who was already familiar with Uhlenbeck's work. Donald Smith put me in touch with Alice Kehoe, a scholar familiar with Blackfeet ethnology, who lives in Wisconsin. Both Genee and Kehoe agreed to write an introduction to Uhlenbeck's 1911 *Original Blackfoot Texts* and his 1912 *New Series of Blackfoot Texts*, which are included in this volume, as stated above. Genee discusses Uhlenbeck's work as a linguist and Kehoe introduces the Blackfeet in general and writes about the mythology recorded by Uhlenbeck.

Appendices B and C are articles by Uhlenbeck's student, J.P.B. de Josselin de Jong, which intertwine with and contribute to this volume.

So publication plans shifted somewhat to the North American continent, requiring that I translate the diary, which I could only do with the unstinting help of Calgary-based translator Penelope Waters. Yola de Lusenet of Edita, the publishing house of the KNAW, kindly provided the Uhlenbeck and De Josselin de Jong publications.

In addition to thanking the people mentioned so far, I would in the first place extend my heartfelt thanks to Mrs. Elsa Heman-Ortt of Israel, who guarded and kept Mrs. W. Uhlenbeck-Melchior's diary for so many years and who, encouraged by Mrs. Cramer of Albuquerque, New Mexico, made sure that it was preserved for posterity. Mrs. Heman also kindly provided information about her and her family's friendship with the Uhlenbecks. Without Mrs. Heman's efforts, this book would not have seen the light. Moving on, thanks to husband Jos Eggermont for providing unrelenting general and financial support, Harry van den Elzen for helping out with proofreading, E. M. Uhlenbeck (1913–2003), great-nephew of the Uhlenbecks, for sharing information about his great-aunt Willy; Petra van den Elzen, Marjan Eggermont, Michiel Eggermont, Jenny Eggermont-Reasbeck, Nicolas Jekill, Colin McDonald, who kindly provided the illustrations for Part II, and Hayo Westra (all in Calgary); Paul Néve and Regina Sprengers (Nijmegen) and Dan O'Donnell (Lethbridge) for listening to my musings about this project and helping out in one or another way; Jo à Campo (Rotterdam) for providing my photograph; Piet Genee (Heemskerk, the Netherlands) for the Uhlenbecks' genealogies; Jos Gabriëls (The Hague), Korrie Koorevaart (Leiden) for providing a copy of Herman Ten Cate's book and the 1917 dissertation of G. J. Geers; Wilt Idema (Boston) for suggesting the Uhlenbeck-Van Gulik connection and providing relevant documentation, as did C. D. Barkman (Zeist, the Netherlands) and Willem van Gulik (Leiden); Hillel Prat (Haifa, Israel) for trying and Alexander Markus (Ber Sheeba, Israel) for locating Mrs. Elsa Heman-Ortt; William Farr (Missoula) for providing Blackfeet photographs; Darrell Robes Kipp (Browning) for showing me around the Blackfeet Reservation; Louise Big Plume (Tsuu T'ina Nation, Alberta), Tom Crane Bear (Siksika Nation, Alberta), Reg, Rose, and Vera Crowshoe and Lowa Beebe (Peigan Nation, Alberta) for their friendship and efforts to familiarize me with Blackfoot and Tsuu T'ina culture long before I started this project. For helping with some of the footnotes, thanks to Wilma Adams and Carol Murray-Tatsey (Browning, Montana), Muriel Bland (Victoria, B.C.), Vera Crowshoe (Peigan Nation, Alberta), Robert C. Gilham, great-great-grandson of Owl Child (Utah), Anke van de Mei-Lombardi (Lugano, Switzerland), Jan Paul Hinrichs, (Leiden), Paul Rosier (Villanova, Pennsylvania), Mary Scriver (Valier, Montana), Gerard Termorshuizen (Leiden), and Paula Veldthuys (Haarlem).

Heartfelt thanks, also, to the staff of the Katholiek Documentatie Centrum (Nijmegen), the Glenbow Archives (Calgary), the Chancery Archives of the Catholic Diocese (Helena, Montana), the Koninklijk Instituut voor Taal-, Land- en Volkenkunde (KITLV), the University Library and the photo archives of the Museum voor Volkenkunde (Leiden), the staff of the Archives of the Dutch Province of Jesuits (Nijmegen), Marquette University Archives (Milwaukee), and the staff of the University of Calgary Press, who showed me what editing is all about.

Introduction to the Blackfeet in Montana

Alice B. Kehoe

Professor and Mrs. Uhlenbeck spent the summer of 1911 among the Amsskaapipikani, the Southern Piegan bands of the Blackfoot alliance, on their Montana reservation. Blackfoot, Nitsitapiksi ("Real People") in their own language, occupied the northwestern High Plains from the North Saskatchewan River to the Yellowstone, and from the Rocky Mountain Front Range to western Saskatchewan and the Montana-North Dakota border area. They grouped loosely into the Siksika ("Blackfoot"), the Kainai ("Many Leaders") or Blood, and the Pikani, divided into the northern Apatohsipikani (North Peigan) and southern Amsskaapipikani (South Piegan). (Pikani is spelled Peigan in Canadian English, Piegan in U.S. English.) Today the Nitsitapiksi say, "Our people were not interested in dominating others or forcing our way of life on them" (Blackfoot Gallery Committee 2001, 54).

Nitsitapiksi Blackfoot have lived in the northwestern Plains for centuries, very possibly millennia (Duke 1991). Their language is a branch of Central Algonquian, but linguists are uncertain of Algonquian's original homeland (Foster 1996, 98–100). Their own reckoning is that the northwestern Plains were given to their ancestors by the Creator (Blackfoot Gallery Committee 2001, 4). First recorded contact with Europeans probably was Henry Kelsey's 1691 meeting with "Archithinue" (Cree word for strangers or foreigners) in southern Saskatchewan: Kelsey, an employee of the Hudson's Bay Company, reported that these bison-hunting, tipi-dwelling people to the west of his route were prosperous and uninterested in journeying to the Bay's distant York Factory (Epp 1993).

European traders came to Blackfeet lands in the mid-eighteenth century, in time to note that the Nitsitapiksi said they had first seen horses when invading Shoshone rode into battle against them, about 1730. The Nitsitapiksi soon obtained horses themselves, using them both in the raids that were Indians' preferred form of warfare and peaceably to transport gear, lodge covers and furnishings, and sacks of food. Driving bison herds into corrals remained the principal means of subsistence, conducted on foot, with mounted chase an alternative mode. That traditional way of life is well described in Uhlenbeck's transcription of "How the Ancient Peigans Lived," told by Jim Blood (this volume).

Map of the Blackfeet Reservation. Courtesy Marjan Eggermont.

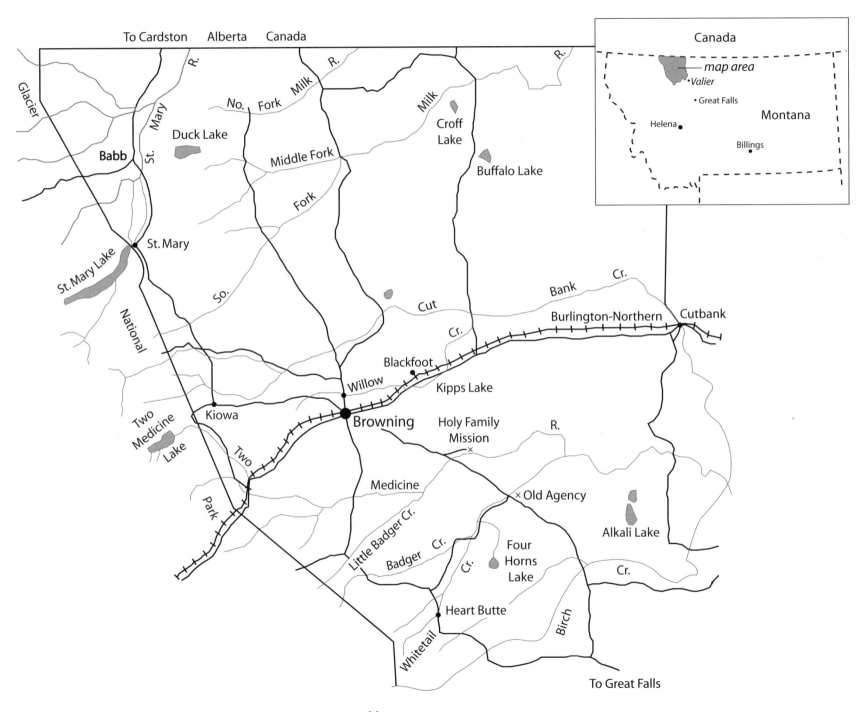

MONTANA 1911

Smallpox devastated the Piegans, and most other nations of the Plains, in 1780–81 and again in 1837 and 1869–70. Fur traders moved in during the 1790s, giving Blackfeet opportunity to profit by provisioning posts with pemmican; before the European-based trade, Blackfeet had sold processed bison to agricultural towns along the Missouri. In 1801 and 1802, Ac ko mok ki (Akai Mokti, "Old Swan," a title), a principal Nitsitapiksi leader, drew maps of the territory he knew, from northern Alberta into Wyoming, and the Missouri watershed as far as Mandan towns in North Dakota, with the intermontane valleys west of Blackfeet lands and the Snake River leading to the Columbia and the Pacific. Peter Fidler, the Hudson's Bay Company factor who asked Ac ko mok ki to draw the maps, annotated them at Ac ko mok ki's dictation with the names of more than two dozen indigenous nations marked with little tipis on their territories (Binnema 1996, 2001a, 2001b). Fidler transmitted the maps to London headquarters, where they were redrawn professionally and published, enabling Thomas Jefferson to obtain a copy and use it to instruct Lewis and Clark on the route they should take once beyond the Mandan towns. Meriwether Lewis followed orders, going up the Marias River in 1806 while Clark continued on the Missouri mainstem. In what is now the middle of the Montana Blackfeet Reservation, Lewis's small party met young Piegan men and camped overnight with them. One tried to filch a rifle, provoking the Americans to fight and Lewis, enraged, to shoot two of the young men fleeing from him. Understandably, Piegan would not tolerate Americans for a generation after this.

In 1831 James Kipp, working for the American Fur Company, built the first trading post in Piegan country, Fort Piegan at the junction of the Marias with the Missouri. It lasted only a year, to be replaced with Fort McKenzie six miles up the Marias.[5]

During Fort McKenzie's first year of operation, Prince Maximilian of Wied, a German scientist, and his artist, Karl Bodmer, spent a month at the post, describing Blackfeet with pen and brush. In 1847 Fort Benton was built on the Missouri at the southern edge of Piegan territory; it prospered as the head of navigation on the Missouri, transshipping bison robes to St. Louis. Some of the Fort Benton employees married Piegan women: for example, the Métis Charles Duvall, husband of Yellow Bird and father of David Duvall, Wissler's collaborator who committed suicide when the Uhlenbecks were dining in an adjacent room of Joe Kipp's hotel (diary, July 10). James Kipp's son Joe had worked for the American Fur Company and then built an unlicensed "whiskey fort," Standoff, on the Belly River in Kainai territory in 1870. Competition from notorious Fort Whoop-Up (where Lethbridge is now) closed that post. Kipp returned to Montana to build other trading posts and eventually, after the bison herds disappeared in the mid-1880s, operated a store and hotel in what became the reservation agency town, Browning – pictured for us by Willy Uhlenbeck.

The United States government negotiated a treaty with Piegans in 1855 in eastern Montana where the Judith River joins the Missouri. Montana east of the Rockies and north of the Missouri had been recognized as Blackfeet in the 1851 treaty signed by Siouan-speaking nations at Fort Laramie on the Platte River (southeast Wyoming), although no Blackfeet had been present. The Judith River Treaty, known as Lame Bull's Treaty after the Piegans' principal leader, outlined what was to be preserved as Blackfeet territory: it defined the Blackfeet's southern boundary as a line from Hell Gate Pass east to and down the Musselshell River, and on along the Missouri to the mouth of the Milk River, with the eastern boundary running straight north from that point to the Canadian border. This treaty took out, from the Laramie Treaty, hunting grounds south of the Musselshell that were to be common to all the Indian nations. Despite usually hunting north of the forty-ninth parallel, Kainai, Siksika, and North Peigan leaders were part of the Judith River Treaty council. They would get a Canadian treaty in 1877, signed at the Bow River.

Lame Bull and other signers agreed to refrain from molesting American settlers, accepting annuity payments for allowing colonization and considering settling down themselves as farmers. The American negotiator warned the Indians that "the Buffalo will not continue forever … bye and bye, the Blackfeet would … have domestic Cattle for food" (quoted in Ewers 1958, 216). This awful prophecy had come to pass by 1884 through a combination of commercial overhunting and drought that destroyed the herds and left the Blackfeet destitute. In 1874 the U.S. Congress unilaterally reduced Blackfeet reserved land by moving the southern boundary north to Birch Creek and the Marias River: then in 1888 it removed a huge area by setting the eastern boundary along the Marias River from its junction with Birch Creek. Finally, in 1896 the U.S. took a western strip along the mountains that promised (falsely) to produce gold; in 1910 this area became Glacier National Park. A last diminution occurred via the allotment of 320 acres per person, a process begun in 1908 and completed in 1912. The Uhlenbecks came during this critical shift from a reservation held by the nation in common to sections allotted to individuals but held in trust by the federal government Bureau of Indian Affairs. In the years to come, after the Uhlenbecks' visit, efforts to divest the Montana Blackfeet Nation of even more of the remnant reservation would bedevil the families the Uhlenbecks had known (Rosier 2001).

By 1911 the Piegans' indigenous way of life – called by the Nitsitapiksi their "dog days" of travelling on foot with dogs bred to carry packs and pull little travois – was nearly two centuries behind them. Throughout the nineteenth century, they battled unceasingly to defend their land, defeated only when their mainstay, the bison herds, astoundingly disappeared. The people then became homesteaders. This word is not customarily applied to Indians, but they cleared land, put up cabins and barns, and managed stock in the same manner as American settlers flooding in after the Civil War (see Kehoe 1996; Wissler 1938; Schultz 1907, 201, on "squawmen" assisting their Indian wives' relatives). It was this ranching way of life the Uhlenbecks saw, modified by the persistence of summer band encampments. Bands had persisted by member families settling in the same localities during the 1880s sedentarization (Ewers 1958, 298–99). Summer is an undemanding season for ranchers, their main job during July and August being periodic haying. From Willy's diary, we get a glimpse of how encampments fit into the ranching economy when the Tatseys go to their allotment for the day on July 23. Willy also describes well the only wage employment available to most Indian men: building irrigation ditches. This, too, is a summer activity meshing with small-scale ranching. The "ditch" was something of a boondoggle, a massive expensive project that ignored the basic and obvious fact that short growing seasons, more than lack of water, doom farming (Ewers 1958, 318; Rosier 2001, 60–61).

Willy Uhlenbeck pictures the Blackfeet as a nation unbowed by political subjugation, constructing a new economy to support its accustomed social relations. She knew men who had fought for their country, women who kept the home fires burning, their children shouldering the burden of reservation life, and little ones who grew up to carry on their heritage in the American twentieth century. More than eighty years after Willy bade goodbye to the Tatseys, Carol Tatsey-Murray, a granddaughter of Joe and Annie's son John, became president of Blackfeet Community College, an institution devoted to revitalizing the Amsskaapipikani.

The confluence of the Marias and Missouri rivers.

6

Marriage announcement in a Dutch newspaper. Courtesy Centraal Bureau voor Genealogie

Getrouwd:
WILHELMINA MARIA
MELCHIOR
en
CHRISTIANUS CORNELIUS
UHLENBECK.
Koedijk, 23 Juli. *1891*
Eenige kennisgeving.

De Heer en Mevrouw UHLEN-
BECK—MELCHIOR bedanken, ook
uit naam hunner Bloedverwanten,
voor de bewijzen van belangstel-
ling, hun bij hun Huwelijk betoond.

The Uhlenbecks and the Burdens of Life
A Biographical Introduction

Klaas van Berkel and Mary Eggermont-Molenaar

When C. C. Uhlenbeck and his wife Willy arrived in 1911 at the reservation of the southern Piegan Indians in Montana, they had been married for almost twenty years. Their twentieth anniversary fell halfway through their stay in Montana, on July 23. When they married in 1891, Uhlenbeck was a young linguist with an insecure future, but during the twenty years he and Willy had been together, he had become a well-respected scholar with an international reputation. He became professor of linguistics at the University of Leiden in 1899 and was elected a member of the prestigious Royal Academy of Sciences in the Netherlands in 1904 at the age of 38. But alongside the successes there were disappointments. Uhlenbeck suffered from almost chronic depression and disliked teaching and lecturing more and more as time went by. And to the distress of both him and his wife, their marriage remained childless. So on the anniversary of their wedding day on July 23, there was not much to celebrate. "A boring day without end," so Willy recorded in her diary. A family member from the Netherlands was kind enough to send them a postcard, but there is no indication at all that for the Uhlenbecks this was a day to remember.

That morning the two of them went out for a walk, and by chance they came across a few children's coffins with their contents exposed because of their dilapidated state. Uhlenbeck's reaction went unrecorded, but in her diary Willy made it clear that for her this chance encounter had a special meaning. On the way back she found a small hexagonal pencil with a chewed-off tip. "As a keepsake to this day," she wrote, "I will take it with me to Holland and I will always carry it in my pocket. I am very happy with this small find."[6] This is a strange remark indeed and it makes us wonder why in the world this small pencil was so important for her. Was there some relation between the sight of the children's coffins or the wrapped skeletons on the one hand and finding that small pencil on the other? Who can tell what this small pencil symbolized for Willy and what kind of unsatisfied desire or existential uneasiness lies hidden beneath this seemingly simple remark about a pencil?

When Wilhelmina Maria ("Willy") Melchior married Uhlenbeck, she was 29 years of age, rather old for a woman in those days.[7] She was born on March 13, 1862 in the village of Koedijk in the Dutch province of North Holland, where her father, Matthijs Nicolaas Melchior

(1825–1895), had been the local family doctor for many years. Matthijs Nicolaas and his wife, Guurtje de Jong, had a total of eleven children, six of whom did not live past childhood. So for Willy, who was the sixth child her mother bore, child mortality was nothing new. We know next to nothing about her youth and can only speculate about her helping her mother or attending a girls' school in the nearby city of Alkmaar.

Christianus Cornelius Uhlenbeck was five years younger than his bride when he married Willy Melchior on July 23 in Koedijk. He was born on October 18, 1866 in the village of Voorburg near The Hague, in the province of South Holland. His family originated in Germany and was partly of noble descent, but in the eighteenth century his fore-fathers had moved to Holland and had developed strong ties with the Dutch East Indies. His grandfather had served as an officer in the Indies before becoming mayor of Voorburg (1828–37); an uncle, Olke Arnoldus Uhlenbeck (1810–1888), had been commander of the Dutch fleet in the Indies; and C.C.'s father, Peter Frederik Uhlenbeck (1816–1882), had also ended up in the Dutch Marine in the East Indies before settling as a pensioner in Voorburg. Of the four children born to his father and his mother, Julie le Roux (1842–?), only Christianus Cornelius ("Kees") reached adulthood. An older brother, born in 1865, only lived a few months as did a younger brother and sister. When C. C. Uhlenbeck was born, his father was 50 and his mother 24. He grew up as a single child and like Willy, his bride, he too knew about child mortality.[8]

Shortly after Kees Uhlenbeck's birth, the family moved to Haarlem, a major city in the province of North Holland, where Uhlenbeck attend-ed grammar school. In 1885, the year in which he passed his final exami-nations, he also published a collection of poems with the Haarlem pub-lisher De Haan, called *Gedachten en Droomen (Thoughts and Dreams)*. The poems seem to have been strongly influenced by the highly roman-tic and somewhat somber poems written by major Dutch poets at that time and they disclose Uhlenbeck's deep disdain of church and religion. Some of his poems also reveal his longing for an aristocratic way of life.

He dreams of being a minstrel of noble descent and mourns the loss of the family estate and fatherland, leaving him only with his honor and his freedom.[9] Finally, it is tempting to see in some of the more gloomy poems the reflection of the depression he had experienced at the age of sixteen, the first of a series of depressive episodes that would haunt him for the rest of his life.

In 1885, Uhlenbeck enrolled as a student at the University of Leiden, where he studied linguistics. His main teacher was J.H.C. Kern, who taught Sanskrit, the language of old India, and acted as Uhlenbeck's advisor. In October 1888 he defended his dissertation entitled *De Verw antschapsbetrekkingen tusschen de Germaansche en Balto-Slavische talen (Correspondences between the Germanic and the Balto-Slavic Languages)*. The dissertation itself was, according to Uhlenbeck himself, rather me-diocre, less remarkable at least than some of the added *stellingen* (propo-sitions) added to it, in which Uhlenbeck ventured original and only later generally accepted ideas about the Basque language (see "A Dutch lin-guist on the Prairies" by Inge Genee in this volume).

In the first years after graduating from Leiden University, it was not altogether clear what direction Uhlenbeck's career would take. First he became a teacher at a local high school, but that was neither a success nor a pleasure. "That stupid school," as he generally described the institution later, was not the sphere of action in which he could feel at home (De Josselin de Jong, 1952, 244). In 1890 he was commissioned by the gov-ernment to make a study trip to Russia in order to investigate archival documents of interest to Dutch history. Uhlenbeck had no real interest in history, but the study trip at least gave him the opportunity to master Russian. Upon his return to the Netherlands he became a member of the Editorial Committee of the *Woordenboek der Nederlandsche Taal (Dictionary of Dutch Language)*, which provided him with rather dull and descriptive work that did not give him great satisfaction. Uhlenbeck cannot have been very happy in those years, but his marriage to Willy Melchior on July 23, 1891 surely must have given him the strength to carry on. Much later, in 1951, his most important student, anthropologist Jan de Josselin de Jong, wrote in his obituary: "Those who have had the privilege of knowing the Uhlenbecks more intimately cannot fail to have wondered how in view of his mental make-up, he could have pursued his vocation, even borne the burdens of life, but for her caring support (1952, 244)."

The year after his wedding, Uhlenbeck published his first substantial study in linguistics. On the recommendation of his thesis advisor J.H.C. Kern, the Royal Academy in Amsterdam accepted Uhlenbeck's book, *Baskische Studiën* (*Basque Studies*), for publication in the proceedings of the division of Arts. This study, in which Uhlenbeck applied Indo-European research methods to aspects of Basque, established his reputation as a linguist, and when a new chair in Sanskrit was established shortly thereafter at the University of Amsterdam, no one was surprised that Uhlenbeck was chosen as the first chair holder and professor, even though his command of Sanskrit was meager, to say the least. On September 26, 1892, Uhlenbeck accepted the chair with a public lecture *De plaats van het Sanskrit in de vergelijkende taalwetenschap* (*The Place of Sanskrit in Comparative Linguistics*). After a short while, Uhlenbeck was also asked to teach Gothic and Anglo-Saxon, and it comes as no surprise that Uhlenbeck later declared that he had never had to work so hard as in his first years in Amsterdam. The newly wedded linguist seemed to have found his goal in life.

The marriage itself, however, remained childless, no doubt to the grief of both Uhlenbeck and his wife. They therefore eagerly accepted the opportunity to start a family in 1899 when a befriended and distantly related couple, the former East Indies administrator Spengler and his wife, suddenly died, and Uhlenbeck became official guardian to the four children from the Spengler marriage. For that reason the Uhlenbecks decided to move from Amsterdam to Hilversum. "You can understand," wrote Uhlenbeck wrote to his former teacher and colleague J. W. Muller, "what a radical change this guardianship has brought in our quiet life....

In July they will live permanently in our house.... We live only for the Spengler children."[10] However, later that year Uhlenbeck became a professor at Leiden University and the Spengler children somehow disappeared from their household although they kept in touch.[11]

In Leiden, Uhlenbeck was appointed as professor in Old Germanic languages, succeeding one of his former tutors, P. J. Cosijn.[12] In his opening lecture, delivered on December 13, 1899, Uhlenbeck with great enthusiasm laid out his plans for the future. He distanced himself from the rigid and in his view sterile approach of the Neogrammarian school and expressed his hope that close cooperation with ethnologists and archeologists would lead to a revival of the *Sturm und Drang* that had characterized the study of languages in the time of Jacob Grimm.[13] Nevertheless, the study of Germanic languages would not prove to be the main focus in Uhlenbeck's work. During his professorship at the University of Amsterdam he had already shown awareness of the idea that a deeper insight into Indo-European languages could only be reached by comparing these languages with languages of other types. Therefore, Uhlenbeck, in the years after his move to Leiden, became an all-round linguist instead of "simply" an expert in Indo-European.

Willy for her part found employment as a volunteer in what we might call upper middle-class philanthropy. In 1903 she was installed as a board member of the *Arme Wees- en Kinderhuis*, a Protestant orphanage, in Leiden. She was a very dedicated board member and, as is apparent from the minutes over the years, she hardly ever skipped a meeting (Haan 1990).[14]

Besides his official tasks in relation to the Old Germanic languages, Uhlenbeck also devoted more and more time to the study of the Basque and Eskimo languages. He published some articles about Basque, but during a visit to the Basque region in southern France, he discovered that he would probably never master this strange language. "Vous n'avez pas les mâchoires (You do not have the [right] jaws)," he was told (De Josselin de Jong 1952, 247). Although this language therefore became

The Arme Wees- en Kinderhuis, *a Protestant orphanage, in Leiden, Hooglandse Kerkgracht 84*

even more intriguing to him, Uhlenbeck decided to put it aside and to concentrate on the language of the Eskimos (i.e., Inuit) in Greenland. This led to an article about the comparative morphology of Eskimoan languages which Uhlenbeck himself considered to be just a rough draft but which was in fact the first scientific treatment on the grouping of these languages (Uhlenbeck 1905).

From the Eskimoan languages, Uhlenbeck turned his attention toward the languages of North American Indians. What started as a mere pastime (Uhlenbeck liked to talk about his "distant American hobbies") gradually became a passion, resulting in a desire to limit his other duties to a bare minimum in order to make as much room as possible for his study of American Indian languages. Teaching becoming more and more a burden to him, Uhlenbeck was still accessible to really interested students, but for those who did not belong to this small group of devotees he was a strange and forbidding figure. He was not willing to adjust his style of teaching to the expectations of these students, who understandably did not like him and depicted the high-strung professor as a neurotic person – talented, but neurotic.[15] Of course Uhlenbeck felt this depreciation and it hurt him, even though he was not willing (or able) to change his habits in the classroom. De Josselin de Jong aptly summarized the result: "Frequent disappointments which wore him out, over-sensitive and emotionally unstable as he was, contributed not a little to his beginning to regard all official business as a heavy burden." De Josselin de Jong added that teaching uninterested students was not the only source of unhappiness: "There may have been other factors, unknown to us, which made him feel ill at ease with himself, at times putting him into such a state of over-fatigue and depression as was unlikely to have been caused by mere strenuous work (1952, 248–49)." Perhaps only his wife, Willy, fully knew about the tensions felt by Uhlenbeck, and maybe even she did not know.

All this did not keep Uhlenbeck from writing an impressive series of articles and books about American Indian languages. His first contribution was a long article in the journal *Anthropos* (in 1908, continued in 1910), "Die einheimischen Sprachen Nord-Amerikas bis zum Rio Grande" (The Indigenous Languages of North America North of the Rio Grande). It was a thorough survey of the fifty four North American language groups identified by Uhlenbeck and served, both for Uhlenbeck himself and for others, as a reliable introduction to the field. Of all the American languages, the Algonquian languages interested him most, and soon he felt the desire to study these languages in

the field, in order to create an empirical basis for further comparative research. Why he chose to go to the Blackfeet Reservation in Montana is not clear. Maybe he was following the advice of one of his American colleagues, George Bird Grinnell or Franz Boas; perhaps the director of the Ethnological Museum in Leiden introduced him to the authorities in Montana. Or, possibly his friend P. D. Chantepie de la Saussaye, a professor of religious studies, connected him with missionaries who were active in the region.[16] Anyhow, in two consecutive years Uhlenbeck travelled to Montana. In the summer of 1910 he was accompanied by his doctoral student, De Josselin de Jong, and the next year by his wife, Willy. That year (1911) De Josselin de Jong was doing research on the Red Lake Reservation in northern Minnesota, where he stayed with his wife, Lien.[17] While Uhlenbeck talked with his informants, recorded their stories, and sometimes played with their children, Willy took care of the tent and their belongings, observed life on the reservation and wrote in her diary whatever she considered to be of interest. Their relationship had its moments of tension, but in the end, Willy's utmost concern was still to remove everything that could interfere with the work of her husband; she wanted to create the best work conditions for him.

The two trips to Montana were very rewarding and resulted in quite a number of important publications about the Blackfoot language. In 1911, based on his first visit, the Dutch Academy published Uhlenbeck's *Original Blackfoot Texts*, followed by *New Blackfoot Texts* the next year. In 1911 Uhlenbeck also delivered a lecture before the Academy, "Geslachtsen Persoonsnamen der Peigans" (Patronymics and Proper Names of the Peigans). Meanwhile, he still had an enormous stack of material intended for a Blackfoot grammar and a Blackfoot dictionary, – two big suitcases with "thousands of cards."[18]

Notwithstanding this rich harvest of the two visits to Montana, the first years after his return to the Netherlands were very difficult indeed for Uhlenbeck. In 1912 he experienced a severe depression and Willy was even forced to give up her position as board member of the

Leiden orphanage in order to devote herself completely to the recovery of her husband. The next year the situation had hardly improved. Uhlenbeck wrote to his former student, C. H. de Goeje: "My wife is completely healthy, but I cannot concentrate myself for a very long time; I forget things, make mistakes and suffer from fatigue, even though it has become slightly better than a year ago. It will probably have to wear off."[19] It would not be the last time that colleagues and students would hear from Uhlenbeck about his emotional miseries and regrets. In the Preface of *Flexion of Substantives in Blackfoot* (1913) Uhlenbeck writes:

In the course of the next years I hope to publish some more monographs on chapters of Blackfoot morphology, leaving the troublesome task of writing a handbook on the whole subject to one of my students, Mr. G. J. Geers. The state of my health will not allow me to work very much for some years coming, and my official duties do not leave me sufficient leisure. If I should [sic] have been the author of a Blackfoot grammar, I would certainly have dedicated it to my Indian friend Joseph Tatsey, to whom I owe a debt of gratitude for his disinterested teaching and interpreting, and without whose help and affection I never could have succeeded in gaining the confidence and affection of such Indians as were able to tell me everything about the good olden times.

In the meantime, however, Uhlenbeck had firmly established himself as an Americanist. It was therefore no surprise that in 1915 the leading German-American anthropologist and linguist Franz Boas invited Uhlenbeck to join the editorial board of the *International Journal of American Linguistics*, a new journal established by Boas and due to appear in 1917. Furthermore, Uhlenbeck had a small but important number of students who specialized in the field of their tutor. In 1913 De Josselin de Jong, who had travelled to Montana in 1910 with Uhlenbeck, earned his doctorate (*cum laude*) with the dissertation *De waardeeringsonderscheiding van "levend" en "levenloos" in het Indogermaansch vergeleken met hetzelfde verschijnsel in enkele Algonkin-talen: ethno-psychologische studie* (The difference in appreciation between "living" and "lifeless" in Indo-Germanic compared to the same phenomenon in some Algonquian languages. Ethnopsychological study*)*. A year later, De Josselin de Jong was able to publish his own corpus of stories, *Blackfoot Texts from the Southern Peigans Blackfoot Reservation Téton County Montana* (followed, the next year, by a commentary; see Uhlenbeck 1915a).[20] Another student, G. J. Geers, earned his doctorate in 1917 with the dissertation *The Adverbial and Prepositional Prefixes in Blackfoot*.[21]

Uhlenbeck's own magnum opus still was to come. Only when he much later happened to meet the talented Robert van Gulik and more or less recruited him as his secretary was he able to publish the two volumes of his *Blackfoot vocabulary* in 1930 and 1934, followed by *A concise Blackfoot-Grammar, based on material from the Southern Peigans* in 1938. All those publications were published by the Royal Netherlands Academy in Amsterdam, of which he was a member.

When Uhlenbeck finally processed what he had harvested during his visits to Montana, he was no longer a professor at Leiden University. Lecturing had become such a burden and the depression and mental breakdowns had become so chronic that Uhlenbeck seriously tried to have himself dismissed, at least temporarily, from teaching (because of "tiredness in his head," as he formulated it in 1918).[22] Events in international politics were not unrelated to his longing for withdrawal. Even though the Netherlands were not actively involved in the First World War – the Dutch remained neutral, albeit with some difficulty – Uhlenbeck did feel the devastating blow that affected the optimism of Western civilization. "To realise his impotence against this collective mania," De Josselin de Jong wrote, "put him in a bitter mood with which he could not easily cope, at the same time strengthening the fatalistic strain in his philosophy of life which throughout had driven him, be it to a less extent, to aloofness (De Josselin de Jong (1952, 250)." He distanced himself more and more from Western civilization and was

The Uhlenbeck's residence in Nijmegen, Berg en Dalseweg 251.
They occupied the house at the right.

more than ever attracted to non-western cultures, the positive qualities of which he saw reflected in their languages.[23]

Finally in 1926, at the age of 60, Uhlenbeck could not bear the burdens of teaching anymore. He informed the curators of the university that he "was declared unfit for State service" and that he would therefore ask the Queen to dismiss him from his professorship. The curators proposed that the government award him with the Order of the Dutch Lion, but for reasons unknown to us, this prestigious order was not presented to him.[24] After his retirement the Uhlenbecks moved to the city of Nijmegen, near the eastern border of the country, where they settled in a house near the woods to the east of the city. In Nijmegen, where three years earlier the Roman Catholic church in the Netherlands had established its own university, Uhlenbeck rekindled the friendship with a colleague of his, the priest, ethnologist, and linguist Father Joseph Schrijnen (who had become professor at the Catholic University of Nijmegen). Together, they organized the First International Congress for Linguists, held in The Hague in 1928. Uhlenbeck was chair of the organizing committee and Schrijnen was secretary.

Pleasant though Nijmegen may have seemed to the Uhlenbecks, they only lived there for a short while. De Josselin de Jong is rather vague about this period in Uhlenbeck's life. He relates how Uhlenbeck got in touch with a few "studious undergraduates who called on him regularly" and then continues: "While after a while this was brought to an end by a body which to them [that is, to these undergraduates] was an authoritative one, he [that is Uhlenbeck] cannot fail to have reflected that at Leyden at least he would have been spared this disappointment, for a disappointment it was. Although this incident in itself might not have caused him to leave Nijmegen, it must have rendered parting easier to him and no doubt to his wife too, when fairly shortly afterwards they moved to Amersfoort (1952, 252)." De Josselin de Jong does not tell us who these undergraduates were, what Uhlenbeck was teaching them or what kind of body finally put an end to this contact. Since he refers to Uhlenbeck's students as "undergraduates", one might think that the university may have been involved in this, but the archives of the University of Nijmegen do not contain any piece of evidence with regard to this "incident."[25] However, there are other sources that may shed some light on this affair, and even though it is not possible to come to definite conclusions, reveal something about Uhlenbecks' stay in Montana, it is worthwhile to dwell a little longer on it.

One of the so-called "studious undergraduates" mentioned by De Josselin de Jong was Robert van Gulik, whom we already met as the one who finally helped Uhlenbeck to finish his Blackfoot grammar and vocabulary. In 1926 Van Gulik was a sixteen-year-old student at the grammar school at Nijmegen; he had lived in the East Indies for many years and for that reason stood somewhat apart from the other schoolboys.[26] Many years later, Van Gulik became a famous diplomat, ambassador, Sinologist, and writer of Chinese detective novels, most of which are still in print. In his autobiographical notes, which he wrote in English (cited in Barkman 1993, 25) he explicitly relates how he met Uhlenbeck and what was the result of their first meeting:

I had the great fortune to meet the famous linguist and Sanskrit scholar, Professor Dr. C. C. Uhlenbeck, who had just retired from Leyden University to settle down with his wife in Nijmegen. Our meeting was brought about by a lucky incident: I had bought in a curio shop a bamboo-leaf inscribed with a script Martin [his friend F. M. Schnitger, later a talented archaeologist] nor I could identify, so I paid a visit to the professor to ask him what it was. He corresponded in every respect to my idea of a learned professor: a thin man with a high stoop and a straggling beard, and the high dome of a bald head. He was very kind, told me that the script was Burmese, and questioned me about my studies. Thereupon he offered me to teach general linguistics and Sanskrit, once every week on Wednesday afternoon, when there were no classes. At first Father [Van Gulik's father] objected, saying this was imposing upon the professor's kindness, but he [Uhlenbeck] replied that upon reconsidering he had not realized how much he would miss lecturing to students, and that moreover he thought he could make me into his special pupil who would in years to come continue his own school of linguistic thought.[27] Soon I went there Saturday afternoons too, and the Uhlenbecks, being childless themselves, came to consider me more or less as their adopted son.[28]

In this way, Uhlenbeck and Van Gulik became very close. As already mentioned, in 1928 Uhlenbeck took Van Gulik along as his personal "secretary" to the International Conference for Linguists in The Hague, and Van Gulik helped Uhlenbeck with the final preparations for the English-Blackfoot (1930) and Blackfoot-English (1934) vocabularies, which were published with Van Gulik as co-author.

When in 1928 the First International Linguistic Congress was held at The Hague and when he was elected President, he took me along as his secretary.… When I was entering the sixth and last grade of the Gymnasium, I had an opportunity for showing Prof. Uhlenbeck my gratitude. He and his wife had formerly lived one year with the Peigan tribe of the North American Algonquin Indians, and for the first time recorded their language; their notes were written on thousands of cards which filled two large suitcases. When he told me that his failing eyesight prevented him from working this material out into a dictionary, I offered to do it for him. He accepted because he thought it would broaden my linguistic insight if I came to know also a language of so-called "primitive people." He gave me a brief course on the structure of the language and on the phonetic system he had used. Father bought a typewriter for me and I set to work. … I had hoped that the Professor would mention my name in the preface as the one who typed out the book; but on receiving the first proofs I saw to my astonished delight that he had put my name next to his on the title-page, as co-author![29]

It certainly was a blow to Uhlenbeck when Van Gulik, after finishing grammar school, decided to enroll at Leiden as a student in Chinese languages and to opt for a career in the diplomatic service (during which he also developed as a Chinese detective story author) and not, as Uhlenbeck had hoped, in linguistics, but their cordial relationship was not broken. As a university student, Van Gulik still regularly visited Uhlenbeck.

In his autobiographical notes Van Gulik gives us the impression that nothing was wrong with this relationship, but one of his Chinese detective novels contains a puzzling episode that seems to refer directly to Uhlenbeck and that at least suggests that relationship was not without its problems. In *The Chinese Lake Murders*, the principal figure, Judge Dee, meets a certain Dr. Djang, who is certainly modelled after Uhlenbeck. Dr. Djang is described as a "tall, well-built man, with a sharp, intelligent face." At age fifty he has already been granted a pension, devotes all his time to his studies, and confines his teaching to two private courses in his own house to a few advanced students. However, there are rumors, so Judge Dee learns, about a certain affair that forced Dr. Djang to resign. "It has been established beyond all possible doubt that the girl student who lodged the complaint was mentally deranged," Dee is told, but still it was the right thing to do for Djang to resign, "because he opined that a professor of the Temple School should never be talked about, even if he were proven completely innocent."

These passages, as well as repeated statements by Judge Dee about homosexuality throughout the other novels, may tempt one to think that

Van Gulik in his novels incorporated references to what had happened with Uhlenbeck (Eggermont-Molenaar 2002). Whether there really was a homosexual relationship between Uhlenbeck and one of his young pupils cannot be established – novels don't offer proofs like archival documents do, and one can never be sure when the author has changed crucial information and when he is relating what has happened. Still it is tempting to speculate on a deeper connection between Uhlenbeck's mental depressions and possible suppressed homosexuality. Such tendencies may have been known to his most intimate pupils, which would explain a curious phrase in De Josselin de Jong's biographical memoir: "To us, who were his pupils, it is not the most important thing who exactly he was, but what he was to us (De Josselin de Jong 1952:256)."

Whatever the case, the "incident" mentioned by De Josselin de Jong and related rumors that went around in Nijmegen were such that in 1930 Uhlenbeck decided to leave the city and to move to Amersfoort, a quiet city in the middle of the country and not far away from Amsterdam, the location of Uhlenbeck's beloved Royal Academy. There he and Willy lived until 1936, when they finally settled in Lugano, Switzerland, in a boarding house called Eugenia, located in the Ruvigliana quarter. Yet while Uhlenbeck left the Netherlands, he did not say farewell to linguistics. He still worked for Boas's *International Journal of American Linguistics*, wrote reviews and articles for several other journals, and was prepared as ever to help promising young scholars. As late as 1948, E. M. Uhlenbeck, a grandnephew, came to visit the old scholar in Lugano before he went to Indonesia to teach Javanese and general linguistics at the University of Batavia (now Jakarta). "I look forward to his stay in Eugenia," Uhlenbeck wrote to former student De Goeje, "even I consider myself to be a rather poor advisor."[30]

In those years, it seemed as though finally the burdens of life had been taken off of Uhlenbeck's shoulders. "With us it is going *cosi, cosi*. A bit old," he told De Goeje in the letter just quoted. The shaky handwriting testifies to this, but, as Uhlenbeck added with some resignation, "Nothing to be done about that." He remained active almost to his last day. His last article, concluding an exchange with the Eskimo expert William Thalbitzer on the interpretation of a number of Eskimo words, was published in 1950. On August 12, 1951, Uhlenbeck died in Lugano. According to De Josselin de Jong, Uhlenbeck's dying before Willy was a blessing for him and would no doubt be accepted by Willy "with complete resignation, realizing that is was better this way (De Josselin de Jong 1952, 244-45)." There is a story that Willy committed suicide not long after Uhlenbeck's death. However, in her letters to family members in Holland up to the year of her death, "aunt Willy" gave no sign of being tired of life and neither does she complain excessively about her age or her health.[31] She finally passed away in Lugano on May 6, 1954, having reached the age of 92.

MRS. UHLENBECK
An Informed Diarist?

Mary Eggermont-Molenaar

Willy Uhlenbeck was not the first to keep a diary while visiting the Blackfeet in which she simultaneously recorded her experiences with them and the activities of an European scholar among them – who happened to be her husband, C. C. Uhlenbeck. In the summer of 1833 Fort McKenzie was visited by the German ethnographer, Maximilian, Prince Wied zum Neuwied, who left his reminiscences of the fort, the fur trade and the battle that took place in August that summer in *Early Western Travels* (vols. 22–24). That same summer American Lieutenant James Bradley must have been in the area. In *Bradley's Journal*, published in *Contributions to the Historical Society of Montana*, Bradley (1900, 3:206) provides vivid descriptions of the same fort and fur trade, the wheelings and dealings of the Blackfeet and sketches a portrait of the Prince Wied zum Neuwied, "nearly seventy years of age ... a man of medium height, rather slender ... speaking very broken English ... and [wearing] the greasiest pair of trousers that ever encased princely legs ... a bachelor and a man of science, and it was in this latter capacity that he had roamed so far from his ancestral home on the Rhine."

Bradley continues: "During the Prince's stay at Fort McKenzie he had an opportunity to watch an Indian Battle ... Thirty lodges ... under Stum-ick es-te-ki-e, Lame Bull, ... attacked 1500 Assiniboines," (ibid., 3:207–208) and goes on to describe Prince Wied as a possible, though not probable, slayer of an Assiniboine.[32]

What Prince Wied and C. C. Uhlenbeck have in common is not "possibly having slayed someone" or "wearing greasy trousers," but having been recorded: Prince Wied by Bradley (1833) and C. C. by his own wife (1911). So, readers of "Bradley's Journal" and of Willy's diary not only get an impression of the community through these writers' eyes, but also of actions of both Prince Wied and C. C. Uhlenbeck and people's reactions to them. It is tempting to compare "Bradley's Journal" and Willy's diary at length and muse over keepers of the land becoming owners of a plot, the buffalo that were and went, the whiskey that came and stayed, the contagious diseases still hovering in 1911, and determination and independence returning. However, we will restrict ourselves to a single quotation about Bradley and how his Journal came about, and

"Snapshot" of Dr. and Mrs. Uhlenbeck in Lugano, Switzerland.

then move on to a discussion of Willy's diary. In the introduction to his diary (Bradley 1896:141) Bradley is introduced as follows:

Lieutenant Bradley was one of the subordinate officers of the Army best known to the citizens of Montana ... and the diary published herewith is but a small part of the manuscripts which he left at his decease. Through the intelligent interest of General Gibbon, who was his commanding officer here, seconded by the efforts of Lieutenant Bradley's wife [Mary Beech], these papers came into the possession of the Historical Society.

Bradley's Journal was saved by his wife and the "intelligent interest" of a general, but how did Willy's diary come into the possession of the Glenbow Archives, and (1900, 3:206) by whose efforts? The staff of the Glenbow Archives informed me that, indeed, there was some correspondence with regard to the arrival of Mrs. Uhlenbeck's diary and then handed me a letter, dated January 16, 1990, to the Curator of the Maxwell Museum of the University of New Mexico, from Mrs. Elsa Heman-Ortt (transcript):[33]

Dear Mrs. Rodee   *16.1.'90*

I thank you very much for your offer to give a "home" to the diary of my dear friend Mrs. W. Uhlenbeck.

Now I have to tell you some personal things to give you a bit understanding of the background of this document.

First of all I ask myself if in your museum of Anthropology the name of Prof. C. C. Uhlenbeck is perhaps already known. Uhlenbeck visited the Blackfeet Indians Reservation twice, about 80 years ago and made a grammatic and a vocabulary of their language. His name was well known in linguistic circles over the world. Special gifts he got from the indians are kept in the anthropology museum in Leiden (Holland).

I remember my conversation with him about this diary, which he judged as so personal and unscientific that it was just good for me to get it – and no more.

As I talked about it with Mrs. Cramer, she thought that maybe the very personal voice could still be worthwhile to be kept for eventual[ly] researchers.[34]

Mr. and Mrs. Uhlenbeck were originally friends of my father and then, perhaps because of the fact that they had no children, a deep friendship grew between them and me.

I send you this little snapshot to give you a slight impression of the two old people. He died in 1951, she some time later.

I'll send you the diary by sea-mail, so it will be still sometime before it will arrive.

I once more thank you for helping me to find this solution.

Yours,
Elsa Heman-Ortt.
Beer Shewa, Israel

The addressee of this letter, Mrs. Rodee, Curator of Southwestern Ethnology at the University of New Mexico, was informed by Hana Samek-Norton that the Archives of the Glenbow Museum in Calgary was "probably the most appropriate home for the personal diaries of Dr. C. C. Uhlenbeck (Letter of March 13, 1990 from Mrs. Rodee to Mr. Dempsey, then Associate Director of the Glenbow Museum)."[35] Hugh Dempsey agreed, writing in his Thank You note to Mrs. Rodee: "When Blackfeet Indians from Montana are undertaking research projects they invariably start with our repository in Calgary" (letter of March 22, 1990).

Only in September 2002 did I succeed in contacting Elsa Heman-Ortt in Israel. In a lengthy letter, dated October 12, 2002, signed by Elsa Heman, she communicated that the friendship of Uhlenbeck with her father stemmed from their elementary school in Haarlem and, "that there were long periods of no contact until the time they came to visit us."[36] Elsa also wrote that Uhlenbeck regretted that her father's books had never been translated into English and that she greatly admired his thinking capacities and his humanitarian ideas. As an example she quoted Uhlenbeck as saying: "Fortunately no horses are used anymore in wartime."[37] Elsa wrote that in 1930 the Uhlenbecks moved from Nijmegen to Amersfoort in order to be closer to their family and that "the renewal of the friendship was strongly coloured by the friendship with us, children." Elsa provided me with a long list of books written by her father. In a subsequent letter dated October 29, 2002, Elsa wrote that the split between her father and Uhlenbeck was caused by the divorce of her parents.

Elsa's father, Felix Louis Ortt, was employed by the Dutch Government Waterworks where he became famous for his development of a tide table.[38] He was also one of the leading so-called Christian Anarchists of his day. He wrote about natural healing, vivisection, art, vegetarianism, spiritualism, sexuality, Tolstoy, art, colony life, disarmament, temperance, pure living and animal protection, and undoubtedly

I am overlooking a few fields of his interests.[39] This busy mind and body was Uhlenbeck's lost friend. It was Ortt's daughter, Elsa, a social worker who worked in Iceland and among the Bedouins, whom Uhlenbeck entrusted with the diary of his wife.[40]

The diary consists of six notebooks, all lines filled with handwritten text and contains 94 entries covering as many days, as well as occasional remarks about the days not covered. The notebooks are written in a steady hand, though sometimes the handwriting flattens somewhat, just like the ears of a cat in distress. We learn that it was cold, or that the "teacher" didn't show up, or we sense that she was overcome with impressions and in a hurry to write them all down. The cover of Notebook One is severely discoloured into gray, while the other five are bluish and gray rimmed. Somewhere, they must have spent some time in a sunnier environment than an archival box. From Montana in 1911 the notebooks moved, along with its author, to Leiden, from there to Nijmegen, then to Amersfoort (where the friendship with the Ortt family was picked up again), and then on to Lugano. The next thing we know is that Elsa took the diary with her to Israel from where it moved to Albuquerque in New Mexico, and subsequently to the Glenbow Archives in Calgary.

Willy clearly had moved to Montana with the intention of keeping a diary covering the period of their stay on the Blackfeet Reservation in Montana. The diary begins with their arrival in Browning on June 8, 1911 and ends with their departure on September 17, exactly one hundred days later. Willy wrote in her native language, Dutch. For someone who apparently had no lengthy, formal education, she had a remarkable command of the language; only a few spelling mistakes or slips of the pen occurred. Punctuation, it must be added, seemed to be the least of her concerns. She used English on a regular basis while in Montana and, as time went on, also some Blackfoot terminology. She did not master English as well as she did Dutch, a fact she was well aware of, as she confided to her diary that she read George Eliot's novel, *Adam Bede*, carefully in order to improve her English. Spelling was a concern to her;

sometimes she later found out what the correct spelling of a particular word or name was and then continued by using the latter.

As for the general content, Willy invariably started her entries by listing the time at which she and her husband got up, and then continued with a weather report. She noted where they had breakfast, supper and dinner, in general what they ate, and whether she liked it or not.[41] When they did not eat in the tipi of their main teacher, Joseph Tatsey, or when it was not he who had been teaching her husband, she also noted what they paid others for their food, for the teaching, and for other services such as transport. She described her own activities and those of her husband, who spent time checking the material he had collected the previous year and who recorded new stories. She wrote about the people who told stories and about those who visited them and what they looked like. She wrote about the people they visited and described the interiors of their *tipis* or cabins. The same goes for the dances and the ceremonies they attended, and their moves from one camping place to another, sitting on top of their belongings in a buggy that sometimes crossed high waters, the passengers desperately holding on. Willy once sighed that she wished that her acquaintances in the Netherlands could see this spectacle: the readers of her diary certainly get the picture.

Invariably each entry ends with a description of how the day ended: whether or not visitors came in the evening, the ambience in their candle-lit tent, the night creeping in on them, the silencing of the sounds outside; she writes about how the night was spent, with or without Uhlenbeck having belly aches, and at what time and how "morning was broken" – by hard winds or rain or sunshine or birds flying against their tent. Willy's depiction of Annie Tatsey, the wife of Uhlenbeck's main informant, Joseph Tatsey, the woman who tirelessly cooked and cared for her own family and the Uhlenbecks and a woman of whom Willie genuinely seemed to be in awe, inspired me to dedicate this whole book to Annie Tatsey and those like her.

With regard to Willy's style of writing, it should be noted first of all that she apparently did not feel bound by many conventional writing rules or regulations. She arbitrarily uses past and present tense and constantly interrupts her descriptions with associations, reminiscences, and occurrences such as people stopping by their tent and subsequent conversation with them, followed by opinions about them. She describes, in the present tense, a good number of events and her thoughts about them after they happened. For the reader this evokes the impression of being an eye-witness and a mind-reader at the same time. Her uninhibited way of looking around and registering everything she sees and hears, registering everything she thinks about, provides the reader with the same unexpected views mountain goats must experience when they jump from one slope to another. C. C. Uhlenbeck judged the diary, according to Mrs. Heman's letter, to be "so personal and unscientific." Mrs. Heman remarked that the diary, "was just good for me to get it – and no more," and Mrs. Cramer had suggested that "maybe the very personal voice could still be worthwhile to be kept for eventual researchers."

In order to evaluate the judgement of these three people, look at the value of the diary – and along with it the performance of C. C. Uhlenbeck – and find a guideline for assessment, I envisioned the Blackfeet Reservation in Montana in 1910. That year, Willie's husband spent some time there with his former student Jan de Josselin de Jong, who in 1922 would become a professor of anthropology in Leiden. From the diary we know that Willie, while in Montana in 1911, exchanged long letters with "our Jan" and his wife Lien, who in the same year spent some time on the Red Lake (Ojibwe) Reservation in Minnesota. She undoubtedly kept the young couple informed about the Uhlenbecks' stay on the Blackfeet Reservation. It is not hard to imagine that the two couples, back in Leiden, often visited each other and shared their fieldwork experiences. Whether De Josselin de Jong ever got to read the diary can't be ascertained, let alone how he would have assessed it. However, "College-dictaat Prof. Dr. J.P.D. de Josseling de Jong. Leiden 1948/49"

(Lecture Notes Prof. Dr. J.B.P. de Josseling de Jong" Leiden 1948/49), provides all kinds of instructions regarding fieldwork, one of them being that fieldworkers should keep diaries. Willy was not a fieldworker but in a sense acted like one because she did just that: she kept a diary. In the following paragraphs we will compare some of her activities and observations, described in the diary, with De Josselin de Jong's lecture notes.

De Josselin de Jong started with the question of the goal of the fieldworker. Dr. C. C. Uhlenbeck formulated his own goal in his presentation, "Geslachts- en Persoonsnamen der Peigans" (Patronymics and Proper Names of the Peigans): "My main objective was to learn the language and to save it from threatened oblivion by recording an accurate description."[42] So Uhlenbeck profiled himself, then and there, in 1911 in Amsterdam, as a salvage linguist and occasional ethnographer.

Willy was no scholar and she pursued no scientific goal. She did not write to test or to promote one theory or another, and she did not compare her observations with those of others. But she did have one set goal: facilitating her husband's work. Still, the question arises, why did she keep a diary? Why do people keep diaries? As a support for later musings and reminiscences? She certainly didn't write out of boredom as she began the diary on her first day on the reservation. The impression one gets from the diary is that she was an avid writer, that writing came naturally to her. She not only spent much time writing her diary but she also kept up a large correspondence with family and friends, which helped her stay in touch. Writing the diary might have had an added benefit for her: it enabled her to stay in touch with her – elusive – self.

While people cried, as they did on the 10th of July because of the suicide of ethnographer David Duvall, she escaped, on paper, into recording her distractions: a walk to the camps, a closer look at the Medicine Lodge, and everyday concerns such as the details of their next move, their next encounter, the state of the buggy (horse-drawn wagon), and so on. Throughout the diary, it is clear that Willy was and had to be strong-willed; she had to deal with a numerous incidences, that she approached as mere challenges and a sound dose of irony. When her husband's work was somehow endangered, though, the irony was replaced by sarcasm. By the end of her husband's fieldwork period, she sometimes seemed to be overcome by feelings of loneliness, by doubts about the progress of her husband's work or anxiety about his mood. Where else could she confide but in her diary?

Furthermore, one also gets the impression that Willy didn't write only for her own current or future benefit. She might secretly have been hoping that one day the diary would be useful as it appears that sometimes she straightens out a few matters for eventual readers. By writing *I do this and I do that*, she gives the reader quite a nice impression of how a genuine, very thrifty, Dutch housewife tackled her duties while living in a tent in a deserted location on one of the windiest places on earth, during the extremely cold and wet summer of 1911. When Willy writes that she did not give a certain child candy again, she explains that she did it "for his education." It is as if she addresses an imaginary reader. By noting her husband's admonition to her that people should not see that she works – shaking out the blankets or so – she reveals something about the relationship of this upper middle class couple to the outside world. Keeping up appearances! By describing next how she solved the problem of "working" without it being seen by outsiders, she also reveals something about the relationship between herself and her husband. Again, it is as if she communicates, not just with herself but with an audience in mind.

Willy profiled herself as the person who greatly facilitated her husband's work; still, in more than one way she also seemed to compete with him. Not only did she list her own activities, but more than once we learn that while she is toiling away, Uhlenbeck is still in bed, while at the same time, by describing the circumstances of her husband's work such as: who told him what story, how much they were paid, etc., Willy unwittingly gave a valuable insight into how her husband's fieldwork came

about. In hind-sight she was a valuable co-worker despite not being recognized as such by her husband.

De Josselin de Jong also discusses the goal of the research: a preliminary exploration of a certain culture, an all-inclusive culture or society, or data with regard to a certain problem, and they state that a particular orientation might influence one's research methods and slant the results in a certain direction. De Josselin de Jong thought it was difficult to expect someone to approach one's field of interest without previous knowledge or experience of it. Again, Uhlenbeck collected data with regard to a certain problem, a language that he and others thought was about to die out. He noted in the above-mentioned 1911 lecture that he recorded oral traditions and stories as well – as he had the opportunity.

Willy must have had some previous knowledge about the reservation and ethnography in general. Her husband had been on the same reservation the previous year: Willy would have gained some background from his stories and possibly from reading or hearing about *Reizen en Onderzoekingen in Noord-Amerika* (*Travels and Researches in North America*) by the Dutch ethnographer Herman F. C. ten Kate (1858–1931), which was published in 1885 in Leiden (Ten Kate 1885, 2004). She had heard of, but maybe not yet read, Grinnell's *Blackfoot Lodge Tales*, which she mentions. From the diary it is clear that she knew about certain aspects of polygamous relationships, about the punishment of unfaithful spouses; that she knew some people by name before she had met them, and that she knew about the boys attending the mission school at the reservation.

De Josselin de Jong does not elaborate much about the implications of having knowledge about the field to be explored. But as we can expect, it does have implications. On August 13 Willy reacted to the behavior of a woman with a cut-off nose with: "However, now it [her nose being cut off by a husband] no longer bothers her, she is lively & cheerful – and she doesn't think that she is ugly at all!" This reflects a secondary, not a primary, shocked reaction, which one might have expected from someone who didn't know about the practice of cutting off noses in cases of adultery. Apart from possibly having heard about it from her husband, she might have read in Ten Kate (1885, 175) that Apaches were polygamous, but that enraged husbands punished adultery by cutting off the nose of an unfaithful spouse.

Evidence of Willy's previous knowledge also occurs in her descriptions of how she and her husband came across burial sites. Willy was not surprised to come across coffins with body parts sticking out; she described meticulously what she saw and, every time she wrote about coming across coffins, stressed that she didn't take anything with her. Did she know about anthropologists of her time who went grave digging and didn't hesitate to take away skulls, items and artifacts? Hovens (1989, 80) notes that in 1900 the Leiden Anatomisch Kabinet had in its possession about 800 skulls from all over the world. Had Willy seen or heard about the collection of 800 skulls and read how Ten Kate bragged about his grave robberies? Ten Kate (1885, 30) describes his plan to rob a grave: "I had to be careful, because who knows to what these normally so peaceful Indians are capable of when they notice that someone had violated the graves of their ancestors…." Ten Kate goes on to describe how he used a hook to pull a skull from a skeleton. This was not his only grave robbery.[43] It certainly looks as if Willy disapproved of these practices!

Another aspect of Willy's descriptions of people also indicates that she can be considered to be an 'informed' diarist. At the time, around 1911, anthropology was largely concerned with "physical" anthropology: it was thought to be important to describe people in every detail, such as the size of their skulls, the length of their noses, the shades of their skin, etc. So, "Measurement" used to be considered an important component of research; possibly addressing the question whether people who looked different could be deemed to be people after all. It seems that Willy knew about this notion of measurement, as she made a point of describing as many of the features of the Indians as she could. In one case she even commented on the width of someone's nails. The appearance of the other white people was not of much interest, since the diary lacks their descriptions.

If descriptions beyond physical aspects were scientifically imperative or not, they occurred. Ten Kate's (1885, 76–77) appreciation of the beautiful Mohave girls and young women, "black hair locks, brown hued, with shiny sly eyes, with her red lips on which often a childlike chuckle plays, the elegant shape of her slender body rendering in its natural simplicity the image of the *peerless dark eyed Indian girl,* so eloquently sung the praises of by Joaquin Miller" is a good example thereof.[44]

Some of Willy's descriptions can be called equally sensual. As Alice Kehoe put in a note to me (fall 2002), "Mary, she had a very active eye for male beauty while her husband didn't seem to be very active sexually." Occasionally, Willy describes young people with an appreciation similar to Ten Kate. On Saturday July 15, Willie noted about one Richard, "Again these narrow, small feet, and beautiful shaped hands and nails and this soft, shiny skin."

De Josselin de Jong continued his lecture with requirements for the technical preparation of his students: fieldworkers should be as independent as possible. However, that is easier said than done. We will see that for food and transport the Uhlenbecks had to depend strongly on their Blackfeet hosts, the Tatsey family. Fieldworkers should know about medical care – Willy had a medical kit and instructions with her and on several occasions she described dispensing medications to her husband as well as to the Blackfeet.

Fieldworkers shouldn't try to develop their own films: Willy found that out the hard way. So far her photographs, which she took with so much care and even tried to develop herself, have not been found. Fortunately, the ones De Josselin de Jong took in 1910 have all survived in the K.I.T.L.V., respectively in the Museum voor Volkenkunde, at Leiden and serve as illustrations to the diary. The best practice, De

Josselin de Jong urged, is to bring an assistant for all these practical matters (1948/49, 3). That is just the role Willy assumed.

We move to the October 22, 1948 lecture. De Josselin de Jong admonished his students to distinguish between impressions and facts: don't assume, for example, that someone who is crying is sad. It was not always easy for Willy to know what to assume when people walked into and out of her tent with hardly a hello or goodbye. Or why they did not apologize for certain behavior or did no say "thanks" for some of her little niceties. Indians did not do that: they did not say "thank you," nor did they say "goodbye." Understanding why was not her job, so we can't blame her for not going around and inquiring. It is too bad that she was not familiar with De Josselin de Jong's notion that "Gratefulness is a cultured emotional reaction in our culture."

One of the greatest frustrations of the Uhlenbecks was that people didn't always keep their appointments. According to the De Josselin de Jong's October 22 lecture, there are cultures where saying "no" is not considered polite. One rather says "yes" and doesn't show up. What we sense from the diary is that their teacher, Tatsey, was very busy and often consulted by many people. Busy with what? Consulted about what? On paper Willy hardly ever wondered and consequently there isn't much mutual understanding about each other's expectations or time frames.

One of De Josselin de Jong's next notions was that anthropologists should come across as people who come to learn. Willy understood that since she always referred to the informants as "the teachers." She also seemed to understand that one should avoid being perceived as someone from the government or the mission, or as a merchant, because people might distrust the use that could be made of the information gathered. In this respect McClintock (1923, 512) illustrates De Josselin de Jong's notion when he states: "The whole question of lifting up the Indian is one of economical, educational, and moral difficulty to both state and church. They are together responsible for its solution, the work of each supplementing the other."

Willy noted a few times that she avoided socializing with non-Indians in order not to jeopardize their relationship with the Indians. Apart from the question whether this would always be the case, she seemed to be aware that it might cause distrust as she actually comments once on the policy of the Indian agent and the priest – on a certain occasion the Blackfeet were not allowed to dance. Still, despite not having associated much with white people we will see at the very end of the diary that their relationship with their hosts at their departure in September 1911 had soured a bit; was not as glorious as the mood that transpires from the picture that the same host family presented to Uhlenbeck the previous year on July 19, 1910. In 1911, on the very last day of their stay on the reservation an argument about how the Uhlenbecks were to be transported to the train (with one or with two buggies) ended with Tatsey's remark: "Now Professor, you shall have it."

Talking about the departure of the Uhlenbecks, the striking similarity between Willy's notes on finally taking off by the Pullman train with the literary rendition of such departure in the short story *Een Geleerde onder de Indianen* (*A Scholar among the Indians*) by the Dutch author Maarten Biesheuvel (1983, 188–94) comes to mind.[45] The scholar from the short story, after having spent some time on an Indian reserve, in the plane, on his way back to Leiden (translated from Dutch): "sees the sun rise above the clouds and thinks about the fate of the Indians. He will earn about twenty thousand guilders because he has recorded a nearly lost language for eternity. He will be the hero but he thinks about that Indian in a cell, somewhere in America and tears well in his eyes. 'Sir, duck's breast or beef,' asks the stewardess."

Compare these few lines with the last ones of Willy's diary, where she describes her feelings when the Pullman train started them on their way back to New York and back home. The instant, though fleeting, feelings of nostalgia for the Indians left behind are shared by the scholar in the short story and Willy and we may guess that her husband would have shared these feelings. Willie's diary can't be denied some literary

This picture was presented to Prof. C. C. Uhlenbeck by Mr. and Mrs. Tatsey. (DJdJ 1910).

merit![46] Biesheuvel told me that he had based the story on his conversations with Dr. A. H. Kuipers, a Dutch linguist who did fieldwork among the Shuswap and Squamisch in British Columbia in the 1960s and 1970s.[47]

Returning to the issue of learning. The Uhlenbecks needed the mission boys for teaching (and to keep them company), so contact with the Jesuit Fathers was unavoidable. From the diary it appears that the relationship with the Fathers in the few days they camped near their Holy Family Mission, even with the Dutch Father Soer, was somewhat cool. We are not sure if this was a personal thing, a notion that one should not associate with clergy, or whether it can be explained by the Uhlenbecks' appreciation of things religious in general. Uhlenbeck had revealed his disregard for clerics in 1885 poems such as "In de Kerk" (In the Church) and "*Al bidt al werkt de Vrome*" (Even when the Pious prays or works). In another poem he confessed to being a heathen, and in his 1899 *Public Lecture*, he sang the praises of the Germanic gods Wodan and Donar (1899, 9). On the other hand, the missionaries might have disliked Uhlenbeck's interest in Blackfoot language and culture, something they were attempting to stamp out.[48] Willy's thoughts about the missionaries' proselytizing efforts shine through in her description of a church scene at the beginning of their stay, on June 11. She doesn't compare her impression with the one of the well-known writer McClintock. Later on in this volume, we do, and it is eerie to see how her description matches McClintock's.

Uhlenbeck came to learn from the Blackfeet. Still, had the relationship with the Jesuit Fathers been more congenial, he could also have learned that in 1894 one of them, Father Bougis, had written a Blackfoot dictionary and would perhaps even have been willing to share the contents with him. He could have learned about the English-Blackfoot translation activities of the Dutch Father Soer; or perhaps even about the Blackfoot grammars, vocabularies and other (religious) texts in Blackfoot produced by Oblate Fathers such as the Fathers Léon Doucet

and Albert Lacombe in the Canadian province of Alberta. If he had knowledge about this, he does not mention it.

Back to the Leiden classroom. De Josselin de Jong advised on etiquette: act as if you are at home, don't give advice when people don't ask for it, don't get involved in conflicts, no pawing, no handing out of presents to acquire goodwill, no intimacy with members of the opposite sex, and don't think that you have to participate in everything. Uhlenbeck once scolded Tatsey's wife about her husband not showing up on time. Fortunately, Tatsey's admirable, gracious reaction the next day prevented the situation from culminating in a conflict. With regard to the advice "act as if you are at home," two almost identical occurrences come to mind. Tatsey's mother died, followed two days later by his ailing daughter. Both times the Uhlenbecks watched the funeral cortège from a distance. At home they would have been invited to participate in the funeral. But they weren't at home, they weren't invited and they didn't know whether they would be welcome. But, instead of observing some time of mourning, they busied themselves with finding other teachers. It is clear from the diary that the couple felt awkward. Uhlenbeck half-heartedly apologized for not showing up. Willy duly noted her husband saying to Tatsey: "We strongly thought about going." A social awkwardness comes across out of this incident – at least the Uhlenbecks could have asked about funeral mores.

This social left-handedness, Willy's meticulous bookkeeping of small loans and the focus of both on getting the fieldwork done and showing no regard for the fact that other people had to do their own work may have contributed to their somewhat uneasy departure.

Visits by Indian people who were not employed as teachers still contributed to Uhlenbeck's work in progress, which might explain the generosity of the thrifty Willy. This leads us to the *Lecture Notes'* other admonishment: don't hand out goodies to acquire goodwill. In the Uhlenbecks' case word must have spread on the reservation about the gigantic quantity of candies and tobacco the Uhlenbecks had stored in their tent. Sometimes people came by to buy some. Willy then went to great length to assure people that they weren't merchants, not here and not in their home country. The impression one gets from reading her comments on being taken for someone who sells candy, is that in their circles (professors and their wives) one didn't sell candy, one just gave it away to friends! It reminds of De Josselin de Jong's remark that the fieldworker who visits to study a certain people will be classified himself by his subjects. Willy was aware of this and certainly did not want to be classified as a merchant's wife!

One more admonishment was: no pawing. Pawing stretches it. Uhlenbeck's way of entertaining the mission boys before or after recording their language and stories, *"Boys' experiences,"* makes one wonder what came first: his interest in spending time with these young people – filling the gap of his childlessness, which he seemed to do throughout his life – or the awareness of the importance of their language for the sake of research. Maybe both – perhaps he was inspired by the title of the journals James Willard Schulz published, such as *Boys' Lives, Youth's Companion* or *The American Boy.* (Schulz 1988, xi). But if the notion was first of all that the language of young people is important (field linguists prefer work with older people, certainly at that time), why didn't

Uhlenbeck, who called himself a salvage linguist, complain about or at least mention somewhere the fact that the same young boys weren't allowed to speak their language in school?[49] The diary and Uhlenbeck's self-profiling as a salvage-linguist provoke all these questions.

About the anthropologist's methods, De Josselin de Jong mentions the direct method (observe and ask questions) and the indirect method (gather data and construct the explored area afterwards). Since Willy only wrote while on the reservation, we will just look at how she handled, unwittingly, the direct method: observe and ask questions. Comparing her descriptions with my own observations of ceremonies, nature, photographs, for example of the gifts she got and described, and keeping in mind Darrel Kipp's letter, quoted in Genee's contribution in Part II of this volume, we can safely say that Willy's observations were largely accurate. Her descriptions are like photographs taken with an unfocused lens. Since she didn't indulge in asking questions and didn't compare or test a theory, we also have to agree with her husband's apparent qualification that the diary is "so unscientific." The fact that the diary is "so very personal" which is true, might have led Uhlenbeck to hand it to a friend instead of sending it along with his other materials to the Leiden archives.

Nevertheless, in my opinion the diary is not only 'good enough' for Mrs. Heman but is also 'worthwhile' and of great importance for 'eventual researchers' with an interest in early twentieth century Blackfeet and Dutch culture. It provides a mountain of material for exploration and for comparison. It provokes a myriad of questions for anthropologists, ethnologists, linguists, Americanists, historians, and anyone with an interest in the art of diary writing, women's studies, early reservation life, or early twentieth-century fieldwork standards. One question: did De Josselin de Jong have Willy's 1911 diary and / of letters and / of conversations with her in mind when he wrote the lecture notes mentioned above?" On October 29, 1948, he told his students that (translated from Dutch), "The best ethnographers from the last quarter of the previous century … just told what they had experienced and observed themselves."

In the translation of Willy Uhlenbeck-Melchior's diary, the punctuation is adapted to today's standards. Willy's use, in her Dutch text, of English and other foreign languages is put in italics. When she uses English verbs but conjugates them in Dutch (e.g., *teachen, geteached*) the conjugation left as she presents it but is placed in italics. In general, I have used italics to mark words that I have copied, rather than translated. Some obvious spelling mistakes in names have been corrected as Willy often wrote names phonetically, in the way she heard them with her Dutch ears. For example, she spelled "Henault" as "Hinaut," "Hatty" as "Hetty," and "Guardipee" as "Guardepie." "Bear Chief" is often written as "Bearchief" or "Bear-chief." I have standardized these names according to their spellings in *Blackfeet Heritage, 1907–1908* (i.e., DeMarce 1980). Her variant spelling of the name "Kjaijoes" has been retained.

In DeMarce (1980) the names and genealogical data of people who received allotments at that time are listed. By the Act of Congress of March 1, 1907, the Piegan could ask for allotments of 40 acres of irrigated lands and 280 acres of grazing lands, or 320 acres of grazing lands. Land not allotted was sold under the Enlarged Homestead Act of 1909.

As already explained, in the United States Peigan are known under the name "Piegan" and Blackfoot are called "Blackfeet." Most names of persons mentioned by Willy were traced by the contributors to DeMarce (1980), which is a compliment to both the accuracy of the people who put this book together and to Willy's observations.

Concepts such as "pemmican" or "bands" will be explained in the Collage of Dr. C. C. Uhlenbeck's work. Readers may wish to move from diary entries to Collage entries of the same date.

I apologize for any terminology that comes across as offensive. Translating renders a text as it is, not as something politically correct. So when Willy writes about *Roodhuiden*, this term can only be translated as *Redskins*. As is commonly known, red does not refer to the skin but to the habit of painting the skin red at certain ceremonies. As far as I know, this ritual happens when people want to be recognized and blessed by their Creator as one of its followers. The irony is that this colloquial term "Redskins" simultaneously reminds us of the Blackfeet's ritual use of red ochre and of the ignorance of the very people trying to understand these people and their culture.

In determining the identity of people mentioned in Willy's diary, I have consulted DeMarce (1980). The information in DeMarce (1980) was compiled approximately three years prior to the writing of the diary. Therefore, I have added three years to the ages of the people mentioned in *Blackfeet Heritage, 1907–1908*.

Part **I**

Mrs. Uhlenbeck's Diary

Blackfoot Reservation, Thursday, June 8 – Sunday, September 17, 1911

Willy's Table of Contents, a loose page tucked into the back of notebook VI,
is used to divide her notebook diary into chapters.

Thursday, June 8.

On Thursday evening, June 8, at 6.57 p.m. we arrived at Browning.[1] It is only a small *depot* right in the middle of the prairie. What a big disappointment that Joseph Tatsey (with whose family we will camp) was not at the station as agreed upon.[2] We telegraphed him the day before from New York about the day and the time of our arrival. Our suitcases weren't there either. That is why we went in Joe Kipp's old car to the village, to the city of Browning, ¾ of an hour down the road.[3] At the *depot* I saw the first Indian. There is a kind of a road between the depot and the small city which has one hundred inhabitants. The rough road makes one shake in quite a strange way and I continue to worry about our camera and the glass plates and I don't understand that nothing broke. We arrived at "Hotel Browning" – a big wooden house of very humble appearance. Joe Kipp, a Mandan, *half breed,* is a widower of advanced age. His *wirtschaft* [business] is being handled by his *menager* [*sic*]. A *mixed* Blood-Peigan girl, dressed completely European, is serving his guests.[4] With her beautiful, black eyes she seems standoffish, looking straight ahead of her. What could we do this evening? We had eaten our *supper* on the train and Tatsey will not come for sure. The telegram to him was sent several days ago; at least, that is what they told us in Browning. However, it was and remains a disappointment. We had expected to see the face of the man whom we had longed to meet for; instead we have to satisfy ourselves with Joe Kipp. Then Uhlenbeck got the idea of taking his Blackfoot texts from his hand luggage and reading aloud from them.

We did not stay in the pub, a somber bare portal where one is not served (strong drinks are not allowed to be imported), without any claim to hygiene, with an enormous rusty stove which, to our amazement, had a big fire in it.[5] Instead we walk on to the office-like residence of Joe Kipp. It is a dirty room with gray sheets and gray half-turned-down bedspread. All kinds of rubbish at the sides and in the corners. We each got a wooden chair. Joe Kipp himself sat down on his bed and then Uhlenbeck read a few stories in Blackfoot. How nice that one under-stood everything. Other Indians, half-breeds, also join in, among them a half-brother of Willy Kennedy, Charlie Potts, a most charming boy of 20 years.[6] It is an agreeable hour. We went to bed about 9:30. Is it clean? Oh, no. In such a case it is best not to look too carefully. The room was spacious and even big, but as dirty as can be. Still I slept very well after having spent so many nights at sea or on the train.

Willy Uhlenbeck-Melchior (1862-1954). | *The Browning railway depot as it now looks.*
A young Crow girl in front of Hotel Browning (DJdJ 1910).

MRS. UHLENBECK'S DIARY

Friday, June 9.

We rose very late at 8:30 and had breakfast in a different room, which appeared to be the "dining room." I have forgotten what we ate. I just remember the big, unclean cup of coffee with dirty egg stains. After breakfast we went shopping. At Mr. Scherburne's we bought a lot of *candy* and a lot of tobacco for fl. 125 for our Indian visitors and also two *buckets* with *sweets* (one with *candy* and one with *peanuts*) for the mission kids. Scherburne has a very large shop, a low, big, wooden building, where there is a lot for sale. I think that he is going to be a rich man, and now he conducts his business with three sons.[7] We talked with the oldest son. We went with Mr. Scherburne to his house to visit his wife. There we found luxury & comfort.

We enter a nice suite with bookcases & curtains & rocking chairs. Then we see his dining room with the table neatly set and we walked past the bathroom and then entered a room with the most splendid Indian artifacts. Headdresses for an *Indian war dress*, beautiful *beadwork* on belts and on moccasins, and still more beautiful *guillwork [sic]* in most splendid colours. What treasures! How did he get them? The walls were hung full of drawings of groups of Indians. These limber figures, sitting together are beautiful. We also saw a nice portrait of Eagle-Calf, a very old Indian with a most characteristic face.[8] It was same Eagle-Calf who was so friendly with Uhlenbeck last year and always came to shake hands. Also a lot of mountain sheep are hung there, all shot by Sherburne's sons.

Then we visited Mrs. Nixon, the wife of the government blacksmith and the mother of Charlie Camp who is now in the Cutbank school.[9] Charlie's youngest sister picks up her *puppy* for us.[10] "*This is my baby*," she said. Uhlenbeck showed his papers to the *agent* and in the waiting room of the *agency* we saw all kinds of Indians. Little Dog, also, an old, small Indian, who said that I am his sister-in-law.[11] This is very friendly, meaning that we might be heading for a "big time," meaning that they trust us. After dinner we walked around and furtively looked at the Indian women, who walked around with children on their backs or ride around.

Later, to pass the time, we went to a baseball diamond. Some small boys said to us, "*Will you come with us, we shall have practice.*" We watched the nice game and the nice boys for a long while. Tatsey, we thought, would still not come. How happy we were when someone immediately told us, upon our returning to the square, "Joe Tatsey has just come in." He had been shopping. We looked for him, asking about. After quite a while, what appeared to us a very long time, I saw him arrive at Scherburne's shop. He looked at me and I looked at him, until Uhlenbeck himself approached him. How friendly he seemed to be, this long, lanky man with his very dark complexion, his black eyes, his shining, black, straight hair, parted in the middle. "*I am come at last, only a little slow,*" he said about himself.[12] On his advice we bought a few blankets.

After that we had *supper* with Joe Kipp. We had to leave before seven. Our two big suitcases were picked up by Joe Kipp already Friday morning, but it was impossible to load them up. The barrels with *candy* also had to stay behind. Tatsey did have his two oldest boys, John and Joe, with him and a second wagon, but it was loaded with all kinds of purchases. We drove with Tatsey himself and were seated well on the second bench of the big *buggy*. Its back was fully loaded with boxes, pieces of stove pipes etc. etc. Tatsey covered us with a blanket and gave us another blanket for a cushion. He tucked everything in tightly and then went *en route*.

The evening is beautiful. The sky splendidly red. The wind calmed down more and more. Now we drove along a road or something that seemed almost a road, then straight across the prairie. We went up and down hills, drive along beautiful cliffs, with sharp curves. We encountered whole herds of horses; sometimes we saw them from a distance and sometimes they ran neighing towards our wagons to gallop away in great haste when they had nearly approached us. The landscape was very beautiful. The hills contrasted sharply against the evening sky. How bumpy is the road. The wagon jolts so much! Will the glass plates survive? I can hardly believe that.

Holy Family Mission. Courtesy of Marquette University Archives.
The remains of the mission building with the present church in the background.

Wilma Adams, daughter of Hattie Guardipee, looking at pictures of her father and grandfather.
Bear Chief (DJdJ 1910). | Willy's sketch of their tent and a tipi.

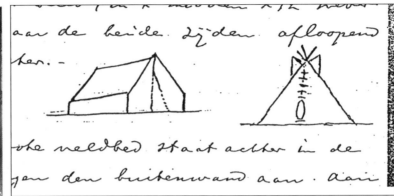

After driving a few hours we saw the mission buildings from a distance and the shrubbery along Two Medicine River.[13] About 9:30 we arrived in deep twilight at Tatsey's tents and are welcomed by Tatsey's wife, his very old mother and Hattie Gardepee, his married daughter.[14] There, for the first time in my life, I was in an Indian dwelling, an Indian tent. There was a big camp bed, on which we had to sit and Hattie Guardipee asked me to take off my coat. A kind of small stove with a crackling fire was burning.

Hattie's little daughter, a few months old, hung in a *cradle* and cried sadly. She took the child out and showed us the white face of the small redskin child.[15] "Yes, *I am proud of her*," she said. We had already talked while sitting on the wagon, with her husband, a big, heavy, handsome Indian with a very friendly and not too serious look. All of Tatsey's small children were already sleeping in their grandmother's tent.[16] We walked around outside a little while, looked at the fabric tied to a little pole and dedicated by Bear Chief to the sun and Uhlenbeck went for a little while to Bear Chief's cabin, which is ten minutes away.[17] He did talk to his friend he had met the previous year, but found him halfway in bed.

Tatsey has three tents, very close together. His own tent, where we will eat three times per day, grandmother's tent and our tent, which is completely new. That same evening we got the big camp bed from Tatsey's tent. He and his wife laid our new blankets on it. He also brought us a blanket for the floor and spreads it out in front of the camp bed. "That will be nice, Mrs. Uhlenbeck," he said. "You cannot sleep on the floor. It is always damp. We are used to it." So here we were in our new house, a long tent, a *square tent*, as one calls these tents, as opposed to the old-fashioned but much nicer Indian tent, the *tipi*. Our tent is about the following size: 4 ¼ meters deep, 3 ¼ meters wide, in the middle 2 ½ meters high, sloping on both sides one meter.

The big camp bed is at the back of the tent, against the outside wall. Later the suitcases and the barrels with *candy* have to be put on both sides. We undress a bit and go to bed and then, lying down, we listen. I heard the grandmother sing *Indian songs* for the baby, who sometimes cried vigorously. I heard the horses run around our tent, neighing gaily, and for a long time I heard the Tatseys chatting among themselves. Then everything became silent and lying down, I looked about our canvas tent. Never will I forget the ride that beautiful evening to one of Tatsey's tents. This first night of our prairie life will never be lost from my memory. We slept gloriously under our new blankets, almost too warm. We did not have sheets yet or pillow covers; they were in our big suitcases.

Two Medicine River.

MRS. UHLENBECK'S DIARY

Saturday, June 10.

On our request Joe Tatsey was going to wake us up at 6:30. But Tatsey's wife was of the opinion that we had to sleep longer after the journey and we did not wake up until 8:00. John brought us a little enamel bucket with water, a small new tin wash bowl, a towel and a piece of soap. We found breakfast prepared and ready in Tatsey's tent. There was again a big fire in the stove. Now there was a very low square table, a very unusual piece of furniture in an Indian tent, set with a white cloth. Bear Chief was already there to welcome me. Bear Chief was in his *Indian hair dress*, his long, thin braids, his primal Indian face. For a long time he shook my hand, all the time looking at me, while he laughed in a most friendly and approving way.

We had breakfast with Tatsey and Bear Chief. We were seated on a little box and have coffee and tea, bread with meager bacon, fried very well, and jelly. Everything was set neatly. For each of us there was a dark gray enamel plate upside down and a matching cup and saucer and a knife and fork. We did not talk for long because we wanted to be at the mission before 9:00 to see Willy and the other mission boys. It is a quarter of an hour from here. Everything is new for me. For the first time I walk over the prairie, see all kinds of plants with whitish leaves; I see bigger or smaller remains of butchered or perished animals.

Before 9:00 we are at the mission. There we first talked with *Father Bougis*, who had arrived 14 days earlier to take the place of *Father Delon*.[18] We talked with *Father Soer* in the parlor and then, after *Father Soer* leaves, Willy enters.[19] He seemed to be a long and supple boy. He is shy, also laughs very shyly; but he looks very friendly. The previous evening Joe Tatsey said, "*Willy is jumping around, saying, now the professor is coming, taking me out of school.*" I also think that he is a very nice boy, but I have only known him a little while. He stayed a while to talk and we were allowed on the grounds and see all the boys, also Lewe Kasoos, Peter Bear Leggings, Jimmy Red Fox & Jimmy Vielle.[20] That was nice and quite different from their sweet little letters. Until 10:00 they were allowed to stay out of school. Willy will, we hope, be together with us for a long time. His father will be sent a letter asking if Willy can stay with us the whole summer holiday.[21] We will pay Tatsey 50 Amer. dollar cents for it. He will sleep with the Tatsey boys and have all his meals with us. That will be nice and I will very soon feel comfortable with him. On our request John and Joe Tatsey have brought the two *buckets* with *candy* and *peanuts* to the mission. The boys are elated with joy. It will be handed out to them at 4:00 when we will come to the mission again and see the distribution for ourselves. So at 10:00 we went again and visited Bear Chief and his wife Elk Yells In The Water, who used to go raiding horses with him. Again Bear Chief shook my hand warmly, again I attentively looked at his broad, dark yellow face, his bony cheekbones, his strong, regular teeth, his somewhat stocky and somewhat too bulky figure.

Bear Chief's wife has pitch black, long hair, which is loose and untidy hanging around her face, parted in the middle. She was wearing a dark blue one-piece cotton dress, the abundance kept together by a broad, copper belt. Just like Bear Chief, she is wearing moccasins. She stood up, shook hands with us and said that Uhlenbeck was her brother and I her sister-in-law. Then we also saw her two little daughters, slight girls of two and four years of age. The smallest was especially very responsive. I took chocolate for them from our tent and the smallest with black and very silky hair, braided into three small, thin braids, repeatedly came back to me to return the empty chocolate papers. We also spoke to their son Sebastian, 16 years old, who in the fall of 1910, after Uhlenbeck's departure, fell from his horse, broke his leg and now has to use two crutches forever, because one leg is much shorter than the other. Bear Chief himself has treated the leg. The boy looks very fragile and lank. "*He looks weak*," Tatsey says about him. Maybe he will not live much longer. He gives us a very friendly look with his dark, soft velvety eyes, and his voice is also soft and friendly. We saw Bear Chief's oldest son, Eddy, 26 years old, a while earlier at the mission.[22] He is a tough guy, a splendid Indian. I remember his brown, leather collar lying around his beautiful neck, his leather high wristbands around his beautifully shaped wrists.

Bear Chief's cabin is rectangular. The front and the back have a small window that I sometimes saw open. There are no curtains. It is made out of logs that lie horizontally. The roof is made of boards and slopes a little bit. Both of the longer walls have a door. Inside, the house is divided into two rooms. Cabins are always built that way. I see a camp bed in both rooms. Apart from the cooking stove I also see a big heating stove at Bear Chief's, which, red and rusty as it is, does not serve as decoration. Both stovepipes stuck separately through the roof. I also see a kind of open cupboard with plates and saucers. We had to sit down immediately on the two wooden chairs. Bear Chief himself lay half-reclined on his bed. Elk Yells-In-The-Water, his wife, was seated on a blanket on the floor and busy peeling thin branches, which look supple.[23] Knife and teeth were her tools. Once she had peeled a branch, she cut it to the right length and straightens it with her teeth. These branches were to serve as cushions in the tipi during the Sun dance week in Browning. Bear Chief gets up, goes to the wall and takes out a little grimy looking bag. It is carefully tied together. He pulls off the little cord and takes out three wooden artifacts, which he brings me with great satisfaction. It is the present which he destined for me a month ago. It is a big wooden drinking bowl with a stem cut out of wood and also an even bigger bowl for soup and a shell-shaped bowl for bread, also hollowed out of wood. All three pieces have colorful drawings: of Indians, *scalps, tipis,* guns, etc. While Bear Chief talked with us, his son Sebastian interpreted. I leave my presents in his cabin, until our suitcases arrive.

MRS. UHLENBECK'S DIARY

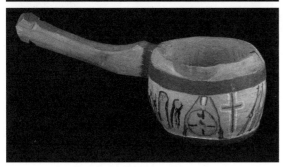

Back at home we soon had to go out for dinner and at 4:00 we were, according to our appointment, at the mission. The boys get half of our treats; they will get the second half later. In their hats the boys get a handful of *candy* and a handful of *peanuts*. When they had finished eating, they tumbled at the high bar and pulled themselves up. We stayed there quite a while. I am already getting used to the boys and know how to distinguish between the five *schrijfindiaantjes*.[24] We had supper with Tatsey and then walked together onto the highest hills. For the first time I saw cacti in the wild, two kinds, the usual one and a spherical one. The spherical one barely pokes up from the ground, no more. The old-fashioned moccasins with long folded up toes serve to protect the feet against the cacti. On top of the hills we had a splendid view of the mountain range and over Two Medicine River. We went to bed at 9:30, without artificial light, with only the light of a beautiful full moon.

Sunday, June 11.

Breakfast with Tatsey at 7:00. First I write a little and at 10:00 we are with Tatsey in the mission church: a small wooden church with a color-fully decorated altar. The men are seated on the right, the women on the left, all on pews. All the mission boys & girls are also seated, as are the teachers and the sisters. Father Soer conducted the service with two choirboys, among them Jimmy Vielle. Later Lewe Kasoos also served; he swayed with the censor. One of the Sisters sang at the organ and sometimes all the girls sang along. Only at the end of the service did everyone sing.

I looked at Tatsey and watched him with his rosary. I also kept look-ing at Bear Chief, who was seated in a corner near the open window. He looked at the beautiful summer weather and played a little with his braids to pass the time. He does not understand a word of the entire ceremony.[25] Also he is not baptized and is one of the many Indians who longs for the *Sandhills.*[26] Next to me an Indian woman was seated. She moves quite a distance when she becomes aware of me. In front of me as well an Indian woman is seated, with a scarf & a blanket and a small boy with thick, medium long, black, untidy hair. On the square in the front we see all the mission children go home in rows. The Indian women also leave the church, carrying their children under blankets on their backs. They firmly hold the ends of the blankets in the front with their hands. A very small child about one year old, for example, clinging firmly to the jacket of the mother or the sister, is also being carried like this. We spoke with Brother Galdes, a Basque.[27] This guy has pretty face; he works in the garden and last year was also very friendly towards Uhlenbeck. We walk back home with Tatsey. On the way we see an Indian grave in the shrubbery near the mission. The coffin is mostly covered by sand, but here and there it is totally uncovered.[28] Tatsey is also being kept back by an Indian on horseback. The talk takes a while; we will wait patiently, which might be the best thing to do. For dinner we got *beacon,* freshly boiled – sliced – cow tongue, small bread buns, which Tatsey's wife bakes herself, cold pears from a tin and cold rice (cooked very wet and

Indian grave about three miles from the mission (DJdJ 1910).

Montana 1911

much too long, but still very tasty) & tea. At 3:30 the five mission friends came visiting. Uhlenbeck had asked permission from Father Soer. It is beautiful, sunny weather. They walk slowly in our direction; we already see them from a distance. They find it too warm to go for a walk, too warm to lie down on the high hills. They would rather stay in our tent, which I now open wide. I am seated on a little empty tin barrel. Peter Bear Leggings & Lewe Kasoos hang on our camp bed. Uhlenbeck is half lying on the floor with Willy & with Jimmy Red Fox and Jimmy Vielle, and is joking with them. I hand out some of our Dutch chocolate and also give them our *hopjes* and peppermint.[29] They look at the small portrait of our queen on the chocolate wrappings and Peter Bear Leggings takes the portrait carefully from the wrapping and puts it in his pocket. The boys were allowed to stay until 6:00. We chat about them after they have walked away, watch them go for some time, and have our supper with Tatsey. Bacon, fried slices of liver & bread with tea. Bear Chief also entered Tatsey's tent and also has his evening meal here when we are finished. Very soon afterwards he enters our tent. He wants to smoke and I give him two packs of tobacco. And then we have a very agreeable evening. Bear Chief is seated on our camp bed, a bit inclined against the wall. Uhlenbeck sits next to him. Tatsey is lying on the floor on the blanket in front of the tent opening with another Indian, a half-blood who is camping here for only a day with a few small children, a few big dogs and a young coyote. The small coyote is tied with a rope on the wagon and is very shy. Tatsey's wife joins us for a while. "*This is good enough for me,*" she says when she is going to sit on the floor after declining my

43

Delegation of 1903 to Washington, D.C. Top row (left to right): Owl Child, Joe Tatsey, Bear Chief, Four Horns, Jack Miller, Mountain Chief. Sitting (left to right): Bill Russell, Little Dog, Curley Bear. Courtesy K. Ross Toole Archives, University of Montana, Missoula

request to take a seat on the camping bed as well. Bear Chief went to lie down on the floor; that is still easier for him. Then Uhlenbeck started to read from his Blackfoot texts in Blackfoot. They take a lot of pleasure in it and Bear Chief is shaking with laughter.

Later Bear Chief also tells about his hunting and adventurous life. With what keen interest I looked at this scene – Bear Chief's facial expression is *second-sighted*. His mouth is nervously moving. His eyes are staring, he moves his hands a lot. He tells about old times, how, while hunting, he thought he saw a buffalo; carefully creeping closer it appeared to be stone. He communicates all of this in deepest earnest. And then he relates how he and Elk Yells In The Water together found a stone in the shape of a boy. They colored the stone and dressed it and many years later – called by the government to New York – he saw this same stone in a museum and he said, "My wife and I, we were the first ones to see this stone."[30]

Tatsey relates that once he saw a very small buffalo of loam, half an arm long, found deep in the ground while ploughing up the soil, where they had been ploughing for many years. And the half-blood Indian told about a skeleton of a prehistoric animal, also found while digging in the soil.[31] While talking and telling they smoke. Later John also joined in and lies down. They left at about 10:00. The moon comes again blood red on the horizon. And when I said, "*Natoos*," Bear Chief had to laugh.[32] What a wonderful evening I have had. How I tried to memorize the face of Bear Chief and Tatsey, as they are totally lost in the stories they are telling. Sometimes I also peered out of the tent. I saw the old grandmother sing lullabies for Cathy, stooping down over the child, sometimes even doubled over.[33] The back of the old woman is very crooked. Sometimes she wants to let walk; but the child does not dare and rather crawls just like the others, the bigger Tatsey children prefer to crawl on the floor. Later I also saw John & Joe Tatsey again on their horses beside their tent. A picturesque group. Tatsey's wife also stands there. Grandmother is seated with Cathy on her lap. Such a group for a photo! That would be a nice souvenir. In the afternoon I took pictures of the mission boys. Nothing will come of it, I think. I will develop them at Badger, my first photographs & then I will make a dark room with a blanket. Now, with the full moon, it is much too light in our tent. I just can't believe that it would ever be dark enough.

Tatsey and his wife, Annie, with their sons Chub and George at a campground near Browning (DJdJ 1910).

Monday, June 12.

Breakfast at 7:00 is bacon, warm small thin pieces of meat, fresh baked buns, coffee and jelly by a glowing stove with John & Charlie Guardipee and with Tatsey.[34] At 8:30 Bear Chief has already entered our tent and chats and smokes a bit. I can now name Tatsey's children. They are Josephine, 21 years: she is not at home. For the time being we will not see her. Then Hattie follows – married to Charlie Guardipee, a very beautiful, slim young woman who is quite polite. However, she does not have that big friendliness like her mother, who is always busy and looks so friendly with her healthy, round face, her beautiful eyes and beautiful teeth. John, the oldest boy, 17 years old, looks like his mother. He is quiet and serious and has a beautiful face, a beautiful figure, though quite small. His leg injury from last year, which made him bedridden for weeks at home and later in a hospital outside the reservation, is completely cured. He never says much, in contrast to Joe – *little Joe* – who is next. A tough, wild, but cheerful, carefree boy who is always very nice to us. He always has something to say and races over the prairie on the wildest horses. Then Lizzy follows. She attends the mission school & will come home for holidays next week and then turns 12 years old. We haven't met her yet. Then follow Robert – or Bob – and Chubby, eight and six years old. Robert is the oldest of the two, but not the most handsome. However, he is the boy who is always with his grandmother and also sleeps in his grandmother's tent. Then Mary Louise follows, a shy, wild girl of five years old. Then George, a very nice young little Indian of about three years old. He is very dark, has

MRS. UHLENBECK'S DIARY

a round little face, with a nose that shall be a beautiful Indian nose in a couple of years. That peculiar line – that beautiful hook is already there. And he has red cheeks, pitch black eyes and hair that hangs untidy today, but yesterday was hanging from his head in small, short braids. I think that he is a most charming child to look at. He wears a light shirt that is tucked into his faded and half worn-out pants. The pants are too long for him and drag under his heels. That is just what makes him so cute. Cathie is the baby; she is well over one year old and is the youngest of Tatsey's ten children. Robert likes to elope once in a while to the Guardipees, which he did on Saturday night, and he was taken back on Sunday.

At 2:00 Uhlenbeck starts to work with Tatsey, but soon Bear Chief also comes. He crouches and has us choose a portrait of his, which were taken when he was in the east. He speaks a lot about his *raids*. Then they would take along dried meat and they survived on it or killed buffaloes on the way and ate that meat. Sometimes days went by when they had no meat and lived on prairie *turnips,* which further down, and still, grow on the prairie. Having no water during the raids was much worse than having no food. When they drank, after having suffered from 24 hours non-stop thirst, they threw up the water again. Bear Chief relates how once he had to pull his friend from the water because otherwise he would have drunk himself to death. While Bear Chief speaks, I observe him again. He has four braids. The top hair at the front is combed to the back and tied together on the top of his head with a dirty string.

At the sides two braids hang forward & two hang down his back. Many Indians wear three braids. The younger ones nearly always have two. His braids are still fine, though they taper off pointedly. On his crown his hair is still dense; it is just a bit greyish at the temples. In one ear he wears a ring, quite big with blue beads. His light cotton shirt is dirty and worn out. The elbows come through. The holes are patched by placing other pieces of other fabric underneath and sewing the edges somewhat. It is this same Indian who sacrificed to the sun on a hill

nearby. There is a short small pole in the ground; attached to it a crosspiece wearing a old, light brown woollen sweater. A grey blanket hangs down to the ground. From the upper arms dangle long colorful pieces of red chequered cotton fabric. They are completely new. Everything is tied together with strings and bouquets of prairie plants and flowers, which are painted, here and there, with a red dye. A white piece of fabric lies on the ground, seemingly blown off the sun offerings. A branch is also stuck in the ground near his *log house.* Pieces of fabric also hang from it. Bear Chief wears moccasins decorated with colorful beads; they are made of antelope leather. His hands are very dark, much darker than Tatsey's hands. His nails are narrow and beautifully shaped and contrast strongly with his dark complexion.

The palms of his hands are nearly white. Bear Chief speaks on and talks about *pemmikan* & how they prepared it. They used to take it with them when they went horse raiding or left on the warpath. They took buffalo meat, boiled it well in a big pot, deboned it, mashed it and saved the marrow. Then they dried the berries, which in the past and currently still grow near the Maria and at Milk River. They would take the fruits, spread them on a buffalo skin, press them out with a stone and dry them in thin layers in the sun, turning the layers over and over. When they were dry enough, then meat and fat and fruits were mixed quickly into a mass. It was excellent food that didn't take up much space. The women & children tasted it first at home and it was also saved for the raids. At that time they did not know about salt yet. Old Mountain Chief, Walter's father, had never been a *chief*.[35] He played around too much and kidnapped others as he happened on them. Painted Wing and Tail Feathers also were never *chiefs*.[36] They were well respected and joined in on the raids, but they did not wish to exercise much influence as this brought along with it many obligations.

While Bear Chief is thus narrating, he suddenly starts to sing. He sings several songs in a steady beat and claps his hands once in a while. The first song is a *scalp song*. And then he goes on to narrate. Apparently he likes to do this. He relives his old times. Going raiding they slept as sheltered as possible. They took branches and bent them toward each other in a tipi shape and covered the big holes with smaller leafed branches and long grass, and at night they lay close to one another and their buffalo skin tunics served as their blankets. When they felt lonely after having been away a long time raiding, the leader sang a song of encouragement. Once, Bear Chief goes on narrating, a strong woman went along on the warpath. All the young Indians were tired. But the strong woman went high on the hill and raised their spirits by singing. One of the younger companions could not take it. So he also stood high on the hill singing encouragement to his brothers, "Soon we will go home; then we will eat cherries and ride the horses we stole from our enemies," etc.[37] He could not allow that courage should come from a woman. However, women did not go often on the *raids*.

Tatsey now tells that there used to be an old medicine man – he died in 1881 – who painted the Indians when they left for war and gave them *medicine*. He also gave *medicine, [said] Bear Chief,* for success with raiding horses and killing enemies. But he also gave them *special medicine* to take along, which they had to use in case they were cornered and surrounded by enemies. That was, namely, a small purse with dirt and *seven tail feathers from an American eagle.* Bear Chief once put some of the dirt in the middle of his hand and blew it over the eagle feathers and he also once applied it to cause a rain shower, a fog and a snowstorm. That same rain, fog and *blizzard* were supposed to enable him to escape.

(Monday). At night we walked around, a nice piece of prairie to the left of Tatsey's tents and we also talked a bit with Sebastian, who is seated in front of the log house in the nice weather. It is still melancholic to see this boy sitting on his chair. He looks so weak. How will he ever grow to be a strong Indian, riding and racing over the wide prairie? Now I take Bear Chief's presents to our tent. John & Joe have picked up our suitcases from Browning. We give all kinds of toys to the Tatsey children, which we brought along for them in our big suitcases. The suitcases stay on the wagon as well as the barrels with *candy*. That is easier with our forthcoming move. I climb onto the wagon, open up one of the suitcases and take the toys out. Joe Tatsey opens the barrel with sweets & I hand some of it out as well. I give each a handful. The second barrel, with the other kind of candies, *the kisses*, stays closed. Joe came and asked me for some *candy* for his grandmother. I now know that the old lady likes it very much and I will treat her more often.

Tuesday, June 13.

Move to "Badgercreek."

We rise quite late; it is nearly 7:30. We have a quick, but very good breakfast. We will *move* to Badger Creek and Tatsey's wife says that it will be quite some time before we get something to eat again. Tatsey and his wife are very busy running around. Grandmother partakes in this. She also carries all kinds of clothes to one of the wagons and shakes the dust out of all kinds of blankets and gathers tent poles. All three tents are taken down quickly and four wagons are being loaded. Each wagon is hitched up with two horses. John with Bobbie & Chubby and all kinds of rubbish are in the front wagon. Hattie is seated on the second; she drives and sometimes nurses the baby. Grandmother with Mary-Louise and George are sitting on top of the wagon with all kinds of bedding and she often takes the little Guardepee on her lap. The old woman wears an old man's headgear and sits completed hunched. Sometimes she really looks very old. I am seated with Tatsey's wife in the third wagon – on the *buggy*, and I have Cathie, her youngest child, on my lap. All of the cattle and horses are driven by Charlie Guardipee & by Joe. The two dogs also walk along. In this way we leave our first camp. I look attentively at several wagons, also at Tatsey's wagon, the fourth one riding behind us and on which Uhlenbeck is also seated. He has an uncomfortable seat, sitting on all kinds of furniture. Tatsey is sitting next to him. We pass the mission and one of the boys is looking to see if any letters have arrived for us.

Completely unexpectedly I suddenly see Two Medicine River in front of me. "*He is awful high, awful high,*" I overhear the Tatseys say to each other. There is a strong current but we still have to wade through. We stand in front of it for quite a while. Tatsey dismounts, says something to his wife. John crosses first. And I have to follow John? Tatsey's wife is asking and immediately she drives down the shore & and we are already splashing through the water. The horses want to drink first. John is in front of us and drives to the opposite side, which is very high. According to his father he chose the wrong direction. Tatsey follows

right behind us and overtakes our vehicle. But soon his wagon stops. One of his horses, that black horse, does not want to go on. Earlier this morning we already saw that it was agitated and Tatsey had already said to Uhlenbeck, "Don't be afraid, professor, he will jump up." But Tatsey's wife firmly overtook the wagon and drove with a firm hand to the opposite side. The shore is also high there. She shouts at the horses again and again: "*Get up – get up!*" The water came into our wagon but before that happened, out of fear of it, I took the little suitcase with the camera on my lap, well, at least beside me on the bench. I think this wading through the river is very peculiar, and it does not seem without danger when the water, as it is now, is that high. Tatsey's wagon, after trying repeatedly, also crosses and now I no longer see Uhlenbeck sitting high on the wagon, completely surrounded by water. Mrs. Tatsey says about the unruly horse, "*He is strong but lazy.*" Now we are on the opposite side. Only Hattie's wagon still has to cross. Tatsey's wife keeps looking anxiously behind her. Grandmother will be afraid, she says. Charlie Guardipee sets himself beside Hattie and he takes the reins and the fourth and last wagon also crosses well. We are waiting for a long time in the bushes. I don't know what for. I think that all the cattle & all the horses have not yet come together. There is a shimmering heat and in the shrubbery at Two Medicine there is no wind at all.

We certainly get a lot of sun on our faces and we don't have our straw hats. Cathie sometimes gets restless and then she wants to be with her mother and she is nursed a few more times. This all happens while driving. After a few hours we finally reach Badger Creek and from a distance we see the camp. I see a lot of tents spread out over a big area. Sometimes we drive very slowly. We are now on a beautiful road over a monotonous prairie. I see again whole herds of horses and also many remains of dead animals. There, in front of us, is the big *ditch camp*.[38] Just Badger Creek still separates us. We also cross this river. It is narrower and not as deep by far; but the bottom is very uneven & rocky and the current is stronger. The camp is beautifully laid out with all kinds of small shrubbery on the shores of the river and the Rocky Mountains in the background. It is 5:00 when we arrive and we left at 11:30. All *ditch camp* horses are just being brought to the river – to Badger. They gallop towards it, some running very fast. All kinds of stuff is unloaded from our wagons. I still have Cathy in my arms. Tatsey's tent is soon set up; after that ours is set up. The third, grandmother's tent, stays on the wagon. Tatsey's wife is again very active. She is exceptionally firm with everything. We have our evening meal at 7:00, after having had our previous meal at 8:00 and we are still not extremely hungry. There is coffee on the table, of which small George poured himself half a cup when the large, high, enamel jug stood on the floor. Fried slices of liver, bacon and bread. Part of the bread had become wet because of the high water that came into the wagon. We also got pears from a can. After that we walk around a bit. Then it started to thunder. The Rockies and the shore of Badger Creek are beautiful. We ask for our big suitcases, which are still on the wagons. They would easily have left them there. Tatsey and Charlie Guardipee, the son-in-law, bring them inside the tent. Now we have our suitcases; we have all kinds of stuff at hand, sheets, covers, etc. Now we also have our lantern, but I haven't taken out the glasses and the little candle is repeatedly blown out. It is windy and it rains hard with the thunder. John and Joe come in for a little while and Joe for the second time picks up matches from his father to light [our candle] again. Now we go to bed, this time blissfully under the sheets.

MRS. UHLENBECK'S DIARY

MONTANA 1911

Wednesday, June 14.

Breakfast with Tatsey.

For the first time potatoes, a bit fried, also bread, bacon and beans from a can. After breakfast I rummage for a long time in our big suitcases. Chubby & George now each get one more flag. They really like that. If we only had more. John gets the big ball. He doesn't think it childish. All bigger Indian boys play with the ball. They all also like to play *baseball.* Earlier we saw John & Joe play with the smaller balls we gave to Bobbie & Chubby. Bill Guardipee, the much younger brother of Charlie, looks us up. Tatsey says about him, *"He is a wild boy, I don't like him."*

Then two Indians come around; one is a very old medicine man. He is quite ugly, wears glasses, has a kind of goiter and is also too fat. *Come up with the Eagle Tail Feathers* is his name, or Brocky.[39] The second Indian is, I think, beautiful. He is about 50 years old, has splendid hair with two shiny, long, heavy braids. Both take their hats off. The medicine man has a white swan wing with him, which he keeps fanning himself with. I give each of them 2 packages of tobacco. They don't smoke, but put it in their pockets. U. reads his Blackfoot texts aloud to them. Sometimes they laugh, especially about the meaning of some clan names, about the *Lone coffeemaker.* Finally they rise. They shake hands with me again and the old medicine man presents me with his swan wing.

It is sometimes warm; sometimes a cool wind is blowing. A small Indian boy of ±10 years of age enters our tent. He has 3 braids and doesn't know a word of English. He only stammers, *"Candy."* But we still don't have our *candy.* Now, Wednesday afternoon, the barrels

Thursday, June 15.

with sweets are still on the wagon. An Indian cannot get himself to do anything and still Tatsey says repeatedly about someone else, that he is *lazy*. We also see the father of the small mission boy. Billie Russel is an extremely fat and ugly man with an exceptionally low & coarse voice.[40] His mother is a full-blooded Blackfoot, not Peigan. His father is a negro. This mix only occurs twice at this reservation. (Before we went to Badger on Tuesday we handed out our scarves to the five mission boys. They could choose & and it made them very happy. And Willy also got a purse. We held the gift distribution in the parlor of the mission. Joe Tatsey will also get one from us and with that our scarves were gone.) Walter Mountain Chief comes at 7:00.[41] That is very nice. I was sitting on the slope with the small Tatseys and suddenly I heard my name. Uhlenbeck had also just arrived and it is good to see how happy Walter is. He immediately asks after Jan de Jong, is not shy at all and I think that he has a handsome face, now that he looks so cheerful.[42] He looks much more cheerful than I had imagined. He says that he will come very often and also promises to come with us to Holland. Tatsey has no time to come with us & and he thinks John is still too young. After Walter, Joe & John drop by for a chat. (In the afternoon Uhlenbeck worked with Tatsey, who, just like me, stood up to see three heavy wagons crossing the Badger. I see many lashings & from a distance I hear, *"Get up!"* When I enter our tent again, Tatsey is seated on the floor; that is the easiest posture for him. Bear Chief also comes in. He came on horseback from his *log house* to visit us again and he tells us a story. I give Tatsey a little stool. He sits on it a while, then slides down & and rather lounges on the floor. Bear Chief, who was first seated on our camp bed, goes to sit on the floor also). After Walter & John with Joe there are no more visitors.

Breakfast with the two of us. Not much fun! For the first time we have some kind of American corn. It is boiled in water and it is no treat. After breakfast Tatsey comes to work. After eating we walk together throughout the whole camp and speak for a little while with Walter's parents & the oldest sister, Kassoos.[43] In the old days old Mountain Chief must have been a very beautiful Indian. He has a distinguished face. His wife, not Walter's mother, is small & slim, has red squinty eyes and also wears a broad, leather-fitted copper belt, as does Bear Chief's wife. She also has copper bracelets around both wrists, 12 thin rings held together with a small plate at one side. In the afternoon Uhlenbeck works with Tatsey; later we walk around a bit in the neighborhood. It thunders somewhat. Splendid sky. *Supper* with Tatsey.

Very soon after our evening meal we get visitors until 10:30. First the same Indian came again, the one who came the other day with Brocky. He shows us his beautiful medal, which hangs from a colorful ribbon, and his crucifix. He stays a very long time. His name is Big Moon.[44] Hattie Guardipee serves a little while as the interpreter. Then a fat Indian of about 35 years of age comes in. Uhlenbeck starts to read aloud his texts. The fat man leaves and I think, "It must certainly bore you," but after a few minutes he comes back with his *women folk*, an old meager woman with a characteristic face and a younger, fatter and cheerful one in her colorful blanket. The women sit down in the opening of the tent. I hand out tobacco and *candy* and Uhlenbeck reads aloud for a long time.[45] The women double up with laughter. After they leave the old Mountain Chief & his wife came on foot to visit us. He limps a bit on one of his legs. Both visitors take a place on our camp bed: she on the left, he on the right. They also eat *candy*. I see that she gives some of her sweets to her husband, who eats them with great enjoyment. He puts the tobacco in his pocket. We regret very much that Tatsey is not there. Bill Guardipee comes but he is of no help. A nice Indian girl helps us: Irene Shoots.[46] She is 12 years old & the daughter of the policeman. She speaks Peigan and English & and is a great help to us. After the

Mountain Chiefs have already left, Big Nose suddenly comes in.[47] He suddenly peers into our tent. He is a nice, shy little boy. Uhlenbeck is joking a lot with him & takes his hat off his head and then Big Nose becomes a bit less shy. Irene is still staying there & David Big Nose also comes in.[48] He is a tall Indian, 19 years old. We sit quite a while by the lantern. It is getting cold. Irene is singing for us and teaches us the refrain of *Redwing:* it sounds delightful. After their departure I try to develop the photograph that I took in the tent of the mission boys last Sunday. It does not work at all. Then I fill the three frames with new plates for the first time. We go to bed around 12:00.

Friday, June 16.

At 7:30 Tatsey himself calls us. Fortunately I was already up. We breakfast without him. He was already up at 4:00. Uhlenbeck works with him from 9 to 11. It is very warm. 92 in the tent. I am sewing his shirt a bit, outside, as well as I can in the shade. We have *dinner* at 11:15. Tatsey's wife wants to go to Birch Creek, to their *log house*, to pick up a few things. After the meal we first walk around a while and then pay a visit to the Mountain Chiefs. The old man nods at us, but just mounts his horse & rides off. In his tent we see his wife, his daughter – the mother of Lewe Kasoos, another old Indian woman, who laughs at everything, and her attractive daughter.

There are many blankets in this tent. The inside is very well set up. Blankets and beds all around. On the floor are all kinds of pieces of fabric, old blankets and pieces of jute. The stove is still burning. There are a few pans on it, including a frying pan with high sides that has a few pieces of fat in it and a piece of meat. The old woman shows us a saddle with wooden stirrups from the old times. Two artifacts to scrape buffalo hides and now cow hides. Young dogs walk in & out and are chased away once in a while with a piece of firewood. All kinds of ornaments and also an eagle wing hang on the wall.

The old woman pours some water in a wash bowl and calmly washes her hands. She rinses them repeatedly. No soap. She takes an old, black piece of fabric and wipes off her hands & also her face with it. She wears the same long, wide and very light-colored piece of clothing (white with big, black seams). The front is very dirty, especially the apron, and here & there it is

MRS. UHLENBECK'S DIARY

in tatters with a few right-angle tears. They don't like to sew or to patch up. On her head she has a very old, worn-out man's hat that makes her even uglier. Further, she has squinty eyes & not many teeth. Her daughter is quite handsome, a genuine Indian face, with lips a bit too fat. We spend quite a nice quarter of an hour there. We had to be back home at 2:00. Then Tatsey shows up. It is warm. Irene hauls water for us from the river. George is sometimes curiously dirty. His dirty, old & and too-long pants have disappeared today without a trace – maybe in the laundry – and now he walks around just dressed in a small shirt-like dress.

Once in a while, when George enters our tent and sits down beside his father, Tatsey straightens this piece of clothing. Grandmother keeps the children busy. Apart from Cathie, Chubby, who was nauseated yesterday, went along to Birch Creek. Now grandmother is not wearing her blue cotton dress. Now she wears a very faded light brown skirt and a very light green jacket, which makes her look quite funny. She again wears the blue hair band. Uhlenbeck works the whole afternoon with Tatsey in order to finish a story because he has to go to Helena for court cases & shall be away certainly for a couple of days.[49] In the evening more visitors dropped by.

Saturday, June 17.

Today John will work with Uhlenbeck for the first time instead of his dad, who shall leave after eating. At first it is very strange for John; he acts somewhat shy and has to sum up all kinds of inflections in Peigan for Uhlenbeck.

We eat something with Tatsey, who is already dressed in a travel outfit: a light blue striped cotton shirt, with which the green silk tie clashes awfully. Tatsey takes three letters and one postcard for me to Browning. Joe brings him there. I look after the *buggy*. We walk around the camp a bit and then again working with John starts. Sometimes he has a hard time staying awake. It is 90° again. We have *supper* together & and then all kinds of visitors drop by, among them Nelson Henault, the stepfather of Peter Bear Leggings.[50] At 9:30 it starts to thunder. This is accompanied by strong wind. The weather soon calms down.

Sunday, June 18.

Beaver dance. We are being painted.

It is beautiful weather. Not too warm. Sunday is a rest day so John has the day off. We are advised that no Grass dance will take place, because there is no big drum in the camp. We are very disappointed about it & we walk through the camp to ask Walter about it. He is not at home but we meet him on horseback and he rides back beside us to our tent & then sits chatting cheerily on our camp bed. Also about Holland. Maybe he will come with us. He likes the idea, if only he could be spared. He stays till mealtime with us and says that a Beaver dance will be held in a tipi quite close to us. "*They will start*," he says, when he is about to leave. Once in a while we hear music. We eat very quickly, close our tent & go there. Arriving at the *tipi* we see many people who are peering inside. We also peer inside & Uhlenbeck tells me that I should go a bit further in. I do this & plan to sit in front of the opening. They nod us inside & we are allowed in the circle.

The *tipi* is large & spacious. Thirty or more people sit close to each other in a circle with their backs close to the *tipi* wall. There are children, among them very small ones, with their mothers; the men sit on the right, the women on the left. Uhlenbeck is seated among the men, I among the women. A few buckets full of a dark fluid stand in the middle of the *tipi*. It appears to be coffee. A little box with crackers and a few tin or can bowls with bread and fruits stands on a piece of sailcloth, all these items are still half covered. Someone puts a small piece of fire on the floor in the circle of the tipi. Branches are being spread over it by an old woman. It is soon smoking and burning merrily.

An Indian sits on the floor in front of a half circle of women. His entire face is painted red and it seems as if his forehead is flattened. The shape of his forehead is completely different from other Indians. He sits the whole afternoon on a blanket, which is half wrapped around his hips, a very normal & certainly not uneasy posture. In front of him a hide lies spread out; it is not big and on it is a square dark brown board, covered in copper nails similar to the belts of the women.[51] To the left lies a massive piece of brown tobacco. It is almost hard. To the right is a big can with matches. Two pipes are lying in front of the board, the tobacco board. One of them has figures of animals on the long stem, among them are beavers. Repeatedly he cuts tobacco from the piece with a knife. On the board he cuts it up as small as possible and then fills his pipe with it and hands this to the woman who sits closest to him and who passes it on to the leader. In the same way the matches are also passed down from person to person. Nobody rises. Nobody walks around. The one who holds the yet unlit pipe is not the one who lights the matches. That is always done by the one who is seated next to him. Everyone (all men) takes turns puffing the pipe. It has a peculiar smell that rises. My clothes are completely impregnated with it. There is also a piece of incense (?) burning on the floor. At least, it smells like incense. All men smoke the pipe. Uhlenbeck also smokes when it is his turn. The men, as well as the women, are wrapped in blankets, but they let them slide down when they sit on the floor. Once in a while they make music. A number of men have rattles, either one or two. They are small rattles, more or less in the shape of an onion tapering off somewhat sharply and with a handle. They make them themselves out of leather. They put pebbles in them & paint them red. They beat the floor with them, powerfully and rhythmically. It makes a monotonous sound that is always recognizable from far away. They still don't start to dance. Though the leader, the holder of the beaver roll, sings and murmurs time and again and sometimes others join in.[52]

The leader repeatedly makes blessing movements. He is middle-aged. Between him and the first woman in the half circle of women is a big package. This is the sacred beaver roll. In it are all kinds of animal skins carefully wrapped: beavers, otters, smaller four-legged animals and birds. Very seriously the package is being opened. A beaver skin is taken out and painted with red paint.

Now the food is being uncovered. We will eat first. Everyone produces tin plates & bowls. All this is also passed down until the woman

who is seated with the food is, so to speak, surrounded by the plates. Now the distribution starts. She takes a very big flat long piece of rectangular bread, bends it over her knee and makes two pieces, again she breaks it in two pieces and then breaks off smaller pieces. She puts one piece on one side of each plate. Now she hands out the fruits. There is one very big bowl full of pears & peaches and its juice (from the cans). With a small bowl she dishes up the fruits and puts on each plate two or three pieces & some juice. She also puts on each plate a few crackers. They are in quite small piles. One woman comes in with a piece of butter. This is also being distributed. Now someone pours the coffee into the bowls and it is passed out. Everyone wants to have some. Some of the people sitting outside also get something.

When everything is distributed & passed out, the empty bowls & the empty buckets are taken away. Then the leader prays and blesses the food. Now they eat & drink and talk & laugh. When this 'eating process' is finished, all empty saucers & plates are passed down again. In my area some women have saved a lot of the food and wrapped it in a dirty or slightly dirty cloth. Now they will start to dance, says a woman who sits beside me who speaks English. She is the wife of Marceau, the police officer, & the sister of Walter. Her name is Rosy.[53] Her husband is seated next to Uhlenbeck & sometimes advises him.[54] And yes, the dancing starts. Very strange. Male and female dancers rise. They elegantly wrap the blanket around their shoulders & dance with very small shuffling paces into the open space left of the middle. Their rhythm with all dancing movements is incredibly steady. It is as if the rocking movement were innate to them. The dancers barely move around. At first the men dance, then the women. The male or female leader holds a sacred beaver pelt in the right hand, he holds it up and the female or male dancers following, assume the same posture. Instead of the sacred beaver pelt, they hold up a slip of their blanket. It is a beautiful group. Ten Indians sing & beat the rattles. A few women near me also keep singing along.

Music without words. Sometimes a single woman suddenly screeches in between. It is a shrill scream that is held a long time at different pitches and in our ears it sounds quite odd.[55] While dancing, some female dancers about 30 years old make eye contact with me as if they want to say "You are my sister," or, when it happens with Uhlenbeck, "You are my brother." Now the consecration to the sun, the face painting, starts. The men are painted on the forehead & chin by the leader: the women are painted by the female leader of the Beaver dance. Uhlenbeck also goes forward to have himself painted & he says that I should not duck it. We also have the middle part of our forehead and chin painted. Uhlenbeck got red dye in his beard. Now we are included in their circle. To duck this would not have been polite. They gave us a place in their midst & we certainly should appreciate this. The dancing took a long time. We were in the *tipi* from 12:30 until after 4:00, all the time sitting on the floor on the same place. They perform several dances, sometimes acting as if they were animals, imitating the buffalo, the bear or the dog. An old Indian woman with her hair hanging down & and a slim face barked & growled peculiarly well, to the great pleasure of the others. Laughing increased when they imitated the buffaloes, imitating the horns with their fingers. When someone standing in front of you makes an animal movement, you were supposed to imitate it. Uhlenbeck did this a few times & is appreciated for it very much. The seriousness diminished by the end of the dance. The ceremony might allow for this. In the end about 10 Indians danced along. The dancing is now finished & they go eat again. Two covered buckets, containing pearl barley and prunes, had been left covered. Well, that is what it looks like. It is a thick, grayish porridge. Little piles are being distributed on plates and passed out again. We leave the *tipi* & talk outside a bit about it. *"You will wash your religion off,"* one Indian says to us, when we say that we intend to go to our *tipi*.[56]

At home we immediately wash off the red dye. It comes off easily. It is a very fine paint. The leader sticks a few fingers in a pouch & puts the powder in the other palm & if necessary he drops some saliva on it, rubs both hands firmly together and paints face & chin with the ball of the hand. The women also smoked a lot. They had other pipes, I believe their own pipes, which are filled again & again by the same Indian. All women continuously walked around the back of the pipe filler. I forgot to do this when I came forward to have myself painted by an elder Indian woman. So for the first time in my life I have seen a Beaver dance, have sat for the first time in my life in a *tipi*. It was a splendid scene, never will I forget it.

In the afternoon it was sometimes quite warm, even very warm & also quite unhygienic. Near me I saw an Indian woman and a child, both with a lot of rashes on their faces. In the early evening we again heard a drum. "Oh," Joe Tatsey said, "a medicine man certainly is busy singing." Later it appears that still another dance has been performed.

We stayed in or next to our tent & still get more visitors, among them Morning Eagle, the old, friendly Indian of ±94 years of age.[57] He came on horseback & was wearing beautiful, colorful *leggings* of light blue flannel, trimmed with scarlet fabric & decorated with beads. He also gets tobacco & *candy*. He ate a bit of the *candy*. The stepfather of Peter Bear Leggings dropped by with two brothers & later Peter himself, who stayed a long time talking.[58] Now Lizzy Tatsey has come home from the mission school, but much to our regret Joe did not bring along Willy Kennedy. He was not allowed because Willy's father has not yet sent a response. His father seems to have remarried lately & might want his children with him on the Milk River, where he has his ranch. Anyway, we hope that Willy will still stay with us, even if it is not for long. Later in the evening we again have visitors. First the youngest Morgan comes and later Irene Shoots, who sings songs. First *Redwing*, then *Rainbow* and then *Life is but a dream*. At 10:00 all the visitors are gone and we go to bed.[59]

58

Belt that Willy used as a hat band. Walter Mountain Chief's present to Willy. Courtesy Rijksmuseum voor Volkenkunde, Leiden

Monday, June 19.

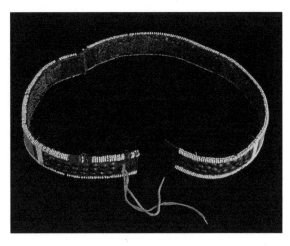

We are still busy getting dressed when Morning Eagle comes along again. He is not yet allowed inside. We first go for a quick breakfast with *hot cakes* and now the ancient man (now on foot with a cane) comes for a little while into our tent. Even so, Uhlenbeck starts working with John. First I am writing outside. But it starts to get windy and I have to go inside because otherwise my papers will blow away. John again reports how he spends his day. He lies on our camp bed & once in a while is sleepy.

Today Joe Tatsey wears a new hat, a grey one, and I no longer recognize him, he now looks so different. Lizzy Tatsey seems to be a sweet girl and looks fresh and very nice. I gave her the beautiful doll and the blue necklace. Today Tatsey's wife will do some laundry for us. Tatsey, we hope, will be back tomorrow from Helena. It is very strange that he is not here even though we speak to many Indians. Last night the Indian New Breast came visiting with wife and child, the same one who in the afternoon also participated in the Beaver dance.[60] I saw her dancing too. I gave them tobacco and *candy*. The little Indian played delightfully with his dog, which time and again tried to snap the sweets from his hand. They did not speak a word of English and did not stay very long. All these different visits were nice, but it does not fill a lot of time. We hope that we will see the mission boys a lot. Sunday night Lewe dropped by for a little while. *"I am in a hurry,"* he shouted & and directly drove off with a few boys. Two on one horse. A very common sight. Lewe laughed a lot; however, just like his uncle/brother Walter, he might not come very often. And we would regret this very much.

After supper we are just sitting in our tent after walking around a bit and Uhlenbeck says, "I don't mind if nobody comes tonight for a change. I don't like it when these Indians we don't know walk in and out; I would rather have no one visit." And then came two of the most cheerful girls, one of them a younger sister of Irene.[61] They speak English quite well, get sweets and both look very tidy and clean. They have just left when Peter's stepfather arrives.[62] Rather, he does not enter, but sticks both hands through the door opening for some *candy*. The man is fond of it. He is 31 years old; his wife, Peter's mother, is 49. She has several children, also married ones, and also grandchildren.[63] "I think that is just right," he says, "that I am so many years younger than she is; now I can work for her and were it the other way around, that would not go." Then Walter arrives and we have a very pleasant and long chat with him. He is tired, he says, and that is why he is lying comfortably on our bed. He acts as if he feels very much at home. A long time later I will be able to imagine Walter lying on the right side of our bed, Uhlenbeck is always seated on the left. I give Walter *candy* & tobacco. Yes, he says, he will eat something first, because the other times I forgot about it. But he does not eat much *candy* and then smokes happily. The tent is closed, which is much cosier.

Around 5:00 or 6:00 there is half a storm. Everything in our tent is covered with dust. Tatsey's wife takes the initiative to look after our tent. She drives new little poles into the ground and also two end poles at the two corners. That makes it much stronger. The wind keeps blowing right in the front. After half an hour the wind calms down a little. With the white swan wing[64] I kind of dust off the bed & suitcases. I arrange everything more or less neatly on the bed and carry the big floor blanket outside. I can no longer stand to see how much sand & mess is on it. I let the blanket air in the wind. Clouds of dust come out. An Indian woman looks at it and laughs at me. That is much better. It isn't like the same tent anymore.

Yes, Walter is quite nice, when I think again about him. You can talk with this Indian about many issues. He contends that he understands what a "life insurance" stands for, etc., etc. We also talk about our Jan with him. He took the small string of beads from his head and gives it to Uhlenbeck for his head & that is why I give Walter another embroidery for his hat, an embroidery I made and took with me for the Indians. It is red on white with a cross-stitch. He appreciates this gift. "It will be a souvenir from you," Walter says. He gives me a belt, which, however, is much too small for a belt, as he sees for himself. I will wear it as a hat band and while he still sits there, I put it around my high, straw hat. Later I get yet another belt, but he has to wear it himself first in the Sundance week; he has to dance with it first. Give this small belt, he says, to one of your *friends* later, but I won't do that; I want to keep it for myself. Walter also liked those little Dutch matches very much and that's why I give him a box. He wears his work clothes; they looks good on him. He was already up since 3:00. It must be hard work for the Indian who works in the *ditch* and has to take care of many horses and lots of cows. With the July feasts I will see Walter dance in his splendid dance outfit.[65] That will be nice!

In the evening the Henaults were around, Walter also asked for and got a loan of 10 dollars. His sister wanted to go to Browning and buy beads with it for the upcoming feasts. During the feast week or earlier, he will return the money. When Walter leaves that evening – he is too tired to stay any longer – I give him some candies for his mother. The old people, especially his father, are so fond of them. When they were visiting us, I saw how he first finished his own sweets and then took some more from his wife's lap and ate them with great enjoyment. The Henaults, no full blooded Indians; they don't look at all like it, are still capable of carrying on a nice conversation. Especially Stephan has a lot to say. Nelson is not so boisterous & the slimmest of the three is very quiet. That fat one, Stephan, talks about the Indians just as Tatsey does. "Yes," he says, "*Bear Chief is a nice man*," and he regrets that he drinks whiskey when he can get it. He also talks about Morning Eagle, the very old Indian with the colorful leggings, who was able to find guns in muddy water when he was young and many Indians who were there witnessed this miracle. He also says nice things about Tatsey's mother. That is what is so nice about these Indians; they can speak so nicely about one another. And he also thinks it very unfortunate that in the summer the Indians waste their money and then suffer in the winter. "*They are starving then*," he says.

When the Henaults left also, George Day Rider came in.[66] What a beautiful Indian! What handsome figure. He is young, about 23. What a beautiful complexion. His black hair hangs neatly over his forehead. And the shape and expression of the face is so beautiful, and so soft & friendly. I am allowed to photograph him; later when George Day Rider has left, Uhlenbeck goes for a stroll. I will change the plates. In the afternoon I photographed the old grandmother with Lizzy, Hatty & child, and the child alone without clothes. I crawl under the dark, grey blanket with the small red lantern. I think that this works well and I file the plates in the carton boxes with the slots that I took with me. If only it weren't so terribly dusty under the blankets & if I had more water, I would like to develop once more. Just taking pictures does not satisfy me. I haven't yet used the tripod. I just do it manually. Does this make sense? When I am done with the plates in the tent, I first make the camp bed. First I air the blankets & sheets & now I go outside where U. is talking to John in half darkness.

Now it is very quiet; no wind at all and a glittering starry sky. Here & there are lit Indian camps. That is a nice sight. John has to go to sleep. He rose very early and he has been teaching U. four to five hours. In this heat sometimes he could not stay awake. On his request U. threw water on John's head & that refreshed him. John is very nice these days. But sitting still for a long time is quite a thing for him. It tires me out,

Tuesday, June 20.

he says. Peter also said Sunday night, "Now my legs are tired from sitting still so long." Then, sitting on our camping bed, he was reading *Bearchief's life story*. We go to bed when it gets dark. In the middle of the night I hear the wind blow hard.

Again we have breakfast together. It will be nice when Tatsey is home again. I think that he will only be coming on Wednesday, because, coming from Browning he might go first to *Birch,* to his *log house*. U. works the whole morning again with John: 1 ½ notebooks already filled by teacher John! Jimmy Vielle, a mission kid, tells "a story about a day at the *mission school*." That is nice & so Jimmy keeps John awake. Joe Tatsey has never *taught*. I don't think that he knows how to & he knows that himself too. Today it is cool, even very cool. In the afternoon 60 to 62. No sun at all. Sometimes some rain, sometimes some thunder. We badly need the rain for the dust. The sky is very gray. In the afternoon Joe Tatsey enters the tent. He will go at once to Browning, to pick up his father. "*You look like a sport*," I say. He wears a light, clean shirt. White with black polka dots. Very unpractical & this for Joe who is so dirty & so untidy. He also wears the leather cuffs again: around his neck our Dutch scarf. And that suits him well.

We received the mail from Charlie Guardipee, who has been to the mission.[67] A letter from Mama, a postcard from Anna Hesseling, a letter & postcard from Jan.[68] He already left "Eugene" by the 15th of June in order to return to Holland. He does not seem happy, returning again to Holland & leaving America so soon. Exactly seven months here & back. John's teaching continues again. Nelson Henault comes in & asks U. to write a letter for him to a shopkeeper in Browning. "*I am too lazy,*" he says about himself. Still he signs it himself. Peter Bear Leggings was hit by a horse and injured a finger of his right hand. That is quite a nuisance for Peter. U. and Peter bring some sweets & tobacco to Morning Eagle, the old Indian. After dinner he, the old Indian, was just napping on the floor. "*Sokàpe,*" he says.[69] The old man was very happy with it. Peter's sister, Mary – her mother always says Mareje – also comes to our tent for a moment. A very nice girl, she laughs in a friendly way, but is very shy. Once in a while I get busy with the belt I am making for Walter. Walter is very happy when he gets something I have made myself.

Wednesday, June 21.

Now it is raining hard. Our tent is only partly open. We have supper together. It is still raining a lot and we stay in our tent. It stops raining at 7:30. We walk around a bit & see Mary Bear Leggings & Irene Shoots and both spend a while in our tent.[70] Now Mary is not so shy anymore. She was allowed to choose a picture & chooses "the evening meal."[71] Now Irene chooses one. She is also a most sweet Indian girl. Her father, *captain of the police*, only speaks Peigan. Her mother also doesn't speak English. With my little brother, she says, I speak English and, she says, "I will keep this picture for a very long time." And then she says that she has read *an awful [sic] nice story* in a book that she got from a sister. It is about a *gipsy girl*. And immediately she runs out of our tent to pick up the book. She brings it back with her. Mary says "that I am that grey." She is not so shy anymore, 10 years old & attending the mission school for three years already & this year she was confirmed. She repairs her own clothes at the mission school & Peter's too. Irene suddenly says, "*Don't you hear, Mary, your mother is calling you*," & yes, there we hear Mareje! Mareje! Mary went at once. Irene stays on, even when the candle is lit. We later undress in the twilight and we go to bed after ten o'clock.

It is nice weather & not warm. For breakfast we have fried potatoes, warm rice & beans for the first time I believe. At dinner only the vegetables are warm: peas & beans. They just serve whatever suits them. And still they laugh when one confuses dinner and supper. While we are having breakfast together, George wakes up. He is only wearing a short, thin shirt. John helps him with his *pan[t]s*. Later Chubby wakes up too. I see our laundry on the lines. I think it hung there all night too. The line goes from tent to tent. After breakfast we stroll around a bit, but I am going to prepare everything: notebook, ink, paper etc. Uhlenbeck comes back with Sam Scabby Robe.[72] What a handsome Indian! What nice, shiny eyes! Maybe too soft, too feminine. He has a beautiful figure, tall, fine and very slim. He has two long, thick braids. He takes off his cowboy hat & sits down on our camping bed. He does not smoke. He eats the candy with gusto.

I am allowed to take his picture; that is a stroke of luck. But then he says that he has to return to his tent first to redo his braids. I tell him that I, too, have a comb. So he sits down on the peanut bucket and I hand him my mirror & my comb. He also asks for some water. I pour some into our wash tin. Then one by one he undoes his heavy braids, combs his hair carefully & wets the hair on the top of his head thoroughly, and then braids it. At the end of the braids again the scarlet band gets wrapped around them about ten times, as tight as possible; the longest hair ends still stick out. I see this quite often even though Sam made an effort to hide the ends completely. Over the forehead, just above the eyes, the hair is short, this is the forelock which is combed back after having been wetted thoroughly. He also does this with great care: time & again checking in the mirror whether the part comes out well enough. The hair is done. He cleans the comb himself, winding the loose hairs around his finger, taking them & putting them carefully in the pocket of his shirt! I had not expected such tidiness from our Indian.

Now he comes outside & I will have the privilege of taking his picture. I take his picture with John and then I take him again alone *en face*

Montana 1911

and *en profile.* And then Sam leaves again. "I will be back tonight with Walter," he says. Now John comes in again and I sit down in the back of the tent and read the pretty story that was brought to me by our Indian friend Irene Shoots. When I have finished the nice story that took place at the Missouri, I diligently start my needlework for Walter. In the tent I hear that, apart from John, Peter Bear Leggings a *teacher.* Peter is nice and narrates a long story about playing *horseshoe* and John apparently thinks Peter's company is a nice change.

I look out over our plateau. Sometimes it is miraculously splendid. The sky is now partly clouded: beautiful woolly clouds, exceptionally beautiful. Now Hatty arrives on horseback, her child on her arm, wrapped in a blanket. She is wearing her dark blue dress again, a cowboy hat on her head. It is a pretty sight. I see her finely shaped profile, so finely shaped. I look at her again & again. She dismounts at the tent of her parents & is about to do our laundry. I guess that she is going to iron. I saw the big, rusty irons on the stove as well as a very big square tin with water, certainly originally for oil or something else. Yesterday I saw the old grandmother and Lizzy from time to time busy with laundry; all kinds of empty tins, *cans* and *buckets* were being put on the stove.

At night there is much like thundering. Mary drops by for a little while with her father. We promise him medicine for his cough and the next morning I hand it to Mary. At night lots of thunder, sometimes strong wind & lots of rain.

Thursday, June 22.

For breakfast beans, peas, stewed prunes & raspberries. It strikes me again that Tatsey's wife does not plan at all; sometimes she hands out too much and then she suddenly does not have enough. From time to time the sky suddenly gets cloudy & it still gets very warm. At 12:00 the thermometer in the open tent is again on 92. Half an hour later it is 80. The temperature changes the whole afternoon. A warm wind is blowing.

From 6:00 to 8:00 thunder with some rain. At 8:00 we walk a long time there & back over the prairie. Just over the mountains, the Rockies, the sky is exceptionally splendid, a crisp-clear, sharp line. The sun peeks for a moment over the little river valley where, there are a few tents & the two tipis where we hear the drumming so often. Opposite the Rockies there are heavy clouds, dark gray clouds. Fierce lightning beams. In the morning Mary came for quite a while. Sometimes she helps with a bit with *teaching* & sometimes John has a lot of fun. In the afternoon they work hard until 5:00. Then Mary comes again, this time with her mother. She is a sturdy, very good-natured Indian woman and she only knows how to say (in Peigan) that her Peter is such a good boy and is very shy. In the evening I shall develop a picture & change the plates. The plate appears to be of Sam with John. Unfortunately the heads are not entirely on it. Still I get more confident making pictures. I develop them under the grey blanket which was very, very dusty. In the light of the little red lantern I can easily see big fluffs of dust in the bowl. It frightens me & later I wonder that something good has come from that plate so far. Outside Uhlenbeck is losing his patience. He wants to come in with a few Indian visitors, Jimmy Shoots & Peter Vielle.[73] A moment earlier Jimmy Shoots was very kind & greeted Uhlenbeck with "*How do you do Mr. Uhlenbeck?*" That was really kind & not at all shy. Uhlenbeck reads a page aloud from his texts; all three are seated around the lantern; I walk in and out with my glass plate, to rinse it. Earlier we had a visit from six Indians. Oliver Day Rider is among them, & he laughs & talks; the younger one, Joe, actually doesn't say anything.[74] There is also an Indian ±50 years old. They eat sweets & smoke. The old Indian keeps his hat in his hand; this is quite polite. He looks very pleased when I give him two packages of tobacco and a handful of sweets. When he leaves he shakes hands. The other Indians don't do this. He has thick, long braids, and is employed at the *ditch* & looks tired. The knees of his pants are patched – very uncommon, but still, just under the knee there is a big tear through which his bare leg shows. Apparently he is ashamed of it. He pulls the tear together & holds his hand in front of it. He also said that the text was so good, continuously repeating the last word. This evening we only get to bed at 11:00. Later it started to thunder badly again and then to lighten a lot. There is no wind with it. Maybe that is why these storms are hanging around so long. It is heard later at the Old Agency that three horses were hit by lightning and killed.[75]

Friday, June 23.

The weather is fine. Not warm & lots of clouds. I take a picture of John, of John with U. & of the three little ones, Bob, Chub & George, + Bobbie stands there each time has his fingers in his mouth. George wants to turn around each time. Still it succeeds because John helps a bit. For the first time I use the tripod & the frosted glass. Tatsey's wife laughs and is looking at us around the corner of her tent. For the second time Chubby brings a nice bouquet of wild roses. They smell lovely; the whole tent smells of them. He has put them again in an empty vegetable tin with fresh water and on the little rose branches are lots of small green leaves. Uhlenbeck & John are quietly working – body parts of the cow – and once in a while they talk about several boys and about the killing of animals. Irene is going with her father & mother to the *Old Agency* and takes Uhlenbeck's letter for Jan with her. Tatsey is still not back. But we get somewhat used to his absence. John progresses in the right direction but still I long to see *the old man,* that is Tatsey, come back.

The Green children are quite rude & sometimes peek right into the front of our tent; they are the only ones who do this.[76] It is a wild group; they always look shabby & very dirty. Among them I always see a very pretty girl of 11 years old. She wears a very tattered dress. Chest & shoulders are completely uncovered. The dress is her only piece of clothing. She is a splendid child. If they had not been looking so cheekily out of their eyes, I would have liked to give them sweets, but I fear that they know no boundaries. They live near us in a small tipi. One very small wagon is their only means of transport. Peter's father's wagons look much better than Tatsey's. Tatsey's *buggy* is bleached by the sun, broken everywhere & patched here & there with ropes & wire and the wood has split everywhere. It is an old run-down wagon & actually dangerous to cross a river in. Sometimes I see a covered *buggy.*

Harness, saddles, everything always just lie outside. When it rains very hard, everything is put under the wagon & then covered with sailcloth. But everything is all over the place. They don't know about thriftiness. John currently wears his rubber boots for three weeks. They al-

ready look worn. They cost five dollars. Is that not dreadful? How can they pay for it? I overheard Tatsey say that it is quite something for him to buy shoes for all his children, but now I understand this. Sometimes John's shoes hold out one whole winter. Joe sometimes is not nice at all. He is a wild Indian; once in a while he is lectured: that is necessary if we want to stay friends with him, but it is not enjoyable. In the late afternoon it gets warm again, even very warm, 90 to 92°. At 5:00 it starts to cool off. It starts to thunder, which goes on for the entire evening with a hard wind.

Saturday, June 24.

First cold afternoon.

I rise at 7:30. The thermometer reads 50°; it is really cold & it is windy & raining hard. About ten o'clock the weather gets nice and I take a picture of Uhlenbeck with John again – because the previous evening I developed the one of *John* too early in the evening. John alone & Peter & Mary Bear Leggings. When Joe leaves at eleven for Browning to pick up his father who seems to have arrived in Browning, he takes with him my letters to Mama & the sisters.[77] The weather is deteriorating again fast. The wind picks up again, it also starts to rain hard & the temperature drops again. In the morning Uhlenbeck does not work with John. John is suffering a *belly-ache* & would rather stroll around & chat. And John promises to write to us later on a regular basis. While it is raining hard, we eat.

John spends the whole afternoon in our tent. The thermometer sinks to 40° & stays that low. Late that evening it is 42°. And it does not go higher. It is most unpleasantly cold in the tent. It is blowing in from all sides around us & at the side of the suitcases a lot of water enters the tent. I pull the suitcases towards me & put thick sticks underneath. U. is so cold in the afternoon that he crawls into his bed at 3.00 with big, thick night socks. John is going to sit at the foot end on his feet to warm them, but this does not help much either. I use the meths burner for the first time, & for warmth and to stay cosy the three of us drink bouillon. It is blowing so hard that Uhlenbeck can hardly hear John, even though they sit next to each other. It is a cold, unpleasant afternoon, but our mood is very good. John is so nice and relates in Peigan everything about his leg injury of last year. We both get along very well with John. At the end of the afternoon Uhlenbeck tells him a brief account of the *Karamasows*.[78] John listens attentively, also to the introduction of *The thousand and one nights*.[79] Later I would like to get a good English translation of the *1001 nights*. U. would love to send this to John later.

At 6:00 we pick up our evening meal. U. is not yet warmed up & I give him a sip of rum. I wrap myself in my raincoat & John closes our tent behind me. From tent to tent there is nothing but puddles. In Tatsey's tent it is warm & cosy; all the children are inside. Only granny is missing. After the evening meal U. also puts on his woollen night suit & I wrap myself in my scarf & we hang around in our tent like that. Then Nelson Henault arrives. He wants to tell a story to Uhlenbeck, but he does not know real Indian stories. That is why he tells about his marriage to his last wife, the mother of Peter & Mary Bear Leggings.[80] He does this very simply & slowly. Uhlenbeck is sometimes bored. Henault coughs badly. I present him with a handful of sweets. "I can live on candy & sweets & pies," he says. And he eats one piece of sweet after another although I advise against it because he is so hoarse & coughs so much. He also gets very cold & keeps shivering. This afternoon he got very wet. When he is done with the wedding story, he leaves at once. He longs for a crackling wood fire.

It has now stopped raining, meaning, as good as stopped. We run around a while on the plain where the puddles have already disappeared. I give U. another big gulp of rum. Only now does he warm up. He still paces up & down outside. In our tent earlier we made all kind of foot movements and I counted to 500. Kicking continuously to get warm. I go home before Uhlenbeck to fix the bed, make it snug & so warm, that once in it, it will be warm. I also put the blanket from the candy barrels on the bed, also all kinds of coats & capes. I am barely finished when U. comes in with Jimmy Shoots & Peter Vielle. They cannot sit on the camp bed this time: it is just too splendidly prepared for the night. The two boys sit on the suitcase, U. & I on the folding chair and on the bucket. The lantern is on the high suitcase. John also drops by & sits beside the lantern. All three eat sweets & Jimmy smokes. When the lantern burns, Jimmy pulls up his high, multicolored collar & U. later says to me that this is only to prevent us from seeing his face. When they have left, I carefully close the tent & we sleep gloriously under all the blankets.

Sunday, June 25.

First Indian Graves. Otter dance.

The thermometer reads 50. It is still very windy, also in the tent. We only rise at 8:00 & only eat breakfast at 8:30. Chubby gives us little animal cutouts, a cow & a few horses. We don't go to our tent, but walk through the whole camp, cross the *ditch* and walk a long time over the hills & through the ravines. On a high hill is a very big Indian graveyard. I count 13 large & small coffins.[81] Most of the coffins are closed or completely empty. Four coffins have their lids completely or partly gone, and the wrapped skeletons are partly visible. The face is uncovered. Some fingers still have rings, one arm still a bracelet. Bodies are wrapped in blankets & animal skins. All kinds of household items lie around: pans, spoons, hair combs, etc. Some of the bodies still wear a necklace of beads and a leather belt studded with copper nails lies beside them.[82]

We don't dare take anything with us. Not one ornament, not one little bone, completely bleached by rain & sunshine. And yet we want to do so very much as a souvenir of this morning. A skull just lies unattached in a coffin, also completely bleached, but we want to but dare not take anything with us. These graves have been terribly vandalized. Some coffins are partly plundered, either by human hands or by cattle searching for food in the months the snow is piled up high. I only pick, as keepsakes, a few flowers that blossom between the coffins. We encounter still another graveyard. It looks like a small log house. The coffins, big & small, all intact, are fenced in & covered with beams. Through the big cracks we count eight coffins. On top is a small coffin, & the white cotton, which here & there sticks out through the coffin, still looks good. We walk back over the hills and drop by old Mountain Chief's. There I see *Indian trunks*. Painted in bright colors, with beautiful forms. Mountain Chief wanted to tell us something about those graves but we did not understand him very well. At 11:30 we are back home. First I write a little, then we go eat. I also take up the old pictures we took with us to give away to the Tatsey's & to Irene. At one thirty it is 64°. We go out. Maybe there is some dancing. Old Eagle Calf rides to the front of our tent on horseback and asks whether we would like to come right away. An Otter dance will take place in the tipi near ours. We are allowed in immediately. Uhlenbeck again between the men, I again sit down among the women. Like the Beaver dance it is again a religious ceremony and also a blessing for the children. Eagle Calf is the leader (the much younger brother of grandmother and Tatsey's uncle). The sacred otter is produced & the blanket unfolded in deep earnest. I distinctly see the whole otter pelt. Eagle Calf repeatedly brushes the head of the animal & paints it & murmurs his prayers over the mouth. The bells, five or six little bells tied together with a string that goes with it, are also painted. They don't use rattles now, but three drums, one fairly big & two smaller ones. The drums are dried above the fire first. Eagle Calf has a pouch with dirt. He shakes it out in front of him on the floor, makes a hole in the middle and sticks two fingers in on all four sides. Now, with the sacrificial tongs he puts a piece of burning brand – from the center fire – in the hole. Herbs are strewn on top of this. It smells like incense. Eagle Calf repeatedly holds his hands above it and brushes his hair on the left & on the right with it. They dance during the singing, but in a sitting posture. Squatted, their bodies adopt the dancing movement.

I love seeing this beautiful, regular, rocking movement. Several women go with their children, older or very young, to the old medicine man and receive a blessing. The woman then takes the otter in her hand, presses it against her heart & murmurs a long time over the head of the animal. Then mother & child were painted. Several older children are also painted. Uhlenbeck gets the sacred otter paint on his forehead as well. Women & children are painted on the face, the hands and partly on the arm. Earlier they ate. Now also food & drinks are ready to be consumed. Both of us get coffee with sugar & cream. Someone also passes out black coffee and sugar & water and I get all kinds of things on a tin plate, pears & gingersnaps. First I have to break a piece of the cracker, have to put it in front of me & can only eat afterwards.[83] I eat

Onlookers observing a ceremony (DJdJ 1910).

a whole cracker & later passed down my plate, saying that I have already had dinner, which is the truth. I drink my cup of coffee down quickly – out of politeness – & a woman then fills it at once. This whole ceremony only takes 1 ¼ hours: so very different than the Beaver dance.

Afterwards we stroll around a while, sit down in our tent a while & are a bit bored. After our evening meal we repeatedly walk through the whole camp, watch the races for a while, – from a distance a nice sight – and in the end we are very disappointed because on this Sunday night no more dances are performed. I enter our tent around 9:30 to change plates & to develop John. It does not turn out very well. The entire plate is dusty. On top of it there is a red stain over the legs. Among other things, I did not have enough water. That caused me the next morning to empty all bottles, to store all the material & decide forever not to develop anymore on the prairie. This is quite a disappointment. In the future I will change the plates late at night, store them carefully and develop everything later at home. Now the idea of giving away portraits is gone completely. I am barely done with the plates when U. comes in with Walter and Henry Hungry, a relative whom U. met further down near other camps.[84] Walter had approached Uhlenbeck & went directly to shake hands with him, while a whole circle of Indians was gathered around them. I give Walter & his cousin *candy* & they eat it. Walter likes our matches again so much, that I promise them to him "when we leave." Shortly before Walter, Nelson Henault dropped in with Mary. Peter appears to be shy. They will *move* on Monday and Peter might leave without saying goodbye to us. How sad for us. That boy used to write so nicely & all by himself, and now that we are near him, he does not show up very often. Walter liked to see the pretty decoration on my hat.

Monday, June 26.

Cool weather. Quite windy. It is a nasty morning for Uhlenbeck because Tatsey is not yet back. Joe will go again to Browning. And also John cannot make it to come and *teach*. He has not said anything, but he is not at home and that is it. At 11:30 Uhlenbeck sees John & talks to him. He will teach in the afternoon. Finally about 3:00 Tatsey comes home!! Finally! He has been away for 10 days. At 5:30 we talk to him. U. works with John & Jimmy Vielle from 2:30 until 5:30. Joe, Wild Bill, Lewe Kasoos & his cousin & Davy Rutherford also show up. They are very noisy in & later around the tent. Only the small Rutherford is quiet, listens & is allowed to stay in.[85] Just after our meal we pay a visit to Mrs. Saintgodard, who was with us the day before.[86] She is with her son-in-law Steward Hazelett. (Her daughter is a little sick and sits on her bed on the floor).[87]

We have the evening meal again with Tatsey. That is nice again. Then we walk around a bit & talk with Racine.[88] His father is a Frenchman from St. Louis; his mother is a full-blooded Peigan. We are seated in our tent. Outside U. meets with Jimmy Shoots & Peter Vielle; they will come but we did not await their visit because we hear loud drumming & singing. We hastily walk towards this & enter the tent. It is dark inside; a fantastic light. In the corner a small candle is burning. Fifteen Indians are sitting & lying on the floor around a big drum & they take turns beating it, always a few drummers at the same time. It is the same kind of drum used for the Grass dances. They drum hard, very hard. It is wild music, sometimes very passionate. One of the players rose immediately upon our entering & gave me the small bench he had been sitting on, then continued drumming. They certainly are polite & forthcoming with us. Very different from last year. It strikes Uhlenbeck all the time. But this does not mean that they always keep us busy. There are long or short moments of exceptionally great satisfaction. In between are times when, at least Uhlenbeck, does not know what to do. It is the waiting & waiting & that makes him very nervous. Apart from the players & singers there are still more Indians, mostly little boys who sit on the floor &

Tuesday, June 27.

hang around. There are no women or girls at all. The tent is completely full. We understand one English word: *One more.* And we get one more song. Some songs sound familiar from the Beaver dance. An Indian song finishes abruptly. At least for our ears. At the end of this evening everyone rises in a wild way. The candle is knocked over & gets extinguished. Everyone goes directly outside. We first have to orient ourselves to where our camp is located. I fix our bed & still change the plates first.

It is cool & rainy. Currently there are two *teachers,* father & son, & one would think that some work would get done. But it does not happen! John contends he has something else to do & we don't see Tatsey at breakfast. He has already gone out. After 10:00 he still does not show up, though he is now in his tent. We keep hearing him talk. They are curious people, *them Indians!* How! You have no idea. Then Tatsey plods along. He says that we will not go to Browning tomorrow the 28th, but only Friday the 30th of June, & now Uhlenbeck arranges with Tatsey how these days should be scheduled & he quietly sits down to work with Tatsey. After having eaten I make a picture of Joe on horseback, Joe on foot, & Joe with Jim Four Horns & Willy Owl Child.[89] Joe is in an exceptionally good mood, now that I have taken his picture three times. Father Owl Child enters our tent with Willy, a boy in poor health who suffers from fits & is so shy that he sometimes covers his face with his hands & suddenly runs out of our tent.[90] After a quarter of an hour the boy comes in again though. Now we no longer address him & I give him some more sweets. He has a very soft face & his four braids hang untidily around his face. Owl Child narrates a short history. Tatsey interprets. Four Horns also drops by and narrates a few short histories. He was in the army & then was a sergeant. He shows us his papers. Now he is old and has loose & greyish hair. They work until 5:30. Then we have a cosy evening meal with Tatsey. In the evening we stroll around. It is almost constantly raining. That is somewhat annoying. Sometimes we play for a moment with the small Tatseys. Especially Mary Louise & George love it & Bob & Chubby are also crazy about it. We don't get visitors. It is cold & damp inside the tent also. We sit together a bit by our lantern and I change the plates again. We don't go to bed late. John is still not at home. He had to drive *ways off,* 15 American miles. One American mile is about 1.8 kilometers.

Wednesday, June 28.

It is rather cold and a strong wind is blowing. We have breakfast alone. We stroll around & meet *Stephan Henault's girl*, a very blond child with a long, gray fluffy coat & a curious scarlet woollen cap that fully covers her blond hair & ends in a point with a tassel behind her back.[91] She addresses us herself. Her father is Nelson's brother, that fat, well-spoken brother. Her mother's name is Stuart, *white woman.*[92] Her grandfather Stuart, she tells us, came from England. Half an hour later she enters our tent. I was looking for something in the suitcase. I feel something scratch on my back; it is the little Mabel.[93] We sit on our camp bed & she tells that she is not *lonesome* at school. She is a busy child & speaks English fluently. She does not know much Peigan. At 10:00, 10:30, Tatsey arrives & Mabel leaves: she wants to help her mother. She shows us a handkerchief tied into a pocket in which she had *a* lot of small beads and a bodice for her doll, already half done with beads, just like the beadwork on belts and on moccasins. *"It is not yet finished,"* she says.

Yesterday I wrote to Lise Bussemaker.[94] The letter is still in our suitcase, I think until Friday, when we hope to go to Browning. After having eaten, while we were walking about the camps, Lewe Kasoos delivered a letter from Mama to us, a reply to my letter from New York. I reflect on Four Horns again: he has such ugly, rough working hands and also big feet, just like us. Tatsey also told us that he is known for his big hands & feet and still Four Horns is known as being full blooded. Uhlenbeck works with Tatsey until it is time for the evening meal. The history of *"The deserted children"* is finished. After our meal we stroll around again & at 2:30 Tatsey returns. However he only worked for a short while and then it is, *"Excuse me, professor,"* & John shall come to replace his father. John does come, but the boy is very sleepy. Tatsey stays away until the evening meal; Uhlenbeck is not very happy about it. We walked for a second time to Kjeijo's tipi; but there is nobody.[95] It is said that Kjeijo can tell stories about the beaver.[96]

That evening Uhlenbeck is in a bad mood. The boys Four Horns & Day Rider enter our tent, eat & smoke something, but don't say much. A rather old Indian woman with black, thick loose-hanging hair and entirely wrapped in a blanket, first stands in front of our tent & then comes in with her little daughter. The child coughs a lot, and looks, though sturdy & robust, unhealthy, puffed lips & and infected eyes. Sometimes she covers her face completely with a cloth. She looks like an unhappy child. Irene Shoots also comes in. They stay a short while. We stroll around again & play a bit with Chubby & Bobbie & George. We also talk briefly with Stephan Henault & his wife & Mabel. Mabel is on horseback with her mother. Then Spearson & Jimmy Vielle enter our tent.[97] I light the lantern & we have a good time. Spearson is a very big Indian boy & a mission kid. Very friendly & outgoing. He also is not shy with me in the least. He looks with U. at the texts, which he had not yet seen. From a distance we hear again the big *drum* just like Sunday night. When the boys leave at 10:00, we walk there. Someone drums and sings, but it is now completely dark in the tent; no candle is burning and it seems not to be that quiet. We stay listening outside and when we walk back to our camp & are already in bed, we hear singing again once in a while.

Thursday, June 29.

The weather is calm & beautiful, not too warm. At 9:00 70° in the tent. Tatsey arrives at 9:30 and they work on the *Seven Stars*. Tomorrow & Friday, John & Joe will go together to Birch and will also store all kinds of stuff that doesn't have to be taken to Browning in a *log house* nearby. We will also have our candy and a big suitcase, the biggest, brought to that log house. Again we will not move on Friday; it is being postponed again & now said to be on Saturday. We will see the dancing, I hope, on Sunday. After the *Sundance week* we will return to Badger. But not to exactly the same spot; it seems more downhill. Yesterday I wrote to Jo van Leeuwen & I am about to start a letter to Haarlem.[98] I sit at the back of our tent & I see the splendid Rockies. The green of the forest there is bright. It is as if I am so close. Last night we saw a herd of 60 horses wade through the creek. In long rows they went galloping & nickering towards the water & in a broad, dense mass they plunged into the Badger. Across the river they first ran for a while further, then, grazing, they spread out. That was a pretty sight. I love to look at such small occurrences. We also saw about 15 mules, beautiful, black, brown & white colored. They don't work at the ditch, but drag lumber & pull the heavy loads to the *reclamation camps.*

We had to pay $2.50 for the laundry!! I think that this is very much. That caused me this morning to wash a few things myself. A few towels, a few handkerchiefs & a cushion cover. That went well. Now it hangs drying on the lines of our tent. Now I am going to sit in front of our tent & I barely sit there long when three horsemen approach me. Again a pretty sight and a nice, cheerful sensation. They are Walter, Sam & the older son Owl Child.[99] They talk & smoke & I will take a picture of them. Walter inquires whether his hair looks good. He runs with his fingers through his tuft & takes Uhlenbeck's straw hat in his hand. Sam takes my sun hat; I think that they do this because of the beautiful bead decorations. First I just photograph Walter alone. Then Walter and Sam. And then, at last, the three of them. It is noontime. Too bad, but we have to go for dinner. In the afternoon, Walter returns. Tatsey goes for a while to his own tent. (I did this – he later says – because otherwise Walter will not feel free.) Because of the rain, we closed the tent & now we notice after a while that Walter's horse is gone. Jim Black Bone, who was also with us talking, notices it.[100] It frightened Walter & as fast as he can, he runs onto the prairie. Now he has to go home on foot & and where is the *saddle horse?* That is quite a trip home, I think. Standing in the rain must have bored him. That evening Walter comes back for a chat. His horse has been found. Now he is riding another one. It is very nice of Walter to come that often.

Friday, June 30.

It rains a bit again & all kinds of Indians are moving. Tatsey is not moving on Saturday, postponement again, for the umpteenth time, we only hear that now. He wants to leave on Sunday to arrive in Browning on Monday and to stay overnight at Two Medicine to let the horses rest. So the plans have been changed again & I suddenly get the idea that it would be better if Walter could move us, we would then certainly arrive on time. Uhlenbeck also thinks this a good idea. We ask Joe to ask Walter, who is at the *reclamation store* to get his cheque, to come & he comes at once with Joe. Walter agrees to move both of us to Browning. He will use his own horses & Tatsey will lend his *buggy*. I hurry to pack a lot of things, because we want to move this afternoon. I am just done packing when Walter returns & stops for a moment in front of our tent, "Professor I will be able to move you *tomorrow*!" Good Walter, Saturday then. He promises to come by early, at 9:00. The weather worsens & worsens. By mealtime the prairie between our tents is flooded. There is a downpour that lasts for a long time. In hindsight it is fortunate that Walter did not depart with us. After supper a lot of water runs into our tent under the suitcases that are sitting on stones & thick branches. We spend quite a miserable hour. No more visitors show up & we already go to bed around 9:00, 9:30.

Saturday, July 1.

Departure to Browning.

It is blowing hard, very hard & it is cold. No chance for rain & that is good enough. At 8:30 Walter comes and mentions that he still has to find his horses. They are gone again. And to Uhlenbeck he says, "Professor, would you mind taking my cheque of 50 dollar and pay me 20 now from it? I would like to buy from this man *a good horse* for 20 dollars." U. does not accept the cheque, but loans Walter another 20 dollars. He now has a debt of 20 dollars. For bringing us to Browning he may discount 4 dollars. Walter is back at 9:30, now with three horses. But now Tatsey's *buggy* is not at home; he rode out with it, thinking surely that Walter would not be back soon. At 10:00 Tatsey is back home. He harnesses at once & we leave. And Tatsey says, I shall not be in Browning before Tuesday. He changes the day of arrival quite often and doesn't even want to stay until the dancing is finished, it appears from what he is saying now, when the three of us are in the little *buggy*! It is awfully cramped. Still, the three of us start up the bench.

Standing closely to the shore of the river, Walter remarks that he still does not have a lash. He wants to pick one up quickly from the shrubbery at Badgers. Uhlenbeck is holding onto the reins for the time being & I then thought, if the horses start to run now & enter the water with us, then Walter would be pretty surprised. But Walter returns with a lash & soon sits up at his place again. We have only driven a little further when it is decided that it is better that Uhlenbeck sits in front of Walter & me on the floor. Now he sits folded up on a blanket, our dark grey bedspread, & Walter repeatedly says, "Hold on to my legs, otherwise you might fall off. Then someone will find you later on the prairie and will think that I murdered you for your money," & Walter enjoys his vivid fantasy.

The first hour I don't like the ride. I don't feel comfortable, also because Uhlenbeck leans over against the splashboards & they look so old & so rickety. I keep thinking that the old *buggy* will break into two pieces, especially now that it is loaded in such an unusual way, and Walter

also says a few times, "*I don't like such a rough buggy.*" It is patched with wire or wrapped with ropes in several places. Actually I don't understand at all how such an unseemly wreck of a wagon can stand such terrible jolts & bumps. After Two Medicine River, which we now cross on the bridge, I enjoy the ride much more. But it is & stays cold, a real cold wind. At the river we see several tents. Also a tent with Walter's mother & sister Kasoos. Lewe's mother waves her hand when I greet her. Walter dismounts a moment & from his mother's tent, who is camping here for the night, he takes oats for his horses. From Two Medicine River until Browning we ride the same road as on June 9 with Tatsey. It is the *trail* from Browning to the mission. "*Professor,*" says Walter, "*take the reins for a moment. I want to get down, lay (on the ground) on the grass & smoke a little.*" And so he does. Uhlenbeck takes Walter's place on the bench & I also dismount & pace up & down. Walter has being lying down and smoking at ease in the grass & approaches the coach with "*Professor, some flowers,*" and Uhlenbeck gets a few pretty, small flowers from the Indian. It is touching of him. I will dry them & take them with me. Later I put a few of the yellow flowers in my purse.

We drive on. Uhlenbeck gets very stiff and will be very happy when we arrive. There is a very strong wind; I also get very cold & the road is miserably bad. Lots of rain the previous day & lots of driving. Potholes & pits & puddles everywhere. Walter sometimes tries to circle around the worst spots. He takes good care of us & I often watch him proudly. It is such a comforting thought to be such good friends with a redskin. Fortunately the journey is over! I will remember this

Sunday, July 2.

ride for a very long time & I still picture Walter in front of me. The old beat-up hat on his head, the scarlet scarf loosely tied around his neck. I look so often at his face, driving through the small lakes & sometimes flying through puddles of mud so everything splashes up in your face.

We halt at Joe Kipp's. We will have to stay there; fortunately we still get something to eat there. We settle into room n°. 8. It is dirty & quite dark, but is level, but as dirty as bad the room we had from Joe Kipp last time, but I don't care. The big oval meat platter that is used instead of a plate, the very big, soapy potatoes and the peas in a sauce of flour & milk & water are an attraction for me. I am in the mood to approve of everything because I am going to watch the Indians dancing. I don't understand it very well myself. After supper Charlie Camp suddenly rushes towards us with his mother. We have to go to her place for a moment and have to promise to return the next day for dinner or at supper time. First we want to decline, but apparently, that doesn't go over well. It would appear as if we were too proud. She says: Charlie wants you to so much. So we promise to come for dinner Sunday at 1:00. We are walking to the *camps,* are being followed continuously by Charley & his younger brother Eddy.[101] Charley still seems to be the same boy as last year. Walking through the *camps* he says to Uhlenbeck, "*Let's go & buy something.*" Uhlenbeck does not like that. Last year it was always, "*Give me a nickle.*" In front of Joe Kipp's hotel we talk to Dr. Grinnell & Mrs. He also comes here to attend the dance parties at Browning & will go with Mrs. to the mountains immediately afterwards. It is the Dr. Grinnell from New York of the *Blackfoot Lodge Tales.*[102] We just sit a bit in our room, afterwards stroll around, meet Walter on a beautifully harnessed horse. Now he wears the hat with my embroidery & I tell him again that it suits him so well and then he laughs so friendly and I see all of his beautiful teeth. We have *supper,* stroll around some more, sit a bit in our room and already go to bed at 9:00.

The weather is good. Not much wind. No sun and thin clouds. After breakfast we walk on the prairie in an easterly direction. Everything is new for me. (We go along the *whisky row.*) It is very beautiful on the prairie & the mountains are splendid. And such a lot of flowers. Often the prairie looks blue because of the *aconites*: lots of low rose bushes, sometimes no higher than ten centimeters & still full of *roses* & buds. The pleasant rose smell blows towards me. The aconite also smells good, very aromatic. Everywhere also small sunflowers & red, scarlet small flowers, which I have never seen before but from the train between Chicago & Browning. I wondered then & did not know whether they were flowers or a kind of seed. I have never seen them at Two Medicine & Badger. We just get back at noon. It has been a glorious morning & I have seen one more part of the prairie where I had not been before.

Walter arrives soon. First he sits on a chair, but the *poor fellow* is not happy at all. He is now allowed onto our bed; I offer it to him. He returns ten dollars to Uhlenbeck so the debt is now 16 dollars. Walter tells a lot: about his own mother, who was so tidy, who did laundry every week & wanted chickens so badly, about both of his marriages. How his first wife left him & his child, whom he had never seen, died young, about his second wife, which went as badly, because he left her etc. etc. Then Walter looks so serious & so sad, as if he wants to cry. Jan, Uhlenbeck & I really like this Indian a lot.[103] We have an idea. As long as Tatsey is not yet here & we are staying in Joe Kipp's inn, we have to walk up & down, then losing a lot of time, & it is very tiring. So we ask Walter whether we can have something to eat with his family. Walter says at once that this is quite possible. We will pay his sister each time (Rosy). So we will have our meals in Rosy's tipi. "If I had a *tipi* of my own," says Walter, "then I would give your meals for free, now I cannot offer that."

Walter has to go because it is 1:00 & we have to go for dinner with Charlie Camp's mother, now remarried to Nixon, the government smithy. We have our dinner there with Nixon himself, his brother, his wife, three girls & the two boys. Beans, tasty potatoes, bacon, bread & cake, prunes

Monday, July 3.

also and rice or pearl barley with raisins & coffee. We stayed there a full hour & thanked them for their great hospitality. Charley ate quietly & did not say much. I do not find this outing very amusing. I rather like being among the redskins than with this half American, half Indian ambience. We went back to our room at Joe Kipp's. Uhlenbeck takes a nap, while I set myself to writing. At four we went to the *camp*, looking to see whether the grand entree would take place. But afterwards it appeared that there will be no grand entree at all. Several Indian wagons arrive at different times. Still, life & movement start to stir in the future dancing grounds. Now we see there are a lot of *tipis*, some sacred *tipis* and others painted with all kinds of animals: buffaloes, elk, otter, leeches. On one, thunder is depicted. It is quite peculiar to see all these ancient tipis that are transferred from generation to generation or are passed on to strangers because of one event or another. I begin to long more & more for tomorrow. In the *camp* Maggy (from Badger) suddenly flies towards me & nearly embraces me. Once back at Joe Kipp's we go to bed early.[104]

We don't rise too late & still there is no breakfast left. So we noticed that Joe Kipp upholds strict order. So we go out & at Sherburne's we buy two mouth organs. One is for Charley Camp, who is already waiting for us at Sherburne's. The other one is destined for Peter Bear Leggings. Having arrived in the *camps*, we stroll around & buy some cakes and eat them while we walk. It is tiring to walk around like this until noon. There is not much to do, but still the place is bristling with Indians. At noon we arrive at Walter's sister's *tipi* (the otter *tipi*). But Walter's sister is not even at home. So there is no way that there is something for us to eat. Walter comes outside & invites us into his parent's *tipi* and we are allowed to sit on Walter's bed. It has a beautiful blanket, with pretty figures & quilted from extremely small pieces of fabric. Actually they are very small strips formed into big squares. Inside the tipi it is also beautifully decorated. All kinds of colored pieces of cotton fabric sewn with other colorful figures are hanging there. The fabric is tightly stretched against the underside of the wall. Also hanging about are all kinds of Indian artifacts. Now we also see how these big, high triangles, which Bear Chief's wife made when we visited her for the first time, are being used as a headrest.

In the *tipi* several women are sitting in a circle. Walter's mother, who does not pay much attention to us, sits there as well. Also Walter's sister, who serves us. On the floor, in front of us, she puts sailcloth. We each get a tin plate, a fork & knife & an enamel cup, into which she pours tea. There is warm meat in small pieces, salt, bread, jelly & sugar. Walter's father also comes in & starts to eat at once. He takes a thick piece of white bread, breaks some off & holds a rather large square piece of meat with his hand, cutting from it on a plate. Apparently the old Indian enjoys it very much. He keeps his headscarf on. Lewe also enters the *tipi* & just takes the meat in his hands, in turn biting from the meat or from the bread, & grandmother squints her small eyes while she holds a big bone with both hands and nibbles the meat off it as she is able to with her old teeth. The *puppies* get the remaining bones. We are tired of all the walking up & down & are allowed to stay and sit on Walter's bed. They indicate to us that we should lie down. We each get a kind of a cushion & I also get covered with a blanket, and both of us fall asleep for a very long time. But Walter is the first to leave; only a few women remain. Grandfather and Lewe also went outside. At 2:00 we wake up & leave at once. We pay Lewe's mother one dollar. Walter thought that half a dollar was fine, but we did not agree. Especially during the holidays they have good use for some money & we don't want to appear stingy. First we walk around for a while in the big circle; then we watch for a few hours at the raising of the *Medicine* [sic] *Lodge*, the large arbor. For wind protection, there is a steady wind, it is cold, there is hardly any sunshine & once in a while a few drops of rain fall, we sit for a long time against a pile of green branches that are ready to be used for covering off the Medicine Lodge.

Suddenly William Kennedy shows up. Uhlenbeck will treat him and gives him a *quarter*; he goes to buy something with it & soon he returns with two bags. He was hungry, he said, because he did not have a meal at noon. He first eats cookies baked with figs in between, not quite such a treat, then fruits, among which are tomatoes, just raw. Willy leaves. He wants to go look for a train and steal a *drive*. We stroll a bit & hear music. Near Mountain Chief's tipi a *Crow dance* is in progress.[105] We watch it for a long time. It is too crowded to get in. Around the tipi it is also crowded with spectators. Indians from several tribes perform the

MRS. UHLENBECK'S DIARY

dances. Among them we see Peigans we know. The non-Peigan women are dressed differently & also their faces are somewhat different. One woman has a disfigured face. She is missing her nose – and wears a nose cloth. She is one of the three Peigan women on the *reservation* whose nose was cut off by her husband because of adultery. She is now remarried and behaves not in the least modestly. The cutting of nose or ears used to be a common & recurring punishment.[106]

Also at this dance animals are honoured; among them we see the *ground squirrel,* & children are now also painted by an old Indian woman. The men have small drums. The women dance alone, but stay while dancing in one spot. They are all beautifully dressed in splendid colors. We talk to Peter & Mary. A moment later Irene also shows up. At 6:00 we meet up with Walter, who comes to watch & listen. He says that his sister has our evening meal ready for us. We enter her *tipi,* which is not as beautiful as her father's is. Again a sailcloth is placed before us on the floor; but it is not very tidy. We sit down on her bed, a bit crouched or crosswise. The blankets are also not as beautiful: very dark blue. We get bread with butter & jelly & coffee & tomatoes. The woman herself and her cousin leave. They say that they want to watch the Crow dance. But we think that they might have done it out of modesty, to leave us to our privacy. A few times someone peers inside and leaves when seeing only white strangers are there. Her son Patrick comes in, he is about eight years old and dressed in a leather *Crow Indian* shirt, beautifully decorated with beads.[107] Later we also see an adult Indian in a very beautiful shirt. We arrange with Walter's sister, who comes in for a moment, that the next day we will have dinner with her at noon & then we will pay her two dollars for the two meals because now she did not have change & so now we don't pay her. We watch the *Crow dance* & talk to Mrs. Grinnell, a moment later also with Mr. Grinnell. Later, when we stroll around, we also talk to Albert Spearson, who is very shy now, and at 8:00 we are back in Browning. This evening hardly anything is going on in the camps. The next day we will go there in time. Then we will

first see the grand entrée, then the first Grass dance and by the evening *the raising of the pole,* meaning that the big, heavy middle beam will be placed in front of the *Medicine Lodge,* the biggest ceremony of the whole week. First confession for the women will take place with the medicine woman, the woman who gives the *Medicine Lodge.* Now she lives in her own tipi near the arbor & fasts for three days. She should be a woman whose behavior and ways are impeccable.

Tuesday, July 4.

Indian Grass dances.

We have breakfast at Joe Kipp's inn. Fried eggs & *hot cakes*. At the post office we find a letter from Anna Hesseling and a postcard from Nelly Hartman. At Sherburne's we change a few dollars in order to get some nickels & quarters. We arrive at the camps when still not much is going on. In between the branches we look up our old spot. It is blowing hard & Uhlenbeck has a bad cold. We sit there a long time. Bear Chief comes along & stays a long time. His face is painted: red cheeks, yellow forehead with an almost round sun circle. Willy also drops by & stays and plays a bit. We get even more visitors. Mrs. Grinnell sits herself down with us and brings along Mrs. Martin with a small boy.[108] Mr. Cole, a *lecturer* from Chicago, starts a conversation with us and is happy to be able to take a picture of Bear Chief & also of Little Dog. He also takes pictures of Willy and Uhlenbeck & Willy alone & he takes a picture of Mrs. Grinnell, Bear Chief & both of us. Later at Walter's *tipi* I take pictures of Walter with Lewe & Walter on horseback. We eat at Rosy's: bread, butter & jelly, coffee & pears.

Gradually Indians start to ride in circles with long, green branches in their hands. They ride in rows. Now around the tree with the sun offering, close to the *Medicine Lodge*, a very big square is being formed by Indians & their wives. A lot of food is piled up there. Meat from one or more cows. About two hundred Indians only now receive the meat. Four or five Indians who are apparently charged with the distribution pass it down in big chunks. Apart from the meat, everyone also receives a portion of sugar, half a bag of flour & crackers. When the distribution is over, an Indian says in Peigan & laughs about it, *"The dogs have separated."* The common formula & final sentence that ends an Indian story. All food is being wrapped in bags & cloths & everyone takes his load home. Some of the chunks of meat weighed as much as eight or ten pounds.

Now gradually a parade starts to form. It does not get long & they still don't sing. We follow them halfway to Browning. Later in Browning I hear them sing. Then we rest in our room & I wash a few handker-chiefs. Then we return to the camps. Old Mountain Chief attempts to call up the dancers. There is also drumming. At least now spectators start to arrive. We sit down in the middle of a big field, on the future dancing ground. A few dancers come up, a few more & still a few more. Now there are many. Someone keeps drumming. Walter also comes in a dancing costume. The upper body is naked & painted light yellow; his face is also yellow, with blue dots & little stars. It is much too cold for Walter to dance with a naked back & chest. His arms are slim & beautifully shaped. His back is straight, his chest is broad. His waist & hips are narrow. Walter looks very sedate. Not the least trace of festive excitement. I only see him laugh once. At the end of the afternoon it is so cold that Walter wraps himself in a blanket & stays seated like that. His sister Rosy is also dancing, sometimes with the big, feather headdress that hangs down to the ground; it is the so-called well-known *war bonnet*. Her face is painted a subtle light yellow with soft red cheeks, everything in a subtle hue. Rosy is apparently flirtatious, just like many other Indian women.

The women dance in close rows. They slowly shuffle along with their sedate faces, which don't match their make-up, their colorful clothes, their colorful hair bands. Actually the men dance much better. Sometimes slow with small, quiet movements, then wild & passionate in peculiar wriggles, twisting the upper body, bending the knees in a stalking movement. Most of the Indians dance alone, just like that, in the crowd. Some dance like that & separate beside one another. Sam is one of the drummers. The big drum is played continuously by three or four men. The sky looks threatening. The dance does not take long. Just one hour. Then we watch a crow-medicine dance in a tipi. At 7:00 or later we have an evening meal with Rosy. We are very cold & warm ourselves in the tipis by the smoking & crackling wood fire that burns in the middle of the floor. The smoke drifts away through the hole above in the tipi but once in a while it drifts down & it becomes stuffy in the Indian dwelling. Uhlenbeck takes off his boots to warm his feet a bit.

Little Dog's wife in front of their tipi (DJdJ 1910).

Because of the cold we each drink two cups of tea. Little Patrick comments about our sailcloth that it is *a funny table.*

We look up the Tatseys and see Josephine for the first time & Bobby & Chub who are wearing new clothes, a yellow *dail*-like fabric. Chub laughs quietly laughs & is very proud of his new pants, which are no longer too long. George acts shy and has already asked for the professor, & Joe is quiet. We don't see John. We ask whether John is allowed to be our guest after Thursday, when Tatsey wants to be back already. I take some stuff from our suitcase, which is still on Tatsey's wagon & climb up onto it. Our blankets are there too & our tent. But tonight we will still sleep at Joe Kipp's. Then our tent does not have to be stored & we will stay with Rosy for dinner. The Tatseys would only be able to take care of us for two days. Tatsey is more or less lying or sitting on his bed & gives us our letters from Jan de Jong & Lien[109] & Prof. La Saussaye. Joe also has letters for us, a letter from Cor & a postcard from Daatje.[110] We leave again & pay a visit to a *tipi* where a Beaver dance is in progress. The Grinnells are already there. Uhlenbeck's cold is a bit better; in the afternoon Mr. Grinnell brought him a bottle with medicine, a remedy for colds. There is a nice light in the *tipi.* The glow from a burning wood fire; sometimes brightly lit, sometimes magical twilight. I sit beside Mrs. Grinnell. She too cannot sit for too long on the floor. You get so stiff that way. It is as if your legs will break. I call it broken on the wheel. At 10:00 we return to Browning. I change the glass plates. To bed at 11:00. There is a lot of noise happening in the hall & also upstairs. We sleep very poorly.

Walter Mountain Chief in dance costume (DJdJ 1910). | Walter Mountain Chief and Sam Scabby Robe (DJdJ 1910).

Wednesday, July 5

Sundance and Erecting of Big Arbor.
Up at 7:45. Hurry, hurry. Not too late for breakfast. Fried eggs, fried bacon & *hot cakes.* At Sherburne's we buy a light green silk necktie for Willy for 1.75 dollars. Once underway walking to the *camps,* we meet up with Walter on horseback. He rides back beside us & promises us all kinds of clothing when the dancing week is over. I pick a few roses for him. He sticks them into the portrait of the *Dutch girl. Fine,* he says, and is very happy with such a small present. We meet up with Rosy's husband & tell him that we will be at their place etc. in the coming days, even if the Tatseys are around. Then we watch a bit at the square, set off for the Grass dance by big, open wooden wagons. Lewe Kasoos comes on horseback with a letter from Walter. Water is indebted for 4 dollars to an Indian; he asks if he can borrow the money & Lewe adds, *"The policeman is after him."* We lend Walter the four dollars & Lewe gets one as a present for himself. He is very happy with that & thinks that it is a lot. We watch for a moment in *the shade* of the fasting woman. They pray around her & rattle incessantly & yell. Then we go back to our hiding place & sit a while longer on the branches. A walking dance starts. Men & women walk in a long row behind each other, or they form a circle. We walk along for quite a while. At noon we eat again at Rosy's. Then a Grass dance takes place. Someone has made a big square of open wagons. We also sit for a few hours on one of these empty wagons. At first there are only a few dancers. In the end surely about 50 men and 50 women dance. Walter's upper body is now not naked. He wears a very light sweater. By the way, his clothes are too colorful & overdone to be considered beautiful; but because of this very Indian like; full of feathers, full of big bells. The purple under-sleeves are an ugly contrast to the wine red silk scarf. His headdress, which juts forwards, hangs down to his loins. Colorful fringes flap on his already colorful *leggings.* A broad triangular ribbon with lots of little mirrors runs over chest & back. Around his waist he has a belt with very big bells. Feathers, very thin & transparent, colored dark purple are on his head. Long, loose

hair falls forward over his shoulders. His face is yellow again with many little figures. In his one hand he holds his little mirror; in the other he holds a big, light wooden hoop. First he dances very slowly, motionless, and he stays beside us. Maybe to obtain our approval, he repeatedly glances at us, for Walter is very vain. First the men dance alone for about one hour; with many or with a few dancing. Then it is the women's turn. They all dance together in one big circle, now also quite slow and shuffling forward very evenly. The drummers are very often with the big drum; they sing incessantly & change places quite often. Each dance is quite short & to us it always seems to end suddenly. Now all the men & women dance together, forming a huge circle, & then very small groups dance again. Now Walter also dances in the center. These appears to be the best dancers. Now Walter dances very wildly. He wrinkles his thin body in the most capricious wriggles. Some women dance along with a baby on their arm.

Poesa's father sits the whole afternoon right in front of us. He wears a very light-colored leather shirt. Very attractive. His *leggings* are red & blue with lots of small, shiny bells, from top to bottom on the outside. His face is decorated with a white circle that runs over his forehead, cheeks & chin. He is also painted white around the eyes. He is one of the most attractive Indians & more subtle than his wife, who has a sharp bird's face. When Poesa is asleep, her mother also dances. Poesa lies under a wagon, the sleeping place for small children & dogs, and another woman is watching him.

The dance is finished; all the people spread out. Now we dismount with stiff knees from our wagon. Now we go to the *Medicine Lodge;* lots of people go there. The medicine woman is seated near the *lodge* under an open *shade.* Her head is decorated with feathers, looking like a crown. She sits motionless, her face as good as covered. The *medicine man* has wrapped himself in a big, black piece of woollen fabric. This is his only piece of clothing. His long, black hair hangs over his face. He is a pitch-black, slim figure with completely naked legs. The big center pole – Y –

is now being decorated in the triangle with long leafy branches, pieces of fabric, rattles etc. Everything is tied onto it with strips of cowhide.

Now large groups of Indians show up the outside the big, round *tipi* area. I count about ten to twelve. The men, about eight to ten, walk in front. Two by two, they each hold up two big branches, which are tied together with a loop at the top. They sing constantly. It sounds beautiful. Now all groups solemnly come a bit forward, meaning to the center of the *Medicine Lodge.* Then they stand motionless again. These groups are still the old *societies,* among them the *Crazy Dogs* (these are not *clans*).[111] Now they approach the center. Now the medicine woman & her train approach the *pole,* which is still lying on the floor. She shuffles on very slowly, is being supported & now prays for quite a long time over the beam. Now all *pole* bearers approach the big center *pole.* They raise the *pole* and amidst loud, anxious screaming & much emotion the thick tree slides into the prepared hole. Now it suddenly becomes quieter. The great tension is over: the ceremony is over. The raising of the big *pole – raising the pole –* is the biggest moment of the whole week. This moment was impressive & I will never forget this situation. Can you imagine that we don't sleep! I hear & see all the Indians in my head.

When I am awake, I hear them sing – Poesa's father stood right beside us with his pole: his wife behind him. He is an Indian who participates very seriously in all ceremonies. For a moment we see Walter walk on the prairie right near his *tipi.* Lewe's mother wants to have her picture taken. I take a picture of her with

MRS. UHLENBECK'S DIARY

Montana 1911

Grass dance at Browning and at the ditch camp (DJdJ 1910).

Medicine man's tent. The smaller tent is to shade onlookers. (DJdJ 1910). | A Crazy Dog with the Stars and Stripes (DJdJ 1910).

Montana 1911

Two members of the Crazy Dog society (DJdJ 1910). | Two Crazy Dogs at the Grass dance near Browning (DJdJ 1910).

a cousin & Sam also joins in, between both women. Sam is dressed as usual & takes off his felt hat & holds it in his hand. Then I take pictures of two more groups of women & girls. Rosy & her husband watch this. We have evening meal with her & look up the Tatseys again. Bear Chief is there also & I hand out candy to all of the small Tatseys. They took our sweets in the empty *candy bucket*, thinking that we would camp this week in our own tent. But nothing came of our tent. John will be our guest when Tatsey once again has left the *fair grounds* at Browning. But actually, it seems as if John does not feel like it. He acts shy. Tatsey does not allow John to be with the Guardipees; he is not allowed to hang around there this week. Now we return to Browning. Very sun-burned & very worn out. Near Joe Kipp's we talk for one moment more with Mrs. Nixon. We go to bed at 9:30 & sleep very poorly. I just lie awake & see all of the scenes in my head.

Thursday, July 6.

Sundance and Erecting of Big Arbor.

We wake up at 8:00. Quickly get dressed & have breakfast immediately. After breakfast I rummage a bit in our room. It leaked badly that night, because upstairs something fell. The dripping of the water also kept me awake. I kept thinking of our hand luggage. We now go to the camps. It is very nice, warm weather. Much better than a few days before, when the old Mountain Chief asked Uhlenbeck to make sure that the weather would be nice the next day. Fortunately, that next morning the weather was better. The old Indian then praised Uhlenbeck & attributed *supernatural* power to him & Walter's father as well as Little Dog laughed approvingly at him. Mountain Chief especially is very busy & though his mood varies and his reliability is doubtful, he does earn praise for his diligence & cheerfulness these days. Before eating I twice take two pictures. Willy twice & one of Irene and her little niece again.

Right after dinner we go to the dancing grounds. Again we climb onto a wagon & soon the dancers arrive. In the afternoon we watch the dancing from 1:00 until after six. Now Bear Chief is also among them. He wears a shirt that looks as if it is made of a striped blanket. His face is painted red with a lot of small figures. He looks very cheerful and enjoys life a lot. We watch several dancers with whom we are familiar now, including White Dog, the older brother of the mission boy.[112] The dwarf also dances along. We leave our seat before the dancing is finished. We can no longer stand this forced position.

While we walk around the grounds, we are advised that another dance is going on. We go there. It appears to be the *Crazy Dog* dance. Only a few male & female dancers: +20 to 25. Small drums. Old Mountain Chief & his wife also dance along. The legs of two dancers are completely naked; the one, who has such a beautiful, tall shape, is beautifully painted. Now the dancers walk forward, stand still, form a square & their dancing starts again. We are so very thoroughly tired that we walk to Rosy's *tipi* & upon finding it closed, seat ourselves down in front of it on the ground. Upon Rosy's return from the Grass dance, which has just finished now, we get tea right away. We also have evening meal there & say at once that we will not return for a noon or an evening meal; it is too tiring for us. In the morning we would rather stay in Browning in order to go directly after having eaten to the dancing ground and be back for an evening meal at Joe Kipp's. We arrive at home very worn out and hang around our room for a while. Actually it is a very miserable hole, but still a place where at least one can rest. But the key to our room has disappeared; we are – very much so – wrongfully blamed for it; we put it in Joe Kipp's office as usual. I change the plates & with the rope from the suitcase I tie the knob of the door to the bed. So it is not possible for someone to just enter our room. In the end we go to bed after talking for quite a while. And after that we both sleep very well, which has not happened for a few nights. We have not seen John Tatsey, who was supposed to be our guest. Strange Indians though. You invite someone, the invitation is accepted and the guest stays away. No trace of John, we don't know where he is hanging out. The previous day this small occurrence happened: Walter approaches us & says, "Can I have 50 cents for Rosy?" Well, U. does not have half a dollar. So Walter receives one dollar. And later we paid Rosy again. So this dollar will be added up on Walter's debt: 16 + 4 + 1 = 21 dollars. Poor boy! How will this ever be straightened out?

Friday, July 7.

Sundance and Erecting of Big Arbor.

We only rise around eight. Hurry & have breakfast at Joe Kipp's. Then we return to our room where I write a long letter to Mama & the sisters & also a postcard to Anna Opheusden. Mrs. Symons cleans our room in our presence; I calmly continue my letter.[113] Right before eating I clean all kinds of things with Sunlight soap. Exactly at noon we finish our meal and afterwards we walk at once to the *camps.* Underway we meet Walter, who has to go to Browning. So we can't take his picture right now. We go to his father's *tipi,* store the glass plates there & walk right away to the *Medicine Lodge.* Quite a few Indians are there already. We also take a seat on the floor, in the back, out of modesty. However, Mountain Chief approaches us right away & places us in the front; now we can see everything quite well.

The sham fights are curious: one person shoots, another dies, a *tipi* is being trashed, a woman in the tipi abducted etc. etc.[114] Lots of blankets and pieces of fabric, in generally new, are being given away as presents by the women, who carefully spread out all the pieces, as if they want to say: "Look, I just give this away." After the pieces have been displayed for a while, they are piled up in order to make room for others just brought in. At the very end of the ceremony a give-away is being held. In this way the less fortunate receive from the fortunate ones.

In the *Medicine Lodge,* the *Sun dancer* is most important; a slim, beautiful figure ±30 years old. Upper body & legs are completely naked as are the arms, & the entire face is painted in a bright yellow. The sharp, beautiful figures on the face are beautiful. He wears a leafy crown around his head. Around his neck is a thin, long, white and wide yellow trimmed cloth. It is draped down his back. It hangs beautifully over his beautiful back, over the slim hips. In his right hand he holds up a (small) feather, from which three tassels hang; in the left he holds a little green branch. He holds up both, as if he wants to display them. In his mouth he has a wooden whistle which is attached to a ribbon around his neck, just like we saw at the Beaver dance. It seems to be made from a little branch. He is seated on the altar made of dense leafy branches and comes forward and dances a repetitive movement right in front of the altar, spreading out his arms or crossing them over his chest continuously. He turns around dancing, each time alternatively turning his chest or his back to the spectators. I can watch this ceremony for a long time, a very long time. Their deep sincerity is also so very striking.

Indians, men & women, keep approaching the Sun dancer; with deep respect they approach the altar. The man presents a pipe. Very soon plumes of smoke rise up: the woman presents a piece of fabric, tied to a branch with a sheaf of green: an offering to the sun. First they pray standing upright. Then the Sun dancer dances a long time for them. Finally they follow the Sun dancer. They also enter the leafy altar & pray there for quite some time. We see father, mother & Poesa also participate in the ceremony in this manner. Later in the afternoon Poe-e-sa again attended the Grass dance with her father & mother. Mountain Chief especially is very busy again. He also dances in a splendid blue shirt, with a headdress and blue *leggings* without pants. Time & time again his sturdy upper legs become visible: it is the almost outdated attire for the Indians. We saw Eagle Calf and Morning Eagle.

We leave the *Medicine Lodge* and watch the *Grass dance* for some more time. Walter participates again, another vest, another headdress. His father is dancing, too. As is Bear Chief. At 5:30 we leave, talk for a moment with John Tatsey, so the Tatseys haven't left yet, take the camera and the glass plates from Walter's *suitcase* and while there was no one in or around Mountain Chief's *tipi,* we are called to Owl Child's where Uhlenbeck manages to have himself understood and then we look up the Tatseys. We only speak with Tatsey's wife and tell her that we would very much like to leave with them. It is too tiring for us and we have seen fully the most important things. We also ask her where John was, why he did not come to Joe Kipp and why he did not let us hear anything from him. She does not answer much but apparently does not approve of John's behavior. We stress that we are going immediately to Joe Kipp's so her

husband or one of her boys knows where to find us in order to discuss the hour of departure.

We are back in Browning at 6:30, have supper and wait for one of the Tatseys. But they stay away and I think, at the earliest, we will go on Monday with Walter to Badger Creek. We have to wait and see. Uhlenbeck has high hopes[115] and he thinks that we might be able to depart earlier. Nobody comes to visit. At 10:00 we go to bed, disappointed. Uhlenbeck coughs quite a lot and does not sleep well. I do, I am totally recovered.

Indian girls near Browning (DJdJ 1910).

Saturday, July 8.

Up at 8:00. Get dressed and have breakfast quickly and off to the post office. Letters from Mama and from Guda. Back home I write a letter to Mrs. Saussaye and the Beets family.[116] Uhlenbeck is resting. I write a little, sitting bent over the drawer cupboard. We don't have a table. We mail the letters and eat. Then I wash the handkerchiefs, hang them in our bedroom and walk to the *camps*. Nothing is going on yet, although it is 2:00. It is cold and bleak. We don't find Walter in his tipi. And the Tatseys seem to have departed. No sign of their *tipi,* no sign of John. Strange Indians, though! So there we are. We go to Bear Chief's *tipi.* Finally we find him. Only Sebastian is at home: the very friendly boy, again so content. He cannot dance and it is too tiring for him to watch it for a long time, he limps on his crutches. He is not quite used to it. Maybe he will make progress. We give him half a dollar, so he can buy some sweets during the holidays. The more eager the Indians are for sweets, the better it is for the white merchant! In Bear Chief's tipi we see that same colored wooden plate made by him; it holds incense in two places. Yesterday he was not in the *Medicine lodge.* He rather dances in the open field and honors the sun in his own tipi, in his own way. A moment later Walter's cousin advises us that Walter talked to her about bringing us back to Badger. This gives us peace of mind. Yes, Walter is a good *kid* and will not disappoint us. We are in a hurry. We would like to be back at the camp in Badger as soon as possible to resume our interrupted life of study. But why all the haste? (As it turned out later, it does not matter.) For Uhlenbeck, riding back with Walter in a *buggy* to Badger means a

MRS. UHLENBECK'S DIARY

Old Chipewyan woman near Browning (DJdJ 1910). | *Young Piegan women (DJdJ 1910).*

MONTANA 1911

miserable ride for many hours because there is no place for him in this means of transport. Again he will be doubled up and crouched over the bumpy road.

We don't think that the Indians will start dancing soon. Anyway, it is so cold, much too cold to sit on the floor. We both are too sick with colds and will rather go to Joe Kipp's, to our room. At Scherburne's we will buy something for the coughing. Generous as Sherburne is we each get a box with cough drops as a present. Uhlenbeck lies down on his bed; I write for a very long time in my diary. It is too bad that it is so cold. For the Medicine Lodge we also find it too cold. I write a long letter to Nella. Shortly before dark I have finished 16 pages. Finally I sat right in front of the window with a piece of cardboard and a sheet of paper on my knee, just as I used to write when on the prairies. When at 9:00 my letter is finished, I read it to Uhlenbeck. Then we go to bed early to compensate for missed sleep. The cough drops, delicious as they are, do help. U. sleeps much better.

Sunday, July 9.

I rise at 7:30. The weather looks quite nice. We dress quickly and have breakfast. We each get a melon and an orange from Mr. Dawson.[117] How kind! It must be because of the key! After breakfast we first walk around a bit, then I write a letter to the regents and a postcard to Mother Bouwman.[118] Uhlenbeck writes again to Jan and a letter of condolence to Prof. Holwerda.[119] Before supper we mail everything. After supper we walk to the *camps*. We try to talk to Walter. He is not around. Still, after old Mountain Chief went in, Uhlenbeck also enters his *tipi*. There is an *interpreter* and Mountain Chief informs us that Walter will come this evening to talk about bringing us back on Monday or on Tuesday. We hope that Walter can bring us back at least on Monday. But I don't believe this. If only we could ride horses, then we would be much more independent.

We go to Bear Chief's tipi once more. "Father is asleep," says Sebastian, who just comes out on his crutches. The younger brother will wake up the elderly man. Then we also go in. Bear Chief calmly stays on his bed and we set ourselves beside him, also on his bed and talk to him. He said that he watched us yesterday in order to give us our Indian names. Now he wants to do it tomorrow. It would be too bad if that does not happen. Not because the honor is so great, but otherwise they would have to describe us. Now they call Uhlenbeck *Tatsey's partner*. In the *camps* nothing will be going on. The *agent* and *Father Carrel* won't allow it, of course.[120] So we walk back to Browning. How often have we walked this distance in the last week? Uhlenbeck lies down on his bed. First I do some needlework and then write in my diary. A day like today is not very agreeable. But there are more such days. It is too windy to walk a lot back & forth. And Browning is always boring, let alone on a Sunday. All the Indians sleep or are *after their horses*. Still I should do something and I start to write to Jan and Lien. I have no other letters left to write. Truus should write us something. Once back at Badger, I will not get to it soon. Because how does one get the letters mailed?

MONTANA 1911

Monday, July 10.

Departure from Browning. Back to Badger. The Tatseys are missing.

Right on time we get up. That is, I do. Before our life in a tent starts again, I want to take a bath in the most primitive way – lack of water, lack of basins. Walking outside after breakfast, near Joe Kipp's blacksmith shop, Lewe approaches us on horseback. What does Lewe want? Wait, again he has a note from Walter who is now asking to borrow four dollars. Lewe changes a ten-dollar bill, gets four for Walter (with a note). For himself Lewe gets half a dollar in order to have some *fun* again on the last day of the *celebration*. Walter now owes us 21 + 4 = 25 dollars. Actually that is far too much. That is why Uhlenbeck again informs Walter that we need this money for our travel back home. We go back to our room. I will write a letter to Truus. A postcard to Hermine Hartevelt and to Lizzy Kunst.[121] Now we sit quietly in our bedroom and don't notice at all what took place in the same inn.

When we go out for dinner, it strikes us that so many Indians from the *camps* are gathered in front of Joe Kipp's house. We don't know why and also don't think about it. We are still having *supper* when a most horrible screaming reaches us and they inform us that David Duvall, the well-known interpreter for Wissler, just shot himself in Joe Kipp's inn.[122] Today is the day that the case for the dissolution of his marriage would have been heard in court. They say that his wife wanted it; she is Marceau's sister.[123] The screaming, sobbing and lamenting of a few Indian women sounds very eerie. Duvall's mother, loudly complaining, sits in Joe Kipp's doorway. Hastily I avoid this crowd and head to our room. I can also hear it there. It affects Uhlenbeck also, but he still wants to go to observe several Indians there. After a while he comes back. We will walk to the camps, that is the best distraction.

More relaxed we look again at the Medicine Lodge. In front of the altar lie all kinds of branches and ribbons, fallen-off pieces of sun offerings. I take a little branch with me for my collection. At the tipi we talk to Walter and also to Lewe and now we learn that, due to the death of

Duvall, there will be no more dancing. The *agent* has prohibited it. So a very sinister end to this week of dancing! But now we should go to Badger right away. Walter is willing to take us there, but his folks are against it, that is his father and his sister Kasoos. They say that Walter should find himself a saddle horse, and Lewe's mother, who is already crying at the sheer thought of Lewe bringing us down, does not allow him to bring us. I do not like Lewe as a driver. Such difficult terrain for such a young boy! In contrast, Uhlenbeck has nothing against it. All Mountain Chiefs make a nervous impression.

A lonely Indian rides through the camps; he also sings songs of lament. Walter says that *it makes me sick*. Finally Walter says: "I will not listen to my father. I will take you and in half an hour I will be at Joe Kipp's." And, Walter says: "*I am mad at my people and I don't feel good, that my people kicked about that boy.*" We walk straightaway back to Browning and halfway meet Dewe Rutherford. He is again the same soft little boy and, talking about Bennet Nobel (the nephew of Duvall whose mother died last year under a train), he says, "*Bennet is a nice little boy.*"[124] Dewe is not a full-blood but has all that attractiveness that renders the Indian so amiable. At the post office again we give the mission as our address, buy stamps, stock some more liquorice and head to our room. First Uhlenbeck pays the invoice, which turns out less than expected, and Mr. Dawson apologizes (!) about the room key, which has been found again. The same Mr. Dawson contended the day before very decidedly that we had mislaid the key. All these days we could not lock our room, neither during the day, nor at night. With a suitcase belt I prevented someone from just walking in at night. And, at Joe Kipp's, strange people show up. All kinds of white trash spend one night or longer at his place. For example that merchant from Strasbourg, who deals in pelts! I disliked his handshake and the sound of his voice, not to mention his face.

Uhlenbeck talks for a brief moment with Mrs. Nixon and says that we are departing. We do not have much fun with Charlie Camp. Actually I do not like that little beggar boy at all. We also talk to Mrs.

Grinnell in front of the house. She has just returned from riding horseback in the mountains. Again she is very friendly and encourages us to be sure to stay with them in New York. We like that a lot. They are such nice people and not at all loud, and Uhlenbeck always finds something to chat about with Dr. Grinnell. In front of the inn is a kind of stretcher. A cloth is spread out on it. It covers the body of Duvall; the shoes stick out from under the cloth. I took in this scene only briefly. After a moment we returned to our room, waiting for Walter. He comes soon, much sooner than I had imagined, but still, there is another problem to be solved – Tatsey's *buggy*, in which we were to drive back, is broken down.

One wheel is broken. That does not surprise us. The old horse wagon suffered a lot on the way here. All those hard, unexpected bumps are not pleasant for the passengers, but for the *buggy* it is the final blow. Uhlenbeck leaves with Walter for a consultation. Joe Kipp does not want to repair it in his workshop and for the government blacksmith to do it, permission from the *agent* must be obtained first. The permission is granted. Now everything will be all right. No, not yet. The repair does not turn out well. Later Walter announces that he has another wagon at his disposal. That took him a lot of effort. But oh, what happiness. Now, this is no ordinary *buggy*, but a *two-seater*, meaning, one with two benches and a kind of cover over it. A woman and a girl will also ride with us and Walter will be allowed to deduct seven dollars from his debt. Walter picks us up at Joe Kipp's. Uhlenbeck and I sit on the second bench. Walter sits alone in the front, because, he says, just outside of Browning another woman will join us. We stop for a long time at the *log house*. Uhlenbeck holds the reins. Walter is gone for quite a long time and returns with Mrs. Powell and her daughter Helen.[125] The front bench of the *buggy* is *crowded*. Walter's saddle horse walks alongside the carriage. Walter does not like it. He gives the reins to the woman and speeds away on his horse. Further on, further down, she says, at the lake, we will see him again. Yes, we have seen this woman before. Her maiden name is Monroe. We saw her again at Rosy's. Helen is 11 years old and is now her only child, and she is a very charming Indian girl. We have to wait for a very long time at the railway track. The freight train seems endless. But, says Helen's mother. "Don't be afraid. I can drive!" Indeed, at the lake Walter joins the carriage. From a distance we could already see him lying in the grass. The saddle horse walks again beside the carriage, jumping & prancing about and along the deep, very uneven wheel ruts. The animal could easily break its legs! Walter doesn't seem to fear that at all and it does not happen.

The weather is beautiful; it could not be better. Never have I appreciated the prairie that much, the high mountains, its deep unexpected ravines. The road chosen by Walter, the shortest, could not be worse. Well, it might be the shortest, but it is also the worst. A couple of times Walter has to get down because one or another piece of harness breaks. They don't have a knife. He gets my very small split knife to cut a strap and a rope. He sticks the little knife in his pocket. A moment later he asks, "Do you have cigarette paper?" Yes, I do, but will have to look for it in the little suitcase. He is prepared to stop for it. Now Walter smokes. He might need the stimulant. Neither he, nor Mrs. Powell and Helen, have eaten anything this morning. The road is now so bad that we have to dismount. "*I don't like to kill you folks,*" says Walter. And later, close to Two Medicine, we have to walk again for quite some time. The woman remains seated close to Walter. One moment we can see them, the other moment they have disappeared in some depression to emerge again after some curves in the road. Nevertheless the walk doesn't bore us at all and Helen is very good company. It is beautiful here and so surprising! Around us the landscape is wild, everywhere *ups and downs*. Two Medicine shimmers and around us is a wealth of wild flowers. Helen picks a bouquet, gives it to me as a present, and in memory of this wonderful evening I will take them with me to Holland!

Now we all mount and drive for a moment through a forest, everywhere high and low greenery, among it even a few large trees! Everywhere

taller and shorter rose bushes. It is a wealth of wild roses, large bloom-
ing aconites, all a light green and nowhere dust. Our horses run up to
their bellies in the rose bushes and Two Medicine is suddenly in front of
us. We wade through the river, which is now considerably less dangerous than with Tatsey at the mission. But ascending the bank it is steep.
After this the road is and remains bad and sometimes the carriage tilts
so much to one side that we repeatedly lean over to the high side in order
not to lose the balance. It is quite strange, normally I am quite anxious
in a carriage, but here on the prairie these unexpected positions don't
scare me that much. I have the weird idea that we will fall soft, if that is
to happen. In hindsight we can't understand that we did not break our
necks. We also drive through Little Badger. Then the road leads through
a kind of *coulee*. In fact you cannot drive through it. Why did it cross
Walter's mind to choose such a path? The previous, long road was very
much better.

"How far do we still have to go Walter?" U. asks. "Ten miles, professor!!!" But that is not true at all. I can just see Badger and a few camps in
the distance. Badger is in front of us. First we have to wade through the
small stream, then a sharp turn and we descend the bumpy, stone slope.
Helen laughs with her face in her hands. I always do that, she says, "*if
I cross.*" I do not like it either. It is such an unusual scene to drive in the
middle of the rapids. It is as if you aren't moving. And the current of the
Badger is fast and its bottom is very uneven. But soon we will arrive at
the Tatscys, and we think, soon we will have our own tent. But where
are the Indian *camps*? The *old campground* is deserted. Just a few tents
around the *reclamation store*. Further down, on the left, we see two more
tents. We drive there and ask a little boy where Joe Tatsey is camping.
The answer is: at Two Medicine. We are amazed and soon we understand that it must be true. At the *store* they also say that Joe Tatsey has
not yet returned and that he has set up his tents in the mission at Two
Medicine. There we are. Two Medicine is too far for the horses, not to
speak of returning to Browning.

The weather happens to be very beautiful. It is exactly 8:00. Soon the
full moon appears, it is beautiful. Spending the night in the low bushes
at Badger would be very romantic. But most certainly, it will also be very
cold. All kinds of wooden sheds belong to the *government store*. In one
nice building only a little bit of oats is stored. Uhlenbeck and I could
spend the night there. Walter & his older & younger cousin will look
for lodging with Indians at the other side on Badger. The *store's* cook still
has something to eat for us. He is a friendly man, a German-speaking
German, from Lake Konstanz, but has already been employed for many
years in America.

I will not soon forget that evening meal. We slide along on the
bolted-down bench. The long tables at both sides are joined together.
Uhlenbeck and I sit next to each other. On the other side, our three
Indians. The cook is really very friendly and fries up potatoes, serves
cold and warm meat, cold apricots, a kind of cake and *ginger snaps*. Bread
and coffee too. Walter no longer has that sour look. But he says: "The
fee for this ride cannot be deducted from my debt, the horses belong to
this woman," and he points to Mrs. Powell. "You have *to pay her* seven
dollars." That is a bit *mean* of Walter. But of course U. pays her. We stroll

Tuesday, July 11.

around a bit. It is so quiet and beautiful at Badger. We follow Walter who drives away with his *folks*. And then we inspect our lodging for the night. An American wife of one of the *ditch* bosses brings us a candle, a towel and a bucket of water.

The room in the shed is quite adequate. In one shed there is straw and a dark grey woollen horsehair blanket. We use our own two blankets also and when it is totally dark, we crawl into the long, narrow drawer. It is miserable. It is absolutely impossible to sit upright in it. My hair is repeatedly tangled in the nails. Finally we still fall asleep. But at 3:00 we go for a walk outside again. It is a beautiful night and so quiet: once in a while I hear a few horses or the water flowing in the river. We don't sleep much. Uhlenbeck worries. He thinks that Tatsey is acting strangely and he still has to do a lot of work in the months ahead of us. We rise early. Small animals in the woods are so noisy that we cannot sleep.

There is not much to do to get dressed. A coat or a skirt is quickly put on, a little washing with water does not take much time either. While I am busy with this, a man comes in. He withdraws quickly as he did not know that the shed now serves as a hotel. When we walk outside at 7:30, Walter and his folks arrive. That is quite kind, they stick to our agreement. We have breakfast again at the cook's; it is all *government* food. U. will pay for everything, 25 Am. cents each time per person. We try to telephone – there is a temporary connection between the mission and the *store*. But no answer so we don't find out Tatsey's whereabouts. Phones again and again. Finally an answer. Tatsey is on his way to Badger! Well, it is about time. If it were only true. We will have to wait and see. Walter departs with his people. We follow him for a long time. He will return, he says, to work at the ditch again and pay his debts.

The rest of the day we can eat at the cook's and if necessary we can spend another night in the shed. We walk, first in the direction of the Rockies, then we follow the bushes along the Badger and sit on the shore of the river, right at a *crossing place*. I find a nice, round, flat pebble and put it in my pocket. At home I will transform it into a paperweight. It is a gorgeous morning. Many flowers, also many orange lilies in these bushes. Here and there we find small strawberries. At noon we eat again at the cook's, with other white laborers from the *ditch*. They don't speak to us, but the cook is friendly and gives us another separate dish. He has also made a little cake for us and he laughs in a very friendly way when we thank him for that. Back at our shed Uhlenbeck lies down in the straw. He is very tired. No wonder. A day with many emotions is behind us. I will work at my diary.

Mrs. Powell repeatedly spoke of us staying with her at her ranch near the mountains. Walter should bring us with his team and stay also. Whether it would be a time for Uhlenbeck to work or for Walter to flirt, we would find out later. It certainly will be beautiful there! But do we have the time and the money? That woman was very nice to us and we like the idea. In the afternoon we visit Mrs. Scorbett, who camps in the bushes at Badger. We get there through a lot of tall grass, through small bushes and over small streams. On the way we talk to her daughter, who is about five years old. Again, such a *forward girl*. Eloquent and street-wise as an adult American and just like Mabel Henault. She is a great help finding our way, that is for sure, but we are more attracted to Mary Bear Leggings with her shy eyes. She, Mrs. Scorbett, shows us the photographs she took herself: very small, but very clear. Her husband is employed at the store, so in government service. She has photographed her daughter who is ±15 years old, in Indian clothes. We walk back again. The little tents there are located in a very picturesque setting, but it bores us to talk for such a long time, restless as we are on this day.

We stroll around on the open plain, have our evening meal at the cook's and some small talk with Mr. Racine & his children.[126] He addresses himself to Uhlenbeck. Being a half-blood himself, he married an Indian girl. On his request we follow him to his tent. It was his son who came last night with the bad news that Tatsey was at Two Medicine. The woman is nice, friendly, fat & rosy and keeps herself occupied with a small child. A few children walk around. She is a much older sister of the Schildt boy, that friendly soft little boy who lived with his grandfather and wanted to grow vegetables.[127] Racine's tent is located in the direction of the *Old Agency*. So we walk back to our shed over the plain and a horseman approaches us. He comes nearer and we recognize him as Walter. What is this? Walter is here again. "*Yes*," he says, "*I come to see if you are lonesome or not. I was not feeling comfortable at my folks.*" Uhlenbeck speaks to him about the work. Walter is on horseback, caressing the brown neck once in a while. Uhlenbeck leans a little against the saddle and the result of the discourse is that Walter will come the next morning at 7:00 to the shed to work. Then we stroll around a bit more and ask permission to spend one more night in the shed. We are allowed to. We had just lain down on the bed of straw that I made up the other way around, when Walter comes again at the door. "I heard you still talking," says Walter, "so you are still up." "No," Uhlenbeck shouts, "I am already

in bed, but wait, I will be with you in a moment. *I sleep in my clothes.*" In a moment he is, indeed, outside with Walter. They both sit down on the wooden doorstep. I listen to the conversation. Weird situation. I stay in bed and it is even more uncomfortable than the previous night. Still it has to stay as is. To turn over the dusty blankets again does not appeal to me. It is too cold to sit for a long time on the doorstep. So Uhlenbeck and Walter pace up and down. I hear the voices again and again either close or at a distance. What is the matter with Walter? Why is he interrupting us for that long? A few hours earlier all the arrangements were set up! He must be acting on his own agenda. Finally Uhlenbeck comes in again. "Oh," he says, "the entire visit from little Walter did not have any other purpose then "*to talk sentiments. I know, that you and your wife love me in your hearts.*" Yes, that certainly does sound sentimental; that is impressive at such a late hour at night, but Uhlenbeck still believes that Walter will share less than he promised and that he will regret for one or another reason that he promised to come and teach. First we discuss it as for the time being we will not be able to sleep. Without any further disturbances the short summer night passes.

Walter Mountain Chief and his girlfriend (DJdJ 1910).

MONTANA 1911

Wednesday, July 12.

Back at the Tatseys.

I am up at 7:00. I am hardly dressed when Walter already arrives. When he sees me I putting my comb in my suitcase, he also wants to use this toiletry item. Of course I hand him my comb. His hair appears to be completely wet. So Walter has already washed. He is very neat & tidy like most Indians. He combs his hair carefully, parts his hair using my pocket mirror. Then Walter has breakfast with us and then Uhlenbeck starts to work with him. I write a long letter to Mama and the Zijlvests and work for a long time on my diary.[128] Uhlenbeck is seated on a attached bench in our shed, Walter on a small unbolted bench, but it is too hard for the Indian so I put a blanket on it. He also finds the table too hard to lean over. So our second blanket is on the table under his arms. Now the teaching goes on. Uhlenbeck works nicely with him and actually I am glad, too, that Walter is here. What else could we do the entire day? At the table Walter is our guest again: *Sauerkraut* with bacon! It is raw, miserable *Sauerkraut*; still I eat it. These days the cook is a beam of sunlight. He takes pleasure in helping us out and he tells us a few things. He is not married, has worked already for many years in America, has a *farm* and has saved quite a sum and will return in a couple of years to his village on Lake Konstanz to live with his sister. He is not Americanized, but still full of *Gemütlichkeit*. After a meal, first a rest. Then back to work again. How sleepy Walter is! Once in a while he lies down on our straw bed, interrupting work. I want to write a letter too, Walter says. "Do you have a pen and paper for me?" It is to Laura Cook, his love. His letter is finished. He is not so naive as to have it read by Uhlenbeck. He closes it, hands

Thursday, July 13.

it to me (of course without a stamp) and says: "Will you take care of it?" Now Walter is again so sleepy. He then falls into a deep sleep. Uhlenbeck and I attentively observe the Indian in deep sleep. When he has slept long enough, Uhlenbeck wakes him up, but he doesn't stay awake for very long. Now Walter is sleepy again. It is unbearable to see how sleepy Walter is. This makes me so nervous, because I feel that it is so irritating for Uhlenbeck. Uhlenbeck and I go outside and stroll up and down. Then Joe Tatsey, little Joe, plods towards us. "Here we are again," he says, as they appear to set up camp close to the previous camping area. I am so glad with the news about the Tatseys being around again! Now everything will be all right. We will have *supper* with Walter once more at the cook's, who does not have change. So Uhlenbeck has to pay the *time-keeper* in another portable wooden building and Tatsey is there also. He is very relaxed with the entire story about the last few days. He planned to come on Tuesday, but first he had no horses and then his wife fell off her horse and that day she was in pain and stiff. Tatsey is with a wagon at the *store* and, at our request, he would never think of it himself, takes our suitcase, our blankets and coats with him. Uhlenbeck carries the tin with boiled water; he just got it from the cook for a slight intestinal indisposition. I carry the inkpot and both of us walk behind the wagon. Our tent is partly set up, just a few small poles, and quite soon Mrs. Tatsey and Josephine carry in the camp bed.[129] John and another stronger Indian have brought in our suitcases and candy barrels. These had partly been stored in a *log house* before our departure for Browning, partly transported in vain to Browning. We arrange everything quickly and that evening we lie down again on our camp bed in our own tent. None of the Tatsey family says much about the misunderstanding, or whatever one might call it. Why would we ask for an explanation? John and Joe act shy, Chubby & Bob don't.

Up at 7:30 and a quick breakfast with Tatsey. Working with Tatsey. I first sew my blouses, which are worn-out at the upper sleeves, from the sun. After that I crochet little stars. After a meal Uhlenbeck works again and I sit for hours down at the creek, at Badger, with several kinds of needlework. I enjoy my knitting, can quietly reflect over the previous days and look out over the undulating prairie, over the white crest of Badger, over the sunny plains around me and feel very happy this afternoon. Josephine comes to haul water. She looks at my knitting. She can't do it. Could I only teach her! Bob & Chub play for a long time at the river and keep me company most pleasantly. We have our evening meal at 6:00 and stroll around a bit, looking time and again for our friend Walter who was supposed to come and work at 7:00. Oh, looking out for somebody who does not show up on time! Walter does not show up the whole evening, as Uhlenbeck suspected. Early, at 9:30, we go to bed.

Friday, July 14.

Up at 7:00. It is already warm in the tent. It will certainly be a really warm day. Uhlenbeck works with Tatsey and discusses future work for a long time. Tatsey says that he does not know many more stories. Is this true! What to do? Uhlenbeck want to collect a whole lot more! I can't understand how this will come out right. Again I have to sew my blouses; they wear out all the time. After a meal, fresh cow tongue with dried apricots, we stroll around until 2:00. In the meantime Tatsey will ask whether the old Mad Plume wants to come and tell stories.[130] After two I take my laundry to the river. I pack everything in Truus' colorful bag. It is easy to carry and nobody can see what I intend to do. To do laundry in the river is not that bad. I also take along the small wash bowl and of course a big piece of Sunlight soap. What could I do here without Sunlight soap? I have never had warm water. Therefore I cannot use the spiritus I brought along.

First I wash a great number of handkerchiefs, stockings and socks and then also Uhlenbeck's cotton cap. It is impossible to make it uglier than it already is. I have to take care not to get my feet wet completely. The shore is quite steep and time and again I have to fill the wash bowl. The laundry is done and I go uphill again and hang everything out on the tent ropes to dry. When I have pinned the last handkerchief, the first ones are already completely dry. There is a lot of sun and quite a strong wind. I am still busy folding when Mabel and her mother pass by on their way to the Tatseys. "*That is a light washing,*" Mabel says. That little one has her nose into everything! When I am totally done, I read a few Dutch newspapers printed in Wisconsin and mailed to us from there. We don't know by whom. I browse in them for quite a while and read among others an article about our arrival in New York and about the objectives of our journey. Then I repair the stockings and socks that are dry and I am just knitting a bit when Mabel returns: "*Gracious me, what are you doing?*" She chats a bit with me, looks at the strange needle work and enters the tent again once Tatsey has left. The child is boisterous and tells about her coming birthday on July 25th, about her watch,

how much it cost and suddenly she asks Uhlenbeck: "How many dollars will you get for the book that you are writing here when you are back in your own country?" and "*Papa and Mama are married for twelve years now and they never split up, but were always together,*" and her mouth keeps going.[131] (At railway stations or on trains, time and again, it always struck us that these young American children are so boisterous and act so wisely.)

Mabel departs again. We have a supper of fried trout. Joe got a spur of diligence and caught them in the Badger and again I regret that, out of laziness, the Indians don't use this food that would be excellent for them.[132] A moment before we leave for our evening meal, Walter arrives on horseback. He looks very uncomfortable. He has a *belly-ache* and feels most miserable. The previous day at work he drank a lot of water. That is what probably caused it. We give him a laudanum tablet. He spits it out right away. Uhlenbeck then breaks a second pill in four pieces and the patient swallows them! How unhappy he is looking. We give him a few big strong peppermints and with them a second laudanum tablet, not to take right now, but later, and walking slowly along with his horse, Walter trudges away. We doctor quite a lot. This morning we gave Tatsey three tablets for his head ache. But we don't like to do this at all. I am especially against it, since I am the one who determines the amount, because I can check this on the medicine list. I am very scared to give too much and it will go from bad to worse.

That evening we stroll around. We also go over the *ditch,* which has a very nice view, but the terrain is very uneven! We still live very lonely, but it is certainly very quiet. This afternoon many *camps* left for a place further down. We saw them pass by on the road to the Old Agency. Nearby the mission, the *ditch* has to be repaired. That is where to go to work, they told us. We see neither John, nor Joe. Certainly *running around*! There is a gorgeous evening sky. We sit for quite a while on our stools behind the tent. (Later, weeks later, I still remember this beautiful evening.) The colorful light spreads splendidly over the Rockies. We go

Saturday, July 15.

to bed without having talked to anyone. It is still quite warm in our tent and there is some lightning. I cannot sleep and stay awake for hours. For a while Uhlenbeck suffers a lot from *bellyache*. He falls asleep late.

Up at 7:00. It thunders a little. Now it is cloudy, then the sun shines. We eat our breakfast alone. Josephine Tatsey will wash a few things for us on Monday. We are sitting on top of the sloping shore of the Badger, on the left away from the bushes, when Lizzy comes to say that her father has arrived to teach. This is the first time that Tatsey is ready for Uhlenbeck when we are not in the tent. We walk there as quickly as we can and they start to work right away and behind the tent I write in my diary and sew a few things. Tatsey took along a letter for Haarlem and a postcard for Jan de Jong and will take care that they move on somehow. How, I don't know. Mad Plume did not show up the other day. He hauls water for the *ditch* workers *(an old water boy!)*. He is a very old, friendly Indian, who always walks around with his grandson, and with whom, when we stayed in the shed, we once talked for a long time, right on the ground near our shed.[133] Mad Plume and his grandson, Walter, Uhlenbeck and I. Of course the old Indian thinks that we come from far away and so it is normal that he tells us how old he is. It has become a warm day, 91° in the tent. Still Uhlenbeck works very hard this afternoon with Tatsey. A few times an Indian enters the tent and something is arranged with Jim Blood on a paid basis.[134] This man knows a lot and will come and tell stories on scheduled days and hours. He is a beautiful Indian, 50 years old. What a gorgeous complexion, what a prominent profile this Indian has. This Saturday night passes very quietly.

Sunday, July 16.

It is warm again. Mrs. Tatsey was ill the whole night; this never happens and Joe says about himself, *"I had heart trouble this night!"* We see John for only one moment when we have breakfast. In the course of this Sunday morning Uhlenbeck and John stroll up and down; he encourages him to visit our tent a little more often, because it is not at all nice to act so shy. We have *dinner* with Tatsey. But it is not very comfortable as we don't see his wife at all. She is lying down in grandmother's tent and Tatsey worries about his wife's illness. After having eaten Jim Blood comes to listen to Blackfoot *stories*. It is very warm in our tent and I see that Uhlenbeck repeatedly wipes his forehead while he reads in Indian *Blue face* and *Clot of Blood*[135] among others. Tatsey's uncle, the old Eagle Calf, also joins in and still another Indian with long, loose hair who laughs a lot about all kinds of sentences. Next week Jim Blood will come and work during the day or after six. When the guests have left, John and Joe enter our tent together. John took a note from Uhlenbeck to Walter, reminding him about his promise to come and work.

Later we get another nice visit. Richard Mad Plume comes, one of the five sons of the old Mad Plume.[136] He is a young, married man of 24, speaking very slowly and very carefully in English sentences. Still it is a great benefit that he is kind of familiar with English. When no interpreter is around and the visitor only speaks Peigan, it is hard on Uhlenbeck, in any case very tiring, because of the great effort to make sentences himself and understand them quickly.

Richard has a strangely attractive appearance. Uhlenbeck reads Blackfoot stories aloud, among them stories Richard does not know, which he finds remarkable and Richard says, "You are reading so well, I can understand everything." That is what it is all about. Uhlenbeck strives for this. And it costs him a lot of energy. With this visitor we spend a very fine hour. He is a real full-blood, the best kind, kind of *New Breast*.[137] Again these narrow, small feet, and beautifully shaped hands and nails and this soft, shiny skin. After Richard has left, Charlie Guardipee brings me a long letter from Go. Outside we see old Eagle Calf, wrapped in a blanket, sitting on the prairie. At *supper* we also see old Guardipee, who sits with his plate on the ground.[138] For starters I don't care much for this long, slim Cree. He has a little moustache, very rough hands and has nothing in common with an Indian such as Richard or Jim Blood. The entire Guardipee family hangs around here for the whole evening. Tatsey does not like it and says: *"I don't like them Crees. They have no brains at all."*

The whole afternoon there is some thunder. In the evening beautiful weather. At dusk the most beautiful colors over the mountains! It is not so warm anymore and there is hardly any wind. We are walking about in the dusk when Carl Schildt and Henry Racine come by our tent.[139] They come in and these two boys of + 13 years old have a very nice chat with us. The mission boy, Carl Schildt, a friend of Willy's, is such a gentle boy. He tells about the severe winters, when life is so hard for the cattle. I shot a cow this winter, he says, *"He was suffering and was weak."* Horses, he says, can withstand it much better. They scratch away the snow and so look for food, but when a cow's nose freezes, they are helpless and perish miserably. He also talks about his old father, who is already 62 years old; *"No one takes care of him,"* and that is why he doesn't want to go to a government school outside the reservation for three years.[140] Henri is also nice: he is two years younger but a bit bigger, though not strong. When the holiday started, says Carl, we were this big, *four feet and two inches.* At first our little candle burned so beautifully, but then it extinguished and I cannot find another that quickly. They will return soon. After ten we go to bed.

Monday, July 17.

At 4:30 in the morning I am awakened by a very strong wind. I get up from my bed and look outside. The sun is just rising splendidly. I look at it feeling a little excited. Too bad that Tatsey's tent is not a bit more to the left. Later on I go to bed again, but we don't sleep anymore. The tent flaps up and down so much and the bed is shaking. Up in time. We have breakfast again without Tatsey. A very cheerless start to the day. Fortunately Tatsey's wife feels much better. She is up and around, but is in grandmother's tent who stays with her daughter in Browning. They did not tell us that grandma had not come back from Browning; they don't do that. They don't think that we would take an interest in it but we had already missed the old woman who is always busy around the tents. Tatsey returns our wooden bucket in which some *candy* is left after our stay in Browning. But it is no longer fit for consumption. They left it on the wagon out in the weather. Everything is wet and sticky. I search for the best pieces and then give the bucket to Joe, who has come to call us for breakfast, saying that I would like it back empty and clean to be used as a seat. After breakfast I give our laundry to Lizzy Tatsey. At my request Marie Louise brings me the broom and I quickly tidy up our tent. That makes a difference. I sweep out grass dragged in, the remains of tobacco and the sweets wrappers. If I only had such an indispensable broom all the time.

Tatsey comes at 9:00. Uhlenbeck quietly works with him, even though he is coughing more and therefor popping *cough drops*. I write in the tent in my diary. The wind calms down and once in a while the sun comes out. At 9:00 it is 60 degrees. But it will get warmer. And yes, at 12:00 it is 84, at 1:00 again 74. I sat for a while outside in front of the tent and read in *Adam Bede*: very slowly and very carefully![141] In order to learn some English. In the afternoon Uhlenbeck works again for a long time with Tatsey. But it is tough. Time and again other Indians come to assist. They all want to talk at the same time. We are still at our evening meal when suddenly I recognize Walter's voice. Walter was somewhat worried about Uhlenbeck's note that he received yesterday and now comes to tell us once more that this week he will come in the evenings to work, and in order to prove his good intention, he unbuckles his beautiful beaded belt and offers it to me. I take off my blouse belt, put on Walter's beautiful Indian belt and will wear it every day.

I have to attach a little iron badge, a numbered badge, onto Walter's watch. He always has to ask for something. It has been raining for quite a while. After Walter's departure it stops and right away we walk around a little, but very soon our little friend Carl Schildt comes along. "*He is just a pet!*" He is allowed to stay until 8:30. He does not want much candy. He is much too modest. Once he has left, we quickly walk around. We are both thoroughly cold. Early to bed. Then we lie nicely in the warmth. At night the wind sometimes blows very strongly.

Tuesday, July 18.

Start of workdays with Jim Blood.

It is raining and the wind is still blowing and it is 50°! Our boots are still damp, which makes our feet cold. It is cold all morning. Tatsey is late, but arrives with Jim Blood, the Indian who will work this week with Uhlenbeck. White Quiver is also around.[142] He certainly has an especially dark complexion. Dark, a very dark copper color and shiny. He wears a dark brown buffalo fur coat. The fur at the outside. A scarf around his head. One more Indian visitor comes in. It makes Uhlenbeck nervous when everyone wants to say a word at the same time. We eat in a hurry. When we are finished, the three Indians also get food at Tatsey's and we also hear them singing in Tatsey's tent. John is not yet back from Seville.[143] Probably stopping at the young Guardipees! That makes father Tatsey very preoccupied and we hardly see him.

After having eaten old Guardipee interprets first, then David Mad Plume happens to drop by and he can help too. Uhlenbeck gets good material. It is very valuable to him. He works for a long time with Jim Blood, who sits on the floor and gestures a lot with his hands. If we could only understand them, that would help. Today I wear Walter's present again, and I show it to our Indian visitors. Old Mad Plume also comes by. That is nice. A beautiful sight, Jim Blood and him beside each other. Our tent is closed, they eat *candy* and smoke and Uhlenbeck works hard until the evening meal. Then Jim receives his two dollar fee and is also invited for an evening meal by Tatsey. Jim also eats very neatly. While Uhlenbeck was still working Walter suddenly comes in with a Blood Indian. But not much notice is taken of Walter & his companion. He sees that Uhlenbeck is busy and knew that in advance. Walter mutters something about not being able to come in the evenings. That is obvious. Because Walter did not come to *teach*, lazy as he is. [143a]

Outside I see Tatsey talking for a while to old Mountain Chief, which makes me think about the boisterous Indian who put out a lot of effort during the dancing week in Browning and played the main role in the sham battle. All his deeds from previous years were mentioned and scenes from them imitated as much as possible. Wasn't it Joe Tatsey that ran like a shot to his father's tent, shouting, "They shot old Mountain Chief, he collapsed in convulsions."[144] Then, when Joe had not been able to stand the scene any longer and had run home. Not knowing and not understanding a sham battle. Joe had never been in a Medicine Lodge, though, and Tatsey says over and over again: "I am proud to be an Indian," but leaves his sons ignorant of ancient customs.[145] I don't approve of Tatsey on this.

It is going to be a beautiful evening. I walk up and down for a long time with Uhlenbeck. This is nice! Chub brings us letters, from Mama and Jan de Jong. And Lien especially relates a lot about the Red Lake reservation.[146] We have good news from Holland. Mr. de Josselin de Jong is doing much better and Theo is engaged to a Scottish girl; he aspires to become a Chinese interpreter and get married before his departure. All the Guardipees are at Tatsey's, certainly because his wife is not yet up and around. This disturbs Tatsey. This evening a fight between Bill & Bob. Bill makes a lot of noise and shouts, *"I will kill you!"* After half an hour all Bill's attention is focused on a handful of sweets. We don't get visitors. In the distance an Indian rides by in the darkness and sings his Indian song. It sounds beautiful; it is always touching. Later, when we go to bed, there is no wind; I like that.

Wednesday, July 19.

At 6:00 prairie birds are continuously landing on our tent. They slide time and again from the sail cloth and climb up again scratching with their claws. Up at 7:00. Now I don't want to hurry so much again. I shine our boots black and shiny. A glum breakfast with the two of us. Cheerlessly little on the table. Josephine even forgets the bread. I saw it somewhere and get it myself. We are still in Tatsey's tent when Jim Blood shows up again. He, Uhlenbeck, starts to work with him right away in one stretch until it is time to eat. Cheerful dinner and very good again. This time too much of everything: some meat, bacon and sweet corn, dried peaches, bread & coffee. Uhlenbeck has it known to Jim that he has to rest for half an hour. Jim is back again, with Tatsey at 1:00. Now they agree to what Jim will deal with. Uhlenbeck makes a list: the work will be done accordingly. Jim knows a lot about ancient times; at heart he is an old Indian and regrets any changes in the new direction. They work in one stretch until 4:30. Ambitious for Uhlenbeck, but also very tiring and for Jim a big effort and boring. If only old Mad Plume could come once again, that would be a change for Jim. Bill and Bob and Chub crawl through the tent opening. This is not our idea. Uhlenbeck cannot deal with these youngsters now. At once I give each of them some candy and as quickly as they came in, they slide outside through the tent opening. In general Uhlenbeck is very pleased with Bill's visits. I don't care for him that much. I think that he is stupid and very arrogant. He is very big and young as he is, very fat. And riding horseback is all he is capable of.

I have a lot of time to spend writing letters. Today is even colder again. This morning at first the sun shone. Now 55° and very windy. It is cheerlessly cold to sit still in the tent for long. If this is still the case after dinner, I should make some tea. At *supper the warm coffee did us well.* It warms us up so I don't make tea. We walk around to get warm again and see Lewe on horseback. He enters our tent after we went in first. If we hadn't done this, we most certainly would not have had him visit us. He is a friendly boy. How his dark, big eyes shine so softly. He is quite shy, otherwise he would certain visit us more. But during the day he hauls water for the ditch workers and makes $1.65. He gives half of it to his grandfather; the other half he has to spend on clothes. That sounds very solid. However, I think that many a *quarter* will be wasted. The entire Mountain Chief family is not geared towards using good judgement. Walter arrives. Lewe is Walter's sister's child and they like each other very much.

Walter greeted us with, *"I get lonesome for you."* Sentiment evokes sentiment and Uhlenbeck diverts Walter and says, "You must be tired and so do you want to rest and not work?" Walter likes this and now promises that he will come and work the entire day on Aug. 2 and 3 and on Aug. 4 he and his folks will move. I am very fond of Walter, but he is a strange Chinese bird. He relates long stories from his life at school and Lewe laughs about it. "Come," Walter addresses Lewe. "Let's go. The sun has already gone down." But that is not true at all. It is only darker because of the fog. But Walter looks around uncomfortably. His *saddle horse* dislikes waiting in fog and rain and has left. Lewe's horse has also disappeared. They tie them so carelessly to the poles! Then Walter runs away at full speed! That is very unlike him. For a long time we watch them.

Later we see Walter back, on his horse. Lewe is still looking for his horse. We walk around a bit more. Wet, cold feet are very uncomfortable. Uhlenbeck keeps walking up and down to keep warm. I *fix* the bed and have just finished when John and Uhlenbeck come in. Joe also steps inside and Bill and Bob too. The last two leave at once after I gave them a few sweets. Joe is shivering once in a while and thinks, with only his shirt on, that it is awfully cold at our place. He goes to his mother to be by the fire & just John stays to talk. He had returned from Browning the previous evening at 12:00. I think of how dark it must be, alone at that time of night on the prairie. At the *bridge* near Two Medicine River are ghosts. "They say that they are there," John repeats once more. "When I go by there, I always sing loudly and so I have never heard them." He is

Thursday, July 20.

tired and sleepy and has to go to Seville early next morning. Uhlenbeck takes some aniseed sucker to warm up and in the bed piled with warm blankets it is more than cosy.

I hear John at 6:00. He had by then already been looking for his horse for quite some time. At 7:00 I get up. Fortunately the sun shines somewhat. It is still 50°. We have breakfast in a hurry because Jim has already arrived on horseback. Before we enter Tatsey's tent I already saw him coming from a distance. Uhlenbeck works hard with him again. Mad Plume comes in at 11:30 for a little while. Jim eats quite a lot of candy; it seems that he likes it a lot. Time and again I put some on a sheet of writing paper in front of him on the floor where he always sits. He has a noon meal with us at Tatsey's, as does the old Guardipee and Bill is up and around again. I take a picture only of Jim, and Mad Plume alone and both of them together. It may not turn out very well. It is too sunny and the middle of the day. At 1 o'clock they go back to work. At 2 o'clock Uhlenbeck asks for tea. I will make it, that will be nice. Each of us gets three very small cups and a piece of chocolate. The tent is open; it is 75° and quite windy. I write again to Jan de Jong and Lien and a postcard to Mrs. De Jong in Leiden.[147] I read, do needlework and write the whole day inside the tent, to give there some distraction, otherwise it is so very quiet for Jim. In the afternoon working hard again with Jim. These are *werthvolle [valuable]* days. But in the evening Uhlenbeck is really quite tired. Walter comes for a short while, does one short story, and nods three Indians in. They just have *candy* and walk out again and Walter says, "I will join them to go have fun." That is the fickle nature of our unpredictable prairie life. The tent is full of visitors, you enjoy their presence and away the Indians go, they come and go; like a quick rain shower. We go to bed soon. It is nice and peaceful.

Friday, July 21.

Up at 7:00. Jim is early again. Now he is on a yellow horse that fortunately does not have a bridle. Otherwise the animal must stand there for hours and hours with a bridle in its mouth. At 12:00 he leads it to the river to let it drink. Indians do so much damage by not letting them drink, out of laziness. I think that it is strange that the animals don't look for water on their own. Can't they find it because the Indian moves around all the time? It is a warm day again, 90° in the afternoon. Uhlenbeck still works uninterrupted. I give them some tea and some chocolate. Josephine brings our laundry at 5:00. We have to pay three dollars for it. What a lot of money! Uhlenbeck calls it greedy, does not appreciate this from Tatsey. But the fees here are high. They earn a lot or nothing at all. There is no middle of the road. However, I will do the laundry myself, because this cannot go on. This evening unstable weather, at night it is somewhat stormy. We both sleep very badly. Tatsey coughs a lot. I hear him over and over again, though there is quite a distance between their tent and ours. I like the barking of the dogs once in a while. I always like to listen to it during sleepless nights. And nothing is more welcome than the sound of galloping and the neighing of horses.

Saturday, July 22.

Up at 7:00. The wind has calmed down and the sun shines again. Quick breakfast, then right away to work with Jim. First I wash the handkerchiefs. They are dry right away. Later I write letters in the tent. There is too much wind, though, to sit outside. Jim can stay on until 4:00, then he wants to move, *lower down* where many camps have gone already and where we will move as well, they say, tomorrow or the day after. That evening the weather gets worse. Miserably cold, a lot of rain, a lot of wind. Chub comes in half wet and keeps us company. That quiet boy does not say a lot and when he tells stories he tells how he managed to hit a bird with a stone and he points to his temple or his forehead. When Joe comes in, Uhlenbeck reads him aloud the story of *Waterbear*, and Joe listens attentively and later wants to hear more stories. I *fix* down our tent firmly and very carefully and I spread the blankets from the two candy barrels on our camp bed to protect us against the wind. Oh, how I would love prairie life so much more, if there wouldn't be wind. I wipe off the thermometer, which is now at 46°, then at 50°. It gets so wet, it just drips down on that spot. At night there is some kind of rodent in our tent. It must be that gopher I see all the time around our tent or it could be a *skunk*. What a horrible smell suddenly. A *skunk* gives himself away at once. Its presence is quite unbearable, all Indians agree as well.

Sunday, July 23.

Nasty day.

No wind, the sun is shining. All our misery is forgotten. The mountains lie splendidly in the west. However, a meager breakfast, bacon with bread, warm rice and syrup. A meager dinner, bacon with bread and syrup and *sweet corn* – which we never eat because we don't like the taste of it. And we don't see Tatsey and there is no trace of his wife. Where is everybody? It seems that just Josephine and Lizzy are around. Yes, all have gone to Birch.[148] Why didn't they ask if we wanted to come along? Today is our 20th anniversary. A boring day with no end. We don't see any of the Tatseys; the two of us quickly eat the three meals. Nobody is at the tent and yesterday also Tatsey did not attend the meals. How cheerless! We can't do without a chat with Tatsey. What is he doing? Why is he so busy? He has his *ranch, his log house* in Birch Creek. We would like to see his place so much.

Uhlenbeck does not feel very well today. *Belly-ache* and lumbar pain. That is what you get from *camping out in fresh air!* After breakfast he has to review the work done yesterday and the day before for over an hour. At 10:30 we go for a stroll, cross the loose plank bridge over the *ditch* and walk towards the very high hills in the distance. We see an elevated spot on the highest hill top. Is it a barren piece of rock? No, no, fortunately not. We come closer and closer and see that it is an Indian grave. Two children's coffins. The fully wrapped skeletons are quite visible. One coffin is intact. On the other one the side wall has given in. This was caused by the big, heavy stones on the lid. We descend the highest hill. I find a green hexagonal pencil with a chewed off tip. I will take it with me to Holland as a souvenir from this morning's walk. I will carry it always in my pocket. I am very happy with this small find. We encounter a wagon. It appears to be the engineer of the ditch and his wife. They ask about Uhlenbeck's book and the engineer writes down the title; he will order a book from Holland from Johannes Müller.[149] After dinner, which I just mentioned, which was so glum and meager, Uhlenbeck slept for a long time. The tent was totally sealed up and 88°.

Even while reading *Adam Bede*, I get sleepy, too. I will make some tea. At 4:30 we stroll around. We see that old Mountain Chief is busy moving. He signals and asks for tobacco. I will give the old chief a good treat and quickly walk to our tent for tobacco and for *candy* for the old woman, Walter's stepmother, who is also seated on the wagon.

She is lucky, she gets nice soft *candy* that I had set aside for Morning Eagle. Because I was in a hurry, I took the package that is ready. Earlier I was looking for Morning Eagle's tent with Chubby. But he might not be here anymore. I have not seen him for the last few days. He might turn up at the new camp. He is fond of having friends and his toothless mouth is fond of our soft sweets. After our evening meal Uhlenbeck writes to our Jan, from whom we did not receive any mail so far. Yesterday I got a letter from Nella and a postcard from Daatje, who remembered our anniversary.

We see so little of the Tatseys today. Are they getting shyer?

We are far from all the other *camps*. This is not living in the *crowd* as Uhlenbeck so dearly desires. It is good that we will move soon. We hope tomorrow and then work with Tatsey on Tuesday! But will this happen? We don't know one hour ahead what will happen, what will take place and everything drawn up with Jim Blood has to be reviewed with Tatsey! How many long working days will this take? Uhlenbeck recorded masses and such nice pieces. Jim is an orator, narrates beautifully, relives the years of his childhood, is very affected by the great disaster of the cold winters: without buffalo meat, without buffalo skins. Bacon is expensive, the square sailcloth tents cold to live in! Chubby comes in late on this Sunday night. He has just returned from Birch. The quiet day is over. Out of boredom we go to bed early.

Monday, July 24.

Departure to White Tail creek
(most beautiful camping).

Up at 7:00. Nice, clear weather. At breakfast we hear that we will move. Maybe even at eleven. First we walk around a little. Tatsey cannot teach. Then Uhlenbeck lies down for a while on his camp bed. I do needlework and repack the two big suitcases. Only at noon do they start to load and at 1:00 all the Tatseys depart in two wagons with father, mother and all the children, leaving both of us and our tent. "I will come soon for you, professor!" says Tatsey, seated on the first wagon with his wife and Cathie. Josephine drives the second wagon; beside her sits Lizzy. On top of all the items to be moved is the old grandmother again with Bob, Chub, Louise & George. Like *puppies* they look for a corner on the still overcrowded wagon. Here we are! Nobody and nothing around us. When will they come to pick us up and where will we go then? What will we think of the place? Will there be a *crowd?* And will we be able to live there? Uhlenbeck told Tatsey once more that he wants this so dearly, but will it really happen for that reason?

The weather is outstanding. We appreciate it a lot. Joe and John arrive at 2.30 each with one wagon. One wagon is both for ourselves and our furniture. John drives on with the second one. At first the candy barrels are loaded onto the wagon, then our large and small suitcases. In fact the big suitcases are much too heavy for Joe, even when John takes the heaviest part, then the camp bed, then the tent itself. The bed is spread out in the open part in the back of the wagon, a few blankets on it and Mr. and Mrs. Uhlenbeck prepare to take a seat! This is quicker said than done. The wagon is so high and there is nothing to hold on. However, I climb onto it. On my lap I have my black velvet purse full of medicine bottles, ink and spiritus and I have to hold my head and need one hand to hold on once in a while, otherwise I might be bounced out on the way.

So, the trip starts. Joe drives and sits in front. It seems he prefers to look for the biggest rocks. We are bounced around! Uhlenbeck is not

happy at all. He hates to be jolted, mutters about the back wheel that is rubbing against his hand, about the camp bed that is coming down a little bit towards us and presses against his back and shoulders. We would walk alongside the wagon, if we did not have to cross White Tail Creek. That's for sure. Right behind us a family, man, wife and children, follow. The two white horses' heads touch us time and again. Uhlenbeck does not like it. But it does not bother me. I hate it when a horse gallops near me and I can't guess which direction it will take with its rider, and I especially don't like it when it is getting dark. Often we dislike different things. I found this ride weird rather than awful and would love it if our acquaintances in Holland could have seen us. In White Tail Creek we stop for a moment. Four Indian boys are busy bathing. I see their dark bodies, their beautiful shoulders with broad chests. "*Some ducks,*" says

Indian boys bathing (DJdJ 1910).

little Joe! Tatsey's camp is already set up. No trace of a crowd! That is a quarter of an hour down further down. "Too many horses there," says Tatsey, "for his small children!" His tents look beautiful in the very tall grass, in a little valley and close to Badger, which at that spot is wide with currents foaming over the big rocks. The low shrubbery gives a nice effect. Outside the small stove is burning; the whole family is gathered around it having their evening meal. We will eat in the tent and the warm tea tastes delicious. Since breakfast we have not had anything yet. But I appreciate that the Indians, when they are moving or driving, skip their meals. What can be simpler! But Uhlenbeck says to Tatsey, "We don't want to camp at Badger. We want to be at White Tail Creek and in the middle of the camp."

Perhaps Tatsey mutters to himself, because now he will have to walk that distance between his tent and our camp time and again. After the evening meal we go to look for a spot; the old and the young Joe get up into our wagon while we walk alongside. And, 15 minutes higher, we see a good spot, close to White Tail, right close and between other tents. It is still warm. However, a beautiful evening. How beautiful these tents look pitched there. How beautiful the Rockies contrast with the clear evening sky. Such high prairie mountains, such large plains, what herds of horses and everywhere children colorfully dressed, women in colorful skirts. Everything gives an impression of *freshness*. It is as if everything is new to me again. We have never been among everyone so much! Tatsey and Joe set up our tent, but don't do a good job. The boys did not take along all the *pegs,* which means that now there are not enough. We encourage

Seventeen-year-old Indian girl and her brother outside the jail (DJdJ 1910).

Joe to come back this evening with more poles. We look around. There are also children swimming in the *creek*. They swim and flounder about. An old Indian is washing himself. A very old woman takes off her *moccasins* and crosses the *creek*. Uplifting scenes! What compensation for the previous day. July 23 will stay as a *sad blank* in our memory. When our tent is fixed I make up the camp bed and arrange all kinds of things from the suitcases. Then we go out for a walk and inspect the terrain! I am in such a good mood! It is so Indian here! We see lots of people, hear lots of voices! I take water from the *creek*. Maggy runs towards me. Maggy whom we saw earlier with Irene.[150] She wants to carry my full bucket. I will make some tea. Nice tea, not strong. That will taste good, after our gorgeous walk in and around and behind the *camps*.

Again we see all kinds of Indians crossing the *creek*; an old woman lifts her apron very high, another one takes a girl under the arms as if she is a bundle of branches and, wrapped in a blanket, an Indian approaches the *creek*. He throws his garment down, washes himself and then, wrapped in the blanket, walks away again towards his tent. Further down we see a *sweat lodge*. What are they doing there? Two Indians are sitting in it. It is open at the side of the sun. They nourish their naked dark bodies in the delicious warmth of the sun and do their prayers. I steal glances at them. Uhlenbeck looks directly at them and enjoys the first experiences of his new location. Jim Blood's *camp* appears to be close to ours. He passes our tent and shouts an Indian greeting. Numerous Indian children around our tent. They watch us anxiously. With his hands in front of his eyes one

MRS. UHLENBECK'S DIARY

Four Indians boys at the ditch camp (DJdJ 1910). | Three Grass dancers at the ditch camp (DJdJ 1910).

Boys playing baseball (DJdJ 1910).

little boy goes running past us. Another one looks for a moment and says a brief greeting. They will get used to us when they see us every day.

Now we are looking for our own tent. The teacups have been cleared away! Walter arrives. He is on horseback, he comes straight from Browning. *"Do you know about my trouble from yesterday? I had a fight."* And then he tells quite a story. Big Beaver's son started on about an old feud from three years ago, when Walter, please note, was a policeman himself. This led to his arrest and now, after his release from Helena, the Indian got very angry again when he was drinking whiskey and feeling excited and suddenly noticed Walter. The Indian is now in jail again in Browning and Walter might be summoned for the case. We follow Walter when he rides away and now know exactly where he lives. The warmth of the day is now absolutely gone. It is getting cold and Uhlenbeck puts on his heavy coat. I put on my coat but already feel a sore throat. We had better go to bed early, when it has quieted down completely around us, in order to rise early. How wonderful! Now we are in a crowd. Now we are living, as it seems, in the middle of a whole village of tents scattered gracefully about.

Maybe we will spend the most wonderful weeks here! We spoke briefly to Jim Red Fox, when we were going from Tatsey's *camp* to our new location. How this slim Indian boy laughs at us in most friendly manner. Later, when other Indians are around, he will pass by us again looking shyly at us. We sleep well in our new terrain. At 5:00 a horse woke me up. He rubs his back time and again against our tent poles. The entire tent is

MRS. UHLENBECK'S DIARY

shaking. Right away I see the shadow of a horse's snout on the tent cloth and hear horse-neighing. Before 6:30 I am already busy with the laundry and now I wash my whole blouse – I don't always do this, sometimes I just wash the collar. I also shine our boots, which is proof that I am in a good mood, and then I quickly get dressed. I have already gone to White Tail for water when Uhlenbeck is only half dressed. What a splendid scene! An aged Indian sits on the shore. He is not dressed and is about ready to take a bath. Shall I return? No, that would be crazy. That would be puritanical. And I don't want water from his rinsed back. So I have to get the water *higher up* and I pass by him. Another Indian, whom I don't know, says something to me. I enjoy this! In high spirits I return to our tent, relaying to Uhlenbeck everything he missed.

Suitcases closed, tent closed and then to Tatsey's for our breakfast. Once we arrive at 8:00, a quarter of an hour later, everything is ready. Meat and bacon and peas. This time peas and not the big green peas, but the kind that I like but that Uhlenbeck cannot handle very well. More than once he suffers from *belly-ache*. There is also jelly. After breakfast, with no Tatsey around, we want to find out where the *reclamation store is to find out something*. Ten minutes further down from Tatsey's *camp* we find the different buildings. Upon our return Mrs. Oolson nods at us.[151] We have to go in. The two rooms in the wooden shed are furnished quite nicely. They live in the front one. There is a heavy cooking stove, just like the government smithy in Browning. As well I count three chairs, a sofa and a few tables. All kinds of colorful pictures on the walls. The bedroom is in the back, with mosquito netting, furnished for warmth[152] and for the cold. They will stay here until mid-January and then work in an office in Helena. They are a young married couple. She lived until her 18th year in New York (the best city in the world). But now the conversation has to come to a halt. Tatsey will be here at 9:00 and we never keep our interpreter waiting even for one minute! Still one more interruption. The old Eagle Calf sit in his open *tipi*. He calls us. In front of the *tipi* we talk for a little while to the old medicine man, Tatsey's uncle.

The old man complains, "My body is not healthy." Tatsey later says, "I believe that; they just butchered a cow themselves, the old man will have eaten too much meat." "It might or it might not," I think by myself, but the old man coughs terribly and he is so short of breath! Now hurry! And walk a bit faster! Indian Joe is already walking in front of us, slow as always with his head bent. We catch up to him and continue on together. In the tent I quickly fix everything so work can start right away.

It is a nice morning for work. But inside it is very warm. Outside it is nicer and I look around in amazement. At the other tent close to us the stove is sitting outside and has a fire lit inside. Lots of smoke rises from the pipe. A few long poles are put over the stove like for a *tipi*. An Indian woman drapes all kinds of pieces of meat on them; they all look like thin slices. She is wearing a white dress. Again and again she rearranges the pieces, cuts and scratches them with a knife and sometimes tastes them too. Oh, how these women can laze away the time. Early in the day they visit and talk and lie down and sit and smoke endlessly. The *little ones* walk around and don't care if their dresses or shirts are tattered, or their faces are dirty. When they *move* they are busy, but the rest of the time life is lazy and relaxed, but when winter comes and they go through times of great misery because of lack of food. Very many Indians work at the *ditch*, which explains all these herds of horses in the immediate surrounding. And dogs! Everywhere! They say that some Indians have around twelve to sixteen. Could they have that many? Well, lots of them wander around. They search out food for themselves. Everywhere they find larger or smaller bones, but they don't have a fat life. So they look skinny, neglected and dirty. It is getting warmer and warmer. The thermometer is at 99°. Too bad that it is not at 100. But Uhlenbeck works quietly with Tatsey. Now I sit in front of the half-open tent. In the evening we watch the *base-ball* game for a long time and Walter came to continue with one *page* of his *story*. He was too tired, the *poor fellow!* Not late to bed.

Wednesday, July 26.[153]

Nice weather. Not too warm. Up at 5:30. Before eight we are already at the Tatseys, who eat breakfast outside in the tall grass close to the hot, burning stove. We take a detour back to our camp and talk again to the sons of Eagle Calf and they get some sweets again.[154] They are nice, timid boys, be it that they never did anything, never learned anything. Jim Blood has to help out again. Tatsey can't solve a difficult part. After eating, Morning Eagle and a woman who speaks Peigan and English arrive. Her husband is Weasel Head, and Jim Blood and Uhlenbeck read them stories out loud.[155] Yesterday Peter and Duck Head spent some time with us.[156] After the visit, when nobody is around, I make some tea. We have just finished everything at 3:00 when Tatsey trots in. Because he is late he does not get anything. Then he works again with Uhlenbeck and Jim Blood also shows up. But the small children outside are sometimes so noisy and run around our tents, maybe proof of rapprochement. In order to finish something Uhlenbeck continues until 5:30. Now there is a very strong wind. After the evening meal I haul rocks from far and near to plug the large cracks. That helps, but it is blowing in the tent. We stroll around a bit. Jim Red Fox and Jim Vielle come along with us. They come inside and we have a nice talk. Timid Red Fox is getting quite used to me. His gentle look is quite different from Jim Vielle's dark, fiery, restless and piercing eyes. They enjoy the *candy*. Then, for the first time, also the *kisses*. Then the policeman Peter comes to talk for a while, but actually he comes for *Bear Chief's life story*, which he wanted to read to his wife. He takes the book along and later that night returns it, intending to borrow another part later. We walk around again and *watch* the *base-ball* players. When it gets dark, I fix the bed. Uhlenbeck comes home holding two Indian girls, Maggie and Lucie, by the hand. I give them sweets. Maggie especially is an old acquaintance of ours. The affectionate girl almost kisses me. I check all the large cracks in the tent. To bed. Quite soon it starts to rain, strong wind and thunder. A troubled start to the night.

Thursday, July 27.

Up at 6:30. Nice weather. To the Tatseys at 7:00 and by then our sleep tent is already transformed into a living room area. After breakfast first a chat with Eagle Calf's wife and a few children, among them Mary Duck Head & Jim White Man in the *log house*, beside the *tipi*. Then a visit to the *tipi*.[157] Old Eagle Calf and his much older friend, the nearly 100-year-old Morning Eagle, are there. The inside of the *tipi* is beautiful; we sit on the ground as well. Now Eagle Calf wears his black headband again. Once in a while Morning Eagle uses his white handkerchief on his eyes which I had earlier presented to him for washing his eyes. Before nine we are in our tent, because Jim Blood will tell *The young man who lived with a beaver*. Walter tells this same story, but according to another tradition. When we walk again in the direction of Eagle Calf's, we should look for the rocks where, in the old times, the buffaloes, being chased, stampeded and died.

This morning they work hard. Then a *big dinner*, tongue and a fruit pie! In the afternoon I do a lot of needlework, read and write. I make tea. Again it is 88°. After a supper of, among other things, rice and jelly, Walter comes with cousin Owl Child and a green-haired Indian who says that he is married and has four children.[158] A moment later it becomes clear that he is only 20 years old, has neither wife nor children, and just wanted to joke. He, as well Owl Child, has a lot of fun with our credulity. Only Walter laughs sourly, an expression that happens more than once. How he looked the previous evening! He had not slept the whole night, he said, and felt miserable. Will I really get moccasins from him and U.? Maybe an Indian trick? If only this could be true! But, thinks Walter to himself, having to tell *stories* is the worst thing that can happen to a human being! We walk to watch the *base-ball* players and Walter goes with us. He is not ashamed to go watch the Indians with us whites. Later Uhlenbeck comes back again with two small kids, who get *candy*. To bed with nice, quiet weather.

Friday, July 28.

Up before 6:30. Hurry. Before 7:30 we are already en route to Tatsey's for breakfast. We meet up with Jim Red Fox, who is riding with another boy to the *Old Agency.* We follow the boys as long as possible. The steep, meandering uphill path lies there so romantic. Out of sight and then in view once more, I long to follow that uphill path myself, longing to know what land lies behind it. Jimmy told us that he will be *around.* Uhlenbeck is always so happy when he sees one of the Red Foxes. After breakfast we head to the *store.* We also pay a visit to Mrs. Olson, this is how you spell the name, at this early hour of the day. At 9:00 we are back in our tent. Jim Blood comes right away. Two other Indians also come to listen for a while. Mabel Henault also comes; she is allowed to come in. The large pile of notebooks filled with writing sparks her interest, All kinds of neighborhood boys are kept outside. Just three are allowed in for a moment to get some *candy.* During *working hours* we have no use at all for all these *kids.* Jim Blood stops at 11:00. *The dogs have separated,* the story is finished – and Tatsey is still not around. That's why we go out for a short walk, continuously watching to see if the *teacher* will show up before it is time to eat. We climb over the *ditch* and high up into the hills. It is a stony slope, often I step from rock to rock. Uhlenbeck stays at the bottom. At the top I don't have a nice view. It is the middle of the day, it is not very clear and there must be a forest fire, at least, that is what it looks like and how it smells. It would be too bad if the forest fire would last a while just like last year, when all views were blocked for days and weeks at a stretch and there was always that *bad smell.*

I receive a postcard from Loe Scheffer. He passed his engineering exam. Also a postcard from Jetje, from Mama a long letter. A bit later they bring me a letter from Anna Marcus from Switzerland. I send a post-card to Scheffer. *Dinner:* radishes, very big ones from the mission garden, and rice with apricots. At 2:00 Tatsey arrives. Once in a while Jim Blood comes and helps and at 4:00 two other Indians also drop by. One is our neighbor who limps; he fell from his horse. He has long hair. It hangs loose and falls far below his waist. Together they sit on the large suitcase and listen to a *history.* Jim sits on the ground, Tatsey on the little chest. They work until the evening meal. We leave with Tatsey and after supper we return straightaway to our tent. Lewe Kasoos and his cousin Peter Step by Mistake, a nice, but shy boy 17 years old, soon arrive.[159] He doesn't speak a word of English, laughs a bit and looks in amazement at my cro-chet work and says to Lewe, "How fast she is doing that." After they have left, we watch the baseball players again for a long time. Joe Tatsey also comes and wrestles once in a while with Lewe or boxes with him. When it gets dark, I go home ahead to fix the bed. I am just finished with it, when Uhlenbeck comes in with Jimmy Four Horns and Day Rider. Both talk and eat a bit. We sit together cosy in candlelight. The visitors leave, we blow out the light and only then prepare for the night. We really don't like the shadows on our tent cloth!

Blackfoot boy from the mission school (DJdJ 1910).

Saturday, July 29.

I only get up at 7:00. That is too late. We have break-fast and find Tatsey in a very bad mood. There is *something wrong with a cow*. John failed to do his duty. By mistake another Indian's cow was butchered, that will cost Tatsey money. We return to our tent and wait and wait, but Tatsey doesn't show up. Uhlenbeck is not at all in a good mood. Oh, the waiting for your *interpreter*! We go eat. Tatsey eats with us. There is a lot of good food, again cow tongue, a sharp contrast to the usual leather-like, thin slices of meat; there are also canned peaches and pears, yes, even rice and bread! How ex-travagant! In a few days there will be hardly anything again. Uhlenbeck says to Tatsey, "John should come to our tent when you are engaged in business." But Tatsey answers: "Don't worry Professor, I will be there at 1:00 and then we will work at one stretch right until 6:00, so 5 hours at one stretch!"

Upon our request Tonny, he calls himself Tony, comes in. He is a beautiful Indian child with a half-naked chest, with pitch-black braids and a timid, attractive ap-pearance. He only stays for a moment to get some sweets. He was the one who ran past us on the first day keeping his hand in front of his eyes. Then the *'pony'* child comes to the front of our tent. He also gets a few candies. The little boy is not that bad, but it is hard to see how he time and again rides that very young pony. Tatsey does arrive at 1:00 & Jim Blood also comes around to listen. I give Jim tobacco and sweets again and he says to Tatsey that he has never seen a white woman who is so friendly towards Indians. Tatsey then adds to me: "*He thinks you are wonderful.*" I am delighted with this praise. Will I succeed in developing a friendship with them and will

MRS. UHLENBECK'S DIARY

Sunday, July 30.

they look for rather than avoid our tent! Jim plays a bit with the pieces of matchsticks on the ground and the blanket. It is as if he wants to make them march like soldiers. There is a very strong wind again & kicking up so much dust! And early this morning it was so splendidly quiet. Jim is neat. He takes up all the matchstick pieces and throws them one by one outside the tent. He also neatly throws the *kisses* wraps outside. The inconvenience of this new kind of sweets the empty wrappings, lying *around* everywhere.

Uhlenbeck works exactly until 6:00 with Tatsey. That was a hard afternoon, but Uhlenbeck does not hand out one quarter of an hour as a present. Tatsey does not go to his *camp,* he has to go *higher up* to other camps for business and will only have *supper* at 10:00. The stomach of an Indian takes it easy. So we eat our evening meal alone. Tatsey's wife and the children are not inside either. We eat what is prepared and I pour tea or coffee. Back in our tent. Walter comes straightaway with Owl Child and Walter says, "Next Sunday I will come and work the whole day!" We walk around a bit. The weather is somber, heavy clouds blow over and it still rains. Walter says, "*I feel lonely* when we have this kind of weather." That very timid boy and another Jimmy enter our tent. They are very shy and pull the tattered, felt hats deep down over their eyes. The boys don't know how old they are and are extremely timid. We go to bed rather early. I am prepared for a storm. I have put a few more stones on and around the poles.

Rain. "Hand game." Tatsey's oldest daughter sick.

That is that. *Sister Margaret's crossing is over at last.* She will be happy about that. This night she crossed over to England.[160] I am up already at 6:30, even though it is Sunday. I have many things to do and maybe Walter will be there already at 9:00. Outside it looks gray. It stayed dry the whole night. Now it slowly starts to rain. That is not very promising. We have breakfast at 8:00. Put on overshoes, take an umbrella along. The Tatseys had not counted on us yet. But everything is ready soon. John still sits on his bed & Joe & Chub & George, still nicely tucked in, pulled the blankets over them once more. After breakfast I head first to our camp. I pick beautiful roses, in bud they are especially beautiful and they smell so lovely. I also have to do some laundry quickly. I have just finished with everything when Uhlenbeck arrives. He quickly goes outside again and has a chat with Mike Big Lake.[161]

He is outside the tent, right in front of us, and he is the father of that healthy three-year-old Indian boy who always sings and sometimes dances so beautifully, when he thinks that nobody sees him.[162] His mother is a sister of Peter & Mary Bear Leggings. This woman also seems so quiet and friendly, just like Peter & Mary's mother. Mike also comes in. He does not smoke, neither he nor his brothers smoke or chew tobacco. But he likes *candy* and for his nice little son and an even younger daughter I give him a few handfuls to take along.[163]

Just when he has left, that nice Jimmy comes by with an even younger brother of about five years old. Both get *kisses.* Then Walter comes. It is 10:00 and both start to work right away. Maybe there is a Crow Medicine dance today and Walter starts by saying that he might want to go there. This is called working a full day. We will wait and see how it turns out. It is rainy and 50°. Walter does not like that at all. After having arrived at 10:00, he leaves already at eleven. "*Now, I must go & shop – for my folks!*" That is too bad!! And in order to placate him I even heated some water and gave him two cups of bouillon, because it was raining so much. Through the rain to eat at Tatsey's. It is very wet everywhere.

I am wearing my overshoes, but it is not possible to avoid the tall grass here and there. I have to take care that the skirt of my dress doesn't get too wet. There is nice macaroni soup; it is prepared because of the wet weather. The soup is scalding hot and in the iron bowl it doesn't cool off very quickly. We return in the rain. Back home Uhlenbeck puts on other socks & boots right away and until 3:00 he sits tightly tucked in under the blankets because of the cold, on the camp bed. Walter was supposed to return at 1:00, but just stayed away. We are very pleased that it is completely dry at 4:00. For Uhlenbeck a day of rain is also very unpleasant; it is the only day of the week that he uses to take a rest. Our part of the prairie is soon passable again. No high grass here and it is located so much higher than Tatsey's camp. Close by, in a tipi, we hear *drumming*. The Crow Medicine dance has started & we will go there and have a look.[164] Because of the damp, Uhlenbeck sat himself down on his handkerchief. One woman had to laugh a lot about it and threw him her blanket. Now both of us have very good seats, that is what Uhlenbeck thought, but before I come in, old Morning Eagle approached Uhlenbeck & sat beside him. That was the end of his own nice seat on the blanket, because, when I came in, I was allowed to sit down next to our old Indian friend & again Uhlenbeck had to be content with the handkerchief.

Due to the damp we did not stay for long. Again I am very impressed, partly because of the ceremony, partly because of the very Indian-like surroundings. We pick up our evening meal. It is not raining and we avoid the big puddles. After our evening meal back to White Tail, and there we got to see something very beautiful, something very fine, something very unexpected. The game that is being played was a *handgame* and is taken from the Gros Ventres.[165] The game is being played in a *shade* fixed to a tent.[166] For over two hours we watched it. It is a childlike game. Little discs are handed out. The people handing them out, here a designated man and a designated woman, later guess in which hand the discs or the little sticks are held. The whole milieu is very interesting to us. There is continuous drumming and Sam made himself very useful. He flirts a

whole lot, that slim, young man. His beautiful eyes are shining. Women & girls all around are being courted. The music makes them restless. Sam just goes on playing, sometimes rubbing his hands through his shiny hair, laughing with his shiny, friendly eyes, which has a bewitching effect on the girls. Oh, that Sam with his quiet face. Today he has a field day and has a lot of fun when he has them guess in which hand he held the *little stick*. And he can make sounds, in the same way the women can! Exactly the same *yells!*

With his hand in front of his mouth! Tatsey also came to have a look and cheerfully watched the game with a happy expression on his face. I have not seen him look this way before. I only know Tatsey with a bent head. We also saw John & Joe. In places tent flaps are turned down. Everywhere visitors stand & watch, lean or stand on some wagons beside the tent. Still I see the player in my head; with monotonous movements he keeps handing out the *little sticks* and time and again the same melody is repeated and he takes his sticks, decorated with tassels, moving them up and down with his right hand. His face is quiet, no cheerful expression is to be seen on it, but for him it should be fun too. Old Mountain Chief is also there. Finally he wants to perform something and time & again he mimics a grizzly bear that is wounded during a chase. That was not a lovely sound. But perhaps remarkably realistic. He also mimics the animal's jumping. Everyone has a lot of fun with it. And Mountain Chief likes to be admired; he likes to play the first fiddle.

The game has ended and we stroll around a bit. The evening is splendid. The evening light falls beautifully over the prairie, over the mountains, over the herds of horses. It has been one of those evenings one will never forget. Such evenings make up for cold weather, any deprivation. Back in our tent we light our candle. Joe & Lewe Kasoos come, and a moment later John & Jimmy Red Fox also. All four stay eat and chat with us. After they have left, the tent is full of *kisses* wraps. But the ending to a somber and unpleasant morning is cheerful.

Monday, July 31.

I rise at 6:00. The weather is beautiful. I want to clean up in the tent and quickly wash socks & stockings, also empty the one *candy* barrel and give it a different spot, etc. etc. so I have a lot of rummaging to do before Uhlenbeck gets up. We leave for breakfast on time. I fill my pompadour workbag with sweets. I give one-third of it to Chubby to pass on to the small Tatseys. I take all the rest along for the children or grandchildren of old Eagle Calf. Then we enter his *log house* beside the *tipi* for the first time. It does not look bad, but cannot be called tidy.

Both housewives and a few children are eating. Eagle Calf sits in his *tipi*. He lives there during the summer months; only when winter arrives does the old man move into his *log house,* but he only likes the old Indian tent, in which he feels at home.

Eagle Calf's first wife died; now he has two left, not sisters, but maybe relatives.[167] That is why the children from these marriages have very different ages. Duck Head, the oldest one, must be 45, Paul, the youngest one, four years old. Little Paul is a beautiful child. We walk further down. Coming back, we enter the *tipi* that is now open. Duck Head & Peter are there with still another woman and a few children. "*Sokapi!*" the old man exclaims, when he learns that we will stay for a few more months. Then quickly back to our tent! John will come and teach. Tatsey wants to go to the *store* for business. Working with John sure goes well. Apart from a few difficulties, he doesn't dislike interpreting the texts that much. But, at noon, he doesn't walk down with us. "*He is too bashful, that fellow!*" We eat with Tatsey. There is a very big *trout* sliced and fried (and caught by Joe). There is cow tongue, peas and stewed fruits; there is also bacon and bread!!

Upon returning to our tent, Uhlenbeck's little friend, Jim War Bonnet, gets some *candy* for himself and his friend.[168] Uhlenbeck works with Tatsey. A few times Indians come by and listen. I don't know them, but I also give them tobacco and sweets. The young, freckled Indian who always wears blue spectacles also comes in. The visitors have left. I make some tea and am about to pour it, when Mabel comes in with

a girlfriend. Mabel laughs heartily about my little stitch ripper – now Uhlenbeck's scratch knife. She looks at it and shouts, "*Gracious me, is it not cute!*" Unexpectedly we get a visit from Father Soer; he stands for a moment in front of our tent, doesn't want to take time to come in because he still has to visit ill people & wants to baptize two more children. But he has letters for us: a letter from Mama, a postcard from Prof. Saussaye, in which he asks that we write him something about ourselves. Fortunately a long letter from me to Mrs. is already underway. There is also a postcard from Jan de Jong about Indian texts. From Holland they told him that his father is doing much better, that he is walking again and even goes downstairs. A little further down is *Brother* Galdes with his *buggy.* Uhlenbeck walks Father Soer back to his carriage, gives him a letter to be sent to Haarlem and starts working with Tatsey. Before we leave for our evening meal, we met up again with *Brother* Galdes. We talk for quite a while with this friendly, most modest Basque. Uhlenbeck finds him the most amiable man in the mission. He has been there already for many years and always talks about the *poor Indians.* He shakes my hand so friendly-like, asking whether I like *camping out* and whether I am *lonesome* or not. Still I hear his "*That is good, that is good!*" after I have reassured him. The two of us have supper & inform him about Josephine's coughing. Lizzy & Chubby come to us this afternoon for some medicine for Josephine. So I give them Doveri tablets and our lozenges. Her cough is very bad & and she doesn't feel good. Lizzy quickly left with the medicine & Chub stayed around until we send him back.

Uhlenbeck wants to rest a little before Tatsey would come back. Back from our supper, Uhlenbeck heads in the direction of the *store.* I go to our *camping place* and write in my diary. Eagle Calf of course calls on Uhlenbeck again. He dearly wanted Uhlenbeck's watch chain to hang on the elk stand that he showed us this morning, but Uhlenbeck acted as if he did not understand. He cannot do without his chain. Now we stroll around a bit, handing out a few candies here & there. Jimmy, Uhlenbeck's friend, gets lots of sweets and also some for his little sisters too. Later this evening Walter drives by with Owl Child. *"I will come to-morrow in the evening to teach you!"* he shouts at us. Lewe comes in with Willy Sanderville (Kjaijoes' son) and Philip Chief; they eat *kisses* and laugh more than talk.[169] Lewe is not easy to deal with. To bed at 10:00. Again there is a forest fire.

Tuesday, August 1.

Lots of rain. No teaching.

At 6:30 it is very dark. It will certainly rain and the forest fire is still burning. Jimmy gets some more sweets. The War Bonnets leave; they are about to pull down their shabby tent.[170] I also give sweets to our neighbor's boy, August Big Lake, and to our naked friend, who is dressed now somewhat because they are also about to *move*. Will a lot of Indian families move today or tomorrow? Nothing is more charming to us than being exactly in the middle of the *crowd*. Uhlenbeck has just started to work with Tatsey, when Walter shows up in front of our tent. Apparently he has something to tell. Uhlenbeck goes outside to him, but that is still not enough. He wants to meet with me, he wants to talk to me and preferably alone. Tatsey goes outside with Uhlenbeck & Walter comes in to present me with presents. He honors me with a few moccasins and a purse. Later Uhlenbeck also gets moccasins. He surprised me a lot and I offer him a few packages of tobacco and a few *kisses*. He certainly sees that I am very happy with his presents. But soon he wants to leave again. His *folks* are *moving* also. But, says Walter, at the end of this week I will come and teach another two or two and a half days. Oh, promises, promises. Walter, Walter, sometimes you are so friendly, so touchingly fond of us, but why do you delay your teaching time and again! Don't you regret the promised candor? And doesn't it upset your inner being!

After Walter's departure Uhlenbeck works uninterrupted with Tatsey until 12:00. Dinner, again fried fish, bacon and bread, pies and dried peaches. After dinner a little stroll. Eagle Calf is always out look-ing for us. He recognizes our voices right away and shouts from his tipi, *"Katojes! Katojes!"*[171] For the time being, that is what he calls Uhlenbeck after the well-known story. We enter the tipi. George Speck, his grand-son, is there also and they speak English very well, and Peigan.[172] The old Indian is again very amiable. He is so accommodating with us. When his son, Jimmy, comes in and also wants to sit down on one of the beds, his father tells him to go outside, to the cattle, he should not be so lazy.[173] So Jimmy leaves, but outside he can be lazy too. Jim does and has never done anything; he is laziness personified and now looks timidly and dully out of his dark, misty eyes.

Old Eagle Calf wants to give us some *paint*. He sends his grandson, George Speck, to the log house. George returns with a cherished package. It looks like a fur pouch. All kinds of sacred artifacts emerge from it: among other items, a very small weasel about 10 cm. long (a small, still entirely white-haired animal), a little wheel with beaded spokes, small bells, a pouch with one big bell attached. He produces the bell, presses it against his chest, first to the right, then to the left. While doing this, he does not see us anymore. There is also a pouch with red paint. He opens it – the leather pouch is tied with a leather strip – and produces a piece [of paint] and some chips. One of his wives arrives with a piece of leather and a leather strip; the piece and the chips are to be wrapped in it. He himself strings the strip around it and knots it with a special knot. That is how Uhlenbeck gets it. We must take it with us to our own country. At sea it will protect us from accidents. Eagle Calf's spirit will be with us and give us a safe journey back home. And then he paints us, first Uhlenbeck, then me. He takes the fine paint grains in his palm, wets them with some saliva. He firmly rubs it with his other hand into a colorful mass. Then he indicates how I have to paint Uhlenbeck back home.

With the sacred sacrificial otter paint on our forehead we leave the old medicine man & return to our own camp. We meet up with Adam, one of his oldest sons, and we show him our painted foreheads. Adam approves of his father's act and says: *"A sie sokapi!"* We are very fond of Adam as well. This big, heavily built Indian has a strikingly handsome face, but he does not speak English; he can neither read nor write. We see him more than once in & around the Tatseys. We see Many Guns (49 years old) at our tent and John Red Fox (16 years old).[174] Both come in. Many Guns is ugly, tall, very slim, with deep-set secretive eyes, but his appearance is still very agreeable and, when he laughs, even very attractive. He also has those very short top teeth. Earlier, he says, I had my hair tied around my waist with my belt, it hung down that long & he points out how long it had been. Now he has ordinary braids. His forehead is also painted; he had a bad dream.

Uhlenbeck reads *Bear Chief's songs* and pieces from *Bear Chief's life story* to Many Guns. John Red Fox is, when needed, *interpreter*. No wonder Many Guns wants to hear that story. More than once he figures in it; in the old times he was always going on *raids*. He and Bear Chief often raided enemy tribes together. A bit later he says: "I will tell you a story too," and he starts to describe a scene from his own war past.[175] Tatsey arrives. I close the tent carefully, especially the crack in the front – the wind blows right through it. Now Uhlenbeck writes down Many Gun's story with Tatsey's English translation beside it. In the meantime John Red Fox leaves; he heard a game of *horseshoes* being played outside. I recognized the sound too. Now Joe plays, too. Many Guns also eats sweets and smokes a bit, but he does not take with him the whole tobacco pouch; therefore, I indicate that he can keep it all. This Indian too is decent. This always strikes us again as remarkable. Uhlenbeck works until 5:30 with Tatsey, who leaves the tent just before us. It starts to rain and very hard too. Too bad, Uhlenbeck wants to go to the *store* and leaves before me. I am the first to arrive at Tatsey's *camps*. What rain! We have to go back home through little ditches and it takes agility not to slide on the slippery slopes. Back home Uhlenbeck at once gets dry socks & boots and takes aniseed oil with sugar. Sometimes his intestines are oversensitive, too bad. He gets into bed and under the blankets. Coats, socks and shoes, I hang everything to air in our tent, hoping for sun the following day. Our tent is such a sight! How wet it is everywhere! It is only 7:30. Were it only nine! Then I would go to bed also. Now I work at my diary.

Today many *camps* left us. We observed this sadly. Before nine I close our wet palace. It is and stays wet. I don't see anyone when I look outside. So, early to bed. Uhlenbeck suffers the whole night from *belly-ache*. Time and again I too wake up and hear small Big Lake cough, a horse neigh or Tonny's dog bark.

Wednesday, August 2.

Argument with interpreter. Many visitors.

It is raining again very hard. I didn't get up until 7:30. All of the clothing is still wet as before and as long as it rains the tent cloth drips with humidity, like a very fine drizzle. Uhlenbeck is not at all in the mood to go out for breakfast. He will eat only a tiny little bit. And it does not cross my mind to go alone through all the damp, "*My shoes are no good*." I would rather make some tea for myself and for breakfast I eat some sweets. Uhlenbeck gets dressed at 8:30, but then gets back under the blankets so he won't suffer cold feet and to give his intestines some rest. At 9:00 Tatsey comes in; he can only stay for a few moments and has to move on for business. Joe also comes. He will pick up some bread at his mother's, just a single piece of bread. At 10:00 Joe is back. He brings a platter with 10 *hotcakes*, some bacon, some tea and sugar. This is too much for breakfast. The weather remains bad and we tell Joe that we have enough food for our noon meal and will only be back at his mother's for our evening meal. In the evening the weather will be better. For breakfast we each have two *hotcakes* and tea. It is not really food for someone with a *belly-ache*.

Time and again I look around for our interpreter. Tatsey stays away, but there are visitors: John Red Fox, Joe Day Rider, a big 17-year-old boy, Little Bull and a small boy, Many Guns, … & son of Bear Chief's partner.[176] I take their pictures. Then they come in again, also Jim Oldman Chief, and I give them *kisses* and tobacco.[177] Five of these young redskins seated on the ground in our tent. If only I could describe this scene! Once they have left at noon, I close our tent from the inside and prepare our noon meal. Again we eat the cakes and drink tea and I also eat bacon. Everything with our hands, because I don't have a fork or a knife. Now each some more tea, sweets for dessert and our dinner is finished. I wrap up the platters. The sun peeks out for a moment; it starts to blow. It seems that the rain is over. We go outside at once, I hang out all the wet clothing. I have to pin everything down carefully because of the wind. I also pin our boots to the lines. I just saw Joe Tatsey drive by. I give him the saucers to take along. He thinks that his father will come to teach. I hope so. Uhlenbeck gets nervous with this staying away. At two 2:00 Uhlenbeck says, "I can't stand this any longer," and he goes to Tatsey's camp, who is not at home, but Tatsey's wife has to listen to how dissatisfied Uhlenbeck is with her spouse. Maybe harsh words, but it is the truth.

In a nasty mood Uhlenbeck returns with me to our tent. At 4:00 Chub peers through a crack in our tent; I immediately recognize his face. He is our big friend, quiet friendly Chubby. For a while he sits quietly beside Uhlenbeck on the camp bed and has some *kisses*. Tatsey shows up at 4:30, not to teach, but to inquire about Uhlenbeck's health. Courteous! Certainly, but Uhlenbeck would rather work at once with Tatsey. It is not pleasant that Chub is around, but now Tatsey hears from Uhlenbeck himself, that it cannot go on like this. Things have to change. Is it better that Tatsey teaches in the mornings and John in the afternoon or vice versa? Chubby leaves, this conversation apparently bores him. Tatsey looks melancholic. He is too busy with his *beef contract* with the government *store*. He says that he can not keep it up. He will think about it, talk with his wife about it and the following morning he will inform us about the new arrangement. If need be, we may have to go to another location and work with another *interpreter*. At the last moment Uhlenbeck shouts after him, "Tatsey, we would rather have you and your son as teachers." After his conversation we too don't feel very happy, but it had to happen.

We close our tent and need a change of scenery. We walk down the prairie, far behind Eagle Calf's tipi, to the future camping area. We only arrive back at Tatsey's by 5:30. When returning along the highway the road is so bad that we backtrack time & again. We had a good evening meal. Cow tongue with peas and prunes. We hardly see Tatsey. Better that way. Only the next morning the decision will be made. We walk back home & get a visit from Bob & Chub. They come in & are allowed to catch some *kisses*. Uhlenbeck plays for quite a while with the *kids*.

Joe comes in with Running Wolf, who wants to hear a *Napi* story.[178] Running Wolf stays to listen; the three Tatsey children leave. Then we look around again, and again all kinds of visitors arrive: John Red Fox comes, then again that same Indian Little Bull who has a gentle but not too intelligent face. Again his beautiful braids falling down his chest. They leave. More visitors, now Albert Spearson, our mission friend, Henry White Dog and a young Indian and his young wife and one more young Indian, whose name I don't know.[179] The policeman, Horn, also comes in.[180]

The lantern is high up on the chest in the center. I light two candles so Uhlenbeck can read for a long time. All smoke from the same package of tobacco, eat a lot of *kisses* and listen very attentively. It is a splendid scene. Attentively I watch the group. The young woman sits on the floor also, leaning with her head against the tent pole, her shimmering eyes so shiny and black, her teeth such a bright white. Her narrow face is lively; doubled up she too listens to the old story. All the Indians love the *Napi* stories and they are impressed and don't understand how a *White man* can recount their stories in their language, right in their own words. It was already 10:30 before everyone left. Of course everyone leaves at the same time. They don't say goodbye when leaving. When they feel very satisfied they say: "Tomorrow I will be back."

We go outside for a little while. All our neighbors have already left us. It is dead quiet around us. Tired from the eventful day, we go to bed & I sleep much better at least than the previous few nights. Before six I hear a soft rain. At 6:30 I see some sunshine. Oh! I am really hoping for a dry, sunny day! Such wet roads, such wet boots and cold feet! I worry a lot about Uhlenbeck.

Thursday, August 3.

Tatsey promises improvement.

I am up at 7:00. It is still raining a bit, but the sun peeks out once in a while and the sky doesn't look that bad. There is no wind at all. I have to clean out the tent thoroughly, I pick up handfuls of the kisses wrappings from the floor. At 8:00 we are at Tatsey's for breakfast. Tatsey is there. His wife is also in. Then Uhlenbeck talks for a long time about the interpreter situation. Tatsey says he will be able to come that morning, it seems that he doesn't want to give everything up. We talk to him about all kinds of possibilities. About Lymans, about Dick Sanderville, about Peter White Man etc., etc.[181] Tatsey says, "I'll come this morning at 9:00." We walk back together to White Tail Creek. Uhlenbeck will say to Tatsey that if need be, he will be content with three hours of teaching per day. He prefers this over having another interpreter.

Tatsey arrives exactly at 9:00. He again agrees to teach each day, now three hours, whether in the morning or in the afternoon. Cancelling without notice must be outlawed. Should he have any spare time, he will volunteer to teach an extra hour. In order to reassure him, we clearly state that he is our favorite *teacher* and then Tatsey says how his wife is worried about when we will leave: "Who will take care of them, how will Mrs. fare." She is a charming woman, modest as ever and she quietly does her things. Imagine if this could be true, image that Uhlenbeck could make progress on a continuing basis! I fervently hope for this. He has such beautiful stories, very valuable data, but the English, the proper translation is lacking. And Tatsey is one of the best, if not the best, *interpreter*! There is still so much to be done and eight weeks pass quickly. Now Uhlenbeck and Tatsey cheerfully co-operate. For me it is wonderful to watch this. Jim Blood pays us a short visit, eats a few *kisses* and leaves right away.

Now the weather is beautiful, a little sun, and it is getting warmer again. At 9:00 it is already 70° in our tent. Yesterday and also in the evening only 54°. Uhlenbeck works on steadily until 12. The three of us walk away together for our meal. I like this; I like it very much to overhear a conversation between Uhlenbeck and Tatsey and actually, I like this quiet Indian very much. *"But you can't trust him!"* We have to keep this in mind, because it will not take long before he cheats again with the hours. The weather is stable and everything dries nicely. After our meal we walk past Pietaunista's tipi.[182] Further down we arrive at the beautiful bushes of the Badger, right on that sharp bend. How often have I 'strode' towards them. We walk down many paths; here & there it is very, very dirty. It seems to be a well-trodden path. Too bad, between all the flowers, all little leafy trees, all this *unreinheit* [dirt]." I regret it, time and again, that these bushes therefore have to lose so much of their charm because of it. *Aconites* blossom here and *Imonikappi*, and I hear a bird. It is not the ordinary prairie bird; *this one is yellow under* its wings. I have never noticed this kind before. Sometimes I walk far *ahead* of Uhlenbeck. He wants to go back, I want to see where this path leads. It ends at the Badger. I thought so. It is a rider's path. The undergrowth has been trampled everywhere for a reason and the horses are used to walking in the shrubbery, bending for nasty low branches. Then we follow the road up for a while; it is the same road where we saw Jim Red Fox on his white horse. We continue on; the prairie is still rising. I then walk on alone to the highest hill and still could see the Badger Creek twice. Also a nice view of our own camp and further to the west over the Rockies. But it seems to be raining already in the northwest. If this is so, our beautiful weather will not last long.

At 2:00 we are back home and I will make some tea. However, I don't get to it, because many visitors

MRS. UHLENBECK'S DIARY

arrive by the time the small amount of water boils. It is starting to rain and now, on the ground in our tent, are seated Lone Eater, Spotted Eagle & Running Crane.[183] Later Crow Eyes also joins us.[184] They want Uhlenbeck to tell them a story, which means that he should read aloud a few old stories. They stay until 5:30. They smoke and eat sweets and have a lot of fun. A short halting sound signifies their approval, as does clapping their hands.

The weather is now awfully wet and the road very bad again. My overshoes repeatedly stick in the mud; I have to take care that I don't slip. I want to avoid that! Crow Eyes is not a charmer. Last year he was already a beggar and he still is one. He is an exception. His sly, squinty eyes peer around. In the morning he was already here. He got tobacco and *candy* then & now he wants some more. I understand that. He is not only looking around, but he also touches everything and when we left he asked for our small folding chairs. And what is in this barrel? And what is this? And he points to my velvet working bag that always hangs on the camp bed, filled with *candy*. I don't give him any more tobacco & only a very few *kisses* and if he is back too soon, I might give him nothing for a change. We get a lot of mail from Joe, a letter from Jan, the first from Beverwijk, from Mama, from Jo v. Leeuwen, from Lizzy Bussemaker, from Mrs. Elisabeth Grinnell & a postcard from Daatje.

After *supper* the weather is equally bad. Uhlenbeck immediately puts on other socks, other boots. I keep the wet shoes on because my feet still aren't cold. Uhlenbeck has just finished getting dressed when Jack Day Rider comes, a big, brown boy with shiny, dark eyes, very big white teeth, of 10 to 12 years, that is what he says, but later it appears that he is ±14 years old, which is what we supposed him to be.[185] He is a son of Mike and a brother of Oliver Day Rider. He brings along George Duck Head, Eagle Calf's grandson.[186] Jack wants to hear a *story*. They listen, catch the candies that Uhlenbeck throws at them and play with a ball. Jack looks like a big, young poodle; of the wildest kind. It rains continuously. Both boys are barefoot, an indication of bad weather! Their feet

are clean, beautifully shaped and small. They laugh about Uhlenbeck's big boots. One pair, wet, is drying. Jack tries them on and has to laugh about the space left. They stayed for a long while, but suddenly slide outside. All Indians are good at it, head forwards, one shoulder tilted through the crack and so they slid outside. I don't have the knack for it, at least not when I wear my big straw hat, or, when I start to first put my foot outside or inside. Now it is nearly dry. We walk around a bit. A few passers-by greet us. Before 9:00 we are back in our tent. Now I get really cold feet too and we go to bed rather early. No wind and no rain. I wake up at 6:30. Outside it is somber. Once in a while some rain.

Friday, August 4.

Many visitors; lots of rain.

I get up at once. I clean the boots. They are still very wet. At 7:45 we are on the road. It doesn't rain very hard and it starts to blow a lot. The road is not that bad. The Tatseys say that we will get a lot of rain again. How awful if this is true! Tatsey communicates an entire murder story: "The young New Breast murdered his father & his stepmother at Two Medicine. He came home drunk, got into an argument with his father with the result mentioned above!!" Once at the *reclamation store* Uhlenbeck talked to this murdered father and he remembers his looks. That same young Indian also murdered someone three years ago and was detained for two years. Tatsey is at our tent before 9:00 and of course he talks once more about the nasty occurrence. His wife worries a lot and has someone tell us to seal our tent well – as if this would make a difference! – and not to let anyone in in the evenings or at night. Actually, we don't intend to do this and I can't do more than put a single pin in the cloth at the entrance. Anyway, the pin lock only serves to keep the wind out and to keep people from looking inside. They wouldn't do that, but it seems a bit too idyllic to be peered at when I am getting dressed, or when I am washing or rummaging through the suitcases.

Uhlenbeck works for a long time with Tatsey. It rains continuously, 50°. I call this nasty weather. *"No fun at all!"* Having to go out for a meal in the rain, to come back in the rain. When it is finally dry we pace back and forth in front of our tent. Uhlenbeck has to sit still for so many hours every day and in the tent there is no room for him at all. He can only stand up straight in the middle. Very soon Indians approach us: Harry Horn, the two brothers Spotted Eagle and No Bear, John Guardipee, Williams and also a few others. For a while we have nine visitors.[187] So with both of us, eleven persons in the tent. *That is crowded.* But because of the cold, very nice. The thermometer rises from 50 to 58. I pass out tobacco. I load the tea platter (the lid from an oval cookie bin) full of sweets and indicate they should help themselves. When nothing is left, I will fill it again.

Uhlenbeck has to tell a story. Sometimes they enjoy themselves very much. Uhlenbeck's wild little friend, Jack, also attends for a while. He is seated on the high, American suitcase and when a moment later some diversion occurs because even more visitors want to come in, he quickly grabs all the *kisses* from the platter. I saw it but of course let it go. The tobacco is passed out again, he also rolls a cigarette & leaves. One moment later the tobacco jar is missing. Undoubtedly Jack took it. A decent Indian wouldn't do this. Seldom, very seldom, do they put packages of tobacco into their own pockets on their own. I always have to tell them to do this and then they gladly accept it, but on their own, they don't want more than one *smoke*. That's why I don't like Jack that much. He is too *forward* for me. I am rather attracted to diffidence and great modesty. This evening we see no more of Jack. Our afternoon visitors stay until 4:30. Once in a while two Spotted Eagles and No Bear, with his red band around his head again, have a lot of fun. They laugh a lot about Napi's greasy mouth, *grease all over!*[188] Are they thinking, how ridiculous! Or are they thinking, what a situation to be in and what fun? A gorgeous afternoon, one of the afternoons that will linger on forever in our memory. But ice cold feet and wet! Bad weather during *supper*.

Tatsey is at home, but already finished his evening meal. So many visitors came for dinner, he said, so I just joined in, otherwise there would be nothing left for me. Tatsey enjoys feeding *crowds*. It is *chique*! After supper we walk around, but it is wet, on the prairie also. Henault, a stepbrother of the other three Henaults, wants to come in for a story. Peter Vielle also comes in and listens, too. After they have left, we stroll around again a little. Johnny approaches us on horseback, comes along with us and pays a very nice visit. That was nice, that was quite a nice end to a busy day. John informs us, among other things, that the terrible murder story appeared not to be not true at all. It is completely made up, perhaps by mistake (?), perhaps out of mischief (?). Fortunately that is so & not otherwise. John goes home at ten and we go to bed. We have been

Saturday, August 5.

sitting cosily by our candlelight; it always strikes me that this light suits being in this tent situation completely. Heavily clouded sky. At night I wake up more than once and it rains time and again.

I am up by about seven. I don't have to do anything to our boots – why would I? It will be wet again? At 8:00 we are at the Tatseys with thoroughly wet feet. The grass is so wet. Why could the Tatseys choose this low camping place! For them it is much too wet also, I would say. We have trout for breakfast, a delicious change from the leathery steaks! Walking back to our camp we meet up for a little while with Henault, Peter's stepfather. We should give him some more *candy*, he shouts to us, he will come for it to our tent. Yes, we know Henault, he is fond of *candy*, he can live on it, he contends. Tatsey only comes after nine. The sun now & then peeks through. How very nice! Will I be able to gloriously dry all of our wet boots and clothes today? I stick my wet feet and the wet hem of my skirt outside, underneath the cloth of the tent. Uhlenbeck continues to work with Tatsey. A moment later I sit outside in my stockings, my feet in the sun; boots etc. etc, are now hanging in the wind. The last appointment with Walter, set up yesterday, is that he will finish the story he started, that he will pay back in cash ten dollars, and then he will pay off his entire debt on Saturday, it is said, when he will come.

Working with Tatsey is difficult. Time and again people drop by to talk to him. And a five-minute conversation seems to be a very long time when you are waiting; Uhlenbeck is always ready to continue, pen in hand. But our tent is en route; they are not that stupid. Indian Joe's camp is too far away for the Indians. But nothing should or might be lost of the real working hours. We are going to eat with Tatsey, who, behind Duck Head's log cabin, is stopped by Dick Sanderville. Sanderville & Tatsey are counsellors for many Indians. After eating we walk back home together. The sun is shining nicely. Now everything around us is warming up and drying nicely. Maybe it is getting too warm; it is already 85°. I go alone to our tent and see from a distance that Walter is circling around it. "*Where is the old man?*" he is asks me, when he sees that I arrive without Uhlenbeck. Uhlenbeck is working with Walter at 1:15, after discussing business first. Walter has no cash. He never has any, we do understand that. He wants to present us with an Indian dress instead.

But we count our money again and prefer the ten dollars cash. We can't figure out exactly how much the journey back will cost us. Then they work on. When the *story* is finished, they talk a while, but he doesn't have much time. He wants to ride with Joe Owl Child to his ranch and stay there until Monday.

During the morning, when Tatsey was around too, Henry White Dog and George Day Rider dropped by for a moment. As soon as Walter has left, I wash our pillow slips and quickly dry them in the sun. Uhlenbeck writes a long letter to Jan, to be sent to Beverwijk. I start a letter to Haarlem and then we walk around a bit. While walking I read letters to Uhlenbeck from Elisabeth Grinnell, Jo v. L. and Lizzie Bussemaker. Unfortunately a sudden rain shower falls and there is some thunder. When it is nearly dry, we go outside again. Right before Jim Blood's (Kainaikoan's) tent, a *sweat lodge* has been erected, entirely covered with cowhides. A few Indians sit in it; outside are four to five little piles of meat. An Indian woman straightens the skins again, puts a few more blankets over it to close it and, with a branch shaped like a fork, she carries three hot stones inside, which have been heated red-hot outside on a fire. While walking we watch from a short distance away. Now enough hot stones have been brought inside. The sweat bath is ready. The woman comes outside again, carefully closes the opening, takes a pipe & contentedly starts to smoke in front of the tent. She enjoys smoking the big, wooden pipe. Her forehead is painted red and for a while she ernestly stays seated, maybe listening to the praying & the singing of the people inside. Jim Blood is among them, we have just seen him going over the prairie, wrapped in a blanket.

When we return from our evening meal, Jim just returns from the *sweatlodge* to his own camp. We sit around for a while in our tent, and walk around again. Then Henry White Dog & Jim Fine Bull come in.[189] Just after they arrive, Jim Gamnon and the Gros Ventre Indian, Aloysious Black Bird, also come.[190] The Gros Ventre is really a very big Indian, but very nice. This spring he joined this reservation. In the winter he will go back to his own tribe. He can talk in Gros Ventre with his grandmother, who lives here among the Peigan. We sit together very cheerfully. Henry White Dog on the camp bed, in the place where the inkpot goes. The Gros Ventre in front of the *candy* barrel. Jimmy Fine Bull on the *candy* bucket. Jim Gammon on the old suitcase. I put something to smoke and a platter full of sweets on the open, big suitcase. First the two boys leave. When Black Bird is about to leave, an older Indian has just arrived in front of our tent. Black Bird speaks in sign language to the Peigan, Mike Bad Old Man, who wants to buy v from us.[191] We have someone tell him that he can get a candle, but that we are no merchants. U. remembers Bad Old Man from the previous year. He is a nice Indian. Now everyone has left. Now it is 9 o'clock. Around us, the prairie is quiet. The ¾ full moon is red. It is beautiful outside. I still have to make up the bed. A clean top sheet and clean pillow slips. What a treat!

Sunday, August 6.

Today Jan is 24 years old. The weather is nice. Lots of clouds, but it doesn't look as if it will rain. We are only at Tatsey's by 8:30. We quickly eat breakfast in order to get back early. A few dogs are extremely excited. *Mistapak! Mistapak!*[192] Uhlenbeck shouts at them and waves with his umbrella. Finally the nice! animals withdraw growling & muttering, regretting that for once they could not bite the whites' legs. A moment later Henault's stepbrother, Eagle Ribs, says, *"One of those dogs wanted to eat you."* Back at our tent I go for water. Uhlenbeck changes something in his work and then starts to write to Prof. La Saussaye. I am busy with my diary when suddenly little George peeks inside through a very little crack. Immediately I recognize his dark face, his flat Indian nose. Chubby is with him. They don't stay for long. They catch some sweets, don't say much, actually hardly anything, they also speak English very poorly and quietly walk away, hand in hand. We go to eat and take three letters along (for Prof. La Saussaye and family & Wiepke, Tatsey will take care of them).[193] After eating we want to go see Mrs. Olson, but the road is too bad. Eagle Calf is outside; I find this Indian really beautiful. How clearly can I see his sharp features in full daylight. It is a well-shaped profile & the red headband suits him well, his shirt falls loosely open on his chest. We follow him inside. Owl Feather, painted entirely in red, also sits down in the *tipi*.[194] One of his wives is inside too. She sews cow skin moccasins. Her thread is dried intestine. She holds it with her teeth and pulls threads from it in this way. Mary Duck Head, the granddaughter, is the *interpreter*.

Twice a bed bug crawls over me. They must have been brought from the log house into the tipi. I shake myself thoroughly when I get outside. In the future, I will still not avoid sitting down on an Indian bed. Uhlenbeck says to Eagle Calf that we have stored his paint pouch very well and he, Eagle Calf, has Mary repeat once more what we already knew, that this paint will protect us. "We have to put it under our cushion and then it will stay with us." Then painted Owl Feather asks for Uhlenbeck's name and Uhlenbeck explains to him the meaning of his

seal ring. It starts to rain. So then we leave. It starts to rain very hard & with wet, but warm feet, we get back to the tent. We make some tea. This was Uhlenbeck's idea. It is delicious. Each of us gets a few cups of warm weak tea. I shut the tent tightly. Then Chub comes again and he brings Bob along. They play a little. Two more boys arrive, Jim White Man & Jack Day Rider. Both are extremely wet and dirty. All four get sweets again, but especially Jim & Jack don't get too many. I do this because of their upbringing! They stay for quite a while, play & talk a bit and walk back in the rain. Uhlenbeck thinks that we should have another warm drink. Now I make some bouillon, *beef tea*. The meths burner does beautifully and now with a big flame. The water heats quickly & it tastes delicious.

The road to Tatsey's is very bad but we are used to it: now we know how to jump from one piece of bush or shrubbery to another in the hollow where the path is completely down-trodden & beat-up. We have a good supper; actually, dinner was very modest too. It is warm near the stove. Hattie Guardipee is there with her baby & sits with mother Tatsey on Josephine's bed. Uhlenbeck drinks lots of weak tea, takes off his shoes and warms his feet by the stove. He calls this his *sweat lodge*. Tatsey is not around. Josephine has had a cold for a few days already, is very listless and often lies in bed. We walk a bit around our tent. Joe Tatsey wants to come in with John Little Bull (18 years old). He is my little friend with his scarlet braid ribbons, his red neck scarf, the ends tied behind his neck and dangling down, the triangular part hanging down the front, his broad brown leather belt & his black shirt. It looks good on him & he is aware of it. The old felt hat suits him well. For a long time I enjoy looking at this beautiful Indian boy. I always find his shiny eyes, his shiny braids so attractive. His father, Tatsey says, liked to ride a white horse; he was vain and he liked to make people laugh.

Tom No Bear (15 years old) is also there.[195] For his age this is a big boy and he has a much more expressive face. He has a yellow complexion and deep-set, secretive small eyes. He is a clown and together

Monday, August 7.

they have great fun saying that he & the 15-year-old are young married men. Joe is also 15, but a lot smaller. Actually, Joe is a bit stocky and will grow up to be a beautiful, slim Peigan. A married Indian also joins with his three children; he sits close to the *candy* barrels. John Head Carrier is 38 years old; he is slim, has a yellow complexion, seems weak and glum.[196] He says that he is old; he does not smoke because it used to make him sick. They want to hear a narration. Little Joe leaves. The others listen. Then, as soon as they have left, we stroll around a little. Soon we have visitors again. Again John Little Bull & Tom No Bear & Jim Williams (20 years old) of the blue spectacles arrive. Right now he is not wearing his spectacles and when he takes off his hat, I see that he has quite a nice and charming face. He also shows he is interested, speaks English quite well and asks a lot about the Peigans and about his own language. He believes that in the north, very far away, there are Peigans still living on rich hunting grounds, just as in ancient times. "Could this be true?" he asks Uhlenbeck. "Do you believe this too?" Then one more visitor arrives, Peter Running Crane (14 years old, a mission boy with big, black eyes and a fresh, naughty, healthy but shy demeanor).[197] Then Uhlenbeck stops reading and talks to Jim Williams. And they are still amazed that Uhlenbeck knows so much about their language. "When you come back again," Jim says, "you will speak it like we do." I light two or three candles on a bucket turned upside down to have some light. After the visitors have left we go to bed because of the cold. Uhlenbeck has ice-cold feet. At night I hear it raining again.

I am awake at six. The sun is shining. I get up at once. I have to rearrange the suitcases. I can't do this during the day. It keeps me busy until after 7:00. This hour I wear a pair of Uhlenbeck's big, dry boots; I push all the wet shoes with their toes under the tent cloth to dry them in the sun. How much I appreciate the sun's drying power! En route at 7:45, without umbrellas. However, heavy clouds float in. We encounter Tatsey & John on a wagon. Tatsey says that our letters are mailed. Almost 8:30 and we are already back at our tent. Now I hang the wet boots on the ropes outside.

I walk cheerfully around with Uhlenbeck; we talk about a next voyage: about Peru & Yukatan, about Persia, about the Eskimos, about Montenegro, about Egypt. I remember this so clearly now, it is as if I can still see the plants and the flowers on the path we walked on during this moment. Suddenly we are interrupted. Tatsey comes and we run back to our tent. Tatsey gets here before us. This has never happened before. The weather will be nice today. I carry everything outside and sit gloriously in the sun. We go along with Tatsey at 12:00. Again a trout dinner. How diligent the Tatsey children are these days, to make an effort to catch fish so often. It makes sense for them to decide to do this, it does not cost them any money. They have to provide beef for themselves by butchering a cow of their own, or take over part of the meat from another Indian and they have to buy bacon from the government, which is remarkably higher priced than beef, but also a much bigger treat!

When we walk around after our meal, John Red Fox, John Horn & Running Wolf soon join us.[198] They talk, eat & smoke and we give John Red Fox some candies for Jimmy. A moment later Running Wolf returns, but with Al Black Bird. *"Just Al,"* he said when we asked him what his name is in English. Tonny Edwards (a delicate, small face with some white blood and very polite, friendly and outgoing) comes along with Francis Vielle, Peter Vielle's older brother. Both brothers are lookalikes; the oldest especially has a somber and somewhat dour demeanor. Uhlenbeck reads a story for the entire group. After they depart the

Big Moon and German painter Julius Seyler, 1913. Courtesy Sigrid Reisch Collection.

weather quickly deteriorates. Heavy clouds pass over. I just have a cup of tea ready when Jack Big Moon arrives. We haven't seen him since Browning. He is in a very good mood, he laughs so friendly, and he has a way of rolling his eyes. His demeanor is very peculiar and not at all pretty. Maybe there is a certain agitation in his expression. Now he talks again busily about the President. His medal shines on his chest again. We have no tea left for him.

Richard Mad Plume also comes. He is a friend of both of us. All the Mad Plumes are loved at the *reservation.* After Big Moon's departure, Richard stays for a very long time. He talks very nicely about his family, about why the little son of his diseased sister is being raised by old Mad Plume, the grandfather. The little boy now calls his own father brother-in-law, *nistamoe* in Peigan, and, Richard continues, he is no longer my brother-in-law, because now he has taken a second wife.[199] Richard regrets that we still have no Indian names. His father, he says, would like to give you a name. Uhlenbeck presents Richard with his business card and Richard promises to write to us some time. On the back of the card I draw the front of our house in Holland. He thinks it is very big.

After Richard has left, we want to get some exercise and take the umbrella & raincoat along. Suddenly a downpour. Lizzy Tatsey motions us inside, though her mother isn't yet ready with this & that for us. Then supper and unending miserable rain. Because of the damp we drink bouillon & I wrap Uhlenbeck in the blankets on the camp bed. I tuck extra coats around his feet. He lies still tucked in like that when at eight Jim Oldman Chief & Jim Williams, the two friends, come in. For eight years they have been big friends; their mothers have always been partners as both stepbrothers are now. Jim Oldman Chief understands English quite well, but he speaks it poorly. We have a very nice evening with them. Al Blackbird comes also. Jim Oldman Chief is in a very good mood from our welcoming reception. He smokes & eats candies & says, "Now we could sing for once." Then a flood of Indian songs. Some are Beaver dance songs, we have heard them before and recognize them for sure. There is only one song that has words. Jim Oldman Chief has a good voice; he is known to be a good singer. One song follows the other. Time and again he puts his hat in front of his face, so I can't watch him too closely. Black Bird sings along on many songs. Gros Ventre Jim sings the Gros Ventre ones alone.[200] They smoke, eat & talk & keep singing all the while. We are proud that three Indians feel so much at ease with us that they even want to sing for us.

Uhlenbeck stays in bed. On the upright suitcase I burn two candles. On the stool I put something to smoke & sweets and time and again I bring other sweets. What a great evening! The three Indians feel so at ease. Big, heavy Black Bird is only nineteen years old. However, it is damp & cold. The thermometer did not get higher than 50°, still it was one of the best evenings during our Indian period. Only at 10.00 do they leave. As soon as our visitors left we went to bed because of the cold. At night I hear it raining again.

MRS. UHLENBECK'S DIARY

Tuesday, August 8.

Up at 7:00. Nasty weather! 50°. Fine drizzle & fog. We get to Tatsey's with wet feet & even wetter when back at our tent. A moment later John comes and says that his father will arrive half an hour late. But we don't have to wait too long. Before 9:30 he is at our tent. He was up at 4:30. Josephine had a bad night. We also saw her again and thought that her cheeks & her eyes were so very shiny. Tatsey worries & says, "It may be consumption; her mother's mother also died of it and many of her family members!!" He dearly wants the government doctor from Browning to come & tries to get him to come. I make some bouillon and try to cheer Tatsey up a bit. If only the fog would leave for a while; I get used to this total dampness, but I am not comfortable with it & I always worry about Uhlenbeck who then suffers a lot from *belly-ache*. The warm bouillon is delicious. Little Chubby comes at 11:00 and the four of us leave at 12:00. A moment earlier Tatsey has just said, "I hear a carriage," & looking out from our tent he sees the doctor's carriage from Browning!! He calls out and stops it and talks to the doctor who has visited Josephine already. The doctor said that it is consumption, he will give her something for her cough and she should drink some cod-liver oil. Maybe drier weather will benefit her! She longs so much for the sun and heat. At the table they are still cheerful, not even so much as in a depressed mood.

Tatsey even seems to be excited and drops piquant sentences. That is how he reacts to the knowledge of having to lose his first and oldest child.

Adam is also there. Yes, Tatsey says, & Eva is not here, etc. etc. and later on, "Adam prefers work over words." Evans is also eating here.[201]

Josephine lies quietly on her bed in a corner of the tent. Time and again I watch her. She tosses from side to side, sometimes she is half-asleep. Now she is also fully dressed and is wearing her shoes. Her feet stick out from under the blankets. How sorry I feel for anyone being so ill. Time and again I think about her and I can't help myself. Tatsey should pick up a camp bed for her somewhere. He even plans to do so, but delays it. Grandmother is also ill; we have not seen her for a few days

now, but this happens more often & that is why we did not worry about it. In the long afternoon we see Charlie Guardipee for only a moment; he is looking for his father-in-law, Joe Tatsey. Joe comes to announce that the evening meal is ready. So we will pick up our meal once again. We find Tatsey in his tent. Now it is nearly dry. For the entire evening 50°. For a long time we walk around a bit. There are no visitors. A quiet day, quite a big difference to yesterday and the day before. Maybe good for a change to have some rest. Then we sit together by our little lantern. I can't knit this way. Coarser needlework works better. At 9:00 we are already in bed. I spread out all our clothes on top of us because of the cold.

At 1:30 I suddenly hear shouting: "Professor!" It is Tatsey; Josephine is much sicker and he wants some whiskey or rum from us. Josephine is so weak, he says, he wants to see if he can revive her a bit. Right away I get up, because I can find our rum better & quicker than Uhlenbeck who really never has anything to do with the suitcases. Quickly I give our entire little bottle of rum to Tatsey – actually there is not that much in it; we have been very sparing with it. How dreadful a situation for this sick girl!

Her care – well meant as it may be – is so extremely primitive. The camping bed has not come. Now she lies again in grandmother's tent & old granny is weak too and, she worries about her granddaughter. How will the girl be tomorrow morning? I look out once more & watch Tatsey; it is a clear, quiet night. The moon has just appeared and the entire prairie is lit up. After being awake for a long time, we fall asleep again. Uhlenbeck wakes me up at 4:00. He has a terrible *belly-ache*. I get up and give him medicine. It calms down and we drowse on.

Wednesday, August 9.

Tatsey's daughter gets sicker. The doctor comes. The old grandmother is also sick.

Up at 7:00. Gray weather, cold, but dry. At 8:00 we are at the Tatseys. They have had quite a time with Josephine. She slept finally a bit and now seems a bit better. She was somewhat revived by a teaspoon of rum with some water & sugar. Tatsey & his wife are very affected now. All the children are rather quiet. Now Josephine lies in grandmother's tent, too. Let her stay there, I think. Moving her so often worries me a lot; I am so afraid that they will let her walk or stand a little & she is too weak, she says that herself. And it is so damp & cold, here in this little valley. Oh Tatsey! Why did you choose this low-lying camp. Maybe it was that which made Josephine so sick. Tatsey comes at 9:30. Earlier he said that he would be half an hour later. He is quiet and not in the mood to teach. He says that Josephine is often completely confused. Jim Blood comes for a moment into the tent. Last night I heard him coughing a lot and his little child was crying a lot. He is riding to the Old Agency and takes letters from us with him, one for Haarlem, one for Mrs. Grinnell, address: Lame Deer, Montana.

At the midday meal we see Josephine again. Now she is lying again in her father's tent. She smiles nicely at us. She doesn't look good. Her cheeks & ears also have a blue color. This worries us a lot & we think that she has a serious pleuritis, maybe *pleurisy* The examination done by the government doctor is extremely basic. Tatsey has asked for the doctor at the *agency*. The doctor comes, stands in the tent opening, looks once at the sick girl who lies in the corner on her[202] bed and without approaching her, without any examination he says to the mother: it must be consumption; I will give her some medicine. He has no time at all to visit grandmother who lies nearby in her own tent and he leaves. If all his visits to the poor, sick Indians go like this, he is a bad doctor.

We are back home, sitting in our closed tent, and time and again think time and again about the Tatseys. Jim Williams comes in, and the son of Big Crow and Paul Running Crane, the younger brother of Peter Running Crane.[203] Later Albert Spearson drops by. He is a real nice boy, but suddenly he wants to leave. It starts to thunder and he wants to be at the Old Agency before the storm hits. When he has left, Walter comes in. Everyone thinks, today the government will pay the *ditch* work wages, and everyone heads this way in vain. Walter has a sour look, but cheers up a bit cheered up for us. We always pay a lot of attention to Walter, as if he were a small child. He has tea with us. There is a downpour. Lewe Kasoos, Willy Kjejijo & Peter Step by Mistake suddenly run in sopping wet. Walter & the boys leave and we are glad when the storm is over. Maybe it will dry up a bit more before *supper*. Josephine is not doing too badly. She does not have good color and now looks very worn-out & complains a lot about her throat. Time and again she rubs her throat, coughs a bit and looks at us gently with her dreamy eyes. Now she looks so much like her father again. Tatsey has that same look; but when he gets excited, then something very special sparkles in that melancholic, introverted face. Lizzy Tatsey comes to us for medicine. Because, Tatsey says, I rather no longer give her what the doctor gave us, it made Josephine much sicker last night. I give *chloras kalium* for gargling and Doveri tablets for coughing and also our last Enzer pastilles and also half a box of cough drops from Sherburne. Bob & Chub walk along with us.

While I am busy preparing the medicine, and writing the prescription, Jim Blood's wife comes by for medicine for their smallest child's eyes.[204] That is why I heard it cry so bitterly these last nights! But I don't have ointment for eyes. I read through Nico's list (our doctor's list) and see that I can give *chloras kalium* for an eye rinsing. With a lot of patience & effort I grind four tablets into a fine powder & give them to Uhlenbeck who goes along with the woman. George Day Rider arrives just then and is *interpreter,* but they won't use the medicine either, either because it was not an ointment, or because they had no bottle. Anyway, Uhlenbeck brings the medicine back again and they don't come to pick it up. John Sandovil, uncle-sayer to Dick Sandovil, comes to visit us.[205]

He is a nice boy & speaks English easily and says: "I should have come earlier." The cohorts Little Bull and No Bear also visit, etc., smoke & talk & leave soon again because we don't pay them enough attention. After John Sandovil has also left again, we sit together again with our candle. George Running Wolf is still with us. He is a slim, beautiful Indian with a very serious face that is charming, but not really very handsome. We hadn't expected that he is only seventeen years old. He doesn't smoke, but eats lots of *candy*. When he wants to leave he takes a coin out of his pocket to buy some sweets from us for his little brother who is five years old. I give him a big handful. Uhlenbeck adds that here and in our own country we never sell anything, but that he can get sweets; it is our pleasure! He accepts this very kindly. We go to bed. This *evening* Uhlenbeck also lay under a blanket. It is thoroughly damp and I am happy that he takes precautions as much as possible.

Thursday, August 10.

At night Tatsey comes for help for his daughter.

Up before 7:00. Beautiful weather! The sun is shining. In the tent everything is still very wet. Before 8:00 we are at Tatsey's. Early in the evening Josephine slept quite a lot and now feels better. When we walk back to our tent, Lizzy runs towards us with a letter from her father. It says that Josephine had become suddenly so stuffed-up again & and therefore he can't come. When she gets better, he will come in the afternoon. So now I will do my laundry, also my blouse. It dries quickly in the sun. The sun feels good on us and again we talk about Persia, about Spain, about a journey to the north. Uhlenbeck is also attracted to Spain's old cities. But he feels even more attraction for Persia. He still wants to experience more in life. Bob comes to pick us up and gets a sweet. We don't like Bobby that much. He doesn't have a lot of brains and always throws things at animals or unmercifully teases their own dogs. We do pity Bob, but his company is very seldom agreeable.

Josephine was asleep when we arrived at Tatsey's. It seems that the Doveri tablet helped a bit & the *chloras kalium* helped her throat somewhat. She is still in grandmother's tent, who is very weak herself, does not eat; the old lady is maybe about 95. She must be between 90 and 100, Tatsey says. Grandmother, reflecting on nearing her end, said this morning: "I hope, that my granddaughter dies before me, then I will not be lonely after I die, but will find her." For the Tatseys it is a very troublesome time. What will the coming days bring? Tatsey comes to teach at 1:00. Walter stops in front of our tent with the two Calf Robe Calf Robe, but when he notices that Uhlenbeck is working, he goes on.[206] Old Mountain Chief passes by & asks for some *candy* for his grandson Lewe. Of course he gets it, but I don't know whether grandfather & grandmother saved it for Lewe or ate it themselves. The old chief is so fond of it, and a real beggar.

An Indian, completely unknown to us, is asking whether we have letters to be mailed. He is on his way to Browning. This is very nice of the man. I give him a letter to Daatje to take. Now it is 75° in our tent.

This warmth is glorious. Uhlenbeck sits again in just his shirt, different than sitting wrapped in blankets. Old Eagle Calf comes at 2:00. He enters our tent making a lot of noise & shouting and stays for a very long time. He sits on the ground beside Tatsey, smokes two cigarettes, which Tatsey makes for his old uncle; then he smokes a pipe using his own tobacco, which smells like incense. Tatsey pulls the old man's chin and laughs a lot about the way his old uncle eats sweets.

Eagle Calf thinks it very weird that I can make tea without a wood fire. He finds my spiritus light so strangely foreign. He watches it closely, listens to Uhlenbeck & Tatsey working, talks a bit to himself & mutters a prayer, "Earth, pity me," & then points down and a moment later he points up, presses his hand firmly against his chest. What is he doing? Was he praying for himself? For Josephine or for his old, sick half-sister? Or for us? At 4:00 the uncle & nephew, Eagle Calf & Tatsey, go home. John Red Fox visits us. This suits us well; he gets some tea too and spoons it up and enjoys it. Then we have our evening meal. The patients are not doing too badly. Josephine is reasonably quiet, grandmother very weak. *Father* Carrel from the mission has been here. He gave her the last sacraments. He prayed for grandmother. She could not receive the last sacraments because she kept vomiting. But also, the old Indian woman would not like it. She wants to go to the *Sand Hills* and she is not able to think like a Catholic. We don't see Tatsey & all children are absent. So it is very quiet and now Josephine stays at her grandmother's. I give the Tatseys even more *chloras kalium*.

After *supper* we walk back to the next new camp area. Over the prairie back & forth. We still trust the road. Oh, it is so glorious, now the weather is so nice. It is as if everything seems less somber. And then all the horses and the mountains! We talk to a nice Cree, David Salloway.[207] He is a mature teenager with an extremely cheerful & carefree demeanor, about 14 years old. In the evening the weather is still nice, but it is cold. We are sitting with the candle lit when Jim Oldman Chief, Jim Williams & George Champagne – stepson of George Horn – come

in.[208] They each sit cheerfully on a seat. The lantern is on the carry-on with the sweets & the tobacco. U. tells them about his student life and about sports in our own country and they tell us about their games. Jim Oldman Chief listens attentively, but again, at the same time, the boy again stares aimlessly. Once in a while there is a little tic of his head, I saw it happen more than once. George Champagne speaks English fluently – a great exception – and speaks more clearly. In contrast, Jim Williams has trouble expressing himself. After they have left, we look around outside once more. How light the entire prairie is. The full moon rises gloriously, just over *that big hill* as Walter called this top. It is one of the highest hill tops on the entire prairie around us. It is quite windy, that is why I rearrange the stones a bit.

Friday, August 11.

Up at 6:30. Cloudy sky, but the sun shines through a bit. I stow away U.'s boots again. For how long? If only the rainy period was over! I soak some laundry with Sunlight soap. At 7:45 we are en route to our breakfast. Josephine is doing quite well & slept quite well; old grandma is and stays very weak. Josephine is also not stuffed-up anymore & she wants to eat something. By 8:30 we are back home again; I quickly wash everything & hang the handkerchiefs on the tent lines. Tatsey comes quite soon & they go to work right away. We have not seen Al Blackbird the last few days. Tatsey now tells us that they have put him behind bars in Browning. *Poor fellow!* He did something wrong, but now we miss the cheerful Gros Ventre. U. works until 12:00. It seems that Josephine is a bit better; the old lady is weak.

After our *dinner* we talk briefly to Mrs. Olson. We can't go into her cabin because her husband is busy doing designing for the *ditch*. Anyway, we did not want to go in. The American engineer – supervisor & his wife might be very nice to us, but we do not want their company. On the contrary, if we want to be friends with the Indians, we have to avoid the whites. Then we talk a bit with Wagner's wife; he is a supervisor for the excavation work. The American engineer-supervisor & his wife treat us quite nicely, but their company is not attractive for us. To the contrary: if we want to be friends with the Indians, we have to avoid the whites. We then have a little chat with Wagner's wife, a supervisor at the ditch works. And we also have another look at our next camp. Somewhere around here we have to end up, we hope, with very many Indian tents.

Back home I make some tea. Jim Whiteman & Joe Tatsey come in for a moment. They stay briefly and only giggle a bit. Then Bob comes to pick us up. I don't want to *encourage* this and only give him one sweet. Bob is not our favorite. I dislike the boy, sometimes even very much, sometimes I only pity him. It is his demeanor; he looks very veiled and he is the worst animal teaser. Our *supper* is not yet ready, Tatsey's wife is being held up by her patients & her visitors. U. and Tatsey pay a visit to a five-year-old, very sick little boy who camps nearby & I play and sit a bit at Badgers with all the little ones. Tatsey eats with us; he always wants to. Later, we walk around for quite a while, & then I sit in front of the tent for some time. U. hears a drum. He can't help himself and investigates. But it does not mean much. John & Louis come and Jack Vielle and cousin Peter, Jimmy Shoots' partner.[209] On the way back from their walk, Mr. & Mrs. Olson approach our tent. They peek briefly inside, but don't want to sit down. They invite us for an evening meal and set it up for next Wednesday, Aug. 16, at 6:00. Later, on request of the Vielles, Uhlenbeck reads the story of *Scarface*, which they did not know. After everyone has left, we look around a bit again. A slight haze hangs over the highest prairie mountains. On that spot it is getting lighter and lighter and after I have been watching for a while, the moon gloriously appears. Around me it is getting gloriously light. It wakes up the horses and they walk around more than on a dark night. To bed at 10:00.

Saturday, August 12.

Beautiful weather. Up at 6:30. Again I soak all kinds of laundry in Sunlight soap. Before 8:00 we are already at Tatsey's. The sick ones are doing reasonably well. Tatsey's sister (62 years old) has come with her daughter and grandson.[210] Little Leo Maude is, I think, 8 years old. We quickly eat breakfast & are back home early. I quickly do the laundry & take advantage of the beautiful weather. I pin everything up on the lines & on the sunny side it dries quickly. When U. works with Tatsey inside the tent, I stand on guard outside for the laundry. The Indians will not take it away, definitely not, but I don't want them to see my laundry, in order to not give them the wrong impression about our tidiness. At 11:30 all the laundry is already quite dry and ironed! Chubby comes into the tent, but he doesn't get anything; he should understand that he is not allowed in during working hours, otherwise time and again one of the Tatsey children comes in.

At *dinner* we meet Tatsey's cousin – I believe it is Maude – and her son Leo Maude. Grandma seems to be a bit stronger. Because of the stove it is burning hot in Tatsey's tent. In ours at 12:00 it was already 90°. In the afternoon a wind starts to blow. We walk back to our tent. The sick (white) little boy has been transported by his father to Conrad; it will have been a long & difficult ride, but if they leave the child in their tent, he certainly will die. I put on tea water & rummage a bit in the old suitcase. I wish that something could be done about its bottom. We can't take the suitcase back with us in this state. We should ask whether the government smith, who repairs all kinds of tools for the ditch, could do it.

We drink a lot of very weak tea. A lot to make up for our cups being very, very small, but on this warm afternoon it is very nice. At 3:00 our tea time is over & John Horn comes by.[211] He thought it was payday. We have *supper* by ourselves & it is boring around Tatsey's camp. We go home quickly. We also walk around a bit & get a visit from Jim Gambler, who stays for quite a long time.[212] Again we see the moon rise. A long letter from Jan de Jong & Lien is very dear to us.

Sunday, August 13.

Many visitors.

Up at 6:30. Beautiful weather. Again I have to do some laundry and a lot of other things. U. only gets up around eight. At nine we are at Tatsey's. After breakfast we walk uphill and get a beautiful view. Days in advance I long for the Sunday morning walk. It is the only day of the week that U. ventures a bit further from our *camp* & I really enjoy being further away from our camp. The great expanse looks so romantic to me; I would dearly like to know what is behind the hills. If only we could ride horses, far, far over the hills!

During *dinnertime* nothing special. Back home I just sit outside for a while. Mad Plume's oldest son, Rattler, comes in.[213] He looks like Richard. He has the same charming face, but he is quite a bit older than Richard is. He stays for a long time. Jim Blood comes by also, as do Jim Four Horns & Oliver Day Rider and Jim Williams. This is a very nice afternoon. Entirely unexpected. Good thing that we were at home. U. is right to want us to stay around his tent, even when I sometimes object to it. After the visitors have left, I make some tea. Now Lewe Kasoos' mother enters our tent. She has come from a Crow Medicine dance, held a few miles from here, and she asks for the pictures with her in them.[214] Actually I don't believe that this is her only purpose. But I haven't been able to develop the plates here and I promise to send her the pictures later. Sam Scabby Robe also drops by, with Patrick Marceau. Sam has been out with her. Sam likes this, *he makes love to any girl* (a married woman is also being called "girl" as long as she doesn't decline the love-making). I give Sam a smoke. By mistake (?) he puts the whole package in his pocket. I give sweets to Lewe's mother & to Patrick. All three leave at 5:15. Sam has a wagon. He says that he wants to work at the ditch after payday, to make money & then he will live in George Day Rider's tent. If this happens, we might see him once in a while.

Supper without Tatsey & this evening no more visitors. Together we sit for quite a while by our candle. This morning we were called to see Sa-aukjie, who is that very ugly Indian, a strange, ugly, small man of about 50 years of age. He danced with horns on his head during the big dance week, as if he doesn't look enough like a devil already. He is in his tent with his wife & his daughter. She, his wife, is one of the very few women who no longer have a nose. It was cut off by the husband due to adultery. In earlier times this punishment was executed more often. However, now it no longer bothers her; she is lively & cheerful – and doesn't think that she is ugly at all! Their daughter is married to John Eagle Head. (They are the young Indian couple who were among our visitors one evening, and she was the one who, listening that long to the old Indian stories, seated against the tent cloth, looked at me once in a while with her black gentle eyes.)[215] In their tent we also met one more Indian woman, who is Curly Bear's wife.[216] She is about 40 years of age, laughs continuously and is very fat.

Monday, August 14.

Tatsey's old mother dies.

Up at 7:30. I can't sleep anyway. Nearly the entire night I was lying looking at the moon or the sun. Beautiful weather. Before 8:30 we are at Tatsey's already. Grandmother is getting weaker. Josephine is reasonably well, but for the time being recovery seems to be out of the question. Yesterday the doctor from Browning, a government doctor, came out on his own. It appears that he was sent by the *agent* because of a complaint made by Tatsey, and he still insists that Josephine suffers from consumption. Tatsey badly wants consent to consult another doctor, before he takes action with regard to his daughter, for example to have her transported to a hospital. Tatsey is at our tent before 9:00. Mr. Evans comes to listen to them working for quite a while. Chubby walks over to visit us with Mary Louise & George. I send back the oldest two right away. George snuggles up against his father. During working hours we have no use for these small kids. We eat dinner with Tatsey. Here & there all kinds of Indians are sitting. Now it is as if it really is payday. We return again early to our tent & visit with Irene Shoots for a while. She was playing with Lizzy and had come along with her father. Early in the afternoon John Red Fox & John Horn also join us. I get them water from the river; they smoke & eat some sweets with utmost modesty. When I put a few pieces in John Red Fox's palm, he says, "That will be enough." By 2:00 they have already left. Nobody comes after that. Supper without Tatsey. Tatsey's wife happens to talk to us quite a bit & says that grandmother is getting weaker. She is nervous, but hides it and quietly goes on her way, always making sure that our food is ready on time. We have just arrived back home, when Joe brings us letters (from Mama & Jo Vreede). Joe doesn't want to come in, because Walter & Owl Child have just arrived. Walter talks to us and he is always a welcome visitor here, because he speaks English quite well. His cousin Owl Child doesn't know a word of English & I can't treat him with sweets. He is the only Indian who doesn't like them, *poor fellow!* Maybe he is suffering from toothache! Walter puts sweets into his pocket & promises Uhlenbeck to pay him off right away, once he has cashed his

Tuesday, August 15.

cheque in Browning. They stay only briefly. We talked for a moment to Albert Spearson who was on horseback. He doesn't want to come with us, but will ride on right away. He points to the Rockies and says, "That is where I have to go & when it gets dark, I am afraid of bears." Albert is not fond of these sweet animals. He talked about them earlier. I don't know whether his fear is well-founded. There are many bears in the Rockies, but Albert lives in the foothills & during the summer months they would hardly scare the Indians. Nobody comes around after that. A quiet evening and Jim Blood has disappeared with his camp. In the afternoon we saw that everything was taken down & loaded up and Jim is checking whether he can get his cheque, while his wife & other female company crouch together & smoke to their hearts' content for hours at a stretch. A quiet evening is looming. If only the same girls from Saturday night would return: Mary Duck Head, Maggy Champagne, Dora Vielle & Lizzy Tatsey and her younger sister.[217] Around our tent everything has been abandoned. We are alone on the great plains.

Up at 7:00. Warm weather. I am hardly dressed when Joe Tatsey comes. Monday night at 7:00 grandmother died – very shortly after our departure – and now his mother can no longer provide for us, at least not our breakfast. Joe says that we will be able to get something at the *store.* So a quiet day is looming! Of course Tatsey will not be able to come & nearly all the Indians have left. We can have breakfast at the *store* & we can also get our other meals there at government prices. We talk briefly to father Vielle & coming back from the *store,* we encounter Tatsey who is on his way to the *store* to send a message to Browning for a coffin for his deceased mother. Tatsey thinks that grandmother could be buried on Wednesday. "I want to do it as soon as possible," he says, "before it gets even warmer." Indian Joe is now very depressed; he lived for so long with granny & granny had seen all her grandchildren being born & now she is dead. He says, I don't know how old she is, but she was between 90 & 100. In case you need money, Uhlenbeck says, you can borrow from me. He declines the offer, but a moment later, through a note, he asks for money that he will pay back on Saturday. He comes around to pick it up.

For days Tatsey will not come and teach. And around us the tents are taken down. We talk with Duck Head. Mary is the interpreter and this afternoon her father will still move us. We will camp behind the store. There are only three Cree *camps* left. It is a busy morning, lots of emotions, walking to & fro & I have to arrange a number of things. To get ahead of things I take the dusty floor blanket & let it air in the wind. Here & there it is full of dust & damp, too. I also put the mouldy carry-on outside in the sun. At 12:00 we have to eat at the *store.* Such a distance to walk and it is twice as far to Tatsey's tents. U. enters the tipi for a moment. The old man says, "My sister has died," and crouching down he mourns the old woman & prays. Duck Head is on time & apart from horse & wagon, he also brings along his wife. He is not a strong Indian, but he has a nice slim build. Still he lifts the big barrels by himself, the big suitcases they carry together.

Further down the prairie, in the direction of the bushes, a few whites are annoyingly curious & come and watch our furniture. They stand right in front & watch cheekily. This is just it: an American will do this, but the Indians are much too modest & have no interest in being importunate. Uhlenbeck gave the women a *speech,* but they did not care & stayed as long as it pleased them. After everything is finished (to my regret not all poles are taken along) both of us walk to our new camping place & the wagon with furniture follows us. The tent is put up quickly & when everything is ready, Duck Head gets two dollars for the transport. His wife has stuck in the poles and the tent is on a nice little plateau. We look out over the Rockies. In this weather a very nice spot. But how will the tent's location do when a west wind blows?

How warm it is this afternoon. In the tent it is soon 90° and I have a lot of tidying up to do. I haul water from the Badger. No longer from the White Tail Creek. And I will make tea right away. Then we sit down quietly and the warm tea is so delicious. At 6:00 we have our evening meal at the *store.* At first the laborers eat, only then do. There is no room for everyone at once and there are not enough plates & forks. The same German cook is here. That man is so friendly to us and that is nice for the first days, which will seem strange. The location of our camp is not bad at all. Uhlenbeck indicated the spot to Duck Head. But there are many holes & potholes right in front & around our tent. In the dark we will have to take care, but it is convenient that my paper bin and sewer are so close. Everything I want to get rid of, I just throw in the big hole, near our tent. As long as Tatsey stays at his old location, we will eat at the cook's and when he comes to teach again, he will receive two dollars daily. Tatsey approves of this arrangement presented by Uhlenbeck. Josephine is not doing very well & she is coughing a lot again. It is a beautiful evening and I sit in awe in front of our tent looking at the mountains. It is a completely new scene, all the peaks of the Rockies are different. In time we go to bed, after having been paid a visit by a young Indian, Jim Fine Bull, who came straightaway to our camp, showed us a few coins & wanted to buy *candy.* We say, again, that he can get sweets, but that we don't sell anything. Uhlenbeck also reads stories to him & Jim shows a lot of interest. He is a superb type of Indian. For a long time I will remember his features, sharp as they are. While busy getting ready for bed, I hear a wagon coming on the high road, from the Old Agency. How did they get down in the darkness? I don't understand it. It is a very bad road & here & there it is very steep. We sleep restlessly and around our tent is a *skunky* smell. That animal has to move, or we will. The smell of a *skunk* is unbearable. During the day we did not notice it.

Wednesday, August 16.

Tatsey's daughter dies. One week no teaching.
Up at 7:00. A gray sky. Breakfast at 8:00. At 9:00 I am working on my diary while Uhlenbeck reviews his new apparatus. John & Joe Tatsey briefly drive by with Wild Bill. They have been looking for flowers, because grandmother is about to be buried. There were letters for us, but John forgot to take them along and will make sure we get them. I sit down & look out for a long while. How we both long to be able to work regularly again. We hope that Tatsey will be able to come again by Friday. If only he could come on Thursday, but that might not be possible & we don't want to hurry him. Tatsey wants to have another camp location as well. That is what we thought. They don't like to stay in the same spot for long after someone has died. I just sit and look out over the spacious prairie & over the Badger.

I see the burial procession approaching. It is quite far away. First I see the open wagon with the coffin without a drape. There old grandmother rides for the last time over the hills, for the last time through the valleys. She does not approve of it, going to the Catholic graveyard, where they are bringing her, and she wants to buried in the Sand Hills. It is a sunny, warm afternoon. Everything looks clear in the light. Far! far behind the open wagon a few *buggies* follow & John rides along on horseback. The different carriages disappear behind a range of hills & reappear and for a long time we hear the death march. Slowly, very slowly the procession heads further on to the mission at Two Medicine and for a long, a very long time, I watch Granny's last journey. A weird mood! An afternoon never to be forgotten.

Joe, who comes by with the letters – from Ab & Nella & a postcard from Jo in England, causes our mood to change. Shortly before her death, Joe saw his grandmother. And then no more. "*It makes me sad,*" he says. "There will be relatives & lamenting," & says Joe, "I can't handle that." Of course Tatsey went along, but his wife stayed at home with sick Josephine, who, according to Joe, was quite well. "She even had a bit of meat." Joe really believes that his sister is doing well & that they will be

able to move soon. After Joe's departure we quietly read the letters. It takes a long time & it is a welcome change. After a while we walk around a bit & buy some sugar at the store. Now we can drink tea again.

Old Eagle Calf approaches our tent on his brown horse. Pietaunesta looks so sadly at us with his old eyes. Today they don't shine. He weeps repeatedly & alternately holds Uhlenbeck's and then my hand. Weeping, he sits down on our bed and stares. "Now my old sister," he thinks, "is at the *Sand Hills*, where the buffaloes are not scarce & where all the Indians are gathered." We try to cheer up the old man. I present him with sweets, give him tobacco. He takes a small whetting stone from his pocket. It is a narrow, rectangular, smooth little stone. Earlier he had drilled a little hole in it. He pulls off the attached old string & he cuts off a piece of elk fringe & ties it to the grindstone. And he presents it to me, after wetting it with saliva & indicating how I to whet a knife on it. I am very happy with this small artifact, much happier than he might imagine.

"Well," Uhlenbeck addresses me, "why don't you present something to the old man! There must be something in our old suitcases that he would like to have!" And then I produce the tea platter cloth that I took along to decorate our tent by spreading it over a suitcase & that I did not use, first because our suitcases are seats and because time and again I have to rummage in them. He is very happy with it and ties it around his head as a headband. They are very much used to headbands, no matter how small. They like to stick a single feather straight up in it. I also think of Anna Hesseling's black-lined handkerchief that I got as a cap. He appreciates this present even more. For a long time he presses the cloth against his chest, then against his naked chest, because now again the shirt falls entirely open and then he loosely puts on the cloth around his neck. And he asks whether Uhlenbeck has half a dollar for him. He gets it, rises & mounts his horse to ride slowly downhill. Not long after he returns he presents Uhlenbeck with a nice fan that has been used in the *sweat lodge*. The fan part is made of buffalo hairs and the handle is richly decorated with beads. And again he asks for some money. Being of the ancient Indians, he wants to give us an Indian name. Uhlenbeck will be called *Omaxkskitsanik* – Big Bull. He calls me *Sakoo-Akè*.[218] In bygone days, years ago, when he still owned a lot of horses, he himself was called *Omaxkskitsanik*. That was the happy period of his life; that is why he gives Uhlenbeck this name. He names me after his mother. She was such a good woman, he says, and he looks at me approvingly. He talks a while longer; sometimes for Uhlenbeck he is incomprehensible and in English, he doesn't understand a word. He leaves again.

Now Uhlenbeck sits again quietly on his bed; I sit outside in the shade on the ground, close to the tent wall to get as much shade as possible. It is warm, very warm. I am very glad that Mr. Olson does not live far away. We have to go there at 6:00, and have our evening meal, but we want to be back home in time for possible evening visitors. I stay seated for some time longer & look out over the prairie: a small Indian boy sings, he walks high up on the highest hills & his Indian song sounds wonderful. And time and again I hear the drum. It must be Pietaunesta in the distance in his tipi. He must be sitting with his Otter bundle, rubbing the sacred otter pelt, muttering & praying, then drumming again, expressing his feelings on this day. Now I have to get up & hurry & will take my black party dress from the suitcase and put it on. How strange this black, silk blouse looks to me. It is quite something, to dress up on the prairie, & I can only see a little bit in the small mirror.

We are just ready to go when Joe approaches on horseback; again he has letters, from Jan among others. Josephine is doing quite well; she ate something again. We have a good time at Mr. Olson's. Their cabin is nice, comfortably & practically furnished, partly living room kitchen, partly bedroom. At first we sit outside for a while with the engineer. He wears a very clean, very light, soft shirt. The collar is loose at the neck & turned down a bit. The sleeves are turned up, the arms half-naked. Inside Mrs. Olson takes care of the evening meal. She does not have servants. For us it is weird that Mr. Olson serves everything. He takes my plate & I get it back completely filled: lean meat and tomato sauce, potato slices

& a cold salad (made of salad, potatoes and beets). For dessert each of us got on a plate a big piece of very strange tasting warm cake, with *berries* they just got from the Guardipee girl. We drank coffee and water. Later we talked outside a bit more, looked again at the pictures on the walls inside & were back home shortly after 8:00. But there was nobody to visit us & for the first time, when I realize that all our Indian friends have left and we might be facing days, perhaps weeks of great loneliness, I feel loneliness and melancholy creeping all over me. And again I worry about Uhlenbeck's work. When will it progress well enough? For quite some time we sit by our candle. And when we go to bed at 10:00, I sleep much better than the few previous nights. The *skunks* have disappeared; we no longer smell them.

Thursday, August 17.

I am up at 7:00. The weather is beautiful. It is still a bit misty, but the Rockies sparkle & it will be a warm day again. We have breakfast at 8:00. Then we walk to the government smithy; he is allowed to repair our suitcase. The smith, a Dane, & the Indian First One, his assistant, come right away to pick it up.[219] Then Uhlenbeck writes to Jan & I write to Mama. When we go out for a meal, we hear that Josephine Tatsey died the previous night at 10:00.

How this unexpected news strikes us! Right away we want to visit the Tatseys and on purpose we don't walk close to Pietaunesta's *tipi,* but still the old man calls us. We stay briefly, don't pass Duck Head's *lodge,* but cross the small stream & so arrive sooner at Tatsey's *camps.* Grandmother's tent has been moved. Their own tents are in the same spot. We arrive unnoticed. There are several women. Grandmother's tent is completely opened up. All the side walls are rolled up high. The warm wind blows through it. In the middle of it lies the body of Josephine; they are still busy wrapping it, and a moment later it lies on a small mound. It is carefully covered with sheets and a few women sit around. Our mood is somber also. The one tall, slim woman talks to us. *"She is happier now than we are,"* she says, talking about Josephine, & time and again she wets the tent cloth to make it cool down.

We don't go in there, but walk on to Tatsey's own tent. We find visitors there also. There are all kinds of small Tatsey children. We walk in & in a corner of the tent we find Tatsey's wife. She is tightly hugging her Cathy, half seated, half lying, she has isolated herself. When she sees us, she gets up, holds my hand for a long time, holds it firmly and talks to us with dignified self-control. She had noticed that Josephine's condition got worse & grandmother's death had set her back even more. Sometimes she had been very stuffy. Mother Tatsey looks at us with her black, friendly eyes and later, much later I still remember what she said: *"I shall never forget her."* Josephine was only 20 years old. She was always very quiet & always around & close by her mother, in great contrast to Hatty, who is one year younger and is now married to Charley

Guardipee. Hatty is charming, her beauty is rare, but her character not easy.

We don't see Tatsey. When we are outside again, we peer around. There, further down under a *buggy,* someone is lying down. Is it rude to disturb him? An Indian also needs to be alone & he hardly finds that in his tent life. Yes it is Tatsey. The poor man is quite sad. "Never," he says, "did I have such occurrences in my family." He speaks softly and is hardly audible and stays seated in the shade of the four-wheel wagon. We leave him alone & think that it will take a long time before he will return with some cheer as our *interpreter.* On the way back, again along the damp lower road, along the little stream, we meet up with Hatty with her child on her arm and a few other women. Hatty gets very nervous when we address her & weeps pitifully. How somber was this whole environment! How glad we are that our tent is far away. Perhaps our presence would now not always be appreciated. Perhaps it would make us too somber as well. Later in the day Joe comes once more & says that the Indian visitors lament so such. Actually, from time to time we can hear it, too. Bear Chief & his wife drive on from Two Medicine & his lamenting also reaches us. In our tent it is warm, 102°. It cools down a few degrees, when we open it wide.

Near the store Uhlenbeck speaks to George Day Rider; if he can make it, he will come and teach in the evenings for one dollar each time. In the afternoon he comes for a short while into our tent, smokes a bit & eats some sweets. He is certainly one of the most beautiful Indians. He has a noble & soft face. And how beautiful his complexion. But I miss the long braids. However, nice strands of hair fall along his forehead; a colorful beaded belt decorates his hat. Later that afternoon, Willy Kjaijoe comes. For quite a while he lies behind our tent in the shade & we sit with him and I make tea. We are content with our visitors. Perhaps it will not get too lonely? At 6:00 we eat our evening meal & talk there with the cook. Later we sit again behind our tent & when Uhlenbeck sees that an Indian and his wife & a small boy go to the *spring,* he ap-

Friday, August 18.

proaches them & has a chat. The man is Chippeway and will drop by sometime.[220]

Really, George Day Rider arrives after all. He has already led his horses further down. He sits himself down beside Uhlenbeck on the bed & working with him is not too bad. He is a slow thinker & doesn't express himself easily, but he is very friendly. At first I stay outside. I do this on purpose not to distract him. Then I light two candles, put one on the carry-on and one on the *candy* barrel, & in this way Uhlenbeck continues working with him. The last 15 minutes we talk. George wants to go to bed early because he has to get up early, at 4:00, to fetch the horses again before the ditch work starts. He receives a dollar for 5/4 hours of teaching and promises to return the following evening. Now we have our big suitcase back again. I hope that is reinforced well enough & that the bottom will hold out. Later we will pay for him. We go to bed at 9:30. First we look around outside a while . The sky is unusually clear. The Milky Way is exceptionally bright.

I am up at 7:00. Beautiful weather, but warm. Nice wind. Breakfast at 8:00. At nine Uhlenbeck leafs through his work & I write in my diary. Mrs. Olson passes by on horseback & says a few words. She wears a heavy, velvet riding costume. To me it seems very warm. She doesn't even know that Josephine has died. Proof that neither she, nor her husband, have a lot of contact with the Indians. Later George Duck Head & Joe First One drop by & get some sweets. *Tendrement,* with their arms around each other's shoulders, they head for the side of the bushes. Time and again an Indian passes by. There aren't many, but I like it. At 12:00 we go and eat. Again it is 103° in our tent, but the thermometer drops to 95 when I roll up the tent wall.

George Running Wolf approaches our tent on horseback; he has visited us several times. He is only 17 years old. It is hard to believe. He has an intelligent and serious talk with us for about one and a half hours. He tells us about his stepfather Joe Kasoos, Lewe's father, who encouraged his stepsons to do manual work. An older brother is now a carpenter. George wants to go to a technical school somewhere, far away, & and also learn a trade. He also lost a brother to consumption, "*the same sickness as Josephine,*" he says.[221] Another of his brothers was murdered, as was the brother of his stepfather. Whiskey played a big role. The murderer was never found, though in both cases an Indian spent quite a time in remand. He cheerfully sits with us, he makes the time fly today, but I don't find George Running Wolf very attractive. He also informs us that there will be Indian dances, outside of the *reservation*, in Valier, about the 5th of September. Especially the younger Indians will go there and he thinks that all kinds of Indians will soon be *around* again, that is, here in our neighborhood.

After his departure I make some tea, which we drink behind our tent. George also mentioned that Josephine will already be buried this afternoon. So after a short while we see a funeral procession for the second time following the same road. Again the procession heads for the graveyard at the mission near Two Medicine River. Again the open wagon is far ahead and is followed again by a few *buggies.* It is a somber spectacle. To what will Tatsey and the other Indians attribute these losses? Consumption with rapid onset occurs often & grandmother was very worn-out & tired & perhaps died of exhaustion. We did not go to Josephine's burial. Tatsey did not invite us, maybe they don't do that, and we were afraid of being rude.[222]

Later in the afternoon I see a boy go to the river with horses. He nods at me & I alert Uhlenbeck who is inside writing a letter to Ab. Uhlenbeck comes outside, and I was right, it is the nice Cree Indian, David. He only returned with his family yesterday, a bit further down near the few Cree camps. He is the *water boy;* his father works with a *team.* He lists the dollars that the family earns on a daily basis. He brags that all his cousins also work and they all live together.

Soon he will drop by. We eat our evening meal at 6:00 & talk for a moment to George Day Rider. He has to look for two of his *saddle horses.* So of course he can't come to *teach. Saddle horses* are troublesome animals. They always disappear or are thought to have disappeared. At 7:00 we are sitting in front of our tent when Adam White Man drives up on with his adopted son Clarence, who is 10 years old.[223] The boy is called *Different Guns.* He is a very gentle, not very handsome little boy, but a full-blooded Indian. He has a yellow paper bag in his hand & time and again he takes something out. In the *store* Adam has apparently treated his son to something yummy. I give father & son some sweets. These also end up in the yellow bag. I also give Adam tobacco. The package is put into his pocket. Still Adam is a nice man; he has white blood, and remarkably enough, he has clear, blue eyes as well – something I have never seen before – doesn't know a word of English, never went to the mission school & reproaches his father that he never learned anything. However, Adam still has something more; he continuously holds it in his hand. It is the colossal vertebra of a prehistoric animal, completely petrified & very heavy. Uhlenbeck gets it as a gift, after Adam has repeated once more: "I am so keen on it," & "two years ago I dug it up

myself." A moment later Adam says, "Now you should give my little boy some money," and we give Different Guns half a dollar. The Indian thinks that this is not enough, but for us, with our Dutch money, everything is expensive. Adam calls me by my Indian name & points out his *ranch* to us far in the distance past Badger Creek. He sends the boy with the horses to the riverbank & then he tells us that they adopted the child when he was only four weeks old. "My wife did it," he says, "at that time we did not have children yet." Now he has two girls.

After their departure, we walk around a bit and when it is dark I change the plates. I am still occupied with it when Uhlenbeck wants to come in with Jim White Man & Jim Fine Bull – the two Jims, who are always in each other's company. They ask for old stories and Uhlenbeck reads them a few. Little Jimmy smokes a lot and sticks the package of tobacco in his pocket. At 10:00 they leave, but come back right away. They can't descend our hill; it's too dark for them. We light the way for them with our lantern. Over the twisting path downhill, until they are on the road. Then I say, "Now you will be able to go on," and point out the light stripe, which is the road, & Uhlenbeck & I return with our light. They will get used to the darkness; it is a starry sky, but we think that they are scared. Ghosts! You never know & the two deaths will make the Indian boys more scared than ever. This evening sunset was of rare beauty. What light over the Rocky Mountains! We only get to bed by 10:30.

Saturday, August 19.

Up at 6:30. Beautiful weather. First I have to do laundry. Breakfast at 8:00, then we walk around quite a while. Then Uhlenbeck rereads his new stories, in order to become more familiar with them for when he has to read them for the Indians on request. For a long time I write in my diary. Before noon Tatsey arrives with Joe. He ascends our hill & talks to us for a while & looks around for a good camp area. Today or tomorrow they want to move to this area. They might choose the elevation near the riverbank, close to the bushes, I think. Tatsey says that his wife was quite calm & that she had slept a bit as well. Yesterday, about one hundred Indians were at the graveyard and Uhlenbeck says that that we had also thought strongly about going. When the Tatseys have their camp close by & on Monday, when Uhlenbeck continues work with Tatsey, we certainly can also eat with them again. The cook tells us that this morning the Indians were fighting, right near his cabins. He was not sure who they were, but they had already been transported to Browning & in any case George Day Rider was not among them. It is warm this afternoon. In the tent it stays at about 95 degrees. First Uhlenbeck sleeps a little while, then I make some tea. We manage to sit just outside the sun in a streak of shade behind our tent. Delicious tea and shade! Uhlenbeck prepares a few new *stories* aloud and I do needle-work and read a bit. The Chippeway Indian from the previous day passes by again. He shouts at us that he is going to move, lower down again. And he points in the direction of George Day Rider's tents and then he also tells about the fight & that George Day Rider had been there & was brought to Browning. George was drunk, he was going around with two bottles of whisky – a prohibited privilege! – bought outside the *reservation* & had been fighting with Gobertz, a half-breed, camped near the Guardipees.[224] "And," the Chippeway added, "Maybe he will get two months." What a disappointment to us. Perhaps we might not see this nice Indian again & Uhlenbeck had counted on his teaching & today I had intended to photograph him. George must have felt so lonely in his tent. Why didn't Sam Scabby Robe come to work & live

with him! Perhaps it would not have happened. It really is a very tough sentence, to be drunk, to fight and then to be *in jail* for two months in Browning. After our evening meal we get all kinds of boy visitors and I take three pictures of Wild Bull, Jim White Man, George Duck Head & Jim Fine Bull. Jim Fine Bull can't stay long and so all the boys leave soon. Still it was a visit that, I don't know why, left a strong impression. This evening, the nice weather, the beautiful evening sky, the gorgeous view right in front of our tent affected me very strongly.

The smallest boys are still around when David Salloway rides by. He joins our group & wrestles with Jim White Man, who loses in the end; in the first place Jim is younger & David is a real wrestler. David's mother and then another woman also come and watch & laugh & look in amazement at my crochet work. David did not go to the mission school, but went outside the *reservation* to Valier. Later this evening the two Jims, Jim Fine Bull & Jim Whiteman; return, then we sit again in our tent by the candle & Uhlenbeck reads to them again from his texts. They want to hear Clot of Blood. With the lantern we bring them again to the main road. We watch the dark shadows and after they have disappeared, we return to our sailcloth roof. I forget to change my plates; right away we go to bed – sleep very, very poorly. When we were about to go in bed, there seemed to be a cat in our tent. Here there are a very few cats, in contrast to dogs. It must have crept in when we brought the kids a little distance away. In the middle of the night Uhlenbeck notices it again; once in a while it is very windy and I am afraid that the tent will be blown over.

Sunday, August 20.

Our tent is turned around.

Both of us are awake again at 6:00. It's still blowing very hard. I can't sleep & get up and time and again I tie the tent's front pole that is tilting. I go outside and with a new suitcase rope I make a firmer support for our tent. Now the wind is from the west, 20, which worried us all week & now it is clear that our tent is facing the wrong direction. When the wind is blowing against the front, it will get blown over. Dust clouds fly inside. This can't stay as it is. Before eight we have eaten our breakfast. I don't tidy up the camp bed. We can't go in and out of our tent, because that would let the wind get inside more. Rather we walk around a bit & hope that our furniture will not be blown from one side to the other.

At Eagle Calf's we meet his married daughter Horn & also Margaret Champagne, who speaks fluent English & excellent Indian.[225] She has already helped Uhlenbeck this afternoon. Her mother tells Uhlenbeck a long story about Gambler, a chief from ancient times.[226] Mother Champagne, now married to Horn, recites nicely; her daughter translates all the time and Margaret recites as well. Also that Duck Head still has that gambling wheel in his possession. If we ask he will certainly show it to us. Margaret comes along with us, but first we have to see the Tatseys who are now camped near Duck Head. They have moved, but only a meter or so. That beautiful grassy valley has become the site of their greatest disaster. On this sunny hour in the afternoon it is warm & dry there, but beware! when damp hours & rainy days come along! They lived there in the water & Uhlenbeck & I keep thinking that this likely meant death for Josephine & that it also shortened the life of Granny. Tatsey will not come to teach on Monday, but on Tuesday. If only that were true! We also talk to Tatsey's wife and Hattie, who both wear black. Both women look glum and stare in front of them.

At Duck Head's we see Tatsey's sister.[227] She is a rather small, lanky woman & looks like her recently deceased mother. We get to see the old *gambling-wheel*. It is a small wheel with colorful little beads on the spokes, with very small bundles of weasel tails hanging down from it. It

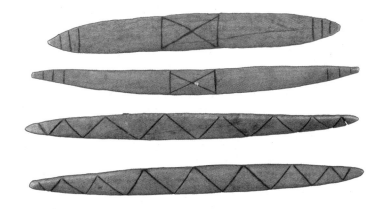

carefully wrapped in its entirety. From a chest he takes a package that is wrapped & wrapped up again. Duck Head also shows us a piece of mouldy wood or root. It is tied to a little branch with a leather strip. Apparently this is also very valuable to him & he carefully stores everything back in the chests. Duck Head's *log house* is furnished much better and is most of all much tidier than the dwelling of his old father, who has two housewives to keep everything tidy! Uhlenbeck says to Duck Head that our tent is nearly blown over and asks him whether, for one dollar, he could turn it around. "Yes," says Duck Head, "I will do that tonight." But we know that there will be delay after delay. Actually he should have told us last week that our tent should be turned. All tents are facing another direction. But the women who are also inside speak up and say that he has to do it now, this morning, because of me; otherwise I will get too cold.

Then Margaret comes along with us and we walk away, but the old man calls us in. He has little Paul, that dear, little, beautiful, supple Indian, dance for us in the under tipi. His little moccasins move elegantly up & down, from time to time he holds his arms akimbo, arching his little child's body. His old father claps his hands rhythmically and sings and I shiver with enjoyment. Then the old man takes all kinds of things from his *log house:* a piece of buffalo hide, a dark brown, beautiful long curly hide, a little gambling wheel, but not as beautiful as the one his son

Duck Head had and a petrified buffalo rib. Finally Uhlenbeck is presented with the buffalo rib. This one also has a hole drilled in it.

When we come outside, both his wives run towards us, rather, to me. One woman presents me with a heavy hammer, it is an old pemmican hammer, one of a type they used to use. The strong buffalo hide is tied firmly to the heavy stone head with intestines. The handle is also wrapped with leather. The entire artifact gives the impression of being very old & used very often. His other wife also brings me a present: slightly bent bone sticks engraved with identical markings. It is a *hand game*, one of the many favorite Indian games. Outside they spread a blanket on the ground, crouch around it, the children from around us, too & they indicate to me that I have to throw the little staves; time and again they laugh about the small success I have with the game & they show me how the staves have to fall down. I am excited about my presents and when we get up & want to go back to our tent, we see from a distance that they are already busy setting it up. Duck Head and his wife are busy with it & John Tatsey also helps for a moment. What a mess it is now. Everything is buried under dust and this morning, before we went out for breakfast, I had not tidied up anything; normally that never happens. Now it is too late for Uhlenbeck to work & I have to rearrange everything, suitcases, barrels, everything is in a place where it cannot stay.

Our little dwelling has to be arranged economically, otherwise it is crowded even without visitors. I want to air the ground blanket too. Uhlenbeck disapproves of that. He doesn't want the Indians to see that I work and yet something has to be done. Nobody does that for me. At 12:00 I am finished. Now the wind, calmed a bit, is blowing against the back wall, leaning halfway, so that is now much better, more solid, but our beautiful view is gone. The last few days we enjoyed so much sitting in the tent with half the front side rolled up. Now we want to go and eat, but all the laborers are still there & we go back. Later we eat with the cook & his help & the cook talks about the small German and Swiss villages with their old houses & narrow streets & suddenly I *sehn* [long] for those windless alleys, for those massive strong houses. After mealtime, when I am working on my diary, Margaret is already around to act as *interpreter.* How will that work out? *That girl is clever though!* She will receive one dollar for one afternoon. For a morning and an afternoon two dollars. I hope now that Uhlenbeck will make some progress. How much I do want this. Waiting irritates him so much; I see this on a daily basis. The teaching progresses: Margaret does a better job than George Day Rider and leaves with the promise to return.

Nobody comes before our evening meal. *And I feel lonesome!* The cook again is a nice contact for me. Long after I am home again, I will still feel for this man. After our evening meal we go around for a stroll. Now the very strong wind is weakening a bit. At 7:00 the old faithful arrive: they are the two Jims. Uhlenbeck reads them *The deserted children.* Still at dusk they left & long, lanky Jimmy says, "When I have finished my work tomorrow, I will come again," And when Uhlenbeck, taking leave from him with, "Goodbye, my younger brother." Jim nods & says, "That is good, that is very good," and while saying this, we see his happy, friendly face. I have *fixed* the tent even better by bringing in more and bigger stones from nearby & farther away. When I walk around alone & I discover a few good stones, I can't refrain from taking them home secretly. I hold them tight against my body & act as if any Indian I encounter will not see them. Now I am more successful at closing the big cracks between the tent wall & the grass. The wind blows less under them and it helps so that poles & ropes don't rub against each other much anymore & make them loose. We go to bed early. For a long time I lie awake. Uhlenbeck falls asleep sooner. The storm wind has lessened a lot and now & then it rains. A single horse with a little bell is a welcome sound to me; it breaks up the long silent night. Early in the morning I hear a lot of horses; they are being led to Badger Creek.

Monday, August 21.

We only wake at a 7:45. That is late, but I had hoped to sleep a bit longer during the morning hours. Our tent is now turned, so our bed is now turned as well and the suitcases etc. also. At the head of the tent, over the camp bed, I hung up and pinned one of our blankets. In the evening I also pin our watch to it & our thermometer now hangs there as well. In the future I will leave the blanket hanging there and instead will use all the coats etc. as covers. Now we will not get that much wind against the back of our heads when in bed. We are late and hurry. Still we have to wait a for a while at the cook's. The Danish helper, a good friend of ours, says that the cook is momentarily at the smithy and can't help us. A moment later we get warm, small, thick cookies (*hot cakes*) and a kind of barley boiled in water for breakfast. The weather is gray, very gray and nasty, 50°.

We are just back at 9:00 when Margaret comes to teach. I go out to look for more stones. Lots at the other side near the high hilltop; carrying them warms me up. They are quite heavy and I take along as many as possible. I make a threshold with the front of four, very big flat stones. Inside I put the cart box; that will do against rain & wind. Uhlenbeck works with Margaret & I write in my diary. Too bad that the sun is hiding for the entire day. A lost day for us, a lost day for Indian hay harvesting, and it will take one more day before they will set up a big camp here again. Yesterday a letter from Mama, and I wrote to the Vogler-Slothouwer ladies, because their sister has died. I also write to Lien & to Jan de Jong and will send this letter to Holland again. One of these days they will leave the Red Lake reservation.

That 50° temperature is really not very pleasant. The day before yesterday it was 100° in the tent. Still, it seems that the sky looks less stormy than yesterday, and the mountains, this morning completely invisible, have appeared again today. Perhaps the Tatseys will not move today; the weather doesn't permit it. I dearly long to know where their new location will be and whether we can eat with them again. Uhlenbeck works with Margaret until 12:00. Then she will eat and return at one. We also eat quickly and from one to three they work diligently together. For the five hours of teaching she receives two dollars & will return Tuesday morning at 9:00. Uhlenbeck is quite satisfied with his teacher, but working with her is tiring. We stroll around a bit and keep watching to see whether any visitors show up. Time & again I think of the Blue Beard fairy tale, "*Sister Anna, isn't anyone coming yet?*"[228]

We have our evening meal with the cook & his helper & later Jim White Man drops by briefly. He only gets a little bit of tobacco & not too many sweets because he comes so often & perhaps we should be sparing with it. He stays briefly and then we also talk for a short while to Jim Fine Bull's father. He is strikingly his son's older edition. Uhlenbeck has already met his father. He is a typical Indian type, sharp features & extremely slim. Then nobody comes anymore. We did get mail: a letter from Mama, from Cor & a postcard from Mrs. De Josselin de Jong Sr. from Oosterbeek.[229] Because of strange clouds above the Rocky Mountains the sky is going completely red. We haven't yet seen such a red color. The sky looks better than yesterday. We are in bed already by 9:00. How I long for a beautiful day tomorrow! We sleep badly; Uhlenbeck has such a bad cold.

Tuesday, August 22.

I get up at 7:00. We have breakfast at 8:00. The weather is beautiful, quiet. It looks gorgeous everywhere. By 9:00 we start looking for Margaret. However, she does not show up. In contrast, Tatsey arrives on horseback; he will teach until 12:00. Margaret will not come at all anymore. Yesterday in the evening, that is Monday, she left with her family for Birch Creek, without saying anything to us. Did she find her job too strenuous? Did her family no longer allow her to help out? Now Uhlenbeck checks with Tatsey the work he did with George Day Rider & with Margaret Champagne. Tatsey reviews a lot and by working hard and very intensively, at 12:00 Uhlenbeck is as far ahead as yesterday at that time, the difference being that the mistakes are removed & everything is now revised correctly. For a while Duck Head came to listen to their work & the whole morning I had to do laundry and make sure that everything dried quickly. Tatsey says that he will come and camp here only at the start of next week. First his wife wants to do a lot of laundry. Tatsey also returns the 100 dollars & Uhlenbeck pays him for another two days teaching, Aug. 13 and 14.

Uhlenbeck pays the *timekeeper* for our meals. We are late for our meal. The cook has already eaten. We are still around when George Running Wolf comes in. It is strange, but I don't recognize him and for a long moment Uhlenbeck wonders whether it is indeed George himself or one of his brothers. We are still talking when the doctor from Browning also comes in with an Indian with beautiful, long braids. We briefly greet the doctor, only exchanging a few words. We do not have much sympathy for him & for that reason don't want to enter into a long *discours* with him. Last year Uhlenbeck talked to him in Browning. We walk around a bit (the same old song). Uhlenbeck reviews his morning's work & I keep up with my diary.

We are quietly sitting when Pietaunesta calls our names from outside. Now he is on foot & has a long stick with him, a blanket wrapped around his hips. He sits down beside Uhlenbeck on the camp bed and I make some bouillon & hand him a cup. He seems to like it. And he looks at the meths burner & at my knitting & crocheting work & the long letter that I just finished. He holds it for an entire moment with his lean hands and then he says, "*Yes, Sakòo-àke is wise!*" But to Uhlenbeck he ascribes supernatural powers otherwise "he could not be so knowledgeable about the Indian language!" And *Sakòo-àke* was also the name of his mother, who was such a good woman. She was the sister of Little Dog's father. So Pietaunesta & Little Dog are first cousins, but don't look like each other at all. Pietaunesta again asks for some money. He says he is hungry! Uhlenbeck finds this very awkward! And Uhlenbeck says again, that we are poor, that we can't give away much money, but have to save our travel money. (Later Uhlenbeck instructs Tatsey to make it clear to his uncle that it is impossible for us to give away so much money. Tatsey says that the old man is not in need – his sons Duck Head & Adam take too good care of him. But his two housewives aren't thrifty & the sons are not always very happy with that.)

The old man is still with us when David comes in with a much younger brother. Dan stares at the sweets which are lying in front of Pietaunesta; he also gets a few pieces & the younger brother runs off as quick as a bunny. David only pays us a short visit & when Pietaunesta leaves and is walking down the hill, I watch his lean figure for a long time. The blanket is draped beautifully over one shoulder. He holds it elegantly under one arm & his red hair band contrasts beautifully with his deeply tanned face. A moment later one of his youngest sons, our friend Jim, comes in. He takes cards from his pocket & wants Uhlenbeck to play with him. This scene seems peculiar to me. Jim is still around when Wild Bill comes in. His horse is outside, but walks away & later Jim holds it for Wild Bill. The little, fat Wild Bill is very excited. With lost of gestures he talks about his brothers & sisters, about the fights at home, and about his much older half-brother in Cutbank he says, "I don't like him, he always thinks that I make his children cry." Bill will

Wednesday, August 23.

return soon. We have *supper*. There are no more visits, we sit at 8:00 by the lantern (50°) and go to bed already at eight thirty, half out of misery. During that night I found it cold. At 5:30 I look at the thermometer: 38°! At 8:00 it is at 50°, at 9:00 70° and at 12:00 84°!

Before eight we have already breakfast. The weather is beautiful and the sun will soon come through, which is actually the case. A few hours later though it is 84°. Again the cook has thick, warm cookies and barley & hot coffee. At eight thirty we walk around a bit. At 9 o'clock Tatsey comes. I am also in the tent, quietly writing a long letter to Mama. George Mad Plume comes to listen for a bit.[230] There are still two younger brothers. Old Mad Plume has five sons; now I know three of them. This Indian again is very modest. He only accepts tobacco & sweets when I clearly urge him to do so. At 12:00 he leaves with Tatsey, actually after twelve. We eat with the cook & his helper & then the cook tells us that he will be leaving. He has been dismissed & preferably as of the second day. He cooks too well & he feeds the laborers too much. They just told him that there will be another cook and that is it. He thinks that he has not been thrifty enough and is very upset by this treatment. He has saved some money, has a *farm* and will go there again. So, tomorrow we will see him for the last time. Now we are very happy again that we will be eating again soon at Tatsey's. How unexpected everything is here. You never know how the day will go.

At the cabin we meet another ±50-year-old American, a free thinker & very unsympathetic. He is a talented speaker & some things he says are not at all stupid. We go for a walk. Uhlenbeck reviews his work; I keep up with my diary. Again we walk around a bit. I hear something! It is, I think, a wagon driving up our hill. I see two horses' muzzles and then a *buggy*. Maybe it is an Indian coming here to camp, but, I don't see tent equipment. Then suddenly we see that it is Bear Chief. Bear Chief, our faithful friend, with his wife & his two daughters.[231] They stop & dismount. I lift the oldest girl from the wagon. The smallest (two years old) starts to cry loudly: that's how much she is frightened by us. Apparently she does not remember our faces. I quickly give her a few sweets & right away she is no longer scared. A moment later she plays peek-a-boo with me behind her mother's back.

Bear Chief sits on our camp bed in his usual corner & smokes a bit. He doesn't eat sweets. He hands them to his wife. The children eat a lot of all the treats. Juice runs in little streams down their little faces. Elk-Yells-in-the-Water continuously picks up the empty sucker wrappings & puts them into her scarf. She wipes the children's mouths with a very dirty cloth and tears off a small strip to tie the stocking of the little girl. Their dresses are very dirty & wet in the front, especially the bodice at the front. Bear Chief's braids are coming loose – and still these four are *on a trip!* They are visiting & have to go further along for hours. Isn't it idyllic, being away from home for just a night or so? Upon Uhlenbeck's request I make tea. They like that; they each drink two cups & the children are allowed to taste from their father & their mother's cup. They also like the meths burner very much & also the very small cups, not enamelled, & the very small spoons. I promise to send the small cups and the spoons to the little girls when we leave. For sure I will remember. Fortunately, I now get the idea to take their pictures. The buggy & the horses form part of the background. I give them a lot of sweets to take along for the road and to each of the girls a piece of chocolate (still left over from our boat trip). They are small children. They laugh at us confidently & Bear Chief's wife looks so friendly at us. They approve of our Indian names & have already called us such. When they drive away, we watch for them as long as possible. They take the steep road up to the Old Agency. This visit was very good for us. We hadn't seen Bear Chief since Browning. Then I first tidy up the tent, wash the cups carefully & walk around again for a little while. When we go for our evening meal at 6:00, it appears to be too early. So we wait some more time & then have our last meal with August Kramer, the man who took such good care of us. (His next address will be August Kramer, Lothair, Montana.) He has prepared beef for us, which is really not that bad, & also fried potatoes. The laborers, who come here for their meals, don't approve of August being sent away. We say goodbye and promise that he will hear from us when we are back in Holland. Then we go home, but I am kind of glum & more than once I think about this evening,[232] about this friendly German.

We walk over our high plain & visit for five minutes with Joe Tatsey and Wild Bill. When an Indian passes by our tent in a wagon, they find this a splendid occasion to ride along with them. Then we don't see anyone else. By eight it is already 50°. Uhlenbeck lies on our camp bed with his feet deep under the blankets. I change some more plates & carefully put all kinds of covers on our bed. And before nine we are already undressed. Now it is nice and warm under the blankets but still we don't sleep well. I have to find the sleeping pills & take one. The weather is nice and calm. At night more than once I hear a horse near our tent & once in a while near our suitcases a rodent gnaws on the empty candy wrappings or whatever it can find.

Thursday, August 24.

I am up at 7:00. It is not as cold as the previous morning. By eight we are already in the dining room. The cook has already left. From a distance on the other side of the Badger we see two wagons. He is sitting on the first wagon beside the driver. He is on his way to Seville and there he will take the train. The new cook has already arrived. Uhlenbeck thinks that he saw him once last year. He is also German, but a totally different type. So far I don't find him attractive. Fortunately our Danish helper is still around. By 8:30 we are already back home. Time and again Wagner's black-and-white young dog follows us, rolling right at our feet & badly wanting to be petted.[233] We walk about until 9:00. Then Tatsey arrives on horseback. Uhlenbeck sets himself to work & I write in my diary. Bill Russell comes in to talk business with Tatsey & it makes Uhlenbeck nervous when the conversation takes such a long time. At 12:00 George Duck Head brings Tatsey's horse and then Tatsey tells us that all these old, big holes around our tents are old wolf holes. For example, the big hole was of a big wolf, the smaller holes were puppies'. Groups of such holes are still found a lot on the prairie. The new cook doesn't seem to be the same as last year. His name is Sager. We always think of the helper, Irvin Charley Eriks, a *pet*. This Irvin sometimes looks like our little Leiden friend, Bart.

During the long afternoon we don't see anyone else, but the weather is nice & we enjoy walking around now and then. When we pick up our evening meal at 6:00, Jim Fine Bill, our friend we spent so many quiet days and evenings with, also arrives. I have just gone into our tent, which I closed up tightly, when I hear a light scratching at the tent. It is Helen Powel and her mother and a stepson. They are camped nearby until Sunday & have been looking for our tent for a long time. She says she is working on a little purse for me. Actually we really like seeing her (she is the woman who with Walter brought us on Monday July 10 from Browning; it was her *team* & then we had to pay her). David Salloway and his brother Camil, the wrestler, also drop by for a moment, as do Bill & Jim White Man and & big Jim, who is shy at first, but who finally ventures in, now that there are other visitors, on Uhlenbeck's repeated request. Big Jim is scared by visitors who don't speak Peigan.

Peter Weasel Head drives the horse-drawn carriage and then Helen & her mother move on again.[234] They promise to come back before their departure from White Tail Creek. Both Jimmies are sitting quietly and ask for a narration. Outside, near our hill, I see little Dick. "*Pochaspott! Pochaspott!*"[235] I shout at him & the small, yellow-painted Indian boy with his four little braids laughs and comes in. Little Dick knows all kinds of ancient stories by memory & sometimes unexpectedly completes half of Uhlenbeck's sentences. Dick has most fun with a "*ghost story*." The three boys leave at dusk & by 8:30 we are already heading for bed. For the first time we both take a sleeping pill. I fall asleep soon, but Uhlenbeck still can't sleep.

Friday, August 25.

I am up before seven. The weather is nice, but windy. We eat breakfast before eight, then we walk around for a little while and I wash a few towels & haul water from the *spring* when Tatsey arrives at 9:00. He walks slowly – Tatsey always does that; with his head down, he climbs uphill & approaches our tent. Two Indians, Calf Robes, also come in. I thought they came to visit us, give them tobacco & sweets, but they have a question for Tatsey and quickly drive on. At 12:00 Tatsey *fixes* our tent somewhat. He pulls a few ropes tighter. "It might rain," he says. We eat with the new cook & with Irvin. At first the blacksmith is there too.

When we go home, Jim White Man trots along with us. I give him his ball that I repaired for him. Then he produces his cards again & draws a bit for us. Jim sits on the bucket and pays great attention to his figures. He draws Indians and horses & Uhlenbeck observes him closely. Now it is blowing very hard & once in a while it rains. The weather quickly deteriorates. Strong winds the entire afternoon & lots of rain, an extremely nasty, cold afternoon. Fortunately Jimmy is here and stays for a long while. It stays between 50° and 47° in our tent. Jim repeatedly takes his ball from his pocket & looks at its patches.

Dick is suddenly at the entrance of our tent, sopping wet. I indicate to him to come in real quickly and Jim tells him to take off the heavy, fur-like shirt. He kept on a black, woollen undershirt. The boys took their hats off. That is quite something, because they prefer to pull the hats deep down over their eyes. Uhlenbeck plays with the boys & Jims draws a lot. Little Dick looks time and again over his shoulder and says, "*Sakòo-aki* should play with us, too." And then I played along with them, too & I give Jim tobacco. I will make some bouillon for the boys. They keep watching what I do. As soon as the bouillon is ready & poured hot into the cups, Jim keeps warning his younger brother. Little Dick still wants to taste it & shouts *Sokapiy! Exkaiik Sokapiy!*[236] The little Indian enjoys it. I try to take a picture of the boys & Uhlenbeck, but of course nothing will come of it. It is much too dark. Suddenly Dick is very excited & tells a long story. "I am Bull Chief; I am on a *raid* & with my knife I stab a Cree to death," and the slender body is all movement.[237] Each moment the child's facial expression changes, he shakes his head, so his braids swing up and down, he claps his hands & he sings several warrior songs. We greatly enjoy watching Dick. He acts exactly like his father. Jim is not half as impulsive, is always *slow* and rather yawns once in a while. Dick also doesn't know any exclamation other than *kot tam!* and *Ko ahat.*[238]

At 5:00 the boys leave. I give them sweets to take along for Paul, the handsome, little brother who danced so beautifully for us in the tipi. We eat our evening meal at 6:00. It is not raining anymore, but it is very wet & very dirty. After *supper* we don't see anyone else. Outside Uhlenbeck paces up & down to get his feet warm. I prefer to stay inside the tent. By 8:30 we are already under the blankets. Now we warm up wonderfully and both of us again take a sleeping pill. It has stopped raining & the wind has calmed down.

Saturday, August 26.

Up at 6:30. I have all kinds of things to do. Once in a while the sun shines. Breakfast by eight. Before nine I have washed the handkerchiefs & the socks & by the time Tatsey arrives I have also looked for fresh flowers. Very often I have flowers in our tent. They are in an empty vegetable tin that I got months ago from Chubby. Uhlenbeck is going to sit with his feet in the sun. It is cold and it stays quite cold; still, I think that the sky is looking better. The band of sun in the tent is now taken up by the fat son-in-law, Charly Guardipee, who of course is here for business, just like Joe who drops by to say that he has found the horses again. Then Johnny, who is on his way to Browning, comes to talk to his father. That is three interruptions. Oh! This makes Uhlenbeck so nervous, especially when Tatsey repeatedly rises to go outside & follow John, to see whether he really drives on, or is still hanging on at the Guardipees.

Finally Johnny is en route & father Tatsey calms down. At 12:00 he leaves. Then we eat and the only peculiarity of the afternoon is that it rained incessantly and blew for hours at a stretch. It is a very cold, very nasty afternoon. We drink very hot tea. At 6:00 I want to warm myself at the cookhouse fire. The *storekeeper* sees this and he brings me a wooden chair – the only chair in the cookhouse. This evening it is dry. Uhlenbeck paces up & down a bit to get warm, but when he comes in later, he is still cold. I heat a big, very flat stone on the meths burner. I unexpectedly treat him with it. So now he sits down on his bed & I wrap his feet and the heated stone in a blanket. By 8:30 our night begins. The only really good place is under the blankets. It is not raining. The wind calms down. 47°.

Sunday, August 27.

I get up before seven. Sometimes the sun shines & the steady wind dries everything. Breakfast at 8:00. Until 12:00 we walk around a lot. We eat with the cook & with Irvin & after our meal we talk a bit to old Owl Child. He gesticulates in a lively manner with his arms & hands. He is a real Indian, such slim hips. Uhlenbeck had already recognized him from a distance. Now the sun is shining deliciously, though it is still cold. Uhlenbeck works that afternoon alone with his notes & I write in my diary. Nothing else happens. Just David Salloway drops by for a moment with his brothers Camil & Dan & the two Gobertz boys, the youngest of which has braids.[239] We have nearly finished our evening meal when we have a brief talk with John or George Running Wolf, John Sanderville, Tony Edwards and John Big Lake.[240] We have a quiet evening & get to sleep rather early.

Monday, August 28.

Up at 7:00. By 8:30 we are back from our breakfast. Tatsey comes at 9:00. He says that they will move tomorrow if his wife is feeling better. When I return from the well, Adam is sitting in our tent. He addresses me again as Sakòo-aki. I give him something to smoke & sweets & our little match box & he puts everything in his pocket & smiles friendly at me. Tatsey works until twelve thirty with Uhlenbeck. John dropped in for a moment & will come and *teach* at 2:00 for one more hour for a halve dollar. However, John only comes at 2:30 and thinks that he is right on time. He was fishing with Joe & Jim White Man. He cheerfully chats & again Uhlenbeck and I come under his spell. *Teaching* progresses *slow*. John finds it difficult. He will receive his personal fee at the end of the week. John likes that better, too & also Uhlenbeck would not have that much change, because we are very thrifty with it. His visit broke up the long afternoon a bit.

We eat our evening meal after six. This cook is always so late. Irvin says, "*I quit tomorrow.*" We regret this very much, but he can't get along with this cook. It is a nice evening. We enjoy walking around. Exquisitely beautiful red sky in all directions & the high gray prairie hills turn shiny green. It looks like lush, young grass. After half an hour all the glow has disappeared. Only in the west a faint shine remains. The new moon is already shining mistily. In the afternoon we got a brief visit from Dennis Boy Chief & the much younger Saingodard.[241] Dennis is the stepbrother of Percy Spotted Bear, who last year fooled Uhlenbeck with his name.[242] We bring two letters to the *timekeeper*.

Tuesday, August 29.

I am up at 7:00. The weather is nice, though the sun is not really out. It is 47°. When we go outside at 8:00 we notice that a forest fire is burning. Not a trace can be seen of the Rocky Mountains. In hindsight Uhlenbeck thinks that there was smoke yesterday, too. The wind is coming from the mountains. I hope that it will change direction soon, so we can see our beautiful Rockies again. We talk for a little while to Irvin. He has to wait for a drive to Seville. At 9:00 Tatsey comes. First Uhlenbeck reviews with him John's work from the previous day. I go outside & walk and read an Eliot. Uhlenbeck makes good progress with Tatsey now. Sometimes a few pages are finished. In case John is prevented from coming in the afternoon, Tatsey will come this afternoon for one more hour. Nothing special during meal time, just inedible salty bouillon soup. Tatsey actually comes at 2:00. His wife is at Birch Creek. I make some bouillon. Tatsey's sister is still around. Just when he is nearly finished with Uhlenbeck, the *storekeeper* comes to talk to him & together they walk downhill. We walk a bit, up & down the hill. At *suppertime* Adam also comes to pick up a meal. He must have some money in his pocket & a fancy for meat & must not have had too much at home. We visit Eagle Calf, who now lives in a square tent beside his log house. He lent his tipi to Bear Chief for the dances in Valier. We walk back home along the higher prairie. It's now blowing very hard. Now no one else comes. Early to bed, but certainly no sleeping. A long and boring night. In the morning it is blowing just as hard. Now the tent is secured tightly and stays in place. All my hard work has shown success!

Wednesday, August 30.

Up at 7:00. Strong wind. It will get warm. Already 70° now. Irvin is still there at breakfast, but everything is very glum and very untidy. When the *store* wagons are back from Seville & leave again, Irvin goes along. Tatsey comes at 9:00. I go sit outside in the wind. Outside it is so warm & it makes me so sleepy. By 12:00 Richard Mad Plume & Mike Big Lake (August's father) drop by briefly & say that they will return later. We go for a meal, see them go in there later also & still later they come to visit. Uhlenbeck has to read a few stories for them. And Richard especially has a lot of fun. A third visitor joins, Running Crane, a young, broadly built, married Indian.[243] John Tatsey comes to teach when the three visitors are still around and they want to stay and listen how this goes. They are modest and only eat a few sweets. They also want to go to the dances in Valier and after that they will camp here.

It has been a very nice visit. Only too bad that it partly coincided with John. We would have enjoyed it twice. Even though Uhlenbeck couldn't work that much with John, it was nice that the boy was with us. Then walking around again, evening meal & to bed on time. There will be no visitors. Now the weather is totally calm, a very different night.

Thursday, August 31.

Up before 7:00. Early breakfast. Before 9:00 we have already walked around for quite a while. I head for the bushes for flowers. There are no more roses there either & the green on the shrubbery is as brown as the creeper at home in the fall. Before 12 I write to Mama & also I start a letter to Jan. It is getting warm. 94° by 12:00. Then a meal & at 2 o'clock Tatsey comes back. John is off to Seville. He stays until 3:30, then goes to the *timekeeper* and if there are letters for us, he will come back to deliver them. When Tatsey isn't in a hurry & chats so amicably, he is always in a good mood & then I am so taken with this man and then I forget again that so often he cuts his teaching short. Tatsey comes back up to our hill with our *mail*. Uhlenbeck went part of the way to meet him and brings me lots of letters, from Mama, from our Jan, from Truus, from Mrs. Saussaye, Anna Boerlage, Go and from Henriëtte van Ophuijsen and still a newspaper from the Hesselings from the Eiffel.[244] What a lot to read! It will last me a long time. We have just finished a first reading of it, when old man Pietaunesta drops by again. He smokes a bit and I give him some sweets, also some for his youngest son.

After six we go out for our evening meal. A Chippeway woman and two small children want to buy some *candy* from us. This same game is repeated that evening. And again we explain that we don't trade, but have sweets in store for our friends. This evening a whole *bunch of kids*: David and his brothers, Wild Bill & Joe First One.[245] A wrestling game between Wild Bill & Camil. Bill soon lost, looks very upset and Joe First One shouts: "*He is just jumping like a chicken!*" Everyone gets some sweets and they roll downhill like a gust of wind. Later in the evening an older Solloway, 20 to 21 years old, also comes to buy candy. That *Solloway outfit* we do like as far as the younger ones are concerned, but the older ones are a plague to us. It is as if we have a *candy store!* We don't sell anything, not now & never & I give him two big handfuls. He is acting shy, that older Solloway. And that is good; then they will be cured of thinking we are *traders*. Here you get an even greater sense of pride than at our little Rijn.[246] Without a lantern & in moonlight we go to bed. It is a quiet night. We still sleep badly though.

Friday, September 1.

Early up. Breakfast before 8:00. Today the eatery is buzzing loudly with flies. That is not very nice. But we don't think about whether or not it is damaging to our health. It appears that, at least here, it can withstand a lot. The sky's clarity here on this high prairie compared to the sky over a city canal is certainly very different! Tatsey comes at 9:00. They will move on Sunday. I hope that is true. Food at the eating place is not great and we think that it is much tidier at Tatsey's. In this regard, the previous cook was also much better. And now Irvin has left as well. We don't find it there cosy anymore. Uhlenbeck & Tatsey work quietly & I sit outside in the shade of the tent & look out over the prairie, over Badger Creek, out to the Rockies, & the beautiful morning makes me appreciate everything to the fullest. In such a mood I enjoy everything around me, beyond description. The herb-like smell of all the plants, the glorious sunlight around me and I sit and look & time and again the high road to the Old Agency seems to me like a fairyland, where I want to be & where I will never be able to get to!

No traces anymore of forest fire. Uhlenbeck pays the *timekeeper* for our meals from Aug. 15 to September 1. For the repair of the suitcases he owes 25 American cents. That is cheap. When going back to Europe, I will pack the old suitcase with light artifacts; otherwise it will certainly not survive. We go for a meal. John has to go to Browning & Tatsey himself will come back this afternoon. The long afternoon teaching hours break up the time for us very much.

Before our evening meal we walk around for a long time and early in the evening Peter Step by Mistake & Jim Fine Bull come in for a while. Uhlenbeck has to read out loud again. What a difference between Peter & Jim. Peter happens to be just fat and robust & big & is completely the opposite of our lean Jim who doesn't have an ounce of fat on his entire body. Peter still has to drive to Owl Child's *log house*. After their departure Camil Salloway and Freddy, the slender mission boy come in. They say that none of them ever swear. "*I don't swear,*" Freddy says. "*I am afraid the devil will get a hold of me,*" and he really means it, this sincere,

sweet Cree half-breed.[247] He has attended the mission school, but now he will go somewhere outside the *reservation,* where they make sugar. And, he says, Carl Schildt *cried* when he left the mission school. He doesn't mention it again and I regret that. Later we talk a bit to David, who is leaning on his horse. David lies on his bed or leans on his horse and preferably doesn't lift a finger, lazy as he is. We go to bed early & in spite of the sleeping pill, don't sleep well at all. Uhlenbeck advises that we try to go to bed later. We will try this once. But when the evenings are cold & dark & without visitors, *I feel lonesome (not for meat like the Indians) but for my bed!*

Saturday, September 2.

Beautiful weather and up early. I have lots to do. Breakfast before 8. A long time before eight thirty I am already busy with laundry & when Tatsey arrives all kinds of clothing are hanging on the lines. At 12:00 everything is dry and put away. Tatsey only stays until 11:00 and will come back in the afternoon for another two hours. His early departure suits Uhlenbeck well, though Uhlenbeck doesn't like all this irregularity, because Painted Wing, that well-known, very old Indian, arrives.[248] Now he is wrapped in his blanket again. Joe Spotted Eagle & James Running Crane also visit. The three visitors stay for a while and Uhlenbeck has to "narrate." Uhlenbeck has to sit right near Painted Wing, close to his ear so the old Peigan can understand him and they laugh time and again. Their gaiety is very amusing to me. They also appreciate the ancient *Napi* histories very much. Outside First One hears laughing, leaves his work & approaches our tent. He sits down between the tent split, crouches and also laughs until the story is over.

For me this is proof that Uhlenbeck is getting quite good in Peigan; otherwise they wouldn't return time and again for a narration. These three Indians also want to go to Valier. It makes Uhlenbeck restless & he would like to go there, too. I prefer to stay in my tent. Indian dances at an area outside the *reservation,* so there will be many white onlookers, don't appeal to me. But Uhlenbeck may go with some Indian & I will stay home & ask if Lizzy Tatsey can sleep here to keep me company. We go out to eat & at 1:00 Tatsey has already arrived; he didn't know the right time. He advises against going to Valier. "Drinking & fighting," he says. "No dancing under the open sky, but in a wooden shed. And, it is not 25, but 40 miles away." So, Uhlenbeck will stay home. A few more very quiet days and then the Valier dancers will return, then they will camp here in order to make some more money working at the *ditch*. We hope so much to spend a glorious time together as an end to these months!

Driving by, on their way to the Old Agency, we see the three oldest sons of Pietaunesta. And later Duck Head says to us that he will go to Valier tomorrow. They can't stay at home, they love the good time and they like so much to be admired and, haying, well, that will be all right. They have no idea about agriculture. About 9:00 or 10:00, they tell me, we start to hay & I try to tell them how, for our farmers, haying time is a time of action. This afternoon Uhlenbeck works for a few hours with Tatsey. When later, to pass the time, we walk around a bit, Sebastian Bear Chief comes by. This is the crippled Sebastian, who last year broke his leg. He dismounts and limps into our tent to quickly sit down on our field bed. We are so happy to see the boy again. Sebastian is such a sweet boy. (Tatsey thinks that he is not good company for his sons, because Sebastian was *in jail* in Browning when he was 13 years old; "*he was running away with a girl*.") But to us this gentle face is very attractive. His parents are on their way to Valier and now he is coming from the Old Agency to pay us a visit. He sits quietly and I give him tobacco & sweets, also some for his sisters. He looks stronger than in June & that makes us very happy. Perhaps in a year he can do without his crutches. Uhlenbeck helps him mount his horse & at a walking pace he rides away.

After that nothing else happened. Take a break! Walk around! Take a break! Evening meal and walk around again. David tells us that he moved & now we can really see that the entire *Cree outfit* has moved to the bushes in the beautiful deep valley where their tents are in sharp profile against the short & tall greenery. David is busy with all the horses, but once in a while he waves at us. It is already dusk when Tatsey comes around. He bought a young horse from Billy Russell & now would like us to lend him 50 dollars against a cheque he has. When John goes to Browning in a few days, he will cash the cheque & then we will get our money back. We lend him a 50-dollar bill; for us that is a large amount of money. Tomorrow, he says, I think I will move, that is supposed to cause us to be a good mood. Then I change the plates and for a long time we sit by our lantern. I also look outside. It is a beautiful, half-cloudy, half-clear moon-lit evening. I see light in several tents in the distance. We now go to bed later and we sleep reasonably well.

Sunday, September 3.

Lots of rain, snow & cold.

I only get up at 7:30. The weather is good, but quite overcast and it will certainly not get to 85° or 90°, like yesterday. Yesterday it thundered a bit also. We only eat breakfast at 8:30 & walk about for the entire morning. Together Camil & David have to transport a big water barrel from the old camp to the new one. They roll it along, laugh and have a lot of fun with it. After twelve we eat our noon meal. The cook says that when we feel cold, we should come and warm up. However, we leave & walk into the coulee where the Crees used to camp & then walk up the highest hills. Upon descending, we see three children a bit further down. We soon recognize Dick White Man & Clarence, & the girl appears to be Adam's oldest daughter. She is called Minnie.[249] We take the three children to our tent to give them sweets. Dick & Clarence beg a lot for tobacco, which they *don't* get. Minnie is very nice, she has dark brown hair & looks like Paulientje from Berkzicht. Of course she knows Peigan very well, but did not speak anything else two years ago. Now knows how to express herself well in English. She learned it at the mission school and stayed with her grandfather. "And I have two grandmothers," she says. She means the two housewives of her grandfather, Pietaunesta.[250]

Upon coming home, it has already rained a bit, otherwise I would have taken pictures of these kids. They go home in the rain, too. There is no wind and it is not cold, but there is a quiet, drizzly, which perhaps will stay around for a very long time. I will make some bouillon & then we should take it easy on this day. Strange idea! Perhaps in four weeks we will be in New York. Perhaps in six weeks we will receive visitors in Leiden! It rained early in the afternoon and late in the afternoon and after our evening meal we come home with soaking wet feet. Jimmy White Man drops in for a moment. Feeling sentimental, I put tobacco & sweets in his pocket. We go to bed quite early.

Monday, September 4.

Rain! Rain! No end. The road is very bad, the grassy slopes extremely slippery. The cook is friendly & he brings me the wooden chair & I gloriously warm myself at the stove. Tatsey doesn't come to teach, but at 11:00 he sends John for a moment to check out how we are doing in our tent. "At ours," says John, "*the water is two inches deep.*" He wears his yellow slicker and is on foot. All the horses have either run away higher up to Badger Creek, or to Birch. Of course it is too wet for Tatsey to come & too cold in our tent. We understand that. At twelve Uhlenbeck & I take turns warming our feet on the stove. The laborers we meet with today are nice. One of them says: "Come to my tent, I have a fire." At the evening meal we again take turns putting our feet on that deliciously warm stove. At the cook's there are a lot of leaks. In this wooden cabin it leaks a lot more than in our tent. It is only starting to drip near our sweets' barrels. For prevention I have put all the *candies* on our bed, then stored them in the wooden bucket, but think it more advisable to store them in one of the suitcases. One thing is very nice; once in a while I can heat a stone. John doesn't return, even though we asked him to do so; he also hasn't brought back the small bottle filled with whiskey that I would have liked to have as medicine. Tatsey himself told me that he had some & that I could have some of it. So Johnny is not coming. The entire Cree *outfit* sits at their fire. We don't see anybody, don't even hear anybody, and somberly sit by our candle. When I fix our bed, which takes a lot of effort, Uhlenbeck's feet, unfortunately, get very cold again and so, because of the cold, he can't fall asleep. All in all we have a very good night & wake up at 7:30. At night it was sometimes dry. Now it is raining again, harder & harder. Why should we hurry?

Tuesday, September 5.

Before eight I get up. I hurry. Everything is cold & wet. 43° We warm ourselves at the cook's. The road is better than yesterday. I think it has been rinsed clean, and we have to cross a few *creeks*. I heat the stones & Uhlenbeck reads a bit in our Baedeker about Chicago and New York. He is too cold to work and I read my own diary for a long time. Tatsey doesn't show up. At 12:00 we eat & warm ourselves again at the stove. Today the cook is friendly & the new assistant sometimes is not too bad either, but still we never like to eat with them and that happens quite a few times. The food is also nice and warm, but the road is extremely bad. We have to wade through the water; there's no sense in being careful anymore.

While still at the cook's, it starts to snow, a half-wet snow, which stays on the ground for the most part. Actually, yesterday I heard someone say, "It already snows in the mountains." Time and again we have to go through all this nasty wetness. Uhlenbeck had an idea to take along to our tent a little stock of food & drinks; then this evening we don't have to go back to the cookhouse. We get a piece of cake and a kind of biscuit. *"That will do,"* I think, for tonight & in the worst case also for tomorrow morning. What a splendid idea Uhlenbeck had; at first I wanted to object to it, stupidly enough.

So, now we are garrisoned in. Then first of all we take off all our wet socks & boots. Delicious, that dry cold! What a wealth & then the heated stones! Each of us gets one. Uhlenbeck gets the very big, flat one & rolls himself in the blankets. I put the yellow piece of carton on the ground, close to our bed, on it my little stove & wrap my feet in my woollen scarf. I wear two pairs of socks. That is delicious. The big night socks are indispensable. Uhlenbeck wears his black pyjamas the entire day. The thermometer goes down to 38°. Now, at 2:00 it is 40°. It keeps snowing & there is not a bit of wind. But I enjoy one thing – here & there I hear drops fall steadily. So it is still thawing and perhaps the snow will soon disappear. The river gets wider and much clearer than normal we hear Badger's water coursing down. Now to cross Two Medicine in

an old *buggy* with two unwilling horses! I wouldn't like that at all. For a long time I worked on my diary & I read a long piece of it to Uhlenbeck, which he always appreciates. And what will I do later? Maybe write to Nella. Uhlenbeck doesn't want any teaching after this week – at least, that is what he thinks now. It is wearing him out too much & sometimes it bores him when it goes so *slow* & then the Indians will have returned. It depends on our redskins how long we will stay here. They dance today! Not in the open field, but in a shed! Stupid Indians, how can you be like that. The whites will watch you & laugh at you and at home they will say that they saw something very weird. And you are eating away your money/drinking/drowning your freedom & you will end up *in jail!* In case the Indians don't return here, we will leave the *reservation* earlier and then spend longer en route. But first we will wait and see & hope for a good time. Maybe tomorrow all the snow will be gone. Maybe tomorrow the sun will shine. Maybe in a few days all kinds of Indian friends will come to our area. Both of us are in a very good mood & take turns praising each other for it. Because, when you think that this is what one calls *camping out in fresh air,* you are *cruelly mistaken.*

I worked a lot on my diary. At 3:00 John Tatsey comes and stays until 5:00. That is nice. Uhlenbeck pays him three dollars for teaching and two dollars as a present. Tatsey likes that. He doesn't say thanks but the young Indian flushes & that clearly indicates his inner emotion.[251] He is very nice & breaks up the time for us a lot, but again he has no whiskey. They moved a little bit further on. It was too wet in their tents. Stupid Indians though. We are doing much better on the high spot.

We have our supper *indoors*. Each a piece of cake & a biscuit. We don't have anything to drink. Because of the cold we have to economize with the methane. It is cold & it stays *pretty cold*, 37° to 38°. We are already in bed at 8:00, not to sleep, but to talk and to get warm. When we wake up a few times at night, it is still snowing a bit. At 7:00 a gray prairie bird flies through our tent. It must have been looking for a hiding place from the snow between the stones & then it ended up in the wrong spot. It flies around for quite a while and then I get up & give it back its freedom. With a stick I make a crack in the door opening, I put a *candy* barrel in front of it & this is how the bird finds its way out. Not with a stick, but with Big Nose! I made an opening in the tent cloth. Now I look outside too. Everything is white. The high road is also white. And I see no Crees, no horses. Everything is dead silent & abandoned. We no longer hear the cows either which were mooing a lot in the distance. Strange of Johnny, not to bring us some whiskey. I would like so much to give Uhlenbeck a bit.

Wednesday, September 6.

Finally I get up. It is after nine. I am just out of my bed when Tatsey shouts, *"Professor, are you staying in bed?"* We say that we will be ready in a moment, he can come back in ten minutes. And he comes back, without an overcoat while it is still lightly snowing, but wearing sturdy rubber boots. We have already eaten breakfast as well, each a cake & a biscuit. But nothing to drink. No question about that. What an ambitious desire! We have to economize with our methane. Tatsey is not coming to teach. For him it is much too nasty in our tent, but he talks for half an hour. He doesn't bring whiskey, because Duck Head, he says, stole his stock of whiskey from suitcases which were stored at Duck Head's. He drank the stock himself, got drunk & was put *in jail* for a day or longer. When he was *sober* again, he was released & went to Valier. Duck Head's wife preferred to stay at home. "You will get drunk again," she had said. "When they put you in *jail*, I take the *team* & drive home."[252] So how will our slender, handsome Indian fare?

After Tatsey has left, I heat the stones & start my letter to Nella. By 12:00 Uhlenbeck comes out from under his blankets. We put on wet socks and wet boots, quite a job, and head for the warm stove in the eating cabin. For a long time we take turns putting our feet on the stove & we talk to the same nice white laborer who invited us the previous day into his tent. We eat with the cook and his helper. Both gentlemen have an indifferent demeanor & any coziness is out of the question. The cook gives us something to take along again because the weather is still as bad, wet snow, which partly stays, partly thaws. We go home with provisions for the evening and for the next morning. Two pieces of apple pie and an old vegetable tin half filled with weak coffee. We arrive again with sopping wet feet. We had to cross quite a few streams. Upon returning to our sailcloth house, which looks so ghastly in this wet environment, we take off all our wet clothes right away & put on the dry socks & boots. That feels wonderful. Then I hurry to heat the stones & Uhlenbeck crawls under the blankets again & reads again in Baedeker. I sit on the wooden bucket again, also have again a heated stone for my feet, & tightly wrap

Thursday, September 7.

my woollen scarf around me. The thermometer is rising, 44°, 48°, even 53°. A ray of sun causes this sudden rise. But it is of short duration and again it drops to 51°. It is no longer snowing now – sometimes it is almost dry, sometimes it rains hard, sometimes strong wind gusts. Perhaps the wind is our savior! If only the weather would change again. I continue to be worried that Uhlenbeck will get sick. I imagine that to suddenly leave this misery would not be possible. Not one Indian would offer to bring us away now. They don't dare drive on the slippery hills. In the afternoon John Tatsey brings us some mail. It is a postcard from Hermine, that has been underway from July 26 until September 6! David & Camil, who appear to be 15 and 12 years old, come with him. The Crees leave right after they got some sweets. John stays for a little while. Later we drink a bit of the coffee. Just to have something to do. The thermometer drops again, 45°, 43°, 40°. It snows and once in a while it hails. Then there is only a little wind. By eight we are already in bed with lovely warm feet. What a success for me! I am proud that Uhlenbeck is not cold. We now lie in lovely warmth. All coats, covers etc. lie on top of us. We talk for a long time. Once in a while it rains again. When we lie awake at night, it is quiet; just Badger Creek is rushing with a faster current. Very early in the morning I hear a horse. Later I hear lots of horses & also a rider. I look at the watch. It is 6:00. I look at the thermometer: 30° and we snuggle deep under the blankets. Later I wake up again and – I see sun rays!

Up near eight. The sun is already shining. Oh! How nice! Will the entire sky clear up? I hurry to look outside and quickly push all wet boots outside in the sun through a crack in the bottom wall and I walk around in the tent on my old overshoes. Then I open up the tent & go outside. And I see the sun, a clear, glorious blue sky, and the Rocky Mountains are shining, forming one white range from the peaks to the ground. Both of us are awestruck. What exceptional beauty & we hadn't expected this. In front of our tent the snow is partly melted & the warm sun will soon dry up everything. Each quarter of an hour it is getting drier around us and then the road will improve soon & at 12:00 be passable again. I heat up yesterday's coffee & our breakfast tasted unusually delicious. Each gets a piece of cake, a hot cup of coffee, & we sit in our open tent in the sun. We sit together, close to the front opening, and are in the best of moods. Our misery seems to be over. I would take three pictures of the Rockies, but the distance is too big.

I also walk around outside in my old overshoes. They keep falling off, because they are much too wide. I don't wear boots. They hang in the sun to dry with all kinds of wet clothing. Uhlenbeck keeps walking around in front of the tent in the sun in order to keep his dry boots dry. Quite a collection of clothing hanging outside. It looks like the stock from a second hand dealer. One hour later we walk down the prairie a bit further. David & Camil & an older Solloway briefly drop by our tent. At 10:30 I heat up a bit more coffee. We walk up the higher hills a bit to get an even better view on the Rockies. At 12:00 we put on our dried up boots again. I take along empty saucers & the coffee tin. The road is not too bad and now there is no need to warm ourselves at the cook's fire. After mealtime we walk around for a while. Glorious, after being locked up for a few days. Now it is 63° in the tent. I quickly wash a few handkerchiefs and a few other pieces. After an hour everything is already dry. Still the wind is chilly. Only in the sun it is so nice. Uhlenbeck lies down on his bed some more & I keep up with my diary. After more than three hours we walk around. No trace of Tatsey! When will he return? We

Indians on horseback near Browning (DJdJ 1910).

are now in a better mood than yesterday & if possible we want to stay here until Sept. 20. If only the Indians would return soon so we can observe them again! We try not to think much about the time ahead of us.

Tatsey doesn't come. Nothing much happens; we stroll around our tent and have our evening meal at the usual time. Right afterwards dusk is falling. But because of the cold we still walk around. The oldest Wagner boy approaches us & asks whether we are cold and whether we would like to visit his mother.[253] We really appreciate this. To the Tatseys it doesn't ring a bell that we have gone through a lot of misery these last few days. They just sit together around their big wood fire & they don't bother even once to provide us with any fire. However, we thank the little boy for his offer & say that we are going to bed soon.

MONTANA 1911

Saturday, September 8.

I am up at 7:00. The sun is shining a little. About 8:00 we eat breakfast and then move on to visit the Tatseys. The situation can't stay like this any longer. It is too *unpleasant* and what is worse: too *irritating*. We meet all kinds of Tatseys, also Tatsey's sister, & small George holds up his hat and thinks, "Why not throw in some sweets." But I have nothing with me. Outside Uhlenbeck speaks for a long time with Tatsey; I see them pace up & down, Tatsey with his head bent deeply. I stay inside and talk a bit to his wife. It is agreed that Tatsey will come from 1:00 until 4:00, after which he will move one tent to the Cree valley, which is lower than our camp. Tatsey's last word is: *"You shall see me this evening!"* Indeed he comes but not until 4:00. He had left at 2:30, in order to move, as it is called. We walk around & look in the direction where Tatsey lives now. We look & look, but he doesn't show up.

We meet up with two Indian women on horseback, off the road, right near the foot of the hill crest. They look beautiful riding in their colorful outfits. The colorful blankets blow jauntily on their white horses. Both their faces are painted red. Hanging from a bag on a horse is a big bundle of grass & all kinds of prairie plants. It is a beautiful group. They would be 40 to 50 years old, these powerful women who look at us in a friendly manner, laugh with us and say a few words to Uhlenbeck. For a long time we watch them. This is again an overall impression of the Peigan. If we could only get this more often! Leaving, leaving suddenly, that is the worst thing.[254]

We walk around a bit more and just when I want to put our night lock on our tent, meaning that I close the flaps a bit more with pins when Camil still wants to come in. He tells us about his old grandfather who is 102! years old & about the city! About Valier and about Jupur.[255] And, he says, in Valier there are 16 shops. And we live there on our own ranch, we have a house with rooms & we all live together, all of the Solloways together. And we have cows and also chickens, even ten eggs per day. He goes on and on talking. This Cree boy is quite different from a Peigan. But Camil is nice & very welcome. After this visit, feeling quite depressed, we go to bed.

Saturday, September 9.

Up at 7:30. No sun. But, when I go outside the mountains still look beautiful. A nice light falls over everything. About 8:00, the breakfast. Then again to the Tatseys. Uhlenbeck now knows exactly what he wants. Either the Tatseys *move* this very day, so we can get our evening meal with them, or we want to leave. Today is no longer possible, but tomorrow, Sunday, to Browning and try to work a bit in Browning! We have made our decision & now it has to be executed. It is either this or that. We come closer and closer to Tatsey's camping place: one tent is taken down, one wagon is fully loaded & just when we arrive the wagon with Tatsey and his wife drives out. So it will really happen. They will be much closer to our location & teaching will start again. We walk on, much further down, to our old camp at White Tail Creek. That makes us good. In this valley we had a wonderful time. Here we lived in the center of the *crowd*, from morning until evening among the Indians. On our return we see Tatsey's tent already in the little Cree valley. The Tatseys just drive on with the empty wagon, to pick up the second load. Now we look at their camp spot, which we can't admire because of the rain. We walk around a bit. Uhlenbeck lies down on his bed, I do needlework. Though not sunny, the air is warmer. With some effort I gather a few more flowers. Because of the days of snow they have all disappeared. At 12:00 we eat at the cook's & say that from now on we will eat at the Tatseys again. Uhlenbeck goes to the Tatsey camp again & talks busily with John & I see them walk onto the high road.

A bit later Tatsey approaches me & asks whether Uhlenbeck wants to work with John this afternoon. Then he will also set up his second tent, fix everything and wait for us with the evening meal. It seems strange that he suddenly depicts this in this way. Because it is not him, but his wife who sets up the tent and it is not him, but his wife who takes care of our evening meal. Actually they seldom or never do what is agreed upon. I see Uhlenbeck and John return from the high road & I communicate to him father Tatsey's wishes. John has letters for me. I get quite a package. For the moment Uhlenbeck has no interest in it. He talks for a long time with his Indian friend. In our *mail* I have a package of photos of Mr. Cole from Chicago (we met this lecturer in Browning), a photo of our own princess, sent to me by Pauline, & letters from Mama, Anna Hesseling, Adolf Edaar (from Norway), from Paulina & Daatje.[256] What a lot for me to read! I sit down behind the tent with my feet in a badger hole. Uhlenbeck works in the tent with John, who is sleepy & hungry. He did not get dinner. He will go first and eat something at his mother's. Our last two biscuits, from the time we were snow-bound, and a few sweets aren't enough for him. He leaves & indeed comes back 10 to 15 minutes later. Now they work again. I believe they deal with *Bear Chief's life story*. Now *from* English *into* Peigan. After John has left, we go again quickly to the Cree valley & have our evening meal there. Everything is orderly & and nice again. A new white sailcloth is on the rustic table which, from all that moving around, appears to be coming apart. Actually their camp location is very picturesque. The bend of the Badger is so beautiful here & the bushes stand out so beautifully. After *supper* we walk around, I change the plates and we go to bed quite early, even though it was not necessary because of the cold.

Sunday, September 10.

Indian graves.

I am up already at seven. The sun is just rising above the highest hill. It is 40° & chilly & damp. Our sheets feel thoroughly wet. Around 8:00 we eat breakfast with Tatsey, who has canned peas & tomatoes for us. He will, even though it is Sunday, come in the afternoon to *teach*. We are still in the Cree valley when old *Morgen Arend* [Morning Eagle] trots up on his tame, white horse. At our request Joe also comes along with us, as *interpreter,* because Morning Eagle doesn't know a word of English & speaks, toothless as he is, very incomprehensibly. And I give the old man quite a supply of sweets, nice soft pieces, and three packages of tobacco. He has also been to Valier, but he did not approve of it: *lots of whisky!* And after our hundred-year-old guest rides away, we close our tent, walk uphill, the very high one and there we see a gorgeous view. To the left & to the right even higher parts of the Rockies and much more prairie area & we can follow the course of the Badger much farther down. In addition we find a few Indian graves, partly destroyed, partly intact. Finding a few strings of bead, a few bracelets beside a grave I pick these up & take them with me to Holland. Never before did we find burial places so high up. I can't describe all directions of my surroundings and even less the mood it evokes. Only a strong feeling of reverence makes me stay here for a long time. I can't decide to leave this quiet, high place which I will never return to, and in my imagination I see the Indian processions pass by: step by step they climb the high hills with their loads. They have to cross great distances to find such a quiet, remote place. They take along all *beigaben* [offerings], all the cover stones have yet to be collected and then the flock slowly descends to their tents & they mourn or envy their dead people![257] Who knows what their mood was? Descending we see more graves. It is as if the dead are put in a leftover *log house*, a previous abode (so left by the inhabitants to allow a resting place for the dead).[258] All kinds of woodwork & parts of wooden partitions are still lying about, jumbled together.

Monday, September 11.

Slowly we descend further & further until we get close to our tent and suddenly see Tatsey approach. So he has changed his plan again and comes now, before the afternoon already, while it was supposed to be in the afternoon. This doesn't suit Uhlenbeck very well. We walk far, he got a mass of impressions & now suddenly work & of course nothing to do in the afternoon. And it is 80° in the tent. When they finish working I show Tatsey our little princess & the pictures of Mr. Cole. Again we get a fresh meal. Rice & raisins, cooked apart. The rice is very cooked & bluish & wet, but Uhlenbeck says time and again to me, *I eat lots;* that is how much he enjoys the tidiness here again. Then we walk back home. A new Cree-outfit drives into the valley. Again the Solloways are here. And closer to our own tent, Frank Guardipee, a distant relative of Ely, is setting up camp.[259] He thinks that soon many Indians will come here and then he wants to trade & sell sweets to them & lemonade. Tatsey says that there will be a lot of noise when many buyers come to his tent and then I can hardly teach! Now, that is not the case yet & perhaps it will never happen, wait and see, we have been doing this already for months. We have a nice *dinner* with Tatsey & in the afternoon he will come and *teach* for another little while. That is unexpectedly very nice. What a prospect! But he does *not* show up. We even eat our evening meal alone, and only when his son has come down does father Tatsey return to his camp. For a moment a little visit from Camil, just in passing. For the rest, no one else. We sit by our candle & go to bed in time. The sky is totally clear. Very beautiful, but for that reason a beautiful sunset didn't happen. Sunshine on thin clouds, that is what is most beautiful here.

I am up at 7:00, 43°. Every morning before the sun is up, it is chilly. Breakfast with Tatsey at 8:00. We will take pictures of him & his wife, there in the valley, and quickly I go and pick up my camera. I hope that these pictures turn out well. Often Tatsey has disappointed us, too often, but still, we love this man and he will make a deep impression upon us for many years to come. David & his entire entourage have to watch when I take pictures. *"How much do you charge?"* David asks & would like to have his picture taken too. But I have no more plates. Tomorrow we will also take a picture of Tatsey's aunt, who stays there. Tatsey comes to *teach* at 9:00 & I write to Mrs. Grinnell in New York & to Berkzicht. At 12:00 I have just finished.

We eat again with the Tatseys, very cheerful, *lots* of vegetables & rice with raisins. Then we walk around a bit & Uhlenbeck reads my letter to Mrs. Grinnell. He approves of the date & everything. We will telegraph from Chicago to New York, hope to arrive there on Sept. 25 & will go to Browning, to pick up her response *poste restante.* Uhlenbeck thanks Mr. Cole for the pictures. We bring our letters to the *timekeeper* & pay him for our last meals from Sept. 1 to 9, in total 13 dollars. We take a bit of a rest and have *supper* at 5:00 without Tatsey & are finished quickly.

Adam arrives on his beautiful black horse & prepares to come in. He didn't have fun in Valier either & he also suffered cold & misery. He does understand some English, but doesn't speak it. We tell him we talked to his daughter Minny & give him lots of sweets & a package of tobacco. After he has left, Joe First One & Irvin Gobert (not Gobertz) arrive, first cousins. No wonder they are look-alikes. Later in the evening Camil & Freddy Nolt & George & Gab (Gabriel) Soloway-Solloway or Solwijs. The two oldest boys, + 20 years old, are quite nice & talkative. The new little neighbor boy, Ely Guardipee, also enters. Just like Camil & Freddy he can't sit still; the boys fly in and out. At 9:00 to bed; a beautiful starry sky, a beautiful clear sky. Later the moon rises. Sleep poorly, despite our sleeping pills.

Tuesday, September 12.

I am already up at a 6:15. I have all kinds of thing to do. 43°. At 7:00 the sun rises beautifully. Breakfast at 8:00 without Tatsey. A moment later we talk to him briefly. He comes at 9:00 and now continues on with the Napi history. I wash all kinds of laundry, now for the last time I think. I still have unused underwear in the suitcase. I save this for our journey back. Uhlenbeck tells Tatsey that we want to leave on Monday Sept. 18 in the morning at 9:00 in a big *buggy* and with a separate wagon for all the suitcases and that we want to cross Two Medicine over the bridge, so, a detour & not through all the water after this period of rain. For this he will receive ten dollars. He approves of all of this & he will take us with John. Now I continue with my diary, sitting behind the tent. The mountain range is very beautiful & even more snowed under than earlier this summer. I will miss this. Never again will I see these mountains, which for months we have had a view of. Work goes on until 12:00. Just Running Crane, with an infected eye that is now improving, and old Day Rider, stepfather of George and father of Joe Day Rider, come in for a while, partly for business with Joe Tatsey, partly to listen. Old Day Rider is also a splendid example of mankind.

Chubby announces, *"Dinner is ready."* It appears to be a message from the widow Duvall-Marceau, who stays with the Tatseys.[260] Mother Tatsey and all the little ones are at Birch Creek. We eat with Tatsey & later, while walking around a bit, we see Green Grass Bull, Tatsey's helper, that stocky broad-faced man looking exactly the same type as Little Dog, who is his relative. He arrives with an adopted brother, also called Green Grass Bull, a *Blood Indian*.[261] This one has beautiful carefully braided braids; he is long & lanky, has narrow eyebrows, *finely & beautifully shaped.* They ask for a history, stay for a long time & laugh a lot. They are still with us when Eagle Calf announces himself by his sounds & singing. Now he is wearing a black shirt, *leggings* and the headband; one blanket is wrapped around his hips. Sometimes he wraps himself entirely in a second blanket. He is on foot, is warm & sometimes stuffy & he stays for a very long time. Apparently he has reserved the afternoon for this. Adam also comes along. The old man stays the longest and asks for tobacco preferably the tobacco, which he is used to smoking, the very hard, flat strips. Later on he calls for my attention. Listen, he concludes, listen *Sakòo-aki*, and he says that sometimes he has lots of bugs, but Paul, that sweet little Indian child, checked him this morning & he mimics a combing movement, and, he says, Paul should check *Sakoo-aki's* hair too! I laugh at that & indicate to him that it is not necessary.

He is still around when Crow Eyes comes in. We don't like this Indian. Perhaps he is an unhappy man; it appears that he has neither a house, nor a family, but his looks are insidious & we distrust his entire demeanor. I only give him a tiny little bit & after looking around for a long while, Crow Eyes leaves again. Then Eagle Calf also leaves & we quickly walk back & forth a little. At the evening meal we don't see anybody. Tatsey isn't there. His wife is not back yet. Back home father Fine Bull comes. I want to give him tobacco; "I don't smoke," he says, "but my wife does smoke," and that is why he would like to get the tobacco. I also give him sweets. He asks for some money, but Uhlenbeck says that we can't deplete our travel money. He is a very good man & worked with Jimmy at the ditch. Both father and son are extremely thin. We think that they are doing badly during the winters. He also has a daughter who smokes, and furthermore has two horses, that is all. At dusk Lizzy & Chubby arrive. Lizzy brings me a bracelet that she crafted for me. They talk a bit & get lots of sweets. Chub can count in English and Peigan until seven or eight. I promise Lizzy some more pictures & and I will also give her a piece of embroidery that I finished here which a few Indians now wear on their hats. I still have + three yards. After this we sit for quite a while by our candle. In the north there is quite a lot of strong lightning. No thunder. To bed at 9:00. 44°.

Wednesday, September 13.

At night it rains more than once. I am up at 6:00. It is blowing steadily. Still 44°. At eight in the little valley for breakfast with Tatsey, who arrives by nine already. It is blowing harder, sometimes sunny, sometimes no sun. Still, at 11:00 in the closed tent it is 66°. Sometimes Uhlenbeck can't quite understand Tatsey because of the noisy wind. I repair my grey woollen blouse & my grey skirt for the journey back. It takes quite a while; then I write in my diary. We eat with Tatsey & in the afternoon nothing else happens. At the evening meal we see only Tatsey's wife. It is blowing very hard & the sky looks very bad. Out of boredom we go to bed early & I hardly sleep at all. A very stormy night, but again the tent withstands it well.

Thursday, September 14.

Up at 6:00. I am going to fit what has to be packed into small suitcases. It is still blowing very hard, but we seem to get used to the wind *in* the tent. I think it is warming up a bit. Maybe Tatsey will come only at 10:00. His sister & aunt presumably will leave and will be brought to Browning by John. He comes to teach for an hour; then they call him away, rather, he says that his business calls him away, and he leaves. Still he returns after half an hour. We eat with him and discuss with him that we will leave one day earlier, so Sunday September 17. He approves of this & he will take us. Tatsey's sister & aunt have not yet left; it has been too cold. They will also stay until Sunday & then we will all leave at the same time. The old aunt will be in our *buggy* & his sister on the wagon with the suitcases or vice versa. Later this afternoon Tatsey comes back for a while to complete three hours. The 50-dollar cheque is not yet cashed, so Uhlenbeck hasn't got back the money he loaned out. But our last week with Tatsey & the journey to Browning can be discounted from it & then we don't have much credit left. The debt to us would be ten dollars, in case Tatsey forgets the entire settlement. But he will have ten dollars and he will give it back to us. For the very last breakfast & something for on the road to Browning we calculate two dollars. We have an evening meal with Tatsey, who is in a hurry. The wind calms down, the sky is getting much better. Between 6:00 and 7:00 we walk onto the high road. The mountains are so beautiful, so clear. We sit by our lantern & go to bed early, hoping for a calm & good night. Both of us sleep much better.

Friday, September 15.

I am up at 6:30. Only later I see the sun. It is quiet, but quite cold. At 8:00 breakfast with Tatsey. When we are finished, George says, "*Where is the plate of the Professor?*" and right away he sits himself down in Uhlenbeck's place. George more often than not behaves like that. Apparently he loves Uhlenbeck a lot. With me he is not so sentimental. Even last year this little boy always talked about de *professor* once he had gone. Later First One comes and asks on behalf of the blacksmith whether our tent is for sale. We tell him that it is Tatsey's property, but we give him a package of 100 sweets for Joe First One. We also call Ely Guardipee inside and he gets the same package for his brothers & sisters in the neighborhood. Tatsey comes to teach at 9:00. Now it is blowing very hard again. Still I have to do laundry for the last time. It blows so hard & the tent shakes so much that Uhlenbeck gets off the shaking camp bed – his usual seat – and sits down on another object, on the wooden bucket. At the same time this is somewhat closer to Tatsey, who always hangs around in the same corner on the ground. Mealtime at 12:00.

Later it is not only getting cold, but it also rains a bit. It is also cold. I heat stones for Uhlenbeck and he wraps himself in the blankets. Quickly I fix all kinds of things for the journey back. I prepare the travel boots, put new soles in them, shine them, glue addresses on the suitcases & prepare packages of sweets for the Tatsey children, for Dick & Paul White Man and a much larger package for the Bear Chief children. Sebastian Bear Chief gets all our packages of tobacco, his little sisters two small cups, two spoons and the platter & also a lot of sweets. We deliver the package for Bear Chief to Tatsey's. John will take care that it will get there.

Just when I am finished with all of the packages, visitors arrive. One is one of Eagle Calf's housewives; the other is Jimmy Fine Bull's mother.[262] Little Paul is riding on his mother's back and bundled in the blankets. How beautiful & loose-limbed this child is. He just sits on his mother's lap & looks around with his sweet eyes; then he quietly falls asleep. His mother has tied my *dish towel* around her head. Fine Bull's wife wears a white, grubby head scarf and wears, I think, about three dresses on top of each other. First I see a light blue dress, then a Scottish check & then the dark blue. "*That will do,*" I think. Both are wrapped in blankets. They stay for a long time, ask for our suitcases. Uhlenbeck tells them when we will leave. They eat lots of sweets. When Fine Bull's wife shows me her tobacco pouch with a pipe in it, she also gets some tobacco. We give sweets to take along for Dick & Paul, & for the old man we now have some of the hard tobacco. His wife gets it for him. I will take pictures of Paul & also of Joe First One and a few other little boys. The women don't want to have their pictures taken. All the boys also come in and when Fine Bull's wife says, that she wants to narrate a history: *Napi and his four wives.* Joe Tatsey is the interpreter. I didn't understand all of it, but I picked out that Napi was acting very weird again. Sometimes Joe wasn't certain how to go about it. The boys listen & once in a while Joe First One knows how to interpret a Peigan word or meaning in English, when Joe Tatsey fails to. Then follows a second story, *Napi and two women.* This story is even weirder & sometimes the boys roared with laughter. Sometimes it is very indecent, but that is how Napi is. Only after five do the visitors leave. Both women also wriggle themselves through a crack in the tent cloth and just disappear with little Paul on her back. Saying goodbye here is very casual & yet they walked long distances, just to say goodbye to us.

It is blowing hard, sometimes very hard. The mountains are barely visible. We eat our evening meal alone & then stay in our tent. Uhlenbeck wraps up again & I heat the stones again. This, again, is very nice & it suits us very well that during the last three weeks we haven't drunk tea or bouillon, but saved all the fuel to heat the stones.

Three boys appear in front of the tent, but I tell them that Uhlenbeck is not at home. A moment later he arrives home with the boys he met on the road. He saw them in the Blacksmith valley. They bought a bottle of lemonade cider in merchant Guardipee's tent & invited Uhlenbeck to "*the first drink.*" "*It taste good,*" Bill said, "*We play drunk.*" Joe First One

Saturday, September 16.

said. Uhlenbeck comes in alone & the boys first finish their bottle down in the valley & they stay for quite a while with our lantern. Only when they want to leave do I give them a few sweets. Joe First One is again very modest and says, *"I don't need them,"* because he already got an entire package. That little First One is an attractive boy & not at all shy. We also talk about the mission boys and he says, *"I like Willy Kennedy a whole lot. He always hands out such a lot. He just takes a few pieces."* This is what is so attractive in these Indian boys. They appreciate each other so much and feel strongly about friendships. It was an enjoyable evening visit. After their departure it is blowing hard. We are cold & take turns with the hot stone when the lantern is lit. Later I go outside to take a look. Over the Rockies a thick bank of fog hangs, but for the rest, the sky is splendidly clear.

What starry nights on the prairie! The Milky Way! It is imprinted on my memory. But always a strong wind. After nine thirty we go to bed & try to fall asleep quickly. The warm stove comes along under the blankets. That is very nice. But in the middle of the night we wake up for a while. It storms & the tent shakes and the sailcloth flaps & sometimes a lot. But the poles hold out, the ropes don't break. That is because everything was new when we arrived in June & because during the day I make sure that the poles are fixed and solid.

About six I am up. I have lots to do & now start to pack for the road. Uhlenbeck wants to get up at 7:30. Around me is the greatest mess. The entire floor is covered. Still he wants to get dressed. I take everything from the floor & put everything on the camp bed & cover the mess a bit in order to continue packing later. We eat breakfast after 8:00. It is still blowing a lot, sometimes very hard. The Rockies are clearly visible. Some fresh snow has fallen but this time only at the peaks & more in the north than in the south. After breakfast we walk around a bit. The sun is shining, but the air is really cold. Then Tatsey comes to teach for the last time. By 12:00 the text still to be reviewed will be finished! Bill & Joe First One want to come in, but Uhlenbeck says to them, "Tatsey is here now; come by this afternoon." If they do so, Uhlenbeck will tell them that he wants to treat them. I hope that this happens, then for this last evening we will enjoy ourselves & we won't feel too *lonesome.* Uhlenbeck will leave a note for Walter that he should pay Tatsey his ten dollars owed to us. It is our intention that Johnny will get them as a present.

How little we have seen of Walter during these last few weeks.[263] He must certainly be ashamed, but that doesn't help us much & we don't see him at all. When Tatsey is here, Young Man Chief & No Coat, both about 50 years old, also come in.[264] The first one is small & skinny, quite ugly with an unattractive demeanor. He is the same Indian who said to Tatsey, "I should earn ten dollars per day & if not, I would never want to tell ancient stories." However, now he is in a good mood and he brings Uhlenbeck a bag with old arrow points and old knives, dug up by him in an ancient *corralling place.* Tatsey's work is finished & we go and eat at 12:00. The two visitors also eat at Tatsey's. They eat a lot of meat. I observe them attentively and quietly. Young Man Chief had eaten a lot of crackers and then still takes a massive piece of meat.

Right after our meal I keep packing. The entire bed is still piled up. I am still sitting in the middle of the mess when the boys come in. Uhlenbeck keeps them around for quite a while. They would like to come back in the evening for a treat. Then they may choose something to eat or something to drink, whatever is for sale at Guardipee. *"I don't feel like eating,"* Joe First One says. *"I want to drink."* They leave again & I finish packing. I am just done when Peter White Man & George Champagne come in. The old father told Peter, "You should go there & say good-bye." We show him the maps of Chicago & New York. Peter gets the nearly falling apart Blackfoot texts, once destined for Walter, because he doesn't show up here anymore. Peter takes the book, folds it & puts it in his pocket. He will bring greetings to his old father from us once more and adds that the weather was too bad to go to his *tipi*. Without Tatsey, no cosy evening meal. He has hay business with a white man and is the *interpreter*. We are hardly back at our tent when the entire band of boys arrives, Joe First One, Wild Bill, Ely Guardipee & a younger brother Willy, and Jim & Dick White Man.[265] Each of them wants cider. Each a big bottle. They will buy it themselves at Guardipee's, who recently did all kinds of business and picked up everything himself. Just Jim & Dick want an orange, which are for sale for 5 American cents. Actually the bottles are much too large. Each of them costs 35 Am. cents. If only they don't get sick from all this sour stuff on this cold day & they aren't at all used to such luxury. Joe has Uhlenbeck taste it too & laughs about the tingling in his nose.

It is also Joe who first thanks Uhlenbeck & then me for the treat. Wild Bill has to drink fast, because otherwise the foam bubbles out of the bottle. I give Jimmy some tobacco. He looks around shyly because the boys can speak fast in English sentences & he can't participate. This exceptional, shy, wild Indian boy can only ride horses and nothing else. He is not foolish, but is slow & he watches drowsily from his pitch-black eyes. In the afternoon the boys have just left when John Tatsey drops in. He doesn't have much time, he has to go *after wood* or *after horses*. Always something, & even this last day Johnny doesn't have the time to sit down quietly with us. In the evening he also doesn't come back. After the boys' visit we sit by our candles. I light three simultaneously to cheer us up. All this light provides a bit of enjoyment. For the last time I *fix* our tent once more. For the last time we go to bed with a strong wind. At night it is also blowing hard. At 6:00 it starts to rain slowly. The winds calm down a bit. Will we be able to leave, if the roads get very bad? And at what time will we go? We insist on leaving early.

Sunday, September 17.

Up at 6:30. I still have to rummage around a lot. At 8:00 Uhlenbeck is at Tatsey's, before I am. I also first close the second large suitcase and tie the rope around it. Everything is completely ready when I go to Tatsey's at 8:30. Uhlenbeck had already had his lonely breakfast; I also eat something quickly. It will be one more hour before we can leave. The weather is too cold for the old aunt & the sister. They will not leave today. Then Tatsey wants to give us *a light waggon* & no *buggy* & also loads the suitcases onto it, & "John," he says, "will drive you & sit in front of you & bring you along like that & so I save a second *team.*" However, Uhlenbeck is very dissatisfied and when Tatsey notices that this discourse is not to our liking, he says*, "Now, Professor, you shall have it."* We ask Tatsey's wife for the food for the road. She doesn't know anything about it and keeps her finger in her mouth, looking shy. It doesn't matter. We can do without it and try to get something later, in Browning.

Joe is asking whether we can come to our own tent to give instructions for the large suitcases. That means walking up & down and it is raining continuously. Joe First One unties the suitcase rope from the tent pole and brings it inside to me. Sometimes it rains hard. We can see less and less of the Rockies. It will be a bad day. We return to Tatsey's camp where we will mount the borrowed big *buggy.* There we will be wrapped up well from the rain. Joe First One is there again. *"Behave yourself, Joe, and be a good boy,"* and Uhlenbeck firmly shakes our mission friend's hand.

Adam also comes to say goodbye. He greets us by our Indian names. For the last time spoken by an Indian mouth. *Omachksistamik* and *Sakoo ake!* It resonates deeply in my soul! Uhlenbeck speaks for one more moment to Adam & sends greetings to the old man. David also comes. We hear that Camil broke his leg. And now we have to say goodbye to all of the Tatseys, big and small. Tatsey has his head bent and doesn't look cheerful. He won't take us himself. But John will be our driver and Joe will take the wagon with the suitcases.

I am the first to mount the high *buggy* and then Tatsey comes to wrap me with coverings, coats and blankets. I can barely move. Uhlenbeck will sit in the front beside John and among other things he gets Tatsey's fur coat around him. Adam still says: "Please blanket Sakoo-aki very well." Everything is ready. We say goodbye and look at them time and again and we drive away on this chilly, wet, fall morning. We leave the Cree valley going along the back of the tent and past the *store.* We get to the Badger through a detour. We have to cross it. Water is splashing on all sides; the stream is very strong, and the bottom here is also very rocky. Then we ride over the high prairie hills, through deep valleys. The road is extremely bad, the weather extremely unpleasant. The sky is dismal and there will be rain and wind until the end of the ride. But John is nice and that is why the cold and all the wetness don't get to us that much. John tells a lot about his life as a boy on the prairie, his young life full of unrest and harassment. Uhlenbeck listens very attentively to him and I quietly wonder time and again about John's open-heartedness.

We have to cross Two Medicine River again, but now we take the bridge. Then the road sometimes gets really bad and really slippery; time and again the horses slip, but John doesn't think it necessary to dismount. He knows his horses so well and he is a good driver. Once in a while we look back at Joe, who follows us, sometimes right behind, then further back. A bit further past Two Medicine we see Green Grass Bull near his *log cabin.* His adopted brother wants to ride along with Joe. He says a few Indian words to Uhlenbeck and for the last time we hear a lively *discours* in Peigan, between him and John.

We left at 9:30, now, about 2:00, we approach the depot, the Browning station. First we pass the rail line. You drive towards it along a slanted slope, going slowly, and we keep looking out to see whether an express train might approach at high speed. Then it even hails, coming down hard on us. The horses want to turn aside, they turn their heads away from the wind and John has to turn to the side and stop. *"It hurts my face,"* he says, as if for us it is just a pleasure to drive in this weather

over the open plain. There is the *depot.* We dismount, cold and stiff. The suitcases are loaded off, checked in against receipts and Uhlenbeck takes out the tickets for us, too. There is a problem. The chief doesn't have tickets for New York in stock. In the meantime I warm myself at the big stove burning inside and then we go with the boys to the *section house* that belongs to the *depot* five minutes further along. There we eat together. There, at Mrs. Clifford's, it is so nice & warm and then the two brothers leave. At least Joe, who is always scared of ghosts, wants to be back home before dark. "In a week," says John, "I will write."[266] We say goodbye and Uhlenbeck watches them for a long time; for a long time he watches Johnny and thinks, *"I like that feller!"* And we, for hours and hours we sit near the warm stove. The express train comes at 10:19. The bright light approaches rapidly, the train stops, the *negro* is ready with his steps, we get in and suddenly we are in the Pullman Car. There is no wind around me, no rain either, but our Indians aren't there anymore. Prairie life belongs to the past.

Part II

THE BLACKFOOT TEXTS

In part II of *Montana 1911: A Professor and his Wife among the Blackfeet*, Uhlenbeck's 1910 and 1911 *Original* and *New Series of Blackfoot Texts* are presented in such order that they match Willy Uhlenbeck's diary entries, so that diary and text mutually inform one another. These *Blackfoot Texts* were published in 1911 and 1912 by Müller, Amsterdam, and later in 1934 by N.V. Noord-Hollandsche Uitgevers-Maatschappij. Now a collage of these two *Texts* in their entirety is published in this volume. I am grateful for the contributions of two scholars, Inge Genee, Assistant Professor of Linguistics at the University of Lethbridge, Canada, and Alice Kehoe, Professor of Anthropology at Marquette University, Milwaukee, U.S.A., who, each from her own discipline, agreed to shine their light on Uhlenbeck's standing in their respective fields. Their contributions precede the collage.

A Dutch Linguist on the Prairies
C. C. Uhlenbeck's Work on Blackfoot[1]

Inge Genee

In 1985 Darrell Kipp and Dorothy Still Smoking, members of Piegan Tribe, Blackfeet Reservation, Montana, decided it was time to do something to try and reverse the ongoing decline of their tribal language, Blackfoot. In 1987 they founded the Piegan Institute, which in 1995 established the *Nizipuhwahsin* Center, an immersion school for 5–12-year-olds. In the period between the founding of the Piegan Institute and the establishment of the school, they researched anything and everything that could aid them in their goal: to save their ancestral language from extinction (Darrel Kipp to Inge Genee, letter of November 11, 1999).[2]

In their search they came across the work of C. C. Uhlenbeck, a Dutch linguist who had published a grammar of their language (Uhlenbeck 1938). Uhlenbeck's grammar was based on fieldwork he conducted in the summers of 1910 and 1911. Kipp and Still Smoking found the grammar to be of great use despite its age. It forms part of the groundwork for Jack Holterman's *A Special Study of the Blackfoot Language* (1996), which in turn is the basis for much of the language curriculum in use today within the *Nizipuhwahsin* immersion school.

How did this Dutch scholar, who was by training neither an anthropologist nor a specialist in North American languages, come to be one of the most important linguists of his generation to work on Blackfoot?

As we saw in Part I, Uhlenbeck and his wife Willy spent the summer of 1911 on the Blackfeet Reservation in Montana, where he was doing fieldwork; she kept a diary of their three months' stay. It was Willy's first visit to Montana, but her husband had already spent the previous summer on the reservation. In 1910 he had been accompanied by his doctoral student Jan de Josselin de Jong. The biographical introduction by Van Berkel and Eggermont-Molenaar describes the general development of Uhlenbeck's academic career and a number of personal events in the Uhlenbecks' lives that are essential to a proper understanding of the background to the diary. Here I position the fieldwork periods in 1910 and 1911 in the broader framework of Uhlenbeck's career as a linguist and the development of his thinking about language and its relation to history, culture, and psychology.[3]

Uhlenbeck had come to the study of Blackfoot indirectly. He was by training an Indo-Europeanist, educated in the nineteenth-century

European tradition of comparative historical linguistics at the University of Leiden, to this day one of the world's leading centers for descriptive and comparative-historical linguistics. His doctoral dissertation tackled a topic within the Indo-European language family: the connections between the Germanic and Balto-Slavic languages (Uhlenbeck 1888). The idea of genetic relationships between languages and their organization into genetic groups, represented as family trees, had become widely popular in the course of the nineteenth century. It was in this framework that Uhlenbeck started working as a linguist in the late 1880s.

The first language family to be thoroughly studied was Indo-European, in those days often called Indo-Germanic or Indo-Aryan. This family contains such well-known subgroups as Germanic, Celtic, Romance, Indo-Iranian, and Balto-Slavic. While the general outlines of the Indo-European family tree were clear by the time Uhlenbeck started his career, there were (and are) still details to be worked out, and this is what Uhlenbeck did in his dissertation and in a number of other specialized articles and monographs.[4]

But Uhlenbeck had an interest in languages outside of the Indo-European family as well, especially those that are structurally unlike Indo-European. He believed that the understanding of Indo-European genetic affiliations could be deepened by comparison with unrelated and structurally distinct languages (e.g., 1901, 171). One such language is Basque, spoken in the mountainous region on the border of Spain and France. It is now commonly accepted that Basque is an isolate – a language with no known relatives. But such was not the case at the time when Uhlenbeck worked. That Basque could not be Indo-European was accepted by most linguists in those days, but the hunt for family members was by no means over. Different options were being explored, and Uhlenbeck contributed to this discussion with a number of publications over the years.[5] Already in some of the *stellingen* ("propositions") attached to his doctoral dissertation (1888), he alluded to Basque: in one of these propositions, he rejected a relationship between Basque and Finno-Ugrian (De Josselin de Jong 1952, 244). His first major publication after receiving his doctorate, "Baskische Studiën" ("Basque Studies") (1892), was published by the prestigious Koninklijke Nederlandse Akademie van Wetenschappen (Royal Netherlands Academy of Sciences) and made his name as a linguist. It also landed him the position of Professor of Sanskrit at the Municipal University of Amsterdam in 1893 at the age of 27, which he held until his appointment as professor of Old Germanic at Leiden in 1899. He stayed in Leiden until his early retirement in 1926 (De Josselin de Jong 1952, 245–51).[6]

From Basque, Uhlenbeck's attention shifted to Eskimo (Inuktitut). Van Berkel and Eggermont-Molenaar draw attention to Uhlenbeck's frustration over his failure to attain fluency in the Basque language, which may have led him to choose a different language for his studies. This will no doubt have played a role, but from a scholarly point of view a clear line can be drawn from his work on Indo-European to that on Basque, Eskimo, and Blackfoot. The choice of these languages was motivated by Uhlenbeck's search for an explanation for observed similarities between genetically unrelated languages. As with Basque, an important issue in the scholarly discussion of the time centered around the possible relationship, genetic or otherwise, of Eskimo (Inuktitut) with other languages. Modern linguistics places Inuktitut in a larger family called Eskimo-Aleut, which contains a number of languages spoken in the arctic from northeast Asia across Alaska and northern Canada and into Greenland (Campbell 1997, 108). Research into more wide-ranging genetic relationships of Eskimo has mostly focused on Uralic and Indo-European, and Uhlenbeck contributed in both those areas.[7]

After Basque and Eskimo, Uhlenbeck focused his attention on North American Native languages. Here he found very fertile ground indeed for his comparative work. Very little was known about the relationships, genetic or otherwise, among the languages of North America, and Uhlenbeck threw himself into this problem to the exclusion of his other work. His interest soon settled on Algonquian, the language family to which Blackfoot belongs. Comparatively much was already known about Algonquian at the time (Uhlenbeck 1909, 21), and it was to become one of the best-researched language families of the New World. In more general terms it was also Uhlenbeck's hope that the study of the languages of *wilde jagervolken* (wild hunting peoples) (1909, 39) would contribute to better insight into universal aspects of human psychology.

As he became increasingly frustrated with the often unreliable data with which he had to work, he decided it was time to do his own fieldwork (De Josselin de Jong 1952, 249). A large overview publication on the languages of native North America (in two parts: 1908, 1910a) as well as some preliminary theoretical and comparative work (1909, 1910b) prepared the ground. He had done fieldwork only once before, when he was working on Basque shortly before 1907 (De Josselin de Jong 1952, 257). As noted earlier, we are not sure why he chose Blackfoot out of the large Algonquian family. Blackfoot is the most western language in this family, which also contains well-known languages such as Micmac, Fox, Cree, Arapaho, Menominee, Cheyenne and Ojibwe, and is more distantly related to the Californian languages Wiyot and Yurok (Ritwan). The exact place of Blackfoot in the Algonquian family tree was and is not without its problems and in some aspects it is rather atypical of an Algonquian language (Goddard 1994, 187–89; Mithun 1999, 335; Uhlenbeck never addressed this problem in his writings, see below). Perhaps Uhlenbeck was attracted to a language that had not been extensively described, as are some of the better-known Central and Eastern Algonquian languages, and did not have a published grammar and dictionary on linguistic principles, so that he would really be able to make an important contribution to the state of knowledge of the Algonquian language family. It is also not clear why he chose the American Blackfeet Reservation in Montana rather than one of the three Canadian reserves just north of the border in Alberta for his work.

The two field trips to Montana in the summers of 1910 and 1911, each lasting three months, produced a wealth of material, from which Uhlenbeck drew for the rest of his career. He also pulled others into this work, publishing two dictionaries together with R. H. van Gulik, while his students G. J. Geers and J.P.B. de Josselin de Jong published independent work on Blackfoot (Geers 1917; De Josselin de Jong 1913a, 1914); Jac. van Ginneken wrote a dissertation on psycholinguistics, one of Uhlenbeck's theoretical interests, under his supervision (Van Ginneken 1907). All of these students later pursued other interests: Van Gulik became a diplomat in China, Geers went to Spain and published extensively on Spanish literature, and De Josselin de Jong became an ethnologist and anthropologist in Leiden and worked, among many other things, on Indonesian language and culture; the Jesuit Van Ginneken later became a professor of Dutch, Indo-European, and Sanskrit at the new Catholic University of Nijmegen in 1923.[8]

The most important of Uhlenbeck's publications on Blackfoot are the text collections (1911a, 1912a), the two dictionaries, published jointly with R. H. van Gulik (Uhlenbeck and Van Gulik 1930, 1934) and the *Concise Blackfoot Grammar* published in 1938. The 1912 texts are the direct result of the 1911 fieldwork. Mrs Uhlenbeck's diary allows us to see how the process of collecting those texts took place and provides additional detail on the informants and the circumstances under which the work proceeded. A selection of those texts is published here along with the matching diary entries, so that diary and texts may mutually inform one another.

The delay of more than a quarter of a century between the original fieldwork and the publication of the *Concise Blackfoot Grammar* (which is not really a concise piece of work by any definition) in 1938 is reflected in the comprehensiveness of this work, which really summarizes all of Uhlenbeck's knowledge of Blackfoot as well as Algonquian as a whole. While work on Blackfoot had been done by others in the intervening years, the grammar is based exclusively on his own fieldwork (1938,

Preface). Uhlenbeck seems always to have been wary of other people's data and wanted his own grammar to be based on data he knew he could trust.

Uhlenbeck's descriptive work was and still is valued by linguists and anthropologists for its careful detail, and his text collections are exemplary for their time. He generally notes meticulously who his informant was for a certain story, frequently distinguishing between an informant and an interpreter, and he also includes genres other than the traditional myths and origin stories – some of the most interesting parts of the 1912 collection are in the chapter called "Boys' Experiences," in which daily events in the lives of some of the "Mission boys" are related, as told by the boys themselves. In combination with Willy's description of the frequent visits of these boys, the reader gets a rather clear picture of what their lives were like, as well as a fascinating view of the use of the Blackfoot language by the younger generation.

This does not mean that Uhlenbeck's work is beyond criticism. It must be said, for instance, that his treatment of the Blackfoot sound system is very poor, even given the transitional state of phonological theory in his time. His analysis of the Blackfoot vowel system is especially disappointing, and one wonders if this had to do with his analytic skills or whether he just did not have a very good ear for vowels.[9]

Uhlenbeck's interest in non-Indo-European languages originally seems to have stemmed from a desire to gain a deeper insight into Indo-European itself (Genee 2003). His earliest formulation of this guiding principle is found in a curiously short two-page article from 1901, which foreshadows his 1916 paper on transitive verbs in North American languages (1916a; see below). After discussing his theory of the case system of early Indo-European, he draws parallels with genetically unrelated languages, mentioning Greenlandic, Dakota, and Basque by name:

In my opinion there can be no doubt that the structure of Indo-Germanic, as we can reconstruct it from the comparison of the different languages, developed out of a polysynthetic, suffixing and infixing structure. To this points the root variation with its endless variability, which can only be explained through the collaboration of the most widely differing factors; … to this points also the mediopassive, which reminds us of the verbs with incorporated dative and object case of Basque and the American languages. Also in our case we can refer to striking parallels in genetically unrelated polysynthetic languages. To say nothing of the languages of the original inhabitants of America, although for instance Greenlandic and Dakota could be referred to, it is common knowledge that the Basques have only the distinction between Agent and Patient, but not that between Nominative and Accusative.[10] (1901, 171)

The languages that belong to the Indo-European language family go back to an ancestor language called Proto-Indo-European (usually called *Oerindogermaans* or "Primitive Indogermanic" by Uhlenbeck and others in his time), which was spoken perhaps seven or eight thousand years ago somewhere in Eurasia. Uhlenbeck, along with others, thought that the early stage of this proto-language was characterized by some structural features that were atypical for an Indo-European language and were in some sense "primitive." In order to provide supporting evidence for the existence of these atypical features, he looked for them in other languages, preferably those of "primitive" cultures, so that his argument for their occurrence in early Proto-Indo-European, which was several thousand years old and therefore, in Uhlenbeck's view, arguably also a "primitive" language, would be more convincing (see Lehmann 1993, 208, 223–24; Schmidt 1979).

In this context Uhlenbeck was interested in languages that classify nouns not in terms of gender (masculine, feminine, neuter) but in terms of animacy, so that a noun is classified as animate or inanimate according to whether or not it is considered to have a soul or spirit.[11] His student J. P. B. de Josselin de Jong's dissertation (1913) is wholly concerned with this issue in Algonquian generally and Blackfoot specifically, and bears strong marks of Uhlenbeck's influence in the way in which Algonquian categories are compared to those found in Indo-European languages.

Uhlenbeck was also interested in languages that distinguish between two types of possession: things that a person possesses inherently and cannot be given away, such as a parent or a limb (called "inalienable possession") and things that a person may possess only temporarily, such as a piece of clothing or worldly power (called "alienable possession").[12] Both animacy and inalienable possession occur in Eskimo and Basque, non-Indo-European languages that Uhlenbeck had studied before Blackfoot. Together with his ideas on inclusive and exclusive *we*, obviation, and centripetal/centrifugal (direct/inverse) verbal flexion, which I cannot discuss here in detail, these phenomena form the theoretical link of these languages with one another as well as with Indo-European.[13]

But the most important aspect of Uhlenbeck's search for structural parallels was the overarching linguistic phenomenon that would later become known as ergativity.[14] In an early article Uhlenbeck concisely defines it as "de congruentie der transitieve verba met hun lijdend voorwerp" ("the agreement of transitive verbs with their object") (1909, 33). Nowadays many linguists distinguish among three ways in which languages can mark the relationship of a verb with its logical subject and object. In a nominative language, such as most Indo-European languages, the verb agrees with its subject, independent of whether it is transitive (has an object) or intransitive (does not have object). Subjects of transitive and intransitive verbs are marked by the same case-form (i.e., the nominative) if the language has case endings. In contrast, in an ergative language such as Basque, the verb agrees with its object if there is one – it will only agree with its subject if there is no object: thus, transitive verbs agree with their object, exactly as in Uhlenbeck's formulation cited above, and intransitive verbs agree with their subject. Therefore, these languages make a formal distinction between types of verbs. If such a language has case-marking, objects of transitive verbs and subjects of intransitive verbs get the same case-form, called "absolutive," while the subject of a transitive verb is marked by a different case, called "ergative." Many languages make use of a combination of nominative and ergative marking, and the distinction may permeate the grammar of a language quite significantly or be a rather superficial, mostly morphological, phenomenon. A third type of language has a semantic basis for its case-marking and/or agreement patterns and is often called "active." In these languages it is the semantic nature of the participants in the verb, namely whether or not they are in control or perform an action, that determines case-marking and agreement.

The Algonquian languages are by modern definition active rather than ergative, a distinction Uhlenbeck also formulated in essence (Lehmann 1993, ix, 208, 223–24). Uhlenbeck focused on the agreement of the Algonquian verb with its objects in some cases, and saw in this phenomenon a parallel with Indo-European passive constructions. This explains his use of the term "passive" in his treatment of the Algonquian material. He struggles with this verb-object agreement in several publications (see especially 1916a), and it is clear that it was one of the questions foremost on his mind while he was conducting his fieldwork in Montana. If we interpret the following passage correctly, he was trying to throw some light on it by asking his informants what the correct translation of certain of these "passive" constructions in Blackfoot was:

> For instance, were one to ask a Prairie-Indian who speaks English whether a certain verbal form in his indigenous language really means "I killed him" or rather "He was killed by me," then he, surprised by such a useless and ignorant question, will answer: "That is just the same," only paying attention to the reality of his being killed through my instrumentality. (1916a, 187–88)

One of his reasons for wanting to do his own fieldwork was no doubt the insufficient data available in print that he needed to analyze this "passivity" expressed in Blackfoot verbal inflection. In one of his theoretical publications from the period just before the fieldwork, it becomes clear that Uhlenbeck saw as a special challenge the attempt to throw some light on "the verb, the infamous Algonquian verb, which – like the Basque verb – has already scared away so many" (1909, 33).

This he wrote just a year before his first fieldwork period. In 1916, with the benefit of his own data collection, Uhlenbeck was ready to synthesize his ideas in "Het passieve karakter van het verbum transitivum of van het *verbum actionis* in talen van Noord-Amerika." ("The Passive Character of the Transitive Verb or the *verbum actionis* in Languages of North America") (1916a; see also De Josselin de Jong 1952, 251). In this article, he attempts to present an integrated treatment of two classes of Algonquian verbal forms that are usually treated separately: "passive" verb forms and the forms that Uhlenbeck calls "centripetal-transitive" (1916a, 188).[15] He refers to his own earlier work on Basque, which exhibits a similar "passivity" in the transitive verb (195).

After presenting a wealth of data from many different and unrelated languages, Uhlenbeck comes to the theoretical point of his argument. Making a basic distinction between two types of passivity, he seeks to reduce them to manifestations of one deeper, underlying psychological category: the distinction between *casus energeticus* and *casus inertiae* (213). In languages like Basque, the manifestation is one of *casus transitivus* (for the subject of the transitive verb) vs. *casus intransitivus* (for the transitive object and the intransitive subject). In languages like Dakota, the manifestation is one of *casus activus* (for the controlling subject of transitive and intransitive verbs) vs. *casus inactivus* (for the object of transitive verbs and the non-controlling subject of intransitive verbs). Modern terminology would call Basque "ergative" and Dakota "active."[16]

Uhlenbeck's theoretical ideas about "the true nature of the energeticus" (213) were criticized almost immediately and rather harshly by Edward Sapir, who in his review of Uhlenbeck's paper significantly advanced the understanding of ergativity and related subjects (Sapir

1917a). Sapir reviewed this and another paper with a similar tendency (Uhlenbeck 1916b, on possession) in the first issue of the *International Journal of American Linguistics* (*IJAL*) (Sapir 1917a,b). While he calls the paper "highly suggestive and important" and refers to Uhlenbeck as "the distinguished Dutch philologist" (1917a, 69), he criticizes almost everything Uhlenbeck says that goes beyond the mere presentation of the data, calling it "ethno-psychological speculation" (Sapir 1917a, 70). Most importantly, he does not believe in the "unity" of the *casus energeticus* and the *casus inertiae* and prefers to see languages that distinguish transitive/intransitive (ergative languages) and languages that distinguish active/inactive (active languages) as essentially two unrelated phenomena, while he also stresses that ergative and passive are not to be equated, given the fact that there are languages in which both exist. He concludes his review with a table summarizing his own analysis of ergativity and related phenomena.[17] The fact that Uhlenbeck was one of the founders and editors of *IJAL*, of which this was the first issue, must have made Sapir's criticism particularly jarring to him.[18]

Perhaps as a result of his very widely ranging work in typologically and genetically different languages, Uhlenbeck developed a general theory concerning the relation among language, culture, and psychology, which he himself called "ethno-psychology" and which may be seen as a sort of psycholinguistic typology *avant la lettre*. Closely related to this is his theory of language contact, then usually called "acculturation." Both of these theories found their best formulations in Uhlenbeck's later work, and his thinking on them is very much transitional in the years around the Montana fieldwork periods; again, they represent issues that occupied him in relation to his work in Indo-European as well as his work in North American languages and Basque. Because he was clearly already playing with both ideas in the early 1900s, it is worthwhile to get a basic understanding of Uhlenbeck's ideas about ethno-psychology and acculturation (see also Genee 2003).

The basic problem behind both theories is the search for an explanation for observed similarities among languages. Such similarities may be lexical, when two or more languages clearly have related vocabulary, or they may be structural, when languages have similarities in their syntactic or morphological structures or in their sound systems. It is not usually difficult to find an explanation for lexical similarities – they are either inherited or borrowed, but structural similarities pose a special problem. When languages show widespread structural similarities, there are in principle three types of explanation possible (excluding chance): the similarities may be caused by genetic factors (the languages share a common ancestor from which they both inherited features); they may be caused by language contact (such as borrowing); or they may be typological (caused by inherent limitations imposed on the structure of human language by the fact that all humans have similar brains and vocal tracts and use language for similar purposes).[19] In Uhlenbeck's time it was standard practice, at least in European linguistics, to attribute similarities in the first instance to genetic relationships. American anthropological linguists, who had to work with much messier, mostly oral, material, developed alternatives to the straightforward family tree model in considering language contact (Uhlenbeck's "acculturation") and human psychology (Uhlenbeck's "ethno-psychology") as possible explanations for similarities among languages.

The basic idea behind acculturation is the realization that the traditional interpretation of genetic relations among languages as a family tree with increasingly more and smaller branches that neatly break away from the mother tongue would entail that the further we go back in time the fewer languages there were and that far back in time languages did not influence each other. Uhlenbeck, along with others in his time, did not think this was a realistic presentation, and developed the idea that some very old similarities among languages could in fact be the result of ancient language contact: "acculturatieve taalmenging" ("acculturative language mixing") (1942, 330) is his later term for this phenomenon (see also De Josselin de Jong 1952, 252–54). The idea can also be found in the work of Franz Boas, with whom Uhlenbeck was on the editorial board of the *International Journal for American Linguistics* and with whom he corresponded. Obviously, the farther back in time we go, the harder it is to make a clear distinction between similarities due to genetic affiliation and those due to language contact. Uhlenbeck thought there were possibilities in this kind of explanation for a number of similarities between language families that have possibly had some historical contact with each other but are not straightforwardly genetically related.[20]

In a personal letter of 1926, Uhlenbeck had this to say about the evolution of his thinking on the matter:

> With the exception of clearly self-contained language families such as e.g., Algonquian, Athapascan, Siouan, etc., it is hardly possible yet to speak of genetic relationship ("oerverwantschap") in North America. The languages have not been sufficiently researched…. To me personally the study of archaic ("primitive") tribes is primarily of psychological importance. My opinions on genetic relationship and borrowing have changed considerably in the course of the past years. I would like to define genetic relatedness as "as good as perfect linguistic acculturation, followed by differentiation." Franz Boas has approximately the same opinion about the large linguistic families of the Old and New World. (Uhlenbeck to Schrijnen, September 8, 1926, KDC Archief Schrijnen nr. 142, Nijmegen University; translation by Inge Genee)

As Uhlenbeck himself remarks here, his opinion that cultural and linguistic borrowing are intimately connected, especially when morphology seems to be borrowed, echoes the thinking of Franz Boas (Darnell and Sherzer 1971; Campbell 1997, 64). Unable to draw a clear line between the two, Uhlenbeck often assumes a mixture of distant genetic relationships and borrowing ("convergence"), for instance in his handling of the Algonquian-Ritwan similarities (Swiggers 1988, 231).[21] While Swiggers

(1988, 231) characterizes this type of explanatory mixture as "somewhat schizophrenic," it is important to realize that at the time there was no systematic methodology for dealing with the distinction between language change through contact (borrowing) and internal change away from a common ancestor – the notion of linguistic area or *Sprachbund* did not yet exist. Uhlenbeck's reluctance to choose among available options in individual cases gives some of his publications an air of indecisiveness, but his ability to always play the devil's advocate and his willingness to allow for the possibility that better explanations may become available with the steady growth of comparative and descriptive data (which also remind us of Boas [Darnell and Sherzer 1971, 21; Campbell 1997, 66]) are also the hallmarks of careful and thorough scholarly investigation.

While Uhlenbeck explicitly allowed for language contact as an explanation for observed structural similarities between languages, he never, as far as I can see, explicitly addressed the question of the problematic position of Blackfoot within the Algonquian family. While Blackfoot has a typically Algonquian structure, the source of much of its lexicon is unknown (e.g., Goddard 1994, 187–89; Mithun 1999, 335). Bakker (2000, 608–10) even suggests that Blackfoot may be a mixed language. Uhlenbeck did not to my knowledge ever consider the possibility that Blackfoot could be non-Algonquian or the result of prehistoric acculturation between Algonquian and a non-Algonquian language, but he did address the problem of the Blackfoot lexicon in a practical way by producing the first list of Blackfoot-Algonquian cognate lexical elements (1924a), which was praised as a breakthrough by Michelson (1925). Given the types of explanations advanced by Uhlenbeck for some of the structural characteristics of Pre-Indo-European, I cannot account for the fact that he never considered language contact as an explanation for the position of Blackfoot within Algonquian. He seems never to have had any doubts about the Algonquian affiliation of the Blackfoot language.

The idea of ancient language contact as an explanation for certain similarities between language families was widely discussed in Uhlenbeck's time. It formed the subject of a long-standing debate between the famous American linguist Edward Sapir and his former teacher the anthropologist Franz Boas (Campbell 1997, 72–76; Darnell and Sherzer 1971, 21; Swadesh 1951; Thomason and Kaufman 1988, 5–8). In summary, Sapir believed that widespread morphological similarities between languages were to be taken as evidence of genetic inheritance. Based on such structural similarities, he went on to propose a small number of very large language families for North America, culminating in the famous "Super-Six Classification" (Campbell 1997, 74–76; also Darnell and Sherzer 1971, 26). Boas, on the other hand, believed that "at a certain time depth it was impossible to distinguish results of borrowing from those of common origin" (Darnell and Sherzer 1971, 25; also Campbell 1997, 63f.). In this debate, Uhlenbeck was clearly closer to Boas than to Sapir. This led him to oppose Sapir when the latter proposed a common genetic origin for Algonquian and Ritwan (1927c, 1939). We now know that Sapir was right and his opponents, including Boas and Uhlenbeck, were wrong (Goddard 1975; Campbell 1997, 70), but it could probably be said that Sapir was, to a certain extent, right for the wrong reasons (Swiggers 1988, 230–31), and neither all of his larger linguistic groupings nor all of the details of his cognate proposals have found acceptance.

Besides historical explanations such as genetic inheritance or language contact, languages may also show quite sweeping and wide-ranging structural similarities as a result of ahistoric factors. Such similarities are studied by the fairly recent sub-field of linguistic typology. Uhlenbeck formulates a number of notions that can be called typology *avant la lettre*; his term for them is "ethno-psychology." In this, as in the issue of language mixing, his thinking is again very close to that of Franz Boas.

In his inaugural lecture on the occasion of his acceptance of the professorship at Leiden (1899), while mostly discussing genetic relationships and diffusion as causes of similarities among Indo-European languages, he already formulated the basic idea behind what he would later come to call "ethno-psychology": "thus we recognize in all the languages of the world the unity of the human mind. Eternally true are the words of the Preacher: 'What is it, that has happened? even the same, which will happen hereafter. What is it, that one has done? even the same, which one will do again hereafter; and nothing new happens under the sun'" (1899, 18). Discussing the phenomenon of inclusive and exclusive *we*, he says in an early article: "But this distinction is likewise not the especial property of the red race and those who practice Indonesian and its relatives are completely familiar with it" (1909, 24).[22]

Uhlenbeck looks for the explanation for these kinds of similarities in a deep, underlying psychological unity of all humankind, which would be reflected in the structural similarities among languages (see also De Josselin de Jong 1952, 254–55). While his formulations strike us now as somewhat out of date and perhaps overly romantic,[23] the idea that typological restrictions and similarities are in some way related to restrictions of the human mind is very modern indeed, and the study of such universals occupies a central position in present-day linguistics.

Uhlenbeck's early ethno-psychological work also has a no-longer-accepted diachronic aspect to it which is best characterized as evolutionary or teleological. It has long been known that typological characteristics are not static but may change over time. In Uhlenbeck's view such typological change is linear and unidirectional and has a natural endpoint. To give an example, this means that a polysynthetic language, such as Basque or Blackfoot, necessarily represents an earlier stage on some developmental scale than an inflectional language, such as Latin or German. Polysynthetic languages, in some essential sense, are more "primitive" than inflectional languages; in Uhlenbeck's words, Basque represents "an older stage of development" (1907, 15), more comparable

with the development stage represented by many of the languages of Native North America, which he admired with romantic determination: "How many a category, of which in our languages only some hardly recognizable survivals can be found, thrives in sprawling fullness in the more youthful languages of America!" (1909, 21). This again explains his interest for the languages of "primitive" peoples as comparative material for his ideas about early Proto-Indo-European.

This "evolutionary-typological orientation" was already opposed by Boas in 1911 (Campbell 1997, 65), and although, as far as I can see, Uhlenbeck did not explicitly retract his ideas, it is perhaps significant that his later work – after the Montana fieldwork, which brought him in contact with real live "primitives" – does not contain strong statements along these lines. His ideas may now strike us as extreme or even shocking, but they were prevalent at the time and strongly codetermined the general view of linguistic history (Campbell 1997, 44).

Like many in his time, Uhlenbeck also assumed there to be a causal relation between linguistic structure and mental processes. He calls the Blackfoot animate/inanimate distinction a "'primitive' (animistic-dynamistic) classification" (1938, 18), implying that this type of noun classification is in some sense lower on the evolutionary linguistic development scale than noun class systems of the Indo-European type, which tend to be based on gender rather than animacy. In discussing the fact that some non-living entities are classed as animate in the (Ojibwe) noun class system, he states in the article quoted earlier, which was published just before his first summer of fieldwork:

The names of numerous objects which do not really have life belong to the living group, but only because they are animate in the animistic perception of the Algonquian. For instance, if grain and bread count as living for him, then that must be because the food, which carries the power of life, cannot be seen by him as anything but the origin of life. In the drum which he beats during religious dances he hears the voice of the spirit, in the rock, which serves him in all his profane and sacred rituals, he feels the presence of the soul matter. (1909, 29–30)

But before we accuse him of some kind of white supremacist ideas, let us read what he adds later in the same paper, after discussing the existence of a special dubitative conjugation of the verb:

Through such characteristics of the grammar we gain insight into the thinking of the Algonquians, a thinking which much more than ours is bound by that which can be perceived by the senses, which is much less than ours capable of realizing the absent, the past, the future. One should not seek in these words a depreciation of the Red man, because I am fully convinced that his world view, restricted by the senses, is not to be explained by his possible inferiority, but by his lesser development. I also feel that the more we penetrate into the so called nature peoples, we will increasingly discover, and it is already present in our own linguistic feeling, that we are ever more – to speak with Trombetti – *realmente fratelli.* (1909, 35–36)

Clearly, Uhlenbeck sees non-Western people as less cultured or less developed, not because they are inherently inferior but because they have not had the benefit of contact with Western civilization – again an idea that is conspicuously absent from his post-fieldwork publications.

While Uhlenbeck seemed unaware of the ethnocentrism of his views on the relationship between language and thought, he did at all times strive to avoid the risks inherent in using a western descriptive grammatical system to describe languages with different grammatical structures, especially after his fieldwork had brought him in contact with the living language:

Our linguistic feeling is misleading. We are always in danger of wanting to find our own habits of thinking also in the primitives, of imposing our own world view on their perspective, which is less developed by abstraction and generalization, less also degenerated by spiritual arrogance. If we truly want to gain insight, we have to look for objective, inner criteria. (1916a, 187–88)

Uhlenbeck's more speculative and theoretical work did not always meet with approval, and much of it is of course now superseded. In this he is not alone, however, and in general he may be seen as representative of his time. While some of Uhlenbeck's ideas now strike us as hopelessly eurocentric, and while the likes of Sapir and Boas attacked some of them already in their own time, they must be seen as part of a larger framework of thinking about the relationships among language, culture, psychology, and ethnicity that was prevalent in the early years of the twentieth century. His focus on non-Indo-European languages was perhaps somewhat unusual for an Indo-Europeanist, but many influential American anthropological linguists were themselves European-trained. Uhlenbeck was to insist all his life on the necessity of applying comparative standards developed in the reconstruction of Indo-European languages to the comparative study of Algonquian. In Campbell's words, "[h]e is representative of the interconnectedness of European and American Indian scholarship" (1997, 385n67).

Uhlenbeck seems to have had some trouble penetrating into the North American linguistic scene. At the end of his career he complained that his work (on the Algonquian/Ritwan issue) had been ignored (1948, 223). There certainly is some truth in this. For example, Bloomfield (1946, 85), in an important general overview of Algonquian, mentions Michelson's (1925) work on Western Algonquian (including Blackfoot) but completely ignores Uhlenbeck's *Concise Blackfoot Grammar* in his comparative discussion, even though he cites it in his bibliography.[24]

Nevertheless, Franz Boas thought highly enough of Uhlenbeck to invite him to the editorial board of the *International Journal of American Linguistics.* Uhlenbeck was invited with the goal of having a European connection, because Boas and Goddard wanted "to make the journal a means of publication not only for American scholars, but also for European scholars in this field" (Boas to Uhlenbeck, letter of October 4, 1915, APS Boas-archive). Many Americanists know the name Uhlenbeck "mostly as a name on the masthead of *IJAL*" (Victor Golla to Inge Genee, email of December 17, 2001). Uhlenbeck's Americanistic work seems to have gained a wider audience mostly indirectly, through Sapir's reviews in *IJAL* discussed above. The dictionaries are still used, possibly more widely than the *Grammar*.

The fact that the *Grammar* now plays a role in the language re-vitalization efforts on the Montana reservation would have pleased Uhlenbeck, who, as noted in Van Berkel and Eggermont-Molenaar's contribution to this volume, saw himself also as a salvage linguist. As Darrell Kipp formulates it in an e-mail (February 15, 2002) to Inge Genee, "Native languages (especially the Blackfeet in Montana) struggle against enormous odds to survive [and] the work of early day linguists such as Uhlenbeck now circles back to assist in the effort." Even the diary of his wife, which Uhlenbeck himself did not regard as important, provides some useful first-hand information on early reservation life and its people: "In reading [the] notes of Mrs. Uhlenbeck I was taken by the descriptions and how they held so true to form as others I had heard re-garding the area" (ibid.).

As we have seen, both Uhlenbeck and his wife seem to have re-mained relative outsiders on the reservation. They were observers of, not participants in, the life of the people they studied. As a result, their understanding of what they observed sometimes appears limited or even superficial. But there is another side to this coin: they did not actively participate in the lives of their informants, but they also did not attempt to change or interpret what they observed. This attitude is evident in the writings of both. As Kehoe (this volume) points out, Uhlenbeck himself recorded and published his Blackfoot texts with a minimum of editorial intervention unusual for his time, which makes them, in all their chop-piness, stand out as valuable recordings of real narratives from the early reservation period – a more truthful account of language in use without the use of a tape-recorder is hard to imagine. His wife, Willy, in her diary likewise refrains from interpretation and editorializing and records everything from little details to big events with the same unfocused lens (see Eggermont-Molenaar, this volume). Even if we would personally sometimes gladly have given up some of her and her husband's detailed recording of events and facts for a glimpse of their own thoughts and emotions, their unedited descriptions are now particularly valuable as a true description of early reservation life and the state of the Blackfoot language almost a century ago. Given the state of decline in which the Blackfoot language finds itself, carefully recorded materials from a time when Blackfoot was still largely the language of everyday life and spoken by many monolinguals can hardly be overrated.

Legendary Histories

Alice Kehoe

Christianus Cornelius Uhlenbeck had two objectives for his research on the Blackfeet Reservation: recording the Blackfoot language and recording Blackfoot narratives. He correctly realized that lists of words and fragments of sentences do not a language make, that extended discourse alone reveals a living language. Requesting dictation from his informants, he might listen to narratives of the dawn of existence, of life in the recent past before the imposition of reservations, and of contemporary happenings. Contrary to common practice of his day, Uhlenbeck resisted labelling some texts "myth" and others "real experiences." This essay compares Uhlenbeck's texts to other publications that do use this common Western distinction, and to general theories of mythology; my purpose is not to undermine Uhlenbeck's work but to reinforce it.

Theories of Myth

In the 1996 *Encyclopedia of Cultural Anthropology*, Michael Carroll categorizes anthropologists' studies of myth into these approaches:

Euhemeristic: Derived from the Classical Greek writer Euhemerus, this construal suggests that events and actions of notable kings were told, over time, as stories of gods.

Degradation: Jakob Grimm and Max Müller theorized that metaphors for natural phenomena, particularly astronomical, over the passage of generations came to be vulgarized into fantastical stories.

Animism: Edward Tylor inferred that "the lower races" believed that natural objects and phenomena were animated by spirits, and that spirits could appear to people in dreams and visions. Social evolution leads "higher races" through polytheism and monotheism to an eventual scientific understanding of the world.

Ritual and myth: W. Robertson Smith, James Frazer, and Jane Harrison represent three generations of scholars premising myths to be narratives providing meaning to rituals. From this perspective, the ritual is the critical behavior binding together members of a society (the word "religion" comes from the Latin *religere*, "to tie together"), with the myth satisfying people's questions about why the ritual is to be performed.

Psychoanalytic: Sigmund Freud claimed that myths expressed repressed sexual urges, Jung that a collective unconscious embedded archetypes phenotypically appearing as various personalities and fears. In these psychoanalytic approaches, myths are seen as projections of subconscious anxieties.

Projections of Society: Franz Boas sought empirical content in myths, hypothesizing that they described social structure and rules for behavior, sometimes directly and often in exaggerated or inverse manner.

Functionalism: Bronislaw Malinowski realized that myths frequently legitimate status claims and government: they are social charters, parallel to chartering documents in literate societies. (An important corollary of the social charter position is that literate societies also construct legitimating myths.)

Structuralism: Claude Lévi-Strauss analyzed myths through content, drawing upon classifications by Vladimir Propp and other scholars propounding motifs, plus relationships of motifs. Basically a syntax of motifs, Lévi-Strauss's work was founded on the premise that humans seek meaning in experiences by constructing narratives. Lévi-Strauss considered himself an heir of Boas, in that myths are keys to societal structures and social behavior.

All of these approaches were known to Uhlenbeck. Structuralism was not yet fully expounded in his time, but he was familiar with scholars who would influence Lévi-Strauss, especially as Lévi-Strauss draws upon formal linguistics for his syntax of motifs.

Against these theoreticians, we see Uhlenbeck devoted to empirical transcriptions. Fortunately for him, Blackfeet did not taboo telling one or another kind of myth in daylight or at night, or at particular seasons (Wissler and Duvall 1908, 17). Uhlenbeck's informants distinguished between tales of ancient times (*akai-*, old) and accounts of recent or contemporary persons (Uhlenbeck 1911b, 5, 1912a,b, 1). Raymond DeMallie

and Douglas Parks, in their survey of Plains tribal traditions and records, classify "oral traditions … into two fundamental categories: true stories that conceptually were history, and fictional stories that were told for entertainment or amusement" (DeMallie and Parks 2001, 1062). This distinction is drawn from the authors' work with Siouans (Lakota, Mandan, Hidatsa) and the Caddoan-speaking Arikara; a somewhat similar distinction was reported for the Plains Cree (Battleford area, Saskatchewan) by Mandelbaum (1940, 284 [p. 220 in the 1979 reprint by the Canadian Plains Research Centre, Regina]). Such a dichotomy cannot be drawn from Blackfeet ethnography. Clark Wissler said the Indian people he talked with seemed to think characters from ancient times had actually lived, and indeed might still be living in the Above World (Wissler and Duvall 1908, 17).

Insight into such a viewpoint comes from the folklorist John Niles, describing (Scottish) folk performers who are convinced that "[a]s long as people remember the dead … the dead live on in them" (Niles 1999, 186). Niles' principal informant explained that in telling a story once learned from an elder, he feels "as if he was just sending me a phone message through his memory to me at the present moment. Now, how could someone be dead when he could sit there beside me and say to me, 'Tell my story'" (Niles 1999, 186). Niles, incidentally, printed a 1906 photograph of ethnomusicologist Frances Densmore recording Piegan leader Mountain Chief, father of Walter Mountain Chief, one of Uhlenbeck's favorite collaborators (Niles 1999, 97).

Particularly today when Indian people are asserting the validity of their nations' heritages of knowledge, academics' category "myth" – "Purely fictional narrative usually involving supernatural persons, etc." (*Oxford English Dictionary*) – is at odds with Blackfeet understanding. Wissler acknowledged selecting for his *Mythology of the Blackfoot*, "narratives in which the tone of the mythical age predominated, or in which the supernatural was the main interest" (Wissler and Duvall 1908, 6). He excluded "typical tales of adventure, … esoteric narratives [and] ordinary humorous tales" (Wissler and Duvall 1908, 6). (He doesn't clarify the designation "esoteric narratives.") Uhlenbeck's linguistic focus fortunately circumvented the conflict between Western academic and Blackfeet assumptions about narratives' truth-status.

John Niles again is helpful, proffering the concept of *heterocosmos*, "a version of reality that helps make the world intelligible and navigable" (Niles 1999, 77, citing Ruthven 1964, 1–15). We need to step back to see our own cosmos from this standpoint. In Collingwood's classic statement, "The historical past is the world of ideas which the present evidence creates in the present. In historical inference we do not move from our present world to a past world; the movement in experience is always a movement within a present world of ideas ... history is not the past as such" (Collingwood 1956,154). Working from this standpoint, Hayden White discovered that

> "history" functioned in the nineteenth century in the way that "God" had done in the Middle Ages or "Nature" had done in the eighteenth century[:] historical reflection ... serve[d] as the very paradigm of realistic discourse ... constituting an image of a current social praxis as the criterion of plausibility by reference to which any given institution, activity, thought ... can be endowed with the aspect of "reality." (White 1987, 101–2)

Radically and concisely, a philosopher states, "positivism, inductivism, pure rationality, scientific proof, and all that, are parts of a myth" (Agassi 1981, 386).

This concept of heterocosmos, then, comes from twentieth-century critiques of historiography. It reverberates upon our own understanding of our world. Uhlenbeck's texts configure a cosmos and human history very real to people living in tipis amid Thunder and Cold, intelligent animals, and strange foreign humans. C. C. and Willy Uhlenbeck tasted and recorded this life throughout the summer of 1911. Because

Uhlenbeck and De Josselin de Jong wanted the language, they let their informants choose content to be presented. The best approach to their texts is to read them as a heterocosm, its elements grouped by the ethnographers but not elicited according to a European academic blueprint.

Blackfoot Texts

Only Uhlenbeck and his student De Josselin de Jong published original Blackfoot texts, narratives faithful to Blackfoot language and style. After their three sets of Blackfoot texts recorded in 1910 and 1911, their publications in English from Blackfoot research are strictly linguistic. Their three volumes thus are raw material for analyzing Blackfoot mythology rather than propounding a theory of myth.

Other visitors to Blackfeet territory have published narratives taken down in English: that is to say, translated during the telling, or told in English. From the early reservation period, we have English versions from field interviews by George Bird Grinnell (1892, 1913, 1961); Clark Wissler and his collaborator, David C. Duvall (1908); Walter McClintock (1910); John Maclean (1889, 1896); and James Willard Schultz (1907, 1962, 1974). Then interest in recording mythology waned. In the mid-twentieth century, Frances Fraser, an Alberta farmwife neighbor to Blackfoot reserves, published two collections of tales she took down (Fraser 1959). Cecile Black Boy of the Montana Blackfeet presented narratives held as part of Painted-tipi Medicine bundles, to accompany an Indian Arts and Crafts Board exhibit of painted tipis (Black Boy 1973). In 1985 Percy Bullchild published a large number of narratives artlessly styled in conversational tone.[25] Harrod (2000, 25–27) points out the "creative rendering" evident in Bullchild's texts. On the Blackfeet Reservation during the 1970s, the Blackfeet Heritage Program published small books of stories by Darnell Rides at the Door (1979), her grandmother Mary Ground (1978), and other elders – Tom Many Guns (1979), George Comes At Night (1978), and a group collected as *Sta-ai-tsi-nix-sin*, "Ghost stories" (LaFromboise

1979). Adolf (Gutohrlein) Hungry Wolf and his wife Beverly Little Bear Hungry Wolf (1973, 1977) drew from tales, ethnographic excerpts now in the public domain, and their experiences to print a series as "Good Medicine Books"; Beverly Hungry Wolf subsequently published descriptions of her Blood grandmothers' and mother's generations (Hungry Wolf 1984, 1996).

A review of Blackfoot narratives should also include Hugh Dempsey's (1994) collection on famous men, presented as histories. Dempsey recalls that when he began collecting data on Blackfoot history in the 1950s, the absence of electricity on the reserves, to say nothing of television, made story-telling a popular pastime. Humorous stories elicited "quite animated" performances: "Often the teller arose and acted out portions of the story or, if he was too feeble, he waved his arms in the air" (Dempsey 1994, 15). Serious accounts of past events demanded that "the teller made sure he adhered strictly to the truth. His reputation depended on the accuracy of the telling. After telling a story, Iron, at that time the oldest man on the Blood Reserve, said to me, 'Many men told lies about their experiences and they died early. I tell only the truth and that's why I'm still alive'" (ibid.).

George Bird Grinnell, Walter McClintock, and Clark Wissler spent time in Blackfeet lodges listening to narrators. Grinnell, primarily a naturalist, collected stories as he collected observations of animals and landscapes. McClintock aimed for a lively and detailed salvage ethnography, describing and photographing life in the summer camps as if the reservations had not yet been imposed. Wissler trained a half-Piegan resident of Browning, David C. Duvall, to carry on ethnography through directives and queries Wissler mailed from New York, once he saw Duvall's competence. Although Duvall had a native speaker's fluency in Pikuni, he apparently took down narratives in English, presumably translating as he wrote. It is ironic that Duvall, who could have recorded volumes in the Blackfoot dialects and given us a range of idiosyncrasies (De Josselin de Jong 1914, 3), provided only English versions, which Wissler then conflated into common-denominator tales (Wissler and Duvall 1908, 6). Uhlenbeck and De Josselin de Jong spent most of their summers working intensively with one narrator, Tatsey for Uhlenbeck and Walter Mountain Chief for De Josselin de Jong. Their texts are unique in being careful transcriptions of Blackfoot language, yet they can't give us the range of either speaking style or story-telling. Uhlenbeck was aware of this challenge, broadening his presentations of discourse by recording boys' unpolished narratives of their ordinary lives.

Who were the narrators of Blackfoot stories? Wissler said only that twenty-one informants provided his narratives (Wissler and Duvall 1908, 6). Neither he nor Duvall, as a rule, attributed stories to particular tellers; one can glean some likely sources from Duvall's letters to Wissler requesting payment in which he listed people he had worked with during a week. Most of Duvall's informants lived, like his mother Yellow Bird, in or near Heart Butte and belonged to Mountain Chief's band (Kehoe 1995, xxiv–xxv; Table 1).

For Wissler's generation of anthropologists around the turn of the twentieth century, each society held its culture, a singular configuration encompassing daily life, language, beliefs, rituals, and material manufactures. The ethnographer's task was to record all this fully, from which the distinctiveness of a society's culture would emerge. At the turn of the twentieth century, anthropologists saw these many distinctive cultures rapidly disappearing under the combined onslaught of high mortality and government programs to force Western practices upon the conquered First Nations. Salvage ethnography selected older men acknowledged to be leaders to dictate remembered pre-reservation practices. Differences among these informants were attributed to individuals' varied experiences and the limitations of memory and ethnographers' field time. It took the advent of postmodern criticism, allied with postcolonial critiques, to foreground interplay between Western interlocutor and First Nation respondent, and to expose the fallacy of premising a singular culture for each society.[26]

Here the concept of heterocosmos becomes particularly useful. Not only did Blackfoot learn cosmological perceptions different from Western ideas, but there were (and are) also differences among individuals, and among communities of this large and widely dispersed alliance. Because revelations are believed to be vouchsafed privately and usually when the recipient is alone, and respect for personal autonomy is a major principle in Blackfoot philosophy (Kehoe 1995b), differences are expected and tolerated. Overall, one can speak of a Blackfoot cosmos, but it is a palimpsest of heterocosmos. That palimpsest includes Christian elements – for example, Noah's Flood, which Wissler says "a well-informed old Piegan man … regarded … as a white man's tale" (Wissler and Duvall 1908, 8). Percy Bullchild adds current geology to his version of Genesis (Bullchild 1985, 37). How much in Uhlenbeck's texts may reflect Christian influence cannot be sorted out; Blackfeet had been proselytized for half a century before Uhlenbeck arrived, and he himself was welcomed and assisted by the priests of Holy Family Mission, whose boy students dictated texts to him ("Boys' experiences"). Bear Chief, who figures prominently in both volumes of Uhlenbeck's texts, donated the land on which that mission and its school were built (Many Guns 1979, 43).

From the standpoint of present-day studies of oral narratives from First Nations, Uhlenbeck (with De Josselin de Jong), of all his contemporaries, is closest to our standards today (Swann 1994, Johnstone 2000; see Whitt 1995 for the "politics of knowledge" issue). Uhlenbeck identified each narrator by name and status, named the interpreter, and then recorded, following 1910 field methods,[27] the spoken narration, followed by a close translation to English. One of the issues Uhlenbeck struggled with was the problem that a word-for-word translation would be at best ungrammatical in English and frequently not really possible because Blackfoot, a polysynthetic language, combines morphemes with considerable phonemic changes, resulting in Blackfoot words equalling phrases in English. (Notice in the published texts how the Blackfoot narrative appears shorter than the parallel English translation.) Even

in his time, some fieldworkers were interposing exact morpheme glosses between the indigenous word and a grammatical English narrative. Perhaps Uhlenbeck had not yet analyzed Blackfoot linguistic structure so fully when he endeavoured to promptly publish the texts; his monograph on Blackfoot grammar did not appear until 1938.

If Uhlenbeck were working today, we would expect him to indicate forte and piano voice (as in musical notation) by writing LARGE and small letters and words, to note pauses and changes in tempo and pitch, and where meter seems part of the aesthetic, to break the narrative into free-verse stanzas (see Swann 1994, xxvii–xxxvi; Swann's anthology is, as he states, the first to select for the "ethnopoetics" mode of translation [1994, xxxv]). Wissler had told Duvall to make their English translations "as much like the real story as possible," but "Of course in rewriting this [narrative] I have put in our own style." Wissler wanted only Duvall's "own copy to be written as nearly in the Indian style as possible" (quoted in Kehoe 1995a, ix), although judging from manuscripts archived in the American Museum, Duvall did not understand this to require the choppy and repetitive usage found in Uhlenbeck's translations (partly, as noted above, due to the radical syntactic differences between Blackfoot and English).

Blackfoot Mythology

The bulk of Uhlenbeck's and De Josselin de Jong's Blackfoot texts are narratives of extraordinary persons and events. Wissler, who published the most thoughtful study of Blackfoot narratives, concluded that Blackfeet value the aesthetic dimension of narratives highly, while appreciating their function as parables for behavior (Wissler and Duvall 1908, 17). Given the assumption in the Blackfoot cosmos that persons can be blessed with more than ordinary power and that Almighty Power manifests in a multitude of forms, the narratives do not violate possibilities of the Blackfoot real world (i.e., they would not be considered fantasy). Hugh Dempsey, an astute and very reputable historian, discussed the problem (for a non-Indian scholar) of factuality and decided that "the approach in this book [Dempsey 1994] has been to accept the Indians' supernatural as reality. It was truth in the minds of the speakers and is delivered here as their truths" (Dempsey 1994, 2).

Wissler discerned a critical distinction among the array of narratives Duvall collected with him. A number of narratives explain the origin of a ritual; in these, "the transfer [of the ritual from the empowering spirit] is the main incident or climax of the narrative" (Wissler and Duvall 1908, 13). Other narratives, he noticed, have another sort of "culminating incident," although, Wissler states, "some kind of relation [to a ritual] is always implied" (ibid.). It was his impression that the second group of narratives "are decidedly classical, and show greater art in composition than those of the primary [group]. The people seem to appreciate them for the sake of their power to charm, while the sacred associations of the primary myths are sufficient to make them respected" (ibid.).[28] "The most suggestive difference," he argues, is that the origin-of-ritual narratives "are not often found in the mythologies of other tribes," while the "classical" narratives are "widely distributed" (ibid.). The tales of Scar-Face and Scabby-Round-Robe seemed to Wissler to partake of "classical" aesthetics but are unique to the Blackfoot; Scar-Face is associated with the Sun dance ritual, and Scabby-Round-Robe is secondarily associated with a Beaver bundle (he lives with beavers for a winter, obtains some of their power, and in the happy ending, is given a chief's younger wife and the chief's Beaver bundle) (ibid., 81–83). The Napi (Old Man) stories are uniquely Blackfoot in their protagonist, but the incidents are common in trickster tales of other cultures, such as the stories told about Coyote.

Uhlenbeck, and particularly Wissler, footnote publications of tales similar to the Blackfoot from other Plains nations. Selecting from these collections, the folklorist Stith Thompson presents "full, well-told example[s]" epitomizing each of the variety of narratives he categorizes

under the headings "Mythological Stories," "Mythological Incidents," "Trickster Tales," "Hero Tales," "Journeys to the Other World," "Animal Wives and Husbands," "Miscellaneous Tales," "Tales Borrowed from Europeans," and "Bible Stories" (Thompson 1966, viii). From Blackfoot sources, Thompson chose "The Trickster's Race" (his XXVII) (Wissler and Duvall 1908, 27–29), "Blood-Clot-Boy" (XLV) (ibid., 53–58), "The Piqued Buffalo-Wife" (LVII) (ibid., 117–20), and "The Bear-Woman" (LXIV) (ibid., 68–70). Thompson's "Comparative Notes" code each tale according to his *Motif-Index of Folk-Literature* (1932–36, in addition to listing its many occurrences in the literature. "The Trickster's Race" is motif K11.5, "Blood-Clot" T541.1, "The Buffalo-Wife" C35, and "The Bear-Woman" B611.1. Note that Thompson's attention to comparable tales overrides Wissler's titles in the second two instances, "The Buffalo-Wife" being Wissler's "[Origins of the] Horns and Matoki" ritual societies, and "The Bear-Woman" his "The Seven Stars" (Ursa Major). The arbitrariness of abstracted categorizations is clearly illustrated in this last case; also illustrated is how this case may obscure interesting questions – with the Seven Stars being Ursa the Bear, how is it that in the tale, the stars are children pursued by their elder sister, the paramour of a bear?[29]

Thompson prepared his "Comparative Notes" as addenda to comparative discussions by Boas, Lowie, Waterman, and Reichard in several volumes of the *Journal of American Folk-Lore* (*JAFL*, vols. xxi, xxvii, xxx, xxxii, xxxiv). He cites sources for his noted occurrences only when they have not already been given by his predecessors in the listed works. Presumably it is for that reason that Uhlenbeck and De Josselin de Jong are cited only six times: Uhlenbeck 1911a, 64 (Old Man and the bullberries), 34 (Blood-Clot), 47 (Sucking monster), 53 ("fee-fi-fo-fum cannibal," the motif Thompson marked for the incident when Sun smells Scar-Face hidden in Sun's tipi), and 1912a, 130 (crane as bridge); De Josselin de Jong 1914, 32 (rolling head). Thompson's identifying Sun smelling Scar-Face as a motif known among Anglos from Jack-in-the-

Beanstalk (the giant smelling Jack) indicates the curious bedfellows created by Thompson's method of categorizing narrative motifs.

There seems then to have been a common repertoire of stories offered upon request for narratives, at least among the Southern Piegan. Uhlenbeck had copies of Grinnell's *Blackfoot Lodge Tales* and Wissler and Duvall's *Mythology of the Blackfoot*, but he doesn't seem to have planned to merely record the Blackfoot texts of these English renditions of stories. His objective was to obtain a full range of the language in use, hence the texts of Mission schoolboys' daily doings following formal narratives by the esteemed elder, Bear-chief.

There are features in many of the narratives reflecting a Blackfoot cosmos. The Above People – Sun, Moon, Morning Star – live like a Blackfoot family. They, and many animals, are more powerful than humans, an observable fact to people familiar with the sun's heat, with the brilliance of full moon and Venus in the clear air of High Plains and mountains, and with grizzlies, wolverines, wolves, herds of bison, hawks and eagles, trumpeter swans, and the uncanny ability of beavers and otters to live underwater as well as on land. Gophers and mice and coyotes may be less powerful, but their bright beady eyes bespeak intelligence as quick as their motions. In this country of immense unbounded distances and dramatic weather, time is a series of events, not a fixed measure, and the shared qualities of human and animal life do not require a Darwin to elucidate. *Mirabile dictu*, a Blackfoot might have said, "wonderful to tell," the adventures of extraordinary people like Scar-Face or more-than-human beings like Clot-of-Blood, the transformed bison foetus (Kehoe 1992, 212–13). Wonderful too, how Power can manifest even as a butte ("A Woman Sacrificed to a Butte," Uhlenbeck 1911a, 63–63), wonderful to tell that there was a man willing to give a woman to that butte – well we can wonder at the callous audacity of career-obsessed strivers, legendary or contemporary!

When we read Uhlenbeck's texts, or any collection from the early reservation period, we must keep in mind that these Blackfeet lived through more than a century of endemic warfare provoked by radical changes in martial technology (horses and guns) and unrelenting pressure from Euroamerican expansion (Binnema 2001). It is no wonder that so many narratives tell of raids and battles; it is interesting that there are relatively few in Uhlenbeck's set, perhaps because he was not expressly asking for history. With or without war, life was beset with dangers: blizzards, treacherous rivers to cross, and large horned or fanged antagonists in the hunt. It was wonderful to tell of humans who survived such threats, and it was reasonable to infer that they had been pitied and blessed by a manifestation of Power.

Balancing narratives with a strong historical flavor – Dempsey's 1994 book is the most striking presentation of such narratives – are stories emphasizing timeless principles and human characteristics. Star stories inform listeners about beings transported to the Above World, quite visible on any cloudless night and conspicuously not dead. Wissler's "ritualistic origins" narratives tie into palpably present Medicine bundles and tipis whose power is still vital and feared. People on the Reservation today suggest that David Duvall was impelled to commit suicide (see the diary for July 10, 1911) because he "fooled around" with Medicine bundles, sending some to New York and getting Tom Kyaio (Kiyo) to perform the great Beaver bundle ritual just for the museum man's publication.

Most timeless of all Blackfoot mythical characters is Dawn [-of-time] Man, Napi. The translation "Old Man" refers to Napi existing at the beginning, the dawn, of the world; a better translation would be "Primordial Man." Darnell Davis Rides At The Door (Darnell Doore) dedicated her 1979 Blackfeet Heritage Program collection, *Napi Stories*, "to those that understand Napi, who lives in us all." Impulsive, sociable, greedy, klutzy, Napi is the spontaneity in every person, always on the brink of disaster but somehow, loveable. The popular story "The Men and the Women" contrasts Primordial Man ("They had no lodges. They wore raw-hides") to Civilized Woman ("their lodges were fine … all were fine inside") (Uhlenbeck 1912a, 107). Magnanimously, the women took Napi's comrades into their camp, civilizing them and their descendants. Napi himself is incorrigible, foolishly rejecting a good woman because "[h]e did not like her clothes." The Woman Chief then reduced him to a pinetree, marvellously phallic and insensate. The women's ruined bison corral (*piskun*) can still be seen, it is said, near Cayley, Alberta. (Forbis [1962] reports archaeological excavations showing first use of the corral two thousand years ago).

"Mythology" is an academic category that was much used when academic dons in black gowns logically contrasted Truth and Error, history and fiction, civilization and "the lower races." A great deal of the Bible is mythology, but in the nineteenth century, only radicals pushed such a view. Scholars such as Wissler at the turn of the twentieth century were expected to discuss mythology when reporting on ancient and on "primitive" peoples; those researchers who carried on fieldwork, like Wissler and Uhlenbeck, expressed their discomfort with the given category, paving the way for later anthropologists to think rather in terms of oral literature. (The word "mythology" does not appear in the long index to Swann's [1994] anthology.) We can't simply drop the word "mythology," because it connects readers to older publications and to comparative literature. We can enjoy those of Uhlenbeck's texts that carry an undertone of *mirabile dictu* – perhaps we can call them legendary histories. And much as the tellers did, we can enjoy stories of Napi, irrepressible Dawn-time Man who lives on in us all. For twenty-first century *Amsskaapipikani* (Southern Piegan), myriads of departed souls twinkle above as they did over the Uhlenbecks in the Montana night. The narratives, too, remain alive.

COLLAGE OF BLACKFOOT TEXTS RECORDED BY C. C. UHLENBECK

Arranged by Mary Eggermont-Molenaar

This Collage contains the complete 1911 and 1912 *Blackfoot Texts* of C. C. Uhlenbeck. As the texts in Blackfoot are not reproduced in this volume, except for one example, his explanation of problems with retaining constructions in Blackfoot is also omitted. In addition this Collage contains one story from De Josselin de Jong's 1914 *Blackfoot Texts*, one story from Wissler (1995[1908]), a few entries from Uhlenbeck's linguistic articles, an article in a French journal, and a *Festschrift*.

My comments, which precede Uhlenbeck's texts, explain their place in the Collage. Matching Uhlenbeck's text with specific dates in his wife's diary required some speculation on my part: it could be this story or another one that he told or was told on a certain date. Uhlenbeck recorded the stories in English; his use of English in the *Original Blackfoot Texts* (hereinafter referred to as "obt") and *New Series of Blackfoot Texts* (hereinafter referred to as "nsbt") should be understood in the light of his desire to stay as close as possible to the Blackfoot texts. On this matter, Uhlenbeck writes in his Preface of *Original Blackfoot Texts*: "The English translation which accompanies the texts, though as literal as possible, does not suffice to obtain a grammatical understanding of all the words and forms contained in them." Please keep in mind that neither Uhlenbeck nor his Blackfoot teachers were native English speakers.

Uhlenbeck uses many square brackets in his *Texts*; when he uses round brackets, it will be indicated. "Addenda et corrigenda" with regard to the English texts, listed by Uhlenbeck in obt, 94, and nsbt, 247, are inserted in the texts, as are the Errata in *Original Blackfoot Texts* (obt, 94–95) and *New Series of Blackfoot Texts* (nsbt, vi).

In nsbt, ix–x, Uhlenbeck provides his readers with:

Some Abbreviations

a, v. Lowie.
aa = American Anthropologist.
blt, v. Grinnell.
cl, v. Dorsey
Dorsey cl = J.O. Dorsey, The Cegiha language, Washingon 1890.
Dorsey to = G.A. Dorsey, Traditions of the Osage, Chicago 1904.
Dorsey tsp = G.A. Dorsey, Traditions of the Skidi Pawnee, Boston-New York 1904

Dorsey-Kroeber ta = G.A. Dorsey and A.L. Kroeber, Traditions of the Arapaho, Chicago 1903.

Duvall, v. Wissler-Duval.

ft, v. Jones.

Grinnell blt = G.B. Grinnell, Blackfoot lodge tales, London 1893.

jaf = Journal of American folklore.

Jones ft = W. Jones, Fox texts, Leyden 1907.

Kroeber, v. Dorsey-Kroeber.

Lowie a = R.H. Lowie, The Assiniboine, New York 1909.

Lowie ns = R.H. Lowie, The Northern Shoshone, New York 1909.

mbi, v. Wissler-Duvall.

Mc Clintock ont = W. Mc Clintock, The old north trail, or life, legends and religion of the Blackfeet Indians, London 1910.

mcbi, v. Wissler.

ns, v. Lowie.

obt, v. Uhlenbeck.

ont, v. Mc Clintock.

Simms tc = S.C. Simms, Traditions of the Crows, Chicago 1903.

slbi, v. Wissler.

ta, v. Dorsey Kroeber.

tc, v. Simms.

to, v. Dorsey.

tsp, v. Dorsey.

Uhlenbeck obt = C. C. Uhlenbeck, *Original Blackfoot texts*, Amsterdam 1911.

Wissler mcbi = C. Wissler, Material culture of the Blackfoot Indians, New York 1910.

Wissler slbi = C. Wissler, The social life of he Blackfoot Indians, New York 1911.

Wissler-Duvall mbi = C. Wissler and D.C. Duvall, Mythology of the Blackfoot Indians, New York 1908.

[Abbreviations added in this volume]

P and P Names = "Patronymics and Proper Names of the Peigans" (translation of Uhlenbeck's lecture "Geslachts- en Persoonsnamen der Peigans").

djbt = *Blackfoot Texts* (by J.P.B. de Josselin de Jong).

AId'E = Archives Internationales d'Ethnographie.

Contents of the Collage

July 20	Blue-face. Another version	nsbt	134–44
July 20	The elk and his wife. First version	nsbt	96–99
July 21	Belly-fat, another version	nsbt	144–66
	Belly-fat	obt	23–34
July 22	The man who was pitied by a water-bear	nsbt	114–20
July 27	The young men and the beavers. First version (Jim B.)	nsbt	72–85
July 28	Medicine-men	nsbt	55–58
July 29	The Old Man and the geese	nsbt	180–82
August 1	Bear-chief's songs	obt	66–68
	An adventure of Many-guns	nsbt	219–20
	Bear-chief's life-story	obt	70–91
August 2	Two adventures of the Old Man	obt	63–65
August 3	Horses found on an island	obt	57–58
	The Old Man and the wolf on the ice	nsbt	170–71
	The Old Man, the elks, and the gophers	nsbt	171–76
August 4	The Old Man and fat	nsbt	177–80
August 5	Horses found	nsbt	204–9
	Boys' experiences, nr. 10	nsbt	236–37
August 6	Red-head	nsbt	123–25
	The Milky way	nsbt	113–14
August 10	The old men, the rock and the kit-fox	nsbt	187–91
	Boys' experiences, nrs. 17, 18,19.	nsbt	242–43
August 11	Scar-face	obt	50–57
August 13	Forms of a nose	A Survey	15
	Nose	English-Blackfoot Vocab.	147
August 15	The men and the women	nsbt	167–70
	The Old Man, the elk-head, and the old women	nsbt	192–95
August 17	A Man saved by a dog	nsbt	199–200
August 18	The Bunched Stars	nsbt	112–13
August 19	Clot-of-Blood	obt	34–50
August 20/22	Ghosts	nsbt	58–64
	A man saved by a child	nsbt	200–202
August 23	Child-birth	nsbt	50–51
	Death and hereafter	nsbt	53–54
August 24	The Wind-maker	nsbt	64
	The Thunder-bird	nsbt	64–65
August 28,	From Bear-chief's life-story	nsbt	211–14
September 5 & 9	Translation in Blackfoot	nsbt	211–14
	Explanation of the graphical system	obt	vi–x
September 2	The Old Man and the girls who were picking strawberries	djbt	23
	-ats-	A Survey	23
	The Old Man and the pine-tree as an arrow	nsbt	182–84
	The Old Man and the buffalo-charm	nsbt	184–87
	The Old Man and the spring-birds	nsbt	195–98
September 10	Tatsey sleep-walking	nsbt	220–21
	Dresses of old women burned	nsbt	203–4
September 12, 13, 14	Horse- and cattle-raising	nsbt	223–25
September 15	Old Man deceived by two women	Wissler and Duval 1908	35–36

Thursday, June 8.

Mrs. Uhlenbeck records that Uhlenback got the idea to read a few Blackfoot texts. These must have been texts he collected the previous year in *Original Blackfoot Texts* (obt). Most of the texts in obt and in *New Series of Blackfoot Texts* (nsbt) are also recorded in Blackfoot language. In this Collage, for reasons of space, the Blackfoot texts are left out. Only the last two stories are provided also in Blackfoot, to give the readers some idea of what this language, as recorded by Uhlenbeck and by De Josselin de Jong, looks like. The first story, The people living in the north, obt, 5, a migration history of the ancient Peigan, was told to Uhlenbeck by Joseph Tatsey, who was, as Uhlenbeck stated in his preface, "an intelligent and broad-minded Indian of Blood descent, living among the southern Peigans, to whom his mother belongs."[30] Tatsey would arrive the next day, June 9. Uhlenbeck dedicated Appendix I of his *Patronymics and Proper Names of the Peigans*, Appendix A to this volume, to Tatsey and his family. Actually all the stories in obt were communicated and explained by Joseph Tatsey, with two exceptions, mentioned hereunder. In the second story, "The origin of the buffaloes," obt, 6–12, Uhlenbeck states in his preface: "The story of the origin of the buffaloes was told to me by Bear-chief (Nínoχkyàio), well-known, even to the whites, as a brave Indian and a leader among his people. The same has been so kind, to sing for me the songs, printed at the end of these texts."

The people living in the north.

The country of the ancient Peigans was long ago very far north. They moved and camped about in it. On this side was a big water. They used to move to it. Then they moved from it again. When they moved one time again this way, they suddenly saw, that the big water was frozen over. Then [the chief] said: We shall move across. That chief went first. He then moved on. All the half crossed. The wife of that chief and his child were in the middle of the ice. His child said to that woman: Mother, there is something very nice. It is sticking out of the ice. Get off [from your horse] for a while, that you get it for me. Then that woman got off. She hit that [thing], [which was] his horn [of the animal which is mentioned afterwards], with a stone-hammer. When she hurt him, then he moved. Then the ice broke down. Right there he started with his head out [of the ice]. When he started, then he was tearing the ice ahead of him. Then this ancient people knew, [that] that one was the water-bull. The half of this people could not cross [the ice having broken down], and now half of the ancient Peigans is living about across [the big water]. And the dogs have separated [after having had their meal; that means: the story is at an end].

[Cf. C. Wissler-D.C. Duvall, Mythology of the Blackfoot Indians, New York 1908, p. 22.]

The origin of the buffaloes.

Long ago the ancient people used to eat roseberries, hard-seed-berries, bark, black alcali. There was a man, [that] camped alone. His wife was picking roseberries about, and there she met a young man. The young man said to her: Have you a daughter, that you are willing to give me? [She said:] I shall go home, I shall tell my daughter's father. If he is pleased, he will perhaps go and tell you. That woman's husband was wise. Then he thought: I shall go and see him, I shall perhaps have use of him. He went to him. When he saw him, he liked him. He said to him: Let us go home together, I shall have you as a son-in-law. That man

Two pages from Willy's diary; description of David Duvall's suicide.

te kunnen hebben. Walter heeft nu van ons 21 + 4 = 25 dollar. Dat is eigenlijk veel te veel. Daarom schrijft Uhlenbeck nog eens aan Walter, dat wij dit geld onmogelijk voor de terugreis kunnen missen. Wij gaan naar onze kamer terug. Aan Truus ga ik een brief schrijven. Aan Hermine Hartevelt en aan Lizzy Kunst een briefkaart. Rustig zitten wij in ons slaapvertrek en bemerken heelemaal niet, wat zich afspeelde in dezelfde herberg. Als wij gaan eten treft het ons wel dadelijk, dat er zooveel indianen uit de Camps, voor Joe Kipp's huis staan. Waarom het is, begrijpen wij niet en denken er eigenlijk ook niet over na. Nog zitten wij te eten, als een aller akeligst geschreeuw tot ons doordringt en men deelt ons mede, dat David Duvall, de bekende interpreter van Wisler, in de herberg van Joe Kipp juist zich zelf heeft doodgeschoten. Op dezen zelfden dag werd het gedrang voorkomen tot ontbinding van zijn huwelijk. Naar men zegt op verzoek

van zijn vrouw, die een zuster van Marcaut is. Heel akelig klinkt dit gegil, het snikken en weeklagen van een paar indianenvrouwen. Duvall's moeder zit luidklagend in Joe Kipp's voorhuis. Haastig ontloop ik deze volte en ga naar onze kamer. Ook daar hoor ik het. Uhlenbeck raakt ook onder den indruk, maar wil er toch heengaan om verschillende indianen gade te slaan. Na een poosje komt hij terug. Wij zullen maar eens naar de Camps gaan wandelen; dit is de beste afleiding. Op ons gemak bekijken wij de medicine lodge nog eens. Voor het altaar liggen allerlei takjes en handjes, afgevallen stukjes van tonaffers. Ik neem ook zoo'n takje mee om te bewaren bij alles wat wij reeds verzameld hebben. Bij de tipi spreken wij Walter en ook Leme en nu vernemen wij, dat er om den dood van Duvall heelemaal niet meer gedanst zal worden. De "agent" heeft het verboden: een heel sinister slot dus aan deze dansweek! Maar

came close to his lodge. He spoke ahead to his wife: Go outside. Here is your son-in-law. It is not good, that you see him. Then that woman went out. She began to build a lodge. She built the lodge with rye-grass, bark, [and] leaves.

They fed him. The things they used to eat, they fed him with. That young married man then ate of the black alcali and the hay. For two nights he just ate the same [black alcali and hay], those other things [the bark and the two kinds of berries] he refused to eat. That man had a suspicion, he knew, that he [his son-in-law] was not the same kind of being as we are. That man was wise. After four nights he went to him. He said to him: What kind of being are you? You are not the same kind of being as I am. Why don't you eat from these bark, roseberries, hard-seed-berries, [which] I eat? Of the two things, which you eat now, hay and black alcali, we don't eat the hay, but we [do] eat the black alcali. Now [go and] hunt. [He said:] Yes, I shall hunt. And he hunted.

He was one night out, where he went to hunt. And he brought the meat from a carcase. It was a person. Then he [the father-in-law] went to his son-in-law. When he knew [that] the one, that he [his son-in-law] had killed, [was a person], he said to him: These pieces of meat, that you have brought from a carcase, for a time I shall not eat of them. [Go] soon [and] hunt, kill some one of your tribe. I shall decide, which of the two, that you will bring pieces of meat from, is best. [He said:] Yes, I shall kill [some one] of my tribe.

He was one night out again. He brought pieces of meat from a carcase, [belonging to] his tribe. [It was] a partner of his, [that] was killed by him. That wise man looked at them again, he knew that they were of different kinds [these pieces and those he saw before]. They then ate of those pieces he had first brought in. They vomited them up. They ate of them alone, but his children did not eat of them. And they ate again of those new pieces. They did not vomit them up. And his children ate, all of them. They did not vomit it up. And he gave his wife and his children again to eat of those last pieces. They did not vomit it up. And they fed

their son-in-law. They gave him to eat of both, of his first pieces and the latter ones. And they had done eating. That man said to his wife: Which of the two [kinds of pieces] that you ate do you like best, these that you vomited up, or these that you did not vomit up? Which will be called buffalo? [She said:] The last pieces which that person brought, he [from whose carcase those pieces were taken] will be called buffalo, and those first pieces which he brought, he [from whose carcase those pieces were taken] will be called person. And then they had finished giving them names.

He said to his son-in-law: Where are you roaming about? He answered him: I roam about under the water. He said to him: Now you have got a name. He said to him [also]: Which may be your name? He answered him: Our name is water-bull. He said to him: What do you eat? He answered him: We eat you, [we eat also] hay and earth, we eat three things. That man said to his son-in-law: Now we shall eat you. And that man picked up fire [that means: a burning fire-stick]. He hit him with it. His son-in-law just picked up that piece of human flesh. He just pressed it under his arm, he ran out, he turned into a buffalo, he jumped into the water.

Next summer his daughter gave birth to a child. Her child was a buffalo-calf. Then that man said: We shall move. That child will not be killed. He will be left here, we are ashamed of him. Yes, there he was left. There was a log, he was left by it. He got to be a year old. Where he stayed, he did not die. And he turned into a person.

He just went in the direction, [he thought] his mother was in. And he was found by two persons, young men. They pitied him very much. They treated him as their younger brother. They took him home with them. And next summer he said to them: You have taken pity on me. Let us go to my father. Then they said: Yes. Then they started. They came there to a lake. They stayed there. Suddenly [two] buffaloes [the boy's father and a companion] came out [of the lake]. They got ashore. They turned into persons. They got far from it [from the lake]. Here that boy followed running. He turned into a buffalo. Then they [the two buffaloes] saw him. They waited for him. When he got near them, he turned into a person.

One of them was his father. He tried to influence him [his father-in-law] by means of [delivering] his companion [that they might eat him]. They met there his son. And those that were behind [the men with whom the boy had come to the lake] rose up. They went towards them [the buffaloes]. One of those who met just ran away. He just ran into that lake. And those people all met. That boy said to his elder brothers [the men he had come with]: Here is he, who is my father. That water-bull said to them: Now you will get something for your visit. We shall go to my father, the chief bull. He stays under the water. That water-bull, one of them, went around [one of the men], and sat down, and he [the man] got on him. Then his son did the same. The other one got on him. When that water-bull and his son started to run, they snorted water. They covered [literally: they did] the [two] riders with it. They [the two riders] did not know, when they [the water-bulls] ran into the water. They were told by the water-bull [the boy's father]: Now get off. And when they looked, they suddenly saw all the people under the water.

They went to the chief of this people. They [the bulls] cried out all over the camp, that they [the visitors] must not [be allowed to] go out. Those persons [the bulls that cried out] said, that they should kill and eat them. That chief then told them: I shall not consent to what my children here say. I shall now camp over there far away. I give you [that means: to the tribe of the two visitors] all the people here [the buffaloes]. I give you half of them, but I don't give you the other half [at this time]. [The old people nowadays still expect the other half of the buffalo-herd coming.] That water-bull [the son-in-law] had the human flesh, [that] had turned into a dog, always under his arm. He just gave that dog secretly to his father. He said to him: When I go out, you must turn that dog loose. The water-bull and his son were ridden again [by the visitors]. Those two persons [the visitors] came out of this water. The father of that water-bull turned that dog loose. That he barked running, that's why these many people all turned into buffaloes. The way those four persons went they all followed running. When they all ran out, they could not go back into the lake. They were given away by that chief. That water-bull and his son turned into persons.

The water-bull was not afraid any more [of his father-in-law, because now he had turned loose the buffaloes]. Then he went straight to his wife. His father-in-law was not angry with him any more. He thought it good, that the buffaloes were turned loose for him. That man said to his son-in-law: What can these buffaloes be killed with? That water-bull said to his father-in-law: They will die by flints. They will be skinned with the same. They [the flints] will be handled on sticks. You will build your corrals to cliffy rocks and steep banks. There they will jump into. You will kill them. He said to his father-in-law: Now I shall eat these buffaloes. I shall not go back to my father. I am very much used to my wife. He said [also] to his father-in-law: When I die, you must put me into the water. I shall turn into a rock. Then the boiling is ended [that means: the story is at an end].

[Cf. C. Wissler-D.C. Duvall, Mythology of the Blackfoot Indians, New York 1908, pp. 128 sq.]

Saturday, June 10.

Uhlenbeck dedicated Appendix III in Patronymics and Proper Names of the Peigans (reproduced in this volume as Appendix A) to Bear Chief's family. In an appendix to obt, 69–70, Uhlenbeck wrote about the same family:

INFORMATION CONCERNING BEAR-CHIEF: GENEALOGICAL NOTES.

Bear-chief (Nínoχkyàio) was born in the year, that the chief Lame-bull (Stámiksistsekai) broke his neck in chasing buffalo (1857). His name in childhood was Takes-the-first-gun (Itóminàmaχka). His mother's brother Red-horn (Ekutsótskina) gave him that name. Red-horn, in charging the enemy, had taken the first gun. Therefore he gave that name to the child. Afterwards his name was changed to Bear-chief, after old Three-sons (Niókskatos), surnamed Big-nose (O´maχksksisi), whose name in childhood had been Bear-chief.

Bear-chief belongs to the Not-laughers. He married four times.

The names of his wives are:

Fly(ing) (Paióta), belonging to the Small-robes.

Good-shield-woman (Mátsauauòtaniàke), belonging to the Small-robes.

Elk-yells-in-the-water (Itsúiinokå`χkumi), a Blood Indian. Her clan is unknown.

Owl-woman (Sépistàke), belonging to the Blood-people. The name Owl-woman was given to her, when she was born, but afterwards she was called Pɑstséu (the meaning of this name is unknown to Bear-chief).

Bear-chief has got seven children (four boys and three girls). Not all of them have got Indian names.

Bear-chief's father's first name, given in childhood, was Mink (Siékaii). This name was given to him by a medicine-man, who had seen a mink in his dream. After he became a chief, he changed his name to Weasel-moccasin (A´paitsikina). He retained this name till his death,

which was caused by the measles. He was considered a great warrior, and distinguished himself during the wars with other Indian tribes.

He married thrice. Bear-chief's mother was called Went-allright-to-the-upper-part-of-the-lodge (A´χsikimoi), and belonged to the Small-soft-grease-people. She was a granddaughter of False-pointing (Kipàái), a great chief, and he remained one, even when he was a very old man. Only Bear-chief's mother had children from Weasel-moccasin. Three sons came to the manly age:

Blanket-robe (Náipistsi), who died after his first raid.

Prairie-chicken-child (Kétokipokàu), afterwards called Weasel-moccasin (A´paitsikina), a great chief who was killed by the Sioux 1879.

Takes-the-first-gun (Itóminàmaχka), afterwards called Bear-chief (Nínoχkyàio).

Bear-chief's grandfather on the father's side was called in childhood Wise-child (Mokákiepòk), and afterwards, when he was a chief, his name was changed to Weasel-moccasin (A´paitsikina). He was also a great warrior. He had four wives. Bear-chief's father's mother was one of them and was named Kill-the-chief (Nánainiki). Bear-chief does not know the name of her parents, nor to which clan she belonged.

Bear-chief's great-grandfather on the father's side was called the Only-old-man (Itámiapì). This must have been his second name. The name which was given to him in childhood is unknown. He was the main chief of the Peigans in his time. The names of his wives are unknown. Nor is it known to Bear-chief who his great-great-grandfather was. The eldest son of the Only-old-man was Red-man (Mekyápi), through whose fault one of the clans obtained the name of Buffalo-chips.[31] Wise-child, Bear-chief's grandfather, was the second son.

Sunday, June 11.

Willy describes a Catholic service. Such description is also to be found in Boys' experiences, nr. 20, nsbt, 243–45. Preface: "Communicated and explained to me by my young friend John Tatsey."

[20] Church. When they enter, they all kneel down and make the sign of the cross. They begin to pray. And then the priest enters, and he begins to pray. They all sit down. And he begins to preach to them. And when he has done preaching, he kneels down again, and he sings, and the girls and the boys all sing. And he goes to sit down, and when the children have done singing, he gets up again, and the boys that serve at the altar get up, they take [the wine and water], that he drinks, and they bring them back, and they kneel down. And after a short while the priest preaches. One of the boys rings the bell, and the people are praying, they all kneel down, they bow their heads down. They ring the bell again. When they have rung the bell five times, then the people put their heads up. The priest preaches again. When he has done praying, the boys take again [the wine and water], that he drinks, and they put them away again. They go back and kneel down again. And they ring the bell again. When they have done ringing, they all sit down, and the priest comes down. He takes off the clothes, he uses while praying, and he puts on different [clothes]. He goes back again, he goes back up to the altar, and the girls and the boys sing again, and one of the boys is swinging the censer. He [the priest] gets up, he puts something in [the censer], then he goes up again, he takes down the Blessed Sacrament, he turns with it to the people, they bow their heads down again. When they have rung the bell again, they put their heads up, they sing again, and when they have done singing, the priest goes out. The people then all go out.

Willy noted on that same day, June 11, that Bear Chief, who attended the service was "one of the many Indians, longing for the Sand Hills." In the Preface of obt, Uhlenbeck wrote that Bear-chief allowed him, "an insight into his religious conceptions, his ecstasies and his dreams. In an Appendix I publish the materials concerning Bear-chief, he himself has made me acquainted with. Nevertheless, but for Joseph Tatsey's interpreting, it would have been impossible to me to profit by Bear-chief's life-experience, ancient lore, and imaginative power, as this gentleman speaks only the language of his warlike ancestry." "Bear-chief's cosmogony" is in obt, 91–93:

Bear-chief's cosmogony.

We are sitting around the table, and Bear-chief is going to tell you the story of the Sun. The Sun and the Moon keep us alive. The Sun has got the earth and the sky all in one room. No white man knows, how big the room of the Sun and the Moon is. The Moon had a child. It was a boy. The Moon told the Sun, that he should give a name to that boy. Then he called him God (A'pistotoki). When the boy was seven years old, the Moon asked the Sun for another child, and the Sun gave her another boy. The Sun told the Moon to give a name to her new-born child. Then she named him the Old Man (Nápi). These two children grew up, so that they could run around. God said to his father: Why don't you make something for me to eat? Then his father gave him the deer as food. Afterwards the youngest son went to his mother, and told her: Get me something to eat. Then she gave him the berries as food. God went over to his father, and told him to put something on the earth to carry the meat home. Then his father put the dog on the earth. Afterwards God said to his father: Why don't you make day-light for us? The Moon heard her boy asking for day-light, and told him, she did not want any day-light. The Sun dug a hole in the ground, and made a trapping-place for catching the deer. One day the Sun told the Moon to go to the trapping-place after the meat of the deer that was caught that night. The Moon said to God, her eldest son: If your father gives you day-light, I am going to kill you. The Moon started out for the trapping-place, but she went in a wrong direction, and so the Sun asked: Where is your mother going to? But the Moon was going to a big tree, that was standing alongside a hill. In that tree lived a snake, with one horn below the eyes, and the reason, why the Moon did not want any day-light, was that she had secret intercourse with that snake. The Sun killed the snake by the heat, saying that the Moon was not strong enough to kill it. When the Moon reached the tree, the snake was all burnt up, and the tree was standing in a blaze. When she came home, she told her eldest son, that there was no hope for him to escape. She said, she would kill the Sun and both her children. The Sun went into his house, and was sitting there. When the Moon came to the door, he shut it with the sky. He had made a hole in the sky, and she put her head through it. Then the Sun got up, and chopped the Moon's head off. The Sun said, that his two sons were to be the rulers of the country. The Sun gave four things to his sons: sand, stones, a fisher's hide, and water. Then it was going to be day. The Sun got up in his room, and stretched his hand north, and made a motion round the room, swinging his arm round, and cut his room in half. The sky spread out, and the earth likewise. The first direction, he pointed to, was the north. That is the reason, the storm always comes from there. After the boys had got the things, which their father gave them, they started off, leaving the dog at home, because they were afraid, it would be drowned in crossing water. Just before they started, the Sun told his boys: Your mother will be only four nights under the ground, and then she will be up again. Her body will be after me, all the time, and so you must take care of the world. Your mother's head will be after you, but you will be saved by means of the things, I gave you. And he said: I shall be in the sky, and when your mother catches me, there is something to

be up in the country. The Sun started off, and the two boys went in another direction. After four nights, the body of the Moon went after the Sun, and the head of the Moon after the two boys. When the head came close to the boys, it told them: There is no hope for you now. But they threw the stones, which their father gave them, back at the head, and the head could not move on as fast as before, because it was bumping against rocks. Then they got far away from the head, but it got through the rocks, and caught the boys up again. When they saw the head nearly overtaking them, they threw the sand and the fisher's hide back at the head. Then the grass and the brush became so thick, that the head could not get through. After they had used these three things, the only thing left to them was the water. So, when the head had found its way through the brushes and was quite close to them, they threw the water back at the head, and then the ocean was there. The head tried to jump over the water, but it got only half-way, and fell down into the middle. And that is the reason, you don't drink the water of the sea: it is so strong, that it killed the head. After the boys had crossed the ocean, God told the Old Man to go back to the place, where the dog was. God himself would go to his father, the Sun. He said, that all things were given to him by his father to put them on the earth, and that all birds and animals, put on the earth, would talk to the Old Man. God told his brother also, that he – the Old Man – was not going to die, but that in summer and in winter he would be changed into some kind of animal. Then God turned the Old Man into a big swan, that was picking bugs along the shore. After that God made a man and a woman out of clay, and put the man on the right wing of the swan, and the woman on the left, so that the Old Man could take them across the sea. God told the Old Man to leave them on the other side of the ocean. When the Old Man had crossed the sea, he flew to the place, where the dog was. Then the Old Man left the shape of a swan, and turned into a man. The dog was very glad to see him. When night came, the Old Man put the man and the woman together, and covered them up, and then the clay turned into living persons.

Now there were four together: the Old Man, the dog, the man and the woman. Then God put all kinds of living things on the earth. They all were fighting together. That the black beetles and the ants were in war together, is the reason, that we have war ourselves. And the reason why people always steal, is that these insects were stealing first. The Old Man made the springs, the rivers, the creeks, and the mountains. And afterwards he turned into a pine, and he will not be seen any more.

[Cf. Father Morice, Transactions of the Canadian Institute, vol. V, pp. 4 sqq. 11. 14, and also the rattle-snake version of the story of the Seven Stars, which has been written down in Blackfoot by J.P.B. de Josselin de Jong, and will be published afterwards. Another version of the same tale has been published in English by C. Wissler-D.C. Duvall, Mythology of the Blackfoot Indians, New York 1908, pp. 68 sqq. Concerning the magic flight in Bear-chief's story cf. also F. Boas, Indianische Sagen von der Nord-Pacifischen Küste Amerikas, Berlin 1895, pp. 99. 164. 224. 240 sq. 268, and P. Ehrenreich, Die Mythen und Legenden der südamerikanischen Urvölker und ihre Beziehungen zu denen Nordamerikas und der alten Welt, Berlin 1905, pp. 83 sqq. A similar flight occurs in the story of "The leader-buffalo". but here the obstacles have lost their original magic character.]

Uhlenbeck reads aloud Blackfoot texts for Tatsey, his wife and Bear Chief. He might have read the third story in obt, 13–18, "The Leader-buffalo."

The Leader-buffalo.

There was a man, [that] had one wife. The ancient Peigans were making a corral. The buffaloes would not run in [into the corral]. That woman went after wood. There were other women, they saw buffaloes coming that way. That only wife said [to the leader-buffalo]: Leader, run well, I shall marry [you]. [This was only meant as a jest.] After a short time the buffaloes jumped [over the bank]. The leader was not injured. The rope broke with which that woman had packed the wood on her back. Her companions left her. There was a young man, [that] wore his robe inside out, he came to her. He told her: Come on, we shall go away. She said to him: Why do you say that? I don't know you. He told her: Make haste, I did not care for those [buffaloes], my father, my mother, my younger brothers. [I only cared for you!] You said: Run well, I shall marry [you]. That woman said: Yes, you are right. Then they went away. The leader said to that woman: Shut your eyes. After a while he said to her: Come on, open your eyes [literally: see]. [When she opened her eyes,] they suddenly sat among the buffaloes.

When his wife did not come, that man began to ask for her. He was told by those women: Yesterday we went with her to get wood. She said: Leader, run well, I shall marry [you]. Then that man knew: My wife is taken away to the buffaloes. He then went to the buffaloes. He came there. He concealed himself. He sat near the river. That woman was told by the leader-buffalo: Go quickly and get me a drink. Here is my horn. [Saying this, he took his horn from his head.] If you meet any person, it will sound. She was just dipping water, [when] she was told by her husband: I come to see you [and to take you home]. She said to him: Wait. Sit there. After a while he sleeps. He sleeps very soundly. I shall come back. She then went home [to the leader-buffalo]. The horn sounded. She was told by her husband [the leader-buffalo]: There was a person, you talked with him. She said to him: No, over there are your younger brothers. They told me, that I must give them a drink. He said to her: Come on, look for lice on my head. A long time she was looking for lice on his head. He fell asleep. That woman rose up. She went to her [former] husband. She said to him: Come on. Then they started to run off.

After a very long time that man looked back. He said to his wife: He is running after us. He was close to them. That woman threw away her moccasin. The [other] buffaloes were there with the leader-buffalo. He had taken them with him. He got to that moccasin. He stopped running. He licked it. All these buffaloes licked it. When they had started again to run, after a long while there was another moccasin [thrown by the woman]. They then did it the same [licked it]. When they had started again to run, again after a long while there was a legging [thrown by the woman]. He [the leader-buffalo] then saw it. He did it the same [licked it]. When they had started again to run, after a short while there was a dress [thrown by the woman]. He [the leader-buffalo] then found it again. That woman said to her husband: I cannot do any more. Over there was a big tree, they ran up into it [for safety]. These buffaloes got to it. When they had run around it, [and] after a long while had started again to run [not finding the trail, and not having discovered that the man and the woman were in the tree], these buffaloes were far away.

And there was a scabby bull, [that] was the last one running. He scratched his back on that tree. That woman said to her husband: I shall spit down on him. He [her husband] told her: No. Don't spit at him. We shall be known from him [by means of him]. Nevertheless she spit at him. That scabby bull looked up. He saw them. He called for Red-scar [this was the name of the leader-buffalo]: Here is your wife. When they [the buffaloes] had made a long run around [in coming back], Red-scar got back to that tree.

He said to these buffaloes: Come on, now try to knock this tree down, each in his turn. Those bulls were butting it [one after another]. That man was shooting at them. It looked, very many of them were killed. Then Red-scar got up. When he shook himself, yellow paint rose up from him [that means: the dust that rose from him was turned into yellow paint]. When he walked towards that tree, he sunk with his feet into the ground. That man said to his wife: Is he used to tell what he will die with? She answered him: He will die by flints. Every time Red-scar

butted that tree, he then stripped off big pieces of it. He nearly felled it. And that man shot down at him. He broke his back with a shot [hitting it in a joint]. These buffaloes fled, making noise with their feet. That man [and his wife] came down. He shot Red-scar more than once, while he was lying [on the ground]. Then there they stood about. His wife was then weeping. He said to her: You loved Red-scar. She answered him: Yes. There she was, then he killed her [that means: he killed her then on the spot]. That man said: That way will be treated the lovers of the wives of other people, and our wives that we know [as having a lover]. And the dogs have separated [that means: the story is at an end].

[Cf. G.B. Grinnell. Blackfoot lodge tales, London 1893, 104 sqq.; C. Wissler-D.C. Duvall, Mythology of the Blackfoot Indians, New York 1908, 109–16, and for some particulars J.O. Dorsey, The Cegiha language, Washington 1890, 157 sqq.]

Later that night, Bear Chief told about the old times. "Wonderful experiences of Bear-chief's" are in nsbt, 214–18. Preface: "Told by Bear-chief, interpreted by Tatsey."

Wonderful experiences of Bear-chief's.

[1] Twenty-eight years ago I went to war to the Cypress hills, I was one of forty in a party, I went afoot. I went on a raid against the Crees. In the morning we came to the Eastern Sweetgrass hills, there was Sage creek [literally: Rough creek]. There was a butte right close to the creek. From there I saw three bulls. I told these my war-companions: Stay here, look at me, I shall shoot those bulls over there. I began to crawl, I came near them, they had no chance to escape me. I got up and aimed at them, then instead of running off they sat down. Then I began to crawl again,

I was getting very near them, my body began to tremble, I was very much afraid of them, I looked at them again, I recognized them, that they had turned into rocks. I got up, I went to them, which were black rocks. They were glittering [in the sun], they were shaped like buffaloes. Those my companions got up, they came near [me], they got to [me]. We saw these rocks, we wondered at them, and we thought, they were holy. I filled my pipe. I then gave it to these my companions. They gave their clothes and [different] things [they had] all to these rocks. I myself just prayed to them. Running-wolf was the eldest. He said to me: Let us go back from here, now there is something dangerous and bad. The reason why these buffaloes now turned into rocks, was that we were shown a warning for the future. Then I turned back home. Late in the summer I went again to war. I was one of thirty in a party, I went in the same direction. I came near to that [place], where these bulls had turned into rocks. I told Little-dog: Let us look on those, that were buffaloes, and were turned into rocks. He [Little-dog] was told by these my companions: He [Bear-chief] was right, they are very wonderful. We just got there [where the buffaloes had been]. They were gone. Where they had been sitting, there were just only deep places. Three sun-flowers were growing there [in those deep places]. I just passed by [after having looked at them]. This is what I know [to be] the first wonderful thing, I have seen in my life-time.

[2] Now, this my first story happened in the lower country, but now this time I was moving about in the mountains. I was hunting there. There were two of our lodges, my lodge and my partner's. He was called Big-top-knot. In the morning I heard, there was a sound. I knew, that this [sound], that I heard, was higher up the river. I just went up to it. When I looked over to it, I saw, there was a person. He was standing near the water, he was small, he had no clothes. I then hid myself, I went around him, I looked up at him, who [then] was a rock. I then went to him, I got there. I told him: Now I shall take you, I shall bring you to my lodge.

I put him on my horse, I sat behind, then I went home. I came to my two wives. And my partner had also two wives and his mother. They all came out to [me]. I gave them that person, [that was] a rock. They took him in into my lodge. My partner's mother was such as these [that are] wise women. She began to paint him about with her paint on his face and his body. She prayed to him, she wrapped him in a piece of cloth. He was one night in my lodge, and next morning we began to make a shelter for him. We broke camp and moved, we left him. There he was on our old camp-ground. I told him, that he should keep watch. And this is the second wonderful thing, that I saw in my life-time.

[3] Now, since then I saw wonderful things a third time. Here on Two-Medicine river, where it enters the forest, I went to chop my poles. I went with my wife and with Medicine-owl. I had done chopping. I went shooting with my wife. High in the mountains I shot two mountain-sheep [literally: big-horns], I killed them. I told her: Over there are two mountain-sheep, that I killed. Now I shall clean my gun. There was a rock, we came to it and sat by it. I had done cleaning [my gun], I put it up against that rock, and then I saw, that [the rock] moved about. I quickly took up my gun. We looked at that rock. It was then breathing aloud, it scared us very much. I told my wife: I shall see its eyes. She forbade me [to try]. I did not listen to her. I touched it with my ramrod, and then it moved faster. It never looked. We recognized it, [that it was] a big frog. We left it. Then we went over to those [mountain-sheep], I had killed. That are the only three wonderful things, I have seen in my life-time.

After having told these three short stories, Bear-chief said to me about Little-dog, whom he had mentioned in the first one: We are the only [true] war-chiefs [living now], myself and Little-dog. Little-dog's father was made a chief on account of his wars, and the whites made him a greater chief; he was the first [Indian of this tribe], that went east; he brought first the white soldiers to this country.

Monday, June 12.

Bear Chief's "Two (scalp) songs" are in nsbt, 210. Preface: "Communicated by Bear-chief, interpreted by Tatsey."

Two songs.
———

1. This song was sung by warriors, when they came back from a raid, having taken the scalp of an enemy.

Peigans, look at us, that you may be afraid of us now.

2. When Indians had been a long time on a raid, and they began to feel lonesome, the leader would sing the following song to cheer them up:

Try hard, all of you, our lodge is not [so] good, that we should love it [that means: it is better to be on the war-path than to be at home].

Painting warriors occurs in "How the ancient Peigans lived," nsbt, 1–38. Preface: "Told by Blood (Káinaikoan), interpreted by Tatsey."

How the ancient Peigans lived.
———

How the ancient Peigans moved about, how they ate, the things they cooked with, the things they had happy times with, how they fought in war, how they played, and how they dressed, the way I heard about them.

Far down on Maria's river [literally: Bear creek], there they stayed till late in the spring. Their horses were really fat, they had done shedding their hair. They [the Peigans] waited for one another. They waited for the bulls, that they had shed their hair. The chiefs talked, they went crying about the camp, they would say: Go about to get lodge-pins. We shall move up [away from the river]. Then they moved up. It was in the Battle-coulee that they camped. In the morning they went round saying: Come on, we shall move. When the buffaloes were far, we overtook them in the Cypress hills; when they were not far, we overtook them in the Small Sweetgrass hills. We would chase the bulls between the Small Sweetgrass hills. The bulls were chased first. And their bodies were oily. They were put straight up [after having been killed]. Their eyes [the bulls' eyes] were dusty. They would rub the knives a little, with them they cut their backs open. They were all skinned from the back down. Then they would throw out their kidneys. And the oil and grease would gather about their navels. They would throw down the yellow back-fat and spread it out. The man would tell his wife: Take and wash the manifold. When she came back, he would say to her: That leg-bone, the oily leg-bone, just break that. It would be broken for him. And the manifold and the marrow of the leg would burst by chewing. He would roll the marrow in the manifold. He would burst it by chewing it.

He had done skinning. Then he began to pack his meat [on a horse]. Then he came home with the meat. Then the woman [his wife] brought it [the horse with the meat] home [to her own parents]. He [her husband] stretched his hand out [that means: gave the meat to his parents-in-law]. And the man [the husband] just sat [inside of his lodge]. His wife came in with the son-in-law's [that means: her husband's] food. The broken boss-rib, the short rib, the gut with the blood in it, the tripe where it is good, with those [four] things he [the son-in-law] was fed [by his parents-in-law]. He was told by his wife: Give an invitation. The old men, those were the ones he invited. The women jerked the skin-meat from the skins which they would make their marks on [the skins that would be used as parfleches]. They made marks on the parfleches, and the long sacks, the real sacks, and the berry-sack. In that way we made use of the hide. The chief then again cried about the camp: When the slices of meat are dry, then we shall move. We shall move down over on Milk river [literally: Little creek]. Close by [that river] are the better buffalo. We shall skin [for lodges]. Again he cried around the camp: We shall move. We shall make a circle [to chase the buffalo]. We shall camp on Bad-water [a lake]. They camped. The lodges were all put up. Everything was quiet in the camp [literally: they – the lodges – were all quiet]. And the chief said: Now begin to catch your horses. Then they went on a hunt. Then they got to the buffalo. They began to get on their horses. Then they chased the buffalo. The carcases were scattered all over. And they began to skin. They would take the teats of the cows with sucklings. There was foam on the back-fat from rubbing. They would go home with the carcases.

The horses that had meat on them would be taken all over [the camp]. They were what the married man presented [to their fathers-in-law]. The cooked ribs, that were all carried about, were the food given to the sons-in-law. Inviters would go about. When a man was still at home, [some people on the outside] then would say: A big herd of buffalo is coming towards the camp. The women would say: Over there is [a buffalo], that the people try to kill, that we may go to get the entrails. No one went ahead of them [the women] for the blood, when they went themselves to the carcases about. They camped a long time, where they got food. All their choice pieces of the meat got dry [during the time they were camping]. Then they dried their skinnings [the hides]. The strong women would quickly get the hair off their hides. The chief said: Come on, we shall move to the Many-berries [a local name]. We shall camp there. There is a young man who went far, he found out [that] the berries are ripe. Come on, you women, you may go for berries. And they had many berry-bags [literally: And many were their berry-bags]. In the evening they all came back from picking berries. The pickings

of that one [bunch of women] were sarvis-berries, goose-berries, white-berries [red-willow-berries]. That were the pickings of that one bunch of women. Their children would be delighted in eating the berries. The women prepared [an oil out of] the brains and the liver, mixed up [to oil the hides with]. There began to be many [hides] for their future lodges. They had done the oiling of the skins.

When they moved again, the chief said: We shall move. We shall camp at Buffalo-head [a local name]. There are many berries [of all kinds], [especially] cherries. They took them. When they had brought them home, they mashed them with the whole seed in them. They were picked for future use [for winter-time]. Then they moved again. The chief said: The buffalo is near the Seven-persons [a local name], we shall camp there, and there we shall chase elk. And there they camped. They gathered in a circle [to chase the elk]. Then they chased [the elk]. And there was much hot pemmican, tripe, guts. The choice parts were back-fat, flanks, belly-fat. They all had plenty of food. The chiefs would come together to decide, which way to move the camp. They did no move about [far], they only ate food. And there they moved about [just a little]. When the hides were all good, then [the chiefs] said: We shall move to the mountains [the Cypress hills]. We shall cut the lodge-poles. Then they started to move. Then they separated [by bands]. Then they would move this way. They camped over there at Long-lakes [a local name]. Then they moved again. The chief said: We shall move to Where-the-Women-society-left-their-lodge-pole [a local name]. And there are some [buffalo], we have still to chase. We moved back [towards the prairie].

The chief said: Come on, we shall move. We shall move to Green lake. And there they camped. Then stray-bulls were chased. They were taken to use their hides for Indian trunks. The women would use their hides to tie their travois with. The hair on the head [of the buffalo] was taken also. It was made into ropes. The same [hides] were also made into hard ropes. And the women made a string from the sinews [this string was used in tanning]. They began to tan the skins for the lodges. [The chief] would say: We shall move. We shall move to Writing-stone [a local name]. There are many berries, [especially] cherries. They camped there. The women did not go far for picking berries. And the mashed cherries were dry. They put them away. They put them in calf-sacks. They were the berries for future use. In winter they would skim the grease with them, they would mix them with their pemmican, and they would make soup with them. [The chief] would say: We shall move up [alongside Milk river] to Woman's-point [a local name]. We shall camp about along the river. The meat about [the camp] is getting scarce. Then we had moved away [from the river]. Buffalo and antelopes commenced again to be shot. The prairie-antelopes were fat like dog-ribs. They had sweet livers. There was nothing, we would just look at [without killing it]. Wolves, badgers, skunks, prairie-antelopes were those, that we bought tobacco with.

[The chief] said: We shall cut our lodge-poles from Cut-bank river. When we were near to [the place], where we would cut our lodge-poles, the women would have completed their lodges. They would have done sewing them. Then they [the Peigans] moved fast. Then they camped. It is Cut-bank river, where they always cut lodge-poles from. They would watch the lodge-poles. When they were all dry, then they would stretch their lodges with them. And they would look like leaf-lodges. And it was late in the fall, the leaves would all be white. They began to eat guts [and] tripe. They began to make soup with them. One never turned his head away from the soup. They would begin to eat even hard-seed-berries. They were careful [literally: hard] women, [that] never would be hungry. Over there [near the mountains] it was, they camped about. Black-tails, deer, elk, moose, those were [the animals], they hunted for. These [people] were camped about [near the mountains], those were [the animals] they killed. When it snowed [first] in the fall, then they began to hurry, that they moved down [to the lower country]. There [down] on the river, there they would be camped about. There they waited, where the buffalo would come the nearest. To that place they

would move. They would carefully look, where they [themselves] would be during the winter. Then they camped in different places all along the river. They would make the corral [for their horses]. In the beginning of the winter they were all happy.

[The chief] would say: The buffalo would not set warm their [unborn] calves [that means: the buffalos would not have another place than their own bodies to hide their calves]. Then they [the people] were happy. When it cleared up, one person would see the buffalo. In the night he came back, and said: The buffalo are close by, they are many. In the morning you will hunt. They were all gone on a hunt. Then they would chase the buffalo. The buffalo's fur was good already. They [the people] liked the big heifers [four years old], [and] the heifers [two years old] very much. With those they wintered [that means: they ate them during the winter]. They would be like as if their hair were brushed. Oh, happy times there would be in the beginning of the winter, from the food that they got. They all came back home. [After] two, three, four, five [days] the buffalo would go away [from the neighbourhood of the Indians]. They [the buffalo] moved back [they would drift away north]. And here, where they were camped, they would just stay. They would be in a hurry for their robes [to tan them]. They jerked the skin-meat from them. Then they scraped them. Then they oiled them with the brains and the liver. Then they greased them. When they were soaked with grease, they had already warm water. Then they would pull the water [from the fire]. They poured the water on them. When they were soaked with water, they would twist them. [When] the water was all out of them [by twisting], then they would untie them. Then they tied them stretched. Then they began to scrape the moisture out of them. They scraped them with a broken stone. They would brush their fur with sticks. It [the hide] was a little dry, then they pulled it on a string. Then they put it down. Then they stretched it by stepping on it [by holding their feet on the ends]. Then they pulled it again on the string. There were some buffalo-bones, they were called shoulder-bones. With those they also scraped the hide.

Then they [the hides] were completed. Then there was nothing to think about [to worry about]. They had done making robes for themselves. The woman, and her husband, and her children, they all had robes for themselves. When they slept, they would sleep as if they were sleeping with fire [the robes were so warm!].

[When] the buffalo was far, the girls would cut a big tree over there. It would fall. She [a girl] would go up to it. Here, where she liked it, she would knock off the bark of it. She would hit it [the tree] lightly. Then she would peel from the same place [where she had been hitting]. The same size [as she had peeled] she would tear in two. She would eat it. It was very sweet. Then the girls and boys – many of them – would go. Over there on the hill-side they dug for false roots [a kind of eatable roots], rattle-sound-roots, [and] make-bleed-roots. Those they ate also. The children never became sick [because those roots were so healthy]. They would find the other [trees] to eat, they took all those trees. They peeled the bark from them. They ate also roseberries, [and] hard-seed-berries. And then there was earth-medicine [black alcali], it was earth. They licked it. All the mouths would be just white from it. That [the earth-medicine] prevented them from being sick [literally: they would not get sick from]. The women kept bull-berries through winter [literally: laid bull-berries over night]. They had them also for berries to use them afterwards. When they had real winter, they would provide for wood. The women would go on foot for wood. They would pack the wood on their back. When the wood was far to get, they would put the travois on a horse. They had covered their saddles from one end to the other [with raw-hide]. They carried wood on them [on the travois and the saddles]. They had profit from the travois. They valued it very much. When they had done carrying wood with it, then they began to coil up the ropes, attached to the travois, [for fear] that they might be eaten [by the dogs]. And the old woman had [also] profit from her dog. She would say: Just put it [the dog] short [that means: just put the travois on its neck]. That way she got her wood.

When she had done getting her wood, then she began to put her leg-bones together. She pulled out her stone to hammer the bones on, [and] her stone-hammer. She put her leg-bones down on her half of a hide. She would say: I shall make grease [from the bones]. Then she began to hammer them. She had already put her real pot on the fire. She would make the soup with one of the leg-bones. She had done hammering them. Then she would put the mashed bones in [the pot]. When it had boiled a long time, then she would pull it from the fire. She had already put the cherries [near her]. She took a horn-spoon. With that she skimmed. She put her skimmed grease in a big real [wooden] bowl. Then she had done skimming [the grease]. She put the cherries in [the bowl]. There was much [literally: far] of the cherries with skimmed grease. She told the women: You must get hot this soup of the leg-bones. Her daughter was already hammering the sirloin-dried-meat. [When] she had done hammering, she gave it to [her mother]. And she [the mother] mixed it [the dried meat] up with the skimmed grease [and cherries]. Then she made it all into one roll. She gave that to her son-in-law. He invited the old men.

It was winter again [it was the second big snow-storm], [and] then they went up to the prairie [from the river] to hunt. The calves were put in the pot [that means: were not too big for being put in the pot]. And then they began to get robes to buy with. Then they chased the buffalo. Even if it was very cold, they chased the buffalo with arrows. When it was extremely cold, they first stuck their hands in the snow, where they were to chase buffalo. They would put them [their hands] under their arms. Then they would put earth on them. Then they chased the buffalo. Those that shot hard would kill two [buffaloes]. They, [the hunters] were just as strong as their arrows. Their horses were of hard endurance, they could stand much cold. When the buffalo were far, [and] when the places where they camped a long time about became to be bad [dirty], then they moved notwithstanding [the cold], even if it was very cold. Their small children all cried for cold. [When] the buffalo were far, when it was really warm weather, the chief would cry out over the camp: We shall go on a hunt. We shall go with pack-horses, and stay for some days. They took the small old lodges. They took them for lodges [on the trip]. They went walking [slowly]. They would use thin willow-sticks for lodge-poles. [Where] men had two wives, their younger wives would go [with them] on a hunt. They [the husbands] took them along. Then they [the younger wives] were called "the chief-woman of the pack-hunt". Those chief-women of the pack-hunt had their faces black on the sides [because they did not wash them]. Then the calves were known, what size they were. According to their [the calves'] different sizes, we tied their shoulder-bones inside of the lodges. From the different sizes [of the shoulder-bones] we knew [the sizes of the calves].

As it was far in the winter, when the calves had hair on them, then it began to be spring. Then they [the calves] were of hated size [that means: they were too big, so that the Indians had to cut them in two]. And then the buffalo's fur was not good. Then they had summer, [and] then it was, [that] they quit getting robes to buy with [because the fur was not good]. Then they began quickly to make robes. The people counted for themselves [the number of the robes]. One person had twenty, thirty, forty robes to buy things with. Those that had not good horses suffered for [want of] something to buy with. They all went on [to the trading-post] to buy powder, hard cartridges, tobacco, white blankets, black blankets; such things they would buy. One blanket costed five robes, one blanket [another one] costed four robes. Powder [one gallon] costed one robe. A hundred cartridges costed two robes. Flints, [and] black gunsprings costed together one robe. Only four [plugs] of tobacco were [to be bought for] one robe. Of white tobacco they got eight [plugs], if it costed two robes. Such things they would buy. Then they would go home from buying. Then they came home after buying. Then they moved up on the prairie [from the river-side]. When they had moved on the prairie, the women had a big supply of lodge-pole-pins.

Then they hunted for the buffalo. They would move to the Cypress hills [literally: Striped earth]. They could not find the buffalo. There were not many places [literally: it was scarce], where they found the bulls. They moved down on the other side of the Wide-gap. The Round forest, that was the place they moved to. They would go to Much-drift-wood, [and] the Big Sandhills [local names] and [then] turn back. They turned back and moved up to Rotten-willow-wood [a local name]. They were moving this way to Buffalo-lip [and] Many-snakes [also local names]. They finally found the buffalo. Then they began to chase the buffalo. Then they moved about that way, where there were many buffalo. Those that hunted far gave the alarm [suspecting the enemy being near]. In the night the chiefs would talk. [They would say:] Do not go far. We have had alarm. Over there, where there are many buffalo, they ran away [scared by some people, enemies of this tribe]. They [the people of the camp] were careful, they would not turn loose their male horses. They would look at the Sun. If he [the Sun] had stripes on each side [the Sun-dogs], if he had often stripes on the sides, then they were very careful. All the horses were not driven far [from the camp]. After a short time the hunters, that did not listen [to the chiefs, and went far from the camp], were charged on [by the enemies]. Then suddenly there would be said: A certain one was killed. He was scalped. His relations began to go about crying. All his relations would suffer. And they would put weeds cut-up with tobacco in a pipe. And they went crying to him [the medicine-man]. To that man, who was walking about, they gave the pipe. They would say to him: Now here is your smoke. Pity me, I have suffered. Pity me, that I may have revenge. Let the nights not be many, that I see [that means: before I see] a scalp.

That man [the medicine-man] would say: We are not women, that we only cry. Then he [the same man] would get on his horse, then he would run around. The people [that followed him] were getting many. They ran near the lodges. The women then yelled. The young men that felt brave yelled. They sang [their war-songs] to themselves. That man [the medicine-man] then would say: We shall also make cry our enemies. Then they began to catch their horses. As they knew their long-winded [literally: hard-winded] horses, [and] hard-runners, they would take those along with them. They started. The warriors went on horseback. They went around, where they were hidden from view. Two strong brave men went ahead to look about. They were the scouts. They went that way, where the coulees were about [they followed the coulees]. They saw the camp [of the enemies]. Then they ran back. When they saw the people [their own party] over there, then they yelled: u' u´ +. The warriors then crowded one another about. They were told: The cranes [that means: the scouts] are coming. They really saw [the enemies]. They [the cranes] made a circle. There was a big [literally: a far-reaching] circle [formed by the main part of the warriors, after they had seen the cranes making a circle]. The leader of the party alone went back to them [the cranes]. He was told the news by them. He was told by them: Close by they [the enemies] are camped. He [the leader] alone told his coups. When they all heard it [that the enemies were camped close by], they were happy. Many of them were singing [war-songs] to themselves. And a brave young man sang words in his song: To-day you will know me. I shall take one of the guns [of the enemies' guns]. If I do not take one of them, then put a woman's dress on me.

Then they [the warriors] would go on. Then they came near to [the enemies]. They sat near by them. They looked at them, that one of them might run out on the prairie. It was not a long time, then two of them [of the enemies] ran out from the camp. Then they [the warriors of the war-party] crowded one another. Then they [the same warriors] got on their horses. They warned each other: Wait, wait! Let us charge on them close [that means: when they are close by]. When they [the two enemies] were close by, then they [the warriors] made a charge on them. The horse of that young man [that sang the song] was fast. That one [that young man] overtook them [the two enemies] first. They [the two enemies] jumped off their horses. That young man had a plume for top-knot. He

also jumped off in front [of them two]. Then they made a charge on one another. He [the Peigan] was shot at by one of them. He [the Peigan] jumped at him in spite [of his shooting]. He took his [the enemy's] gun from him. He killed him. That way he got a gun. One of them [of the two enemies] had arrows. And another [Peigan] took his quiver and arrows [from him]. And the other people took his scalp. There they [the enemies] were, there they [the Peigans] killed them. They [the enemies who were scalped] had only their ears left. Then they [the Peigans] ran to escape. They ran home. They were not chased by him [by the enemy], they were not found by him. Then they had a good scalp-dance [before they arrived in the camp of the Peigans]. [When] they were near the camp, then they camped. They put up shades. Then they tied up their scalps. Then they mashed up char-coal. They blacked their faces with it. They ran down the coulees. When the lodges were close by, that one that had a relative killed [by the enemy] blacked his face all over. Then they [the returning warriors] gave a signal to the circle-camp. Then all the people [in the camp] crowded each other about. Then they [the returning warriors] were known: We shall have a circle in sight. Then they [the people in the camp] made a rush out. We ran singing scalp-songs. Then they [the returning warriors] ran through the camp. We were shooting. We began to run across one another.

And that one that got a gun ran ahead [of his companions]. When he ran into the camp, we – all the people – were shooting. Then he told what he had done: There he lies, where I shot him down. I took his gun from him. And then the women yelled for him. He then entered his lodge. After a short while the Women-society gathered. They [the women of that society] went to him. They came to the lodge of him who had killed [an enemy] and counted coup. They had there a happy dance. All his relations gave presents for him [to the dancing women]. Horses [and] things were the presents they made. And the Women-society also would go to the other one who had taken the quiver and arrows and counted coup. They also had a happy dance for him [in his honour].

There were many things given to them [to the dancing women] by him [by his relations] for presents. And the Women-society would also have a happy dance for still another one who killed an enemy. And there were many things again given to them by him [by his relations]. They hurried one another: Come on, make haste, all of you, men, that we may have the scalp-dance. You must put paint on the faces of your wives. They [your wives] will shake their heads [dance]. They [the men] put on the war-bonnets, the war-bonnets with tails down the back [literally: the war-bonnets standing straight up], [and] the horn-war-bonnets. They [the men] would put on shields, they would pack them on their backs. They would also pack medicine-pipes on their backs. They put sleigh-bells on their necks. They also put on weasel-tail-suits. Some of them would use spears as canes while dancing, others would use bows as canes while dancing, and the wife of him who had taken the gun would use that gun as a cane while dancing. And there was a big scalp-dance. Now the women began to shake their heads [to dance]. They already held their fans. They [the fans] looked like snow-birds [literally: shoulder-bone-tail-feathers]. That young man that took the gun was just led round about through the crowd by an old man. And he [this old man] was singing old man's songs [praises] to him.

And he was pursued by those people, one of whom he had killed. [They came near the Peigan camp.] Then they [the Peigans] made a charge on them. Then they [the Peigans] had a fight with them. All the women ran out fast. They put their robes on the lodges, on high where the lodge-poles were tied together. They [the Peigans] continued to fight during the day. They [the women] only heard the sound of the guns. The guns were only heard. In the evening they would stop. Then they quit fighting. The dead were taken home. They [the dead] were laid across on horses. They put the rich ones inside of their own lodges. In the forests their lodges were put up. There they were put inside, when they were killed. Their horses [the horses of the dead] were killed [near them, that they might accompany their masters], and all the things that

belonged to them were put in there [in the lodges]. All their horses, that were not killed, had their tails and manes cut. Their mothers had their little fingers chopped off. And their wives had also their little fingers cut. Their sisters had also their little fingers cut. They [the women] would cut their legs [just skin-deep]. They would cut off their hair. The widow suffered most [of all]. The father of the dead married man stuck himself. He stuck himself with arrows. That he might suffer more, that man would cut also his upper-legs. He had his hair all cut off. The companions of the dead one all suffered in the same way.

They [the Peigans] moved to Maria's river [Bear creek]. And there would be some young men saying: Let us go on a raid. Then they [some others] said: Yes. Then they began to have moccasins [made]. Then they would tell their sisters: Make me moccasins, sew ten pair of moccasins for me. Then they [the sisters] began to put the soles on them. Then he [the young man] was given things to patch up his moccasins. He would put an awl [and] a sinew in his awl-case. He would sew the awl to his bullet-sack. All the things that he would take were complete. They [the young men] built sweat-lodges for those that they knew to be old medicine-men. Then they would put tobacco in a pipe. They would say to that old man: You have a sweat-lodge [built for you]. Then they would be told by him: I shall go there, I shall sweat there. Then he would go in, at the upper end [of the sweat-lodge] he would sit. Then he [the young man] would hand him his smoke: Here is your smoke. That is your pipe. This is your horse [he says this giving him one]. Try hard, paint my face. He [the old man] would say prayers for him, that he might get a horse, that he might go about on his raids allright. [The old man would say:] And over there, a little way from the camp [of the enemy], you will get a horse. Among the lodges you will take [the horses] that are tied. I give you a striped one. Then he [the old man] had done putting paint on his [the young man's] face. He [the old man] would give him his top-knots [tail-feathers] to carry them. Then they began to roll their things up. His rope, his whip, his moccasins, his buffalo-skin [to patch up his moccasins], those were the things, he would roll together. Then they began to hurry each other. They stood in front of one of the lodges. They took hold of the parfleches. They drummed on them, they rattled their sticks on them. The women sang with them. Then they [the young men] scattered in different directions. Then they went home to get their things.

And that way over there they started during the night. Then they camped in the night. In the morning then they started again. Then they came to a river. They began to float pieces of ice. Two of them then began to strip their clothes off. They just put on their fire-steels, [and] their rotten pieces of wood [to make fire with] as top-knots [that these might not be wet]. They went on ahead across the river to build a fire. They built a fire. They had built a big fire. And those others all went in [the water]. They had each of them a hold of their raft. Two of them were the leaders. They were nearly frozen in the water, because the water was so cold. It was winter when they went on the raid. They pulled their raft ashore. Then they began to dress up. They had done warming themselves. Then they left the fire. They came to the forest. There they camped. They began to clear the snow, which was deep. They had done clearing the snow, then they would make a lodge. They would make a lodge of sticks. They would put in rye-grass for beds. Because it was so cold, they did not go on. Then the leader said: Go and hunt. We shall not go on, it is very cold. Then two of them hunted. They were not far, then they saw a few buffalo-cows. One of them went up to shoot. It was a very fat buffalo-cow [literally: a bear-cow], what he killed. They began to skin. Then they began to tie the pieces of meat together [to pack them], and the rest [what they could not pack on their backs] they dragged along [on the snow]. Then they began to go. They came near their lodge. They called ahead for help. There were three that stretched their hands back [that means: that went back to the two hunters to help them to bring in the meat]. And there they were, they came back with the meat. They sat happy.

They put some of the entrails on a piece of bark for the leader, that he might eat them. These young men then began to make roasts in a hurry. The ribs of one side were staked up [near the fire]. They [the ribs] would shoot their juice into the fire. They [the ribs] looked like a short-back butte. All their roasts were cooked. They put them on willows, those they use for plates. On those they put their cooked meat. And then they split the ribs. Then they broke the ends of the ribs. All of them would provide the leader first. In the morning the younger ones among them would make the fire. Then they went on. It was not cold then. It was a fine day. They went happy about. One would run ahead, that he might see people of the other tribe. Then they shot again [something to eat]. Then they took half of the hide. Then they camped. They all packed the pieces of meat [on their backs]. One of them took the crow-guts. They cut the boss-ribs off. Then they began to make their lodge. They got through building their lodge. One of the young men began to cut the meat off from the skin. He put stones of small size all in the fire. He began to sharpen sticks, forked sticks. He put them on four corners. He hung the hide on [the four sticks]. He poured water [on the hide]. He just cut the meat down to the ends of the boss-ribs. He then put them [the boss-ribs] in the pot [meaning: on the hide]. With that stick, the forked stick, he put one of the stones in the pot. He put five more stones all in the pot. Then the hide-pot began to boil. It boiled over. Then he pulled out half of the stones. Then he put again some more stones in the pot. He pulled them out again. Then he put again some more stones in the pot to make it boil harder. They [the boiling pots] do not listen [that means: do not quit boiling], when they once start to boil. They had done boiling meat, and from those [the boiled boss-ribs] they got all they wanted to eat.

In the night a young man began to prepare [to cook] the crow-guts. He made them holy. They were cooked. They began to cool the guts. Then they prayed. [The guts] were given to the last one [the man sitting on the end]. Then he prayed with them [with the guts]. He said: May

I get a horse from those people, we are going to, a fine one, a good one [and] may we get them [the horses] allright. When we get back home, I will talk from myself to a [certain] woman over there at home, that I may become her relation [meaning: her husband]. This [piece of gut], [that] I shall bite off, is she [represents that woman, or, rather, is dedicated to her]. Those others would all say the same. After a short while they found the enemy. Then they went on. [The leader] would say to one of the young men: Go on ahead as a scout. And that way over there he went off on a run. He [the leader] told him what to do: If you do not see anything over there, I will get there [meaning: you must wait there for me]. Then [the leader and his party] came there. Then he [the leader] would say to him [the scout]: Did you suspect anything? He was told by [the scout]: Where there are many of them, there these buffalo stampede [because there are people near]. Let us be careful. To-day there must be nobody shooting [literally: that he might shoot]. We shall try hard, that we get close over there, where the buffalo stampede. There we shall sleep about. Come on, now quickly make a fire, that we may cook. We shall not make a fire, where we are to sleep. Cook here food enough, that you will carry with you. This night we shall travel on during the night. Close before day-light we shall camp. Then we shall sleep.

The sun went down, then they went instead [of going in day-time], they went during the night. They would sit down now and then [to rest]. Then they would go again. After they had travelled a long time, they would sit down again. Then they began to smoke. When they had done smoking, then they started again. Towards morning, [when] the morning-star was coming up, then we would camp. They would clear the snow. There they lay down [literally: they doubled up]. They slept a while. Then it was early in the morning. And two of them were called upon: Run on ahead. After you have run a long time, then we shall go on [and follow up]. They did not make fire. And they ate the food that they carried. It [the food] was frozen hard. [When] they had done eating about, then they started. During the time of his sleep the leader

was singing. He had a dream. He said [when he woke up]: The one that painted my face, told me: Be careful. I give you a great many horses. If you are careful, it will be good. I still give you a striped horse. You will cut him loose [from his stake]. His companions were many. This is what that one, that had a dream, said [to them]. These boys were all happy from that dream of his. Then they went on. They were still travelling. They suddenly saw the scouts running. Then they [the war-party] stopped. Then they saw them [the scouts] running in a circle, while they were yelling: uwú+. There they [the war-party] were, [there] they stopped. They made a pile of buffalo-chips, and the leader went back to meet them [the scouts, who would come up and run around those buffalo-chips and knock them over, so that the war-party immediately knew, that they had seen the enemy]. He said to them: Did you really see [the enemy]? They told him: We really saw [him]. He is close by still chasing buffalo. He [the leader] began to look about the forest.

There they made a small fire. Then we began to put on other moccasins. [When] they had done putting on their moccasins, they began to stretch out their ropes. They smoothed the earth. They pulled a charcoal from the fire. On that they made their incense. They began to untie their top-knots. They held them over there over their incense. Then they prayed: Pity me, I am very poor. May I go straight to a good horse. And they painted their faces with the paint. [When] they had done painting their faces, they sang [war-songs] to themselves. When the sun was over on that side, late in the evening, then they began to run towards the camp [to steal horses]. The sun was down, then they tried hard. After a short while, in the night, they would come up to [the camp]. They would hear the dogs bark. They would sit by it [by the camp]. They would wait for him [for the enemy], that he might go to sleep. They would look at him [from where they sat]. One [of the war-party] would find out about the horse-corral. He would tell him [the leader]: They have a very strong corral. [The leader said:] We shall go to tear the corral somewhere about. That young man [that had made a vow] then would take out his knife, he would begin to sharpen it. He would say: even if he [the owner of the horse] holds the rope in his hands, that is tied to [the horse], I shall cut him [the horse] loose. I shall cut his [the owner's] fingers.

Now he [the enemy] was asleep. The leader would say: I shall take one [of you] with me [to the camp]. The two [the leader and the other one] went towards [the camp]. They got to the lodges, and they began to look about, where it was the weakest part [of the corral]. There they would tear it [the corral] down. Then they would enter the corral, and the leader would begin to look at the many horses. A good striped horse, such a one he had found. He pulled out his knife. He cut him [the horse] loose. Then he also cut loose another good horse. He led [his horses] out. He told his younger brothers over there: He [the enemy] is really asleep. Four [of you] must go again. And the other one with whom he went to the camp was also back. He had also two [horses] that he cut loose. And then they ran for escape. They were all together. They still were running for escape. Over there in a coulee they came to many horses. Then they drove them. And then it was cold. It was foggy. It was that leader himself, that caused a change of the weather of the day, that he might not be found by those people he stole from. During the night he tried hard, he made his flight all night. In the morning he tried hard again, that he might get far away. Finally it was night, [and] while they were making their escape, after a long time, during the night, they all got off from their horses just for a moment. They smoked. It [the tobacco] was all burned up. Then they began to get on their horses again. Then they started again to make their escape.

Finally it was morning again. The sun was rising high. [The leader said:] now, begin to get off about [just where you stop]. We are already far off. We have [now] really camped [that means: we can now stay here for a while, and cook our food]. [Afterwards the leader would say:] Now, get on your horses again. [Our people] must be singing praise-songs to us [now]. Then they started again. They drove their horses on foot, because it was cold. And when they got tired, then they saw the

buffalo. He [the leader] told that young man [that had made a vow]: Taste for yourself now [that means: try your horse's speed by chasing the buffalo]. He caught his horse. He got on it. He chased the buffalo. He overtook a very fat buffalo-cow [literally: a bear-cow]. He killed it. They all came up to him. Then they skinned it. They cut one side in different pieces. They took those for a seat [putting them on their horses instead of a saddle]. From the same [half of the hide] it was, [that] they made stirrups. Then they came to a forest. Then they made fire. Then they cooked. Then they made a hole in the ice. With their knives they made a hole in the ice. When they had done eating, then they drank. Then they went away.

And they met some people [Indians] who were travelling to trade. They asked them [the traders] where their [own] lodges were. They were told by [the traders]: It is at Sweet-roots [a local name], where your lodges are. These Peigans camped along in different places. They [the war-party] saw their [own] lodges. Then they made a fire. Then they began to paint the faces of their horses. They would come in sight of the camp in a circle. They [the Peigans] put red stripes on the faces of white-faced horses. The red paint looks plain on white horses. When they had done painting their horses, they came up in sight [of the camp] in a circle. They sang while they were running. They worded their songs: I run in a circle. That way they worded their songs. Then they were heard. And then all the people ran out on a charge to them. [Now all the people would say:] We run in a circle. The old men then sang their praises. Then their relations, their fathers would come to them. They were kissed by all of them. They separated going home to their lodges. They gave horses to their sisters. They also gave horses to their elder brothers. Their fathers went about the camp to invite the people. Then [when the people were together] they began to tell the news, how they went [on their trip], how they travelled about, how they got horses, how they cut loose the horses. About those things they told the news. And then they were given a big meal of berry-pemmican.

Then the strong warrior was picked out, that he might be a son-in-law. A chief's daughter, a child of plenty, was driven home to that young man. He gave ten head of horses [to the girl's father]. That many he gave for his wife. In the same way the man, that had him for son-in-law, also gave the holy things [he owned] to his son-in-law. And in winter-time he [the son-in-law] would get food for him. He [the father-in-law] had him for a child. He called him his son. And the young-married man called him father. The old women were very much ashamed of [their sons-in-law]. They could not see them. When the young-married man went on a hunt, he took his wife with him. When the young-married man came back with the meat, he only got off [his horse]. His wife would just take all the horses that carried the meat to her father's lodge. Those were the ones that he gave to his father-in-law [properly he did not give the horses, but only the meat carried by them]. That woman [the mother-in-law] would pull the meat down [from the horses]. All the choicest parts of the meat he gave to his father-in-law. And if the girl [the young-married woman] was foolish, if she had a side-husband, then he [her husband] would kill her. He would not be ashamed of her father, his father-in-law.

In summer they [the Peigans] had a dance. They called their dance "scrape-leg-dance". The chiefs went through the camp crying, that they would have a dance: Come on, make haste, that we may have a scrape-leg-dance. They called some other dances of theirs their "main-dances". Their warriors owned those [main-dances]. The women gambled. It was with bones, that they gambled. There were four of them [of those bones]. This is the length of the bones. This way they threw them. [Saying the last two sentences Blood showed me, how long the bones were, and how they were thrown]. They called two of them "snakes". The other two, if they turned over, were called "six". If the two turned over twice, then they were called "falling on the edge". Another [game] [that] the women [had] [is as follows]: they peeled sticks. They were long sticks. They played a stake-game with them. It was called the "stake-game." That is

the way, the women played. The men had a wonderful game. They had ten [sticks] for pointers. The [stick] of [the players on] one [side] was long, it was a hider [to be hidden in the hand]. And the [stick] of those on the other side was short. Those were the [sticks], they hid. A good player won the game. There were some that dreamed about the stick-game. They [those that had such dreams] were called the "wonderful hiders".

Then they had another game. They put sticks on each end. They knocked [the ground] smooth. Then they threw loose earth [over that ground] in good shape [so that it was level]. They put buffalo-chips on the back-side [of the sticks]. I heard, [that] they split beaver-teeth in two [to make the circle of the gambling-wheel]. They put them [those teeth] together. Then they wrapped them together. They took [the bark] off from the red willows. That way [Blood said this, while he was showing to me, how] they cut [the willow-bark] in different pieces. With those they made the counters. That is the way, they made the gambling-wheel. With arrow-shooting they started the wheel-game. They [the players] put their clothes on a bet. They were clothes of old lodges. They put their leggings also on a bet. On those they used counters. [When] they had done putting them about [when they had done putting a value on each article], then they began to roll the wheel and shoot against one another. They would say: We will [stop and] have a drink for a moment. And others would say: Is it deep? [that means: if you do not shoot, it is a go!] If it was not deep on the other side, [one] would have none, if he happened to forget, that it should be deep [that means: if the other one did not shoot, his partner would have no points, if he happened to forget to shoot]. [When] they would begin to play the wheel-game, their partners were sitting over there. They sat for the things that they put a bet on [to keep counters]. When they gained a point, they [the others] would say to them: Give me one point. And the other one would also gain a point. He would say to his partner: Partner, give me two points. When they beat one another, [the one that lost] was made to walk the prairie [that means: he had to put a bet on things, he had not with him, but in his lodge]. [Then he would say:] Let me begin to make my bets. His robe was a cow-skin. A young man would also put on a bet his arrows, his saddles – they were [so-called] prairie-chicken-traps –, the belly-part of his robe – his saddle-blanket –, his outside-top-saddle-blanket; those were the things he put on a bet. That was the way, the people of long ago used to bet, [and] used to play.

[Some of the following particulars refer, of course, to a more remote period than that, of which Blood has given a picture in the foregoing pages.] The robes of the old women were made of strips [sewed together]. Their dresses were made of old lodges. They used to sew them with the sinews of the buffalo. Bones were their awls. Very few [of the ancient Peigans] had antelope-dresses. All the other people wore old lodges for clothing. From an old lodge they made their leggings. Their robes were made from the hides of young buffalo [literally: were young buffalo]. They were buffalo killed in the fall of the year. Stones were their pots. From those they got their food. Bones were their scrapers. Sticks [and] stones were things, they [also] scraped with. Their arrow-points were stones, they were flints. Their knives were flint. There were no horses. They packed their lodges on dogs. There [on the dogs] they would put them. Some of the people put their beddings also on [dogs]. And they packed the other things themselves [on their own backs]. In summer-time they moved about. Those were the people, [that] were always corralling. From that they got plenty to eat. When it would soon be winter, they were already near [the places], where the fowl changed their feathers. Around the lakes they began to pick up the wings. The men had their arrow-sticks and their round sand-stones [to smooth the arrows] as useful things. When it was winter, they used to move down [to the river]. They would not camp away from all these corrals [and] cliffs of rocks. They used to have hard-seed-berries for the winter. They also used to have roseberries for the winter. And there were some [roots] that were called sweet-roots. And there were others, [called] turnips, they

were all over. In winter the men had strips of robes for caps. That is what I know about them, what I heard about them [about the people of the olden times]. I do not know very well about them [this refers to the things, he only knows by tradition].

[Cf. Wissler's monographs mcbi and slbi, and also the alphabetical indexes of Grinnell blt and McClintock ont].

Monday, June 12.

In 1910 Tatsey told Uhlenbeck another story about ancient Piegans and how a few of their lodges came about, obt, 58–60.

The two buffalo-lodges.

The ancient Peigans lived north. The Elk river was close by. They moved. There were two persons, young men, [who] took their arrow-sticks. They went ahead. They said: Let us sit by the river. There they were. They began to shave their arrow-sticks. They sat there a long time. One looked into the water. He said to his partner: Partner, don't you see something here, where the water goes round? He answered him: No. He said to him: I see, there is a black-buffalo-painted lodge. I shall go in [into the water]. Look at me. Then he got up. Then, higher up [the river], he went in.

Under [the water] he then saw that lodge. He entered. There were two persons, the owners [of the lodge], a man and his wife. He [the man] said to him: You are welcome. He [the young man] sat down. He [the man] said to him: My son, now that you have seen my lodge, I shall give it to you. Look here on the inside and the outside. Fix it that way. In the future you will get profit by it. That way I give my lodge to you. Then that young man went out. Then he went ashore. He sat by his partner. He said to him: Did you see me? He answered him: I saw you, when you went into that lodge. He said [also] to him: Partner, [when] you went out [of the lodge], did you see there inside [in the water] another lodge, yellow-buffalo-painted? And there it is. It is there yet. He answered his partner: Yes, I saw it. Go on, partner, go in [into the water]. Then he got up. And then, higher up [the river], at the same place [as his partner went], he went in.

He was seen by his partner. He entered. There were two persons, the owners [of the lodge], a man and his wife. He [that man] said to him: You are welcome. And sit there. He said [also] to him: My son, now that you have seen my lodge, I shall give it to you. Look here on the inside and the outside. Fix it that way. In the future you will have profit from it. That way I give my lodge to you. Then that young man went out. He then went ashore. He sat by his partner. He said to him: Partner, our lodges are the same. Let it not be a long time, [before] we shall fix these lodges, which are given to us. If it is a long time, this man [who gave the lodges] may get angry with us. And they went home.

It was not after a long time, [that] they married. They immediately fixed their lodges, the one with a black buffalo painted on it, and the other with a yellow buffalo painted on it. These two persons lived there. From these [lodges] started the buffalo-painted lodges. And [now] it is complete [the story is at an end].

[Cf. G.B. Grinnell, American Anthropologist, N.S., vol. 3, pp. 658 sqq., and C. Wissler-D.C. Duvall, Mythology of the Blackfoot Indians, New York 1908, pp. 94 sq.]

Tuesday, June 13.

Grandmother is moved along with the family. In 1910 Tatsey told Uhlenbeck about a troublesome grandmother, who was not moved along, obt, 62.

An old woman left on a camp-ground.

The ancient Peigans moved from the place where they had camped a long time. There was an old woman, a very old woman, she was troublesome to her children. She was just left by them. She then got up. She walked that way on the road. When she was tired, she then crawled on her hands and on her knees. There was a war-party, [that] came round the old camp. They then followed the road that way. Ahead of them they saw, [that] there was something black. The leader of the war-party said to his companions: Let us walk fast. That one is moving. Then they came to that, which was a very old woman. She was crawling. He said to her: Poor thing, where is she going to? She said to him: My children left me. He said to his companions: We shall take her to the lodges. We shall carry her on our back, each in his turn. They carried her to the lodges. She said to the leader of the war-party: My son, I give you my old-woman's-age [that you may be as old as I am]. And he kept her until she died. That's all.

Wednesday, June 14.

Uhlenbeck reads to Brocky and his friend "Names of Clans," in obt, 1–4. Preface: "I have to add that Bear-chief and old Mountain-chief (Nínaistɑ́ku) gave their assistance in collecting the details about the origin of some clan-names. Still there are quite a few more, on which I could not get any information as to their origin."[32]

Names of Clans.

1. Fat-melters they were named long ago, because they liked to eat fat. As they were always melting fat, even when they had supplies [of meat], they were melting.
2. Not-laughers they were called long ago, because they were laughers. People reversed their names, [calling them] Not-laughers.
3. Long ago there was a chief, called Red-man. Then there was another chief, with whose [literally: his] wife he [Red-man] ran away. They went to the Crows. When they got there to the Crows, he said to his wife: What is it you will ride with? She told him: Medicine-bags, and a shield, and something to cover [those things]. And – [he asked her] – what colour [of horse] will you ride on? And [what colour of horse] will you put your pack on? I shall ride – [she said] – on a black-striped back. I shall put my pack on a bay-striped back. What – [he said] – will you use as a saddle? I shall use as a saddle – [she said] – a saddle with two sides up. And then they started home. When they were close to their camp, they camped. That woman was afraid of her former husband. She said to Red-man: I fear, my husband will kill me. He said to her: No, he will not do you any harm. Here are buffalo-chips. Take them. When he is angry, throw then one into the fire. Say every time: Here is a buffalo-chip. When all have been thrown in – there are four of them – he will not do you any harm. He will be glad, that he got horses, and that he got a shield and [having got] those medicine-

bags. Since that time they [that means: the clan of the former husband] were called Buffalo-chips.

4. Small-robes they were called, because their robes were small.

5. The chief of the Bug-people was bad [he had syphilis], he was eaten [by bugs, which according to the Indians were the cause of syphilis]. Then these were called Bug-people.

6. Lone-eaters they were called, [because of] their chasing [the buffalo] by themselves, and their eating by themselves [without inviting others]. They are stingy people.

7. All-medicine-men they were called, because they all acted as medicine-men. Even the young ones doctored. They got All-chiefs as another name, because they all acted as chiefs. Even the young ones acted as chiefs.

8. Blood-people they were called a long, long time ago, [because] their chief's pleasure was his chasing [the buffalo] and getting the blood. He never failed in all his chases [of buffalo] to save the blood, [because] he liked to eat it. From the blood they were called Blood-people.

9. Black-patch-people they were called, because they were dirty-looking. They used to patch their moccasins.

10. Eat-before-others they were called, [because] their chief never invited [anybody to feast with him], as before all the people got up, they had done eating. When his younger brothers were going to war, they ate by themselves. When their companions [belonging to other clans] got up early, they were suddenly seen by them, [that] they had already done eating. They are called from it: Eat-before-others.

11. The Skunks were nearly all bad [that means: they had syphilis]. There were many single women; they were all bad. Because they smelt bad, these people were called Skunks, [for] they were eaten [by bugs, that were supposed to be the cause of syphilis].

12. Because they were mean and fighting, the Pelicans camped alone.

When they moved to the [other] ancient Peigans, they got into fight, and they moved away. From that they were called Pelicans [the proper meaning of moχkámi "pelican" is a "bunch by themselves"].

13. Hard-top-knots they were called, [because] their chiefs were all medicine-pipe-owners and wore the top-knot. From that these people were called Hard-top-knots.

14. Lone-coffee-makers they were called, [because] their chief's wife used to make coffee for herself alone in a small coffee-pot.

15. Black-door's they were called, because their lodges had small doors. They made them black with grease [by rubbing them every time they went in].

16. There was a rough-mouth chief, [that] had a moustache, and his children were then called Rough-mouth's.

17. The father of the Short-neck's had a very short neck [literally: his neck was very short]. They all resembled him. Therefore these people were called Short-neck's.

18. The chief of the White-breast's, [called] Iron-shirt, had a sister. That woman was white-headed. She was a bad woman, she was a whore. She was called White-breast [on account of] her having white hair and [because she had] an albino-breast.

19. The chief of the Lone-fighters was very quarrelsome. He was always thinking of having a fight. When he fought, all his children and younger brothers helped him. They were then known by the people, that they were fighters. Therefore they were called Lone-fighters.

On this day, June 14, Walter Mountainchief showed up, and directly asked for De Josselin de Jong. Uhlenbeck dedicated Patronymics and Proper Names of the Peigans, Appendix II, to him and his family. See Appendix A of this volume. Another Blackfoot text Uhlenbeck might have read to Brocky and his friend could have been "A woman sacrificed to a butte," obt., 62–63.

A woman sacrificed to a butte.

There was a man, [that] slept on the Small Sweetgrass hills. He saw in a dream, there was a man. That was the one, which he slept on [viz. the butte]. He [the butte] said to him: I don't pity anybody. Now, if you give me a woman, I shall pity you. He said to him: Yes, I shall give you [a woman]. When he woke up, he went home. He took his youngest wife to that butte. They stood on it. Then he said: Partner, here is the woman, I give you. [He killed her.] Since that time that man became a great medicine-man in war [that means: he became a great warrior with super-natural power]. He became a chief by it.

Bear Chief's story late that night might have been another version of "The elk and his wife," nsbt, 99–101. Preface: "Told by Bear-chief (Nínoxkyàio), interpreted by Tatsey."

The elk and his wife. Another version.

There was an elk-bull, and his wife was a female elk, and he was jealous of her. She ran away from that elk-bull. He called on the crow. He said to him: Look for my wife. He was told by him: Yes, I shall look for her.

That crow then started to fly away. He flew to [a place], where there were many elks. Then he saw there one [female] elk, sitting [literally: she sat] by herself, away from the others. He flew to her, he lighted down on her back. She jumped up. Then he knew, [that] it was the elk-bull's wife. The crow then flew back. He said to the elk-bull: There is your wife, I have found her. Then he [the crow] went with him [to her], then they came to her. That elk-cow saw, that her husband had come. Then she told her husband: Now this is the reason why I went away. It was bad, that you falsely said to me, [that] I was stealing a young man [that means: that I had sexual intercourse with a young man]. She told her husband: Here is a big tree. If you knock it down, you are right, [that] I steal a young man. If you don't knock it down, if I knock it down, I am right, [that] I do not steal a young man. And that elk-bull used his full medicine-power, and butted it. He could not knock down that tree.

And that elk-cow got up. She asked her husband: Will you call on some one for help? That elk-bull said to the crow: Go and tell the moose-bull [to come and help me]. The crow flew to him, and brought him back. And that moose kicked the tree. He could not fell it by kicking it. And that elk-cow said to them: You have not been right. She herself butted the tree. She felled the whole of it. And the wise woman, that elk-cow, was told by the moose: You are a wise woman, here are my hoofs, I help you with them. Tie them to your wooden pin. And the crow told the elk-bull: Here are my tail-feathers. Your wife there is already a wise woman, you will be with her, when she makes the medicine-lodge. You will wear them [the feathers] on your head. And this is it, that the medicine-lodge started from. And that is all.

[Cf. The first version of this story above, and the reference given at the end of it.][33]

Thursday, June 15.

The funny story Uhlenbeck may have been reading to the thick man and his womanfolk is "Whom-the-buffalo-inquires-after," obt, 65–66.

Whom-the-buffalo-inquires-after.

There was a man, [who] was named Wolf-going-west. He was secretly called Whom-the-buffalo-inquires-after [because of the following incident]. There were two persons, women he had intercourse with, talking about him. There was another woman, [who] went to them. She said to them: What are you talking about? Why are you laughing? They told her: There is a Whom-the-buffalo-inquires-after, we are laughing at him. [There was no such man in the camp, but the women invented that name, not wishing to betray Wolf-going-west.]

Friday, June 16.

Uhlenbeck works with Tatsey to finish a story. It might have been the one in nsbt, 66. Preface: Told and interpreted by Tatsey.

The Chinook and the blizzard.

The ancient Peigans were camping about in the lower country. That winter there was a river, they would go up from to hunt. Spring was near. There was a chief that hunted. He looked west. He saw a man [coming]. He [that man] was running east. He had all his hair tied in front as a top-knot. As he [that man] ran, this snow was melting. A warm wind came to him [to the chief]. That chief then knew him: That is the Old Man. He [the Old Man] had run far [past the chief]. Then he [the Old Man] went back. From there he [the chief] saw him [last]. When he [the chief] came home, he began to tell about him. That is why we say now, when in winter-time [literally: in winters], there is an oily [warm] wind [the chinook]: The Old Man has run down [from the Mountains].

The same [people], that were camping, went all up on a hunt. It was far away on the prairie, where they chased the buffalo. There was one chief, [that] was looking north. He said: Make haste, there comes a person on foot, he is running this way. They had all done skinning. Then they came together [in one place]. Then the person on foot came running too close. That chief said: Wait, let us look at him; what will he do? He [the man on foot] was near by, he just ran close by them. All those that hunted saw him. His leggings were of cow-skin, his shirt was the same. He was shooting his arrows ahead. He was looking back. He had run past them, and there came a blizzard. Those that were hunting nearly all froze. Then he was known: That is he, that makes the winter. Then he was called the Good Old Man. Because he was a bad person, he was called the reverse of it. Now every winter [literally: all winters] we say: The Good Old Man makes winter. And the Old Man makes the oily [warm] wind. Winter comes from the north. The oily wind comes from the west. The Old Man and the Good Old Man chase each other back. In spring the Old Man has the victory. And that is what we know about the Old Man and the Good Old Man.

Saturday, June 17.

John Tatsey provides Peigan inflexions. Examples of such inflexions are found in many of Uhlenbeck's papers, such as in Some General Aspects of Blackfoot Morphology (1914:33, 35; English translations by Inge Genee).

Blackfoot	English translation
nitsíksipau(a)	"I bite him/her"
kitsíksipau(a)	"you bite him/her"
siksipíu(aie)	"he/she bites him/her"
nitsíksipoko	"I am bitten (by somebody)"
kitsíksipoko	"you are bitten (by somebody)"
síksipáu	"he/she is bitten (by somebody)"

Another example is from the 1916 paper in Dutch "*Het passieve karakter van het verbum transitivum of van het verbum actionis in talen van Noord-Amerika*," where we find the following forms on p. 189 (the translations into Dutch are by C. C. Uhlenbeck, who did not indicate that "he" can also be read as "she." English translations are by Inge Genee):

Blackfoot	Dutch translation	English translation
nitáinoko	"ik word gezien"	"I am seen"
kitáinoko	"jij wordt gezien"	"you are seen"
nitáinok	"hij ziet mij"	"he/she sees me"
kitáinok	"hij ziet jou"	"he/she sees you"
nitáinoau	"ik zie hem"	"I see him/her"
kitáinoau	"jij ziet hem"	"you see him/her"
áinoau	"hij wordt gezien"	"he/she is seen"

[*Editor*: Actually, Uhlenbeck had planned to publish his "materials on Blackfoot grammar" before the end of 1913. In the Preface to obt, v, he wrote on this matter]:

Sunday, June 18.

During my stay in Blackfoot reservation, from the 11th of May till the 15th of August 1910, I collected vast materials on Blackfoot grammar, and if I am not thwarted by unforeseen circumstances, I shall publish them before the end of 1913. These grammatical materials were written down from the mouth of many people, mostly boys and young fellows, who were kind enough to allow me in their leisure-hours to interrogate them about intricate matters. With gratitude I remember the afternoons spent with some of the Mission boys, or the evenings in my tent, when surrounded by young Indians, I wrote down my notes, sitting on a trunk, by the light of a lantern. With gratitude I remember many of their faces and their names, though it would be scarcely possible to retain all of them in my memory. Afterwards all my notes were verified by Joseph Tatsey, and so I am quite sure, I have a sound basis for a scientific description of the Blackfoot language.

Though I was recommended by the Dutch Government and by the Royal Academy of Amsterdam, the American authorities did not do very much to facilitate my connections with the Indians, and my linguistic investigations among them. The more I appreciate the generous help, I received from the Reverend Fathers of the Holy Family Mission, the more I am grateful for the true friendship, which was shown to me by some educated members of the noble Peigan tribe.[34]

The Uhlenbecks miss the Grass dance but do attend a Beaver bundle opening. One beaver story is in nsbt, 93–95, "The woman and the Beaver." Preface: "Told and interpreted by Walter Mountain-Chief."[35]

The woman and the beaver.

There was a man, [who] camped alone. He liked trapping about [literally: his liking was his trapping about]. Then he came to St. Mary's lake. Then he camped there. [After] he had camped there a long time, he was trapping a beaver. Then his youngest wife went after water. She came to [the place], where she was to get her water. She saw, there was a young man, who was standing [by her]. He told her: I have come to see you [and to get you]. And that woman told him: I don't know you. And he told her: No, let us go home together. Now I made think your husband [by means of my supernatural power], that he should camp here on St. Mary's lake, so that he might trap about. For your sake I made him think, that he should camp here, so that I might go away with you. Now don't refuse [literally: don't say a word]. He told her: Now, shut your eyes. And that woman shut her eyes. Then she was brought in under the water. It was St. Mary's lake. After a while he, who brought her in the water, told her: Now, open your eyes [literally: look]. And she opened her eyes [looked]. Then she saw, [that] it was a lodge, she was sitting in. It was a big lodge. She married the young man, who brought her in the water.

Then her [former] husband and her elder sister, who were looking for her, did not know, how she was gone [what had become of her]. And it was near winter, and her husband moved away. Then it was winter. And [when] it was summer, her husband came back to camp, where he had camped before. And that woman was told by her [new] husband: Now your husband has come again. You shall go ashore over there [to your husband's lodge], you shall come back again. Then she went ashore. She had already a child born. That child was a little beaver. Her new husband was a beaver. Then she came to her [former] husband's lodge. She, being outside, said through [the lodge] [to her elder sister who was in]: My elder sister, I have come. Make incense, I shall come in, that you may see me. And they made incense, and there was a song for it, when she was going in [to make her entrance holy]. And [when] she was going to sit down, there was another song for it. Then she told them the story, how she had disappeared. Her husband was not angry with her, when she told him, that she had married a beaver. Her husband respected her as holy. Then she told him: I shall go back again [to my home in the water]. Then she went home again.

And her husband the beaver asked her: Was your husband angry with that child? She told him: He pitied it very much, he was not angry with it. Then she was told by her husband: Now because your husband pitied my son, you shall go back to him. Now I shall give you something, that you may go back with to your husband, because he pitied my son. Then she was given his beaver-rolls by him. The she went back to her husband. She told him: These beaver-rolls are given to you by my husband [the beaver]. He took them. And then, when he slept, the beaver taught him [in his dream], how he must sing [at the beaver-dance]. That is how he came to have the beaver-rolls [literally: to have water]. Then he knew, how he must sing. He said to the Sun, the Moon, [and] the Morning-star: teach me twice seven songs. They then taught him [the twice seven songs]. When they had done teaching him, he was told by the Sun: Now when the [new] moon is there, then sing these [songs], that I have taught you. That is how it was, that [the beaver-medicine] came to the beaver-roll-owners [literally: water-owners].

[Cf. Wissler-Duvall mbi 74 sqq.]

Monday, June 19.

John again reports how he spends his day. These accounts are in Boys' experiences, 1–7 and 9, nsbt, 225–35. Preface: "With only a few exceptions communicated and explained to me by my young friend John Tatsey."

[1] Friday in the morning I got up at five o'clock. I built a fire, I took my hat and my coat. I walked to [the place], where I had tied my horse. I cut him loose, I brought him home, I put the saddle on him. I then walked in, I put wood on the stove. Then I went out again, I got on my horse, I went out on horseback. I drove the cattle out [of the corral]. And when they began to eat, I went up to a rock. I got off my horse, I sat down [on the rock], I looked round down from there. Men on horseback were running all over, they looked for their horses. And after a while I walked down, I drove our horses, I drove them home. We cut [two] work-horses loose, we put the harness on them. And I walked in. I began to eat. I went out again, I got in the waggon, I drove down, I loaded up some meat. I went back, I took an axe and a knife and a book. Then I started out again. I began to cut the meat, I was selling it, and they finally bought it all. I then went back down, I took the harness off the horses, I entered. I began to count the money I got [for the beef], there were forty dollars. I then put the harness on the horse, I went on horseback, and I was running around about Birch creek [looking for horses], and it looks very fine [over there]. But I did not stay there very long. I then went back, and they [all the fellows] were working on the ditch. I then came back. They had all stopped [working]. I then took the harness off the horses. I entered, I went out again, I went to the river. And I talked with my elder sister. She then walked away. She told me: Come up [to my camp] after a while. I entered [my own camp], I ate [supper]. When I had done eating, I then went to those white men. I then went to them there, and there was a lot of people, I then walked over to them. And it was dark. I came back again, and I then entered my brother-in-law's

camp. He was playing violine. Then I went back to my own camp. I then entered, and all were asleep. I then went to bed, I went to sleep again.

[**2**] Sunday in the morning I got up, I went after the horses, I got in [the camp] with the horses. I got a saddle-horse, I just put the saddle on him. I rode higher up, I walked around. I came back again, I went to tie up my horses, I changed saddle-horses. I then started out to Birch creek. I went there, I chased the cattle, [and] the horses. And after a while I came back again to a house. I then went in. And after a while there was a rider coming, he was driving horses. He drove them into the corral, he caught them and brought them out. I myself went in [into the corral], I began to rope the horses. After I got through roping, I drove them out. I got on my horse. We rode over to a cow, we then drove it, we ran it up [the road]. We got quite a way out, it would not go straight. I roped it round the neck. And the other boy roped it round the leg. We threw it down. Then it got up again. We started it out again. We got quite a way out again, it was tired. Then we left it. And I roped there also another one. We threw it also down. I tied its legs up. And [the other boy's] horse stepped into the rope. He [that horse] then ran around, he broke the rope, he then ran away. I caught him. I nearly died from laughing. We then went back to [the place], where the cow was lying, and one rope was loose, and the other one was just about to come off. And that boy got off [his horse]. He was going to give me the rope. And [the other rope] came off. I chased it again, we roped it again, we then sat by it. We rolled a cigarette, we did not have any matches, we were looking for some. I found one. We then went [on horseback] to a house. We entered, we built a fire, and so we got to light our cigarettes. Then we smoked. And when I had got through smoking, we went again [on horseback]. We then came to Blackfoot creek, we walked around [on horseback] in the water. It was getting late, we started again this way. And we got here. I turned my horse loose. Then I went in. Then I ate. When I was through eating, I walked out. And I entered this [other] tent here. I talked with

that white man, he was telling me stories about the dance [in the afternoon], how it had been. And after a short while I went out. I walked up, and I entered a tent, and there were people sitting in it. I sat by one of them, I then was talking with him. And it was dark, I then went home, and they had gone all to bed. I went to bed myself. And there ended my running around, [that had begun] on Sunday-morning.

[**3**] After I had got through teaching, I went.[36] And there I was nailing the tongue of a waggon. And when I got through nailing it, I went in, that I might eat. Then I ate. When I had done eating, then I went out again. I began to nail it [the tongue] again. After I was through nailing it, I was tying it. When I had done tying it, I went in again. I then took a certain piece of paper. Then I went to my brother-in-law's tent. Then I went in. I then gave him that piece of paper. He was looking at it. When he had done looking, then he gave me some money. I then went to the store. Then I went in. I asked a man: Is there any butter? He said: There is none. I asked him again: Are there any fruit-cans? And he said: There are none. And I told him: [Give me] one package of matches. And he gave them then to me. Then I went out. Then I went over to the blacksmith's shop. I sat behind it. And after a short while there a boy came along, he told me: Help me for a while to hook up my team. Then I helped him. When I had done helping him, we got in [into the waggon]. Then we went higher up. We left the waggon. Then we went down [afoot]. And there was another wagon, we hooked up our team to that one. Then I came to my camp. I got to it. I took water, I poured it out on my head. And here I entered. I began to tell you stories about what I had done, which you wrote down. And that is all.

[**4**] Sunday in the morning I got up. I went to catch a horse, I went to Medicine-wolf's house. There I found my horses. I drove them. When I had driven them back to camp, I caught some of them. After I had put the harness on them, I tied them up. I saddled up, I got on my horse, I

went to my brother-in-law's tent. I came there, I went in, I stayed there and some other boys came there. And some girls rode [on our horses]. And after a while they [these girls] went back. I caught my horse. I then went to our horses, I drove them, I drove them again to camp. I then tied up my horse, I went home. I turned my saddle-horse loose. Then I went to my brother-in-law's tent, I then went again, I caught his horses, I put the harness on them. Then I went with the waggon across [the creek]. They butchered. Then we came back, we sold the meat. About ten o'clock it was very dark. I turned the horses loose. I went in, I stayed there a while. We ate. When we had done eating, I went home. When I came home, I looked at the clock. It was already twelve o'clock. I then went to bed. In the morning I got up about seven o' clock. I got up, then I went again to my brother-in-law's tent. I got there again, I ate breakfast there. When I had done eating, then I went to catch his horses. After I had put the harness on them, I went with the waggon higher up. I stopped then, and women began to buy the meat. One of them said: Cut it right here. So I cut it there, and she was looking at it. She said: I will not take it. I told her: I never told you, that you should take it. If I think, that I shall not give you any, [then] I shall not give you any. And after a while she came back. She said: Give me some. I then left them. Then I went back, and I got here.

[5] I saw Willy yesterday, I just greeted him, [but] I did not talk with him. I then went again to Bear-chief's house, I got there. When I had done eating, I told Sebastian: Come with me. Then we went, we got there [at Seville]. We left the meat. Then we went back again, and we got to a lake. It then began to rain, it rained hard. Then we went slowly. We finally got back home [at Bear-chief's]. I then went straight on up to the bridge. Then I slept. And in the morning I started again, and I got here. I then began to walk around.

[6] Monday in the evening they began to drum. The people here thought, the Grass dancers might be dancing. There were a great many people [singing in a tent]. The man, who owned the tent, said: Sing four [songs] more, that you may quit then. And [when] their four songs were finished, they separated.

[7] [How I lived "up the round".] Then we started at the bridge and [went over] to the Old Agency. We ate dinner there. And then we went to Birch creek. I then caught a black horse. We went over to eat something. There is the house of a partner of mine. We went there to eat. When we were through eating, then we started out again, and we got over there to Fish's springs. And in the morning we caught horses, we all rode out then. I was the last one, I kicked the horse I rode, he began to buck with me, I was about to fall off. He stopped bucking. We were running then. And there might be about seven hundred head of cattle. We began to cut out [the strays] [from the cattle] that we drove. And we began to brand the calves. When we got through, we went home to the camp. We turned the horses loose, then we ate. And in the morning at four o'clock we got up, and then we rode out again. We drove back again, we went home to eat. When we had done eating, we caught some more horses. When we got through working, then we went back to camp. When we got there, two horses ran off. I chased them. The horse I rode began to buck with me again. I then turned him loose. In the morning we moved camp, and we camped there at the Old Agency. In the afternoon I again took that bay horse, I got on him, he was bucking again. And my father came, he was whipping the horse I rode. Then we ran out. And it rained. We had done working then, we went home. In the morning we moved camp again. We then camped near Owl-child's lake. We had done working. And in the morning we rode out to Black-tail creek. We were branding again. At two o'clock we went home. And in the morning we moved camp to Heart butte. We camped there. And when we had done working, we moved camp again, and [now] to Badger

creek. Where the ditch comes out [of Badger creek], there we camped. And next morning we again moved camp, and [now] to Little Badger creek. And we stayed there two days, [and] then it snowed, and I then went home. I went to the Mission. And [when] I had stayed there three days, then I went to White-calf's hay-ground, and they were camped there already. And after two days we moved camp again. And then we camped near the old bull-corral. Then we gathered all the cattle up. And next morning we moved camp again. Near Dancer's home on the other side of the hill, there was a lake. We camped there. And there were a few boys, with whom [literally: with them] I went. There were some cows, we were going to drive them. We drove them far, we were going to rope them. And myself, I roped a steer, that was going there, round its horns. And then my rope got tangled up on my saddle. That steer ran away, I then fell off, it kicked me. I got a hold of him. And he ran over me. We then went back, we moved camp, and we camped near the ditch-workers. And in the morning we moved camp again. And then we camped by a spring. I was watching some cows, [that] there were. I went to sleep, and it might be about one hour, that I was sleeping. I woke up, I went home to the camp, I ate, I stayed there then. And in the morning we moved camp again, and we camped in a deep coulee, where they cut hay. And in the morning we moved camp again. We then camped near New-woman's husband's lake. Next morning we moved camp again. And then we camped way up near the old station over there. And in the morning we moved camp again, and we camped then near Browning [literally: Creek]. And we did not stay there very long. We moved camp again. Then we camped near Kipp's springs. And next day in the afternoon we quit working. My father [and myself] then went home. And that is all.

[**9**] [How I go trapping.] In the afternoon I am going. I take my traps and a cow-head, I carry them along. And when I have gone quite a way off, then I put the head down, and I put the traps around it. I stake them.

Then I go back, I take some fish, I go and get another pair of traps. Then I come to the river. I put the traps. Then I go home. And in the morning I go to my traps. I go there, and there will be a kit-fox. And then I go over to my other trap. I then get to it also, I then have trapped a mink too. One week, I was trapping, I sent twelve [skins], that I had caught by trapping, down [to Minneapolis]. I got fifteen dollars for them.

Monday, June 19.

"Fat" Stephan talks about Indians and about Morning Eagle who could find guns in muddy water. The story, "Morning-eagle diving for guns" is in nsbt, 210–11. Preface: "Told by Bear-chief, interpreted by Tatsey."

Morning-eagle diving for guns.

Morning-eagle was pitied by two, the thunder and the false-thunder [a kind of bird]. They were called false-thunders, because they were strong and because they caught fishes.

A long time ago I saw Morning-eagle over there on Maria's river [literally: Bear creek]. There was a man called Black-eagle, he lost his guns in the river. This river was full [that means: the water was high]. He was told by that Black-eagle: Look for my guns in the water. If you find them, you will own them. Then he went in [into the water]. Then he whistled [imitating those birds, called false-thunders, that they might help him], and dived in, and it was a long time, that he dived [literally: his diving]. Far down he came out [of the water]. He had found those guns. Many people saw him, when he dived in, and when he found those guns. And that is all.

Tuesday, June 20.

Jimmy Vielle and other mission kids tell stories about the Holy Family Mission school. They are in Boys' experiences, nrs. 14 and 15. nsbt, 239–41. Preface: "For n°. 15 and n°. 16 I am obliged to a smaller boy called James Vielle, whom I could not understand without John's help. James Vielle pronounces ks regularly as ts, as many of the younger people do, but I have not expressed this peculiarity in writing down his stories." Nr. 14 must be a story of one of the Mission kids and nr. 15 is Jimmy's story.

[14] [How I fought, when I was at school.] I had three fights. This is how I came to have a fight with one [fellow]. We were eating and he spilled my coffee [literally: my drink]. I told him: Spill it again. So he spilled it all. I told him: I shall hit you, when we have done eating. We then went over there. When we entered, I looked for him. When I found him, I told him: Do you know, what you have done, where we were eating? He said: I know it. Then I hit him. I made his nose bleed. And I hit him just about three times. He said: It is enough, you hurt me. Then I let him alone. And this is how I got into a fight with that other [fellow]. He was hitting my younger brother. Therefore I fought him. We fought a long time between ourselves, and then the prefect [literally: the one that watches us] entered. He took hold of us and separated us, and he hit both of us with his glove. And this is how I got into a fight with still another [fellow]. It was the first time we fought, then we were sent to the corner. We stayed there. When we were through dinner, then I fought him again. And then it was, [that] I licked him. And [till] now [it did not happen], that I fought again [that means: and since that time I had no more fights].

[15] [Jimmy at school.] I am called Jimmy. At six o'clock the bell rings, we get up, we wash our faces, and when we get ready, we go down, we say our prayers, and when we have done saying our prayers, we go back

up again, we fix up our beds, we go right back down, we run around [in the yard]. The prefect [literally: the one that is watching us] blows the whistle. We go to eat [breakfast], we eat a whole lot, then we go out, we are sweeping. When we have done working, we play. We play a game with horse-shoes, we steal pegs, we are kicking the can. At nine o'clock we go to school. We are hit over the head with a stick once in a while. We then begin to write, we read in our books. And when we are soon going out, we draw a bucking horse, and swine, and dogs, and there are many other things, we draw. Then we go out. And we go out and stay there about ten minutes, and then we go to eat [dinner]. When we have done eating, we chew chewing-tobacco. (Jimmy chews on the sly, he smokes tobacco.) Half past one we go to school, and at three o'clock we come out [of school]. Half past three we go in again, and at four o'clock we come out [of school]. We run around outside. And at six o'clock we go to eat [supper]. Ten minutes after eight we go to bed. (Jimmy had a dream, he was breaking a black horse, and [when] he got thrown off, then he woke up. He stayed awake for a while, looking around, he went to sleep again.)

Friday, June 23.

John Tatsey and Uhlenbeck work on body parts of the cow. They are to be found in "A Survey of the Non-Pronominal and Non-Formative Affixes of the Blackfoot Verb," on pp. 101 and 120. In its Preface, Uhlenbeck thanks "the regretted Joseph Tatsey and his son John."

p. 101:

-pisak – *hind-part, thigh*, cf. oápisàkists – *its hind-quarters (e.g. of a cow.* itaitapisakiu – *he would hold his hind-part to (the side from where the wind blew)*
nbt. 176.

akaiitapisaksitòkaie – *he then was suddenly shot by him (4 p.) in the thigh, so that there was a gap in it* nbt. 182.

p. 120:

hind-part (his) oómoχtotsopop ("his where-we-sit-on") – *the hindquarters of a cow and other quadrupeds are called oápisàkists. Cf. –pisak-, and thing, upper leg.*

Saturday, June 24.

John Tatsey's stories about his sore leg, about how he makes a fire and about his mother baking bread are in Boys' experiences, nrs. 11,12 and 13, nsbt, 237–39.

[11] [How I make fire.] I then make shavings, I light them. And I put small pieces of wood on top [of the shavings]. Then it burns.

[12] How my mother bakes bread. She then takes flour, and she puts it in her pan. And [also] salt and baking-powder. And she puts water in [the pan]. She begins to knead it, and she puts it in [the stove]. And when it is done, she takes it out [of the stove], and we eat it. And that is all.

[13] [My sickness.] The first time, that my leg pained, we went over to our ranch. And when we got back, then next morning we went over to Blackfoot station. We went back then. When we got home, I went to bed. And in the morning I tried to get up. I could not get up. I looked at my leg, and it was swollen. They were doctoring me. And about one week it mattered. They opened it. It was one day and a half, that the matter was running. And I could not sleep at all from it. During one month it pained. And it stopped. And it was another month, that I did not get up. In the first part of Christmas-month [i.e. December] I got up. The first thing I then did was to ride, I went to the Mission, I got there, I came back. We then moved up to the bridge, we camped there. Next morning we moved back down again. We then camped by the Mission. In [the month] When-the-geese-come [i.e. March] we moved over to our ranch. One month we stayed at home. We then moved back [to Two-Medicine river]. We camped by Bad-John's house. The third day of this last month they brought me away to Conrad [literally: Where-they-used-to-freight-the-flour-from]. Then they brought me there. It was three months, that I stayed there. In [the first part of] haying-time [i.e. the beginning of August] I came back home, and then I have seen you. I did not know

you, when my father told me your name. In the afternoon I saw you there at the door, I was standing there, you came in, and you asked my father: Is that one another boy of yours? He told you: Yes. You came up to me, you shook hands with me. About two weeks [afterwards] you went away. I then felt lonesome for you, that you went away. And that is all.

Nelson Henault's story about his marriage was apparently too boring and did not make it into the nsbt. According to Willy it was not a "real Indian story." Still, nsbt, 51–53, has two stories about marriage. Preface: "told and interpreted by Tatsey."

Marriage.

The fine young men of the ancient Peigans, when they were to marry, never asked for a wife. The daughter of the chief, that had to have him for son-in-law, would be dressed up. He would give all the finery, that belonged to him, to his daughter. He would send all good horses with her. Everybody would know, [that] a certain person had a wife sent to him. And he would be known, that he was a fine man. And his father-in-law would also be known, that he was a chief. And the young man would be helped by his father [to give presents to the chief who was to be his father-in-law]. The horses and the other things, that he [the future son-in-law] would give, were just as good [as the presents he received]. All the people would see just the same, what that young man had given. Just the same that young-married man would also give [presents] to his wife's male relatives. If, in the future, his wife was foolish [did something wrong], he would not be ashamed, he would kill her [that means:

shame would not prevent him to kill her]. If he did not kill her, [and] if he was right [in saying], [that] his wife was stealing a young man [that means: that his wife secretly had a lover], she would be killed by her male relatives. If they did not kill her, they would cut off her nose. Of others they cut off their ears. Other men had three or four wives. If one or may-be two of his wives were bad, he would throw them out-of-doors. They would not come back. Even if they were chief's daughters, he would not be ashamed; he would do, what he wanted to do. He gave plenty for his wife [that means: he paid richly for her, and therefore he was entitled to do with her just what he wanted].

Ordinary people would ask for a wife. If he [the wooer] was liked, he would be taken for son-in-law by that man [the girl's father]. He [the wooer] would give presents. If he was disliked by that girl, his wife, the same way he would throw her out of doors. He would take back what he had given for presents. When people took back what they had given for presents, that meant, [that] one was giving up his wife. There were in the olden times people who took their wives by force, that was the way, they got a wife. Such ones, we said, were bad people.

[Cf. Grinnell blt 211 sqq., McClintock ont 184 sqq., Wissler slbi 9 sqq.]

The other story about marriage is in nsbt, 221–23. This story is told by the stepfather of Peter Bearleggings, nicknamed White-whiskers. Preface: "Communicated and interpreted by the man himself, a half-breed who does not want his white man's name to be mentioned."

How a certain man came to be married.

I am called Little-plume, and I am called also For-nothing-many-guns. I then went to Two-Medicine river, where Came-up-over-the-hill-with-the-eagle-tail-feathers stayed. I came there, there was a horse, I went to catch him. Then Snake-people-woman [the wife of the man just mentioned] said: I will get you a wife. I told her: You are fooling. She said: No, I don't fool. I asked her: Who [is it]? She said: Charging-home. I said to her: Yes, I shall go home now. And two days after New-year I shall come back here again. She said: Yes. Then it came to time, [that] I came there again. I asked her [Snake-people-woman]: What does she say? She answered: She does not say anything. [Snake-people-woman] told me: In the morning I will tell her again. Then [having been told by Snake-people-woman, that she ought to marry me] she said: Yes. Then I told [Snake-people-woman]: I will go and get the waggon, I will bring her home with it. She said: Go ahead. Then I went home. I got the waggon, and I came back with it. When I got back in the evening, [Charging-home] said: I don't like to go [literally: that I shall go] to your home. And now we shall stay here. [I said:] Yes, I shall bring my waggon home. She said: Yes. Then I went home. In the evening I got there. Then I slept. And after a while I got back to be married [literally: for my going to be married]. And she consented, that I should remain with her together. Then I stayed there, I stayed there the whole winter. And in summer I got married by the priest. It was in the church. And then we lived together allright till now, and it is now [just the same], that there is nothing to part us yet. And now I began to work on the ditch. And [last] Sunday I took Mary and White-whiskers [my step-children] out of school [and brought them] here. They are staying now here with their mother. And to-day, [this] Saturday, there is awfully much rain, it is cold. Some [of the people] have got no wood [to make a fire]. And this is the end of my story.

Sunday, June 25.

Uhlenbeck attended the Otter ceremony at Eagle Calf's the previous year too. His account of it appeared in English in "Festschrift: Vilhelm Thomsen, zur Vollendung des siebzigsten Lebensjahres am 25." Januar 1912, 74–77. Big Beaver's story in Blackfoot is left out.

The Origin of the Otter-Lodge.

The following text was communicated to me by a middle-aged Peigan, named Big Beaver (Oʹmαχksksìskstaki), whom I visited in his otter-painted lodge, at Browning June 24, 1910. Another full-blood Peigan, Johnny Ground, acted as interpreter, and afterwards some corrections in the text and the translation were made by my Indian friend Joseph Tatsey.

This Otter-lodge is a beautiful white tepee, ornamented with coloured pictures, representing otters, the water, and the mountains. It is called in Blackfoot Ámonisikokàup (Otter-lodge), or Ámonisauàstàmiop (Otter-flag-lodge). I give some particulars, as much as possible, in Johnny Ground's own words:

The otter-lodge is a big lodge. There are buffalo-hoofs on both sides of the ears. When you go out of the lodge, you shake the buffalo-hoofs. They are tied inside. And then there is a big pipe, that belongs to the lodge. And the tobacco-board is tacked all over with brass-tacks. On the tobacco-bag is a buffalo-robe, and on the back and on the tail it is beaded. That is the otter's tobacco-bag. And the pipe-stick is ornamented with porcupine-quills of two colours. And inside the bags, that belong to the lodge, are seven petrified rocks, and the bags are put over the inside of the lodge, and some juniper, sweet-grass and elk-food bushes are put under the bags. And they take some kind of white paint, and

pour it over the centre of the lodge, and spread it out, and then they take down the petrified rocks from the lodge-pole, and put them down on the juniper, sweet-grass and elk-food bushes. And they put cow-fat all over the petrified rocks, and rub them in their hands with red paint, and then they will say their prayers to them when they are wishing for money, horses, clothes, or something else. And all the people will kiss them, and they have got some songs. Those petrified rocks are called buffalo-rocks.' [The Peigans, when speaking English, always use rock instead of stone.]

Joseph Tatsey, however, says, that kissing the buffalo-stones was not practiced in the former times, but that the people rubbed them all over their heads and shoulders. Originally buffalo-stones did not belong to any sacred lodge. Such stones gave the owner the power to call the buffalo, that they might run over the cliff into the corral. A story about the origin of these stones has been published in English by G.B. Grinnell, Blackfoot lodge tales, pp. 124 sq., and by C. Wissler, Mythology of the Blackfoot Indians, pp. 85 sqq.; in Blackfoot and English by the author of the present paper in his *Original Blackfoot Texts*, pp. 12 sq. Another version of the Otter-lodge story is given in English by C. Wissler, op. cit., p. 92. Cf. about the sacred lodges of the Blackfoot tribes G.B. Grinnell, American Anthropologist, New Series, vol. 3, pp. 650 sqq.; C. Wissler, Mythology of the Blackfoot Indians, pp. 92 sqq., and Material culture of the Blackfoot Indians, pp. 99 sqq.; W. Mc Clintock, The old north trail, pp. 207 sqq.; and my remarks on the subject Versl. en Meded. der Kon. Akad. v. Wetenschappen, Afd. Letterk., 4ᵉ Reeks, Deel XI, pp. 22 sqq.[37]

[Big Beaver said:] An old man slept, near a river he slept, in the night. That old man was very poor. [He had a dream] an otter pitied him. It [the otter] gave him its lodge. It [the otter] said to him: It [the lodge] is medicine [that means: it has supernatural power], you will get profit by it [in the future]. Look on high the otter-flag. That is medicine. Here is my whistle, my yellow paint, my cooked paint; they belong to the lodge.

There at the upper end is a place for burning the incense. There is elk-food, juniper, sweet-grass. Take some fire. We use for incense juniper, elk-food, sweet-grass. And that is all. I give it to the old man. [And the otter said:] Let us put our hands above the incense, [let us put them over] over nose, and the tops of our heads. [And let us say:] Pity me, I am poor, help me! This lodge here is medicine. Hear me! [And the otter said:] [Here] is a small cup. Pour some water in it. Paint your face with yellow paint. Scratch your face to make stripes. Wear the whistle round your neck. It [the whistle] has the yellow paint on it. Take some green grass. Set the otter [that means: the otter-flag] on this. Take the otter-flag from on-high, take it down, set it on the green grass. [The old man said:] I took it [the otter-flag], I took it in my arms. On the otter's face were some bells, on its feet were tied some bells. And it had some eagles-tail-feathers on its back. That was on its back [and] on its tail. And I took it, I prayed to it, that it might pity me. [Big Beaver said:] I shall sing [the songs, the old man was taught by the otter, the first of which is as follows: I live in water. I say my prayers. My family is born in water. They are growing well and live. The water is medicine. And singing another song, the otter shook its tail, dived into the water, and when it came out, it whistled. I was not able to secure the text of these songs in Blackfoot.] The old man did his buffalo-robe upside down. He rubbed the paint over the robe. He knelt down, he went through the motion in the centre [of the lodge]. He took a stick, a forked stick, he stuck it in the upper end of the lodge, and then the otter [that means the otter-flag] was put on top. It sat on top. [And then the otter – the giver of the lodge – told the old man:] Now issue out the food(s) to the women, the children, the men – they are tired –, so that they may eat. When they have done eating, it will commence again. It will commence. We shall shoot the otter [that means: the otter-flag]. Sit with a saddle, a blanket, bedding, clothes, a hat, a bow, a telescope, a bridle. We shall shoot that otter. It sits on-high. We shall shoot it down. It will be done with. We shall put it away. We shall quit. It will be hung up in a bag. Put the paints away, put them with it [that means: with the

otter]. Put the paints with the otter into the bag. We have finished, and we shall put it [the otter] away. It will stay in its lodge. It [the lodge] is medicine and that is all.

Leiden. Christianus Cornelius Uhlenbeck

Uhlenbeck announces in the Festschrift article that "another version of the otter story" is to be found in his obt, 12 sq. It is "The Origin of the buffalo-stones" on 12–13.

The origin of the buffalo-stones.

Long ago the ancient Peigans were camped about. They were nearly all dead, for [want of] something to eat. They did not know, where the buffaloes went. There was a poor second wife, [that] went after wood. While she cut wood, she heard there some one singing. She looked for him. There were big willows. She saw, there was a buffalo-stone. She took it. She put it in her bosom. She went home. She said to her husband: Invite the men. I shall sing and pray. That man said [to his first wife]: Dress your younger sister up, set her at the upper end of the lodge.

These men all came in. That man said to them: This my wife will sing and pray. That woman said: Try to get even a small piece of fat. That small piece of fat was given to her. She said: I shall sing. I shall grease [and] paint this buffalo-stone. She made incense. She sang. She said: This night I shall cause to come [animals for food]. Tell all the people, to tie the mouths of all their dogs up [that they don't bark and scare the buffalo]. Harden this corral. Before day-light two persons must go out to lead the buffalo. Then she had finished her singing and praying. Then she said another thing: Fix your lodges well. It will be cold. When the men got up in the morning, they looked out. They suddenly

Monday, June 26.

saw, that there were bulls standing all over the camp. They suddenly saw, that buffaloes were jumping off [from the bank] into that corral. And that's it [the whole story].

[Cf. G.B. Grinnell, Blackfoot lodge tales, London 1893, pp. 125 sq., and C. Wissler-D.C. Duvall, Mythology of the Blackfoot Indians, New York 1908, pp. 85 sqq.]

Uhlenbeck works from 2.30 until 5.30 with John Tatsey and Jimmy Vielle: Boys' experiences, nr. 16, nsbt, 241–43.

[16] [Jimmy in camp.] Tuesday in the morning I got up, I washed my face, I ate. When I was through eating, I went to my horse, I went to catch him. When I brought him to camp, I saddled him up. I then went higher up. I was hunting [for a horse], I had a hard time to find him. When I had found him, then I roped him. He [the horse I had roped] pulled my saddle off [the horse I was riding]. And [after having been pulled down with the saddle] I got up, I saddled him [the horse I had roped] up, and I led the other one along. I went with another boy. He caught a horse. We then ran home. When we got home, we watered our horses. When we had done watering our horses, we fed them with oats. When they had done eating, we turned them loose. The workmen quit [working]. I took the harness off my elder brother's team. We fed them [the team-horses], and we ate. When we had done eating, we turned them loose, we hobbled them, we went back home. We then played around. It was dark, we went to bed. I began to dream, I roped a bear, I fell off [my horse], I woke up. And that is all.

Tuesday, June 27.

Owl Child "himself" tells a short story. Preface: "Told by Owl-child (Sépistòkòs), interpreted by Tatsey." nsbt, 67–68.

Goose-chief.

———

There was a party of warriors, they were killed. They were not known [it was not known what had become of them]. After a very long time they were seen, they were only bodies, they flew [to the camp]. Their hands were cut off, their feet were also cut off. And they were scalped. Then they were known, [that] these were those, that did not come. Those, that had seen them, then died [from the sight]. That is why the ancient Peigans were afraid of them. Only once they were seen, they were never seen any more. Since that time they were all called Goose-chiefs [after the leader of the party].

After Owl Child, Four Horns shows up and narrates some of his experiences. Preface: "Told by Four Horns (Nisoótskina), interpreted by Tatsey." nsbt, 218–19.

Wonderful experiences of Four-horns'.

———

[1] I was camping on Maria's river [literally: Bear creek] in a shady place. In the night I went out, I went on the prairie. I did not know, where I was going to. I could not see, I could not see with my eyes, there was a person, that caused that I could not see [literally: from him I could not see]. He was very short. And he went away. He was getting larger, he rose up in the air. Then I could see again. I then came home to my lodge. In that way happened this wonderful and dangerous thing. And thus was this first wonderful experience of mine.

[2] On the other side of Birch creek I was travelling about. When I started to go home, I lost my way. In the night I saw a person. He walked ahead of me. I did not know, what kind of person he was. I came to this river. It was deep. I could not see [how it had happened], [but] I was standing on the other side of the river. My leg was not wet [that means: my legs were not wet]. I did not know, how I came across the river. That person went away from there. I did not see him any more. He was burning in a blaze, when he went away. And that is all, I saw of him. I myself went home then. And that is all.

Wednesday, June 28.

Uhlenbeck finishes with Tatsey the story of "The deserted children," nsbt, 126–34. Preface: "Told and interpreted by Tatsey" (On August 20 he will read this story for "both Jims.").

The deserted children.

Long ago the ancient Peigans were all camped together. All the children went out to play. A chief's-child found some sea-shells. All these children crowded together and took them away. That chief's-child ran home crying. He told his father: I found there some sea-shells. The children crowded together and took them away. I did not get any of them. That chief then went out. He cried over the camp. He told these people: My son found there some sea-shells. He did not get any of them. Those children took them away. Now let us move. We shall push the grass up [to cover the tracks]. Then they moved. That chief stood back alone. They all moved. He pushed the grass up with the lodge-pole. After a long while these big girls said to their younger brothers and sisters: Go home and get something to eat [for us all]. They all started to run [home]. After a long while a poor boy with sore eyes [literally: his eyes were sore] came back. He told the girls: Oh, my elder sisters, our lodges have disappeared. They threw dust in his eyes, and told him: You are lying. He said to them: No, I am right, our lodges have disappeared. They told him: When the children come back, we shall know, if the lodges are still there. We shall fill your eyes with dust. After a short while the children came back. They told their elder sisters: We are deserted. Our lodges have disappeared.

Then they all went home. When they came in sight [of the place where the lodges had been], they only saw the deserted camp-ground. They walked about. After a while they found the trail [of their parents who had moved]. They followed it. They found a long round stone. They said: Mother, here is your long round stone [used as a whet-stone]. Again after a while they found a lodge-pole. They said in the same way: Mother, here is your lodge-pole. Then they suddenly heard, there was an old woman. They were told by her: This way. Then they were happy. Then they came, where the old woman was. Her pet-animal was a bear. They told her: Grandmother, forbid your dog to bite us [literally: that he might bite us]. And she forbade her dog. She told them: Come right in, my children, sit down over here. [When] it was night, she told them: My children, lie all of you with the head to the centre of the lodge. There are a great many mice, [so there is danger] that they might bite your hair off. One girl told her younger brother: Don't sleep now, I am very much afraid of that old women. Watch her. You [must] bite the end of my ear, when she is going to kill us. All of them slept. That old woman got up. She began to cut their heads off. That boy bit his elder sister. She jumped up, she told that old woman: Oh mother, pity me. Let us live, you will have use of us [she means only herself and her little brother]. She was told by [the old woman]: Come on, go and get me water to put it in the pot. Leave that younger brother of yours here. She answered her: No, mother, my younger brother is very dirty, he will dirty you. He is not heavy, I will pack him on my back.

She saw, that the old woman was boiling those children, whose heads she had cut off. After a while that old woman told her again: Go after water. I will boil [some more of these children's meat]. She then packed her younger brother on her back. She came to the river. She saw there a water-bull. She told him: Help us, this water-bull here, pity us, take us across. He told her: Yes, look on my head for lice, just for a while. And she began to look for lice on his head. She told him: Oh, your lice taste good. He told her: Come on, sit down on my back. That girl said to an elk-head there [on the shore of the river]: If you hear, that that old woman calls for me, tell her then: Wait, I am wiping my younger brother. [In the mean time] I shall be far away. She got on the water-bull, she crossed, she ran away [with her little brother]. After a while that old woman called the girl. She told her: Hurry up. That elk-head said to her: Wait, I am wiping my younger brother. She [the old woman] said to her: Oh yes, I shall go after [you]. She came to the river, she did not see the girl. She came to that elk-head, she told it: This is the one, that was always saying: I am wiping my younger brother. She broke the head. [Therefore elk-heads do not talk nowadays any more.] She said to the water-bull: Why does not this one take me across? And she was told by him: Look on my head for lice, just for a while. She came and sat by him. She said to him: Oh, your lice have a bad-death-dirty taste [i.e. a damned dirty taste]. He told her: Come on, sit on the nether part of my back. He went in [the water]. He came swimming to the middle of the water. He said: I am going to throw my back sideways. He dived with her. That is the way, that that old woman died. [If that old woman had not been killed off, there would be still such women nowadays.]

That girl and her younger brother went very far off. It was night, [when] they saw the lodges. It was dark, they went among the lodges. They began to look into [each lodge]. They found their [own] lodge. From the door [the girl] said to their mother: Mother, here is your boy. That man [their father] said [to his wife]: Ah, you must have a child [that means: I won't have anything to do with those children of yours, I don't acknowledge them as my own]. He said to his wife: Go out and see it. That woman went out, she saw her daughter and her son. She was told by [her daughter]: Mother, I am very tired. Here is your son. Then she [the woman] entered, she told her husband: Here are some of the children, that were deserted. That girl then forced her way into her father's and her mother's lodge. That man jumped out. He said: Some of the deserted [children] have come here. In the morning they moved all together. That girl and her younger brother were tied to a tree. There was an old woman, her dog was called Curly, it was a wise [dog]. That old woman said to Curly: Here is some pemmican. Hide it over there in the forest. And hide yourself. I shall call you. Don't come out [then]. When

these Peigans move, go over there to that girl and her younger brother. Go and turn them loose, and give this pemmican to them, they will eat it. They are poor. When these Peigans have moved far, then follow up. The chief looked back [towards the camp-ground], if there might be some people, who would untie those children. It was night, Curly came to [the old woman]. He was asked by his old woman: Did you turn loose those children? He told her: Yes.

It was after a long time, [that] the Peigans, where they camped about, nearly died for [want of] something to eat. They did not find the buffalo. That girl and her younger brother were picking up things, that were left, about the old camp-ground. They began to make a shelter. After a long while that boy told his elder sister: Now I shall make a buffalo-corral. There is [a reason to have] your ear [open]. Even if you hear, that people are making noise, don't look out, I will throw a kidney at you. That boy then went away. After a long while that girl heard, that many people made noise. She heard, [that] the people said: Look, over there is a big buffalo, he will jump over the cliff. The dogs howled all over [the camp], the children made noise. That girl looked out, there was no person [to be seen]. Her younger brother entered. She was told by him: You are disobedient, why did you look out? Now I shall lead the buffalo again. Try hard, don't look out. If you look out again, I will not pity you again. I shall leave you right here. I shall go to our tribe. Now, I shall lead the buffalo again. There is [a reason to have] your ear [open]. Don't look again. Then that young man went away. After a long while, when the people and the children made noise and the dogs howled, then that girl tried hard, she did not look out. After a long while she slept. Her younger brother threw a kidney to her in the lodge. He said to her: Here is a kidney. She got up. They [the boy and his sister] commenced to scatter pieces of meat over those old camp-grounds. They filled them up [with pieces of meat]. Her younger brother told her: Now, make pemmican. I shall pack it on Curly's back.

[When] it was done, that young man looked for the ancient Peigans, and he found them. [When] it was night, he looked into each of the lodges. He saw Curly. He [Curly] was sitting by the camp-fire, he nearly died for [want of] something to eat. He [the boy] said to him into the lodge: Curly, here is something that you can eat. Curly threw his head up. That old woman said to [the boy]: Alas, why does he [i.e. why do you] tell him something false? He is awfully hungry. That young man entered. He said to that old woman: Here is pemmican, that you can eat with Curly. He said also to her: Tell your son-in-law, that these Peigans can move back. Let them come back and camp again in their old camp-grounds. They will get something to eat. I made a buffalo-corral. Now I shall go home [to the shelter he made before]. That old woman told her daughter: Of those [two] children, that were tied back [to the tree], this is what the boy [one of them two] says. He [the son-in-law] cried over the camp. He said: That [boy], that was deserted, says this, that we should move back. Then they moved back to their old camp-grounds. They all came back and camped in their old camp-grounds. He did not put any meat in his father's old camp-ground. That young man told his elder sister: [Take] two muscles of buffalo-legs, [and] cook them hard. Hang up a piece of back-fat over there at the upper end of the lodge. His father and his mother entered his lodge. [The boy and his sister] were told by them: I am glad to see my children. That young man told his father: Lick up to that piece of back-fat [on high]. [When] he raised his head, he [the boy] hit him on the throat with one of the muscles of buffalo-legs. There that one was, he killed him. He told his mother also: Lick up to that piece of back-fat [on high]. [When] she raised her head, he hit her [also] with [one of those muscles]. And there she was, he killed her too. He killed his father and his mother. And the dogs have separated [after having had their meal].

[Cf. Grinnell blt 50 sqq., Wissler-Duvall mbi 138 sqq., Grinnell jaf XVI, 108 sqq., Dorsey cl 83 sqq., Dorsey tsp 97 sqq., Dorsey-Kroeber ta 293 sq., Lowie a 142 sqq.]

Tatsey and Uhlenbeck work on "The Seven Stars," nsbt, 101–12. Preface: "Told and interpreted by Tatsey."

The Seven Stars.

There were few of the ancient Peigans in a camp. These were camping. There was a girl, [whose] father was a chief, she did not [want to] marry. These Peigans camped a long time. That girl used to go after wood with her younger sisters. When they came to the forest, she told her younger sisters: Look for wood right here, I shall go over there into the forest. Wait for me. Then she went into the forest. When she came out, her younger sisters began to suspect her. Her hair was all unraveled. Again after a while she said once more to her younger sisters: Come on, let us go and get wood. They came again to that [place], where they used to get wood. Again she told her younger sisters the same: Look for wood right here. When you have done getting wood, wait for me. There was one girl, [who] was meddlesome. She said to her companions: Do you suspect our elder sister? When she comes back from over there, where she goes into the forest, her hair is unraveled. There is something, that she does. Now I shall know about her. And she entered the forest after her, where she [the elder sister] was yet playing with a big bear. She [the meddlesome girl] came back out of the forest. She told her companions: Our elder sister is a very dangerous person. There is a bear, she goes to. She is still playing with him. After a short while she [the elder sister] came [to her younger sisters]. They were told by her: Come on, let us go home. Over there they got home. That meddlesome girl told her father: There is a bear, where we go for wood, our elder sister is always playing with him.

That man went out. He told these Peigans: Begin to prepare your bows and your arrows. Now here in this bunch of timber your brother-in-law, my son-in-law, a big bear, is sitting. We shall go and try to kill him. Then they went. These Peigans commenced to shoot him. They killed him after a hard fight. That man said: We shall burn him up. Then they burned him up. That girl said to her younger sister: A bad death to her [meaning: to you], it is you, that he died from. Go over there, where that bear was killed. Take a small piece of his hide. That girl then went over there, where he had been burned up. She found his foot. She then took a small piece of his hide. She took it home, then she gave it to her elder sister. After a short while she [the elder sister] went into the forest, and fixed that piece of skin. She was already pitied [and given power] by the bear [when he was alive]. She had fixed up the hide [so that it was complete again]. She told her younger sisters: Let us go over there near the shore among the willows. I shall act to you as if I were a bear. She told them: There are your ears [that means: there is a reason to have your ears open, to be on your guard]. Don't put your hands in my kidneys [that means: don't touch me near the kidneys]. She went into the forest. She covered herself with the bear-skin. She sat down [in the brushes]. Her younger sisters went into the brushes. She would chase them out of the brushes. She would go back into the forest again. She would do the same to them [chasing them out] ever and again. After a short while she went into the forest again. Then she sat down. They all went again into the brushes. She would not get up.

The same meddlesome [girl] went up to her. She stuck her hands near [her elder sister's] kidneys. When she [the elder sister] jumped up, there was a very big one, a big bear [she had turned into it]. They were chased by [that bear]. Each of them was bitten through the skull by [the bear]. That meddlesome [girl] could run fast. She was not caught by [the bear]. There was a dog [a bitch], [that] had a shelter built over her, she just had a litter of pups. That girl jumped in [into the dog's shelter]. She told her: You, this dog here, help me – my elder sister has turned into a bear –, that she might not hurt me. The bear was bitten by the dog. She [the bear] ran straight on. She killed each one of these people [camping

there]. And she came back, she came to her younger sister [after having turned again into a person]. She told her: Now, come out, I shall not hurt you. They entered their own lodge. She was told by her younger sister: My elder sister, don't hurt me, you will have use of me. They had been there a long time. That girl went to get water. Her brothers had gone to war. She met them, where she got the water. They told her: What happened to the lodges? Why are there no people about them? She told them: Oh, my elder brothers, our elder sister had a bear for a lover. He was killed. She has turned into a bear. She has massacred this whole camp. I myself have been saved by a dog. She [our elder sister] is very dangerous. Now she is still at home. She has turned again into a person. If she knows you, she will kill you. They told her: Here is a rabbit. Take it, that you may eat it. Try to find out from her, what will cause her death. Don't tell her, that we are staying here. When you know, what will cause her death, then tell us.

Then that girl went home. She entered. She was told by her elder sister: You have persons about you. Who gave you this rabbit? She answered her: There is nobody. I shot it myself at the watering-place. There it was sitting. I shot it with this willow-spear. She was told by her: Yes, put it up there by the door. Shoot at it with that willow-spear. If you hit exactly in the same place as it was wounded before [literally: in the same wound], then you are speaking the truth. That girl prayed to the willow-spear. She shot the rabbit, she hit exactly in the same place, as it was wounded before [in the same wound]. She was told by her elder sister: Yes, you are speaking the truth. Now, eat it. She [the younger sister] began to cook it. And then she began to eat. She said to her elder sister: Here is some for you to eat. She was told by her: Now, I pity you, so that you may eat it alone. That young girl was wise. She then saved a piece. After a short while she said to her elder sister: Now we are always living here alone. I am afraid. Now I shall ask you: what is it, that would cause your death? She answered her: Don't be afraid. I can only die by awls. After a while she told her younger sister: I have not eaten any of the rabbit. She was told by her: No, my elder sister, here is some, I saved for you. She told her: No, I said it just for fun, I pity you, just eat it. That girl went again for water. She saw again her elder brothers. She said to them: Our elder sister says: I would die by awls.

They told her: Now when you go home, go to each of those camps. Get all the awls. When it is night, stick them outside of your lodge in front of the door. In the morning, if she says again "I have not eaten any of the rabbit", tell her then "I have eaten it up". Then run outside of the lodge. We shall be standing there already. In the morning that girl said again to her younger sister: I have not eaten any of the rabbit. She answered her: I have eaten it up. What [harm] will she [meaning: you] do? She ran out [of the lodge]. She [the elder sister] ran after her, she turned into a bear. She jumped on the awls. Then she could move only sitting [not able to get up or to move forward, because her feet were full of awls]. Those boys came in sight. There she was, they killed her [then and there]. The eldest [brother] told his younger brothers: Go and get some wood, we shall burn up our elder sister. Then they burned her up and went away. When they travelled, they came after a long while to a lodge. They went in. There were no people. Outside there was a woman. She told them: I am glad to see my younger brothers. Don't go away again. Stay here. I shall keep the lodge for you. Don't try [literally: think] to see me [literally: that you may see me], when I am working. Go and hunt. Then they would go out and hunt. When they came home, their food would all be ready.

After a long while the youngest of the brothers [literally: their younger brother], [who] was called Breast-man, told them: I am very much afraid of our elder sister. Every night she is always yelling over there on that tree. Now when we go hunt again, I shall stay here. I will know her [that means: I will know, what she is doing it for]. In the morning their elder sister told them: Go again and hunt. Then they went away. When Breast-man was out of sight, he turned into a bug. Then he ran into the lodge, to the upper part of it, among the trash [that was lying there].

He crept in among it, and he saw his elder sister, she had turned into a person [really being a ghost]. Then she swept their lodge there. She said: This is not a bug, it is Breast-man. She threw him towards the door. He crawled in again. After a long while that woman looked out. She said: They must be far away. I am very much afraid of Breast-man, that he might see me. Then she pulled her robe in sight, it was an elk-hide. She spread it out. She began to call the chiefs of the ancient Peigans by name. She said repeatedly: This a certain one's scalp. Now I have pretty near enough of my scalps [that means: now I will soon have scalps enough to ornament my robe]. Now those my younger brothers are seven. She called their names. Here I will sew that one's scalp. Here I will sew Breast-man's thick bunch of hair. [Now] Breast-man knew about her, [that] she killed persons. He crawled out from the lodge. He went that way, where his elder brothers had gone to hunt.

He met them. He told them: Our elder sister is very dangerous. Now I know her, [that] she kills our chiefs. I heard her, that she called their names. I saw her robe, it was an elk-hide. She sews the scalps of the persons, that she killed, on the robe. Now she called all of us by name. She will kill us also. She will complete her scalp-robe with our scalps. Now when we go again to hunt, we shall leave our game out on the prairie. When she goes to fetch the carcase, then we shall make our escape. Then they came home. They were told by their elder sister: I don't think, that Breast-man went to hunt. He must have been staying here [in the lodge]. She was told by her younger brothers: No, he went with us. After a short while she told them again: Go on, hunt again. Then they started on a hunt. They came home. They told her: My elder sister, go and get the carcase. Then she started. When she had gone a little way, she would run back. Breast-man was wonderful [had wonderful power], he could see through lodges. He told his elder brothers: Keep quiet, there is our elder sister. She comes back to look at us. There was a hole [in the cover of the lodge], through which she peeped in repeatedly. Then she would again run away. After a short while he told his elder brothers: She has gone for good. Let us burn this her lodge. And let us make our escape. Then they burned it [the lodge] up, and they ran away.

That woman looked back. She saw smoke. She ran home fast. When she ran inside, she said: That must be Breast-man, he has caused that I am to be pitied. Her lodge burned up. Those boys were far already. She followed. Breast-man told his elder brothers: Try hard [to make your escape], she is after us. When she came near them, they saw her. She would throw her wooden pin ahead, then she would go faster [than the pin, and she would pick it up and throw it again]. They also would shoot their arrows ahead, then they would be far away [moving faster than the arrows]. There was a tree, they ran to it. She was very close to them. They ran up [into the tree]. They sat [on the tree] according to their sizes [literally: as they were big]. Breast-man sat the highest up [being the youngest]. Then she came there. She said to them: Where will you escape? Breast-man will never escape. She went up to them. The eldest one sat the lowest down. She knocked him down first. She knocked each one down, [in the same order] as they were sitting up [in the tree]. There were only two [boys left] between Breast-man [and the woman]. There was a bird, [that] flew to him, [and] said to him: Breast-man, her top-knot. He then understood [what the bird meant by these words]: He tells me [literally: that he tells me], that I must shoot her there [on a bump] on top of her head. He then began to lick his arrow. She began to walk up to him [climbing the tree]. Then he shot at her bump-head. He then shot her down. And he came down.

He pulled his elder brothers together. He shot one of his four arrows in the air. He told them: Look out, my elder brothers, I might shoot you by accident. They just shook their legs. He shot another [arrow], and then they moved about. He shot another [arrow], and they nearly got up. The fourth time [he shot] they all jumped up. He said to them: Now, where shall we go? They told him: We don't know it. He said to them: We have no place to go. What shall we be? One said: Let us turn into rocks. They said to him: We shall be treated badly, the people will break us. Another one then said: Let us turn into trees. They told him also: It will be bad just the same, the people will chop us for wood. Another one then said: Let us turn into grass. They told him: The buffalo will eat us, and we shall be burned up [the people used to burn the old grass on the prairie; then the new grass would be green and fresh]. And the eldest said: Now, Breast-man, you must say now, what we shall be. He told them: Yes, I think then, that we should go to heaven. The people will have morning from us. They told him: That is the best of all. He told them: Come on, shut your eyes. When I tell you, then open your eyes [literally: look]. Then they went up to heaven. And now when the Seven [Stars] [the Dipper, or Great Bear constellation] have their heads up, then we have morning. By the side of the middle one of these three [the "handle" of the Dipper] is a small [star] scarcely to be seen [literally: is scarcely seen], that is the bird, that advised Breast-man [what to do]. And that is all, I know about them. [The meddlesome women originate from the meddlesome girl in this story, and if the other girl, that had a bear for a lover, had not been killed, the same thing would happen still to-day. One thing is upheld by the he-bears still now, that is that they do not kill a woman.]

[Cf. Wissler-Duvall mbi 68 sqq., McClintock ont 488 sq., Michelson jaf XXIV, 244 sqq., Dorsey cl 287sqq., Dorsey-Kroeber ta 238 sq., Lowie a 161. 177 sqq., and also note in Uhlenbeck obt 93, to which the following two references are to be added: Grinnell jaf VI, 44 sqq. XVI, 108 sqq. Cf. also Dorsey-Kroeber ta 152 sq.]

Tuesday, July 4.

Uhlenbeck records stories about the Sun dance, nsbt, 68–71. Preface: "Told by Blood, interpreted by Tatsey." See also "Social Organization of the Southern Peigans," by De Josselin de Jong (Appendix B of this volume).

The Sun-dance.

There may happen something important, and a wise woman will say: We shall pray. She will pray to the Sun. She will say to him: May my husband and my relations be saved. I will make a medicine-lodge. All the people will have something to look at. When they [the Peigans] gather for the circle-camp, when the berries are not yet ripe, then they camp in a circle. They begin to take the tongues, when there are happy times [i.e. when the buffalo are plentiful]. They are just camped about. When there are plenty of buffalo, then they begin to take the tongues. Then they gather lots of berries, when they are ripe. They look about for high forest, where to build the medicine-lodge. The women that make the medicine-lodge [of course, one woman every year] do not drink during four days. When they are getting near to the time to put up the central pole, they have found a place where to build the medicine-lodge. If the buffalo are far away, the fine young-married men are called on to chase the buffalo, that they skin them for the hides, which we use to tie the central lodge-pole with. And those [hides] will be put there in one place. Now those, that will cut the hides for ropes, that we may put up the central pole, come to the front. All the societies will be called on, that they may go and get [the willows for] the sweat-lodges. They will have a meeting between themselves, they will look for good willows. From there [where the willows are good], they will cut them. They cut a hundred of them.

From that [moment] everything is getting ready for the medicine-lodge to be built. Those that make the sweat-lodges are given to eat one of the parfleches [full of] tongues. They pray with them [with the tongues]. In the night there will be sung to those that make the medicine-lodge [the "medicine-woman" and her husband]. The people will be told: Be quiet, there will be sung to those that make the medicine-lodge. The whole camp is quiet in the night. And in the morning they move camp to where the medicine-lodge is to be built. Then they camp, and then they begin to hurry each other: [Make haste] that you may cut your lodge-poles. Other persons [than those that cut the lodge-poles] are those that cut the central pole. The women have already made the soup of berries. They will carry [the soup] to their husbands. When there is plenty of food, we cut [the dried meat] with the heavy bull-back-fat. The women begin to catch for themselves the fine horses of their husbands. They [the women] dress up. With them [the fine horses and the fine clothes] they drag the small trees [for the medicine-lodge]. When they have dragged the small trees, then those that make the medicine-lodge will be taken out. Some lodges are all put in a row. There the tongues are brought. Then wise women will come there. They are the ones, [that] untie [the tongues]. They are the ones, [that] take [them]. They pray with them to the Sun. They first feed their husbands, that they might get to be real old women, [and] real old men. They also feed the earth, they also feed their relations. Then they stop. And all the people is told: Tie the lodge-poles for yourselves. With those we raise the central pole. When we have raised the central pole, we tie it with those hides [i.e. with ropes of those hides].

In the evening all the societies will enter [the medicine-lodge]. They will have a dance with a hole [in the ground]. In the morning Little-crooked-horn will be the Sun-dancer. That is he, that will be the Sun-dancer. The old men with their daughters beat the drum on half a hide. They are the ones, [that] give the dance with a hole [in the ground]. When they are old and crazy, and when they tell lots of false coups, the chiefs think, that they [the people] will praise them. They think also, that they will get another wife. They are bad old men. Then they begin to bring in the soups. Berry-soups, back-fat(s), bull-back-fat(s), those are the things they cook. They are carried to them [to the societies]. That is what I know about, how we used to have the medicine-lodge in the olden times. Now we only have our medicine-lodges with all things got from the whites. The Sun-dancer is given a pipe. The sacrifices are given to him. He then paints the faces [of the people]. That is the way I understand the medicine-lodge.

[Cf. Grinnell blt 263 sqq., McClintock ont 192 sqq.]

Wednesday, July 5.

Willy notes about the old societies, among them the Crazy-dogs, "These are not clans," she adds. Uhlenbeck, about the Societies, nsbt. 43–44. Preface: "Based on Blood's knowledge of the subject, communicated and interpreted by Tatsey."

NOTE ON THE SOCIETIES.

Long ago the young men, before they entered any society, were going together according to their being of the same age. They were called Birds. They would be initiated, the Doves were the ones that initiated them. They were four years with it [in that society]. Then they initiated their younger brothers. They themselves were initiated by the Flies. They were four years again with it [in that society]. And again they initiated their younger brothers. And they themselves were initiated by the Braves. They were four years again with it [in that society]. Again they initiated their younger brothers. They themselves became Brave-dogs [Crazy-dogs]. They were four years with it [in that society]. Again they initiated their younger brothers. They themselves became Tails. They were four years again with it [in that society]. Again they initiated their younger brothers. They themselves became Crow-carriers. They were four years again with it [in that society]. Again they initiated their younger brothers. And they themselves became Dogs. That is all that Blood knows about the societies. Before he was [born], there were societies that were called the Bulls, the Catchers [the Soldiers], and the Kit-foxes. Now there are two pipes still in existence. They were the pipes of the Catchers. The Kit-foxes had a kit-fox-hide and a tied bent stick. Forty years ago the Kit-foxes were seen the last time. The chief of the Tails had a coat of weasel-fur.

[Cf. Grinnell, blt 104 sqq. 219 sqq., Wissler-Duvall mbi 105 sqq., Wissler slbi 25 sq., McClintock ont 445 sqq., and especially Lowie a 75 sqq., where the different problems relating to the age-societies of the Plains Indians are discussed.]

Jim Blood told about his own society, nsbt, 44–50. Preface: "Told by Blood, interpreted by Tatsey."

The Doves and the Braves.

When I was eight years old, I joined a society, I became a Dove. I then knew this about it, that it was a very happy thing. I did not think, that it would be lonesome in the future, as I knew, that those were happy times, when my partners danced. They were told by the chiefs, that they should watch the buffalo, that there would be no person out of all the people, that would start to chase the buffalo. They were the watchmen. And [if] a man would chase the buffalo, he would hide. The buffalo would all run away [scared by the man that chased them secretly]. [When] a man was chasing the buffalo [by himself], he was seen by the Doves, he was chased by them, he was caught by them, he was thrown down off his horse by them. And their chief tore his clothes [viz. of the man that was chasing by himself] to pieces. All his clothes were torn to pieces. He was just naked [literally: he just had a body], [when] he came to his lodge. There was no person, that might become angry [when he had been treated that way]. It was his own foolishness, that he had his clothes torn. They [the Doves] went by themselves, when they [the Peigans] were camped in a circle. In the centre [of the circle] was their lodge, it was built out of two lodges.

They were ordered by their chief [as follows]. Their oldest partner told their partners, that they should all come to him [the chief]. And so they [the Doves] were invited [to their chief's lodge] [by mouth of the oldest partner]. They all entered Crow's-tail-feather's lodge [Crow's – tail-feather was the name of their chief]. They decided, that they would have a dance. Next morning the Doves would have a dance. Next morning they danced. [When] they had the dance, they put the paint all over their bodies. With their arrows and their top-knots they sat outside in a circle. Their oldest partners were the ones that made them dance. Those at the upper end were the chiefs. One of them had a coyote-skin and an arrow. Another of them had a rattle, and he had also an arrow. And two of them were called the Yellow Doves. And there were two in the lower part of the circle, that were [called] the Bear-Doves. They danced four times.

When [the dances] were completed, all the people would run away. They [the Doves] made a charge on [the place], where the women got water. There it was, [that] they made a charge. They shot at the water-bags. Then they [those bags] leaked. When they stopped [shooting], then they went around the circle-camp. They shot at the dogs. They did not shoot at the bob-tailed ones. They were afraid of them [of the bob-tailed dogs]. When they stopped, they began to take something that they might eat, choice meat. There was their lodge, the lodge in the centre. They brought everything, that they would eat, in [to their lodge]. The Yellow Doves cooked, the Bear-Doves were the ones, that they [the Doves] fed first. In one summer they danced four times. They stopped. The older members of the society relied on them [the young Doves]. They [the young Doves] were told by them [the older members], that they should watch all the people. Then they fixed up their arrows [and] their top-knots. [When] they had stopped their dancing, they were not dangerous. They separated, they moved to the mountains, they did not dance any more [during that summer]. In winter the only thing they chased was the buffalo.

I was thirteen years old, when I became a member of the society of the Braves. They gave a pipe to one another. He [the youth that entered the society] put in the tobacco with other weeds. He entered the lodge. He gave the pipe to a Brave. When he had given him the pipe, he said to him: Give me your Brave-badge. And the Brave answered him: Yes, I give it you. He [the Brave] told him: Now, touch the earth. Put sage there [on the earth]. We shall use sweet-grass for incense. You will make your incense with the buffalo-chip-fire. We shall make the paint liquid in the cup of water. Then [the Brave] told him: Now take off your clothes. And the young man [that entered the society] took off his clothes. And the paint was in the liquid. And he took it. And he put the paint all over his body. With the black paint, the black liquid, he was painted that way beneath each eye, that it looked like tears. There was a round hole cut in the back-part of his robe. Even if his robe was very good, there would be a hole cut in it. His moccasins were the only thing, that was left on him. All his partners were treated the same way. The Braves had done being initiated.

The chief of the Braves had a rattle. There were [two] White Braves, and there were [two] owners of water-bags, and one owner of a willow-switch, and there were two Bear-Braves. They were very mean. And [when] they [these Bear-Braves] danced, the things that belonged to them, they were dancing with, were sticks, and a knife at the end [of each stick]. There they put [the knife]. With those things they danced. They stuck them [the sticks] in the ground. When the Bear-Braves danced, then they pulled out those [sticks] that they had stuck in [the ground]. [The people] were very much afraid of them. They would quit. [When] they had done dancing, they ran to the waters of lakes. Even if their moccasins were good, they threw them away. [When] they went back [to] the circle-camp, they went around. The older members were standing there. They [the Braves] gave orders [to the main camp] not to go about [out of their lodges]. They would tear them [the people] to pieces [if they did not obey]. The Braves were going around to get leggings. [They would say:] Be quiet, the medicine-lodge-makers [the woman, that gives the medicine-lodge, and her husband] are going to sing. You must not make noise. To-morrow in the morning we shall move.

And the Braves alone would look for the buffalo, where there were the most. That way [as they were told by the Braves] they [the Peigans] would move. They [after having moved] were camped. The Braves had seen the buffalo. When they came back, they talked among themselves.

They said: There was none [no buffalo] standing about, [not] even one. Then we just knew, that there were many buffalo. All the people were happy then. Thus they [the Braves] would say. When they said "There are many buffalo", then there were no buffalo. All the people then just knew, that there were no buffalo. And [when] they would catch a person, he would say to them: Here are my things. I give them to you. Tear them up. [Then] they would not tear them. If he said to them "Do not tear them", then they would tear them. And [therefore] some person would tell them: Tear them up, tear my things up. And some other person would ask him [the spokesman of the Braves] for one or another thing: Give it to me. Then he [the spokesman of the Braves] would not give it. If he [that person] said "Do not give it to me," then he would give it to him in a hurry. A Brave was a person with whom everything was reversed. He was a person with whom everything was most reversed. What belonged to one Brave [that means: what is said about a Brave in general], that kind of people they were all. The Braves were people with whom everything was reversed. [When] they had done dancing, they separated. They took each of them their own things with which they had danced. The same way [as the Doves did] they [the Braves] would move to the mountains. And four times in one summer were their dances, and then they separated. And the dogs are scratching the ground [after having eaten] [that means: the story is at an end].

[Cf. Grinnell blt 222 sq., Wissler-Duvall mbi 105 sq., McClintock ont 449 sq. 455 sqq.]

Monday, July 10.

The Uhlenbecks were invited to visit the Grinnells. They accepted the invitation and indeed went to New York, as is apparent from the Introduction to "Some Blackfoot Song Texts," in Archives Internationales d'Ethnographie 23: 241–42. (The Blackfoot text is not included in this volume.)

Some Blackfoot Song Texts by C. C. Uhlenbeck

On my return from Blackfoot reservation in 1911 I stayed a few days at the hospitable house of dr. G.B. Grinnell, the distinguished author on the culture and folklore of the Plains tribes. Then he had the kindness to give me the following short song texts, recorded by him phonographically in 1897, with the permission to transcribe them, to translate them in my own way, and to publish them. I accepted this gift with gratitude, the more because the number of such song texts recorded by myself was rather small (see *Original Blackfoot Texts*, 66–68 and *A New Series of Blackfoot Texts*, 210).[38]

1. Smoking song of Beaver medicine, sung when the pipe is unwrapped.
   Sit up, man, that you may smoke!

2. Another smoking song.
   Get up, that you may smoke!

3. First song of Beaver medicine.
   In summer, when I go out, if I see then [anything dangerous], I am saved, I dive.

4. Crow Water song.

Why are the people talking around? Now there are many horses coming this way. Here they are, I took them.

5. Peigan Water song.
   [The one who is] on high had pity on me. Why are the people talking around? I have supernatural power.

6. War song [the mother of a certain young girl supposed to be speaking).
   Though I was going to have him for son-in-law, now I shall marry [him] [myself]. I all at once admire him (?)

7. Crazy Dog Society song.
   It is bad to be old.

8. War song (?)
   … , do not feel uneasy about me, I shall be eating berries on my way home.

9. Camp song.
   He came in with the dog travois.

10. Song of unknown character (perhaps referring to a buffalo-stone).
    The stone says: Take me.

11. Song of unknown character.
    I am hungry.

12. Song they used to sing when they came in sight of the enemy's camp and prepared to make the charge.
    His [that means: their] children, let us take them now.

13. Song said to have been sung by a party of Blood Indians who returned from war and found the people in their own camp still asleep.

Eastern Bloods, you are still asleep, we shall arrive.

14. Love song.

As I hunger for even a very old woman [, the more I hunger for the love of young ones].

15. Joke song.

A skunk with a bare (?) backbone.

16. Kit-fox trapping song.

May I trap a kit-fox!

17. Eagle song of the Beaver medicine.

Man, I am an eagle; man, I alone have supernatural power.

18. Triumph song [the defeated enemy supposed to be speaking].

What is the matter with us? We arrive, we come here, we are all crying.

19. Brave Society dance song.

The Bloods will die [i.e. get killed] because of their own foolishness.

20. Dove Society song.

Doves, all of you, try hard!

Wednesday, July 12.

"The young man and the beavers," nsbt, 85–92. Preface: "Another version. told by Walter Mountain-chief, whose Indian name is Black-horse-rider (Síkimiåχkitopi), interpreted by Tatsey."

The young man and the beavers.

(Another version)

There was a poor boy, he was called Round-cut-scabby-robe. The ancient Peigans were shaking their heads [dancing]. And there was a poor second wife, she was his sweetheart. She dressed like him, the way he dressed. For shame he went away. He slept about. He slept about, that he might have a dream. He was taken in into the water by some beavers. There was a lodge, a real lodge [there in the water]. He was adopted by the beaver-chief. He [the beaver-chief] became a person. And his wife and his children also turned into persons. And that one, that had the same age as he [as Round-cut-scabby-robe] then became a partner to him. And Round-cut-scabby-robe then stayed there. It was in winter there in the beaver-lodge, and his adoptive father had counters [to count the moons and the days]. They were sticks. He [Round-cut-scabby-robe] would see him [his adoptive father] from time to time. Always after a long while he [the adoptive father] would put aside one of those sticks. And then after a long while he was told by [his adoptive father]: My son, the time, that it will be spring, is getting very near. And after a long while he saw, that the beaver went out. After a long while he entered. He [Round-cut-scabby-robe] then was told by him: My son, spring is getting very near. Now the rivers will flow clear [of ice].

And then after a long while all the beavers went out. And when they entered after a long while, he [Round-cut-scabby-robe] suddenly saw, there was a beaver-child, that entered with a leaf [as a sign of the spring].

He [Round-cut-scabby-robe] was very happy, when he saw it. Then Round-cut-scabby-robe was in a hurry to go home. Then he was told by his [adoptive] father: Now, my son, the summer has come. He answered him: I will go home, I am in a hurry. He was told by [the beaver-chief]: Yes, to-morrow you may go home. He was very happy, that he was going home. He was told by his partner: Now this night, partner, my father will ask you, which [thing] you will take, when you will go home. Tell him then, that you will take that stick cut by beavers. And tell him also, that he should give you that youngest one [that came in with the leaf], and the incense-maker, and sweetgrass, that you can make incense with. Next morning he was told by his [adoptive] father: Now my son, now you are going home. Say, what I shall give you. Then he told him: Give me three things, your counters over there, and that stick cut by beavers. And you will also give me that youngest beaver. Then he was told by [the beaver-chief]: Ask me for something else. You will have no profit of that child of mine. He answered him: No, give me that one. And when he had asked four times, that he might give him [the beaver-child], then he was told by him: Yes, you may take him now. I am stingy for that one, but now I give him to you. And then he was given power with each thing [that was given to him].

And [when] he was given power with each thing, then he was told by [the beaver-chief]: Now you are going home. Now shut your eyes. And he shut his eyes. And after a long time he was told by [the beaver-chief]: Now open your eyes. When he looked, he was standing out [of the water] on the bank. And then he started to go home. And after a long while he came to the lodges. There was one, [that] came out from the camp, he [Round-cut-scabby-robe] was seen by him. He said to [the man from the camp]: Don't come up to me. Now go right back to the camp, that you say to the people there, [that] I have come back, that they might make a sweat-lodge for me. Then that one, whom he had asked to do so, went back to the camp. Then there was a sweat-lodge made for him. And some one went after him and told him, that he might come to

the camp. Then he went to the camp. And then he came to the sweat-lodge. Then he took a sweat. And then he told the news about how he had wintered with those beavers. And after a long while he said to the ancient Peigans: We shall go on a raid. Then they went on a raid. And after a long while they came to the snake Indians. The ancient Peigans never used to kill [the enemies]. They only used to see one another [the different tribes each standing on one side of a river]. They would become chiefs, because they saw the people of another tribe [without having a fight].

Then Round-cut-scabby-robe said: I will kill the chief of the Snake Indians. And he was forbidden by all to kill him [literally: that he might not kill him]. He said: I will kill him. He said to his partner [one of the Peigans]: Don't move from this place, where we stand. I shall come back here. When I have killed him, I will dive down with him, and these people will think, that I will come out of the water below. And then he dived in to the water towards the other side of the river. [When] he was seen by the Snake Indians, that he dived in, then they all ran to the edge of the river. And he was nearly diving across [to the other shore], and then he jumped up, then he stood up in the water. And the chief of the Snake Indians went in to the water towards him. He [that chief] had a big arrow. And Round-cut-scabby-robe took that stick cut by beavers. The Snake Indian came close to him. And Round-cut-scabby-robe sang his war-song. The words of his song were: My father, try hard. And he was shot at by the Snake Indian. When he was shot at, then he yelled. He threw the stick cut by beavers in front of him. That [stick] was it, [that] he [the Snake Indian] hit [with his arrow]. The he [Round-cut-scabby-robe] took it [the arrow] away from him. With that big arrow he then killed him. And he took him by his hair. And the Snake Indians cried in a rush, when their chief was held by his hair. And Round-cut-scabby-robe dived with him down the river. And his party made a charge down the river [on the dead chief]. They then thought, [that] he would come up out of the water below. And where his partner stayed, there he then came up out of the water. And he scalped him. And he gave half [of the scalp] to his partner.

Then he went home. And after a long while they came, in a circle, in sight of the camp. And that poor second wife was still picking rose-berries. She was told: There comes Round-cut-scabby-robe. He killed [one] out [of the enemies]. He is far ahead [of the others]. And then that woman spilled her roseberries. And she ran home to her lodge. There [in the lodge] was her husband, [who] was the owner of beaver-rolls [literally: water-owner]. Then her face was fixed up [with paint] by him, and then she went back to Round-cut-scabby-robe. [From that time] her husband was Round-cut-scabby-robe. Then she was given by him the scalp and the big arrow. She was told by him: I present your [former] husband with them [with the scalp and the big arrow]. And the owner of the beaver-rolls then gave him in return his younger wife, and his lodge, and his beaver-rolls. And that summer he went three times again on a raid [literally: and then three summer-times he went again on a raid]. And on these raids he each time counted a coup. Finally he [the owner of the beaver-rolls] gave him in return [all] his wives. Then [Round-cut-scabby-robe] had the owner of the beaver-rolls, as a single man instead of himself, staying with him in the same lodge. Then Round-cut-scabby-robe became a chief of all [the people]. And then after a long while the ancient Peigans had a famine. They suffered very much for something to eat. Then there was a chief, [who] said: Now we shall go in a circle after buffalo. And after we have made the circle after buffalo, then we shall sing. Round-cut-scabby-robe was then painted in the face. And they sang to him and to those beaver-rolls [he had in front of him]. Then they got through singing to him, [and] then he rolled them [the beaver-rolls] up. His partner [the former owner of the rolls] had had four wives. His lodge was big. Every time Round-cut-scabby-robe had gone to war, he had been given by him [one of] his wives in payment [for his pres-ents]. He finally had been given by him all his wives in payment [for his presents], and he had also received in payment his lodge and his beaver-

rolls. Then [the former husband] just stayed around instead [of Round-cut-scabby-robe, who was now the owner of everything].

And then Scar-face was to have the medicine-lodge. He was told by his partner Round-cut-scabby-robe: I think, this my war-bonnet be-comes you well. Make the medicine-lodge with it. And there was also a pin and a forked stick [to make incense with], those were the three [things], that were lent to [Scar-face] by his partner. And that is why now the medicine-lodge-makers [the women, that give the medicine-lodge: one woman every year] wear the war-bonnet. And that is why the medicine-lodge-makers use the forked stick as a cane. Those were [the things], they lent to each other [that means: Round-cut-scabby-robe lent to Scar-face]. And Round-cut-scabby-robe then put that beaver-skin and that stick cut by beavers in his beaver-rolls. And now the owners of the beaver-rolls [literally: water-owners] still own those [things]. And that war-bonnet, that he [Round-cut-scabby-robe] lent to his partner, he then gave it to him. And he then [also] gave him the pin and the forked stick. And that is why the medicine-lodge-makers still now have many beaver-songs [literally: water-owner-songs] that they sing. Round-cut-scabby-robe's partner Scar-face paid him back seven songs, that are sung when the people are going to the medicine-lodge, seven moon-songs, and seven elk-songs. That way he paid him back in songs. And those three [sets of seven songs] were given to him by [Scar-face]. And that is why the owners of the beaver-rolls still now sing [those songs]. As soon as the [new] moon is there, they always sing moon-songs. They sing thrice seven songs to the moon. And now these owners of the beaver-rolls still sing to her. And now the boiling is ended.

[Cf. the first version above, and the references given at the end of it.] **The "first version above" is in this collage under July 27.**

Sunday, July 16.

Uhlenbeck reads "Blue-face" and "Clot-of-blood" to Jim Blood and Eagle Calf: obt, 18–23 and 34–50 resp.

Blue-face.
———

The ancient Peigans were corralling. There was a fine young man, [that] was called Blue-face. These buffaloes were running around inside [the corral]. There was a scabby buffalo-cow. Blue-face touched her with his arrow. He said [at the same time]: Look here this. And the fat ones were killed. They were all killed. Then the lean ones were driven out. There she was, that scabby buffalo-cow.

Blue-face was not married. He had a lodge of his own. After a long time they had another buffalo-corralling. Blue-face invited [his friends]. It was night, they were still smoking. There a boy entered. His robe was a yellow calf[-robe]. He went then to Blue-face. He sat by him. The [invited] men then went out. Blue-face said to him: Little boy, why did you enter? He answered him: My mother told me: Blue-face is your father. That's why I entered. He said to him: Where is your mother? He answered him: She sits here outside. He told him: Tell her, that she should enter. When he saw that woman, then he thought: She is very fine. He said to her: Sit here. He said to her [also]: What are you talking about [to your son, telling him, that I am his father]? I don't know you. She told him: A long time ago, then here was a corral. I was running around inside. You then touched me with your arrow. From that I had a child. Blue-face said to her: You are right. I know you.

It was a long time, that he had her as a wife. His wife told him: You treat me badly. I shall tell you one thing. Don't hit me with fire. After a long time Blue-face's partner was sitting in his lodge [on a visit]. It smoked there in his lodge. His wife did everything, she could, to that lodge [to drive the smoke out]. He ever and again said to her: Go out and steer the ears of the lodge. And it was still smoking. His partner went out [home]. He grabbed there [a burning stick from the] fire, he hit his wife with it. She then jumped out. Her son was just a little behind her. They turned again into buffaloes. Blue-face, jumping, followed them, which were buffaloes. All the people saw them.

After a short time Blue-face said to his partner: Partner, I shall go to get my wife back. If I don't come [back], say then to your pets [these pets were magpies], that they must look for me. If they find only one hair of my head, let them bring it. Bring me back to life by magic. [After] he had shown him about [those magical performances, which would bring him back to life], he went away. [After that] he would come to buffaloes, [and then] he would sit a long time [looking at them], [but] he did not see his wife. Then he would go away. Once more he came where buffaloes were. There was a creek, where these buffaloes used to drink. He sat by. All the calves there went to drink. He was looking at them. They had finished drinking. They began to ascend. His son walked behind. He [the father] was already seen by him. He [the son] then came to him. He turned then into a person. He [the father] said to him: Boy, I come to see you [both], your mother [and yourself]. He answered him: Sit there for a moment. I shall go and tell my mother. He [the boy] then ran off.

After a while that woman came to her husband. He told her: Come on, let us go home. She said to him: My father and my elder brothers say to you [that you must come]. They then went in, where these buffaloes were. He came there. He was told by his brothers-in-law: We shall dance four times. If you recognize your son, then when these dances are completed, your wife and your son will go home with you. Now to-night we shall dance.

He was secretly told by his son: My father, they dance all night. Don't sleep. When I dance by you, I shall have one ear down. They then began to dance. After a very long while he [the father] was told by his father-in-law: Tell me, which is your son? He caught him as he went by [recognizing him by his ear down]. He said to him [his father-in-law]:

And here he is. They danced all night. He repeatedly was told the same by his father-in-law. Next morning he was secretly told by his son: My father, try as well as you can, don't sleep at all. Then the buffaloes began to dance there again. He was again told by his son: When I dance by you, I shall have one eye shut. They danced a long time. [His father-in-law] said to him: Which is your son? He got up and caught him. He said to him [his father-in-law]: Here he is. [His father-in-law] said to him: You are right. All night he was told the same [by his father-in-law]. In the morning they stopped [dancing].

Then it was another night, he was again secretly told by his son: When I dance by you, I shall have one leg up. They danced a long time. He was told by his father-in-law: Which is your son? He caught him, when he went by. He said to him [his father-in-law]: Here he is. [His father-in-law] said to him: You are right. All night he was told the same [by his father-in-law]. When it was nearly morning, he slept. His son kicked him [to wake him up]. And in the morning they stopped [dancing]. He was told by his son: Oh my father, pity me, don't sleep. Now it is [only] one [night more], they will dance. If you don't sleep, we shall go home to-morrow. Now when we dance again, when I dance by you, I shall kick up. Then it was another night, they began to dance again. They danced a long time. He was told by his father-in-law: Which is your son? He said to him: Here he is. [His father-in-law] said to him: You are right. After a while he slept, and his son kicked him, when he danced by. And again and again he was told by his father-in-law: Which is your son? He always said to him: And here he is.

It was nearly day, his son went on kicking him. His father-in-law came to him. He said to him: Which is your son? He did not say anything. He [the father-in-law] then said [to the buffaloes]: Your brother-in-law has fallen asleep. His son kicked him again. He did not wake up. These buffaloes ran over him. He was tramped to pieces.

After a long time his partner said to those magpies: look out again for my partner. If you find only one hair, bring it here. They had gone a long time, they came flying with a small piece of his scalp. [Then] he performed, what his partner had told him. He then returned to life [literally: he then again became a person]. He said to him: I shall never marry again. And the dogs have separated [that means: the story is at an end].

[Cf. C. Wissler-D.C. Duvall, Mythology of the Blackfoot Indians, New York 1908, pp. 117 sqq. and J.O. Dorsey, the Cegiha language, Washington 1890, pp. 138 sqq. 141 sq. 145 sqq. 157 sqq.]

Clot-of-Blood.

A man, who had three wives, [and] his father-in-law and his wife were camping together [either family having its own lodge]. Every night all the buffaloes would come there in the bend of the river. In the morning he always said to his father-in-law: Come on, let us go and make noise with our feet [to scare the buffaloes]. They then went. That man said to his father-in-law: Go on and run. I shall stay here. The old man then drove the buffaloes up. When they were running by, that man [the son-in-law] would kill the fat ones. And his father–in-law would come to him [expecting some food]. He [the son-in-law] would say to him: Go on, old man, go home and tell the women to come out, you can later eat of the entrails. He was starving his parents-in-law. That old man would say to his daughters [the three wives of his son-in law were sisters]: You are wanted [by your husband] to stretch your hands out [to bring in the meat]. He [the old man] then went home. His wife said to him: Did your son-in-law give you any [meat]? He would say to her: He might give us some, when his wives bring his pieces of the carcases. [But] he would not give them anything, that they might eat.

Every morning again their son-in-law would say: Where is the old man? He would answer him: Here I am. And he would say to him:

Come on, let us go again and make noise with our feet. Then they would get to the place, where he [the son-in-law] used to sit. That man would say to his father-in-law: Go on, old man, run in again. And the old man again drove the buffaloes up. And that man [the son-in-law] would kill the fattest cows. His father-in-law would come to him. He then always said to him: Go on, old man, go and tell the women to come out, you can later eat of the entrails. And that old man would go home. He then always said to his daughters: You are wanted [by your husband] to stretch your hands out [to bring in the meat]. He then always said the same [as before] to his old woman.

Then it was a long time, that his son-in-law treated them that way. The youngest of his daughters was it, [that] used to feed them. She used to throw the round pieces of meat quickly at them. One morning that man said again: Come on, old man, let us go again and make noise with our feet. Then they started to that same place, where that man used to sit. They got there. He said again to his father-in-law: Go on, old man, run in again. The old man again drove the buffaloes up. [While] he was still walking in the buffalo-trail, he suddenly saw a big clot of blood. He feigned to fall by it. He pulled his arrows out [of the quiver]. He then put that clot of blood in [the quiver], and he put his arrows on top of it. He came to his son-in-law. He [the son-in-law] said to him: What were you doing over there? Why were you seen about during such a long time? He answered him: No, [I was not doing anything wrong], I fell down, and my arrows were spilled. I was putting them away [in my quiver]. That's why I stayed a long time. He said to him: Go home and tell the women to come out. He then went home. The old man said to his daughters: You are wanted to stretch your hands out [to bring the meat].

He then went to his lodge. He came near it. He said ahead to his old woman: Old woman, put the stone-pot in the fire, you have got something to eat. She answered him: How is that! It must have been given to him by his son-in-law. He said to her: No. Old woman, here is a clot of blood. I found it. And he went in. He pulled that clot of blood out [of

the quiver]. He said to his old woman: Make haste with it, that we may eat it. Our son-in-law might come. That old woman put it in [the pot]. That, which she used for boiling, [that means: the pot] got very hot. Something suddenly cried from the water. Here was a child. That old man said to his old woman: Old woman, throw him out. We shall live by means of him. When the old woman pulled him out, she said to her old man, that it was a boy. Then she wrapped him up.

And her son-in-law and his wives came home with the pieces of the carcases. That man heard, [that] here was a child crying. He said to his youngest wife: Go and see it. If this child is a boy, say to them [the old folks], that they kill him, [but] if it is a girl, that they wrap her up. That woman came back into the lodge. She said to her husband: It is a girl. That man said to his second wife: I don't believe that one. Go you also. What is it? She came back into the lodge. She said to him: It is a girl. He said to that one, he sat by [his eldest wife]: I don't believe these. Go you and see it. Then that woman went into her father's lodge. She said to her mother: What is that child? My husband wants to know what it is [literally: is thinking, that he may know it]. Her mother told her: Oh, he [my son-in-law] has got another wife. It is a girl. Then that woman went home. When she entered over there, she said to her husband: You got another wife. It is a girl. That man said: Go and give your old boiled bones to your mother, that she might make soup with them. The youngest wife put in a round piece of meat with the bones. She said to her mother: These are [the things], that you can boil.

Then night came. That child [Clot-of-blood] said to his mother: Hold me to all these lodge-poles. Begin holding me from the door-lodge-pole [that means: hold me first to the door-lodge-pole]. That old woman then held him to each one. [When] she held him to the last one, then he jumped down. They [the old folks] were told by him: I am very hungry, give me to eat. That old woman said to him: Oh, my boy, your brother-in-law over there is starving us. She then cooked a piece of that round meat for him. He said to them: Where do you kill [animals]? That old man said to him: Here, higher up the river. He [Clot-of-blood] said to him: Before daylight we shall go and make noise with our feet.

Then they started in the night. That old man said to his son: Right here stays your brother-in-law. His son told him: Go on, run in. That old man again drove the buffaloes up. They began to run by that young man. He killed the fattest cow. His old man came to him. He [Clot-of-blood] said to him: Old man, just sit there, I shall skin it. And that [other] man [the son-in-law] got up. He then took his arrows. He went to the lodge of his father-in-law. He said: Where is that old man? The old woman told him: It is a long time, that he started. He said to her: Yes, it is a long time, that he started. I have a mind to begin with you [that means: to kill you first]. And he went to the place, where he used to make noise with his feet. That old man said to his son: There my son-in-law comes. His son told him: Just eat [that means: just go on eating of the breast-fat]. He said to him: I am very much afraid of your brother-in-law. He said to him: Don't be afraid, he will do you no harm. What your son-in-law says, you must repeat right after him. His son-in-law came close to him. He [the old man] was told ahead by him [the son-in-law, who did not see Clot-of-blood, because he was concealed behind the carcase]: Aha, there is nobody to prevent me from killing you [literally: that you may not die for me]. He said back to him. Aha, there is nobody to prevent me from killing you. He teased him by eating that brisket. He [the son-in-law] said to him [the old man]: That one eating is living the last of his life. The old man said to his son-in-law: Jump up, he is very close. He [the son] said to him: Wait, talk back to him. He is living the last of his life, who is coming this way. He was shot at from a distance by his son-in-law, he as nearly hit by him. He said to his son: Help me, he might hit me, jump up. He [the son-in-law] was just about to get to the [old] man. And Clot-of-blood jumped up. He said to him [his brother-in-law]: Aha, it must be a long time, that he has treated my old man that way. He was told by his brother-in-law: Yes, he is treated badly [but only in fun]. He was thought [by me]: I just scare you for a

while. Clot-of-blood walked towards him. He [his brother-in-law] was shot by him. There he was killed by him.

Clot-of-blood said to the old man: And, old man, take only the choicest parts of this carcase. After a while be owner of your son-in-law's happy things. They then went home. He said to the old man: Now, old man, which of these your children pities you? He answered him: The youngest one, she is it, [that] pities us. She throws secretly of the round pieces of meat to us. Clot-of-blood then went into his brother-in-law's lodge. He said to the youngest: You must trouble yourself about [that means: take care of] our father and our mother. And then he killed those others. He said to his old man and his old woman: Here is now your lodge. Which way are there any people? They said to him: This way, higher up the river. He said to them: To-morrow I shall go higher up visiting.

There he went. He then got to those, who were camping [that means: to the main camp of the ancient Peigans]. They were corralling. The lodge, he went into, was an old-woman's-lodge. They [the old women] told him: that one is a man's-lodge, where you ought to go in. Here we are all old women. He said to them: No, I don't care for man's-lodges, I am an old-woman's-child. They fed him. He said to them: How is that? You are corralling. Why do you give me then to eat [meat] with round fat [fat of the guts]? They told him: Oh, my son, why do you say [that] aloud? These bears might hear you. They take all the choicest parts. He said to them: What kind of people are they? They told him: They are bears. They take the wives of the people here away by force. He said to them: I shall go and lead the buffalo in the morning. Go early on high [to the bank]. He then [in the morning] said aloud: People here, you might go and touch [the buffalo, you want, with your arrows], the corral is full. The old women then went up. There he was, their son Clot-of-blood. All the people began to skin. Clot-of-blood killed the fattest one. He began to skin it. He was told by the old women: Alas, those bears will not fail to come. He said to them: Why did you say [that]?

They told him: I should be sorry to lose the back-fat of this carcase. He said to them: Sit there. There will be none, that will take this back-fat away from you.

The old women said to him: There they are, those bears. He said to them: Don't think about it. That bear-cub [that was coming] looked about for those pieces of fat. He would bite them down. He [the cub] came to him [Clot-of-blood]. He [Clot-of-blood] said to him [the cub]: Yes, what are you going to do? Why do you just stand by those pieces of back-fat? He answered him: My mother told me, that I should gather up these pieces of back-fat. Clot-of-blood went to him and cut him across the face. He just was crying, while running home. That bear said to his mother: There is a man. [When] I was about to take those pieces of fat, he cut me across the face. His father told him: Take us over there, he may cut *me* across the face. The old women said to their son: Those are coming, they all are coming. That she-bear went stretching. Her husband was coming behind. He [too] went stretching. Clot-of-blood went back to them. He first jumped to the she-bear. He stabbed her. And he made another jump to the he-bear. And he killed both of them. He said to those old women: Come on, let us go home. He just took them over to the lodges. He said to them: Which is the lodge of those bears? They told him: Over there in the centre is a bear-painted lodge. They entered it. Some other bears still sat there. He said to them: Go out. When they jumped out by him, he stabbed them. He did not stab only one. He said to him: There can be more bears from you in the future [I won't kill you]. He said to his old women: Here is your lodge [the bear-painted lodge]. He said to the people here: Come here, that you take your wives out.

Then the people here were afraid of him, after he had killed these bears. He said to those old women: Which way are there any more lodges? They told him: And here, higher up the river. He then started to go. It was night, [when] he went among the lodges. There was an old-woman's-lodge, he then entered it. The old women said to him: Young man,

which way are you travelling? He ought to go into the man's-lodges. He said to them: I am visiting about. I am an old-woman's-child, I don't go into man's-lodges. They put [pieces of meat] by him, that he might eat. He said to them: Yes, you are corralling. Why do you give me then to eat [meat] with round fat [fat of the guts]? And they said to him: Oh, young man, the owners of the snake-painted lodge might hear you. They take all the fat pieces. He said to them: I shall go and lead the buffalo in the morning. Come early. Then he went out to lead the buffalo. Then all this people came to that corral. There were his old women. That one, that he killed, was fat again. Then he skinned it. He said to his old women: Let us only take the back-fat, and let us go home. Then they were sorry to lose the carcase. He said to them: After a while you must own the happy things of the owners of the snake-painted lodge. Then they went home.

After his old women had fed him, he said to them: I shall visit the Big-snake-man. He just entered that lodge. At the upper end he sat down. These women all sat there [not the old women, but women, who had been made captives by the snake]. They said to him: Oh, before that man wakes up – why did you come in? He kills people – you had better go out. He said to them: No, I shall not go out. That very big snake lay coiled in the upper part. And he [Clot-of-blood] then took the berry-flavoured water [that was standing there]. He drunk that flavoured water. He stuck him [the Big-snake-man] with his knife. He said to him: Why do you sleep? You had better fill your pipe. He then woke up. He immediately rattled. And these others all woke up. He [Clot-of-blood] said to him: Oh, [when you do] like that, you are acting, as if you wanted to fight. He [the snake] stuck his head high up. And he [Clot-of-blood] cut his head off with the flint-knife [he had]. And he cut the head off of each of those others. One crawled out. He [Clot-of-blood] said: From that one more snakes will come. And he said to this people: Come here, that you take your wives out.

He brought his old women in [into the snake-painted lodge]. He said to them: Here is your lodge. Where are more lodges? He was told by them: And this way. He said to them: I shall go visiting to-morrow. They told him: There is [a reason, to have] your ear [open]. There is the Inhaler. Don't go by him on the westside, he will suck you in. Go by him on the eastside. He then went. He got close. He thought: I shall wonder what he will do to me. I shall go on the westside. It was not yet a long while, [when] he heard, that he grunted. He feigned to be sucked in by the wind. He got near him. He saw his mouth. He jumped in into it. When he was standing inside, he saw all the persons [the being had inhaled]. Some were dead, and others were still alive. He said to them: We shall dance. These here [meaning: you] must be crazy [not knowing the way to get out]. He had seen, [that] there high up was the heart of the Inhaler. He put on that flint-knife as a top-knot. He said to them: Come on, you that can, get up. Just from where you lie, shake your head. He just jumped straight up. It was not long, [before] the heart of the Inhaler fell on top of them. He cut [a hole] between his ribs. There was [the opening], [where] they went out. Then they went to these lodges. They said to the people: Go over there to that Inhaler, that you may take your kinsmen out. I have killed him.

He went in to those old women. [After] he had eaten, he said to them: I am visiting. Where are there more lodges? He was told by them: This way, lower down [the river]. There is [a reason, to have] your ear [open]. Over there is a woman, she slides. Don't go there, even if she says to you: Come here, let us slide together for a while. That woman kills people. He then started. He suddenly saw that woman. She said to him: Young man, come here for a while, let us slide together. He said to her: No, I am in a hurry. She told him: It won't be long. He went finally. He said to her: You must slide first, I shall see you. As she started to slide, he threw out his flint-knife. He cut that rope. That woman just fell down there into a whirlpool [where she immediately was torn to pieces by fishes]. He killed her.

He then went. He suddenly saw again [a person, this time it was] a young man. He was told by him: Partner, let us wrestle for a while. He said to him: Yes. He had seen there a flint-knife, it was sticking out a little. When they scuffled, he [Clot-of-blood] threw him on his back against it. He then killed him.

He then went. He saw there a woman. She said to him: Young man over there, come here for a while, let us play at "Sioux-women". He said to her: Yes. She told him: Stand over there. I shall throw my ball [that I have] here [in my hand] over [to you]. He said to her: No, I shall throw it first. And then, when he threw it first, he just smashed her head. She then died. He went back to those lodges. He went in again to his old women. He said to them: Old women, warmed by fire, I killed all those, that treated you badly. Now I shall go south. There was a young man. He [Clot-of-Blood] then went with him.

Then they went south. They were [going] a long time, then they came to a big lake. Then they sat by the shore. He was told by his partner: Partner, this lake is very dangerous. There are people in it. Here is another place, where many of us have died. He [Clot-of-blood] said to him: Over there it looks black, let us go there. Then they got up. They went to him [the being that was looking black]. He was told by his partner: Partner, you must not stir this one, lying there, the Blood-sucker. This is his, this lake. He told him [his partner]: Partner, I shall kill him, because he kills you [that means: your people]. He touched him with his flint-knife. He then started to crawl. It was a long time, before he got into the water. He [Clot-of-blood] said to his partner: I shall go into the water with him. Just stay now here. Look, when this water turns to blood, then I am killed, and then you must go to that hill. Stay there. You will see a cloud in the skies, [a sign that] the Thunder will help me. He will throw this one, that killed me, out [of the water]. And he will scatter this lake. It will never be water again. Then you must go from there.

That young men then sat down. Then he would see, that this water rose high, there in the middle. He then would know: My partner is still fighting that person of the water. After a very long time he then saw, that this water was turning to blood [literally: the turning-to-blood of this water]. Then he knew: My partner is killed. He went to that hill. He then sat there. He looked up. He saw there a cloud. Then the Thunder began to throw lightning. After a short while there was lightning, and the Thunder clattered. Then he saw, that there was a big black thing in the middle of this lake, that rose up high. He [the Thunder] then threw it east, right on the prairie, and this lake was then no water any more. Then he went in [into the place where there had been a lake], where his partner was. His bones were just there. He then went home, and it is he, [who] showed the snake-lodges and bear-lodges [that means: who showed the way of arranging and painting them].

He [Clot-of-blood] is the same one, [that caused, that] there are no rattle-snakes [literally: big snakes] and bears in this country. They fled to the mountains, those that Clot-of-blood let live. He killed the Inhaler, the Wrestler, and the Slider. And the dogs have separated [that means: the story is at an end].

[Cf. G.B. Grinnell, Blackfoot lodge tales, London 1893, pp. 29 sqq.; C. Wissler-D.C. Duvall, Mythology of the Blackfoot Indians, New York 1908, pp. 53 sqq.; S.R. Riggs, Dakota grammar, texts, and ethnography, Washington 1893, pp. 101 sqq. For the incident of the Inhaler cf. W. Matthews, Ethnography and philology of the Hidatsa Indians, Washington 1877, pp. 67 sq.; J.O. Dorsey, The Cegiha language, Washington 1890, p. 31; S.R. Riggs, op. c., p. 91].

Carl "Schelt" tells about the severe winters. Uhlenbeck possibly recorded Schelt's story under Boys' experiences, no. 8. nsbt, 235, as Boys' experiences are told to him "with a few

exceptions by John Tatsey." Story no. 8 might be one of the "few exceptions."

[8] How I live in winter-time. When the first snow comes, I don't go out walking. When it is not snowing, I take my gun, then I go, and I begin to track up jack-rabbits. I don't go far. They run away. And when they are not gone far yet, I shoot them. They don't go much farther. They stop. And when I get close to them, they fall down. One day [I kill] sometimes one, other days I kill three of them. That is how many they are [that I can kill]. Then I go to the brush, then I go in. Now I begin to look for bush-rabbits. Those are the ones, I have a hard time to find. I hunt prairie-chickens too. And I kill only two of them. Other times I don't go out hunting, then I take my skates, I begin to skate on the ice, I go long ways down. Pretty late in the evening I get back home. Then I begin to chop wood [literally: to go after wood]. When I have done chopping, I go in, I go to sleep. And when I wake up, then I go to the stable. I feed the horses, I take them to the water, I then put them back in [the stable], I go home, I eat. When I have done eating, I walk around a little. I then go to bed. And that is all I know about a day.

Tatsey also told Uhlenbeck about snow, nsbt, p. 58. Preface: "Told and interpreted by Tatsey".

Snowblindness.

The germs of the snow make their appearance in the spring with the last big snow. They cannot be seen. They are insects from the snow. They are very small. When we travel about in the snow, then they will fly in into

Tuesday, July 18.

our eyes. Then they eat us, then we are blind. We chew sinews [till they are] soft and wet. We put those in our eyes and pull them along. They [the insects] stick to them [the sinews]. Then we can see again. When the snow is all gone, then these snow-germs turn into grasshoppers. That is the way, the Peigans of long ago were eaten by them. From them [the ancient Peigans] we learned, how we are to cure them. and that is all.

Uhlenbeck works for a long time with Jim Blood. White Quiver is also around. "How they chased the Buffalo," nsbt, 38–41, was "Communicated by Tatsey and Blood, with the help of White-quiver (Ksiksínopa) and Green Grass Bull (Otsímmokuistɑmik), interpreted by Tatsey."

How they chased the buffalo

The chief, that called the people together to build the buffalo-corral, had only certain persons [medicine-men] sitting with him in his lodge [and praying for good luck in corralling]. He would pick out the strongest man. That was the buffalo-leader. The chief, with whom certain persons were staying, would say: We will fix up the corral. Out of big logs they built the fence up [against the cliffs]. They built it high, [so that] the buffalo could not jump out [of the corral]. When they had completed this [corral], then they began to put up small piles of stones, where the buffalo were standing most. That is the way, they put them [the stones]. Behind those [piles of stones] all the people were hiding. And before day-light the buffalo-leader began to run. Another man then went up high, that is the one [that] looked about. When he saw the buffalo, he said down [to the people]: They [the buffalo] are coming. Come on up [to the corral], that you may hide [behind the stone-piles]. That chief, that had certain persons sitting with him, said to those, that were hiding: Do not hold your heads up. The buffalo-leader ran on one side. When the buffalo ran between those piles of stones, then the buffalo-leader ran to the side, where those were that sat at the end. Then they scared [the buffalo] with the leg-parts of their robes. As they [the buffalo] ran farther ahead, they [the men that were hiding] rose up and scared them. And they jumped up at the same time. And [the buffalo] jumped over [the cliff]. And then two persons cried: òwú'.

When the corral was full, the chief, with whom certain persons were staying, said: Know your arrows well, you will shoot what you want. All the people climbed up to the corral. From there they shot down. When the buffalo were running around, they would not kill them all. They only killed the bulls that they needed. And to the others they opened the corral. And they ran out. And all the people went in [to the corral]. They began to skin the carcases. They looked for their [own] arrow. The back-fat [and] all the choice parts of the meat of the animal that they skinned, viz. the tongues, the [unborn] calves, the ribs, the boss-ribs, the flank parts, were given to the chief, with whom certain persons were sitting. And that was all, that the chief, with whom certain persons were staying, now ate. The lodge [the chief's lodge] was big. A young man would hold a stick into the lodge [to ask for some food]. By those that gave away the food [the chief's wives] he [the begging young man] was given from all this [choice] meat. He stuck it all on the stick. He ate it. They all went after the carcases with the dogs' travois. They brought that meat home. And then they cut it for dried meat. They dried the back-fat. That is what they ate with it [with the dried meat]. They dried all the fresh-cut meat [spread out on sticks]. When the sirloins were dried, she [the woman] mashed the leg-bones [and] the back-bone. She would put them in her pot. She boiled them then, and she skimmed the grease. And there was much grease [literally: and the grease was big]. She would cook the sirloins. That is what she made the pemmican of. She fed her children with the grease.

And they gave that pemmican to the chief, with whom certain persons were staying. All the people gave him the pemmican. The pemmican was put away in parfleches. In the spring [the chief] was singing with that pemmican, [when] he was eating it. Then he quit. He was eating all he had. That was the reason that they [his provisions] were all gone. And in summer he quit [eating his provisions]. In summer, when he moved away, when they were looking for the buffalo on the prairie, where there were many of them [of the buffalo], they were all standing around them. Two persons then would start for a run. They would lead out the buffalo. All foot-men would stand around the buffalo. And that was called the "circle". It was the same as [when the people were standing around] the buffalo-corral. And now the dogs have separated [that means: the story is at an end].

[Cf. Grinnell blt. 227 sqq. And Wissler mcbi 33 sqq.]

After dinner old Guardipee interprets: "How their lodges were made," nsbt, 42–43. Preface: "Communicated by Tatsey, with the help of Elie Gardepie and Green-grass-bull and interpreted by Tatsey."

How their lodges were made.

Long ago, in spring, the Peigans moved lower down [to the lower country]. A married man would chase the buffalo, he then would skin [the hides], he would build his lodge with. His wives would jerk the meat off what he skinned. Then they would stretch them [the hides] out to dry. When they became dry, they pulled the stakes up for them. They turned them upside down, and they rolled them up. They put them in an old lodge. In the morning they made a thick mat, [and then] they turned them over on it. They began to scrape the hair-side. When they had done scraping, they rubbed them with brains, and they soaked them. They squeezed the water out of them. When they were beginning to dry, they would spread them and tie them. Then they began to rub them. The women would break stones. With those they were rubbing [the hides]. And then they began to pull them on the string. When the women had finished them, they cut them so that they would fit together. Then they sewed them together. With them they made their lodges. They cut it [the lodge] even, down to the bottom. They sewed the picket-pin-holders to it. When his lodge was finished, they went to the mountains. They chopped their poles. When he had done chopping the poles, he put his lodge up. We called it: "he has a new lodge". That is what I know about the lodges.

[Cf. Wissler mcbi 63 sq. 99 sqq.]

Wednesday, July 19.

Jim Blood came and worked the entire day with Uhlenbeck. He might have laid the groundwork for "A Woman who killed herself," nsbt, 202–3. Preface: "Based on Bloods information, told and interpreted by Tatsey," and "The man who was pitied by wolves," nsbt, 120–23. Preface: "Told by Blood and interpreted by Tatsey."

A woman who killed herself.

The ancient Peigans had the medicine-lodge. There was a woman, [who] had a side-husband [i.e. a lover]. [One day] when these Peigans were having a happy time, that one, her side-husband, was looking at this medicine-lodge. There was a post, he stood up against it. And he laid his face on it. The paint on his face showed on the post. The Peigans had done making the medicine-lodge. That young man went on a raid. It was not long, then he was killed. Then he was immediately known, that he was killed. These Peigans moved away from there. It was not long, then they moved around [that means: they turned back]. They camped near that medicine-lodge. That woman, that had had [that young man as] a side-husband, was treated badly by her husband. She told him: You have treated me badly a very long time. She called [the name of] her side-husband. She told her husband: Now I am very glad, that I may see my side-husband soon. Then she went after wood. Then she went to the medicine-lodge. She got near it. She sang. She sang words about her side-husband: Where is he, I had bodily contact with? She then came up to that post, where she had seen him before. There was a person already sitting inside of the medicine-lodge. By him she was heard, how she sang and how she talked and cried about her side-husband, the one that was killed. Then she went up on the post, by which she had been crying. She sat on top of it. She tied a rope to [the post], and she put it around her neck. Then she jumped down. And that person got up and ran to her. When he got to her, she was already dead. Her husband over there was running [towards her], his wife was already dead. It was that other person, [that] was telling about her, what she talked about and how she came to die. And that is all.

[A similar suicide is recorded by McClintock ont 317 sq.]

The man who was pitied by wolves &c.

A man, his two wives, [and] his three children were very hungry. They had nothing to eat. The winter had come. He was hunting about, he did not find any buffalo. And he had suffered very much for something to eat. They moved camp. He looked for his people. Then he camped. It snowed during the night. The snow was deep. [While] they were still sitting [in their lodge], they heard, [some one] was knocking the snow off himself. He told his wife: Look out. When she looked [out], there were many people, young men. They all had wolf-robes. All of them had packed meat on their back. Then they began to go in [to the lodge]. They said to him: There is some food, go out and get it. There were tongues, boss-ribs, ribs, flanks, a breast, as they are the choicest [parts of the buffalo]. In that way he was brought these things to eat. [The chief of the young men] told him: Over there is somebody corralling. He says to you, he already knows you, [that] you are hungry, [and for that reason he wants you,] that you move over there [where he is]. [When you come there,] everybody will give you some food. And this night, when he got something to eat [from those young men], he was saved by having something to eat. He was happy, having eaten his fill.

These many young men would go to sleep. Some of them were going to make a fire outside. That lodge there was very small. That man told them: It does not matter [that means: there is no objection against it],

that you all sleep in here. And one of the young men told him: It does not matter, that they sleep outside. All of them went out. That man said to his wives: Do you know them? [When he did not get any answer, he said:] Who is a fool? Women [are fools]. [Then the women said:] We don't know them. That man told [his wives]: They are no human beings. They are false persons. Then they slept. And in the morning he told them [the young man]: It is very cold, so we will not move. They told him: It does not matter, move [anyhow]. These many people will pack your lodge-poles. He said to them: Yes, who is the chief [that means: your chief]? [They answered:] Big-wolf is a chief, Old-coyote is a chief, Red-fox is a chief, Kit-fox is a chief, Big-skunk is a chief. Those are the chiefs.

He moved and came to them. They invited him. Big-wolf invited him. Old-coyote invited him also. And Red-fox invited him also. Kit-fox invited him also. Big-skunk invited him also. They all gave him food, that he might eat. They said to him: Just sit there. To-morrow we will corral. You will be given choice parts of meat. Then he suddenly heard, that they made noise. They made the buffalo jump off the cliff. What was brought to him after a long while, were all the choice parts of the meat. And then he had plenty of food. [When] spring was getting near, he was invited by Big-wolf. He was told by him: Be prepared to go quickly. I [that means: we, the whole tribe] am going to separate. These people are no persons. You have been given choice parts of meat. When it was morning, there was nobody at all in the lodges. They all went to enter their holes [being wolves, coyotes &c.]. [Big-wolf] said to him: We belong over there in that other place. They [the man and his family] moved. That man was an owner of beaver-rolls. He got to his tribe. They [the Peigans] were very hungry. From him they got something to eat. He said to [his tribe]: We will move to the buffalo-corral over there. We will take the carcases. From that we shall have something to eat. They moved and came there, and they were all saved by having something to eat. He became a chief, because he found the food. And now the boiling is ended.

In 1910 Tatsey narrated a wolverine story: obt, 60–61.

The wolverine.

There was a young man, [that] hunted in the mountains. He killed there an elk. He started to skin it, and he cut it to pieces. He stood up, [and] then he suddenly saw, there was a woman. She came [to where he was skinning]. He said to her: Sit down here. He washed the entrails. He said to her: Will you eat of these? She said to him: Yes, I shall eat of them. She held, what she was eating, with her fingers' ends. That young man looked at her. He thought, that she was a good-looking woman. He said to her: Where is your home? She answered him: I live in these mountains. Over there is my home. That young man said to her: I am not married. She said to him: Then we shall live together.

They built a lodge there, where he skinned. They lived there a long time. That man beat his wife. She went out. After a while that man followed her. He saw her, the way she was walking. He walked fast. When he got near her, she disappeared into this cliff of rocks. When he got there, he could not find her. He just saw there a hole. He sat by it. He saw wolverines. Then he knew: This my wife is not a real woman. From there he went home. When he got close to those lodges, he became sick [literally: he became not a person], because he smelt fire. Then he entered. He got very sick. He said to his people: Such kind of woman I was living with, that I shall die through her. Then he died. That is why nowadays we are afraid of wolverines.

[Cf. C. Wissler-D.C. Duvall, Mythology of the Blackfoot Indians, New York 1908, p. 162.]

Thursday, July 20.

Uhlenbeck and Jim Blood possibly worked on "Blue-face, another version," nsbt, 134–44. Preface: "Told by Blood, interpreted by Tatsey."

Blue-face.

[Another version.]

These ancient people were camped. There was a fine young man, he was not married. They had happy times [that means: they had plenty to eat]. [When] summer was coming close, then he told his partner: Let us go and hunt about. And there they were, they then were walking about. They had not got anything yet. They came to a scabby buffalo-cow. She was stuck [in the snow]. They were punching her. They were trying to make, that she might jump out [of the snow]. And that young man had tied his quill-ornament to that stick [he was punching with]. Then it [that ornament] fell off [from the stick] by the side of [the buffalo-cow]. Then they went away. They hunted the buffalo. And there they [the buffalo] were, they jumped over the cliff. They [the two partners] were sitting on the edge [of the cliff]. They were laughing at the scabby buffalo-cow. They said: Now to-night, if it is a cold night, the scabby buffalo-cow will freeze. Then they went home. That night that young man had invited [some people]. He was telling the men about that scabby buffalo-cow. He said to them: Now to-night she will not be saved. She will freeze.

Then it became summer. Then it was some time in the fall, the leaves were yellow. They were coming near [the place], where they had been corralling. All the buffaloes had calves already. All their calves were big already. And that scabby buffalo-cow was then saved, [which] that young man this last winter had been talking about, that she would freeze. There was nothing the matter with her [that means: there was nothing wrong with her], she was saved. The scabby buffalo-cow then had a calf. A bull-calf was her child. Then it was big. The scabby buffalo-cow then told her child: We shall go and look for your father. And they started. Then they came to those people [the Peigans]. Then she told her son: Come on, go and look now for your father. I will stay here in the forest [waiting for you]. That boy said to his mother: I shall not know him. That woman told him: You will know him. Here on his face he is blue [literally: blue-faced]. That boy then went.

Then he entered that lodge. When he looked, there was that blue-faced one, while he [the boy] was walking still. He went to the upper end of the lodge. He then sat by him [i.e. by his father]. He did not make himself known [to his father]. That boy then went out. When he went towards the door, he [Blue-face] could not see his [the boy's] feet. A yellow buffalo-calf's hide was his robe. Then he went out. He said to his mother: I have found my father. Over there he is staying. In the morning his son entered again. He was walking to him again. He sat down by him again. [His father] asked him: Little boy, why do you come in? He answered him: No, my mother told me, that I should go and look for you. Now I have found you. [His father asked:] Little boy, what are you talking about? [The boy said:] My mother told me: Go and look for your father, he is blue-faced. [The father inquired:] How is your mother called? [The boy said:] Buffalo-woman. [His father] told him: Go and tell her [to come here]. [When going out], he walked on top of the bed-sticks. Over there near the door he made a misstep. [His father] then saw his track. He had split hoofs.

He came to his mother [and said to her:] My father told you [to come]. [She answered:] Yes, we shall go. Then she entered. When Blue-face looked, [he] never [had seen] such a fine-looking woman [before]. Far down was her hair. She had just yellow hair. Her robe then was very fine. She told him: Here are [moccasins], put them on your feet. They looked just like the roof of a buffalo-mouth. All her clothes were good. Then he asked her. He said to her: I don't know you, that you are my

wife. Now you suddenly surprise me, [saying] that you are my wife. Where did you become my wife? She told him: Do you remember, where I was sitting now last winter? You came there, [you and] your partner. You [both of you] were punching me. Then your quill-ornament fell off by my side. From that I had a child. After long thinking he knew about it. He said to her: Yes, I remember it. Then he lived with her about. And she was very strong in her work. Her robe-making, her sewing, all [of it] was good. He loved her very much. She told him: Pity me. When you strike me here on my head, even if you cut gashes in my head, I shall not care for it. Now I love you very much. I will tell you one thing: Don't hit me with fire. That is the only thing, I am afraid of.

He had invited [some people] in the morning. [The lodge] was smoking. She was told by her husband: Go out and steer the ears. She could not fix it [the lodge]. She would go out again. Then she began again to steer the ears of the lodge. He finally got angry. Blue-face told these men: That is all [that means: you have had your food and your smoke, so you can go]. Then they went out. His wife came in. He said to her: How did you steer the ears of the lodge about? [She answered:] I kept trying to steer the ears of the lodge about. And over there he grabbed up a burning fire-stick. He hit her with it. She just jumped to her robe [to get it]. Then she jumped out. She ran away. The dogs barked. The people on the outside said: There goes a buffalo running away. Blue-face jumped out. He saw his wife running away [literally: his wife's running away], and then he entered [his lodge]. Four nights passed, [and] then he got lonesome. Then he thought of his wife. After a long while he went to look for her. He told his partner: When I have been gone four nights, if I don't come back, then I am killed. Then go and look for me. Try to find a piece of my body. Then Blue-face went away.

He had travelled a long time. He then got a partner, it was a wolf. He was told by [the wolf]: Partner, where are you going [literally: what is the matter with you]? He told him: I am looking for my wife. She went this way. That wolf said: I will go with you. Then he went with him. He was looking for the buffalo. Then they saw, there were many buffaloes. He [Blue-face] was told by his partner: Stay right here. I shall look for her. The wolf then ran towards [the buffalo]. He came back after having looked for her. He had not found her. He came back to his partner [Blue-face]. He told him: She is not there. Then they went away again. Then there were again many buffaloes. The wolf then went to them again. Then he began to look for her again. She was not there. He said to his partner: She is not there. Then they went away again. Then they suddenly saw, there were a great many [buffaloes], they were all lying down. He [Blue-face] was told by his partner: Stay right here. There are a great many, I shall be gone a long time, while I am looking for her. Then the wolf went away. He had not seen just half of them [he had only looked through half of the buffalo-herd]. He went back to his partner. He told him: I did not find her. I will look for her among the other half. When I come back, you will know, if she is there, or if she is not there. Then he came [back] to him [again]. He told him: There she is, I found her. I shall arrange [the place], where you will stay this coming night. Then he ran towards [the creek], where the buffalo would come down. There he dug a hole. He came back to him again. He told him: Now prepare yourself. Put the manure of the buffalo all over your body.

Then he was led on by [the wolf]. It was night. Then they came to that hole. And there Blue-face stayed. Then it was morning. He sat there. The sun was rising high. He saw his boy. He said to him: Little boy, come here. He came to [his father]. He [Blue-face] told him: I have come to look for you [and your mother]. Where is your mother? [The boy answered:] she stays over there. [His father told him:] Go and tell her, that she must come here. And that calf then went away. He came to his mother. He told her: My father has come. He tells you, that you [literally: she] must come to him. Then they went to him. Then she saw her husband. He told her: I have come to look for you. Let us go. She told hem: I shall tell my father [and] my brothers: My husband has come. She was told by her father: Yes, let him come. Then [Blue-face] was told

by his son: you must go to him [to your father-in-law]. Then he came to him. He [the father-in-law] told him: Four times we shall have a dance. You will not sleep. You will catch your boy. If you [always] catch him right [without mistaking another buffalo-calf for him], you will take your wife home with you. If you sleep, you will be treated badly.

Then these buffaloes danced. He was asked by his father-in-law: Which is your son? [He said:] Here he is. He was told by him: Yes, you are right, it is your son. Then they danced again. He was asked by him the same: Which is your son? [He said:] And here he is. [He was told by him:] Yes, you are right, that is your son. During one night's dance it was four times, that he caught his boy. The next dance, another night, he was told by his son: My father, I shall be watched [by all the other buffaloes]. I will shut one of my eyes [while dancing]. [His father-in-law said to him:] When they are dancing in a circle, then look for your boy. He will dance by [you]. He caught him [when passing by]. [He was told by his father-in-law:] Yes, you are right. All the calves shut one of their eyes [while dancing]. He was told by [his boy]: I will keep down one of my ears. The same way the calves kept one ear down. He was again told by [his boy]: I will throw my leg out in front. All the calves threw their leg out in front. The next dance he was told by him: I shall kick you. This was the last night [literally: they – the nights – were complete]. He fell asleep. When he was asleep, [the boy] would kick him. Then he caught him. All these calves kicked him. Then he would [try to] catch him. He would catch another one [than his son]. Then he slept. He was kicked by [the calves]. He would catch another one. He could not catch his boy, because he was so sleepy. And he slept. When he was going to sleep, he quickly fell over. And all these buffaloes began to run around in a circle. Then they began to run over him. He was trampled to death. They continued to run around in a circle. And then he was all trampled to small pieces. There was nothing left of his body. He was trampled to nothing. There was nothing left of his body. In the earth there must be pieces of his body. And then the buffalo stampeded. Then they ran all in different directions.

And then he was known by his partner: My partner has been killed. I shall look about for him. Then he started. Walking about, he then followed [Blue-face's] road, the way he had gone. Then he came to [the place], where he was killed. He was looking about for his body, that he might find some of it. He did not find any part of it. And over there at some distance he again looked about. He kept looking about farther away. He had done [looking] for him. He followed the buffalo-trail. There was a small muddy place. He crossed it. When he had crossed it, then he heard somebody groaning. He began to look about on the earth. He could not see it. Over there in a buffalo-step [i.e. a buffalo-hoof-mark] there was lying something, it was between buffalo-hoofs. It was that big [saying this, Blood showed me with his hands how big it was], what he found there, [a piece of] a blue face. That was what happened to be found of him. That was what was groaning. Then he went home. Then he came there. There were already four sweat-lodges. He then entered one. It [the piece of the face] was a little bigger [now]. They then also went out of another [sweat-lodge]. And then it was big. They then went into another [sweat-lodge]. There he [i.e. his body] was completed. Then they entered the fourth one. Then he was completed altogether, then he became a person again. Then it was, that his whole face turned blue [before that, only part of it had been blue]. In that way I heard about him.

[Cf. Uhlenbeck obt 18 sqq., and the references given obt 23, to which may be added: Dorsey tsp 284 sqq., Dorsey-Kroeber ta 388 sqq., Simms tc 289 sq., Lowie a 199.]

Walter comes in and does one story, the first version of "The elk and his wife," nsbt, 96–99. Preface: "Told and interpreted by Walter Mountain Chief."

The elk and his wife. First version.

There were elks, they were married to each other. And the elk's wife was taken away by a young man [who was also an elk]. Then he looked for his wife. And after a long while he was tired. There was a moose, he [the elk] met him, [and] told him: Partner, now let us go together to look for my wife. Then he [the elk] went together with him. And there was a crow, he [the elk] told him also: Younger brother, let us go together to look for my wife. Then he [the elk] went [also] with him. There the three went together. They went about to the Porcupine hills [literally: Porcupine-tails]. The crow would be ahead and fly about, where there were many elks, and then he would fly back, and then he would say to that elk-bull: Here are elks. And they would go to them, and [the elk-bull] would look for his wife among them, and he would not find her, and then they would go on again. Then they came to the Porcupine hills, and the crow was flying ahead again, and he saw, there were elks, and he flew around them. He saw there the elk-bull's wife. And the crow flew back again. He told the elk-bull: And over there is your wife.

There they stopped by a big cotton-tree. And the elk-bull said: If this big tree is the one, who has run away with my wife, I shall treat him this way. And then he ran up to that tree, and hooked it. He just shook it. And next was the moose to try his power [literally: tried his power]. While he was walking up to the tree, his feet just sunk in into the ground. And when he came to it, he kicked the tree with his leg, and his leg went clear through [the tree], far out [on the other side]. And [when] they had done this, they went away. Then they came to the elks.

Then he saw his wife. He told the one who had run away with his wife: Now I come to see my wife. And he answered him: Yes, now we shall gamble for our wife. And the one who wins her, that is the one who will have her as a wife for good. And he said to him: Yes. And the one whose wife had been taken away from him was told by the one who had run away with his wife: We shall gamble about this big pine-tree here. And he, whose wife had been taken away, ran up to it. He hooked the pine-tree. He did not shake it any way. And then the one, who had taken away his wife, hooked it. He threw the pine-tree down. Then they were afraid of him. They were told by him: If you show fight, I shall treat you this way. Then they were afraid of him, and they went away.

And they went far. And the crow told them [the two others]: Now you are not powerful. I myself would have conquered him, if I had been in the gambling. He was told by them: How could you have conquered him? He told them: I would have sat on his horns, and from there I would have burst one of his eyes. With my bill I would have burst it. And I would have burst his other eye too. When he [the crow] had done saying so, the elk-bull was very sorry, that the crow had not done it. He was told by the moose: Now let us go back, that we pay him [for the woman, so that he may let her go]. I shall pay him my hoofs. And the elk-bull will pay him his horns. And the crow will pay him some of his feathers. Then they went back and they came there. Then they paid him. Then they were told by him: There she is, that you can go back with her. Then the elk-bull had got his wife back.

And that young man [the other elk] went travelling about. He came to a man who camped alone. It was the one, that had the beaver-rolls [literally: the water]. He was welcomed by him [by that man], and after he had done eating there, he gave him those crow-tail-feathers, and those hoofs, and those pieces of the elk-horns. And he told that owner of the beaver-rolls: Now you have treated me well, and I thought, that these things, which I gave you, would be valuable to you. Put them in your beaver-rolls, that you may dance with them. Then the owner of the beaver-rolls took them, and then the young man went out. Then the man was told by his wife: It is good, [that] you tell the young man, that he must give you the songs belonging to them [to the things, he gave you]. And the man told his wife: You are right. Run after him, before he goes far, that you tell him, that he must come back. And that woman ran after him. She told him, that he [literally: you] must come back. Then that young man went back, and he was told by that owner of the beaver-rolls: Teach [literally: show] me the songs belonging to them. Then he taught [showed] him these [songs]. And still now the owners of the beaver-rolls have dances with these three things.

[Cf. The other version, printed below, and also Wissler-Duvall mbi 83 sqq.] **In this collage "another version" of "The Elk and his wife" is under June 14.**

Friday, July 21.

Jim Blood might have given "another version" of "Belly-fat," nsbt, 144–66. Preface: "Told by Blood, interpreted by Tatsey."

Belly-fat.

———

[Another version.] How Belly-fat came to be. There was an old man. There were three of them, his daughter, his old wife, and the old man [himself]. He had no son. They suffered very much for something to eat. After a long while her [the old woman's] daughter went after water. There by the water suddenly lay a rabbit, by the place where they got water. She took it. She went home, and she carried her water home. She entered. She told her father [and] her mother: Here I killed a rabbit. And the old woman was very glad, that she had to eat a rabbit, and that old man was glad just the same. Then they ate it up. Next morning she went again after water, and there was a young antelope. Then she again packed it on her back, by the place where she got water. Then she took it again. Then she carried the water home. She said again to her mother: Here is a young antelope. [While] it was jumping into the river, I pulled it back. And her father was glad, because he had to eat soft meat. They ate a little from it. They were afraid, that they would eat it up too soon. In two nights they ate it up. They suffered again for something to eat.

She again went after water. At the same place, where she got water, there lay suddenly a doe. She was a long time pulling that one about. She went home. She did not pull it far [from where she had found it]. She ran home for help. Then she went home to tell her mother, that she might help her to carry it. They carried it to their lodge. Then they began to skin it. When they first cut through the hide, it [the doe] was very fat. That old man was getting food from his daughter instead [of supporting his family himself]. The ribs were just as fat as dog-ribs. Then they ate it

up again. Then she went again after water. At the same place, where she got water, there was a big young buffalo-cow. She just pulled it ashore. Then again she went home for help. All of them went, [she herself,] her father and her mother. They began to skin. And then that was a big animal, they ate a long time from it. After a long while, then they had eaten it all up. That old man had a suspicion. He thought, [that] there must be some one, that gave it to her. He told his old woman: I shall watch our daughter. He falsely said: I shall hunt. Where she got water, there on one side he hid himself lying low.

After a short while he suddenly saw, there was a big person, who carried a cow on his back. He unloaded it [from his back]. When he had unloaded it, he rested and cried. He said: I wonder, if they are fat, I am tired now [with bringing food to them]. I am going to eat them. He stood down in the water. Then he went away. That old man went home. He entered. He told his old woman: Take quickly [our things together]. There is no such danger as that, how we are getting our food. We are being fattened. The things that were given to our daughter, those will cause us to be eaten. They ran away for escape. Then it was night. They were running all the night. Then it became morning. Then they kept on running for escape. Their daughter would run back to look back, then she would run after them. It was afternoon. Then he [the giant] overtook them. The old folks were out of breath by running. They had froth at the mouth from running. They saw him, that was chasing them. They told their daughter: Try to make your escape. We have done growing [that means: we have lived our full life]. She ran away, she tried to make her escape. She left her father [and] her mother.

Where she was running, she saw a man. He was shaving his arrowsticks and his bow. She just ran by his side. She prayed to him. She said to this man: Pity me, hide me, I shall marry [you]. My father and my mother may be killed by him. He is a man-eater. He told her: Yes, run farther on in that direction. Then run back. Run back [literally: run through] the same way [you went] [to the place where you started from].

Then he took her. He put her in his belt, he put her right there. After a short while the giant came to him. The man was seen by [the giant]. He [the giant] tracked her up to him. Her tracks were up to him [to the man who concealed her], her tracks went past him. [The giant] came there. He asked [that man]: Did you see any person? He answered him: No, I did not see any. Then he [the giant] went past him. He went to [the place], where she had turned back. He came also back [not seeing any tracks farther]. He then came to that man. He said to [that man]: She stays right here, give me her. I will eat her. I am very tired, I am very angry with them [i.e. with the girl and her old folks]. He kept saying to him: I am telling you, she went this way. He was telling him: No, she stays right here. Give me her now. I will eat her.

[The giant] became angry with him, he said to him: If you don't give me her, then I will eat you too. That man said to him: Get away from me. He gave him two warnings [literally: marks]. [The giant] was just about to attack him. When [the giant] was not going away, [that man] took his bow. He hit him there on top of the head. He knocked him in two. Then he killed him. He took the girl out [of his belt]. He told the girl: I shall make these, your mother [and] your father, alive with my arrows. There they were, they had not been dead a long time. The man-eater then had swallowed them. Then that man made them alive. That girl pitied her mother and her father. She was crying. Four times he shot his arrows up [in the air]. [After his first shot] he took another one of his arrows. The same way he shot up again. The second time [he shot] they did not seem to be moving. The third time, he shot, they moved. And then he shot up again with his blunt arrow-point. [That man] cried: Out of the way, there the blunt arrow-point is coming down, it might hurt you [literally: that you might be shot by it]. Then they jumped up and went away. The girl told her father and her mother: By this one we are saved.

When they [the old folks] went away, that man told his parents-in-law: Go to your tribe. Then he had got another wife [viz. that girl]. He then went to his lodge. Then he came there. And then he suddenly saw that woman [viz. his first wife]. That man said to his first wife: Pity her, you are very mean, I pity that girl very much. She has still a father, she has still a mother [that means: she is not a poor orphan, and therefore she deserves to be respected]. Then that man hunted. He was strong at getting his food. He had lived with her [with that girl] a long time [already]. He told her wisely, he told her: Be careful, that wife of mine is very bad. She kills the wives that I get. That girl was thought of a great deal by him. She [the first wife] was secretly jealous of her. She [the girl] forgot the warning given her [literally: what she had been told wisely]. [The first wife] said to her: Let us go to that butte over there, that we sit there, so that we may look for our husband. He will come back with the carcase. [While they were sitting on that butte, the first wife] told her: Look for a while on my head for lice. Then that girl looked for lice on her head. She had done looking for lice on her elder sister's head [that means: on the first wife's head]. And [now] she herself had her elder sister to look on her head for lice. That girl then went to sleep. There was a bone, an antler, with that she killed her husband's younger wives. When [that girl] was asleep, she drove it into her ear. She then concealed her. Then she went home.

Her husband came. He asked her: Where is that woman? She told her husband – she was crying –, that she [the second wife] must have been lonesome. Then she was known by her husband, that she was lying. She was told by him: You will not get rid of her. Where did you kill her? Then she denied it hard. She was told by him: I shall look round for her. Then he looked round for her. He found her. And the same way he doctored before, that way he doctored her too. That man took his [second] wife home. She had become a person again. He told his [second] wife: I shall tell you, how you can kill her. Try to throw her into the water. She [the second wife] was staying a long time [in that man's lodge]. And [one day] it was very hot. She told her elder sister: Let us go to swim. She [the first wife] was wise. Then she [the second wife] was told by her:

I never swim. She said to her [to the first wife]: Just come along with me [while I am swimming]. She was told by her [by the first wife]: Yes. Then they went to the river. Then they came there.

And the younger one went into the water. She swam about in the water. Her elder sister did not consent to go in. She could not persuade her to go in. She told her: It is very good here in the water. Finally she took her moccasins off. [The younger one] told her: Just hang your feet over the bank. And [then] she just touched the water [with her feet]. When [the younger one] swam to her, she ran away. And [the younger one] approached her to get a hold of her, that she might persuade her [to go into the water]. She finally succeeded in getting a hold of her. Then she swam near the bank. There [the first wife] sat. She got a hold of her. She threw her into the water. She threw her in, where the water was deepest, and as soon as she touched the water, she turned into a crow [literally: who, as soon as he touched the water, turned into a crow]. She [that crow] started for the shore with her wings spread. She caught [the crow]. She pulled [the crow's] head under the water. She drowned her. Then she went home. Her husband came. The animal, he had killed, was very fat. He asked her: Where is the Crow-woman? She answered him: You said, that I should kill her. I have drowned her. She was told by her husband: Let us move. Her brother is very mean. Then he moved. Then he camped. He camped a long time. And he said to his wife: That brother of hers is very bad. Don't talk out of the lodge, when you hear some one saying "Which way?"

And there that man was camping. It was near, that the winter would come. He hunted again. That woman suddenly heard somebody saying "Which way?" Then he was going around. She did not say anything. Four times he went around. He then went away. She did not think anything more of him outside. He went far away. She took an awl. She made a hole in her lodge. From there she looked out. As soon as she saw him, he stopped. He looked at her. He said to her: She [meaning: you] invited me to come back. Then he went back. He then came to the door. Then

he entered. When he entered, then he rattled. He had his lungs all full of earth [because they were hanging down]. His short ribs, those were his legs. He was only the breast-part [of a man]. He was called Short-ribs. That was that Crow-woman's brother. Over there he sat down. She gave him something to eat. She gave him something to eat from [a wooden bowl or something of that kind]. He refused to eat from it. He said: I never use such things to eat from. She said to him: My moccasins. He said to her: Pretty near. [She said:] My legging. [He said:] Pretty near. [She said:] My dress. [He said:] Pretty near. [She said:] My belly. He said to her: Yes, that is it, that I eat from. Then she lay down on her back. He went and sat by her. He began to eat. She saw, that his food fell through [his body down to the ground]. He cut her belly open. He told her: I made a slip-cut. Then that woman died. Then Short-ribs took one [child] out [of her body]. He put it down right near the fire. He called [that boy] Ashes-chief. And [he called] the other one Stuck-behind-chief. Short-ribs ran away for safety.

That man came back with the carcase. Then he knew: My wife is killed. Then he tracked Short-ribs, his brother-in-law. Then he followed him. He saw him. [Short-ribs] went to a forest. He said to [Short-ribs]: Now I have caught you, there is nobody to prevent me from killing you. Then he lifted him up, he put him over a stump. And in that way he killed him. He went home. When he entered, he heard, there were children. Then he took them. He then went to the river. There he left one to the beavers. He told [one of the beavers]: Raise him for me. And he went away to a big rock. There it was, that he left the other one. He told [the big rock]: Raise him for me. Then he went away. He then went to his tribe for one winter. When it became summer, he went to look for his children. His lodge was still there. He did not feel content with his lodge. When he came there, he then suddenly saw a boy. He tried to catch him. He [the boy] made just bubbles in the water [by diving in to escape]. [The man] began to think about [how to catch his boys]. He knew [literally: knew them], how he could catch them.

Then he saw, there was a beaver-hole, from there he stuck his arrows, he stuck them to his lodge. In the same way he stuck arrows from the big rock [to his lodge]. He heard, some [boys] were saying: Partner, jump out, here are some arrows, that we can take them. That man had already hidden himself from them. They came to him. He ran after them. He reached and caught one of them. He said to him: You are my child. Taste me [by biting]. He was told by [the boy]: Yes, you are right, You are my father. They went to his lodge. Then they entered. He [the boy] told him: My partner is very careful. He said to [his boy]: Try and persuade him [to come here]. I shall lie here in front of the door. I will turn into a log. Tell him: Let us shoot at this log. That one boy [whom he had caught first] began to shoot at his father. He said to his partner: Partner, go out [of the big rock]. Then [his partner] came to him. He said to [his partner]: Over there is a log. Let us shoot at it. That one shot at [his father]. He was told by [his partner]: That log is a person. He told him: No, it is a log. And the other one said: Yes, it is a person. [The first boy said:] Let us take his arrows. He was told by [the other one]: No, I am afraid of that man. [Finally] he was going to take one of his arrows. That man got up and ran after him. He caught him. [The boy] struggled about. And he said to [the boy]: You are my child. Taste me. [The boy said:] Yes, he is right, he is my father.

Then they went home to their lodge. Then they entered. They said: Where is our mother? They were told by their father: Over there she is, she has been killed. She has already turned into bones. They told their father: Put the pot in the fire. Put the tongue, the tripe, the back-fat, the knee of [the killed animal] in the pot. [These] four were the things, he put in the pot. They told their father: Go out, don't see us. We shall make our mother alive. Then that man went out. Then they got up. They began to put their mother together. They then exchanged her arms [by mistake]. They looked at their pot. It began to boil. It boiled over. One of them said to her: Mother, your pot will boil over. The other one told her the same: It is nearly boiling over. The first one told her again:

Mother, it is nearly boiling over. Then their mother moved. They told her in a hurry, that she should jump up. They had already laid by a stick, that she could stir [the boiling] with. One of them called his mother: Jump up. Your pot is boiling. She jumped up. She quickly picked up that stick with her left hand. Then they suddenly saw, that she was stirring [the pot]. Then she was left-handed. Then they were told by her: Oh, my children must be very poor, they must be awfully hungry. Their mother became again a person. They told their father: There is our mother. She is saved. That man was always happy, that he had his wife again.

Then he told his children: Don't go far away. Here, close by, [you may] roll [the gambling-wheel] about to one another. Don't roll your wheel eastward. One of them would not listen. He told his partner: Let us roll it eastward. He was told by his partner: Our father says: Don't roll it eastward. By little and little they rolled it eastward. And the wheel rolled faster. They could not catch it. Then it circled round to an old woman's lodge. It fell down near the door, just in front of it. Then the old woman jumped suddenly out. Then she took it. That old woman said: My children, come here, here is your wheel. In a hurry they went to take it. They were told by her: Well, come in. Your wheel is lying in the upper part of the lodge, that you come and take it. Then they entered. They were told by her: Sit down there. We shall smoke. One of them said to her: I don't smoke. He was told by her: Only one time you will smoke with me. He said to her: Yes. Then they began to smoke. Her pipe was a ghost-head [i.e. a skull]. He said to her: [Wait] that I quickly make a fire. He put a rotten log on the fire. There in the lodge was nothing to be seen for smoke. [The boys said to each other:] Which is strongest, her puff of smoke, or the smoke [of the rotten log]? Ashes-chief put his wheel over his head. There was the end of the smoke [that means: the smoke did not come lower than the wheel]. And Stuck-behind-chief's top-knot was a plume. The smoke ended there also. That old woman said to them: Do you still sit there? [They answered:] There is nothing wrong with us. After a long while they did not hear her move about. They told her:

do you still sit there? They were told by her: We shall quit smoking. She talked from far down her breast. After a short while the other one also said to her: Are you still sitting there? She then did not talk [any more]. They killed her instead [of being killed by her]. They went out.

Then they went home. Then they were known by their father, that they had killed that old woman. They came home. They told the news to their father, how they killed that old woman. That man was pitied [i.e. protected] by them [by that old woman, and by the blue-bird]. He told his children: You do not listen. Don't shoot the blue-bird. They walked about through the forest. The same Ashes-chief saw the blue-bird too. He said to his partner: There is a very nice one. I will shoot it. His partner forbade him. He told him: That one is the blue-bird, our father told us about, that we should not shoot. He would not listen. He shot it in spite of [his partner]. He immediately shot it. Then it fell. Then it suddenly hung on a branch. He was told by his partner: Let us go home. He said to him: I shall take it. And he climbed up. He was nearly taking it. It went up higher, without knowing how. [The partner said:] Now, come down. He would say: Wait, I am nearly taking it. This tree was growing higher. And it was very high. [The partner said:] Now, come down. [He answered:] Wait, I am nearly taking it. He was told by his partner: I don't see you any more. He [the disappearing boy] did not say anything. His partner's clothes all fell down to him [the partner below]. Then he knew: My partner is taken up to heaven. [Some people say, that this boy is the Morning-star, and that the parents of the twins are the Sun and the Moon.] He then took his [i.e. his partner's] clothes. Then he wrapped them up in a bundle. There was a patch of rye-grass. There he lay crying: My partner! He became small again. He cried himself small.

And those ancient people [the ancient Peigans] were moving. Then they came to camp near him. And there was an old woman walking about. She was looking for wood. She was picking up sticks. She heard, somebody was saying: My partner! She did not see him. She finally found

him, who was lying there, and who had a big belly. He had gummy eyes. She picked him up. He said to her: Mother, take good care of my partner's clothes. Put my own clothes in the same [bundle]. Wrap them up. Then she took him. She said to him: The poor thing, belly-fat [that means: a child sprung from an unknown belly]! Then she went home. When she came there, she said to her daughter: [Look] this here, I got belly-fat. These people were suffering very much for something to eat. That woman [the daughter] told the news to her husband. She told him: The old woman found belly-fat. That man told his wife: We shall have profit from him.

Belly-fat's old woman was very hungry. He told her: I am hungry. She said to him: The poor thing Belly-fat is to be pitied. There is no food. He asked her: Are there any buffalo-skins? He was told by her: Your elder sister is the owner of one. He said to her: Go and take it. And that old woman went and took it. She entered with it. [He told her:] Stand it up near the door. Scare it four times with the leg of your buffalo-robe. He took his arrows. She scared it four times, which was [that means: which turned then into] a young buffalo-cow. She [that cow] was nearly breaking her tail [by bending it too much]. Belly-fat put his arrow to the bow-string. He shot her. Then he shot her some times more. Then she died. Then he commenced to skin. He had done skinning. His sister took care of half of the carcase. They filled up their stomachs. Then she [the young woman] went home. She entered her lodge. Her husband said to her: Where did you get something to skin? She said to him: It is an animal killed by Belly-fat. It is from him, that we got something to eat. That man said to his wife: I told you [before], we shall have profit from him. That is one way, that he showed, what person he was.

And then there was a chief [who] said: [The person] who kills the black-fox, I shall take him for son-in-law. Everybody went, where they trapped. He said to his old woman: Make me a trap. She said to him: The poor thing, he thinks, that he might get a wife. And over there he went to trap. He put his trap on one side of the road. Then he went home. Then he came there. Then it was night. When it was just getting day-light, he got up. He went to his trap. He came there. [A man called] Crow-arrow had already taken [the black-fox]. [Belly-fat] went home. He said to his brother-in-law: Crow-arrow stole my trapping. His brother-in-law went over to the chief. He said to him: It is Belly-fat's trapping, Crow-arrow stole it from him. And [then] the girl [i.e. the chief's daughter] was driven to Belly-fat [to marry him]. And she entered. Then he was seen by her. She vomited from him. Then she went home. She hated him, who was bad [to look at]. His belly was big. He had sore eyes.

In the night that chief was talking. He said: [The person] who in the morning kills that white prairie-chicken, I shall take him for son-in-law. In the morning the white prairie-chicken sat in the centre [of the camp] [on a tree]. All the people then shot up at it. Belly-fat told his old woman: Make a curly arrow for me. She said to him: The poor thing, he thinks, that he might get a wife. She made for him two curly arrows, one with a blunt point. And he went. The people said about him: Out of the way, Belly-fat will shoot it. Crow-arrow was not far away from him. [Belly-fat] shot up. [The people said:] Pretty near. He nearly shot it. He shot up again, [this time] with the other arrow, the blunt one. He shot [the prairie-chicken]. He shot it down. Crow-arrow stuck his arrow instead of [Belly-fat's]. He was seen by all, that he stole. Then they all said: Belly-fat killed the white prairie-chicken. And it was the youngest girl [chief's daughter], that he married. She entered. She washed him.

In the night that chief said: He [Belly-fat] caught in corralling a white buffalo and a beaver-furred buffalo. And these people, the strong young men, all came back from corralling. They did not find any buffalo. They all came back without having anything. They suffered very much for something to eat. Now comes the story of his corralling [literally: later on his corralling]. Belly-fat then told his old woman: Make me a pair of scabby moccasins. And there he started. He came back from corralling, and he told her: When I am away a long time, then tell my brother-in-law [that he may cry it out to the people]: Belly-fat has been

on a run a long time. He went corralling, [so] that you [that is: all the people] may lie down and hide. And over there he, who was a wonderful person, was already on a run a long time. There he began to fix up buffalo-chips. He put them in a long row. He put a white stone among them, and there was also a blue stone [he put there]. Four times he ran out. When they [the buffalo-chips] began to run, they turned into buffaloes. He ran on one side [of the row of stone-piles]. The hiders already sat [behind the stone-piles]. [The buffaloes] ran between the stone-piles. Then they jumped off [the cliff]. After he had made the corralling, he was just sitting on top, from where they jumped off. Belly-fat told his wife [from on high]: Prepare yourself well. Then he went down. And he shot that white buffalo [that is the white stone, that had turned into a buffalo]. He shot it more than once. And he shot the other one, the beaver-furred one [that is the blue stone, that had turned into a buffalo], too. Then he killed it. He told his brother-in-law: Skin [both of] them. I shall go home for a while. I shall go home to dress up.

Then he went home. Then he entered his lodge. He told his old woman: Give me my clothes. His arrows were all ornamented with eagle-tail-feathers. He was pulling off his clothes one by one. He fixed his body up again. His hair – we are told – was way down [to his belt]. His hair was yellow. There was none as good-looking as he was fine [to look at]. And his wife was just as fine-looking. And he then went to the corral. His [two] buffalo-hides were already skinned. Those wonderful [buffalo-hides] were his bed-robes. He said to his wife: Take hold of [the two robes] over there. Here are my arrows, brush them [the robes] with them. When you have done brushing them, throw them among the people over there, where there are many people skinning. They all rushed for them. That one, that had vomited from him [and who had married Crow-arrow], came to him. She said to him: With which [arrows] shall I brush? He said to her: Brush with those sticks lying there. What is the matter with Crow-arrow? Brush with his arrows. She cried, because she was ashamed. She threw Crow-arrow's arrows [among the people, after having brushed with them]. No one took them.

Crow-arrow became angry about it. He went away. He took his wife with him. He took all the buffalo. They [the buffalo] went into a hole. There were no more buffalo standing outside. All the buffalo, all of them went in. Crow-arrow took away from Belly-fat his wonderful power. Then the winter came on, and all the people suffered for something to eat. The Old Man sent all the birds on an errand. He told them: Look for the buffalo. They were not found. That man [Crow-arrow] was wise. He kept the buffalo shut up. He would shoot at the birds, that sat by [him]. Then they would fly away. In the night there was a hole in [Crow-arrow's] lodge. From there a bird looked in. That man saw [the bird]. He told his wife: Over there is a person. She said to him: There is none. [He said:] No, it is an eye. That woman threw a stick at [the eye]. [The bird] did not fly away. That man took a fire-stick. He burned its eye with the stick. In that way he was found out by [the bird], that he was hiding the buffalo. And [the bird] flew away.

The Old Man was told the news: There is a man, who [literally: he] hides the buffalo under the ground. The Old Man told these people: Now move. Then they all moved. The Old Man turned into a puppy. He ran around the old camp-ground. He howled. And it was the daughter of that man Crow-arrow, [that] went to the old camp-ground. She saw, there was a puppy. She took it. She packed it on her back. She went home with it. She entered her lodge with it. Her father told her: Take it away and let it loose. It is no dog, it is a person. It is the Old Man. The girl cried for it [i.e. for the puppy]. His wife scolded that man for

it. He said: We shall kill one of the buffalo. That man went in [to the hole]. He was going to kill one of them. He killed one of them. And they ate the raw entrails, being happy. The girl carried the puppy on her back. She told her father: This puppy of mine will look upon the buffalo [from on high into the hole]. She was told by him: Allright. The puppy jumped down from here [from the edge of the hole into it]. It ran inside. It began to bark. The buffalo all ran out. When they were running out, then the last ones were the bulls. And the puppy bit one of them in the belly [and hung there]. It was hiding there. And that man was angry. He was going to kill the puppy, [when] it would run out by [him]. And the buffalo were running far. That man became poor instead [of the ancient Peigans], for [want of] something to eat. And that is all.

[Cf. Uhlenbeck obt 23 sqq., and the references given obt 34, to which may be added: Dorsey tsp 88 sqq., Dorsey-Kroeber ta 341 sqq., Simms tc 303 sqq., Lowie a 134 sqq. 168 sq. 176, Lowie ns 274 sq. 280 sqq., Lowie jaf XXI, 97 sqq. The first pages remind us of Dorsey-Kroeber ta 8 sqq. 278 sqq., Dorsey to 19 sqq. For the last part of the story cf. also Grinnell blt 145 sqq., Dorsey-Kroeber ta 275 sqq. Cf. also Simms tc 290 sqq.]

In 1910 Tatsey gave Uhlenbeck the following version of "Belly-fat," obt, 23–34.

Belly-fat

There was a man, [that] camped alone. They were only two, he and his wife. He hunted every day. After a long while he was going to hunt. He said to his wife: Listen, there is [a reason, to have] your ear [open]. There is a man. If he comes saying "Which way?", don't look out at him. He will go round our lodge here. He will always say: Which way? Don't look at him. Don't think thus: There is the door. Then that man went away.

That woman suddenly heard, [that] this man [of whom her husband had spoken to her] was saying: Which way? She did not look at him. He got there finally [to that lodge]. Then he went round her lodge. He always said the same. That woman thought: He is crazy. There is the door, does he not see? And then he entered.

She said to him: And over there in the upper part of the lodge [is a place for you to sit down]. He sat down. She sat before him. He told her: On these [wooden things] I don't put my food. She said to him: Put your food on my legging. He answered her: It is pretty near [the place I want to put my food on]. She said again to him: You will put your food on my dress. He answered her: It is pretty near. She said again to him: Put your food on my belly. He answered her: That is the kind of thing I put my food on. That woman lay down on her back. Then he started to eat. He had not eaten long, [when] he made a mis-cut. The woman then died. She had twins. He pulled one out. Then he put him near the edge of the fire. He will be called – he said – Ashes-chief. And he then pulled out the other. This one – he said – is Stuck-behind-chief [because he put him behind the sides of the tent]. That [man called] Short-ribs then went out. [He had got this name, because he had no legs, and his body ended with the short ribs.]

And that man [the husband] came with pieces of the carcase [of the animal he had killed]. When his wife would not come out, then he knew: And that must have been Short-ribs. He has made me poor. When he entered, he saw his wife, while she lay there, and that one child. He then suddenly heard this one, [that] cried from behind. He then laid his wife aside. He went out with those children. Over there were beavers. He said to them: Help me, quickly raise this one [Stuck-behind-chief] for me. And the other one [Ashes-chief], [he took him to] a big rock. He said to it: Help me, quickly raise this one for me. And then he went home.

After a short time we went away. He stayed out during the winter. Next summer he went home. When he came there, his wife had already turned into bones. Those children had already got big. They were playing outside. He walked towards them. They then fled inside from him [one to the beavers, and the other into the big rock]. He then went home. He then made arrows. Next morning he stuck them along the way, where those boys used to go. When they came out to play again, they saw those arrows. That Big-rock-child was on the lead. He was told by his partner: We shall be caught by them. He said to him: No, there is no person about. Then that man walked up to them, then he jumped up. He then caught that one boy. He said to him: Boy, taste me [by biting]. You are my child [literally: I have you as a child]. He was tasted by him. [The boy] told him: Yes, you are right. He said to him: Try to persuade your partner, that he comes here.

That boy then ran over to his partner. He [who had tasted his father] said to him: Come on, partner, let us walk about, that way. He answered him: I am very afraid of that man. He said to him: He is our father, he will not do you any harm. He finally persuaded him. Then they went away. They played arrow-sticking-game. Big-rock-child was told by Beaver-child: There is that man. He answered him: No, it is a rotten log. He [Beaver-child] said to him: Then let us play arrow-sticking-game on it. They would throw [arrows] at it. Then their arrows were all gone. When they began to gather them up, that man [their father] jumped up. He then caught Beaver-child. He said to him: Taste me. You are my child. He answered him [after having tasted him]: Your are right. He said to them: Come on, let us go home.

When they entered [his lodge], he said to them: My children, there is your mother. It is a long time, that she was killed. There was a bad one, she was killed by him. They told him: Father, [go and] hunt. We shall bring her to life again [literally: We shall make her]. He then hunted. Those boys shot their arrows up in the air. They said to their mother: Go out of the way [of the arrows falling straight down after having been shot up], mother, it might hit you. The other said to her: Your pot [of meat] is nearly boiling over. At the same time he [his brother] shot up into the air. They said again to her [:Go out of the way]. Then she moved. When they shot their arrows the third time up in the air, then she sat up. [They shot] four times, then she got up. They said to her: Our father might soon be here with the pieces of the carcase. Make haste with the boiled meat. Then their father came. When he entered, that man said to his wife: You are left-handed [being right-handed before]. He was told by his children: We put one bone wrong.

After a long time he said to his children: I pray you, don't roll that gambling-wheel [with which you are playing] eastward. Those boys then said: Why did our father say, that we should not roll that gambling-wheel east-ward? And they then began to roll it. They continually wanted to stop it, that it might tumble over on its side [literally: that it might die]. It had rolled far. It was going round like a [wounded] buffalo. There was a big rock [to which it was rolling]. It rolled in into a door on the east-side. They looked in. They were suddenly told by an old woman: Come in, my children. Then they entered. They were told [by the woman]: We shall smoke. That pipe of hers was a skull. Stuck-behind-chief said to his partner: Partner, we shall smoke with our old woman. He pulled out his round smoothed stone. That old woman lit her pipe. They had smoked a long time. [Then] Stuck-behind-chief rubbed his round smoothed stone. The old woman said to them: My children, are you still smoking? They said to her: We are nearly smothered from smoke. She told them: We shall smoke once more. After a very long time Stuck-behind-chief said to that old woman: Are you still smoking? She told him: My son, here is your gambling-wheel. It is enough, let us stop smoking. Now go home. He said to his partner: Sit there in the door. He smoked harder. He finally killed the old woman. When they had smothered her, then they went home. [The boys themselves had not been smothered, because they were saved by Stuck-behind-chief's rubbing the round smoothed stone]. They were told by their father: I said to you [literally: they were told]: Don't roll your gambling-wheel eastward. They said to him: We have killed that old woman.

They were told again [by their father]: There is a spotted bird. Don't shoot it. Again they went about, shooting [different animals]. Ashes-chief said: There is the one, our father told us about. I shall shoot it. He was told by his partner: No, our father forbade us. He then said: I shall shoot it. What will it do? When he had hit it with an arrow, it [the wounded bird] then hung there on a branch. The same one [who had shot] went up [to fetch the bird]. He was told by his partner: Partner, come down. Let it lie there. He said to him: No I shall take it. It was always getting higher [while Ashes-chief climbed after it]. He was told by his partner: Partner, I nearly don't see you any more. Let it go. He said to him: Wait, partner, I nearly take it. And then he was not seen by his partner. After a long while his clothes fell down by his partner. He then took them. There was a log, he lay down on the side of it. He wept [and by weeping he became a baby again].

And the ancient Peigans, they all came and camped there. There was an old woman, she went after wood. She heard him from that log. This was a child. She looked round for him, which was a little child. Then she took him. She put him in her bosom. When she came home with the wood, she said to her daughter: Girl, here is a little one. I got belly-fat [that means: a child sprung from an unknown belly]. It was after a while, he became big again.

The ancient Piegans had been camping a long time. There was a chief. One of his two daughters never would marry. He said: There is a prairie-chicken. It will sit on this tree. He [who] kills it, I shall have him as a son-in-law. They all shot up at it. It was not killed. Belly-fat [formerly Stuck-behind-chief] said to his old woman: Make haste, make a curly arrow for me. I shall go and kill that prairie-chicken. The old woman said to her son [Belly-fat]: Oh, my son is crazy. He will never be able to kill it. Then her daughter came in. She said to her: Your younger brother here said that [that he will kill the prairie-chicken]. And that girl went home [she was married and had a home of her own]. She said to her husband: My younger brother there says, that he wants curly arrows to be made for him. That girl laughed, when she was saying it to her husband. He answered her: He is not a person of no account. I shall make arrows for him. They were made ready. That girl gave them to Belly-fat. He then went towards that tree. These people [who were shooting] all said to him: There is Belly-fat. Go out of the way. He will shoot. He was laughed at by all. He was wiping about his eyes. He said: I shall shoot a while. He shot at it. This people said: Pretty near.

[A man called] Crow-arrow then knew, that he was a queer person. He [Belly-fat] was going to shoot again. He [Crow-arrow] came near him. Then he [Belly-fat] shot again. He [Crow-arrow] shot at the same time with him. The prairie-chicken suddenly fell. Crow-arrow jumped over to it [the prairie-chicken]. He took his arrow and stuck it in the place of Belly-fat's arrow. Crow-arrow said: I hit it. Belly-fat's brother-in-law then claimed it for him. That chief said: Because we all are gathered around it [and disagree about the person who hit the bird], I shall again say something else to-morrow. He said again: There is a black fox. He [who] traps it, I shall take him as a son-in-law.

Crow-arrow knew, that Belly-fat was fortunate. He always watched him. Belly-fat said to his brother-in-law: Quickly make a trap for me. Put it there on one side of the trail. Next morning Crow-arrow went again to Belly-fat's trap. He stole that black fox. He said to the chief: Here is the black fox. Belly-fat's brother-in-law was walking by him. He said to the chief: He is not speaking the truth. Belly-fat is that one, who trapped it. The chief said to her [to his daughter]: Go on, go and marry Belly-fat. That girl then went. [When] she saw Belly-fat, she then vomited from [seeing] him. She then went to Crow-arrow. That one, she married him. Her younger sister said: I shall marry [him]. Then she entered. She said to that old woman: Where is your son? I shall marry [him]. She was told by her: Here he is. He is still sleeping. She [the girl] said to him: Get up! He got up. She then washed his face.

After a short time these Peigans were hungry. Belly-fat said to his wife: Tell your father, that he must harden this corral, I shall take a run

to lead the buffalo. That chief then cried out: Harden this corral. My son-in-law will take a run to lead the buffalo. It [the corral] was made ready. Belly-fat said to his wife: I shall start during the night. Tell your father: There is a white buffalo-calf, that he may skin it well. We shall have it [that means: its hide] for a bed. He [Belly-fat] then went to the corral. He gathered the buffalo-chips. He put them in a row. There were very many of them. There was a white stone, he put it among these buffalo-chips. [When] it was plain day-light, he drove them. When the buffaloes suddenly started to run, then they jumped over the bank. The corral was full. That chief got up. When he went out, he saw over there a big lodge. That was the lodge of his son-in-law Belly-fat. He went over there. He said to his daughter: Girl, there is your husband. He is sitting in sight [on a hill]. Go and tell him, that he may eat. He [Belly-fat] went in. He said to him [to the chief]: [Take care,] that that white buffalo-calf may have no blood on it. It is a holy buffalo. I shall have it for a bed.

Of these Peigans there was none as good as Belly-fat. His lodge was better [than all the other lodges]. All inside it was all decorated with otter-skins and mountain-lion-skins. His wife was just the same as good [as he was]. All the Peigans went to skin. Belly-fat just sat there only [without doing anything]. That white buffalo-calf was skinned for him. He said to his wife: Put it there aloft [on poles in the corral]. Then get me a drink of water. [In the meantime] Crow-arrow's wife came to him [to Belly-fat]. She gave him water. He said to her: No, I shall not drink it. My wife will soon be here. She went to get water for me. Over there is Crow-arrow, your husband. Go and give him a drink. She answered him: No, I shall marry you. He told her: Go away, I nearly vomit from you, [I am afraid] that you might make us dirty.

Belly-fat said to his wife: Brush the hair of your robe [the white buffalo-hide] with these eagle-arrows. When you are through with them, then throw them away. She then brushed this white buffalo-calf. She then threw away these eagle-arrows. All the men rushed for them. His sister-in-law again came to him. She said to him: With which [arrows] shall I brush? He told her: With some stick [lying] there, that you can look about for [that means: You can pick up a stick, lying around there, to brush with]. Then that woman was angry. She went to Crow-arrow. She said to him: With which [arrows] shall I brush? He told her: With these my arrows here. When you are through with them, throw them away. [When] that woman had done brushing, she threw away those crow-arrows. All the boys rushed for them. These Peigans then went home [from the corral to their lodges].

Belly-fat was long talked about. Crow-arrow was then offended. He said to his wife: We shall go somewhere to an unknown place. That is all I know of Short-ribs and Belly-fat.

[Cf. C. Wissler-D.C. Duvall, Mythology of the Blackfoot Indians, New York 1908, pp. 40 sqq.; W. Matthews, Ethnography and philology of the Hidatsa Indians, Washington 1877, pp. 63 sqq.; J.O. Dorsey, The Cegiha language, Washington 1890, pp. 604 sqq.]

Saturday, July 22

Young Joe Tatsey comes in and Uhlenbeck reads him the story of "The man who was pitied by a water-bear," nsbt, 114–20. Preface: "Told by Blood, interpreted by Tatsey."

The man who was pitied by a water-bear.

There was a man, [who] was always moving. He was pitied by a water-bear. He was told by him: Feed me with your children. When he was camped near, he went swimming early in the morning. [Each time] he took [one of] his children with him to the river. When he stopped [swimming], then he caught [one of] his children. Then he threw them in the water. The water-bear jumped up already. He caught them. He then dived again in the water with them. Then the man would go home. When he entered, he would ask: Where is the boy? He was told by his wife [that means: by one of his wives]: You took him along with you. Why don't you know, where he is? He did the same thing to his three children. The water-bear was it [again], he fed with the youngest one. That woman [the younger wife] loved him [that boy] very much. She watched her husband. He went again swimming. She ran after him. She suddenly saw, that the water-bear jumped up. The man threw the child again in the water to the water-bear. He had killed all his children.

That woman went home crying. She said to her elder sister [the elder wife]: I saw our husband, what he was doing to our children [that means: I saw, what our husband was doing to our children]. She was told by her elder sister: Don't cry any more. We shall prepare to do away with him. That man entered. He said: Where is the child? He was told [by one of his wives]: I don't know him [that means: I don't know where he is]. That man said: I shall go and hunt. Over there he was hunting. The eldest woman asked her younger sister: What is it, you are pitied by? The younger one told her: I am pitied by gophers. And you, and what are you pitied by? [The elder one said:] By moles. There on a hill [that man] liked to sit [literally: it was his liking to sit there]. There the women dug a hole. In the night they quit [digging a hole]. Their husband came home in the night. In the morning he hunted again. Then the women went to that hill. They again were digging a hole. It was getting thin on top. There was a buffalo-head, there he used to sit on. In the evening he came back. [When] he had finished his meal, he went to the hill. [The women] prepared to take the things they needed with them. They looked out at him through a hole in the lodge. They said to him: Alas, alas, alas [meaning, that he was getting nearer and nearer to the place, where he would fall through]. He stood by [the buffalo-head]. He began to look about. Then he sat down. Then he fell through. And the women ran for escape.

He was yelling: Help me, help me. There was a wolf, he heard, there was a person calling for help. He said to the wolf: Pity me, pull me up. He was told by [the wolf]: Yes, I shall dig a hole. The wolf began to dig a hole. And after a long while, towards morning, the wolf quit [digging]. It was very thin, that he did not dig. The wolf howled "uuu," four times he howled [literally: four were his howlings]. All the wolves came. The wolves, the coyotes, the kit-foxes, the foxes, the badgers, [all of them came to the wolf, and] said to him: Now, why did you invite us? He told them: Here is a person, I pity him very much. He [who] takes him out, he is to have him for a child. He is to have him travelling about with him. He [the wolf] told them: Now, start in to dig the holes. I will look at you, when all your tails are out of sight. He began to go around them. All their tails were out of sight. The wolf had already dug his hole. Then he entered [the hole]. He tried hard for a while, he caught him. He pulled him out. He told the others: You might wear your claws out for nothing. Now they all came out [of their holes]. All these wolves then went away.

That person then travelled about among the wolves. There was a young wolf [literally: a new-breast], [that] had just come. He said: There

is a buffalo-corral. My companions were snared. And that person told his father, the wolf: Let us go over to that buffalo-corral. In the night they started. Then they came to the corral. He told the wolves: I shall go in first. I shall let down the snares. Then he entered [the corral]. Then he began to find out [literally: to know about] [how the snares were fixed]. They were all made out of raw-hides. He let them down. Then he went out [of the corral]. He told his father: Now, let them all come in, that they might eat. Then they all entered the buffalo-corral. The wolves then began to eat the carcases. It was not good, what they had to eat [i.e. there was no plenty of good meat]. They just fought over it. And these people [the Peigans that were corralling] were happy, when they heard the wolves [thinking that many of them were snared]. In the morning all these wolves ran away. And the people all went over. They began to look at their snares. Then they saw them [the snares], that they were all lying there for nothing. Then they suspected them [the snares]. In the night he [the wolf-person] howled: Uuu, I was taken a captive by wolves. He said that, because his food was not good. What he had got to eat, was bad. The people said [to one another]: Put good food [in the corral], that we might know this one, who is howling.

[When] it was night again, they all [the wolves] ran [towards the corral]. That person said to his father, the wolf: I shall go in first. Then he entered. He began to look at the snares. He let them down. Then he began to know the food(s), the pemmican(s), the fat(s), the dried meat(s), the back-fat(s). He was happy over the food [he found there]. They all entered. Then they began to eat. They were fighting and biting each other, because they were happy to get something to eat. In the beginning of the day they all ran out [to the prairie]. And [when] in the morning the people came again to look at their snares, they were all put down again. Then they knew, [that] it was a person, that treated the snares badly. The food, that was put there, was all eaten up. They said [to one another]: Now this coming night we shall watch it [the buffalo-corral].

Thursday, July 27.

In the night they sat all around this buffalo-corral. They all lay low [so that they could not be seen]. Then they saw among these wolves a person walking with them. There they all came up to [the corral]. That person entered. Then [the people] all walked in a circle [around him]. He began again to put down the snares. Then he was chased. He was caught. Here he was, he was just jumping about. He just clattered his teeth. His eyes were burning. He had turned into a wolf about his eyes. He had begun to have hair on his face. [Also] about his fingers he had turned into a wolf. He was taken home to the lodges. He entered [a lodge]. They all entered the same [lodge]. He was to tell the news. Then he was asked by the chief: How did you come to travel about among the wolves? He told him: Yes, my wives dug a hole for me. These wolves pulled me out. I told them: You will have profit from me. I was the one, that let down the snares. I am used to these wolves. I shall not be a real person again. I have turned into a wolf now. Let me loose. Now I will not do harm any more to the buffalo-corrals. And now the boiling is ended.

[Cf. Wissler-Duvall mbi 148 sqq. The latter part of this story corresponds to Dorsey-Kroeber ta 190 sqq.]

Jim Blood tells "The young man and the beavers. First version." It is in nsbt, 72–85. Preface: "Told by Blood, interpreted by Tatsey." Walter told this story too, but in "another tradition" (see July 12).

The young man and the beavers.

[First version.]

[When] long ago the ancient Peigans were dancing, the women dressed like their lovers, how they [the lovers] dressed. [When] the women danced, they stood in a circle. The young men [and] the men were all standing behind [on the outside of the circle]. And there they saw, that those young men were imitated in dressing by [the women]. And then they [the young men] were all yelled at [by the people]. Then he [such a young man] was known by all: Yes, that is his sweetheart. Then he was known [that a certain woman loved him]. There were some [young men] that came later than others. They were young men that were ashamed. And when the men knew their wives, [that] a certain young man was her lover, that man [such a husband] was always very glad. The women would be afraid. They were encouraged by their husbands, that they might dance. And then they were not afraid, because they were encouraged [by their husbands]. They [the women] admired and imitated each other [in having a lover and dressing like him]. When the women all knew, that they must dress like their side-husbands, then they were not afraid. Then they all thought, that they might have many of those, they had to imitate in dressing.

There was a man, whose [literally: his] wives were the only ones that did not dance. And over there [on the opposite side of the lodge] one [of his wives], his second wife, was his poor wife. To that one he said: Why don't you go and dance? There might be some one, that you might dance for. You may dance, you are the only one that does not dance. He was told by her: Yes, I shall dance. Now when we have a dance, I shall dance. After a short while they hurried one another: Now, hurry up, those that have a new way of dressing [in imitation of some young men], that we can see them, how they will dress. When they all stood in a circle, then those that had a new way of dressing came forward inside of the circle, and then the people made very much noise about them. There was one that came forward. She had earth on her cheeks, She had a narrow strip of a buffalo-robe for a bonnet, magpie-tail-feathers were the ornament of her bonnet. She had each corner of her robe cut. She had cut it around. Her robe looked, as if it were scabby. That women dressed that way. Then she came forward to the centre. When he saw her, that young man [whom she had imitated in dressing] was going away already. He told his partner: Tell me later on, what she says. And then she was yelled at. When that woman talked, she said: When the rivers are warm, I shall show the people, that my lover is a warrior. Then her husband knew, whom she dressed like [who was the young man she loved]. And then all these people knew, that she danced for Round-cut-scabby-robe. That one was her lover. That way he used to dress. [When] they had done dancing, then all went home. Then his partner looked for him. He was found by him, while he was staying in his lodge. [He asked his partner:] Now, what did that women say? He was told by [his partner]: Partner, she said: When the rivers are warm, I shall show the people, that my lover is a warrior. Then Round-cut-scabby-robe said: I shall go to an unknown place, because I am ashamed.

Then he began to take things [with him]. Then he started. He was not known, where he went. Yes, – he [had] told his partner – look for me later on, that you may find me, where my body has dried up. It was not far, where he went. There in the middle of a lake beavers had a den. Near the edge of the water he began to dig a hole in the earth. He made a shade. And there he stayed in. Then he began to cry. Nights [and] days he always cried, because he acted as an unhappy person [that the beavers

might pity him]. While he was asleep, then suddenly a boy came to him. He was told by [that boy]: My father tells you, that you must go to him. Then he looked up. [The boy in his dream] was walking on the water. Then he thought to himself: How shall I be able to go there [to the beaver-den]? Then he was afraid to go there. Then he slept again. Then he was told again by [that boy]: My father invites you. Then he looked up. Then he saw him [the boy] again, that he was swimming in the water. He [the boy] would always swim to the beaver-den. Those times, when he could not think how to go, he began to cry. He then slept again. He was again told the same: My father invites you. He was known by [the beaver-chief], that he would not be able to go there. He was told by the boy: Look at one of my steps. Step in it. Then he followed him [the boy]. He did not sink in the water. Then he came to the beaver-den. The boy then entered. And he himself asked: How shall I enter? The chief then called to him from within: Now come right in. Shut your eyes. Then enter. Then he entered. He had his eyes shut.

[When he opened his eyes,] he suddenly saw three persons in a big lodge, the chief, his wife, [and] his son. He was told by [the chief]: What are you travelling for? He said to him: I am very poor. There was a woman, she dressed like me. I am very much ashamed. I do not know yet about wars. She says, that when the rivers are warm, she will show the people that I am a warrior. He was told by [the chief]: These are my things. Take, which of them you like [literally: think]. He answered him: I shall not take it. I love my younger brother very much. I shall take him [and nothing else]. After a short while he was told by [the chief]: These are my things. They are all strong [they all have supernatural power]. Of those I invited you to take one. He answered him the same [as before]: I love my younger brother very much. I shall take him [and nothing else]. He was told by [the chief]: He is my only child [the meaning is: he is the only of my children, I care for very much, he is my pet-child], it is not good, that you take him away from me. He [the young beaver] was then given to him by [the chief], [on condition] that he [Round-cut-scabby-robe] should stay with him [the chief] during the winter. Then he [Round-cut-scabby-robe] thought: Where is [the food], [that] I shall have to eat now during the winter. Then he [the chief] knew his thoughts. Then he told him: There is plenty of food, that you will have to eat. Then he [Round-cut-scabby-robe] was happy. He said to him [the chief]: Yes, I am travelling, because I am poor. There is nothing the matter [i.e. there is no objection], I shall stay here. He was told by [the chief]: In spring you will go back. Then he stayed that winter. He was told by [the chief]: Your partner is looking for you. Go out, go out on the prairie, that you may tell him: There is nothing the matter [i.e. there is nothing wrong] with the place where I am staying.

Then he went out on the prairie. Then he suddenly saw his partner. They were happy to meet one another. He [the partner] told him: When the leaves are close by [that means: when the leaves are out], these people will go on a raid. Round-cut-scabby-robe said to his partner: When it is close to the time, that they will start, then come here again. Don't worry yourself [about me]. And then there his partner went. He [the partner] was on his way home. He himself [Round-cut-scabby-robe] then went to his lodge [the beaver-den]. Then he entered. And he told the news to his father, the beaver-chief: My partner told me: It has been a long time, that I have looked for you. I told him: There is nothing the matter [nothing wrong] with the place where I am staying. Then come here again [when it is close to the time, that the people will start on a raid]. And that winter he stayed there. Then he was taught the beaver-songs, [that is:] the beaver-roll-songs [literally: the songs of the water-owners]. He was given the power [of the beaver-rolls]. He learned it then [right away when it was shown to him]. When the [new] moon was seen, then he [the beaver-chief] would sing. Then he [Round-cut-scabby-robe] was given seven sticks. They were sticks of that size [saying this, Blood showed me the size of the sticks]. He was told by the chief: When the [new] moon is seen, then lay one stick pointing to [the moon]. And these [seven sticks] were the moons. Every new moon Round-cut-scabby-robe

would always lay one of them pointing to [the moon]. He counted the moons, when he was to go home. All the moons were in, when he was to go home. Then he was told by the beaver-chief: You will go home. These are my things. Now take from them. They are things that belong to the wars. He answered him: I will not take from them. I will go home with my younger brother. I love him very much. Every morning [the beaver-chief] would give him one of his medicines. Round-cut-scabby-robe tried hard, that he might take his younger brother. Finally he was told by [the beaver-chief]: Yes, now I give your younger brother to you. [The beaver-chief] [also] gave him supernatural power with water.

His partner came to him. The same day [that his partner came] they saw each other. Then he went home. He started. And there was his younger brother [the young beaver], he then wore him round his neck. He was not living any more, it was only his hide. Then he came to his tribe. They all were going on a raid. He did not go among them. He then walked on one side [of them]. [He and] his partner were only two [walked together]. They went ahead. They came in sight of a big river. They saw the camp [of the enemy]. They ran back again. Then they told the happy news to the people behind. They told them: Here on the other side [of the river] he [the enemy] is camping. Then they [the war-party] just travelled on. Then they sat in sight [of the enemy's camp]. And those people [the enemies] then began to rush. And these people [the war-party] went down to the river. Then they came there. And over there the enemies came all to the shore of the river. Then they just sat there [each party facing the other one]. And Round-cut-scabby-robe [and] his partner then went away [from the rest of the party]. He told [his partner]: Over there is [a man] standing up. I will kill him. Then he began to strip himself [of his clothes]. Then he went in to the river. He told his partner: Stay right here. I shall come here. I shall feign to dive down stream with him [with the killed enemy]. He made [ready] his supernatural power with water [so that he might dive in as a beaver and swim under the water]. Then he began to whistle. He had his younger brother round his neck. And he started to swim. And on the other side the enemies all yelled. He got near [the other shore]. Over there he dived under the water. Then he suddenly threw up his head out of the water right in front [of the enemy].

The chief, the man of the other tribe, saw him. He [that chief] jumped into the water towards Round-cut-scabby-robe. The water of the river reached around his [that chief's] waist. And that man of the other tribe thought, that he might get closer to him. A big arrow was his [that chief's] arrow. Then he [Round-cut-scabby-robe] went in deeper. Then he [that chief] walked after him. Then he [Round-cut-scabby-robe] was shot at by [that chief]. Then he [Round-cut-scabby-robe] gave a yell. Then his younger brother, which [beaver-skin] had turned into a stick cut by beavers, was hit [by the shot]. Then it [that stick] was hit in the centre. And then he [Round-cut-scabby-robe] pulled it out. Then he [that chief] was jumping away from him. He [Round-cut-scabby-robe] walked right up to him. It was his [that chief's] own arrow, that he [Round-cut-scabby-robe] shot him with. He shot him then right in his back. Then he took hold of him by his hair, and then he swam in the water with him [at the surface]. And then the ancient Peigans gave a yell. And the people of the other tribe were crying. He [Round-cut-scabby-robe] swam to the middle [of the river], and then he dived with him [the killed chief]. And these people [the Peigans] all charged down the river [on that killed chief]. And he [Round-cut-scabby-robe] had already told his partner: Stay right here. And there close to his partner he threw his head up out of the water with him [with that killed chief]. Then he put him right on the shore. His partner just hit him [the dead chief] then. He [the partner] took also half of the scalp. And then all the people also ran up to him [to the dead chief]. Then they began to make coups on him.

And then they all started home. And then Round-cut-scabby-robe had shown the people, that he was a warrior. He was far ahead of the others [in going home]. He got near the lodges. Again he went ahead.

He also first found out [where] the lodges [were]. Then he ran back. Then he told the news to the leader of the war-party: Here close by is our tribe. To-day we shall make the circle [in approaching the camp]. Then they all started. They came up in sight on a hill. He [the leader] made a sign [to the camp]: Over that way I came. It [the trip] was good. And the people made a rush [crowding one another]. When they [the war-party] had started down, then Round-cut-scabby-robe was far ahead of the others. His partner was right behind him. And the people there [in the camp] then sent a messenger, that he might go back [to the war-party] and find out [who they were]. Then the boy [the messenger] came up to them. He then knew, that it was Round-cut-scabby-robe and his partner. He ran again over there [to the camp]. He told them: It is Round-cut-scabby-robe and his partner. And that man, his [other] partner [the husband of Round-cut-scabby-robe's sweetheart] began to look for his wife. He found her, where she was still picking rotten [literally: scabby] roseberries. He told her: Your husband [meaning Round-cut-scabby-robe] is coming. Then she spilled her roseberries. Her clothes were all bad. That poor second wife's elder sister had fine clothes. Those were given to her by [her elder sister]. Then they [the people of the camp] started back [to meet the war-party]. That girl was standing far ahead. Then she shook hands with him [Round-cut-scabby-robe] with a kiss. Then he gave her his coup, the big arrow [and] his scalp. Then that girl gave them to her real husband. She gave him those. And then they began to have the scalp-dance. That man [the real husband] told him: We shall go to my lodge. Then he [Round-cut-scabby-robe] entered. And over there he sat down. Then he was told by [the husband]: Partner, here is our wife. I give her to you in payment [literally: I put her in the place, viz. of the presents you gave to me]. And here is my lodge, I also pay that to you. [And also] one of my dogs, the yellow one. And in that way he paid him three things, that woman, his lodge, his yellow dog.

Then Round-cut-scabby-robe went again [on a raid]. He did not go far. Then he found people of another tribe. Then he killed them again.

He took arrows for a coup. Then he went home. He also took a scalp. He came back to his camp. He sat in sight on a hill. He stood up. He made a sign: Over that way I came. It [the trip] was good. He started [down]. He was far ahead [of his party]. Then he was known, that it was Round-cut-scabby-robe [and] his partner. Then he looked about for his wife [that was given to him by her former husband]. She came to him. Then he gave her the quiver and arrows, [and] the scalp. [She gave them also to her former husband.] He paid him again one of his wives. He paid him also his beaver-rolls. And [now] he had only one [wife] left. Then [Round-cut-scabby-robe] went on another raid. And there he went. And he went far away. He finally found [the enemy]. Then he made another charge on them. Again he killed one of them. He took also his spear [and] his scalp. From those [coups] he became a chief. For all his companions he cut a small piece of the scalp for each. They were very happy, when they were near home. And then he came home. And his partner [the former husband] saw him again. He [Round-cut-scabby-robe] gave him the spear also. And he [the husband] paid him his wife again. And then he [Round-cut-scabby-robe] left him without a wife. He had paid him all his wives. And he [Round-cut-scabby-robe] had him for a single man with him. And Round-cut-scabby-robe became the only chief [of the tribe]. He had had a beaver-dream [in which power was given to him]. And that partner of his [the former husband] had given his beaver-rolls to him. That way I heard about it, [how] he then became the owner of the beaver-rolls [literally: water-owner]. And he is the one, who showed [the people], how the beavers should dance. And now the dogs have separated [after having had their meal].

[Cf. Grinnell blt 117 sqq., Wissler-Duvall mbi 81 sqq., McClintock ont 104 sqq., Michelson jaf XXIV, 238 sqq. Another version of the same story follows here immediately.] **"Another version," the one by Walter Mountain Chief, is in this collage under July 12.**

Friday, July 28.

Jim Blood teaches and is later assisted by John Tatsey. "Medicine-men," nsbt, 55–58. Preface: "Told by Blood, completed and interpreted by Tatsey."

Medicine-men.

A medicine-man. The dream of that man, and what he profited by it.

[1] A man was pitied by a bear. He was told by [the bear]: There is no one, whom I pity. Now you are the only one, I pity you. How the bear in [his] dream called himself, was "Water-bear". He was told by [the bear]: My son, I give my body to you. Even if an arrow touches you, it will not go in to your body. Do not be afraid of arrows. Do not be afraid of a man belonging to another tribe. If he was shot at, he would not be shot through [his body]. If he was shot through [the body], he would use the power of the bear [given to him by the bear]. He would be saved. He was very strong [having supernatural power], because he [the bear] pitied him. He would be given again by [the bear], that he could doctor the sick people. One [bear-]claw was given to him by [the bear], that he might fix it, that he might perform [his doctoring] with it. When he doctored, if he was satisfied [by things given to him in pay for it], he would act like [a bear] in doctoring [literally: he would doctor from him, i.e. from the bear]. He would stick the claw in the ground [after having taken it from his neck, or out of his medicine-bag]. There [where he stuck the claw], he would find roots. With those he would doctor. With those he would cure [a sick person], that he [the sick one] might get stronger from it. In that way he was again given [power] by [the bear]. In that way he profited from the bear, he was pitied by. He was not pitied by him [in that way], that he might be able to take bows

and arrow [nowadays it would mean: to take guns]. And now the dogs have separated [after having had their meal].

[2] An old man, an ancient Peigan, a medicine-man, was also pitied by bears. He was called Went-to-the-bear. He was very dangerous. He had a bear-knife [a knife given by a bear]. He would not be seen [he was invisible] in the war. He was told by that bear: There will be no blood about your body. This his [own] tribe was afraid of him just the same [as his enemies]. He walked just the same way as the bear. That one profited much from his dream. When we were at war, the bear-knife was his only knife, he fought with in the war. When he saw persons [enemies], he made charges upon them, even if they were shooting back at him. He would just catch them. He would catch them by their hair. Then he began to stab them. He would just kill them with that [knife]. He killed seven persons with his knife. He used the power of the bears [given to him by the bears]. He died from his old age. To-day his knife is still here. That was one, that profited from his dream. He had many profits from his dream. When he gave it [the power] away, he had again profit from his dream, from those to whom he gave [the power]. That is the end.

[3] A man slept by a buffalo-corral. There he had a dream. He was told by a bull in his dream: Forbid these people. You will profit from my body. He was told by [the bull]: You have done poorly to these my children [by chasing them over the cliff]. Burn up this buffalo-corral. Here is my medicine, I give it to you. [When] a person is wounded [literally: those that are wounded], even if it is a bad case, how he is shot, you can cure him. His elbow-hair was given to him by [the bull]. His tail, earth, [and] red earth were also given to him by [the bull]. He had much profit from his dream. From that [dream] he made medicines. He was also pitied by the earth. He was told by [the earth]: Do not go to war, only doctor. If you go to war, it will never fail, you will be shot. You will

not die from it, when you are shot. You will die from old age. From his dream he never failed in times of war, he was shot every time, he would not be shot through the body. That is what I know about it.

[Cf. in general Grinnell blt 191 sq., and for N°. 2 Wissler-Duvall mbi 95 sqq.]

Saturday, July 29.

Tatsey works five hours at a stretch, Jim Blood is around. Possibly this resulted in: "The Old Man and the Geese," nsbt, 180–82. Preface: "Told by Jim Blood and interpreted by Tatsey."

The Old Man and the geese.

He went slowly up to a lake in this country here. And he saw them [the geese], he was seen by them, they all ran into [the lake]. The Old Man just sat there. He began to think about, what he should do to them. He knew, what he should do. Then he took earth and a long stick. He tied some earth to [the end of] that stick. Then he went away. He was dragging that earth. He went over to those many geese. He went on one side of them, he went past them. They all ran away from him. He just went past them. He went far. Their chief sent one goose: Overtake the Old Man, ask him: What is it, that you are dragging? [The messenger] was told by [the Old Man]: We dance with it. The goose went back. He told his chief: It is what we dance with. [The chief] said again to [that goose]: Go and overtake him, that he might make us dance. And [the messenger] came again to the Old Man, and said to him: Go back, that you might make us dance. He was told by [the Old Man]: I shall not go back. Let them come here. I shall not go to that lake. It is very far. Just where I am sitting [now], I will make them dance. He coaxed them far away [literally: he floated them far]. For that reason he was not near the water, that many of them might have escaped him [if he had made them dance close to the lake]. They all went to him. He was always hungry. He finally persuaded them.

They came to him. He showed them, how they should stand. Then they stood in their places. And he went to one of them. He felt that one's breast. He was feeling their breasts with his hands. The fat-breasted ones stood all by themselves. The fat ones and the lean ones stood separately. In the centre stood the Old Man with the stick and the earth. There he lied. He said: This is it, that we dance with. He said: Shut your eyes, all of you. He beat on that stick with another stick. And he made them dance. And over there on the farthest end [of the circle formed by the geese] stood one of them [and] looked al little out of one of his eyes. And that one saw [the Old Man]. He ran away. [The Old Man] hit them with that stick alongside of their necks. And they all ran far away to the water. And then he was hitting them. He let the lean ones go. That way he succeeded in killing them. He made a fire. He plucked the feathers. He then ate his fill, just as he liked. He sat with grease all over his mouth. This is the short gut [that means: this is the end of the story].

[Cf. Michelson jaf XXIV 248, Dorsey-Kroeber ta 59 sqq., Jones ft 279 sq., Dorsey to 9 sq., Lowie a 111 sq.]

Tuesday, August 1.

"Bearchief's songs" are recorded in obt, 66–68. For the origins of these songs, see below where obt, 78, is indicated.

Bear-chief's songs

1. This song was communicated to Bear-chief by Big-plume (O'mαχksàpop). It is called "The song of the horse-stealing" (pono kå´mitaikamosìniχ´ksin).
Sun, look on us, have pity on us, help us!

2. This song was revealed to Bear-chief by the Sun.
My son, don't fear, I give you protection of life.

3. Bear-chief was taught this song by Big-plume. It is a help against incantations of jealous people. With "my kindred above", mentioned in it, the Sun (Nató's), the Moon (Kokúmikesum), and the Morning-star, (Ipisóaχs) are meant.
This earth hears me, my kindred above sees me.

4. This is a war-song which Bear-chief sings, when he hears the sound of gun-shots.
The guns can see me, I can see the bullets, they are birds, they curve.

5. The song which follows was communicated to Bear-chief by his father, Weasel-moccasin (A'paitsikina). Bear-chief used to sing it, when he saw the camp of the enemies, in making a raid. Together with this song belongs a buckskin-string, which was given to Bear-chief by his father, when he taught him the song. Bear-chief uses the buckskin-string to tie his hair with. He was also instructed by his father always to take his moccasins off, and turn them inside out, when going into the camp of the enemies. The song was revealed to Bear-chief's father in a dream.
In the nights I am not seen, the dogs are my partners [that means: they never bark at me].

6. Every night when Bear-chief goes to sleep he sings the following song to avert misfortune. He was taught this song by Under-bull (Stáχtsisɑ̀mik), who was also called Black-came-up (Síkotamisò).
When I sleep during the nights, I see all, how it lies [that means: I see all things in the future].

7. The following morning-song was also given to Bear-chief by Under-bull.
Old man on high [= Sun], help me, that I may be saved from my dream! Give me a good day! I pray you, pity me!

8. Big-plume taught Bear-chief the following song, which was sung by Bear-chief's women every night during his absence on a raid. Bear-chief used to sing it with his women, the night before he started, that they might know it well. The Indians, that are mentioned, are the jealous men who use charms against him.
All Indians tell lies. All Indians, you can tell lies, you can talk, [but] you will see me a long time! You will always see Bear-chief!

9. This song was revealed to Bear-chief by the Dove (Kαkóa).
All the people on high are my kindred, and all the people of this earth are my kindred.

10. As before.
God, [I pray you], pity me, hear me, help me! Take what I say! [that means: accept my prayer!]

11. As before

My partner, who does not pity you? I don't pity him!

12. As before

My partner, I pity all the people.

13. This song was revealed to Bear-chief by the Sun.

My son, my road is holy. My son, my paint is holy too.

14. This song was revealed to Bear-chief by the Moon.

My son, [the people] on high are holy. My son, [the people of] this earth are holy too. It is me, [that] can see through the night.

15. This is the song of the One-that-sets-in-the-west (Nímistsitaupi)

My younger brother, all the moving beings, they all see me. My younger brother, all the moving beings, they all are my children.

The story of Many-guns is recorded in nsbt, 219–20. Preface: "Told by Many-guns (Akáinamaχka), interpreted by Tatsey." According to Willy, "John Red Fox interpreted when needed."

An adventure of Many-guns'.

Many-guns told me: Bear-chief was going. He took us on a raid. We were four. We got near the Crees. There was a creek, we crossed it. It was frozen under [the surface]. My legs floated away [from under me]. My rope floated away. And there was an antelope-skin, it was my robe, it also floated away. I then went ashore. Then we started on the raid.

Bear-chief and Bear-head had already caught [horses]. Then they began to drive these many horses. I myself had no rope. I then just ran into the middle of these many horses. I then suddenly saw, that they were just jumping out. I then knew, that it was a spring, they were jumping from. There was one light-coloured horse, I ran after him. I got up to him. I jumped on him. I then sat ready on him. He then ran out [on the prairie] with [me]. I had no means to rein him. He ran among these many horses. Bear-chief [and Bear-head] said to me: How did you catch him? I told them: My whole body was my rope, I just jumped on him. Then they gave me a rope. I used it as a bridle. When I looked at the horse, [then I saw, that] his face was painted. It was red paint, he was painted with. Among the Peigans of nowadays and the people of long ago there has been nobody, that caught a horse that way. I am the only one myself, that has [literally: I have] done that. Bear-chief and Bear-head are still alive. They are the ones, that [literally: they] know about it. It is I myself, Weasel-moccasin [Many-guns is his name given in childhood, but his name of later years is Weasel-moccasin].

[Cf. Uhlenbeck obt 84.]

Uhlenbeck reads to Many Guns parts of "Bear Chief's Life-story," obt, 70–91. Many Guns figures in it from obt, 81 on. In obt, 78, the origin of "Bear Chief's songs" is explained. These two pages are marked in the text beneath.

Bear-chief's life-story

[obt, 70.] Bear-chief was about 17 years old when he went to war against the Gros Ventres. He took the scalp of a Gros-Ventre who was killed by another man. In that first raid the chief he followed was Gambler (A′ikaχtsiua).

After that it happened, that some Nez-Percés came stealing horses from a corral, belonging to Bear-chief's brother Weasel-moccasin (A′paitsikina). Weasel-moccasin shot one of the Nez-Percés, and Bear-chief followed him, and stabbed the wounded Nez-Percé with his butcher-knife. Then he found a crucifix on the dead man. This was the first time Bear-chief saw a crucifix. From this time he began to think on performing great deeds.

The next raid, against the Crees, he followed his brother Weasel-moccasin. Then Bear-chief was about 18. As the leader of some other men he went up to a lodge, where the Crees were dancing the Tea dance, and shot through the lodge, and killed one man. His companions killed two men, and wounded three women. None of these women died. He saw one of the women that was shot in the face.

That same summer he went a second time against the Crees, following Weasel-moccasin, and when they got near the Cree camp, Weasel-moccasin said to his seven companions, that instead of making raids on the Crees, they would make a peace-treaty with them. They went in to the lodge of the Cree chief Big-bear. Weasel-moccasin told Big-bear: I have come here, that my people and your people, who have been at war for a long time, may have peace. We have killed one another, and have taken horses from one another, and now I wish that to be finished. Big-bear consented. This was the first treaty, the Peigans and the Crees ever had (1875). In the same year Weasel-moccasin made a treaty with the Gros-Ventres. When Weasel-moccasin went to meet the Gros-Ventres, Bear-chief was with his brother. After his brother he shook hands with the Gros-Ventres. From this time, till his brother was killed (1879), he has done no deeds, because the Peigans were then at peace. In 1878 Bear-chief was with Weasel-moccasin when he camped with the Peigans on Middle creek. Then Joe Kipp, a Mandan half-breed, was staying with Bear-chief in Weasel-moccasin's lodge, trading with the Indians.

Towards the spring of 1879 they left the camp for a buffalo-hunt, taking many horses and small lodges with them. They were accompanied by the women. During a night the Sioux made a raid on them, and stole horses. Chief Big-plume (O′maχksàpop) led the Peigans to chase the Sioux. They overtook the Sioux on Beaver creek. There were seven Sioux. Weasel-moccasin and his followers ran after these Sioux, he himself being on a swift horse before them all. When Weasel-moccasin was near the Sioux, he dismounted to fight. He soon got shot about the heart, and died on the way to the camp. The Peigans killed six of the seven Sioux. One Sioux escaped. Bear-chief was not with Weasel-moccasin when he died. He had stayed at home. They buried Weasel-moccasin right were he died. Then Bear-chief was about 22 years old. He mourned a long time for his brother. He said to his tribe, that he would be killed by the same tribe that had killed his brother.

In the summer of 1879 Bear-chief and Big-lodge-pole (O′maχksinistamiua) travelled a long time, and came to the camp of Sitting-bull, a Sioux chief, and stole many horses. Then, after having travelled one whole night, they came about noon accidentally to the camps of two Sioux chiefs. They went into the lodge of one of these chiefs, called Crazy-horse, because it was the biggest of the lodges. Craze-horse and two of his women were in the lodge. When they entered, the women ran out. Crazy-horse would run also, with his gun in his hand. Bear-chief and Big-lodge-pole caught him, and shook hands with him, and motioned to him to sit down and be quiet. So Crazy-horse sat down on his bed with his gun on his shoulder. Then the Sioux people without made a rush for the lodge, where they were, with all their arms. They raised the sides of the lodge all up, so that Bear-chief and his companion could be seen from without. The Sioux made signs to Bear-chief and his friend, why they had come to them. Bear-chief made signs back, that the winter before the Sioux had killed his brother, and that Bear-chief now had brought his body to the Sioux, that they might kill him also. But he made understood by signs, that he would defend himself. It was about noon when they entered the lodge, and till dark the Sioux were talking among themselves. Then two chiefs came into the lodge of Crazy-horse, who was always sitting there, the gun on his shoulder. The two Peigans had also their gun leaned against their shoulder. The two chiefs that entered were Red-cloud and White-hat. Both of them went up to Bear-chief and shook hands with him. Then Bear-chief laid his gun down between his legs. Crazy-horse commanded then, that the people should leave. He also commanded his wives to give Bear-chief and his friend a drink of water. After that they gave them a smoke. Then they smoked with each other the medicine-pipe. Then there was given something to eat, which Bear-chief and his companion took as a sign of friendship. Then the two Peigans laid their guns at their side. The horses with which they had come into the camp had been taken away from them. They did not sleep that night, being together with Crazy-horse and the other two chiefs in Crazy-horse's lodge. They were afraid that, if they slept, somebody would come and kill them. In the morning Bear-chief took his gun. He went out from the lodge, followed by Crazy-horse and another Sioux chief. Then they went together on horseback to the other Sioux camp. When they came right close, Bear-chief saw the horses which had been taken away from him and his companion. They were tied to a lodge-door. Bear-chief took his butcher-knife, and cut the ropes which were tied around their necks. When he started to lead them off, the Sioux crowded around him. They had their guns, and some of them threatened to shoot him. Bear-chief pulled his six-shooter out of its cover. Then they made signs to him not to shoot. Then Crazy-horse rode up, and helped him to lead the horses back to his (Crazy-horse's) lodge. When they got back to that lodge, the people had pulled their lodges down, ready to move. Bear-chief saw a great crowd, standing round Crazy-horse's lodge (which had not yet been pulled down). All the people of both Sioux camps made an attempt to take the horses away from them. Then Crazy-horse and that other chief, who had gone with the two Peigans, got angry with their own people. They hit the horses

of the people on the head with their whips, and made them stand back. One of the Sioux jumped, and took Big-lodge-pole's gun away from him. Bear-chief ran after him, and caught him by the neck, and threw him back, and took the gun away from him, and gave it back to Big-lodge-pole. Then Crazy-horse made signs to Bear-chief and his friend, to get on their horses, and to leave the camp. The two Sioux chiefs escorted them. When they had come out of the camp on a hill, they got off and shook hands. Bear-chief and his companion returned to their camp. The trip to the Sioux and back had taken 67 days.

When they had come to their own camp, they stayed there five nights, and then they returned to the Sioux camp. Now they were four, and Little-dog (Imitáikoăn) was their leader. When they came down in the Sioux country, they saw a rider at a distance. Bear-chief was sent over to see, to which tribe that rider belonged. The rider did not ride away, and Bear-chief rode up to him. He caught the rider's horse by the bridle, and he held him, until his three companions came up. They wanted to kill him, but Bear-chief said, he recognized the man as one of the Sioux. He had made a promise to the Sun, that during that summer he would not kill any Sioux. The others insisted on killing him, and the Sioux was so much scared, that he acted like a child. The Sioux made signs to the Peigans, that his lodge was just on the other side of a high butte, and that they must come to his lodge. When they got near the lodge, Bear-chief made his companions stay behind, and went up to see, how many lodges there were. There was only one. Bear-chief went inside the lodge. There were two women, one child, a very old man, and a young man. Bear-chief hit all of them a little blow with a stick. The same he had done to the Sioux, they had met first. It was a sign that nobody else had any claim or right on them. Then the others came up. Little-dog begged Bear-chief to kill the man, so that they might take the women. Little-dog wanted the women, who were very fine-looking. But Bear-chief objected. He had obtained a claim on the man and his family by hitting them all with a stick. Then they left the lodge, without harming them, and travelled all that day and night. They discovered a camp towards the morning. Close to the camp they found out, that there were Red river (Cree) half-breeds. They went back, and stayed until sunrise. Then they went again to the camp, and asked those half-breeds, where Sitting-bull's camp was. Little-dog and one of the half-breeds rode away from the camp, and after a while they came back. Little-dog told Bear-chief and his companions, that the Sioux camp was very near. At sun-down they left the Crees, and went to the Sioux camp. This camp was nearly eight miles long. When they got near the camp, Bear-chief's companions were afraid to go in to steal horses. He himself went in, right to the lodges, and cut two horses loose from the stakes to which they were tied. He took them out to his companions. He did that four different times, each time stealing two horses. He had taken away eight horses. When he had got them, he and his companions started off to escape. Next morning they rode into a camp of ten lodges. They supposed, that these belonged to some of those Crees, but they soon found out, that they were Sioux. The Sioux tried to take the stolen horses away from them. The Peigans said, they would fight for the horses, and then the Sioux left them alone. After that they had no trouble on their way home.

A little while after they got back, he started again for the same Sioux, as the leader of five other Indians. When they got near to the Sioux country, they saw a man on horseback, long ways off. They approached, without being observed, and sneaked round. Bear-chief told the others: I shall go up, and meet him. He went alone, and when he came close to him, he recognized him as one of the Sioux, he had met in Crazy-horse's camp. The Sioux had killed two antelopes. They shook hands with each other. Then Bear-chief's companions came up. He told them not to do any harm to that Sioux. The Sioux gave them some meat. After they had let the Sioux go, they cooked their meat in a brush. When night came, they went to the camp of the Sioux. Bear-chief went right to the lodges, and cut two horses loose. The Sioux knew, that they were in the neighourhood, and therefore the Peigans did not dare to steal more

horses from them. They went home. Bear-chief gave one of the horses to Little-dog.

Little-dog said to Bear-chief: I am going to the Sioux to make a raid. On that trip Little-dog was the leader, but Bear-chief was one of the party. When they got near the Sioux country, they met some of the Cree half-breeds. They stayed in the Cree camp till noon. Then there came a man along on horseback. Bear-chief jumped out, and saw, that it was an old man. That old man was Red-rock, the chief of the Sioux that were moving. He had a double-barrel shot-gun with him. He captured him, before the others could do so. Little-dog wanted to kill him. Bear-chief said, that the time of his vow had not yet expired, but that he afterwards might kill the Sioux. They let that Sioux go, and went to the Sioux camp. There were nine in their party, but only four of them – amongst whom Bear-chief – started right for the lodges. Before they got there, Little-dog told two of the Peigans to go back. They would not do it, and Little-dog pushed them back. In the meantime Bear-chief went up to the lodges, and stole one horse. He had just done that, when he heard gun-shots. These gun-shots were fired by the two Peigans, whom Little-dog had offended, to warn the Sioux. Bear-chef had just time enough to jump on his horse and run away, whilst the Sioux from all directions came, and shot at him. The Peigans went home with one stolen horse.

When they got home, they remained in the camp a few days. Bear-chief was the leader of three other men. They went again to the Sioux. When they got near the Sioux country, they camped in the evening at the mouth of Milk river. They had built a fire, for it was snowing a little. They sat around the fire. Then they heard lots of people talking. They jumped up. Some of them tried to put the fire out. The people were already too close. The leader came up to the fire, and Bear-chief met him. He told him: Partner, I am a Peigan. You shall not be harmed. The other answered: You are a Peigan. My name is Gros-Ventre-boy, and I am an Assiniboin. After they had spoken to each other, he asked Gros-Ventre-boy for some meat, because the Assiniboins had a good supply of buffalo-meat, and he got some. And he called to his companions to come up and eat the meat. When they had done cooking, they all ate of the meat. They went to the Assiniboin camp. When they got to the lodges, it was snowing very hard. Bear-chief went up to the lodges, and stole four horses. When he came back to his companions, he told them, that the Assiniboins had not tied up all their horses, so that they could find some more, if they searched the hills. In doing so, they found 17 head more. They went home with 21 head, and had no trouble any more.

After a few days Bear-chief went as the leader of a new party. They were nine. When they got to the Sioux country, they saw from a high hill, where the camp was. They were about to make a charge on the camp, when they saw some Sioux, chasing buffalo, right below the hill. The Peigans stayed in their camp till twilight. Then they saw that Sioux party, which had been chasing buffalo, camping for the night. They went up, near the camp, Bear-chief telling the others, that he was going to see, how they had their horses fixed. Instead of coming back to tell them, he cut three horses loose. And he saw, where he other horses were loose, and he went there with the three, he had stolen, and drove 27 other horses out to his party. Before he got to his companions, he met two horses, and two saddled and bridled mules. He took them also, so that he returned to his party with 34 head. They got home allright with those 34 head.

[**obt, 76.**] A few days after that there were eleven in a party. Bearchief was the leader. There were ten full-bloods and one half-breed. Before they got to the Sioux country, they saw from a distance two riders, who rode towards the timber of the river. They charged, and then the riders jumped off from their horses, and fled into the brush. The Peigans saw, that they were white men and said to the half-breed, that he should call to them to come out and not to shoot at them, because the Peigans were friends of the white men. They came out, and the Peigans saw, that they had pack-horses. They asked the white men, where they were going. The white men said, that they were trading whiskey to the Sioux. The half-breed told the white men: If you give me some of your clothes, I shall go with you and help you trade. They gave him some clothes, and then the half-breed told the Peigans to stay there till night, and to make a raid on the Sioux in the night, for they would be drunk from the whiskey. After a while they got near the camp, and they heard the Sioux making noise, so that they knew, that they were drunk. Bear-chief saw an Indian, who was tying his horse, wishing to get some more whiskey. Bear-chief stole that horse, and his companions went through the camp, and took 39 head. They started off, and left the half-breed in the Sioux-camp. The half-breed overtook them, and told them, that the Sioux had bought whiskey for lots of horses and some robes. The Sioux went after the white men and the half-breed, blaming them for their losing those 40 head. The Sioux took all the horses away from the white men, and they had a fight. One of the white men got a flesh-wound on his leg. The Peigans returned to their camp.

After a few days, he was sleeping in the night, and a person appeared to him in a dream, and told him not to go on a raid, before the green grass had come up. So he stayed at home. Not long before he had had other dreams, when he was on the prairie, during one of his raids. A very fine-looking young man came to him, and said to him: A man far off on the hill invites you to come to his lodge. Bear-chief asked the young man: Who is he? The young man answered: His name is Dove (Καkóa). Bear-chief did not go to the lodge, but woke up. Next night the same young man appeared to him, and gave him the same invitation. Bear-chief woke up, just as the night before. This happened every night. The fourth night he went with the young man. When they came to a high hill, he saw a very high round butte, far from where they were. They went to that high butte and to the top of it. Whilst they stood there, a part of the butte slipped down, and it seemed quite a while, that it was going down. It went in four different slides. When it stopped, it brought them to a place in the shape of a lodge. They entered, but Bear-chief found out, that it was a solid rock. There were two men and one woman. They all were very fine-looking. The young man pointed out to Bear-chief: There is the Dove. He will help you, because you are poor. The young man pointed out to Bear-chief the other man: There is the Sun. That man was all painted up, from his head all over his body to his feet, with red paint. The same young man pointed out to Bear-chief: There is the mother of the Dove. Her name is the Old Woman (Kipitáke) [the Moon]. The young man told him: My name is the One-that-sets-in-the-west (Nímistsitaupi). The old man [the Sun] first spoke to his son [the Dove], saying: Now help your partner. And the Dove said: I put my partner to the trouble of coming to my lodge. The Dove told Bear-chief: All the people of the high, and all the people of the earth are my friends. And all the time Bear-chief was wondering, how he could get out. And when he looked up, he saw the sky. The Dove told his mother, the Old Woman: Paint my partner's face. And the Old Woman told Bear-chief to come to her. She painted his face by putting a strip across his forehead, and two small strips on each cheek. The paint, with which she painted his face, was red. After that he went back to his seat, and his partner, the Dove, got up and walked around him and took an eagle-tail-feather, and tied it to the back of Bear-chief's hair.

[obt, 78.] He told him: I give you this, that all the people may be your friends. All the raids, you will make, you will always have success. I shall give you one song. Then the Dove walked around him four times, and then sang the song: All the people on high are my kindred, and all the people of this earth are my kindred. All of a sudden the Dove and Bear-chief were both standing on a high butte. When he woke up, he was inside his own lodge. Till this day he believes in that dream [which has strongly been influenced by notions of Christianity, and by the story of Scar-face, though Bear-chief himself seems not to be aware of it], and he uses the song of the Dove as a protection for his family [the Dove has taught him some more songs, which have been printed above]. That dream has given him good luck in everything, he has undertaken. And

the reason, why he has confidence in paint, is that he was painted in his dream. Bear-chief had some more dreams, in which the Sun, the Moon, and the One-that-sets-in-the-west gave him songs [which are printed in this volume]. He had all those dreams in the same lodge.

Early in the spring of 1880, Bear-chief and five others met some Cree half-breeds, who were drinking whiskey. These half-breeds caught Bear-chief's horse, and he told one of his party, who was a boy: Run away, go back to the camp. You might be killed. His other companions came near. The Crees commenced to shoot at Bear-chief's companions. Those of the Crees, who had hold of his horse, tried to pull him down. They succeeded, and then they attempted to take his gun away from him. In the meantime he took his six-shooter out, and he shot four of them down. His companions were at the same time fighting with others. One of the Peigans was shot through the arm, and had that arm broken. They came safe back to the camp, and started afterwards for the Sioux. Bear-chief's vow to the Sun of not killing Sioux had expired.

The party consisted of three Peigans, and four Crows. When they got to the Sioux, they discovered one Sioux lodge, and they waited until dark. Then they stole all the horses, which were to be seen, and having done that, they waited there until daylight. Then they made a charge on the lodge, and they all shot. One man tried to run out with a gun, but Bear-chief standing at the door shot him right through the head. He took the gun, the man had had in his hand. One of his party jumped into the lodge, and killed two Sioux, whilst they were in bed. Bear-chief followed him into the lodge and took another gun, which he found there. They killed only the men, of whom one escaped. They left the women and the children unhurt. They came home allright.

[obt, 79.] A few days later they started on a new trip. Bear-chief was the leader. There were four Peigans, and seventy Crows. The Sioux were looking out for enemies, and saw the party coming. Then they made a charge on Bear-chief and his people. The Crows did their very best to escape. Bear-chief and the three other Peigans stayed behind and fought the Sioux. This was about noon, when the Sioux made a charge on them, and it was late in the evening, before they stopped fighting. They started home that evening, and travelled all night. Early in the morning Bear-chief killed a buffalo-cow. They skinned it, and commenced their breakfast. Whilst they were eating, they saw on a high bank, just above them, a rider. He spoke to Bear-chief's people, and before they could answer him, two more jumped up at his side, and shot at Bear-chief' companions. But then, seeing that there were so many, they ran away. They were Sioux. The Crows went after those Sioux. Bear-chief and the three other went in the opposite direction, where they saw one rider, a Sioux. This rider fled into the brushes. The others did not want to help him, but Bear-chief alone followed him, and shot at him, every time he saw him through the brush, till the Sioux went out into the prairie, where he as hard to get at. Bear-chief rode up to him, and the Sioux would shoot him, but Bear-chief's horse kicked the gun out of the Sioux' hands, and ran over him. The Sioux got up, and took his gun. He shot at Bear-chief twice, and the third time the gun refused to work. Then Bear-chief attacked him with a butcher-knife, cut him over his face, and near his heart, and cut off his head before he died. Then all the Crows, the whole seventy, came up. In the meantime Bear-chief's three companions, that stood upon a hill, had taken eight horses from the Sioux, who was fighting Bear-chief. They travelled night and day to get home.

The Crows were very glad, that a Sioux had been killed, though they did not kill him themselves. Then the Peigans held a counsel, and invited Bear-chief among them. The chiefs told Bear-chief that he had done many daring deeds, and that he was already a chief on account of those, but that they now would give him a new name, instead of Takes-the-first-gun (Itóminàmaχka), the name he had borne till that moment. It was decided upon, that he should be called Bear-chief (Nínoχkyàio), after old Big-nose. And then they had scalp-dances every night, for a week or more.

A few days after that there were five in a party. Bear-chief was the leader. They went to the Sioux. They saw the camp at a long distance. He told his party to stay behind, whilst he himself would go on a high butte to locate the camp. Afterwards they should come up to him. But he waited and waited, and they did not come. He waited until dark, and when they failed to come, he started for the camp, but he could not find it. He walked a long time about, seeking for the camp, and at last he returned to his hiding-place, and stayed there all the day. And at night he started again for the camp. This night there was clear moon-light, and still he could not find the camp, though he was seeking for it all the night. He had to go back to his hiding-place. During the next day he prayed to the holy medicine-pipe, and said, that he would use that pipe to dance with, if it would grant him, that he might steal some horses. That pipe, Bear-chief prayed to, was the only pipe in this tribe, which might be used at the Round dance, when they were dancing all round the outside of the circle camp. It was given to the tribe by an elk. That night he started early by moon-light. Then he found the camp, and he could plainly see the women cooking outside of their lodges. As soon as the women went into the lodges, Bear-chief went to the camp, and cut loose the rope of a bay horse. The owner was near, and gave the alarm. Then all the people came out with their guns. He jumped on the bay horse, and left his own horse, with saddle, bridle, and blanket, and made his escape. He travelled all night and all day. When he camped in the evening, it rained very hard, and it continued to rain during the night. He had no blanket. His only cover was a buckskin shirt. The following morning, when he was on his way home, he met a party of Indians who had stolen horses. He asked them, if they were strangers to him. They did not say anything, but commenced to shoot at him. He ran away. Perhaps they were Sioux. They chased him till a hollow place in a big hill, where there was some brush. Then he came out of the brush, and they shot at each other from a long distance. They left him, and it rained very hard. He got on his horse, and started to ride away. He came to Bear river, and then he was almost frozen by the cold rain. Then he came to the camp of 12 white men, who had been chasing buffalo. One of these white men recognized him as Big-nose's adoptive son. Bear-chief's wet clothes were taken off from him, and dry blankets were given to him instead. They gave him half a cup full of whiskey to drink. They made him lie down, and covered him up with some more robes. He stayed there with the white men two nights, and then he started home. His companions came to their leader. They had not come to him on the butte, because they had lost their way. When everything was allright, they had the medicine-pipe-dance.

Some time afterwards Bear-chief was the leader of ten in a party. Among them were two Gros-Ventres. When they got near the Sioux, three of them started for the lodges, Bear-chief being one of them. There was clear moon-light, and people were sitting in different places of the camp. His companions were afraid, and would not go into the camp to steal. Bear-chief went up to a lodge. There he saw the owner sitting among his horses, smoking his pipe. Bear-chief went to the door, where one black horse was tied to a stake. He led that horse away from the lodge. The owner did not seem to see him. So Bear-chief ran away with the horse, and came home allright.

Late in that summer they started again, Bear-chief as leader, and four others. He stole two horses from the Sioux camp, and his companions stole 14 head out from the hills. They got home allright.

[obt, 81] About the middle of the following winter they started anew. There were five in a party, and Bear-chief was the leader. They had a hard time on that trip, for it was very cold. On their way home, crossing the Missouri river, Bear-chief broke through the ice, and went under, but his horse, struggling hard, pushed him up through the hole. Many-Guns (Akáinamàχka) was near by, and threw a rope to Bear-chief, and pulled him out of the water. His horse was drowned. They got home with eight horses, stolen from the Sioux. They had taken many more, but they had to leave them on account of the big snow.

A few days after they got home, there were six in a party that started on a raid. They got to the Sioux, who had put their lodges in a circle, very close together. Inside the camp were the horses. He and one of his companions went to a place, where there were two lodges, and the Sioux had ropes between the lodges. Bear-chief and his companion cut the ropes. He himself stole two horses, and his companion one. Then they went out of the camp, and started home.

In the spring of 1881 he, as the leader of four others, pursued the Crees who had stolen horses from them. They overtook them on Milk river, but could not find their own horses. Instead of them they stole 27 head from the Crees. They got home allright with all the horses.

From 1880 till the spring of 1881 the Peigans had been on friendly terms with the Crows. In the spring of 1881 the Peigans left the Crows, and started home for their own country. They camped on Arrow creek after several days of move. Some Crow Indians overtook them there, and stayed with them. When they moved, the Peigans went north, and the Crows, who had stayed with them, back south. In the meantime there was one Peigan family staying with the Crows, and that family was now moving north. They met those other Crows, who were going south. The Crows killed the Peigan and his wife, and from that day the peace was broken. Bear-chief did not do anything else during 1881.

But in the spring of 1882 he was the leader of a party of 14. They went to the Crows, and got there in the morning. They did not go up to the lodges, but they got six horses, just a little way from the camp. The Crows had seen, that they took these horses. So they chased the Peigans, and overtook them not far from the main camp. The Peigans came to a hill. Bear-chief stood at the bottom of the hill, and told the others to go on top and dig pit-holes, where they would be safe from the bullets. While he was staying there, he was fighting the Crows single-handed. He had three belts. When he had used the cartridges within them, he went up to the top of the hill, where his companions were. When he got there, he saw that they had dug the holes. But one of his companions had been shot near the hip-bone. They had killed one Crow Indian, and one horse. After that the Crows set the timber afire, which was close to the hill. There was plenty of grass. It burned till it was quite close to them, and it was very smoky and hot. Bear-chief, after filling up his belts with cartridges, got out from the holes. They fought all the rest of the day. And when the night came, they had only one horse left of the six, they had stolen. And when the night came, they had only one horse left of the six, they had stolen. The rest were all killed. Then Bear-chief's companions came out of the holes, one at a time, to sneak away. Bear-chief put the wounded man on his one horse, and then he led it away. They made their escape. Next morning they found, that they were far away from the place where they had had a fight. Bear-chief selected three men from his companions. He told the rest of them, that they should go home with the wounded man. He himself and the three others went to the Cheyennes. When they got to the Cheyennes, 120 head of horses were out on the hills. They took them with them. And after they had gone two nights, Bear-chief told two of his companions to take the horses and go home with them. He and his one companion saw a trail of some moving tribe. He told his companion, that they should follow that trail two nights, and they overtook these Indians. There were only two lodges. They had 21 head of horses, and Bear-chief and his companion took them all. These Indians were Red-tattoo people. Then Bear-chief and his companion overtook their friends, who were going home with the 120 stolen horses, mentioned before. When they got together, they turned their horses loose during the night. Next morning some of the horses were gone. Two of Bear-chief's companions went back to look for them. In the meantime Bear-chief and his one companion sat on a hill. They saw many Indians coming right close to them. There was no hiding-place. So they went right on the level prairie, and tied their horses together. They put their blankets down in a heap. That meant fight. Right where they had the blankets in a heap, the Indians rode close up to them, and dismounted. There they had a fight, but it did not last very long. Bear-

chief and his companion wounded one of the other Indians, and these left them after that, taking with them the horses, the Peigans had stolen before. Then Bear-chief and his friend got on their horses, and rode off. They did not see the other Peigans, These, on their way back, saw the enemies, and one of them fled into the brushes to hide himself, whilst the other fled straight ahead. This one, that fled ahead, ran right square into the moving camp, and there the other Indians caught him. Bear-chief and his companion, on their way home, saw five lodges, with the horses inside a corral. He and his friend went up to where the horses were, and tore down some of the poles. Bear-chief went inside, and led two of the best horses out of the corral. He gave one of them to his companion, and he told him, that they should start. With day-light they came to a little river. There they cooked their breakfast. After they had eaten, Bear-chief told his companion: Get the horses, and water them, and let us then go on. The companion started out to where the horses were. Many white cowboys met him. They all pulled their guns, and they pointed them at Bear-chief's friend. He called to Bear-chief for help. Bear-chief immediately took his gun, and ran up to his companion, and pointed his rifle at the cowboys. These held up their guns, and also their other hands at the same time. He motioned to them to put their guns away. Then the cowboys shook hands with them, and made signs to them, to go with them to their camp. Bear-chief made signs, that the cowboys should go ahead, and that he and his companion would come after them. When the cowboys went to their camp, Bear-chief and his friend went in the opposite direction. They went safely home, and Bear-chief was glad to see his wife, whom he had married before this last trip. The one who had hidden himself in the brushes came home two days later, and the other who had been captured came home after some time. Afterwards they found out, that the Indians, they had a fight with, were the same that had captured their companion. They were Flat-heads.

Afterwards there were six in a party, Bear-chief as leader. They went to the Bears's Paw mountains. They stole 22 horses from the Assiniboins.

They travelled backwards, and on their way, after having eating a hearty meal, Many-guns had the diarrhoea. And that night he had not the time to get up soon enough, so that he dirted the stomach of his companion. So both of them had to get up. The same night all started, and they came to a creek with high banks, and Bear-chief told Many-guns to take the lead in crossing the creek. The horse was used to go. It was dark. Bear-chief whipped the horse for Many-guns. The horse made a jump, and threw Many-guns right into the creek. And in the water Many-guns lost his blanket. He followed the creek a short way without finding his blanket. Towards day-light, when they had crossed the creek, and it was getting cold, Many-guns was all wet. He shook hands with Bear-chief and said: Old man, give me your blanket for the rain. Bear-chief gave his blanket, and after that they got home allright.

Then there were seven in a party, and Bear-chef was the leader. They went to the Cypress hills. From the tops of those hills, they saw ten lodges and seven other tents in a valley. They went to the lodges, and there was a hill quite close to them, and not far from the camp was a lake where the horses stood. Bear-chief said: I shall go down to the horses, and you stay here. If they discover me, you must shoot at the lodges as fast as you can. Before Bear-chief reached the horses, they discovered him. He gave the signal, and his companions began to shoot. Then he ran back to the centre of the camp, and shot a few times himself at the lodges. In the meantime his companions went over to where the horses were, and took the whole band. They had 38 head. He never heard, if they injured the people by shooting at their lodges. When they got all together, they divided the horses, and they got home allright.

After a few days chief Little-plume (Kináksàpop) and three others came to Bear-chief's lodge. Little-plume told him: We know, that you often go on a raid, and therefore we ask you to go now with us. He told Little-plume: I have just returned a few days ago, but I shall follow you. You must lead the party. Little-plume started off. Bear-chief and Many-guns followed him. So there were now six in the party. Every night, when Little-plume slept, he had the nightmare, which was a sign, that something serious might happen to him. Bear-chief advised him to go home. He did not follow this advice. When they came to the Cypress hills, they slept in some cabins, built by the Cree half-breeds, and that night Little-plume got again his nightmare. His companions threw water on his face and body, but he did not wake up. Then they put burnt buffalo-hair under his nose, but it was a long time before he woke up. He awoke after all kinds of hides had been burnt in the cabin. That day they went on, and saw two circle camps of the Crees. In the evening, when they got close to the camps, Little-plume said: A man has discovered us. Little-plume and his three fist companions ran away back to the hills. Bear-chief and Many-guns went to the lodges, as close as they could get. Bear-chief told Many-guns to hold his horse, and went up to one of the lodges. A man and his wife came out. Bear-chief stood amongst the horses, so that the man did not see him. He cut one horse loose. It was a wonder, that they did not see him. He went to another lodge, and cut another horse loose from its stake. After that he had some trouble in getting out. The horses did not want to go out. He managed it after a while. Then they started home. He overtook Little-plume with his companions.

In the spring of 1883 there were five in a party. Bear-chief was the leader. They went to the Cypress hills. There were three lodges, and there were six head of horses standing by themselves. Bear-chief and Iron-necklace (Míkskìmekin) stole the six horses, and told their companions to start home him with them. Bear-chief and Iron-necklace went to the main camp. When it was day-light, they could see the camp close by. They waited there, and thought, they would have to wait till night. But to their surprise they saw four young men driving a band of horses straight in their direction. Bear-chief and Iron-necklace hid deeper in the brush. The four young men drove the horses right to a grassy spot. Then they turned the horses loose, and went back to their camp. As soon as they went out of sight, Bear-chief and Iron-necklace drove the horses away. There were 21 head. They came home with them allright.

After this trip Bear-chief got his second wife. She was the widow of a man who had been killed in 1882. He moved with his two wives and Many-guns to the Sweetgrass hills, and wintered there.

In the spring of 1884 some cowboys came to his camp, and reported that a band of Crees had come over and had stolen their horses. The cowboys went back home from there. Bear-chief and Many-guns followed those Crees. Bear-chief left his two wives just where they camped on Willow creek. The Crees were just one day ahead of Bear-chief and Many-guns. In the night they went to the Cree lodges, but did not find the horses of the cowboys. Still they found 12 head of the Cree horses. They stole them, and brought them home allright. Bear-chief gave his share of the horses to his wives.

He camped a long time on Maria's river without undertaking a raid. Still in the same spring Bear-chief and seven others went to the Cypress hills. He and another man went up to the lodges of the Crees. He went first and cut two horses loose. When he came back to his companion, he held the two horses, he had stolen, and the other two, on which they rode. His companion went up to the lodges, and cut also two horses loose. When they came back to the other fellows, the man, who had gone with him to the Cree camp, started right home. Bear-chief and the others went to the hills, and stayed in the brush till the next night. He and another Indian, called Crow (Sapó), Bear-chief taking the lead, went up to the lodges. Bear-chief stole two horses, and went back to Crow, and told him, that he should go also to cut the rope of two horses. Crow went up to the lodges, and stole two horses. They went back on the hills with the stolen horses, and stayed there all day. During the day they saw another camp, not far from the camps, they had visited. Late in the evening he could see the people driving their horses out on the hills. They went there in the night, and drove a band of 57 horses away. Then they went home. On their way back they found 18 horses, that belonged to white men, and took them, the horses not being guarded. Before they got home, they found out, that among the 57 horses there were nine head that belonged to those cowboys, who came to report, that their horses had been taken away by the Crees. As soon as he came back to his camp, he returned the nine horses to the cowboys, who gave him some money as a recompense.

For the horses taken from the white men, the soldiers of Fort Assiniboin came up, and arrested Bear-chief for stealing. The officer, who arrested him, had Elie Gardepie, a Cree-halfbreed, as an interpreter. They took him out of his lodge, and brought him to the tent of the commanding officer. As soon as he came in, he was very happy, for he knew the commanding officer very well. The commanding officer called him by his brother's name, which was Prairie-chicken-child. Bear-chief's brother had been hired by the commanding officer as a scout, and captured some of the Nez-Percé's during the Nez Percé war in 1877. Since that time the commanding officer was Prairie-chicken-child's (Weasel-moccasin's) friend. Now he said to Bear-chief, that he had commanded his arrest, but that he intended to release him. Bear-chief told the officer, that two of the 18 horses had been left by him on the road, because they were tired. The officer commanded, that his soldiers should go, and take the 16 horses, that they had picked up on the road. The soldiers went into the hills with Gardepie as a guide, and brought them to the commanding officer's camp. The officer commanded Gardepie to bring them before his tent, for Bear-chief to identify them. Then he told Bear-chief: You must leave off these raids. Stay at home, and behave yourself. Be like your brother and help the whites. The officer also wished to take the horses, which the Peigans had stolen from the Crees, but Bear-chief refused this, because the Crees had been making raids on the Peigans for years. The commanding officer released him, only taking the 16 head.

After that the soldiers camped near the Sweetgrass hills to watch the Crees, so that they could not steal any more cattle from the Peigans.

Bear-chief went over to the Sweetgrass hills, and then the Peigans moved to this reservation, his first wife leaving him, and coming up here.

Some time after that a part of the Peigans came also to the Sweetgrass hills, and after a while, Bear-chief taking the lead, there was a party of ten men going to the Cypress hills. Afterwards Bear-chief was told by some Crees, that the night before Bear-chief came to the Cypress hills a medicine-man of the Crees had had a dream, that the man who had stolen the horses from the Crees was again on his road. He said to the Crees, that if his medicine [= natósiu, that means the same thing that he Iroquois call *orenda*] was stronger than Bear-chief's, he would be able to kill him; else his best horse would be taken away by Bear-chief.[39] Bear-chief and his nine companions came close up to the lodges, and then they could see two Crees coming from the lodges, and lying down on the prairie as guards. Bear-chief's companions were afraid to steal horses. Bear-chief was aware, that there were three Crees lying on the ground as guards. He told his people, that he would go to steal horses, but that they must shoot, if the Crees discovered him. It was towards the morning. He started to the three Crees, that were lying down, having covered their heads with their blankets. As he past [*sic*] by them, he heard them talking, but he did not stop, and went to the central lodge. Not far from it he saw a man, who sat down. Bear-chief walked slowly. That man got up again, and went into the central lodge. Bear-chief followed him. He could hear the man inside, cleaning his pipe by blowing through it. He noticed two men outside of the lodge, leaning with their backs against it. They must have been asleep. He came to the front-part of the lodge, where he saw two other persons lying about. They were sound asleep. He could hear them snore. At the same time he saw a buckskin pinto horse, tied to the door-lodge-pole. He went quickly, and cut the horse loose from the pole. He took the horse back to his companions. Nobody had seen him. From there they all went home.

After a few days he started on a new raid. There were 18 in the party. When they got to the Cree camp, he and Many-tail-feathers (Akå´χsoatsìmiua) went to the lodges, and each of them got two horses. In the meantime his companions took 9 head on the hills. Then they went home.

Afterwards they started five in a party, again Bear-chief as leader. They made a raid on one Cree lodge. Bear-chief cut one horse from its stake, and his companions took five horses on the hills. They did not yet go home, but went the opposite way. Before morning they came to five lodges. There were only five head of horses to be seen, and they took them. In the morning they went in another direction. After the sun was up, they came to another camp of Crees, who had just turned their horses loose. Bear-chief and his companions drove all these horses – 20 head – away from them, the Crees following them afoot. They got home allright with the stolen horses.

In the winter he and three others went to the Cypress hills. They got to the camp of the Crees, and waited until dark. They started for the lodges. In crossing the river to the Cree camp, Many-guns fell into the water, and was pulled down by the rope of his gun. But Bear-chief jumped in, and saved Many-guns, catching him by the hair. Before they reached the lodges, they found 23 horses. They took them, and started home. They arrived allright. Then they stayed at home till after Christmas. Bearchief's first child was born on Christmas morning. He did not know about Christmas, but Joe Kipp – the Mandan half-breed – who had invited him to a Christmas dinner, told him.

Early in the spring of 1885 he went as the leader of a party of 30. They came to a lodge. There were only two horses. Bear-Chief took them. They tried in vain to discover the Cree camp. So they had to go home with only two horses.

Afterwards Bear-chief and two other fellows started for the Cypress hills. Next day they saw two men, driving a band of horses towards the Cypress hills. Bear-chief and his companions intended to kill them, and waited for them in a coulee, until the two riders came right close to them. All three jumped up, aiming with their guns at these fellows. One of them was a Peigan half-breed, and the other a Cree half-breed. The Cree half-breed ran off, right on the hills. They talked with the Peigan half-breed. He told, where he stole the horses from his own people. Bear-chief took four of the best horses, and his friends took two horses, each of them, and told the Peigan half-breed, that he could go on now, but must never come back to steal horses from his own people. The reason, that Bear-chief did not kill him, and left him most of the stolen horses, was that he was a kinsman of Bear-chief's. Bear-chief went home, and took his third wife, his second wife staying with him also.

Some time later he started out, and he had his third wife with him, and nobody else. Every morning he sang his war-song, and without being asked, his wife joined him in singing it. It was "The song of the horse-stealing": Sun, look on us, have pity on us, help us! This song was given to him, a long time ago, by chief Big-plume. When Bear-chief and his wife were on this trip, a fire had started somewhere west, and the country was very smoky, so that they could hardly see far ahead. They were travelling down a small river, and all of a sudden they came to a large prairie, alongside the river, where there was a very big camp of Crees. The Crees saw Bear-chief and his wife, but did not mistrust them. They went to the brush, where they stayed all day, and watched the movements of the people. Late in the afternoon Bear-chief painted himself and his wife, and put one eagle-tail-feather on her hair. It is not often, that a woman of this tribe will go out on a raid. So it was a great honour to Bear-chief to have such a wife. He told his wife: We now shall go to the camp, you in the lead, and I behind, and if we see any one, you must turn and run, and make your escape to our camp. I shall stay and fight. When Bear-chief told her this, she was very much frightened. Bear-chief sang another song, before he went up to the lodges with his wife, immediately after he had talked to her. This song was given to him in a dream by the Sun. The words are: My son, don't fear, I give you protection of life. He told his wife to go to a lodge with light in it, without stopping. She was, however, going to stop, because she saw a woman

going out to get some wood, but Bear-chief told her to go on. The night was very dark. When she got to the lodge, she dismounted, and cut two horses loose. He told her: Go out, the way we came in. I am going to get some more horses. And he cut five more horses loose from another lodge. The Crees were not yet all asleep. He started with his five head, and overtook his wife. They drove the horses, and they found four horses more, that were hobbled. He cut the hobbles loose, and now they drove 11 head. They came home, and their camp was down at Fort Conrad. Bear-chief's wife gave one of her horses to Joe Kipp.

After that the Flatheads came over, and stole horses from the Peigans. The Peigans chased them. Big-plume was their leader. Bear-chief found four of the Flathead horses. He took them all, and gave them to Big-plume. Then Bear-chief continued the chase, but he had to return without seeing the Flatheads. They came home.

A few days later there were five in a party, Bear-chief being the leader. They went to the Assiniboins, and got to their camp. They saw nine head of horses near the lodges. He took five, and his companions took the other four. They got home allright.

Afterwards there were eight in a party, that started for the Sioux country, Bear-chief being the leader. That evening the Sioux discovered them by seeing them from a long distance. Bear-chief and his friends knew, that they had been discovered. They had to be very careful, and approached the lodges from another direction. Bear-chief took two horses from a lodge, and on the hill they found 24 horses more, which they took with them. They stayed out a very long time. In the meantime his wives became very uneasy. On their way back they came to some Cree half-breeds. It was day-time. They took 11 head of horses from the Crees. Then they came home allright.

Some time afterwards he called all the chiefs together to come to his lodge. They all ate together. He filled the pipe, and gave them to smoke. He told them: I have called you together to tell you, that I have made my last raid on the enemies. I have worked very hard to gain honour. Now I shall never go on another raid. And from now on I shall follow the ways of the white men. The chiefs proposed, that he should go with them all to the Indian agent, and tell him the same thing. The agent was very happy, to hear Bear-chief saying, that he had left off making raids. The agent gave to the chiefs a big supply of groceries. From that moment all the Peigans left off making raids.

Since that time Bear-chief lived quietly in the Reservation. In 1887 he built a log-house, and afterwards he had two log-houses, one for winter, and one for summer. Since 1909 he has lived all the time in another log-house, half a mile from Holy Family Mission. He has not been baptized, though his parents were. He often goes to church, but still puts rags in a tree as a sacrifice to the Sun. His ideas about the creation of the world are an interesting mixture of Christianity and Peigan tradition. Bear-chief told us his cosmogony, a young Indian, called Philip Arrow-top, being interpreter.[40]

Wednesday, August 2.

Joe and Running Wolf come to listen to a Napi (or Old Man) story. There are several of these stories, for example, obt, 63–65.

Two adventures of the Old Man.

There was a time, the Old Man was walking about down [a river]. On top of a hill at the side of the river he thought: I shall look over the hill [down to the river]. Lower down on the side of the hill he saw a bear. He [the bear] was digging [for roots]. He [the Old Man] ran back [from the bank over which he had peeped] around to him. He gently looked over the hill at him. He said to him: He is slick behind. And he [the Old Man] threw his face down [ducked his head, so that the bear could not see him]. Then he again gently looked over the hill at him. He said again to him: He is slick behind. He [the Old Man] was seen by him. He threw his face down again. Four times he said to him: He is slick behind. Then he was chased up the hill by him. There he went. He was chased by him lower down. There was a big rock, he ran to it. He was chased around it by him. It was a long time, that he was chased. They had tramped around the rock, so that there was a deep hole around it. He [the Old Man] was very much afraid. He kicked into the ground, there was a buffalo-horn. He picked it up. He turned about [to show fight, having got the buffalo-horn as a weapon]. He held it to his head as if it were his horn. He [the bear] jumped around. He immediately shit. He [the Old Man] said to the bear: That way you [bears] will do, when you are scared. [And he said] to this rock: That way [as you are now, with a hole around you] you [rocks] can be seen in the future [that means: you will look like that in the future].

Then it was, that he [the Old Man] got thirsty. He thought: I shall go to the river. I shall drink. He then went. Near the edge of the water

Thursday, August 3.

he sat down on his knees. He was about to drink. He then saw [the reflection of] bullberries [in the water]. He began to strip himself [of his clothes]. He dived in [meaning to fetch those reflected bullberries out of the water]. He then floated aloft. Then he got out of the water again. When he looked in again into the water, [the bullberries] were still there. He then went to get a stone. He came back. He tied that stone to his neck. Then he dived again. He then sunk to the bottom [being heavy, with the stone tied to his neck]. He felt about [with his hands to catch the bullberries]. He got nothing. And he was about to be drowned. Then, being in the water, he broke [the string], that he wore round his neck, [to which the stone was tied]. He needed a long time to get ashore. Then he lay on his back. When he looked up, he [saw the bullberries themselves, which he first had seen reflected in the river, and] said: Alas, for these I was nearly drowned. He jumped up. He quickly took up a stick. He began to thrash them all. He said to them: That way the people will thrash you for their home-use. That's all.

[Cf. G.B. Grinnell, Blackfoot lodge tales, London 1893, p. 157, and C. Wissler-D.C. Duvall, Mythology of the Blackfoot Indians, New York 1908, p. 32 and p. 29.]

Lone Eater, Spotted Eagle, Running Crane and Crow Eyes want Uhlenbeck to read them a few old stories. Examples of old stories are "Horses found on an island," obt, 57–58; "The Old Man and the wolf on the ice," nsbt, 170–71 and "The Old Man, the elks, and the gophers," nsbt, 171–77. Preface on both stories: "Told and interpreted by Tatsey."

Horses found on an island.

The ancient people, the ancient Peigans all went west. They came to mountains. They went over them. They came to a very big lake. In the centre was a mountain. [The tribe] was sitting by [the lake]. After a long while the chief said to his companions: I shall go to that mountain. Wait here for me. And then they tied logs together [as a raft]. He got in [into the water]. He paddled them [the logs which were tied together] in. After a very long time he came to that mountain. He then started up. He came there on high. He looked down all around. He suddenly saw there many horses. They stood on the westside. In the morning he started back. It was nearly night, [when] he came to his companions. He said to them: On that mountain there are many horses. To-morrow half of them [of the Peigans] will stay here. With those others I shall go in [into the lake]. Then they went from there. It was nearly night, [when] they came back to that mountain. They got up very early. Some of them went east. The others went on the westside. And they started to drive these many horses [to the water]. All these many horses jumped in. Those people [who had been left behind] walked about on the [other] shore. They caught those horses [as fast as they came ashore]. Half of them swam back. Only a few got ashore. Those [others] all were drowned. They went home with all these, they had caught.

The Old Man and the wolf on the ice.

There the Old Man travelled about down a river. It was late in the fall. That river began to freeze over. In the morning he was still walking along [that river]. He saw, there was a wolf on the ice, [who] would run and quickly turn around. He would pick up something here and there, and swallow it. The Old Man said: What is he doing? He [the Old man] ran around out of sight towards him, he came near him, he saw him. What he was picking up and swallowing, were pieces of fresh tallow. [The Old Man] cried, walking towards him [and saying]: Oh, oh, let me do in that way. He was told by [the wolf]: Come on, Old Man, it is not important. When we are hungry, we say in the mornings, where the ice is smooth – then he started off [and] said: Ice must begin to crack, ice must begin to crack, hù + wí', hù + wí'. He would just knock fresh pieces of tallow out [of the ice], and then he would quickly turn around and pick up pieces here and there and swallow them. He was told by [the wolf] told him: We do it only once [a day]. And there the Old Man went. He had gone out of sight. He went on the ice, and then he did, as he was told by [the wolf]. He just knocked pieces of fresh tallow out [of the ice], and then he would quickly turn around and pick up pieces here and there and swallow them. Then he went again. He came again on other ice. Then he again walked over it. He would keep saying: Ice begin to crack, ice begin to crack. He could not knock out fresh pieces of tallow. He got angry. He was angry jumping up. He then broke through the ice. He was nearly drowned. He had a hard time to get out of the water. And that was another mistake, he made.

[Cf. McClintock ont 343, Simms tc 287 sq.]

The Old Man, the elks, and the gophers.

There the Old Man was again travelling about. Just at dark he saw there many elks. Then he cried, walking towards them [and saying]: Oh, oh, let me do in that way. He was told by their chief: Come on, my elder brother, it is not important. We are leading each other [while I, the chief, carry the fire]. The Old Man told the elk: Go on, that I may see you, how you do it. The Old Man himself began to look about this high cliff [for a place to get down]. He found, where he could go down. He was told by them: Come on, now you must take the lead. The two pieces of bark [the fire, mentioned about] were burning. And he started. He was striking them together, that they might spark. He came to where this bank was highest. He threw the fire down [over the cliff]. From where it was lowest, he himself jumped down. And from another place he came up. He told them: come on, my younger brothers, just jump from it, it is very funny. Now, why I did not come soon, was that I laughed hard. Over there, where I jumped, the earth is very soft. Then they began to jump. They were nearly all gone. There was one, it was a doe, she was big with calves. He was told by her: My elder brother, I had better not jump, [for] I might get hurt. He told her: Yes, now go away, that there might be some elks in the future from you.

Then he went down. Then he began to put up a lodge [out of trees and leaves]. He had done making a lodge. Then he began to skin all these elks. He then skinned them. Then he had plenty of meat [cut up and hung]. He had tongues for flags. He had done cutting meat [for dried meat]. He was lying on his back in his lodge. There was a coyote, [that] came there. He had his leg tied [with a bandage], he nearly fell on his face [from limping]. He was told by [the coyote]: My elder brother, give me to eat. He told him: Ah, I ought to hit you on the face. He was told by [the coyote]: Come on, my elder brother, give me even burned [stuff] to eat. He answered him: We must first run a race together. He was told by [the coyote]: My leg hurts me. Let it not be far. And there they went away [to the place where they would start from]. [The coyote] would say to him: From here, my elder brother. He would answer him: From that ridge over there. And when they came there, he was again told by [the coyote]: From here. He would say to him: Over there from that other ridge. They had got very far. He said to [the coyote]: Now, from here we shall start to run. Then they started to run. The coyote began to bite his leg loose. Then he ran after the Old Man. He then just ran past him. The Old Man then would say: Oh, my younger brother, leave me some of my choice pieces. The coyote had got to that brush-lodge already a long time.

He then howled. The wolves and coyotes, the bears, the badgers, the skunks, the mice, all were there complete. Then the coyote ate [all] the good pieces. What the bears ate, was the skimmed grease. The coyote said to the mice: Run up. Those tongues, that is what you must eat. They [all the animals] were about to separate. At last the rabbits came there. They had nothing to eat. They then only greased their shoulders with some of the oil [that was left]. And they [the different animals] ran away separately. Why the bears, the wolves, the badgers, the foxes, the skunks are fat nowadays, is that they ate the Old Man's choice pieces [of meat] and his skimmed grease. The mice are not fat, [because] they ate the tongues. They were helped by the ants to eat [the tongues]. The rabbits got nothing to eat, they only greased their shoulders. There [between their shoulders] is the only place, where they have fat nowadays. That they do not eat meat, is because they did not eat from the Old Man's choice pieces. And when the Old Man came to [his lodge] and entered, he saw that his food was eaten up. He looked up. He said: They did not do it completely. There are those flags of mine [left]. He pulled those tongues down. He would say [each time he was pulling down one of them]: This one is a scarred tongue. He would throw it away. Finally they were all scarred tongues [because the mice and the ants had eaten from them]. He threw them all away.

And there he started again. He saw, there were gophers, they were burying each other [in hot ashes]. He went to them crying [and saying]: Oh, oh, let me do in that way. They said to him: Come on, my elder brother, it is not important. He said to them: Come on, bury one another [in the ashes]. When they buried one another, then they [that were buried] would squeal. Then they threw each other out [of the ashes]. They told him: Come on, my elder brother, we will bury you. He was just buried, and then he squealed. He was thrown out. He told them: My younger brothers, because you are many, just let me bury you all at once. They said to him: Yes. They all lay in there. One of them [standing away from the fire] said to him: My elder brother, I am not with them [that means: I don't take part in their play]. And [the Old Man] covered them up. He told that one [that was standing away from the fire]: Just go away, that there will be some gophers from you in the future. Those others kept on squealing. The Old Man then went away to get layers from the red willows [to put the gophers on]. They were cooked. He pulled them from [the fire]. He began to eat them. He ate his fill with good relish.

He said: I will just sleep a little. He told his anus [literally: takes-gun-on-both-sides]: Be careful. If some one comes, wake me up. He lay down. After a short while [his anus] made noise. He jumped up. He saw, there was a bird. He said: Ah, for that one he makes noise. Then he slept again. Then he slept soundly. [His anus] kept on making noise. He did not wake up. There came a bob-cat to those gophers. He ate them all. Then he went away. And [the Old Man] woke up. When he looked, [then he saw, that] all his food was eaten up [literally: all my foods are eaten up]. He said to his anus: I told you, that you should be careful. Now all my food is eaten up. And he followed the bob-cat, who was lying on a flat rock. He caught him. He said to him: Now I have you, there is nothing to prevent me from killing you. He made plenty of fire [i.e. a big fire]. He began to knock his [the bob-cat's] face back. And he stretched out his belly, and he stretched out his hind-legs too.

That is why they [the bob-cats] are long-legged, and long-bodied, [and] short-faced. He would throw him in the fire. He [the bob-cat] would just jump over [the fire]. He only scorched his [the bob-cat's] fur yellow. That is why the bob-cats are yellow nowadays. He told him: In that way you will look in the future. When you run, if people say to you "You have left your fringes behind", then you must stop [literally: then stop].

And he went to that fire, he had made. He wiped his anus with a fire-stick. When the burned place began to hurt, he would hold his hind-part to the side, from where the wind blew. He was saying: Let it blow harder. After a short while the wind blew [harder]. He began to be carried by the wind. He would tear up the roots of what he caught hold of. A long time he was carried about by the wind. He caught hold of birches. [Hanging] on those he was blown about by the wind. After a long while the wind stopped blowing. He got up [from the place where he lay, when the wind had stopped]. He said to them [the birches]: I was happy, being blown about, they had to be there [that means: if you had not been there, I might be happy still, being blown about]. He took out his knife. He cut notches in them. He told them: In that way you will look in the future. That is why the birches now look, as if there were notches cut in them. And that is all.

[Cf. Grinnell blt 155 sq. 158. 171 sqq., Wissler-Duvall mbi 25 sqq. 27 sqq. 38 sq., McClintock ont 338 sqq. 340 sq., Dorsey-Kroeber ta 60. 61 sq. 69, Simms tc 285, Jones ft 284 sqq., Lowie a 111. 113. 115 sq. 127, Lowie ns 274].

Friday, August 4.

Uhlenbeck tells the story about Napi's greasy mouth and abundance to Harry Horn, the two brothers Spotted Eagle, No Bear, John Gardipe, Williams, his "wild friend Jack" and a few more. Perhaps it is the story in nsbt, 177–80. Preface: "Told by Blood, interpreted by Tatsey."

The Old Man and Fat.

The Old Man went, he travelled about. He met a person. When he saw him, his shirt was belly-fat, his hat was a buffalo-flank, his leggings were back-fat, his moccasins were kidney-fat, his bow was the short rib of a buffalo, his arrows were guts, white earth, one kind of earth he had, was grease, and the other [kind of earth he had], a reddish earth, was pemmican [white and red earth were used to paint the robes]. Then [the Old Man] said to him: Where is the earth? [that means: where does that earth come from?] Give me some of it. He gave him some of it. He gave of both kinds of his earth to the Old Man. The Old Man went away, he went out of sight. He began to eat the both kinds of earth, he ate them up. He ran again around after him, being out of sight. He met him again. He said again to him: I went to get some of this earth, give me some of both kinds. He gave it him again. Then [the Old Man] went away, then he ate them [the both kinds of earth] again. Then he ate them up. He ran again around after him, being out of sight. Then he met him again. It was the same one. The Old Man was the same, [and] that Fat was the same [as when they met a while ago]. [The Old Man] met him. He said to him: Give me both kinds of earth. While [Fat] took from it, [the Old Man] did not look at anything else but all his [i.e. Fat's] clothes. He was looking at those [and nothing else]. [Fat] gave his earth again to the Old Man. His white earth was grease, and the red earth was pemmican. When

Saturday, August 5.

[the Old man] had met him four times, then his earth was all gone. The Old Man had eaten up the grease. He then went away.

He again went around to him, being out of sight. He saw Fat again. And he said to him: Where are you going? He was told by him: This way I am now going about on a visit. Then [the Old man] said to him: He looks [meaning: you look] like that one, I know [my wife has connections with]. He was told by him: No, I am not [that person]. The Old Man had already taken a stick. He said to him: No, you are the one. I shall kill you. He threw the stick up. [Fat] ran away. And he ran after him. He overtook him. Fat shot at him with his arrows. He shot at the Old Man. Fat then ran away. He threw away his hat, he also threw away his moccasins, he also threw away his leggings, he also threw away his shirt. He just had a body [and no clothes on it, i.e. he was just naked]. [The Old man] would not quit [pursuing] him. He tried hard, that he might catch him. [Fat] was tired. He overtook him over there in a coulee. [Fat] jumped up. Where he jumped, he burst into pieces, who was [nothing but] a great quantity of grease. The Old Man went over to that grease. He ate it. [When] he had eaten that earth [i.e. that grease], then he went back. He took his shirt, his leggings, his hat, his moccasins. He just went back gathering them up. And now the boiling is ended [the story is at an end].

[Cf. Simms tc 285 sq. Cf. also Dorsey-Kroeber ta 69.]

Breakfast with trout. One of these days, John Tatsey must have told Uhlenbeck "How I go fishing." Boys' experiences, nr.10, nsbt, 236–37

[10] [How I go fishing.] I then go, I then take my fish-pole. Then I get to the river. I throw my fish-line in [into the water]. I then walk down to [a place], where it is deep. I fish there. I catch about two. I go farther on, I begin to fish again. When I am long ways off, then my grass-hoppers are all gone. I begin to catch some. When I have caught quite a few grass-hoppers, I go back to the river. I begin to fish again, and there are lots of fish, and they are wild, and I don't catch a great many, just about ten. It may be, I catch more of them. I get tired, then go back, I will finally get home. When I get home, I clean the fish. And when we go to eat, I take flour, and I put the fish into it. I put the frying-pan on the fire. And I put some grease in the frying-pan. And when it [the pan] is hot, I put the fish in the frying-pan. And when they are all cooked, we eat them. And when we have done eating, I get pretty full. And now the boiling is ended [that means: the story is at an end].

Uhlenbeck first works with Tatsey. It could have been a story that Jim Blood told him earlier, as Willy Uhlenbeck noted on July 23 that "everything drawn up with Jim Blood has to be reviewed with Tatsey!" So maybe it was "Horses found," nsbt, 204–9. Preface: "Told by Blood and interpreted by Joseph Tatsey." Later that day, Uhlenbeck finishes another story with Walter Mountain Chief, likely one of the beaver stories, or "The Elk and his wife," as on July 20 he then only came for a short while.

Horses found.

How I heard the news [i.e. the story]. There was a person, [who] was very poor. He was not known [by anybody], where he went. Then he was travelling about on this prairie. After he had wintered, he was known, [that] he might have died. Then he stayed out also during the summer. Then he was travelling about, [where] there were not many people. Then he was shown [by somebody] in his dream [what to do]. And then he was told by [that person]: Try to get over to that lake. There you will get something. Then he started. How many times did he sleep [before he got to that lake]? [Nobody knows.] Then he got there. Then he was told by the person in his dream: There are your ears [that means: there is a reason to be on your guard]. Don't dodge from him. There is a man, [that] will do some dangerous thing to you. There is none, that he would pity. You are the only one now, that I pity. Therefore I told you to go [literally: that you must go]. Try hard during the night, that you may be close by in the morning. He [the man in the lake] will know you, [that] there is a person, when the water sounds. Don't dodge.

He [the man in the lake] went out [of the water]. He was riding on horseback. Then he ran towards him [towards the poor man]. [When] he got close to him, he whipped [his horse]. Then he did not run from him. Then he knew, that he was very much to be pitied: There is nothing to prevent, [that] I shall die now in the morning. Then he did not run from him. Then [the rider] was going to run over him. The horse jumped over him. Over there [the rider] ran past him, and turned back to him. When he got close to him, he whipped [his horse] the same [as before]. He tried to make him dodge [literally: that he dodged]. Four times he then ran over him, [and] then he got off [his horse] by him. Then he told him: Get up, that we may go home together. Here is my horse, ride on [him]. Then he rode on [him]. He [the man from the lake] was leading his horse. He then took him [the poor man] into

the water. Right in the centre [of the water] he had his lodge. Then he [the poor man] came there. Then he entered. Then he was told by [that person]: Sit down over there. And how many nights will you sleep [in this lodge]? He answered him: I shall not sleep here, I shall go away again. He was told by [that person]: Yes, it is good [that you are going away]. Now, here are my things. Take, what you like [literally: think]. He said to him: Yes, over there near the door are hoofs, I shall take those. He was told by [that person]: They are not good, they are bad. Don't take them. These [other things] are good, take from them. He said to him: No, I shall take those hoofs. He was told by [that person]: Yes, you are very wise. There is nobody, that I would pity. Now you are the only one, I pity you. Now, I give them to you. Now the coming night you will go away. If you had said, that you would sleep here two [nights] or one [night], those [nights] would have been winters. He was wise, that he said: I shall not sleep here.

[When] it was evening, he [the owner of the lodge] took those hoofs. Then that man went out with them. Then he rattled with them. Then many horses all ran towards [the lodge]. Then they all stood about. There was a grey mare. A [rope of] raw-hide was round her neck. Then he caught her. Then she was given by him to [the poor man] [with the words]: Here are those hoofs [belonging together with the mare]. He told him also: These horses are all colts of this mare. Don't sleep during four nights and days, don't look back. Look only in the direction, you are travelling. The fourth night in the morning, before [the sun] has risen, you must rattle with these hoofs. Don't let this mare loose. Hold her fast.

He started in the night. And then he travelled on. Finally it was morning. Then he was travelling still during the day. Finally it was night again. During the night he then travelled again. Finally it was morning again. During the day he then was travelling still. Then it was night again. During the night he then was travelling still. And then, [when] it was getting day-light, he took the hoofs. He began to rattle with them. Then he felt, that the earth was shaking. And his horse was neighing hard [literally: was suffering with neighing]. All [the horses] overtook him. Then they all ran past him. Then he turned his horse loose. Then he slept. Then he was sleeping this whole day. Late in the evening he woke up. Then he went away. He then rode one of his horses. Then he went on, and he was leading that mare, the grey mare. And her colts [all the horses] ran by her. After a short while, when night came, he camped. He slept again. In the morning the horses were gone [literally: not to be seen]. Then he took those hoofs, he rattled with them. His horses ran all again to him. He caught that mare again. Then he started again. During the day he then travelled. He could not ride well [because he had no saddle]. [Therefore] he would just travel on foot. And he would not let loose that one mare. Then he camped again. He picketed her. There he tied her. Then he slept near her. He was told by her: The lodges [of the Peigans] are near. To-morrow you will come there. Then it was morning. Then he caught his horse. And he did not drive those other horses.

He then was travelling during the day. He was still travelling, then he suddenly saw the lodges. One of his horses was a big, bob-tailed, bay horse. Another one was white, also bob-tailed. Those two were the best of all these horses. He had been told by that man [he got the horses from]: These many horses will not be all gone, as long as you [the whole Peigan people] exist. He came to his lodge. All the people always crowded around the horses. They were curious to see them. Then he was known, where he had been. He had been thought, that he was dead. Then he suddenly came back. Then these people moved. Then he lent the horses to these people. They then were afraid of them. They could not ride them, [because] they were afraid of them. He then showed them the ropes. He used them for bridles for them [i.e. for the people]. He then put them [the people] on the horses. Then they started to ride off. Some of them fell off. It was not long, then they learned how to ride [literally: how they might ride]. Then they were all good [riders]. He gave horses to his relations. When they all knew them [the horses], they took care of them. And these horses [that we have to-day] are from those horses [that that man brought with him from the lake]. And now to-day I tell it to you, the way that I heard it. I tell it to you as an old story. And now the boiling is ended [that means: the story is at an end].

[Cf. Uhlenbeck obt 57 sq.]

Sunday, August 6.

The Uhlenbecks spend time in Eagle Calf's tent and Mary Duck Head interprets. In nsbt is one story, "The Milky Way," nsbt, 113–14, that according to the Preface is: "Told by Chief-all-over (Motúinau), interpreted by Tatsey." Was Eagle Calf, the much younger brother of Tatsey's mother, also called Chief-all-over? In any case, Uhlenbeck refers to him (his clan affiliation) as such; cf. the following paragraph in Uhlenbeck's P and P Names (Appendix A in this volume): "A very old woman called O'taitsìua (Weasel-body), whose father was a white man, is supposed to belong to the clan of her mother, the Motúiinaiks (All-chiefs). O'taitsìua herself was married to a Blood Indian from the I'tskinàiks (Horn-people), and Joseph Tatsey, a son from this marriage who lives among the Peigan, also belongs to the Motúiinaiks."[41] In any case, the story follows hereunder.

The Milky Way.
———

I do not know, why the Wolf-road [the Milky Way] was called [by that name]. These Peigans do not talk about the Wolf-road. The people on the other side of the mountains told me about it. One of the [ancient] Peigans killed bad people; that is his road. He killed the Inhaler. He said to these people [the Peigans]: I killed that one, that treated you badly. Go over there, that you take out those, who are yet alive. There are many, that are yet alive, a few are dead, some more may die yet. Clot-of-Blood was the one, [who] said this. And that is his road. In these mountains was the Inhaler's house, it was a mountain. These Peigans called it the Mountain-with-outlets-on-all-sides.

[Cf. Grinnell blt 102, McClintock ont 324. 498, and, for the story of Clot-of-Blood, Uhlenbeck obt 34 sqq. And the references given obt 50, to which Dorsey tsp 80 sqq., Dorsey-Kroeber ta 298 sqq., Lowie a 135 are to be added.]

Uhlenbeck tells a story to a number of people, No Bear, Joe, a married Indian with three children, and John Head Carrier. Perhaps he read the one about "Red Head," the leader of the ancient Peigans, nsbt, 123–25. Preface: "Told by Bear-chief, interpreted by Tatsey." Note: One Red-head is listed also under the All-chiefs clan; see Appendix B to this volume.

Red-head.
———

There was a young man of the ancient Peigans, he had no clan, he camped about alone. That young man killed the Peigans. He had a mother. His mother was called Crow-woman. His pets were crows and magpies. [Women] would come to that young man, they came to marry him. His pets used to tell Red-head [this was the name of that young man]: Kill that woman. There was a chief of the ancient Peigans, whose [literally: his] daughter did not [want to] marry. There was a good-looking young man, he went towards that girl. He said to her: Let us be together. She told him: If you kill Red-head, I shall marry [you]. And that young man was pitied by wolverines. And that Red-head could not be killed. That young man told the girl: Yes, I shall kill Red-head. That young man sharpened [literally: put in order] an elk-horn [that he had]. It got to be very sharp, he put it away along the calf-side of his leg. He went to Red-head. He came close to him. He turned into a woman. He was [now] a very good-looking woman. Then he came there in the night, he did not enter. Then he hid himself near by, where that old woman [Red-head's mother] had got her water. Before day-light he [Red-head] went to hunt, and that old woman went after morning-water [that means: went early after water]. That woman [viz. the young man who had turned into a woman] got up, she kissed her [Red-head's mother]. She [that young man] said to that old woman: Mother, help me, I have come, that I might marry your son. I am not married. She was told by that old woman: My son kills his wives. His pets are the ones [that tell him to do so]. Now I shall help you. She [that young man] went home with her.

When they entered, these crows and magpies told that old woman Crow-woman: She has a man's eyes, and she has a man's legs. They flew towards him [Red-head]. There he was, he came home with the pieces of the carcase. They flew to him, they told Red-head: There is one with a man's eyes and with a man's legs, kill him. Red-head came home, his mother went out to meet him. She told him: Listen to me, now I get tired. Your pets eat awfully much. Don't kill her. There is a woman, she came in. That old woman entered, and her son came in the last. She [Red-head's mother] stood before that woman. Her son finally went to the upper part of the lodge, he was seated already. And that woman [the young man] went to the upper part of the lodge. She kissed him, she gave him moccasins, ornamented with quills, and pemmican, mixed with medicine, that he might love her. And he ate that pemmican, and he liked her. She cheated him. Those pets never slept. They told Red-head: She is not a woman, she has a man's eyes, and she has a man's legs. Four nights passed, and his pets got tired. They flew away, they were watching about, if there were some people coming [that they might tell Red-head to kill them].

Five nights passed, and in the morning that woman was told by Red-head: Let us go into that forest over there, that you may look on my head for lice. It was not a long while, then he fell asleep. That woman put his head down, and took the elk-horn, she hammered it in into his ear, and she killed him, and she scalped him, and she ran away. She was far away. And those magpies flew to [the lodge]. They said to that old woman: This one [meaning: you] may die a bad death, Red-head is killed. You used to say "she is a woman". Then that old woman ran.

And she saw her son, [that] he was killed. That old woman was told by the magpies: We let you go [that means: we won't have anything to do with you]. We shall go to the forest, and the crows will go to the hills. And that young man [that had been turned into a woman, and who had taken now his own shape] then came home. He came up going in a circle [and showing his scalp]. He then gave his scalp to that girl. Then she married him, and then he took his father-in-law's chieftainship. And from that time he was the leader of the ancient Peigans, while they were moving. And now the boiling is ended.

[Cf. Wissler-Duvall mbi 129 sqq. Cf. also Dorsey-Kroeber ta 126 sqq. 133 sqq.]

Thursday, August 10.

Eagle Calf might have been listening to "The Old Man, the rock, and the kit-fox," nsbt, 187–91. Preface: "Told and interpreted by Joseph Tatsey."

The Old Man, the rock, and the kit-fox.

There was the Old Man and his younger brother the kit-fox, they were travelling about. It is over north, [that] this story belongs. There was a river, there they were travelling about. They went on the prairie. He told his younger brother: Let us go over to the other river. They had got far on the prairie. Then they came to a big rock. It was warm. He said to that big rock: Have this here for a robe. He covered [the rock] up with his robe. And [he and] his younger brother went on. They had got far. He saw, there was a rain coming. He told his younger brother: Run back, tell the rock, that I want to use his robe just for the rain. Then his younger brother ran away. He was not going long, then he came back. He told [the Old Man]: He [the rock] was saying: He has already given it to me. And the rain was coming near. He told [his younger brother]: Run back again, tell him, I want to use it just for the rain. Then he ran back again. He was not going long, then he came back again. He told [the Old Man]: He was saying: I will not give it to him, he has already given it to me. He told his younger brother: Run back again, tell him, that he must give it to you. I will take it back. Then he ran back again. He was not going long, he came back again. He told [the Old Man]: He was saying: What has been given to big rocks, that is never taken back from them. He told his younger brother: Wait for me here. I shall go back and take my robe. Then he came to the big rock. He said to him: He has [i.e. you have] always been staying out in the rain, [and now] he thinks, that he ought to have a robe. Then he jerked the cover from him,

and ran back to his younger brother. He told his younger brother: Come on, let us travel faster.

They had travelled a long time, they heard, there was a roaring sound. He told his younger brother: Go back and look. Then he ran back. [The Old Man] himself had already started to run for escape. He was overtaken by his younger brother. He was told by him: That big rock is after us. They ran faster. His younger brother was fast [i.e. faster than the Old Man himself]. He would go back and look. When he overtook [the Old Man], then he would say to him: He keeps on getting closer to us. [After] they had been running a long time, the Old Man saw [the rock]. And his younger brother got out of breath. The big rock came very close to them. The kit-fox ran into [a hole]. And the Old Man was chased by [the rock]. He saw some young buffalo-bulls. He told them: Help, my younger brothers, here comes one chasing me. Then he ran past them. He saw them plainly, that they were mashed down [by the rock]. [The rock] was getting closer to him. He saw, there were night-hawks flying home. He told them: Help, my younger brothers, this big rock has chased me very hard. Then they would sail down towards [the rock]. And then they would fart at it, they would blow off a piece of it every time. After a short while they blew it in two. Then the Old Man stopped running. Then he began to look at the rock. He saw, those bulls were lying inside of the rock. Then he fixed them up [that means: he made them alive again]. They became buffaloes again. And he went back to look for his younger brother. He came to [the place], where he had run into [a hole]. It was covered up, so that there was no opening left [literally: it was knocked shut]. Then he dug after him. [His younger brother] came out. [The Old Man] said to him: Come on, let us go on again.

They went down alongside the river. He found the young ones of the night-hawks. He took them. He told them: I was happily chased by that big rock. Their [i.e. your] mothers had to blow it in two [that means: if your mothers had not blown it in two, I might be happy still, being chased by that big rock]. Then he began to split their mouths wider. He told them: In that way you will look in the future. In such rocky places, that is where you will be in the future. He then went on again. The night-hawks came flying home. They said to their children: Ah, ah, you must have eaten raw food, you are with bloody mouths. [The young ones] told them: No, that Old Man split our mouths wider. He said: I was happily chased by that big rock. Their mothers had to blow it in two. That was the reason, that he split our mouths wider. They said: Which way has he gone? [The young ones] told them: He went north. Then they flew after him. He was still travelling. They overtook him. Then they began to fart down at him. He used his robe as a shield. Each time he would cut out a piece of it [where it was soiled by the night-hawks]. He finally cut it all up. He ran into a lake for safety. He lay with only his mouth sticking out [of the water]. And he was left by them in safety. Then he came out of the water.

And [he and] his younger brother then wintered together. Spring was near. Then he pulled out his [i.e. his younger brother's] fur. He was then short-furred. [The Old Man] told him: when it is this time of the year, you will look in this way in the future. And that night the blizzard [literally: one who makes raids] came. [The Old Man] told his younger brother: This tripe is warm, I shall cover you up with it. He had done covering him. It was night then. In the morning, when he looked at his younger brother, he was already frozen with his face twisted. He said to him: Ah, [I wonder], what he is laughing at. My younger brother has always been a laugher. And that one was frozen with his face twisted. That is why in spring the kit-foxes are short-furred and yellow. And now the dogs are scratching the ground [after having had their meal].

[Cf. Grinnell 165 sq., Wissler-Duvall mbi 24 sq. 37, McClintock ont 342, Dorsey-Kroeber ta 65 sqq., Lowie a 108. 120, Lowie ns 262 sqq.]

John Oldmanchief, Jim Williams and George Champane enter and tell about the games they play. In Boys' experiences, nrs. 17, 18, and 19, nsbt, 242–43 are about games. According to the Preface, N°. 18 was started by "another young boy, Peter Bear-leggings, whose Indian name is White-whiskers (A′pssùyi), but brought to an end by John. N°. 19 was told and interpreted by Peter Bear-leggings."

[17] [Base-ball.] They are even on both sides, they are nine on each side, and nine go out to the field, and they all get ready. And one of those others takes the first strike. If he hits the ball [with the bat], he will run first. If the first runner beats the ball, then he will not be out. And the second will strike. And if he hits the ball, then he will run. And the other one runs the second time. And the other [base] will get to it. Then the third one will strike. If he does not hit the ball, he strikes three times, and he will be out. Another [fellow] will strike. If he hits the ball, then the other one, [that] struck first, will get back to the home-base. And these strikers will go out to the field. And the others will come in and strike. One of them will strike first. If he hits the ball, he will run. If the ball gets ahead of him, then he will be out. And if the next [striker] does not hit the ball, if it goes straight up in the air, if somebody catches it, then he will be out. And the next one strikes. And if he does not hit it, if he has completed his [three] strikes, and if the catcher catches it, then he will be out. And there will be three out. And they will go back out to the field. And the others will come back to strike. And if those others [that were out last] have run their [three] runs, then they will win the game. And that is all.

[18] [Horse-shoes.] [When I was] at school, I played. We played a game with horse-shoes. I beat them [the other fellows]. The first one that counts up to eleven, that is the one that wins the game. If he throws the horse-shoe into the stake, it counts five. And if it leans against the stake,

we count one [horse-shoe] three. And when [we have] eleven, then we win the game.

[**19**] [Kicked by a mare.] I am called White-whiskers. I went down, I then went through the water. I went to our ranch. I was looking for the horses. Then I caught my horse [a mare], I saddled her, I got on her, and she was trying to kick me. I then started, and her colt ran back. I got on the other horse, I started to drive her [the mare I rode first], I started to chase her. And I gave some dried meat to a certain woman [literally: to a woman, that there was]. Then I went up. I started to whip my horse [the mare], and she kicked me, and she kicked my finger hitting it exactly. I drove her up. Then I came to my tent, and he [my step-father] put tobacco on my finger. They tied it up. I then washed my finger.

Friday, August 11.

Uhlenbeck reads "Scarface" to Jim, Louis and Jack Veille: obt, 50–57.

Scar-face.

———

All ancient Peigans were camped [in a circle]. There was a chief's child, a woman, [that] would not marry. Everybody wanted to marry her. She refused [all of them]. There was a young man, [who] had a ridge-scar on his face. He was called Scar-face [literally: Ridge]. He said to his younger sister: Tell that girl, that I want to marry her. She said to that girl: My elder brother tells you, that you should marry him. She said to her: Who is your elder brother? Scar-face, she was told by [the younger sister]. [The chief's daughter said to her:] I don't refuse your elder brother. Tell him: When his scar is seen no more, I shall marry [him]. That girl went home. She wept. Her elder brother said to her: Why do you weep? She said to him: I am ashamed of what that woman said to me. She says: When your scar is seen no more, she will marry [you].

Then Scar-face went to where the Sun rises. He went that way. After a very long time he came to an old woman. She said to him: What do you walk for? He said to her: I am going for this my scar. She told him: I don't know it. Over there it looks blue [a mountain-ridge]. Down on the other side of it lives an old woman. Perhaps she will know it. Here are my moccasins, stick your feet in them. When you arrive, put them with the fore-ends back. Then he started to go.

He arrived. He put off those moccasins. They went back [to their owner]. That old woman said to him: What do you walk for? He said to her: For this my scar. She told him: Over there it looks blue. Down on the other side of it lives an old woman. Perhaps she knows your scar [how to get rid of it]. Put your feet in my moccasins. When you arrive, put them back [with the fore-ends behind]. Then he came to that old woman. Then he pulled off his moccasins. They went back. That old woman said to him: What do you travel about for? He said to her: I am going for this my scar. She told him: I don't know it. Over there it looks blue. Down on the other side of it lives an old woman. She will tell you, where you can go. She will know, [what] can mend your scar. Put on my moccasins. When you arrive, put them with the fore-ends back. He started again.

He arrived. He put off the moccasins. They went back. She [the old woman to whom he came] said to him: My son, what do you travel about for? He said to her: I am going for this my scar. She told him: Yes, I don't know it. I shall tell you, where you can go. That one knows it. Go on, when it is night. Over there it looks blue. Try to get down on the other side of it during the night. There is a lake. When you arrive at the shore, then you must dig the sand. There you must lie in [that means: in the hole you have dug], [so] that you are sticking out with your mouth. It is very hot. The whole day you will lie. There the Sun has a lodge. In the evening he comes home. In the morning his son [the Morning-star, Ipisóaχs] comes out. When you see him, then get up. He will tell you, how you can live.

It was nearly morning, [when] he saw that young man [the Morning-star]. He was told by him: Partner, let us go there, I shall hide you. My father will soon go [round the world]. [After] he [the Sun] went, they entered his [the Sun's] lodge. And then the Sun came again. He said to his wife: It smells human. He was told by her: Over there is [concealed] that one, your son's partner. He said to her: Ah, I told him, that he should never get a partner [any more]. Make incense. And she made incense. He said to his wife: That's enough, let my son [Scar-face] come out. He told him: My son, be prudent. Your friend's partners are killed.

It was a long time, [before] he [Scar-face] was told by his partner: Partner, let us travel that way, to that big lake. [When] they came there, they were chased by a crane. He [Scar-face] said to his partner: Run away, I shall not be harmed. He took a stick. He killed four of those

cranes. His partner got home. His father said to him: I told you, that you should never have a partner [any more]. They are killed. He said to him: I shall go over there on the hill. I don't think, that my partner is killed. He went [over there]. He saw his partner. He was told by him: Partner, I have killed four [of them], that treated you badly [killing your partners]. He [Morning-star] told him: Let us take them home. When they came near [the Sun's lodge], that young man [Morning-star] went ahead. He said to his father: He has killed four [of them]. He [the Sun] praised him. He [Morning-star] was told by his father: Your friend has become a chief.

After a long time Scar-face was told by the Sun: My son, what did you travel for? He said to him: I asked a woman to marry [me]. I was told by her: When your scar heals, when it is all gone, I shall marry [you]. He [the Sun] told him: Yes, I can mend it. He said to his old woman [his wife]: Make four sweat-lodges for me. I shall mend our son [Scar-face]. There were four sweat-lodges. He told his sons [that means: his son and his son's partner Scar-face]: We shall go into this [sweat-lodge]. He rubbed Scar-face with an eagle-tail-feather. He said to his old woman: Which [of the two] is your son? She told him: This one. He said to her: You are right. They entered the second sweat-lodge. He rubbed him again. He said to her: Look here, which is your son? She told him: This one. He said to her: You are right. They entered another [sweat-lodge]. He rubbed Scar-face again. He said again to his old woman: Which is your son? She told him: This one. He said to her: You are right. They entered another [sweat-lodge]. He tried hard to rub [literally: that he rubs] his son [Scar-face]. He [the Sun] [now] stopped [rubbing]. He said to his old woman: Which is your son? She told him: This one. He said to her: You said wrong "This one". This son of yours [not your own boy, but Scar-face], this [will be called] False-Morning-star.

And after a long time False-Morning-star said to his partner: I shall go home. He was told by him: Here is my whistle. And he was told by the old man [the Sun]: What the people will give to me hereafter, they will do it this way [the Sun says this after having shown to the young man how to make incense and to perform the sacrifice]. He was told by the old woman: Here is my cloak [of elk-skin], my hat, [and] my wooden pin. In summer they will have the medicine-lodge. Show it to your tribe [how to make the medicine-lodge]. And then this is all, we have to give you. He was told by his partner: Partner, we shall go over there, to that hole, I shall let you down. When you arrive in your country, give me that woman [that has scorned you]. With this my whistle you will whistle. Then that woman will come [to you]. And this sinew here, throw it into [the fire]. Say [then to me]: Partner, there goes your wife. He answered him: Yes [I shall do just as you told me]. He was told by his partner: Shut your eyes. When you feel the ground, [then] open your eyes [literally: see]. Then he started down. He came here on the ground. He sat there on a butte. He was not far from the lodges.

He was seen. The chief said to the camp: There is a person. He is not of this [people] here. Let there be some one, [that] goes to see him. There was a young man, [that] went over to him. He came near him. He was told by him [Scar-face]: Go back again. Tell my kinsmen and my brother-in-law, that he must make a sweat-lodge. [Then] I shall go in [into that lodge]. That young man went home. He said to his [Scar-face's] brother-in-law: There is Scar-face. [He wants] that you make a sweat-lodge for him. Then he will go in. [When] he had built the sweat-lodge, he [Scar-face] then came [to him]. He [Scar-face] went out [of the sweat-lodge, after having been there for a while]. He [the brother-in-law] was told by him [Scar-face]: This way you will do in the future. He [the brother-in-law] then was shown everything which had been given to him [Scar-face] by the Sun and his wife. And Scar-face went home. He saw that woman, that refused him. He whistled with his whistle. That woman walked over to him. She said to him: You whistle. She told him [also]: I shall marry [you]. He said to her: Go out [from here], you might make me dirty. You are a bad woman. I cannot marry you. After a long while he whistled again. She went in again. He said to her: Why do

you always come in? Go out from here. [When] she came to her lodge, he burned the sinew, so that it crisped up. [At the same moment] that woman was taken with a cramp. She then died. Scar-face said upwards: Partner, there goes your wife. That's all.

[Cf. G.B. Grinnell, Blackfoot lodge tales, London 1893, pp. 93 sqq., and C. Wissler-D.C. Duvall, Mythology of the Blackfoot Indians, New York 1908, pp. 61 sqq. For the scar cf. J.O. Dorsey, The Cegiha language, Washington 1890, p. 606, and for the magic moccasins J.O. Dorsey, op. c., p. 285.]

Note of Uhlenbeck in obt, 94–95, under Addenda et corrigenda: "When my texts were already being printed, a new book on the Blackfeet appeared: W. McClintock, The old north trail, or life, legends and religion of the Blackfeet Indians, London 1910. McClintock (pp. 491 sqq.) gives the tale of Scar-face, though different in many respects from Joseph Tatsey's version (pp. 50 sqq. of the present volume). One of the 'Two adventures of the Old Man,' recorded in my texts, is also to be found in McClintock (p. 345). This author also (pp. 488 sq.) gives a version of the 'Seven stars' (cf. my note on p. 93, at the end of 'Bear-chief's cosmogony')."

Sunday, August 13.

Uhlenbeck also had an eye for the different forms noses can have. In "A Survey of the Non-Pronominal and Non-Formative Affixes of the Blackfoot," (1920, 15), he noted:

"-ani *nose*. I'kaikaχkani(ua) Nose-cut-already-off (a woman's name), káχkanitsiu he cuts off his (another person's) nose. The independent word for nose is moχksisís.

(Cf. Uhlenbeck and Van Gulik 1934, 104): I'kaikaχkaniua) an. *Nose-cut-off-already*, a woman's name."

Uhlenbeck and Van Gulik (130, 147) noted:

"nose *moχksisís* in., pl. moχksisists; *-ani, -ksis-*; he cuts off his (another person's nose) *káχkanitsiu*; Nose-cut-already-off (a woman's name) *Ikaikaχkani (ua)*; Has-nose-woman (a woman's name) *Nåχkåχksisake (ua)*".

Tuesday, August 15.

Uhlenbeck reads two stories to Jim Fine Bull, maybe "The Men and the women," nsbt, 167–70, and "The Old Man, the elk-head, and the old women," nsbt, 192–95.

The men and the women.

The men and the women of the ancient Peigans did not live about together in the beginning. The women lived about on the Porcupine hills [literally: Porcupine-tails] and made buffalo-corrals. Their lodges were fine. Their clothes were cow-skins. Their moccasins were of the same. They tanned the buffalo-hides, those were their robes. They would cut the meat in slices. In summer they picked berries. They used those [berries] in winter. Their lodges all were fine inside. And their things were just as fine. One was the chief of the women. That one led them about. And that one led them to make buffalo-corrals.

Now, the men were living about in the south. They were very poor. They made corrals. They had no lodges. They wore raw-hides [of buffalo] and antelope-hides for robes. They wore [the hide around] the gamble-joint of the buffalo for moccasins. They did not know, how they should make lodges. They did not know, how they should tan the buffalo-hides. They did not know too, how they should cut dried meat, [or] how they should sew their clothes. After a long while their chief told them: Let us look for the women. One useful thing of theirs were their [the men's] bows and arrows. They had [also] flint-knives. Those were the things, they had. And they went north over that way. They came to the Porcupine hills. There they stayed about. Then they found out, where the women were camping.

Their [the men's] chief Wolf-robe told them: Over there on that hill we shall sit in sight of those women. Then they came there. It was on the river, that the women were camped. Their [the women's] chief told them: Over there near the corral are the men sitting in sight. All these women were cutting meat. Their chief did not take off the clothes, she was cutting the meat with. They were told by her: I shall go up there first. I shall take my choice [from them]. When I come back, you will go up one by one. Now we will take husbands. Then she started up. Then she went up to all these men. She asked them: Which is your chief? [The men said:] This one here, Wolf-robe. She told him: Now we will take you for husbands. And then she walked to that Wolf-robe. She caught him. Then she started to pull him up. Then he pulled back. Then she let him loose. He did not like her clothes. Then she went back down. Then she entered her lodge. Then she began to dress up. When she came out again, there was no such fine-looking woman [as she was]. Then she went up again. She got near the men. Wolf-robe jumped up already. She then walked away from him. And then he went in front of her. Then she went away from him again. It was another man, that that woman caught. Then she took him down to their [the women's] lodges. They came there. She said to him: Here is your lodge.

She told all these women: Now begin to go up. That one, that is very tall, [called] Wolf-robe, that is the Old Man. Don't take him for husband. And bring all those others down. That Wolf-robe would come in front of every one of these women, that came there. They would just walk away from him. [The women] would bring the others down. All these men were taken down. And there that Wolf-robe was standing up alone. He was told by that chief-woman: Turn into a pine-tree, right there where you stand. He got angry. He commenced to knock down that buffalo-corral. And then he turned into a pine-tree. And now till this day that buffalo-corral is still there, just as he knocked it down. And he himself there turned into a pine-tree. In that way all these men and all these women came to be together. And that is what I know about them.

[Cf. Wissler-Duvall mbi 21 sq. 39, McClintock ont 346 sq. 440, Lowie a 105 sq. Cf. also Dorsey-Kroeber ta 105 sqq.]

The Old Man, the elk-head, and the old women.

There was the Old Man, he was travelling about down this river. He heard, [that] over there in the rose-bushes some ones were saying: Mice, swing [i.e. move] the eyes, if one goes to sleep while dancing, the hair of his head will be bitten off. He saw, there were mice, they were dancing in an elk-head. He said to them: Oh, oh, let me do in that way. They told him: Now, my elder brother, just put your head in [into the elk-head] from there and shake it. They told him: My elder brother, there is [a reason to have] your ear [open]. Don't sleep. While we are dancing, we don't sleep. They began to dance. They were singing: Mice, swing the eyes, if one goes to sleep while dancing, the hair of his head will be bitten off. At first the Old Man shook his head hard. Towards morning he would sleep at times. They would say to him: Try hard, my elder brother, we have nearly done dancing. And he slept soundly. Then they began to bite off his hair. They bit off all his hair. Then they ran out separately [out of the elk-head]. After a long while he woke up. When he tried to pull his head out, it was stuck in the elk-head. He got up with it [with the elk-head]. Then he travelled about. He was already going straight for a high bank. Where the river was deepest, [there] he was still walking. He fell over [into the water]. He swam down the river. Then the ancient Peigans were camping down the river. There were women sitting [near]. They said: There comes an elk-bull swimming down the river. When he heard them [say that], he yelled like an elk. All the men threw their ropes in at him. When he was pulled ashore, he was recognized: There is the Old Man, [I wonder] what he has done. The old women were told by [the men]: Come on, you must prepare to break his [elk-]head. They [the old women] went home to get their stone-hammers. they came back, they sat on each side of him, they broke his [elk-]head. When he held up his head, the people ran away from him, because he looked so horrible.

He was taken home by those old women. They told him: We will have him [i.e. you] for a young man, we will have profit from him.

It was a long time [that he had been camping] about [with the old women], [when] he told them: I will go out and corral rabbits. It was far away to the forest. There he walked about. He began to pull the hair from his robe. He began to cut his body. Then blood began to show about there, where he stood. He went home. He told those old women: Go on, go and get the carcase. Leave those your children here, I shall watch them. Follow my trail. There in the forest you will find the black-tail deer, that I killed. Then they started. After a short while the Old Man got up. He took out his knife. He said: It is not good, that old women have children. He cut off the heads of those little children. He put their heads back [in the same place], where they had been sleeping. And he boiled their bodies [in the pot]. After a short while those old women came back. They told him: [The black-tail] that you have killed, is not there. It only left bloody tracks. He said to them: Now, you have got something to eat. Don't wake up those your children, they are still sleeping. Just eat. A young antelope ran by, right here, I killed it. Here it is, I put it in the pot. I will go out for wood just for a while to make fire. He began to throw in sticks, he filled up the door. He told them: Eat your children yourselves. They jumped over to their children. When they threw the robes from them, only their heads rolled down. Then they began to throw away the sticks [from the door].

They chased him. They came close to him. There was a beaver-hole, he ran into it. Those old women came there. They could not go in there. Then they sat crying by the opening of that beaver-hole. The Old Man then crawled through the hole. From there at the other end he came out. He again changed his appearance to them. He came to them. He said to them: Ah, old women, what are you doing, why do you sit crying? They told him: It is the Old Man again, that killed our children, here he has run in. He said to them: Ah, I hate the Old Man. Wait, I will go in there. He then went in there. Inside he hammered and yelled for himself.

And he himself cut his face and his body. And he came out. He said to them: Now, old women, I have killed him in there, you may prepare to pull him out. Just go in there, both of you. They crawled in. He built a big fire near the opening [of the hole]. He then smothered them. And that is all.

[Cf. Wissler-Duvall mbi 32 sqq., McClintock ont 341 sq., Dorsey-Kroeber ta 101 sqq., 107 sqq., Lowie a 116 sq. 124.]

Thursday, August 17.

The day Josephine died, George Day Rider came along. His teaching resulted in "A man saved by a dog," nsbt, 199–200. Preface: "Told by Blood, interpreted by George Day-rider and Tatsey."

A man saved by a dog.

There was a man, [who] was camping alone. He was hunting about. He got some meat [once in a while], [part of the time] he got hardly anything to eat. There, where he camped about in summer, where he camped a long time, he went out hunting again. He came back with the meat. They ate with delight. In the night they were secretly approached by people of another tribe. It was late in the night. There was a dog, [that] had pups. Its pups were just big enough to run around. The dog went in the night to get a drink. The people of the different tribe were already sitting [waiting for an attack on the camp]. The dog then was drinking. And then, [when] it was going back on the trail, it was shot by a man of the different tribe. It just howled. It ran home to its lodge. It jumped in [to the lodge]. It was groaning after having got inside [of the lodge]. It was talking to its pups. It told them: The poor things, they are sitting with pitiful faces. They will have their guts torn out. In that way [the dog] was yelling to them.

The man jumped up [from his bed]. He said to [the dog]: What is [the matter]? He was told by it: I was shot in the teats. The arrow is still there [in the wound]. The man said to [the dog] I shall pull it out. The dog said to him: There are many people. The man said to [the dog]: Try and run away. Where there are not so many people, that way we shall go. We shall run away from them. We shall take your pups. The dog went out to find out [where the enemy was]. And where there were not so many people, that way they ran away far. The dog was on the lead. They had not gone far yet, [when] their lodge was yelled at [by the people of the different tribe]. Their lodge was torn down. His dog saved [that man's] life. [Since that time] he loved [the dog]. And that is the short gut [of the story].

Friday, August 18.

Tatsey's daughter is buried this day. Both Jims (White Man & Fine Bull) drop by and ask for old stories. Among others Uhlenbeck perhaps read them "The Bunched Stars," nsbt, 112–13. Preface: "Told and interpreted by Tatsey."

The Bunched Stars.

Long ago the ancient Peigans were all camping together. It was in the spring of the year, they were running buffalo [that means: they were driving the buffalo over the cliffs]. There were some boys, [who] told their fathers: Give us skins of yellow calves for robes. And those men were running buffalo, they killed them, and they came back with the pieces of the carcases. When they came, they had not got skins for their children. These boys went by themselves. They did not go with all the [other children]. They said to one another: It is bad, that our fathers did not get skins for robes for us. They were offended. One said: Let us go away. And another one said: We shall have no place to go. And one said: Where shall we go? And another one said: Let us go on high. Our people will then know from it, that when there are yellow calves, they will not see us. Since that time [literally: now] the Bunched Stars [the Pleiades] are there in the fall of the year. In the spring the Bunched Stars are not seen, [for] then there are yellow calves.

[Cf. Wissler-Duvall mbi 71 sq., and McClintock ont 490].

Saturday, August 19.

Uhlenbeck reads to Jim Fine Bull and Jim Whiteman "Clot-of-Blood" again. On July 16 he started to read this story to Jim Blood. At that time Willy Uhlenbeck noted that Uhlenbeck was wiping off his forehead.

Sunday, August 20.

Uhlenbeck reads to the two Jims "The deserted children" again. On June 28 he finished this story with Tatsey.

Margaret Champagne works with Uhlenbeck on "Ghosts," nsbt, 58–64, and "A man saved by a child," nsbt, 200–202. Preface on both stories: "Told by Blood and interpreted by Margaret Champagne and Tatsey."

Ghosts
—

There are haunting spirits. That are those, we are afraid of. When medicine-men die, those are the ones, [that] are bad. We are shot at by them, they do not stay away from us. They know those that are sick, they do not stay away from them. They are seen about by those that are sick. When a sick person goes out in the night from the lodges, he will be shot by [a ghost]. He will enter. Then he will go to sleep. Then he will die. Then he will be known, [that] a ghost killed him. That is one thing, that they [the ghosts] do. When they are still sitting in the night, the people will hear, that they whistle. When a person is going to sleep, then he will go out. He will be shot by a ghost. Then he will breathe as if he were going to be smothered. He will be asked: What is the matter with you? [He will answer:] I have seen a person right here outside [of the lodge]. Then he will be known, that he is shot by [a ghost].

And a medicine-man, an old man, is known, [that] he knows the ghost-shots very well. Then they go and ask for him. They will give him fine things, if he comes soon to doctor. [The medicine-man says:] Yes, I shall come. Then he will take his drum. They have already a stone in the fire [in the lodge where he is going to doctor]. Then he takes paint, he puts some of it on his hands. He puts some [paint] on his face. Then he will take off his shirt. [The medicine-man always paints himself up, and takes off his shirt, when he is going to doctor.] Then the sick person will lie on his back. Then he [the medicine-man] will find out, what is the matter with him. Then he will feel the place [where the sick person has been shot]. [Then he will say:] It is right here, what is the cause that he cannot breathe. He has drummed already. Some [medicine-men] will lance with a grass. They are going to suck it [the grass]. They will throw it [the shot] out. They are going to spit it out in their hands. [They will say:] here it is, look at it, which is hair [used by the ghosts to shoot with]. In the middle [of that hair] is a cockle-bur. Some other ghosts shoot with finger-nails. They [the ghosts] go around in the night. If people eat during the night, that is another thing, they [the ghosts] do not like. They pull their mouths [viz. of the people who eat during the night] crooked. Old women lance with a flint right there [where the mouth is crooked]. From there they pull it out [what the ghosts have done]. Those [the ghosts] are the ones that kill [the people].

[Sometimes] [the ghosts] pity them. Then they [the people] dream. [In their dream] they [the ghosts] show them [what to do]. They [the people] will sleep in thick forests. Then [the ghosts] bother them. Then they [the ghosts] will pull off their robes. They [the ghosts] hit them. They hit them with sticks. When they bother them too much, then [the people] look for them. There are none [that means: they cannot find them], that are bothering them. They put some tobacco in their pipes. Then they tell them: Pity me, take this and smoke it. I am very poor, pity me. Then [after having offered the pipe to the ghost] they go again to sleep. The same way they [the ghosts] start to hit them again. Then they look out for them again. There are none, that are bothering them. Then they know them: It is a ghost, that hits me. The same way they put some more tobacco in their pipes. They pray to them [to the ghosts]. Finally they start to cry, that he [the ghost] might pity them. Then they are ordered away by [the ghost]: Go away. If he [the person] does not go away [before], he will be pitied by [the ghost], [when the ghost says] the fourth time [the word: Go away]. When he sleeps, he sees him [the ghost]. He [the ghost] tells him: I give you, that you may doctor, [and] I give you also the ghost-shots [i.e. the power to inflict them]. And now you know it, that I give you, that you may doctor the people.

Other ghosts will yell. Then they are heard, that they yell. It was in the olden times, [that] the ghosts were very dangerous. They would kill the sick. Of some other people they would pull back their tongues [into their throats]. And some of the people, they had done that to, would be saved. They [the ghosts] are afraid of anything that smells bad, [e.g.] hair that smells bad when it is burned. They would throw the robes of some people, that were sleeping about, eastward. They are seen in the night, as if they were burning. If we are riding around in the night, they scare the horses too. Then the people will fall off. They are heard, that they laugh. The make the noise: ü ü ü ü. [When] they laugh, they laugh as if they were whistling. They will also enter the lodges. They make noise by hitting the lodge-poles. They are all over the world. The rivers and the forests, there it is, that they stay about.

When some sick people are going to die – if they are dying in the night –, if the next morning, when the sun rises high, [the sick person] sees his robe, then he will be allright. Somebody [who] is dying, will be saved. After a short while [the sick] will always hear ghosts. When [a sick person] is still sitting in the night, then he will hear, that his name is called. Somebody [a ghost] outside will tell him: Let us go. He [the sick person] will say to [the ghost]: Go by yourself. And some others, before they can see well, will see, there is a person coming in. Then he will see clearly that one, that has done something to him. There will be nothing the matter with his eyes, [but after having seen the ghost] he will not see any more. And another person, who is always sick, when he is still sitting in the lodge [during the night], will see him [the ghost] through the lodge outside. Then [afterwards] he will be out of his mind. He will be trying to catch something [being out of his mind]. He will not have his right mind any more. He has seen the person, that has done something to him. That is why he is out of his mind. When he has seen him

[once], then he sees him all the time. He [the ghost] does not stay away from him. Everybody doctored him [but it has been of no use]. A still harder thing, he [the ghost] does to him, is, that he takes him away [i.e. that he makes him die].

That are the things, [the ghosts] have done. Now we are mixed up with them [i.e. they are everywhere among us], [so] we do not mind them any more. In the olden times [the people] used to take their [the ghosts'] hair. They took it again, they put it in a sack. When some people's children, that they loved very much, died, then, where they were buried, just their bones were left. They [the people] took all the bones. It [the child's bones] was complete. They tied them [the bones] up in a piece of cloth. They kept them as a relic. And now the dogs have separated [after having had their meal].

[Cf. Grinnell blt 273 sqq.]

A man saved by a child.

There was a man, [who] was also camping alone. He was very strong [that means: he had a great success], whenever he went out to get something to eat. He had always plenty of food to eat with delight. He also caught eagles. He then would take the good tail-feathers and fix them up. He had lots of them. He camped a very long time. And he, that man, told his two wives and the child, that was a boy: Now hammer the bones. We shall move. During the night you must make grease of them. Then they started to make grease. In the night the man was fixing his arrows. He was fixing them up well [with the tail-feathers]. The child would give somebody outside a taste [of the grease by means of a stick]. He [the man] asked [his wives]: Do you have any suspicion of that child? That woman said: No. The man said: The child is dipping it [the stick] in that grease. Then [the person outside] went slowly in [to the lodge].

He made a sign to [the man] [and said to him]: This night there are a great many people about. I am the scout. Get your things ready. Run that way higher up. The man gave the tail-feathers to that person of another tribe. He was told by him: Wrap them up in something bad [that nobody will think, that it is something of value]. Put them over there by the door. Hurry up. I pity this child, because he gave me to lick [the grease from the stick]. Then they ran for escape. Towards morning their lodge was torn down. In that way they were all saved. They had made their escape. They had been told by him [i.e. by that man of the other tribe] [what to do]. They [the enemies] took everything from their lodge. He [the man that had saved them] took the tail-feathers over there by the door. There was another man with him, by whom [literally: by him] he was suspected. He was told by [that other man]: You must have entered [here before]. He denied it. And now the boiling is ended [that means: the story is at an end].

Wednesday, August 23.

Tatsey came from 9:00 to 12:00. He might have told Uhlenbeck about "Child-birth," nsbt, 50–51, and "Death and hereafter," nsbt, 53–54. Preface on both stories: "Told and interpreted by Tatsey."

Child-birth.

Long ago women, that were about to give birth to a child, did not give birth to it in their own lodges. Outside [of their lodge] there was a shade built for them. Some [of the women] went to their fathers' lodges. In the same way there was a shade built for them [near their fathers' lodges]. When they had given birth to a child, they were safe after nine days. The reason why the women did not give birth to a child in their [own] lodges, [was that] the man and the young men were afraid of those that had just given birth to a child. The ancient people used to say, [that] the young men were not strong [would have no endurance], if they entered in a place [where there were] women that had just given birth to a child.

[Cf. Wissler slbi 28.]

Death and hereafter.

Long ago old men and old women doctored the sick persons [even nowadays such doctoring is practiced]. Some of them doctored with drums. They sang to themselves, and beat the drum. And some doctored by giving something to drink. If the sick person died, he was wrapped into buffalo-robes and cow-skins. He was put up aloft [on top of] the mountains. When there were no mountains, he was tied to bent trees. That was the way, [that] common people were buried. And when the chiefs and the chiefs' children got sick, they were doctored by everybody. When they died, the chiefs were dressed up [in their finest clothes]. They wore shirts of weasel-tails and human hair. Their leggings were just the same [weasel-tails and human hair]. Some of them had scarlet paint all over their faces. Some others had yellow paint all over their faces. When it was a young man, the dead person was dressed the same way. When it was a girl, her dress was buckskin. It was with elk-teeth. There where they died, their lodge was put up; it was fixed up inside [just as if people were going to live there]. A man and a young man had willow-pillows put on each side of them [one at the head, and one at the feet]. The same way a girl was laid down. They were put in the lodge, their faces were not covered up. We said [in the case of] those, that were laid that way, "a dead man's lodge".

Our ancestors, from long times ago, used to tell us, that, when we die, there is [a place] over there in the north, [where] we go to, [which] is called the "Big Sand-hills". Now the old people still say, that we go to the Big Sand-hills. They say, [that] these ghost-people are chasing buffalo. Antelopes are there, and the berries are plentiful, and the things that we eat are plentiful. The ghost-people have a happy time. They still invite each other. And all their holy things are still there. That is how I am told about them.

[Cf. Grinnell blt 193 sq. 273. 44 sq. 62. 94. 127 sqq. 132 sqq., Wissler-Duvall mbi 163, McClintock ont 148 sqq. 164 sq.]

Thursday, August 24.

The two Jimmy's stay on and ask for stories. Uhlenbeck might have read to them "The Wind-maker, nsbt, 64" and "The Thunder-bird," nsbt, 64–66.

The Wind-maker.

Long ago there was a chief, [who] camped on Cut-bank river. In the morning the wind did not blow. He went to the mountains. On a butte there were pine-trees. There he sat in the shade. From there he looked about over the country. He was looking to the mountains. He suddenly saw, there was a person, [who] walked up towards him. He [that person] came near him. He saw him [that person]. There was hair all over his body. Only from his knees down he did not have any hair. He had split hoofs. His ears were big and long. He [that person] stood by him. And he [the chief] began to pray to him. Then he [that person] did not do him any harm. Then [that person] turned away from him. As he started to go away, he shook his ears. Then immediately the wind blew hard. And as he shook his ears harder, the wind blew harder. That [chief] was the only one, [who] saw the Wind-maker. He [that chief] was called Big-snake.

[Cf. Grinnell blt 259, McClintock ont 60 sqq.]

The Thunder-bird.

Long ago there was an old man, [who] was called Four-bears. When he was a young man, the Peigans were camping on Elk river. It was in summer. The long-time-rain had commenced. In the morning, when he went for the horses [to bring them in into the camp], he came to this river. He saw, there was a bird, [that] was sitting [near the edge of the water]. He walked towards it. When he was looking at it, then he knew [that] the bird did not belong to this country. Its feathers were all of different colours, its bill was green-coloured, its legs were coloured the same. It had three claws. It would not open its eyes [literally: look]. He then took it. Then he took it home. When he entered, all the chiefs were invited. They all entered. The bird sat at the upper end of the lodge. He told these chiefs: Now, here is a bird, that you may look at it [to know], what it is. It was not known [nobody could tell what kind of bird it was]. After a long while Four-bears pushed it. When it opened its eyes [literally: looked], then it flashed lightning. The door lay open. It flew towards the door. When it opened its eyes [literally: looked] again, then it flashed lightning again. When it flew, then the thunder roared. That way the thunder was seen.

[Cf. Grinnell blt 259, McClintock ont 425 sq.]

Saturday, September 2.

When Uhlenbeck is reading more Napi stories, the visitors laugh and laugh. Maybe, as there were only male visitors around, Uhlenbeck read them one of the racy stories, "The Old Man and the girls who were picking strawberries" from De Josselin de Jong's This is a story from De Josselin de Jong's 1914 *Blackfoot Texts*. In 1938 Uhlenbeck would analyse one of the words from this text in "A Survey of the Non-Pronominal and Non-Formative Affixes of the Blackfoot," on p. 23. De Josselin de Jong's Blackfoot translation is added. We will first look at this story and Uhlenbeck's analysis and then continue with three less racy stories: "The Old Man and a pine-tree as an arrow," nsbt, 182–84, and "The Old Man and the buffalo-charm," nsbt, 184–87. Preface on both stories: "Told by Blood and interpreted by Tatsey." The third story is "The Old Man and the spring-birds," nsbt, 195–98. Preface: "Told and interpreted by Tatsey."

The Old Man and the girls who were picking strawberries.

by J.P.B. de Josselin de Jong.

Nàpiuaa etsetóto améksim akékoαn áusseea otsistsénea. Opά nnea ixtsetάnistotsim ostsitséni kiméma amékse akékoäks ot- sítàusspi ixtsítspesauχtoma opάnni. Itsinímiauaie amékse akékoäks Etanéaua: Amómαie ómαχkostsistsena, άχkonasαtotå`kstixpa. Ketásαtotåkstsìmiua. Túkskαm etαnéua: Aχkúnitαst,alphàtsesopa. Etsetístαtseseauaiea. Túkskαm etspάχkeua. Ketsístapepiksèaua.

The Old Man came to some girls [who] were picking strawberries. He rubbed his penis with strawberries and where those girls were picking he stuck his penis out of the ground. Those girls saw it [viz. the penis]. They said: There is a great big strawberry, let us bite it. Then they bit it. One [of them] said: Let us sit down on it. Then they sat down on it with their vulvae. He pushed up one of them. Then they ran away.

Uhlenbeck (1938, 23)

-ats- (-ɑts-) vulva. The independent word for her vulva is ópistɑnàni. ɑχkúnitɑstɑtseopa let us sit down on it with our vulvae djbt, 23. etsetístɑtseauaiea (itsitɑtsisiaunaie'a) then they sat down on it with their vulvae djbt, 23. istsiaχkematseua (ixtsiaχkematsiua) he pricked her in her vulva with it (djbt.52).

The Old Man and the pine-tree as an arrow.

The Old man went along. He saw a spring-bird [literally: summer-bird], sitting [literally: sat] on a pine-tree. An antler was it, he sat with. [The Old Man] came to him. He said to him: What is that, that you are sitting with? He was told by [the bird]: It is my bow. [Then he asked:] And what do you do with that, that you are sitting on? [The bird] told him: It is my arrow. He said to him: You are claiming very much for yourself. You cannot lift that pine-tree. He said to [the bird]: Try to shoot at me. He was told by him: Come on, walk away [some paces back, that I may shoot at you]. He asked [the bird]: Here? He was told by him: Farther away. [He asked again:] Here? [Again he was told:] Farther away. He went again farther off. He asked him again: Here? [Again he was told:] Farther away. [The Old Man] then got angry. He went away, being angry. [After a long while] he did not remember his anger any

more. He had gone very far. Then he suddenly heard a roaring noise. He looked up. He saw the pine-tree. He began to be ready to jump about [to escape the arrow]. While he was jumping about, the arrow was going in the same direction [as he himself]. He saw, there was a hole. He jumped into it [for safety]. He was overtaken by [the pine-tree]. He was shot by [the bird]. He was suddenly shot by him in the thigh, so that there was a gap in it.

[The bird] sat down on his arrow, the pine-tree. [He had flown after his arrow with the same speed.] [After] he was shot by [the bird], [the Old Man] said to him: My younger brother, give it to me. He was told by him: I give it to you [together with the bow]. He was told by him [also]: Whenever we think [that means: whenever we feel inclined to do so], then we shoot with [the pine-tree]. We will not often shoot with it. It can be used to shoot at everything, that we can eat. Four times [a day], [but] with long intervals, we can shoot with it. He had not gone far, he shot with it, and he sat down on it. After a short while he shot again with it. He could not kill with it [because he was using it only for sport]. He just shot with it, that he might have a ride on it. Four times he shot with it. The fourth time, when he tried to pick it up, he could not lift it. He had completed, what was given to him [that means: he had shot as often as was allowed to him]. He had made again a mistake for himself. And there it [the pine-tree] was, he left it [right there]. And, being angry, he threw his bow away. And now the boiling is ended [that means: the story is at an end].

[Cf. McClintock ont 344, Dorsey-Kroeber ta 54 sq.]

The Old Man and the buffalo-charm.

There he went again. He walked about. He came to a man. He [that man] was singing a medicine-song [to coax the buffalo to come]. [The

Old Man] said to him: What are you doing? He was told by him: I am singing a medicine-song [to coax the buffalo to come]. [The Old Man] said to him: Now, go ahead and start to sing the medicine-song. And he started to sing the medicine-song. He began to say: *E'ɛ'ɛ'ɛ'*, let [buffalo] fall down on each side of me, let [buffalo] fall down on each side of me. And buffalo fell down on each side of him. [The Old Man] said to him: My younger brother, give it to me. He was told by him: It is not important. Whenever we are hungry, then we sing the medicine-song. There is [a reason to have] your ear [open]. Don't say: I am hit between the ears. And there [the Old Man] went away. He was looking for the very best place on the bank. And there he sat down. And he began to say: *E'ɛ'ɛ'ɛ'*, let [buffalo] fall down on each side of me, let [buffalo] fall down on each side of me. He made a good corralling. Then he went down [to the buffaloes, that had jumped over the cliff]. He began to look for the fattest cows. He skinned those [cows]. There he stayed. He began to make a shade. He went out [of his shade] to get a little of the meat to cook it. He went away again. He did not go far. He came again to [a place], where he could sing the medicine-song. Over there on a big high bank he was already sitting down again. He began to say: *E'ɛ'ɛ'ɛ'*, let [buffalo] fall down on each side of me, let [buffalo] fall down on each side of me. He went away again. He had not gone far [after having had another good corralling], he sang again the medicine-song. Four times he sang the medicine-song. And there he sang again: *E'ɛ'ɛ'ɛ',* let [buffalo] fall down on each side of me, let [buffalo] fall down on each side of me. And then he remembered [the word, that he was forbidden to say]. And he said: I am hit between the ears. He was trampled down by the buffaloes. It was already winter then. And there he was knocked over the bank. He had turned into a white calf, and lay on top [of the pile of buffaloes].

And the ancient people [the ancient Peigans] were moving about. They all were camping in the forest here. There was an old woman, she was getting wood about. She found all these buffaloes, that had fallen

[off the bank]. There she suddenly saw a wonderful calf. She took that one. She brought it home. She took it therefore, [that] it would be her son's robe. And she told her son-in-law: Over there are buffalo, all fell [off the bank], that you may skin them. Give part of them to the people camping hereabout. Inside of her lodge she had sticks spread out on high [to hang the meat on]. It was on high, that she put [the buffalo-calf] on top [of the sticks]. [The calf that was nearly frozen] was thawing [now]. That boy was delighted over his skin [the skin, that would be his robe]. He was always rolling about on his back. He looked up at [the calf-skin]. It spit down on him. He said to his mother: My skin here is spitting on me. He was told by his mother: It was frozen with spittle on its mouth [and now that spittle is thawing and falling down]. He said again to her: Mother, it is making faces down on me. She told him: Oh, it was just frozen with its face twisted. It was thawed all over. That boy lay on his back right under his skin. Then [the calf] cleared [the sticks] and jumped down on [the boy's] belly. It sounded like a gun, when it [the belly] burst. Then [the calf] ran out [of the lodge]. Then it was known, [that] it was the Old Man. He then ran away for escape. That way the Old Man had turned into a wonderful calf. And the dogs have separated [after having had their meal].

The Old Man and the spring-birds.

There was the Old Man, he was travelling about again. He entered a forest of big trees in this country here. He saw, there were spring-birds [literally: summer-birds]. When they said "Spring-bird," then their eyes would fall out. There was a tree, it was a very dry tree [i.e. a dead tree], they [their eyes] would fall cleanly in it. When they said "Back in, spring-bird", then they would fall cleanly back again to them. He went towards them crying [and saying]: Oh, oh, let me do in that way.

They told him: Now, my elder brother, it is not important. Once [a day] we say it in forests of big trees, [when] we are happy. Then he went away. He had just gone out of sight. Over there was a big tree. He said "Spring-bird", [and then] his eyes fell cleanly out [on the tree]. Then he said again "Back in, spring-bird". [and] then his eyes fell back in again. Then he went away. There in a forest of big trees he came again to a tree. He said again "Spring-bird", [and then] his eyes cleanly fell out [on the tree]. He kept on saying "Back in, spring-bird", [but] they did not fall back in again. He had no eyes any more.

Then he went away. He went on the prairie. He stood about, making signs. There was a woman, she saw him. She said: He is making signs to me. She went over to him. She came to him. She asked him: Why do you make signs to me? He told her: You might lead me about, the germs of the snow [supposed to be the cause of snowblindness] have eaten my eyes. She said to him: Yes. He told her: Take me over to that river there, let us make a shelter there. Then he had a hold of her. He was taken into the forest by her. Then they began to make a shelter. He was told by that woman: There are buffalo coming this way. He said to her: Here is my arrow. Only hold it towards these buffalo. Then say: Now. [She pointed the arrow at the buffalo, and then he shot.] He killed one of them. Then they had something to eat. The Old Man told her: I give you these buffalo-hoofs, don't let them go [i.e. don't lose them], you will have no child. [He said this, fooling her, because he wanted, that she should have on her something that rattled, that he might know, where she was.] Where her shoulders came together [i.e. between her shoulders], there he tied them. After a short while he said to that woman: Look on my head for lice for a while. She had looked a long time on his head, [and then] he fell asleep. Then she lifted the cover from his eyes. Then she saw, [that] he had no eyes. She gently laid his head down [from her lap]. Then she got up. She went out. Then he woke up. He asked her: What are you going to do? Then she went away running. He chased her. He nearly caught her. That woman then knew: He hears these hoofs, that is why

he nearly catches me. Then she broke them loose. She got near, where [the river] was deepest. She threw them to the bank [of the river]. When the Old Man heard them, then [thinking, that the woman was there, he went in that direction, and] fell over the bank. And that woman made her escape from him [literally: and then he saved that woman]. He himself had a hard time to get out of the water.

Then he went on again. He came to a round hill. He said: Yes, this is that round hill [literally: his round hill]. There was a coyote, [that] came to him. He [that coyote] would make him smell his claw with a rotten toe. [The Old Man] would say: Yes, this is that old corralling-place. Then he was known by [the coyote], that he could not see. Then [the coyote] would stand in front of him. [The Old Man] then would tread on him. He would say to [the coyote]: Yes, I see you. Then he caught him. He put one of [the coyote's] eyes in [his own socket]. Then he himself could see. He was one-eyed. He said to [the coyote]: I will give it back to you again. Then he could see. He then went back to the forest of big trees. There on that tree were his eyes, they were still there. Then he took them. Then he put them back [in his sockets]. He gave that coyote his eye back. That is the way, that it was told.

[Cf. Grinnell blt 153 sq., Wissler-Duvall mbi 29 sq., Dorsey-Kroeber ta 50 sqq., Lowie a 117 sqq., Lowie ns 272 sq.]

August 28, September 5 and 9.

John Tatsey works with Uhlenbeck. He must have been translating back into Blackfoot "Bear-chief's life story." The
English version thereof is in obt, 76–77 (in this volume under
August 1). The translation in Blacfoot is in nsbt, 211–14 and
titled "From Bearchief's life-story." Preface: "Translated back
into Blackfoot by Tatsey's oldest boy, John." This translation
into Blackfoot is followed by Uhlenbeck's "Explanation of the
graphical system," obt, vi–x.

From Bear-chief's life-story.

1.   Mátsistapakàuo ksistsikuísts nitsikóputsi souíiks. Nínockyàio
ítomo. Kepitápii nitsítapìkoaiks ki túkskama anáukitapìkoan.
Sauumáitautocsau Pinápisinai otáuacsini, itsíppiainoyìau nátsitapìi
ic´kitòpii itápockitòpii atsòàskui niétactai. Itákàuyiau, ki omíksi
ic´kitòpiks itsinísuiauanìau, ki itsístsàpiksiau. Omíksi Pekánikoaiks
itsinóyiauaiks, otsápikoanasaiks, ki itanístsiau omí anáukitapìkoan,
mácksinic´katacsaiks, mácksàkapucsaiks, máckstaiskunaksau, Pekániua
óksòkoa nápikoaiks. Otáisakapucsau, omíksi Pekánikoaiks itunnóyiau,
otsikétaiiskximàniaiks. Itsópoactsìsatsìau omíksi nápikoaiks, otáitapoc-
piaiks. Itaníau: Pinápisinaua nitá´cpummokinàna nápiàckèists. Omá
anáukitapìkoan itanístsiu omíksi nápikoaiks: Tockókinoàiniki kisókà-
soaists, nitákocpokiuò, kitákitspummòcpuau. Itockótsiauaie asókàsi, ki
omá anáukitapìkoan itanístsiu omíksi Pekánikoaiks: A´nnòm ákaitàupik,
áikòkus istákaipiskoctòk amóm Pinápisinàu, ákoctatsèiua nápiàcke.
A´ipstsiksisámo itáistockim akékànists, ki itóctoyìau Pinápisinài otáiist-
sèkinsaie, ki sotámisksinoyìauaie, otauátsisaie. Nínockyàio itsinóyiu omí
nitsítapìkoan, áiisksipistsènyai otàs, istáiinyài, máckatockòtaksiaie nápiàcke. Nínockyàioa kámosatsìu omím ponokå´mitai, ki otocpokómiks

ic´tsítokòyi amóistsi moyísts, okámosoaiks ponoká´mitaiks niíppi
pic´ksékopùtsi. Sotámomatòiau, itsítskitsìau omí anáukitapìkoan omíst-
sim Pinápisinàuyists. Omá anáukitapìkoan itsitsítsiuaiks, ki itanístsiu-
uaiks: Omám Pinápisinànam ic´púmmau nápiàcke ponoká´mitaiks ki
imoiániks. Itocpókiuòiau omíksisk nápikoaiksk ki omí anáukiapìkoan,
áutoimìanaiks, omoctátsacsau nisíppiks ótàsoàuaiks. Itótomoyiauaiks
omíksim ponoká´mitaiks, ki itáuauackautsèiau. Túkskama omíksi nápikoaiks itóau ockátsi. Omíksi Pekánikoaiks sotámoctackàiiau.

2.   MátsipucsapakauòksistsikuístsmátsitsitàkomatapòNínockyàio.
Nisúitapìi Pekánikoaiks ki ic´kitsíkippitapìi Isapóiikoaiks. Pinápisinài
áukakiosatsìau okactómoai, ki itsinóíyiauaiks otáistauauackàniaiks.
Itákaàtseiau Nínockyàioi ki otocpokómiksai. Omíksi Isapóiikoaiks iiká-
kimàiau, máckotsimmotàniau. Nínockyàio ki omíksi matsóksaipeká-
nikoaiks anatóctsik ic´tóiau ki áuackautsìmiau Pinápisinài. Autamákíc´t
átsikaiksistsiku otsítsaipiskoctòk Pinápisinài, ki áiikotàko itsíkyaiaik-
sistauackautsèiau. Sotámackàiiau ánni atákuyi, ki paiánnauatòiau.
Ksiskaniáutunìi Nínockyàioa itsínikiu skéini. Itsíitsiau ki sotámomatàpi-
oyiau. Otsákiauyisau, itsinóyiau omí ic´kitópi itótamiaipuyìnai omí ákik-
sackuyi. Itsítsipsatsiu Nínockyàioi otsitapímiks, ki áckaukaksepuyìau
nátsitapìi stámsokatsitotsipucpaipìii, ki ítskunakatsìau Nínockyàioi
otocpóksìmiks. Otáinoàcsauaiks, otákaitapìsaiks, itsístapukskàsiau.
Pinápisinaikoaniaiks. Omíksi Isapóiikoaiks ic´pókiuòiau omíksisk
Pinápisinaikoaiks. Nínockyàioa ki omíksi stsíkiks misksíppotapòiau, ki
itsinóyiau ic´kitópi Pinápisinaikoáninai. Omà ic´kitópiuai istsíppiksiu.
Omíksi stsíkiks mátskàkspummoyìuaiksauaie, ki Nínockyàio nitisitá-
piiu ic´tsápoaie, ki ánistsinoàsai áiskunakatsìuaie, otáisàkapipiks omá
Pinápisinaikoan, itsauátockotoctoàtau. Nínockyàio itsitápoctocpàtski-
mauaie, ki omá Pinápisinaikoan itáskunakatsìuaie, ki Nínockyàioa
ótàs saiékatsìuaie onámai. Stámipotoyìu omá Pinápisinaikoan. Omá
ponoká´mita itapócpatskuyiuaie. Stámipuau omám Pinápisinaikoan
itótoyiu onámai. Nátokyaiaskùnakatsiu Nínockyàioi, ki ómoctsoks-

kacpi onámai itsáuatockotoctskùnakiu. Nínockyàio ic´tsítoctauàtsiuaie ómacksistoáninai, ki soksipískskiuaie, ki imatátsistsinimaie úskitsipacpi, ki itsíkackokitsìuaie, otsauumáinisaie. Isapóiikoaiks itackánauto ic´kitsíkippitapìi. Nitúyi Nínockyàioa otocpokómiks niuókskaitapìi itockítaipuyìau omí nitúmmoi, ki itótakìau nánisoyimi ótàsiks omím Pinápisinaikoànim, ómam áitskamiu Nínockyàioi. Auauatóiau kokúsi ki ksistsikús, máckotackàiisau.

From Bear-chief's life-story

1.   A few days after that there were eleven in a war-party. Bear-chief was the leader. There were ten full-bloods and one half-breed. Before they got to the Sioux country, they saw from a distance two riders, who rode towards the timber on the river. They charged, and then the riders jumped off their horses, and fled into the brush. The Peigans saw, that they were white men, and said to the half-breed, that he should call to them to come out [and] not to shoot at them, because the Peigans were friends of the white men. When they came out, the Peigans saw, that they had pack-horses. They asked the white men, where they were going. They said: We are trading whiskey to the Sioux. The half-breed told the white men: If you give me some of your clothes, I shall go with you, I shall help you trade. They gave him some clothes, and then the half-breed told the Peigans: Stay here for a while, make a raid on the Sioux in the night, they will be drunk from the whiskey. After a short while they got near the camp, and they heard the Sioux making noise, and then they knew, that they were drunk. Bear-chief saw an Indian, who was tying his horse, wishing to get some more whiskey. Bear-chief stole that horse, and his companions went through the camp, stealing 39 horses. Then they started off, they left the half-breed in the Sioux camp. The half-breed overtook them, and told them: The Sioux have bought whiskey for horses and robes. They went after the white men and the half-breed, blaming them, because they had lost 40 head of their horses. They took those horses from them, and they had a fight. One of the white men was shot in his leg. The Peigans then returned home. [Cf. Uhlenbeck obt, 76 sq]

2.   A few days later Bear-chief started on a new trip. There were four Peigans and seventy Crows. The Sioux were looking out for enemies, and saw the war-party coming. Then they made a charge on Bear-chief and his companions. The Crows did their very best to escape. Bear-chief and the three other Peigans stayed behind and fought the Sioux. It was about noon, [when] the Sioux made a charge on them, and it was late in the evening, before they stopped fighting. They then started home that evening, and travelled all night. Early in the morning Bear-chief killed a buffalo-cow. They skinned it and then they commenced to eat. Whilst they were eating still, they saw a rider, standing on a high bank, just above them. He spoke to Bear-chief's people, and before they could answer, two more jumped up at his side and shot at Bear-chief's companions. [But] when they saw, that there were so many, they ran away. They were Sioux. The Crows went after those Sioux. Bear-chief and the [three] others went in the opposite direction, and saw there a rider, a Sioux. That rider fled into the brushes. The others did not want to help him, but Bear-chief alone followed him, and shot at him, every time he saw him through the brush, till the Sioux went out on the prairie, [and] then he was hard to get at. Bear-chief rode up to him, and the Sioux would shoot him, but Bear-chief's horse kicked his gun. Then the Sioux let it loose. The horse then ran over him. Then the Sioux got up, [and] took his gun. He shot at Bear-chief twice, but the third time his gun refused to work. Then Bear-chief attacked him with a butcher-knife, and cut him over his face, and stabbed him near his heart, and cut off his head, before he died. Then the Crows, the whole seventy, came up. At the same time Bear-chief's three companions were standing on a

hill and took eight horses from the Sioux, who was fighting Bear-chief. They travelled night and day to get home.
[Cf. Uhlenbeck obt, 79].

EXPLANATION OF THE GRAPHICAL SYSTEM (OBT. VI–X)

In writing the Blackfoot language I make use of the Latin alphabet, only adding the signs *ä* and *å*, and taking α, ε and χ from the Greek. a modification of χ is χ′.

There are only a few constant long vowels in Peigan, but vowels with principal or secondary stress are usually longer than the unaccentuated, and accentuated vowels may be incidentally prolonged to a degree, uncommon in most of the European languages. Under these circumstances I did not think it desirable to use the makron. Perhaps one might consistently put it on *å* in open syllables with principal or secondary stress, and on *ä* in every condition (e.g., *ä′nak å`si*).

Only a few times I have indicated the shortness of a vowel, because most unaccentuated vowels are shorter than those with principal or secondary stress. Constantly short is the *a* of the suffix –*koǎn* (in *akékoa′n* &c.), and in some other cases (as *Mékyaˇksi*). It is also short before χ, and before *mm, nn*, even when it is accentuated, but in these cases I did not express the shortness graphically. In general all vowels are short before *mm, nn*, and therefore it is unnecessary to indicate the shortness in every particular case.

In Blackfoot a consonant in the body of a word often belongs both to the preceding and the following syllable, and then we might write it double as well as single. Only rarely I express this gemination in writing, because in most cases it is not constant. Where it is very emphatic, as in some cases with *mm, nn, ss*, I write doubles.

When *i, u*, and the diphthongs with *i, u* as second component stand before a vowel, it would be correct to insert *y, w*, but I prefer to simplify the orthography by omitting these graphical signs of the intermediate semi-vowels, where they may be missed without danger of misunderstanding. So I write *kyáio, otáuaχsin* instead of *kyáiyo, otáuwaχsin*, which spelling would be more proper from a phonetical point of view.

A common sound in Blackfoot is the glottal stop, which may be expressed by the Greek sign for the spiritus lenis. I only write it in a few words, where it is always to be observed. Perhaps I might have written it in some cases more, e.g. in *aito'tó'* and other forms of the same verb. Of course I omit it before initial vowels, even in the beginning of a sentence, where it – just as in German – constantly is heard.

The attentive reader of these texts will soon be aware, that the same word in the same grammatical form is not always spelt in the same way. There are many vacillations in the sounding of this language (e.g. in putting in, or omitting χ and χ′ before explosives, and before *s*), and I thought it better to express these vacillations in my way of spelling, than to efface them by an arbitrary uniform orthograpy. Particulars will be given in my Morphology of the Blackfoot language.

I have only to add, that I indicate the principal stress in a word by means of the acutus, and the secondary stress or stresses by means of the gravis. In the accentuation too, as well as in the sounding, there is much inconstancy in Blackfoot.

VOWELS

a It has nearly the sound of German *a*, sometimes long, and sometimes short. When it is long, it sounds like *a* in German *Rat, Tag*. When it is short, it is more like the sound of *a* in German *Mann*. It is most times long, when it has a principal or secondary stress. In other cases it will be short. Only exceptionally, viz. where *a* is constantly short, and where there might be some danger of mispronunciation, I write *a*ˇ.

*a*ˇ See *a*.

ä It is nearly always long, and has the sound of French *ê* in *être*, *gêne*. It is usually a contraction of the diphtong *ai* (*äi*). In these texts I have always written *ai*, though perhaps it would have been better to write sometimes *ä*, and sometimes *ai*, according to the pronunciation of the moment. There are in the language some words with a constant long *ä* (not alternating with *ai*), but such do not occur in the present texts.

å This is a sound between *a* and *o*. When it is short, it is pretty near to *o*, and then there are often vacillations between *å* and *o* (though also between *å* and *a*, *å* and α). When it is long, it is very near to a long *a*. Short *å* sounds like German *o* in *mochte*. Long *å* is like English *a* in *fall*, but not so very different from Blackfoot *a*, or from English *a* in *father*. In closed syllables *å* is generally short, in open syllables with a principal or a secondary stress it is long.

α It has almost the sound of English *u* in *but*. The Peigans often waver between *a* and α. Nearly always α is short.

e Long *e* sounds like German *ee* in *Seele*, while short *e* has nearly the sound of *é* in French *fermé*. But, be it long or short, it is always more inclining to *i*, than either German *ee*, or French *é* will be. When *e* has a principal or a secondary stress, it will be long. In other cases it is short.

ε A short vowel, with the sound of German *e* in *Messer, kennen*. It seldom occurs. In the name *Oko* ε′ *sau* (Belly-fat) – as in some other cases – ε has sprung from *ai* (cf. *mokoáni* and *isáu*). In kε′ nni &c. it has originated from *ia*.

i A sound between French *é* and French *i*. When it has a principal or a secondary stress, it will sometimes be long. In other cases it is short. Before vowels it is apt to be reduced to the semi-vowel *y*, but generally I have retained the sign *i*.

o When it has a principal or secondary stress, it is long, and then it sounds like German *o* in *rot*. When it is not accentuated, it has the same sound, though shorter in duration. In unaccentuated syllables Peigan pronunciation often wavers between *o* and *å*. On the other side, even in accentuated syllables, there are vacillations between *o* and *u*.

u A sound between German *o* in rot and *u* in *rufen*. When it is short, which will be in unaccentuated syllables, it sounds much like English *u* in *full*, or like Northern German *u* in *Zunft*. Before vowels it will often be reduced to the semi-vowel *w*, but generally I have retained the symbol *u*.

DIPHTHONGS

Blackfoot has many combinations of vowels, such as *ai, au, ei, eu, iu, oi, ui, uo*, but only *ai* and *au* may be considered as true diphthongs, though even these are apt to split up into *a + i*, and *a + u*. Sometimes they lose their second component, so that only *a* is left.

ai The first component of this diphthong has been more or less influenced by the following *i*, so that the original diphthong *ai* often sounds like *äi*, or even, the second component having altogether or nearly altogether disappeared, like a long *ä*. In my texts I write almost everywhere *ai*. Only where the final result of the monophthongation has been ε, I write this vowel with its own sign. But I write *a* instead of *ai*, when the second component has disappeared without affecting the first one.

au This diphthong sounds like German *au* in *Baum, Haus*. It easily passes into *o*, or into *å*. Sometimes the second component will disappear, so that only the first one remains.

SEMI-VOWELS

y It sounds like English *y* in *yell, year*. It often originates from *i* before another vowel. I seldom use the sign *y*, retaining in most cases the symbol *i*. The semi-vowel *y* is always heard between *i* and a following vowel, but then I did not think it necessary to express it in writing.

w The same sound as English *w*. Most times it has sprung from antevocalic *u*. Generally I have preferred to retain the sign *u*. Between *u* and a following vowel *w* is always heard, but not written in these texts.

Consonants

m As in English *more*.

n As in English *never*.

p As in French *père*, not as in English *put*.

t *As in French tuer*, not as in English *to*. Before *i* it has been assibilated to *ts*. Somebody, a white man of course, told me, that the Peigans have also an emphatic *t*, but I am sure, he was mistaken. Sometimes a glottal stop occurs before *t*, e.g., in *aito'tó',* and in the imperative-ending -*'t*, and this may give the impression, that the *t* itself is emphatic. But the same glottal stop will be found before other consonants (cf. *mí'ni, ní'sa, kó's, áiko'ko'* &c.).

k Before *i* (*y*), *e*, and ε (from *ia*) it sounds like French *qu* in *qui*, but somewhat more palatalized. In other cases it has the same sound as French *qu* in *quand*. Blackfoot *k* never has the value of English *c* in *cut*. Before *i* we often find *ks*, originating from *k*.

χ It has exactly the same sound as German *ch* in *ach*.

χ´ Originating from χ *after i*, it has exactly the same sound as German *ch* in *ich*.

' Glottal stop. I write it only in a few cases, though it is very often heard in the language.

h As English *h* in *hand*. This sound only occurs in some interjections.

s A kind of voiceless sibilant, pronounced more backward than English *s*.

Sunday, September 10.

Tatsey is teaching before dinner, to the dismay of Willy because he was supposed to teach in the afternoon. Perhaps Tatsey told Uhlenbeck about his sleep-walking long ago, nsbt, 220–21, and about "The dresses of the old woman," nsbt, 203–4. Preface on both stories: "Told and interpreted by Tatsey."

Tatsey's sleep-walking.

Long ago, when I was small – I then was ten years old –, one night when I slept, I got the nightmare. I then got up, I went out, I went down that river. There was an uncle of mine, he was called Dwarf. I went to his lodge in the night. He asked me: What is the matter with you? I did not say anything. I only scratched my head. He threw water on me. When I woke up, I was so much scared, [that] I trembled from it. I did not know the way, I came. I said to him: My uncle, just take me home, I am very much afraid. He laughed at me therefore. He told me: You came alone, Now go back the same way as you came. I said to him: Pity me, I am very much afraid, take me home. He then went with me. It was very dark. I came near my tent. He told me: Go on, run home. Then I went away home. And he then also went home. And that way was my nightmare.

Dresses of old women burned.

The Peigans of not long ago were camped in the lower country. In the night some young men were going about singing. It was late in the night, [when] they stopped near an old-women's lodge. They said to each other:

I wonder what these old women will be doing. They are sitting up late in the night. One [of the young men] looked in. He made signs to his partner: Come here. By [the light of] their fire those old women were searching for lice on their dresses. Those young men said to each other: Let us get a lodge-pole, that we push their dresses in [into the fire]. They opened the door easily. They held those lodge-poles in. Those old women were still holding their dresses [near the fire]. The young men then pushed [the dresses] in. Then they burned up. Next morning [the old women] said to their daughters: Give us some dresses. During the night there were some young men, they burned up our dresses. And that is all I know about these old women.

Tatsey teaches occasionally. Was he finishing the last story in the nsbt, the one about horse- and cattle-raising on pp. 223–25. Preface: "Told and interpreted by Tatsey."

Horse- and cattle-raising.

Long ago, when there were still buffalo, we took very good care of our horses. We would not ride the mares hard, when they were with foal. We called the male horses, that were not cut, stallions. They were not broken [to anything], that is why they had good colts. In winter, if the mares, we went to hunt with, had a heavy load, when we came home with the meat, we would rub their bellies with our hands, and we would smoke them [i.e. their nostrils] with big turnips. Therefrom they did not lose their colts [literally: therefrom they held their colts hard, i.e. inside their bodies]. From that we had good horses, that we watered the horses all the time. And that we put them on good grass, that is why they were fat. In summer we did not ride our male horses hard. In winter we chased the buffalo with them. And these other [horses], that we call the "hard-dogs," are those, that pack the lodges and the poles, the dried meat, the robes, and [all] these things that are heavy. The mares ran loose about, that is why they had good colts. As we owned horses separately, so we drove them [also] separately. What the horses ate over there in the lower country, was all good, that is why they were hard [and] strong. Our horses were not big. They beat these big horses of nowadays, because they were hard.

When the buffalo were gone, the whites drove us up here. They began to feed us with beef, bacon, coffee and sugar, flour. They gave us blankets, [and] clothing too. In the first place we did not like these kinds of food and clothing, and we could not do anything. The buffalo were gone. We had no place to go to, we became stationary. It was not long afterwards, then the Government [literally: our grandfather] gave us many mares. The Government gave us big horses [i.e. stallions] too. We took very good care of them. A few years afterwards we had many horses. The Government knew then, [that] we took good care of our horses. Then they gave us cattle too. They gave us bulls too. Just the same as we looked after the horses, we looked also after the cattle. In summer we cut the grass. We built houses for our cattle. We fed them with hay. In summer we drove them out. They began to have calves. After a little while in summer we branded the calves. From that we knew our own. We had a great many cattle, [and] horses. Our houses were log-cabins. The Government gave us cooking-stoves and heating-stoves. We were not hungry. Inside our houses were good, with lots of bedding and blankets and anything, that makes houses good [literally: houses are good from].

Alas, now came that, we were to become poor from. The Government took our ration-tickets [literally: we draw our rations with] away from us. They did not give us anything more for nothing. These whites came over there into our agency. There they were, they built houses. We buy from them. After not many years our cattle and our good horses were all gone to them. They are the ones, that broke us. Now we beat [the time], when long ago we first started to go the white man's way, in being poor [literally: as we are poor]. Now we are broken. These traders will not let us get anything on credit. And that is all.

Friday, September 15.

Fine Bull's wife recounts the story of Napi and four women and also tells Napi and two women. Willy notes: "It is very indecent." An indecent story about Napi and two women can be found in Wissler and Duvall, 1908, 35–36. Anyway, after Fine Bull's wife has left, Uhlenbeck wraps himself again in the blankets and it seems that Mrs. Fine Bull's stories did not make it into the nsbt. Because Uhlenbeck was too cold? Because Napi was too indecent? We will have to satisfy ourselves with Wissler and Duvall's recording!

Old Man deceived by Two Women

Now all the women knew that Old Man was a very bad character, and they always tried to avoid him. One day two women out picking berries saw Old Man coming, but saw no way to avoid him. So they decided to play dead. As Old Man was going along, he saw the two women lying on the ground, stopped, and said, "Poor women! These are nice women. It is too bad they are dead." Then he touched one of them, "Oh, they have just died! They are still warm; something must have killed them. I wonder what it was." So he turned them over and over, but found no wounds. Then he began to remove their clothes, examining their bodies carefully. Finally he saw the vulva. "Oh!" said he, "no wonder they died. Here are the wounds. They have been stabbed by a dagger." Then he put his finger in one of the wounds, took it out and smelled it. "No," he said, "it was not by a dagger that they were killed. They were shot by a gun, because I smell the burnt powder. Well," said he, "I pity these, poor women. They were too young to die. I must try to doctor them back to life again." So he took one of them on his back to carry her away to the doctoring place. One of her arms hung over his shoulder, and as she pretended to be dead, she allowed it to swing freely so that, as they went along, her hand beat his nose, making it bleed. At last, when Old Man came to a suitable place for doctoring, he put the woman down, and started back for the other one; but when he was halfway, both women jumped up and ran away. Then Old Man called out, "Oh, I thought you were dead! Don't run away. Come, play dead again."

References

Agassi, Joseph. 1981. *Science and Society*. Dordrecht: Reidel.

Aimard, Gustave. 1879 [1861]. Prairie-Flower. In *Beadles's Dime Library*. Vol. II, no. 24. New York: Beadle & Adams, Publishers. Abbreviated translation of *Balle-Franche*. Paris: Amyot, 1861.

Asad, Talal, ed. 1973. *Anthropology and the Colonial Encounter*. London: Ithaca Press.

Bakker, Peter. 2000. Rapid language change: Creolization, intertwining, convergence. In *Time Depth in Historical Linguistics*. Volume 2. Edited by Colin Renfrew, April McMahon and Larry Trask. Cambridge: The McDonald Institute for Archaeological Research, 585–620.

Barkman, D. D. and H. de Vries-Van der Hoeven. 1993. *Een man van drie levens. Biografie van diplomaat, schrijver, geleerde Robert van Gulik*. Amsterdam: Forum.

Biesheuvel, J.M.A. 1983. Een Geleerde onder de Indianen. In *De Steen der Wijzen*. Amsterdam: Meulenhoff, 188–94.

Binnema, Theodore. 1996. "Old Swan, Big Man, and the Siksika Bands, 1794–1815." *Canadian Historical Review* 77, 1–32.

———. 2001a. "How Does a Map Mean?" In *From Rupert's Land to Canada*, ed. Theodore Binnema, Gerhard J. Ens, and R.C. Macleod, 201–24. Edmonton: University of Alberta Press.

———. 2001b. *Common and Contested Ground: A Human and Environmental History of the Northwestern Plains*. Norman: University of Oklahoma Press.

Black, Hugh M. 1960. *The History of the Holy Family Mission Family, Montana, from 1890–1935. A Dissertation*. St. Paul, Minnesota.

Black Boy, Cecile. 1973. Blackfeet Tipi Legends. In *Painted Tipis*, catalog of exhibition published by Oklahoma Indian Arts en Crafts Cooperative. Anadarko: Southern Plains Indian Museum and Crafts Center.

Blackfeet Tribal Business Council and Roxanne DeMarce. 1998. *Blackfeet Genealogy, Treasures and Gifts*. Blackfeet Nation, Browning, Montana. U.S.A.

Blackfoot Gallery Committee. 2001. *Nitsitapiisinni: The Story of the Blackfoot People*. Toronto: Key Porter Books.

Bloomfield, Leonard. 1946. Algonquian. In *Linguistic Structures of Native America*. Edited by Harry Hoijer. New York: Viking Fund Publications in Anthropology 6:85–129.

Bouda, K. 1951. C. C. Uhlenbeck. *Eusko Jakintza* 5:237–40.

Bougis, Peter A.J. 1894. *A Grammar and Guide of the Blackfoot Language*. Spokane, Washington: Pacific Northwest Indian Center.

Bradley, James H. 1966 [1900]. Affairs at Fort Benton. From 1831 to 1869. In *Contributions to the Historical Society of Montana*. Vol. III. New York: J.S. Canner & Company, 201–87.

———. 1966 [1917]. Book F. Characteristics of the Blackfeet. In *Contributions to the Historical Society of Montana*. Vol. IX. New York: J.S. Canner & Company, 255–87.

———. 1966 [1917]. Establishment of Ft. Piegan as Told me by James Kipp. In *Contributions to the Historical Society of Montana*. Vol. VIII. New York: J.S. Canner & Company, 244–50.

A Brief Biography of Lieutenant Bradley. 1986. In *Contributions to the Historical Society of Montana*. Vol. II: Helena, Montana: State Publishing Company, 140–41.

Bullchild, Percy. 1985. *The Sun Came Down*. San Francisco: Harper & Row.

Campbell, Lyle. 1997. *American Indian Languages. The Historical Linguistics of Native America*. Oxford: Oxford University Press.

Carroll, Michael P. 1996. Myth. In *Encyclopedia of Cultural Anthropology*. Edited by David Levinson and Melvin Ember. New York: Henry Holt, 827–31.

Chantepie de la Saussaye, P.D. 1904. *Het Leven van Nicolaas Beets*. Haarlem: De Erven F. Bohn.

Chen Chih-Mai. 1968. *In Memory of the Last Chinese Dr. R.H. van Gulik. Sinologue Extraordinaire*. Cited from http://www.taiwancomputer.com/company/tony/van4.htm (30/11/01) (originally published in *Hemisphere*).

Chittenden, Hiram Martin, and Alfred Talbot Richardson, eds. 1905. *Life, Letters and Travels of Father Pierre-Jean de Smet, S. J. 1801-1873. New* York: Harper.

Clifford, James, and George E. Marcus. Eds. 1986. *Writing Culture: The Poetics and Politics of Ethnography*. Berkely: University of California Press.

Collingwood, Robin Guy. 1956 [1946]. *The Idea of History*. New York: Oxford University Press.

Comes At Night, George. 1978. *Roaming Days: Warrior Stories*. Browning: Blackfeet Heritage Program.

Croce, Randy. 1983. *The Drum is the Heart*. (Script to video/slide/-tape/filmstrip versions). Browning: Blackfeet Media Department.

Crowshoe, Reg, and Sybille Manneschmidt. 2002. *Akak'stiman: A Blackfoot Framework for Decision-Making and Mediation Processes*. Calgary: University of Calgary Press.

Darnell, Regna. 1990. *Edward Sapir: Linguist, Anthropologist, Humanist*. Berkeley: University of California Press.

Darnell, Regna, and Joel Sherzer. 1971. Areal linguistic studies in North America: a historical perspective. *International Journal of American Linguistics* 37:20–28.

De Mallie, Raymond J. and Douglas R. Parks. 2001. Tribal Traditions and Records. In *Handbook of North American Indians, Plains Volume*. Edited by Raymond J. DeMallie. Washington, DC: Smithsonian Institution Press, 1062–1073.

DeMarce, Roxanne, ed. 1980. *Blackfoot Heritage, Allotment 1907–1908*. Browning: Blackfoot Heritage Program.

Dempsey, Hugh A. 1965. *A Blackfoot Winter Count*. Calgary: Glenbow Museum [reprint 1988. Occasional Paper no. 1.].

———. 1972. *Crowfoot: Chief of the Blackfeet*. Edmonton: Hurtig.

———. 1994. *The Amazing Death of Calf Shirt*. Saskatoon: Fifth House.

———. 2002. *Firewater. The Impact of the Whisky Trade on the Blackfoot Nation*. Saskatoon: Fifth House.

Diettert, G. A. 1992. *Grinnell's Glacier. George Bird Grinnell and Glacier National Park*. Missoula, Montana: Mountain Press.

Dixon, R.M.W. 1994 *Ergativity*. Cambridge: Cambridge University Press.

Duke, Philip G. 1991. *Points in Time*. Niwot, CO: University Press of Colorado.

Duvall, David C. 1904–11. Papers. Handwritten copies. Calgary: Glenbow Archives.

Effert, F. R. 1992. *J.P.B. de Josselin de Jong. Curator and Archaeologist. a Study of His Early Career (1910–1935)*. Leiden: Centre of Non-Western Studies.

Eggermont-Molenaar, M.J.H., ed. 2000. Encounters with the Inhabitants of "Alberta" in 1792–1793 as recorded by Peter Fidler, Surveyor. *Yumtzilob* 12(1–2):7–54.

———. 2001. The Dime-ing of a Novel. How Balle-Franche was transformed into Prairie-Flower. *Dime Novel Round Up* 70(4):137–42.

———. 2002. "Portret van een Professor: Een Nijmeegs incident geprojecteerd in een Chinese Tempelschool?" ("Portrait of a Professor: An Incident in Nijmegen Projected in a Chinese Temple School?") *Canadian Journal of Netherlandic Studies* 23 (Fall 2002): 19–28.

Eggermont-Molenaar, M.J.H., and Paul Callens, eds. 2005 (in press). *Missionaries among Miners, Migrants and Blackfoot: the Van Tighem Brothers' Diaries, Alberta 1876 – 1917*. Calgary: University of Calgary Press.

Epp, Henry, ed. 1993. *Three Hundred Prairie Years: Henry Kelsey's "Inland Country of Good Report."* Regina: Canadian Plains Research Centre.

Ewers, John C. 1955. *The Horse in Blackfoot Indian Culture*. Smithsonian Institution, Bureau of American Ethnology Bulletin 159. Washington: Government Printing Office.

———. 1958. *The Blackfeet: Raiders on the Northwestern Plains*. Norman: University of Oklahoma Press.

Farr, William E. 1984. *The Reservation Blackfeet.1882–1945*. Seattle: University of Washington Press.

———. 1993. Troubled Bundles in Montana. *The Magazine of Western History*. (Autumn):1–17.

Fidler, Peter. 1991. *A Southern Alberta Bicentennial: A Look at Peter Fidler's Journal*. Ed. Bruce Haig. Lethbridge, Alberta: Historical Research Centre. An edition of Fidler's *Journal of a Journey over Land from Buckingham House to the Rocky Mountains in 1792 &3*.

Foley, Michael F. n.d. *An Historical Analysis of the Administration of the Blackfeet Indian Reservation by the United States, 1855–1950's*. Indian Claims Commission. Docket Number 279-D. Montana: Archives Catholic Diocese Helena.

Forbis, Richard G. 1962. The Old Women's Buffalo Jump, Alberta. *National Museums of Canada Bulletin* 180:56–124.

Fortescue, Michael. 1998. *Language Relations Across Bering Strait. Reappraising the Archaeological and Linguistic Evidence*. London/New York: Cassel.

Foster, Michael K. 1997. Language and the Culture History of North America. In *Handbook of North American Indians*, vol. 17. Edited by Ives Goddard. Washington, DC: Smithsonian Institution Press, 64–110.

Frantz, Donald G. 1991. *Blackfoot Grammar*. Toronto: University of Toronto Press.

Frantz, Donald G. and Norma Jean Russell. 1989. *Blackfoot Dictionary of Stems, Roots, and Affixes*. Toronto: University of Toronto Press.

Fraser, Frances. 1990. *The Bear Who Stole the Chinook: Tales from the Blackfoot*. Vancouver: Douglas and McIntyre.

Garraty, John A., ed. 1999. *American National Biography*. Oxford: Oxford University Press.

Geers, Gerardus Johannes. 1917. *The Adverbial and Prepositional Prefixes in Blackfoot.* Doctoral Dissertation, University of Leiden. Leiden: N.V. Boekdrukkerij.

Geertz, Clifford. 1988. *De Antropoloog als Schrijver.* Kok Agora, Kampen, 1989. (Translation of *Works and Lives: The Anthropologist as Author.* Stanford: Stanford University Press)

Genee, Inge. 2003. An Indo-Europeanist on the Prairies: C. C. Uhlenbeck's Work on Algonquian and Indo-European. In *Papers of the Thirty-Fourth Algonquian Conference.* Edited by H.C. Wolfart. Winnipeg: University of Manitoba, 147–63.

Ginneken, Jac. van. 1907. *Principes de linguistique psychologique: Essai synthétique.* Amsterdam: E. van der Vecht.

Goddard, Ives. 1975. Algonquian, Wiyot and Yurok: Proving a Distant Linguistic Relationship. In *Linguistics and Anthropology: In Honor of C.F. Voegelin.* Edited by Dale Kinkade, Kenneth Hale and Oscar Werner. Lisse: Peter de Ridder, 249–62.

———. 1994. The west-to-east cline in Algonquian dialectology. In *Actes du Vingt-Cinquième Congrès des Algonquinistes.* Edited by W. Cowan. Ottawa: Carleton University, 187–211.

Gold, Douglas. 1963. *A Schoolmaster with the Blackfeet Indians.* Caldwell, Idaho: The Caxton Printers.

Golla, Victor, ed. 1984. *The Sapir-Kroeber correspondence.* Berkeley: University of California, Department of Linguistics.

Graham, Jessie D. (Schultz). 1979. In the Lodge of the Matokiks: The Women's Buffalo Society of the Blood Indians. In *Lifeways of Intermontane and Plains Montana Indians.* Edited by Leslie B. Davis. Occasional Papers of the Museum of the Rockies, no. 1. Bozeman: Montana State University, 27–32.

Grinnell, George Bird. 1892. *Blackfoot Lodge Tales.* New York: Charles Scribner's Sons. [reprint University of Nebraska Press, 1962] American Anthropologists o.s., 1896, 9:286–87; n.s. 1899, 1:194–96; 1901, 3:650–68 ["The Lodges of the Blackfoot"].

———. 1913. *Blackfeet Indian Stories.* New York: Charles Scribner's Sons.

———. 1961. *Pawnee, Blackfoot and Cheyenne.* Selected by Dee Brown. New York: Charles Scribner's Sons.

Ground, Mary. 1978. *Grass Woman Stories.* Browning: Blackfeet Heritage Program.

Gulik, R.H. van. 1977. *The Chinese Lake Murders.* Chicago: University of Chicago Press.

Haan, S.W.M.A. den. 1990. *Inventaris van het archief van het Heilige Geest- of Arme Wees- en Kinderhuis te Leiden, 1334–1979.* In: Leidse Inventarissen. 7. HG Weeshuis 117 [Oct. 31, 1904–May 1910] and 118 [June 1910–May 12, 1924]. Leiden: Municipal Archives.

Harrod, Howard L. 1971. *Mission Among the Blackfeet.* Norman: University of Oklahoma Press.

———. 1995. *Becoming and Remaining a People: Native American Religions on the Northern Plains.* Tucson: University of Arizona Press.

———. 2000. *The Animals Came Dancing.* Tucson: University of Arizona Press.

Heman-Ortt, Elsa. Letter to Mrs. Rodee. Case file # M 8116 (90/79). Calgary: Glenbow Archives.

Hinsley, Jr., Curtis M. 1981. *Savages and Scientists. The Smithsonian Institution and the Development of American Anthropology, 1846–1910.* Washington, DC: Smithsonian Institution Press.

Hofstee, Wim. 1991. The French Connection: Gerardus van der Leeuw and the Concept of Primitive Mentality, 127–37. In: *Religionswissenschaft und Kulturkritik.* Herausgegeben von Hans G. Kippenberg und Brigitte Luchesi. diagonal-Verlag. Marburg.

Hovens, P. Herman. 1989. *F.C. ten Kate Jr. (1858–1931) en de Anthropologie der Noord-Amerikaanse Indianen.* Dissertation. Meppel: Krips Repro.

Howard, H. P. 1971. *Sacajawea.* Norman: University of Oklahoma Press.

Hungry Wolf, Adolf (Gutohrlein). 1973. *The Good Medicine Book.* New York: Warner.

———. 1977. (with Beverly Hungry Wolf) *Blackfoot Craftworker's Book.* Invermere, B.C.: Good Medicine Books.

Hungry Wolf, Beverly. 1984. *The Ways of My Grandmothers.* New York: William Morrow.

———. 1996. *Daughters of the Buffalo Women.* Canada: Canadian Caboose Press.

Jackson, John C. 2000. *The Piikani Blackfeet.* Montana: Mountain Press Publishing Company.

———. 2003. *Jemmy Jock Bird. Marginal Man on the Blackfoot Frontier.* Calgary: University of Calgary Press.

Johnstone, Barbara. 2000. The Individual Voice in Language. *Annual Review of Anthropology* 29:405–24.

Josselin de Jong, J.P.B. de. 1912a. Dansen der Peigans. *Onze Eeuw. Maandschrift voor Staatkunde, Letteren, Wetenschap en Kunst* 12(3):201–300, 369–94.

———. 1912b. Social Organization of the Southern Peigans. *Internationales Archiv für Ethnographie.* 20:191–97.

———. 1913. *De waarderingsonderscheiding van "levend" en "levenloos" in het Indogermaans vergeleken met hetzelfde verschijnsel in enkele Algonkin-talen. Ethno-psychologische studie.* Doctoral dissertation University of Leiden.

———. 1913. *Original Odzibwe-Texts with English Translation, Notes and Vocabulary Collected and Published by J.P.B. de Josselin de Jong.* Baessler-Archiv.Beiträge zur Völkerkunde. Herausgegeben aus Mitteln des Baessler-Instituts unter Mitwirkung der Direktoren der Ethnologischen Abteilungen des Königlichen Museums für Völkerkunde in Berlin redigiert von P. Ehrenreich. Beiheft V. Leipzig und Berlin. Druk und verlag von B.G. Teubner.

———. 1914. *Blackfoot Texts From the Southern Peigans Blackfoot Reservation Teton County Montana.* With the Help of Black-Horse-Rider. Verhandelingen der Koninklijke Akademie van Wetenschappen the Amsterdam, Afdeeling Letterkunde, NR XIV, nr 4. Amsterdam: Johannes Müller.

———. 1951. Herdenking van Christianus Cornelius Uhlenbeck (18 October 1866–12 Augustus 1951). In *Jaarboek der Koninklijke Nederlandse Akademie van Wetenschappen,* 1951–1952, 280–98.

———. 1952. In Memoriam Christianus Cornelius Uhlenbeck (18th October 1866–12th August 1951). *Lingua* 3, 1:243–66. Also in: Thomas Sebeok. Ed. 1966. *Portraits of Linguists*, 253–66.

———. n.d. College-dictaat. (Lecture Notes 1948/1949, S 14626/OR). Leiden: Koninklijk Instituut voor Taal-, Land- en Volkenkunde.

Kehoe, Alice Beck. 1990. Primal Gaia: Primitivism and Plastic Medicine Men. In *The Invented Indian*. Edited by J.A. Clifton. New Brunswick NJ: Transaction Books, 93–209.

———. 1991. Contests of Power in Blackfoot Life and Mythology. In *Contests*. Edited by A. Duff-Cooper. Cosmos 6:115–24, Edinburgh.

———. 1992. Clot-of-Blood. In *Earth and Sky*. Edited by C.R. Farrer and R. A. Williamson. Albuquerque: University of New Mexico Press, 207–14.

———. 1993. Maintaining the Road of Life. In *Violence, Resistance, and Survival in the Americas: Native Americans and the Legacy of Conquest*. Edited by William B. Taylor and Franklin Pease. Washington: Smithsonian Institution Press, 193–207.

———. 1995a. "Introduction." In: *Mythology of the Blackoot*, compiled and translated by Clark Wissler and D.C. Duvall. Lincoln: University of Nebraska Press, v–xxxiii.

———. 1995b. Blackfoot Persons. In *Women and Power in Native America*. Edited by Laura F. Klein and Lillian A. Ackerman. Norman: University of Oklahoma Press, 113–25.

———. 1996. "Transcribing Insima, a Blackfoot 'Old Lady.'" In: *Reading Beyond Words: Native History in Context*, ed. Jennifer S. H. Brown and Elizabeth Vibert. Peterborough, ON: Broadview Press, 381–402.

Kehoe, Th. F. 1960. Stone Tipi Rings in North-Central Montana and the Adjacent Portion of Alberta, Canada: Their Historical, Ethnological, and Archeological Aspects. In *Anthropological Papers*, Bulletin 173:417–73. Anthropological papers No. 62. Washington DC: Government Printing Office.

Kuiper, F.B.J. 1966. Herdenking van Jan Petrus Benjamin de Josselin de Jong (13 maart 1886–15 november 1964). *Jaarboek Koninklijke Nederlandse Akademie van Wetenschappen* 1965–1966, 397.

Holterman, Jack. 1996. *A Special Study of the Blackfoot Language, 1932–1997*. Browning: The Piegan Institute.

LaFromboise, Mary Ellen. 1979. *Sta-ai-tsi-nix-sin Ghost Stories*. Browning: Blackfeet Heritage Program.

Lancaster, Richard. 1966. *Piegan*. New York: Doubleday.

Lehmann, Winfred P. 1993. *Theoretical Bases of Indo-European Linguistics*. London: Routledge.

Lewis, Oscar. 1995. Manly Hearted Women Among the North Piegan. *American Anthropologist* 43(2):173–87.

———. 1941. *The Effects of White Contact Upon Blackfoot Culture*. Monograph 6, American Ethnological Society. Seattle: University of Washington Press.

Little Bear. 1996. The Massacre of the Maria's. In *Our Hearts Fell to the Ground. Plains Indian Views of How the West Was Lost*. Edited with an Introduction by Colin G. Calloway. Boston and New York: Bedford St. Martin's Press.

Locher, G. W. 1965. J.P.B. de Josselin de Jong (13 maart 1886–15 november 1964). *Mens en Maatschappij* 40(1):36–47.

Long Standing Bear Chief (Harold E. Gray). 1992. *Ni-Kso-Ko-Was: Blackfoot Spirituality, Traditions, Values and Beliefs*. Browning: Spirit Talk Press.

Lupson, Arnold ("Eagle Tail"). 1923. *The Sarcee Indians of Alberta*. s.n.

Luraghi, Silvia. 1988. Reconstructing Proto-Indo-European as an ergative language: a test. *Journal of Indo-European Studies* 15:359–79.

Maclean, John. n.d. *Papers on the Language and Customs of the Blackfeet Indians*. Calgary: Glenbow Archives.

———. c1896. *Canadian Savage Folk. The Native Tribes of Canada*. Toronto: Briggs. Reprint 1971.

———. 1892. *The Indians of Canada, their Manners and Customs*. Toronto: Briggs.

Maes, André. n.d. *Een Nieuwe Wereld. Latijns Amerika ontdekt, veroverd, bekeerd*. Unpublished paper. Nijmegen.

Mandelbaum, David G. 1940. *The Plains Cree*. New York: American Museum of Natural History, Anthropological Papers, vol. XXXVII, Pt. II, 153–316.

Many Guns, Tom. 1979. *Pinto Horse Rider*. Browning: Blackfeet Heritage Program.

McClintock, Walter. n.d. *The Blackfoot Beaver Bundle*. Southwest Museum Leaflets, numbers 2 & 3. California: Southwest Museum.

———. 1910. *The Old North Trail*. London: MacMillan. Reprinted with an introduction by Sidner J. Larson, Lincoln: University of Nebraska Press. Bison Books, 1992.

———. 1923. *Old Indian Trails*. New York: Houghton Mifflin.

McFee, Malcolm. 1972. *Modern Blackfeet: Montanans on a Reservation*. New York: Holt, Rinehart and Winston.

Michelson, Truman. 1925. Notes on some word-comparisons between Blackfoot and other Algonquian languages. *International Journal of American Linguistics* 3(1–4):233–55.

Middleton, S. H. 1952. *Indian Chiefs: Ancient and Modern*. Lethbridge: Lethbridge Herald.

Mink, Louis O. 1978. Narrative Form as a Cognitive Instrument. In *The Writing of History: Literary Form and Historical Understanding*. Edited by Robert H. Canary and Henry Kozicki. Madison: University of Wisconsin Press, 129–49.

Mithun, Marianne. 1999. *The Languages of Native North America*. Cambridge: Cambridge University Press.

Morice, A. G. (Rev. O.M.I.). Transactions of the Canadian Institute. Session 1892–92. *Notes on the Western Dénés*. (footnote on p. 12) Read 4th November, 1893.

Niles, John D. 1999. *Homo Narrans: The Poetics and Anthropology of Oral Literature*. Philadelphia: University of Pennsylvania Press.

Noordegraaf, Jan. 2002. Dutch linguists between Humboldt and Saussure. The case of Jac. van Ginneken (1877–1945). *Historiographia Linguistica* 29(1–2):145–63.

Oostendorp, H. Th. 1968. In memoriam Gerardus Johannes Geers. *Jaarboek van de Maatschappij der Nederlandse Letterkunde te Leiden 1967–1968*, 69–77.

Orr, Robert. 2001. Review of Brigitte Bauer: *Archaic Syntax in Indo-European: The Spread of Transitivity in Latin and French*. Berlin: Mouton de Gruyter. *Journal of Indo-European Studies* 29(¾):420–35.

Ortt, Felix. 1898. *Christelijk Anarchisme*. Haarlem: Drukkerij "Vrede."

Rep, Jelte. 1977. *Englandspiel. Spionagetragedie in bezet Nederland, 1942–1944* (Englandspiel. Espionage Tragedy in Occupied Netherlands, 1942–1944). Van Holkema & Warendorf. Bussum.

Rides At The Door, Darnell Davis. 1979. *Napi Stories*. Browning: Blackfeet Heritage Program.

Rogier, L. J. 1967. Herdenking van P.Geyl (15 december 1887–31 december 1966). Akademie van Wetenschappen afd. Letterkunde. Nieuwe Reeks, Deel 30, no. 12. NV. Noord-Hollandsche Uitgevers Maatschappij. Amsterdam, 397–412.

Rosier, Paul C. 2001. *Rebirth of the Blackfeet Nation, 1912–1954*. Lincoln: University of Nebraska Press.

Russell, Andy. 1987. *The Life of a River*. Toronto: McClelland and Stewart.

Ruthven, K. K. 1964. *Critical Assumptions*. Cambridge: Cambridge University Press.

Samek, Hana. 1987. *The Blackfoot Confederacy 1880–1920*. Albuquerque: University of New Mexico Press.

Sapir, Edward. 1917a. Review of C. C. Uhlenbeck, "Het passieve karakter van het verbum transitivum of van het verbum actionis in talen van Noord-Amerika." *International Journal of American Linguistics* 1:82–86. Also in *The Collected Works of Edward Sapir. V: American Indian Languages*, vol. I. Edited by William Bright. 1990. Berlin/New York: Mouton de Gruyter, 69–74.

————. 1917b. Review of C. C. Uhlenbeck, "Het identificeerend karakter der possessieve flexie in talen van Noord-Amerika." *International Journal of American Linguistics* 1:86–90. Also in *The Collected Works of Edward Sapir. V: American Indian Languages*, vol I. Edited by William Bright. 1990. Berlin/New York: Mouton de Gruyter, 75–80.

Schmidt, K. H. 1979. Reconstructing Active and Ergative Stages of Pre-Indo-European. In *Ergativity: Towards a Theory of Grammatical Relations*. Edited by F. Planck. New York: Academic Press, 333–45.

Schoenberg, Wilfred P. 1959. "St. Peter's Mission," *The Register* (Helena Diocese Edition), Dec. 13, 4.

Schuchardt, Hugo. 1895. Über den passiven Charakter des Transitivs in den kaukasischen Sprachen. *Ber. Ak. Wien, Phil.-Hist. Klasse*, 133:1.

————. 1913. Über den aktivischen und passivischen Charakter des Transitivs. *Indogermanische Forschungen* 18:528–31.

Schultz, James Willard. 1907. *My Life as an Indian*. New York: Forest and Stream [reprint Fawcett, New York 1956].

————. 1962. *Blackfeet and Buffalo*. Edited by Keith C. Seele. Norman: University of Oklahoma Press.

————. 1974. *Why Gone Those Times? Blackfoot Tales*. Edited by Eugene Lee Silliman. Norman: University of Oklahoma Press.

————. 1988. *Recently Discovered Tales of Life Among The Indians*. Compiled and Edited by Warren L. Hanna. Missoula: Mountain Press.

Schultz, James W. and Jessie L. Donaldson [Schultz]. 1930. *The Sun God's Children*. New York: Houghton Mifflin.

Scriver, Bob. 1990. *The Blackfeet. Artists of the Northern Plains*. The Scriver Collection of Blackfeet Indian Artifacts and Related Objects, 1894–1990. Kansas City: The Lowell Press.

Soer, Al. S.J. 1910. The Piëgans. Letters from Indian Missionaries. *The Indian Sentinel* 1910:17–23.

Steward, Julian H. 1934. *The Blackfoot*. (Typescript for possible exhibits, Office of Field education, NPS). Berkely: National Park service.

Stocken, Canon H.W. Gibbon. 1976. *Among the Blackfoot and Sarcee*. Calgary: Glenbow Alberta Institute.

Swadesh, Morris. 1951. Diffusional cumulation and archaic residue as historical explanation. *Southwestern Journal of Anthropology* 7:1–21.

Swann, Brian. 1994. Introduction. In *Coming to Light: Contemporary Translations of the Native Literature of North America*. New York: Vintage Random House, xii–xlvi.

Swiggers, Pierre. 1988. Theoretical Implications of C. C. Uhlenbeck's Algonquian Studies. *Papers of the Algonquian Conference* 19, Edited by William Cowan, 225–34.

Tatsey, John. 1971. *The Black Moccasin*. Compiled and edited by Paul T. DeVore. Spokane, Washington: The Curtis Art Gallery.

Taylor, Colin F. and Hugh Dempsey. 1999. *White Eagle Tail. Arnold Lupson and 30 Years among the Sarcee, Blackfoot and Stoney Indians on the North American Plains*. London: Vega, 16–19.

Ten Kate, Herman F. C. 1885. *Reizen en onderzoekingen in Noord Amerika*, Leiden: E.J. Brill.

————. *Travels and Inquiries in North America, 1882–1883*. Trans. and ed. Pieter Hovens, William J. Orr, Louis A. Hieb, and Southwest Center University of Arizona. University of New Mexico Press, 2004.

Thalbitzer, W. 1944. Uhlenbeck's Eskimo-Indoeuropean Hypothesis. A Critical revision. *Travaux de Cercle Linguistique de Copenhague* 1:66–96.

Thomason, Sarah. 2001. *Language Contact: An Introduction*. Edinburgh: Edinburgh University Press.

Thomason, Sarah Grey and Terrence Kaufman. 1988. *Language Contact, Creolization, and Genetic Linguistics*. Berkeley: University of California Press.

Thompson, Stith. 1932–36. *Motif-Index of Folk-Literature*. Helsinki.

————. 1966 [1929]. *Tales of the North American Indians*. Bloomington: Indiana University Press.

Tomkins, William. 1926. *Universal Sign Language of the Plains Indians of North America*. s.n. See also http://www.manataka.org/page311.html.

Uhlenbeck, C. C. 1885. *Gedachten en Droomen*. Haarlem: I. de Haan.

———. 1888. *De verwantschapsbetrekkingen tusschen de Germaansche en Balto-slavische talen.* Doctoral Dissertation, Leiden University.

———. 1892. Baskische Studiën. *Verslagen en Mededelingen der Koninklijke Akademie van Wetenschappen, Afdeeling Letterkunde*, 3e Reeks VIII, 179–228.

———. 1899. *De onderlinge verhouding der Oudgermaansche tongvallen en hunne plaats in den Indogermaanschen taalstam.* Rede bij de aanvaarding van het hoogleeraarsambt in de faculteit der Letteren en Wijsbegeerte aan de Rijks-Universiteit te Leiden. Leiden: Brill.

———. 1901. Agens und Patiens im Kasusystem der Indogermanischen Sprachen. *Indogermanische Forschungen* 12:170–71.

———. 1903. *Beiträge zu einer vergleichenden lautlehre der baskischen dialecte.* Verhandelingen der Koninklijke Akademie van Wetenschappen te Amsterdam, Afdeeling Letterkunde, Nieuwe Reeks, V, 1. Amsterdam: Johannes Müller.

———. 1905. *De woordafleidende suffixen van het Baskisch. Eene bijdrage tot de kennis der Baskische woordvorming.* Verhandelingen der Koninklijke Akademie van Wetenschappen te Amsterdam, Afdeeling Letterkunde, Nieuwe Reeks, VI. Amsterdam: Johannes Müller.

———. 1907. Karakteristiek der Baskische grammatica. *Verslagen en Mededeelingen der Koninklijke Akademie van Wetenschappen, Afdeeling Letteren*, 4e Reeks, VIII, 4–42.

———. 1908. Die einheimischen Sprachen Nord-Amerikas bis zum Rio Grande. *Anthropos* 3:773–99.

———. 1909. Grammatische onderscheidingen in het Algonkisch, voornamelijk gedemonstreerd aan het Otchipwe-dialect. *Verslagen en Mededeelingen der Koninklijke Akademie van Wetenschappen, Afdeeling Letterkunde*, 4e Reeks, X, 20–39.

———. 1910a. Zu den einheimischen Sprachen Nord-Amerikas. *Anthropos* 5:779–86.

———. 1910b. *Ontwerp van eene vergelijkende vormleer van enige Algonkintalen.* Verhandelingen der Koninklijke Akademie van Wetenschappen, Afdeeling Letterkunde, Nieuwe Reeks, XI. Amsterdam: Johannes Müller.

———. 1911a. *Original Blackfoot Texts. From the Southern Peigans Blackfoot Reservation, Teton County, Montana. With the help of Joseph Tatsey.* Verhandelingen der Koninklijke Akademie van Wetenschappen te Amsterdam, Afdeeling Letterkunde, Nieuwe Reeks, XII, no 1. Amsterdam: Johannes Müller.

———. 1911b. Geslachts- en Persoonsnamen der Peigans. *Verslagen en Mededeelingen der Koninklijke Akademie van Wetenschappen, Afdeeling Letterkunde*, 4e Reeks, XI, 4–29, Amsterdam: Johannes Müller.

———. 1912a. *A new series of Blackfoot texts, from the Southern Peigans, Blackfoot Reservation, Teton County, Montana. With the help of Joseph Tatsey.* Verhandelingen der Koninklijke Nederlandse Akademie van Wetenschappen te Amsterdam, Afdeeling Letterkunde, Nieuwe Reeks, XIII, no 1. Amsterdam: Johannes Müller.

———. 1912b. The Origin of the Otterlodge. In *Festschrift Vilhem Thomsen*. Leipzig: Otto Haarassowitc, 74–77.

———. 1912c. Exogamy of the Peigans. *Internationales Achiv für Ethnographie* 20:254.

———. 1913a. De vormen van het Blackfoot. *Verslagen en Mededeelingen der Koninklijke Akademie van Wetenschappen, Afdeeling Letteren*, 4e Reeks, XII, 174–219.

———. 1913b. *Flexion of Substantives in Blackfoot: A Preliminary Sketch.* Verhandelingen der Koninklijke Nederlandse Akademie van Wetenschappen te Amsterdam, Afdeeling Letterkunde. Nieuwe Reeks, Deel XIV, no. 1. Amsterdam: Noord-Hollandse Uitgeversmaatschappij.

———. 1914. *Some general aspects of Blackfoot morphology. A contribution to Algonquian linguistics.* Verhandelingen der Koninklijke Nederlandse Akademie van Wetenschappen te Amsterdam, Afdeeling Letterkunde. Nieuwe Reeks, XIV, no. 5. Amsterdam: Johannes Müller.

———. 1915a. *Philological notes to Dr. J.P.B. de Josselin de Jong's Blackfoot texts.* Verhandelingen der Koninklijke Nederlandse Akademie van Wetenschappen te Amsterdam, Afdeeling Letterkunde. Nieuwe Reeks, XVI, no. 1. Amsterdam: Johannes Müller.

———. 1915b. Miscellaneous reviews. *Internationales Archiv für Ethnographie* 22:268–72.

———. 1916a. Het passieve karakter van het verbum transitivum of van het verbum actionis in talen van Noord-Amerika. *Verslagen en Mededeelingen der Koninklijke Akademie van Wetenschappen, Afdeeling Letterkunde*, 5e Reeks, II, 187–216.

———. 1916b. Het identificeerend karakter der possessieve flexie in talen van Noord-Amerika. *Verslagen en Mededeelingen der Koninklijke Akademie van Wetenschappen, Afdeeling Letterkunde*, 5e Reeks, II, 345–71.

———. 1916c. Die Uhlenbeck's. Eine alte Velberter Familie. Velbert, Rheinland. 14 Juni, 1916. In *Festschrift zur Jahrtausend der Stadt Velbert, 1925.* (2.21.165/203). The Hague: Algemeen Rijks Archief, 7–28.

———. 1916d. Some Blackfoot Songtexts. *Archives Internationales d'Ethnographie* 23:241–42.

———. 1920. *A Survey of the Non-Pronominal and Non-Formative Affixes of the Blackfoot Verb: A Contribution to the Knowledge of Algonquian Word-Formation.* Verhandelingen der Koninklijke Nederlandse Akademie van Wetenschappen te Amsterdam, Afdeeling Letterkunde. Nieuwe Reeks, Deel XX.

———. 1923. Over een mogelijke verwantschap van het Baskisch met de Palaeo-Kaukasische talen. *Mededeelingen der Koninklijke Akademie van Wetenschappen, Afdeeling Letterkunde*, 105–37.

———. 1924a. Some word-comparisons between Blackfoot and other Algonquian languages. *International Journal of American Linguistics* 3(1):103–8.

———. 1924b. Blackfoot *imitá(ua)*, dog. *International Journal of American Linguistics* 3:236.

———. 1925a. Nieuwe woorden in het Blackfoot. *Mededeelingen der Koninklijke Akademie van Wetenschappen*, Deel 59, Serie A: 199–215.

———. 1925b. Review of "H. Schuchardt, Primitiae Linguae Vasconum. Einführung ins Baskische." *Revue Internationale des Études Basques* 16(3):365–67.

———. 1925c. Le tchouktche et le basque. *Revue Internationale des Études Basques* 16(1).

———. 1927a. Baskisch *elkar*. *Mededeelingen der Koninklijke Akademie van Wetenschappen, Afdeeling Letterkunde*: 179–81.

———. 1927b. De afwezigheid der datief-conceptie in het Blackfoot. In *Symbolis grammaticis in honorem Ioannis Radowski*, 71–82.

———. 1927c. Algonkisch-klinkende woorden in het Wiyot. *Mededeelingen der Koninklijke Akademie van Wetenschappen* 63:233–58.

———. 1930. The Basque Words for "Woman." In *A Grammatical Miscellany Offered to Otto Jespersen on His Seventieth Birthday*. Copenhagen: Einar Munksgaard, and London: Allen and Unwin, 419–27.

———. 1932. De jongste denkbeelden over den oorsprong der Basken. *Mededeelingen der Koninklijke Akademie van Wetenschappen, Afdeeling Letterkunde*, Deel 74, Serie B, no. 1, 1–10.

———. 1935a. Oer-Indogermaansch en Oer-Indogermanen. *Mededeelingen der Koninklijke Akademie van Wetenschappen, Afdeeling Letterkunde*, Deel 77, Serie A, no. 4, 125–48.

———. 1935b. Eskimo en Oer-Indogermaansch. *Mededeelingen der Koninklijke Nederlandsche Akademie van Wetenschappen, Afdeeling Letterkunde*, Deel 77, Serie A, no. 4, 179–96.

———. 1936. *Opmerkingen over het Eskimo-Probleem*. Jaarboek der KNAW 28, maart 1936.

———. 1936. Letters to "Dick." [Dick Uhlenbeck] (2.21.165/203). The Hague: Algemeen Rijks Archief.

———. 1938. *A concise Blackfoot grammar, based on materials from the southern Peigans*. Verhandelingen der Koninklijke Nederlandsche Akademie van Wetenschappen te Amsterdam, Afdeeling Letterkunde, Nieuwe Reeks, Deel XLI. Amsterdam: Noord-Hollandse Uitgevers-maatschappij.

———. 1939. Grammatische invloed van het Algonkisch op het Wiyot en het Yurok. *Mededeelingen der Koninklijke Nederlandsche Akademie van Wetenschappen, Afdeeling Letterkunde*, Nieuwe Reeks, Deel 2, no. 3, 41–49.

———. 1941. *Oude Aziatische contacten van het Eskimo*. Mededeelingen der Nederlandsche Akademie van Wetenschappen, Afdeeling Letterkunde, Nieuwe Reeks, Deel 4, no. 7.

———. 1942. De oudere lagen van den Baskischen woordschat. *Mededeelingen der Koninklijke Akademie van Wetenschappen, Afdeeling Letterkunde*, 327–76.

———. 1946. Gestaafde en vermeende affiniteiten van het Baskisch. *Mededeelingen der Koninklijke Nederlandsche Akademie van Wetenschappen Afdeeling Letterkunde*, Amsterdam: Johannes Müller, 13–24.

———. 1948. Present general trends in the grouping of American Aboriginal languages. *Lingua* 1:219–24.

Uhlenbeck, C. C., and R.H. van Gulik. 1930. *An English-Blackfoot vocabulary, based on material from the southern Peigans*. Verhandelingen der Koninklijke Akademie van Wetenschappen te Amsterdam, Afdeeling Letterkunde. Nieuwe Reeks, Deel XXIX, Amsterdam: Noord-Hollandse Uitgevers-maatschappij.

———. 1934. *A Blackfoot-English Vocabulary, Based on Material from the Southern Peigans*. Verhandelingen der Koninklijke Akademie van Wetenschappen te Amsterdam, Afdeeling Letterkunde, Nieuwe Reeks, Deel XXXIII. Amsterdam: Noord-Hollandse Uitgevers-maatschappij.

Uhlenbeck–Melchior, W. M. *Blackfoot Reservation Donderdag 8 juni-Zondag 17 september 1911*. Ms. M8116, Calgary: Glenbow Archives.

Wallace W. S., ed. 1932. *John McLean's Notes of a Twenty-Five Years's Service in the Hudson's Bay Territory*. Toronto: The Champlain Society.

White, Hayden V. 1973. *Metahistory*. Baltimore: Johns Hopkins University Press.

———. 1987. *The Content of the Form*. Baltimore: Johns Hopkins University Press.

Whitt, Laurie Anne. 1995. Indigenous Peoples and the Cultural Politics of Knowlege. In *Issues in Native American Cultural Identity*. Edited by Michael K. Green. New York: Peter Lang, 223–71.

Wied zum Neuwied, Maximilian, Prince of. 1905 [1843]. *Early Western Travels, 1748–1846*, vol. XXIII, Pt. II. In *Travels in the Interior of North America*. Edited with Notes, Introductions, Index, etc., by Reuben G. Thwaites, LL.D. in Early Western Travels. Cleveland: A.H. Clark, 1904–1905, vol. 22–24.

Wilson, E. F. *Report on the Sarcee Indians*. London: British Association for the Advancement of Science. 1886–1890. 58th Meeting, 4th Report.

Wissler, Clark. 1971 [1938]. *Red Man Reservations*. New York: Collier.

———, ed. 1916. Blackfoot Societies. In *Anthropological Papers of the American Museum of Natural History*. Vol. XI. Societies of the Plains Indians. New York: The American Museum of Natural History.

Wissler, Clark and D. C. Duvall. *Mythology of the Blackfoot Indian*. Anthropological Papers vol. II, Pt. 1, 1–163. New York: American Museum of Natural History.

Wissler, Clark and D. C. Duvall. 1995 [1908]. *Mythology of the Blackfoot Indian*. Lincoln: University of Nebraska Press. Bison Book reprints.

Appendix A:
Patronymics and Proper Names of the Peigans[1]

Contribution by Mr. C. C. Uhlenbeck

In the northwest corner of Montana and farther to the North, beyond the Canadian border, there are three small tribes, which speak one and the same language and are ethnologically known under the name Blackfeet. In fact this name only belongs to the Siksika of the Blackfoot reserve in Alberta, but for a long time the name has also been used to indicate the Kaina or Blood Indians and the Pekáni or Peigan. The latter people live partly in Alberta and partly on the Blackfoot reservation in Teton county, Montana, where I recently stayed for three months with Mr. J.P.B. de Josselin de Jong. In this relatively short period we succeeded in compiling extensive grammatical material on which the scientific grammar of the South Peigan dialect may be based. At the same time we had the opportunity to record oral traditions and stories from Indian storytellers. Although the grammar may only be completed in about three years, already at the last meeting I was able to offer for publication to the Academy a bundle of *Original Blackfoot Texts*, with an English translation. Although my main objective was to learn the language and to save it from threatened oblivion by recording an accurate description, I also had an opportunity to observe the life of the Indians, knowing well that knowledge of the language without understanding the people will remain lacking and fruitless. In order to show you my grateful acknowledgement for your friendly recommendation to the High Government, I would like to communicate today my observations on the terrain bordering the field of glottology and ethnology, the field of onomastics.

Much is known about Blackfoot-speaking tribes through the publications of Maclean, Grinnell, Wissler and McClintock. However, in this meeting I will not refer to them or other ethnologists, but will restrict myself to the partly new facts that I learned by communicating with the Indians. This restriction forces me to mention only the South Peigan, among whom De Josselin de Jong and I lived, thereby excluding the Blood Indians and the Blackfeet in a stricter sense, about whom I can say nothing from my own experience. If circumstances are favorable, I hope to visit these tribes in the future. By restricting myself to our own material I obtain the advantage that my lecture, when published, will be an independent source, which is even more important because the information obtained by me differs in several regards from the information from other sources.

Before I commence with my actual subject, the family and personal names of the Peigan, you will certainly expect to hear something from me about the place of the Blackfoot among the aboriginal peoples of North America. I will start by telling you that the Blackfeet belong to the large Algonquian family, which at one time spread over an enormous area before it had to yield to the all-destroying white men. So the Blackfeet are related to the Micmacs and the Delawares, the Crees and the Chippeways, the Cheyenne and the Arapahoes, to mention only a few of the wide range of tribes, many of which have disappeared from the earth, "swept away like the buffalo." It is not that the Blackfeet themselves realize this relationship. If one says, for example, to a Peigan that his language is related to Chippeway and Cree, he shrugs and will contend that he cannot perceive one word of similarity, not knowing that a science exists that can unravel the original similarity of that which has been differentiated since ages past. The Peigan also doesn't like to hear about the relationship with the Cree, whom he considers more or less as inferior and of whom he says disapprovingly that they eat horse meat, yes, that they eat everything and don't even scorn a skunk. Whether a particularly close relationship exists between the Blackfeet and one or another tribe has not yet been established. It has certainly not been permissible to assume there is such a close relationship between the Blackfeet and the Fox Indians, because the Fox, with regard to lexicon and grammar, are much closer to Chippeway, Potawatomi, Ottawa, and Cree, not to mention a few other dialects that hardly differ from Fox. Only when all living Algonquian languages have been well researched may it be possible to obtain a clear understanding of the relationship between the Blackfoot and their Eastern relations. Only then, and with the help of prehistoric history, may we be able to trace the routes along which the Algonquian tribes spread through eastern woods and the central area to the undulating prairies of the West. In general the Algonquian tradi-

tions indicate an origin from the North, and also the people who speak Blackfoot reminisce about a far, northern fatherland. In this regard, the Indian Joseph Tatsey told me the following:

Long ago the country of the ancient Peigan was very far in the North. They moved to and fro in that land. In the south was a big lake. They used to move there and then move away from it again. Once when they went south again, they suddenly saw that the big water was frozen. The chief said: We will cross it. The chief went first. He went over. Half of the tribe reached the other side. The wife and the child of the chief were still in the middle of the ice. The child said to the woman: Mother, there is something very beautiful. It sticks out from the ice. Please get off your horse and get it for me. So the woman dismounted from her horse. She hit the thing, which was the horn of an animal, with a stone hammer. When she hit the animal, it started to move. That caused the ice to break. Out of that very place the animal emerged with its head from the ice. When the animal started to move, it tore up the ice in front of him. Then the ancient people knew that it was the water bull. Half of the people could no longer cross because the ice was broken up, so that is why at present half of the ancient Peigan live across the big water.

A critical treatment of this tradition would make me stray from fulfilling the task I have presently taken upon myself. That is why I prefer to begin by relating to you something about the division of the tribe and show you the great differences existing between the clans of the Peigan and those of numerous other tribes in North America.

On our trip we arrived at the Tuscarora reservation near Niagara Falls. When we asked a Tuscarora to which clan he or she belonged, the answer was invariably "I am a bear" or "I am an eel," or something like that. And when we asked further about the clan of the parents, then it seemed that generally the father and mother were members of different clans, but that the clan of the mother was also the one of her children. So we found clans that were closely related to animals, and clans to which one belonged because of maternal lineage and whose members were not allowed to marry among themselves.

How different are the circumstances on the Blackfoot reservation! Exogamy can also be witnessed with Peigan families, but to my knowledge a relationship between a certain clan and some animal does not exist.[2] That someone belongs to a clan because of his mother occurs once in a while, but this is due to certain circumstances. A very old woman called O′taitsìua (Weasel-body), whose father was a white man, is supposed to belong to the clan of her mother, the Motúiinaiks (All-chiefs). O′taitsìua herself was married to a Blood Indian from the I′tskinàiks (Horn-people), and Joseph Tatsey, a son from this marriage who lives among the Peigan, also belongs to the Motúiinaiks, because his father was not a member of one of the Peigan families.

I mentioned the Tuscaroras because I have personally been in touch with them, but what I related about them also holds true for the rest of the Six Nations, as well as for the Iroquois tribes which don't belong to this League of Nations. Matriarchy is found in many Algonquian tribes, but as just mentioned the Peigans have male lineage. According to information from others, this also holds true for the Blood and the Blackfeet proper, who, with the Peigan, form the group of Blackfoot speakers. Based on my personal observation, I can confirm that they are divided into a number of families carrying very peculiar names, which are totally different from totem names such as "Wolf" and "Beaver" and "Bear" and "Raven," as one encounters with so many other peoples of North America. These Peigan families are patriarchal and the inherited chiefdom, as far as chiefdom is inheritable, nearly always follows the male lineage. One is primarily a child of the father, although lineage in the matriarchal line is not undervalued either. Members of the same clan generally don't marry each other and sexual relations with available relatives on the father's or mother's side is considered to be abhorrent. Only the clan of the Iχ′púχsimaiks (Fat-melters) makes an exception

to the rule of exogamy. They marry one another, which causes them to be seen by members of other clans as a shameless people. Joseph Tatsey said about them that they don't hesitate to use coarse language in the presence of their female relatives, and Síkimi-å`χkitopi (Blackhorse-rider, officially called Walter Mountain-Chief) expressed himself to De Josselin de Jong with an equally negative comment.

It appears that the Peigan usually criticize one another and judge one another in case of immediate cause. This tendency emerges clearly in the names of the clans, which are derisive without exception. There are about thirty such family names known, but I can advise you about only nineteen as to how they acquired their names. Please allow me to subsequently deal with these nineteen names.

I will start with the Iχ′púχsimaiks (Fat-melters), which I just mentioned. As reported, they loved melted fat and they were always busy melting fat, even if they had meat in abundance. Because of this peculiarity, they were given the nickname Iχ′púχsimaiks.

With the name of the Kατáiimiks (Not-laughers) it is a bit different. They were ironically named so because they always laughed. It appears that the Kατáiimiks were perceived as outgoing and loose, though they were not accused of such indecencies as the Iχ′púχsimaiks. Síkimi-å`χkitopi especially characterizes women from the Kατáiimiks in an unflattering way. They love, he contends, to play around with men other than the ones they married and, no less than the men, they love alcohol and have a tendency to get drunk.

There is a romance, about which I will tell you everything, linked to the name of the Kàmiχ′táiks (Buffalo-chips).

A long time ago – Joseph Tatsey told me – there was a chief named Mekyápi (Red-old-man), who ran off with the wife of another chief. They went to the Crows. When they arrived, Mekyápi said to the woman, Which one do you want to ride? She answered him: With the Medicine bags and a shield and something to cover these things with.

He also asked her: On which color horse do you want to ride? And on what color horse would you like to load your pack? She said: I will ride a black-striped back and I will load my pack on a brown-striped back. He asked again: And what will you use for a saddle? She answered: I will use a saddle with the two sides up. Then they went back to the Peigan. When they were close to the camp, they stayed overnight. That woman was afraid of her former husband. She said to Mekyápi: I am afraid that my husband will kill me. He told her: No, he will not harm you. Here are four pieces of buffalo pies. Take them. If he is angry, throw them in the fire. Say each time: Here is a piece of buffalo chips. When all four are thrown into the fire, he will not harm you anymore. He will be glad to have got the horses, and a shield, and the medicine bags. The woman did everything that Mekyápi had told her and since that time the clan of her husband was called Kàmiχʹtáiks.

This story is very interesting because Mekyápi was an historical person, who more than one hundred years ago, was known among the Peigans as the most beautiful youngster. Mekyápi was a great uncle of Nínoχkyàio (Bear-chief), who is now fifty-three years old and lives not far from the Holy Family Mission in a poor cabin lodge, in which surroundings he ties pieces of fabric as offerings for the sun. Nínoχkyàio confirmed the history which I just related. This story about the origin of the name Kàmiχʹtáiks was not known to Sikimi-åʹχkitopi, who has been De Josselin de Jong's teacher for a long time. He simply said that they have this name due to the fact that they don't like to haul wood and would rather use pieces of buffalo chips as fuel.

I can be much shorter about the Ináksiks (Small-robes) who, according to Síkimi-åʹχkitopi, used to cut buffalo skins in small pieces and use them as clothing.

It is said that two other clans derive their names from syphilis. The Isksínaitapìks (Bug-people) were given their name because all of them, starting with their chief, were affected by syphilis and this disease was attributed to insects, which slowly ate the patients from the inside out. Joseph Tatsey and Nínoχkyàio were not sure about this tradition, but the same story was told to me by Nínaistáku (Mountain-chief), the father of Síkimi-åʹχkitopi.

The second clan that seemed to have derived its name from syphilis, is the A'pekaïks (Skunks), about which it is said that even the unmarried women suffered from syphilis. The A'pekaïks were given their name because of the offensive smell they spread around in former days. Just as in the case of the Isksínaitapìks they have an animal name but, even when one does not tend to accept the syphilis story, it would still not be acceptable to connect these cases with the Iroquois' "Eels," "Bears," etc. etc., because not one custom or tradition ties the Isksínaitapìks and the A'pekaïks with insects and skunks in a mystical-genetic connection.

From their names three other clans are characterized as being stingy. The first were the Nitáuyiks (Lone-eaters), who went hunting for buffaloes alone, without the other clans, and invited no one to their dinners. It is also said that even among themselves, they did not deny their egotistical traits.

Almost the same thing is said about the Siniksístsauyiks (Eat-before-others). They were called this because they always rose early and had their meals finished before other clans were around. They acted like this to avoid sharing their meal with others.

A small group that has separated from the Nitáuyiks and currently is considered to be a new clan has the modern name of Nitáisiksikimisimaiks (Lone-coffee-makers). It is said that the wife of their chief had the habit of making coffee for herself in a small coffee pot. So here we have a third case where a Peigan clan is shamed by a name as being selfish and stingy.

The Moχkámiks (Pelicans) were also egotistical and could not camp with the other Peigan, because they always ended up feuding. That is why they used to set up their tents isolated from the rest. That is what the tradition tells, and as with the Isksínaitapiks and the A'pekaïks, there is no reason to associate this animal family name with a totem. We have here common nicknames without a mysterious background.

Like the Moχkámiks, the Nitáitskaiks (Lone-fighters), who separated only recently from the Iχ´púχsimaiks, are known as being very troublesome. Their chief was always fighting, and when he fought, his children and younger brothers helped him. They were called Nitáitskaiks because they were constantly fighting others.

One other clan had two different names that were related to mutual rivalry, which was a characteristic of this clan. They were first called Motátosiks (All-medicine-men) because all of them, even the youngsters, worked as medicine men. Later they got the name Motúiinaiks (All-chiefs) because each one of them, even when still young, behaved as a chief.

However, the Aápaitapìks (Blood-people) owe their name to a quite innocent peculiarity. Their chief, when he killed a buffalo, used to make sure that none of the blood, which he liked very much, was lost. Nínaist àku and Síkimi-å`χkitopi, whom I mentioned above, belong to this family. Because this is so curious, I will tell you about the characteristic Síkimi-å`χkitopi ascribed to his own family: "In the old times most members of this family were tough and brave and rich, and all were good-natured and honest. They also liked lewd conversations, but they never married their own relatives. At present they still amuse themselves with lewd language, but these days they no longer do so in the presence of women. Most are still friendly and honest, but some are not honest, though they are never in big trouble (because of killing someone or theft). They don't like a relative to be cornered during a fight, but they will always defend them. But this never occurs. Currently, a few of the women are very decent but most are not. They may drink whiskey, smoke and lie, just like the men. They are also fond of men." The behavior of Síkimi-å`χkitopi himself demonstrates that the Aápaitapìks like to defend their relatives or friends in a fight. Sometime before we arrived at the reservation he took a white man, who had insulted an Indian and threw him down and stomped him in the face, for which he was incarcerated for some time in the Agency prison. He had not yet been released for long, when I happened to get in touch with him in an Indian camp. Since then he has served us with utmost loyalty and self-negation.

In the past the Sikátsìpamaiks (Black-patch-people) were known for looking dirty. Because they were always wearing patched moccasins, they were called the Sikátsìpamaiks.

The Myåχkínaiaiks (Hard-top-knots) are so named because all of their chiefs possessed "medicine-pipes" and they wore their hair in a topknot.

The Síkoχkitsimaiks (Black-doors), a new group that only separated recently from the Sikátsìpamaiks, derive their name from the fact that their tents had narrow entrances that were very dirty because upon entering and leaving they always rubbed on the sides of the opening to the tent.

The Itstsúyiks (Rough-mouths) are a young branch of the Aápaitapìks. According to Nínaistàku they are named after their chief, who, unlike the habits of Indians, wore a moustache.

The Saχkókiniks (Short-necks) got their name because of their short necks, which distinguished them from other clans. They also don't belong to old families, but only sprouted recently from another clan.

The last family name, the origin of which I became familiar with, is Kaiékaukèkiniks (White-breasts). This new clan was so named because their chief, Míkskimisokàsimi (Iron-shirt), had a sister of low morals who was an albino. The same chief, Míkskimisokàsimi, at the birth of Nínaistàku, now 62, gave him the name Matsinámaχkai (Takes-a-good-gun), so you can see that the Kaiékaukèkiniks only got their name a short while ago. Though they don't belong to the old families, the name of the Kàmiχ´táiks, which is considered to be an old clan, dates, as I have just shown, from the end of the eighteenth or beginning of the nineteenth century. And although I intended to just communicate the facts to you and leave the assessment of it to your greater prudence, I can't refrain from remarking that all Peigan family names give me the impression that they are relatively young, while the grouping of the tribe in exogamic clans seems to carry the stamp of being ancient. Did the old family once carry other names and have these been set aside only recently by the current nicknames? Is the disappearance of supposedly earlier names and the emergence of new ones connected to the great changes that the people speaking Blackfoot have had to go through since the acquisition of the horse? Because in this time, covering only a few generations, the Blackfoot's ancestors went from stealthily creeping up on wildlife, to being reckless horse-riders, galloping far and wide through the prairies, a change that must have transformed their entire existence. Anyone who has seen the Peigan's straight, tall stature, "*als wär es ein adlig Geschlecht*" [as if they were of noble blood], and has seen how unequalled they are in their taming of the most stubborn bronco can scarcely imagine that they descended from wanderers on foot. Still, this is undoubtedly the case. The Peigan themselves even know this, as will become apparent from the following story: "The old Peigan all moved to the west. They came up close to some mountains. They crossed them. They came upon a big lake. In the middle of it was a mountain. The tribe sat down on the lakeshore. After a while the leader said to his companions: I will go to that mountain. Wait here for me. And they tied pieces of timber together and made a raft. He went into the water. He paddled swiftly on the lake. After a very long time he arrived at the mountain. He started to climb it. He got to the top. He looked down and on all sides around him. Suddenly he saw some horses. They were on the westside. In the morning he started his return. It was almost midnight when he reached his companions. He said to them: On the mountain are many horses. Tomorrow morning half of the tribe must stay here. I will take the others with me. Then they left. It was almost nightfall when they got to the mountain again. The next morning they arose very early. Some of them went east. The others went west. They started to steer the horses toward the water. All of the horses jumped into the water. The ones staying on the shore moved up and down along the lake. They caught the horses that came back ashore. Half of the horses swam back. Only a few came ashore. The others drowned. They, the Peigan, went home with the horses they caught." This story certainly relates to the first horses that the Peigan possessed. Though it assumes that the horse is a familiar animal to them, it depicts the Peigan on foot along the shore in order to catch the horses coming ashore. Consistent with this is the traditional story that a distinguished woman among the Peigan, who died over a century ago at a very old age, was the first to possess a great number of horses. The words composing the name 'horse' in Blackfoot also indicate a recent origin. Apparently "ponoká´mita" is composed of the words for elk and dog. We probably don't have to be reminded that the horse is not a native animal to America. However, elaborate guesswork regarding the influence of the Blackfoot's transformation to an equine society is not intended here and I see that I wander off too far from my topic. Before bidding farewell to the clans, I will try to give you an impression of the different ways a person is named. Again without the help of Joseph Tatsey and Síkimi-å`χkitopi, it would not have been possible to gather such extensive data as we now have at our disposal. I have already mentioned some things about the character of Síkimi-å`χkitopi. As far as concerns Joseph Tatsey, I will only communicate that I have not met anyone on the reservation who was his superior with regard to his inborn civility and distinguished bearing. What both men communicated could be continuously verified by comparing the facts that we both learned from all sides. I will restrict myself to the essentials and only clarify the rules followed for giving names, with a few examples. In case the father cannot name his child himself, he goes to a well-known warrior, or a medicine man, or an older woman. The warrior, more often a chief, will name the child, even when it is a girl, after one brave deed or another that he once performed; in choosing a name the medicine-man is guided by a vision; the old woman hears sounds murmured in the bushes along the shore and derives the name from these sounds. A girl keeps the name she receives at birth, in general for the rest of her life, but a boy could take on another name as soon as he had stolen horses, killed an enemy or had distinguished himself by another manly deed. It seldom happens that a man changes his name more than once and sometimes, not unlike the old Beggars (*Geuzen*), he takes on a snappy nickname, which he gets through some personal peculiar circumstance.[3] I will get back to these nicknames that became first names, but first I will give you examples of names that are bestowed upon a child at birth.

A name given by a medicine man was Siékaii (Mink), as Nínoχkyàio's father was called in his early childhood, because the medicine man who gave the name had seen a mink in his dream. Two other names are Páiautaisètsikòai (Came-back-walking-with-the-rattles) and Åχká naioχtòai (Hurt-by-all). This last name is a girl's name and is, like the previous one mentioned, connected with the rattling buffalo hoofs that were used by the medicine-man as a rattle. A name given by an old woman to one of her grandsons is Anátsepiståχkumi (Yells-as-a-pretty-owl).

Lots of names are given by warriors. Nínoχkyàio got his first name Itóminàmaχka (Takes-the-first-gun) from his uncle on his mother's side Ekutsótskina (Red-horn), who, when attacking the enemy, had captured the first gun. At birth Nínaistàku was called, as I already told you in another context, Matsinámaχkai (Takes-a-good-gun), an allusion to the fact that Míkskimisokàsimi, who gave him this name, had taken a new gun from the tent of a Snake Indian. Of the same nature is the name Akáinamàχka (Many-guns) and, the boy's name Nátokotsìnamaχk (Takes-two-guns) is also tied to the capturing of guns. Nátokotsinamaiàke (Takes-two-guns-woman) is the female counterpart. The name Nátokesapàpistàtsis (Two-spears) indicates that spears have been captured by the name-giver and Sapαpístasàke (Spear-woman) is the female variant. A son, daughter and cousin of Nínaistà ku have names that recall the fortunate theft of a black horse that was

captured in broad daylight from the Crows by Nínaistàku. The chief gave a number of names, partly to his own children and grandchildren, partly to strangers, and they were names that alluded to events from, by Indian standards, a very honorable warrior career.

In De Josselin de Jong's notes I find the following piece of information about Nínaistàku giving a name to one of his grandsons: "Before he named him, he spoke like this: In my younger days I often made mischief around the camps, but I never got into trouble by it. Then he told, that he stole lots of things and horses from his enemies. That he fought in many wars, with many different tribes, and that he was known by many different tribes. That he always got out of danger without being much hurt. That he was shot but twice. He then said: Now, my enemies had very good chances to kill me. I do not see how they could possibly miss me when they were standing in front of me, shooting at me with their guns. All the different tribes heard my voice and would recognize my voice every time we had war. This yelling during the fight I did because I always thought: It would be better for me to get killed by a gun in a quick way. Now I shall give my grandson the name of 'Every-body-heard.' May he have good luck, get no illness, may he not get into trouble among his own people and be useful and honest when grown-up" [De Josselin de Jong 1914, 113]. The bestowing of a name always occurs in such a solemn manner, and when a warrior acts as a name giver, he will never fail to elaborately recount the event to which the name alludes. All names given at birth, either by the father or by another man who has distinguished himself in war or by magical medicine, or by an old woman who hears voices in the mysterious sounds of nature, have a prophetic meaning.

The youngster, who had been proven by his deeds to be a man, was entitled to trade the name, which he had had since his earliest childhood for a new one. I speak here of the past, because the warring with other tribes stopped a quarter of a century ago. Nínoχkyàio told me that, after he had performed a number of brave deeds, he did away with

Itóminàmaχka, the name from his childhood. During one raid he got in a fight with a Dakota whom he killed with a butcher's knife after a gunfight. According to his own words he first gave him a cut to the face and stabbed him near his heart and then he finished him off by cutting off his head. Then the chiefs of the Peigan gathered to discuss it and invited Nínoχkyàio, still called Itóminàmaχka. They told him that he had performed many brave deeds and that therefore he was considered to be a chief, but the moment had arrived to give him a new name. One chief decided that he would be called Nínoχkyàio, after the old Niókskatos (Three-suns), better known by his nickname O'maχksiksisi (Big-nose), who during his childhood had been called Nínoχkyàio (Bear-chief). Thereafter the Peigan held scalp dances one week long.

However, Nínaistàku traded his name more then once. We were told that upon birth he was given the name Matsinámaχkai. When he was fifteen years old, he went on the warrior path and got the name O'maχk'atsì (Big-brave), but the next raid he was called Natósunistài (Sun-calf). Only after a fight with the Cree, in which the Cree chief was killed did he get the name Nínaistàku (Mountain-chief), which he kept since then. Nínaistàku was also the last name of his father. Before he took this name, he was subsequently called Naiístotstsòi (Charges-from-two-sides), Akétsikin (Woman-shoe) and Iχ'tɑtsíkiaupi (Sits-in-the-middle). In passing I would like to mention that not only the father with the same name of Nínaistàku, but also his grandfather Kipitáisuiekàksin (The-old-woman-stretched-a-leg) and his great-grandfather U`nistaiíso (Calf-boss-ribs) had been Peigan chiefs. Nínoχkyàio could boast as well that he is a fourth generation chief in the direct male lineage.

One nice example of a name change among the Blood Indians, who belong, just as the Peigan do, to the Blackfoot speaking people, I derive from a tradition in Joseph Tatsey's family. His great-grandfather, a Blood chief, at birth was called Imótsina (Man-of-massacre). When he had killed an Indian of another tribe during a certain fight, some held the opinion that he was a chief, but others said: "He did not qualify for it." This event caused Imótsina to change his name to Kɑtáiatàχsi (Not-really-good). His son and his grandson later, when they later became chief, did away with the names of their childhood in order to also call themselves Kɑtáiatàχsi. Joseph Tatsey was given this name at birth, but that name is never used for him.

However, this tradition, which in fact is away from my topic as it belongs to the Blood and not to the Peigan, brings us gradually to an interesting category of names that were originally nicknames. If someone heard that someone else called him a ridiculing nickname, he then looked for an opportunity to distinguish himself. If he succeeded and all the members of his tribe had witnessed that he was not a coward, he took on this nickname, which had now lost its nasty character, in the presence of all, as a first name. In case the nickname alluded to vices other than cowardice, a brave deed was still the only means to get rid of the defamation. If someone knew that he had been given a nickname, and he later did not attempt to get rid of the defamation connected with it, he remained subject to contempt and sarcasm the rest of his life. Just as in the names of clans, in the nicknames of persons a strong tendency emerges towards scornful reference of such individual peculiarities that according to prevailing concepts are considered to be inferior.

A certain man who always chased buffaloes but never gave any part of the kill to others, got the nickname A'uàkima (After-buffalo). After he had defeated an enemy, he took this nickname as his first name. Another was called Iníkaiotàs (Fast-buffalo-horse), because at the buffalo chase his horse outran all others, but he was always in the rear when chasing enemies. When he was told he had been given this nickname, he was ashamed and tried through bravery to regain the esteem of the members of his tribe. He killed an enemy and returned with his bows and arrows in his quiver. Only then did he take Iníkaiotàs as his real name. The great warrior who was called in his childhood Pítaisiksinɑm (Black-eagle), was nicknamed I'ksisakauyi (Meat-eater) because he liked to always eat meat. After killing an enemy he declared he wanted his nickname instead of his earlier name, and as I′ksisakauyi he became famous among his people.

Very often someone got a nickname because of a liaison with someone else's wife. The following is a case of this nature. A young man, Makúiimåχsin (Wolf-going-west), had sex with a married Indian woman of his own tribe. Two other women, with whom he also had relationships, got to know this and joked about it. Then a third woman came along and asked what they were talking about that was so funny. They did not want to betray him and said: We talk about Einíotasopoχtsisàk (Whom-the-buffalo-inquires-after) and have a lot of fun about him. Well, there was no one in the camp with such a name, but the woman did not let herself be fooled. She let this rest until she had found out whom they referred to with this peculiar name and soon Makúiimåχsin, when absent, was called Einíotasopoχtsisàk by the entire camp. He found out about this, and as a real Peigan he left, in order to silence the derision by acquiring fame as a warrior. He returned with the bow and arrows of a defeated enemy, and in the presence of his tribe members, he traded the name Makúiimåχsin for Einíotasopoχtsisàk. Later he was given the nickname Osoχkóminau (Pimple-man), which he declared to be his in the same way after performing a memorable act. That is how I was told this story; although maybe not every detail is passed on totally correctly, without doubt it is in essence true. I communicate this to you because it is characteristic of the old Indian mores.

I could continue on for quite a while about the names of the Peigan, but even when I multiply the facts presented for consideration, they would still all fit in the system revealed and it would not yield any new points of view. Why tax your attention any longer? Before finishing I would like to tell you something about the names of certain sacred tents, which in some cases belonged for several generations to the same family. This causes one to think that there had to be an inherent connection between the name of the tent and the family that resided in it for so long. As most of these tents are named after animals, it brings totems to mind. In connection with this I would like to point out that, because of the Beaver dance, the Peigan worship several animals. However, let me tell you immediately that these tents, even if they are often passed down from father to son, are still not connected at all to one particular family or even to one particular lineage, but may be traded indifferently to any new owner. According to legend such tents were given by one or another animal to the first owner, which caused him to be obliged to honor the animal or whatever being with a certain ritual. When the tent was transferred to a new owner, the obligation of this ritual was transferred to the new owner. From this I gather that we are not dealing with totems but with the worship of animals or other beings, which were not assumed to be genetically connected with the worshipper. At most we could assume that a mystic personal tie existed between the donor of the tent and the first owner. However, I don't feel certain about this religious-historical field and rather than ponder these facts, I submit them for your judgement. In the days of the Sun dance I saw several of the sacred tents and De Josselin de Jong photographed a few of them. Though the original cover of buffalo skin has been replaced by linen from the white men, the old symbols of sacred figures are colorfully drawn on this modern cover. I have become familiar with the names of fourteen of these tents of which two came to the Peigan from other tribes. The twelve aboriginal names are Siksínikokàup (Black-buffalo-lodge), Otaχkúinikokàup (Yellow-buffalo-lodge), Kyáiekokaup (Bear-lodge), Pitséksinaikokàup (Snake-lodge), A′monisikokàup (Otter-lodge), Ponokáikokàup (Elk-lodge), Maistókokàup (Crow bird-lodge), Ksíststaχkikokàup (Beaver-lodge), O′maχkskimikokàup) (Big-rock-lodge), Mistáksikokàup (Mountain-lodge), O′maχksikiχ′tsipikokàup (Big-striped-lodge), Ikå tsikokàup (Loop-lodge). To these we have to add Ponokå′mitaikokàup (Horse-lodge) from the Crows and Otskóyis (Blue-lodge), which according to tradition was given to a Blackfoot proper by Ksistsikúma, the thunder, and only shortly are with the Peigans. Though two of the aboriginal tents, Kyáiekokàup and Pitséksinaikokàup, would have been conquered from bears and snakes by the fairytale hero Katoyís (Clot-of-Blood), in general such lodges are considered to be mystical gifts. I only know the tradition with regard to the details of a few tent origins, but I was assured that the granting of such a tent by one being or another in general took place in a dream. Among others, this is the case with the A'monisikokàup, which belongs to O'maχksksìststɑki (Big-beaver), and which according to his own words was given a few generations ago by an otter to an old man who was sleeping on the shore of a river. But sometimes it happened that this gift came to someone who was awake, as will become clear to you from the story about the origin of both buffalo tents, with which I would like to close my lecture:

The ancient Peigan lived in the north. Moose River was near by. They moved. There were two young men. They took their arrows. They went ahead. They said: Let us sit down by the river. There they sat. They started to prepare their arrows. They sat there a long while. One of them looked into the water. He said to his friend: Don't you see anything there, where the water twirls? His friend answered: No. He again said to him: I see a tent there, painted with a black buffalo. I will go into it. Look at me. Then he stood up. A bit further down the shore he went into the river. Then he saw the tent under water. He went in. There were two persons, the owners of the tent. They were a man and a woman. The man said to him: You are welcome. The young man sat down. The man said to him: My son, because you saw my tent, I will give it to you. Pay attention to the inside and the outside. Furnish it like this. Later it will give you an advantage. So I give you my tent. Then the young man went outside. He went ashore. He sat down with his friend. He said to him: Did you watch me? His friend answered: I saw you, when you went into that tent. And he also said: When you left the tent, did you see another tent in the water, one painted with a yellow buffalo? There it is! It is still there. The other answered: Yes, I saw that tent. Come on friend, go inside. He stood up and went upstream to the same place. Then he went

into the river. His friend saw him. He entered that tent. There were two persons, owners of the tent. The man said to him: You are welcome. Sit down. My son, because you have seen my tent, I will give it to you. Pay attention to the inside and the outside. Furnish the tent like this. Later it will give you an advantage. So I give you my tent. Then the young man went outside. He went ashore. He sat down with his friend. He said to him: Our tents are the same. Let's not wait to furnish the tents given to us. When we wait too long, the man will get angry with us. And they left. After a short while they got married. Right away they furnished their tents, the one painted with the black buffalo, the other painted with a yellow buffalo. The two persons lived there. Both tents were painted with buffaloes from the beginning. And this, so my Indian narrator finished, is the whole story.

Uhlenbeck's footnote: With regard to the origin of the Blackfoot speaking tribes, compare with G.B. Grinnell, Blackfoot Lodge Tales, London 1893, pp.; 177 sqq.; C. Wissler, Material Culture of the Blackfoot Indians, New-York 1910, pp. 5 sqq.; with regard to the names of the clans, G.B. Grinnell, Blackfoot Lodge Tales, sqq. 208 sqq.; J. Maclean, Social Organization of the Blackfoot Indians (Transactions of the Canadian Institute, vol. IV, pp. 249 sqq.); W. Mc Clintock, The Old North Trail, London 1910, pp. 200 sqq.; with regard to the family names W. Mc Clintock, op. cit., pp. 395 sqq.; on the sacred tents G.B. Grinnell, American Anthropologist, New Series, vol. 3, pp. 650 sqq.; C. Wissler-D.C. Duvall, Mythology of the Blackfoot Indians, New-York 1908, pp. 92 sqq.; C. Wissler, Material Culture of the Blackfoot Indians, p. 99 sqq.; W. Mc Clintock, op cit. pp. 207 sqq.

Appendices
[to Patronymics and Proper Names of the Peigans]

I. Joseph Tatsey's family

Joseph Tatsey was born on March 19, 1865 and at birth he was named Kαtáiatàχsi (Not-really-good). He is married to Annie Langley, the daughter of a white man, named Lewis Langley, and a Peigan woman named A'skχsàiniχ'ki (Always-singing). This Peigan woman was a sister of the well-known chief Niókskatos (Three-suns), who also had the name O'mαχksksisi (Big-nose), who as a child bore the name Nínoχkyàio (Bear-chief). A maternal grandson of Niókskatos, Lewis Reevis, with the name O'mαχksksisi, now a boy of about nine years of age, sacrificed many hours of play to be interrogated by me about language. Niókskatos belonged to the Iχ'púχsimaiks (Fat-melters).

Because his father was a Blood Indian, Joseph Tatsey is supposed to belong to his mother's clan, the Motúiinaiks (All-chiefs). His mother's name is O'taitsìua (Weasel-body), from which the name Tatsey is adopted into English. O'taitsìua is the daughter of a white man, named John Libby, and of a Peigan woman, Suiinámaiàke (Fringe-woman), who belonged to the clan of the Motúiinaiks. O'taitsìua belongs to her mother's clan because her father was a white man. After the death of John Libby, Suiinámaiàke married chief O'mαχksàpop (Big-plume). A son from this marriage was also given the name O'mαχksàpop and was a well-known chief among the Peigan. He appears in "Bear-chief's life-story," which I will publish in an Appendix of *Original Blackfoot Texts*.

In his childhood Joseph Tatsey's father was called Imótsina (Man-of-massacre). As I mentioned, he was a Blood Indian. When he became a chief, he changed his name to Kαtáiatàχsi. Because of his lineage in the male line, he belonged to the Blood clan of the I'tskinàiks (Horn-people).

In his childhood Joseph Tatsey's paternal grandfather was called Kíχ'tsipùnista (Spotted-calf). When he became a chief among the Blood Indians, he took the name Kαtáiatàχsi. He had two brothers, Mekyáisto (Red-crow) and O'tskápini (Glass-eyes), which were the names they used after becoming chiefs. One son of Mekyáisto is named Nínaikèsum (Chief-sun) and is currently a chief among the Blood Indians.

The great-grandfather of Joseph Tatsey on his father's side was called Imótsina as a child. When he became a chief, he used the name Kαtáiatàχsi.

II. Family of Nínaistàku.

Nínaistàku (Mountain-chief) was born on or about 1848 and belongs to the Aápaitapìks (Blood-people). Upon his birth he received the name Matsinámaχkai (Takes-a-good-gun). This name was given to him by chief Míkskimisokàsimi (Iron-shirt). Subsequently he was called O'mαχk'atsì (Big-brave), Natósunistài (Sun-calf), Nínaistàku. He is one of the most distinguished chiefs among the Peigan. Of his ten brothers, no less than nine attained the rank of chief. The only one who did not is called Sépistokos (Owl-child), but he is also very influential among the members of his tribe. Of Nínaistàku's children I just mention Síkimi-å'χkitopi (Black-horse-rider). Because of the information he provided, De Josselin de Jong and I owe him a lot. A maternal grandson of Nínaist àku is Lewis Cassous, a fourteen-year-old student of the Mission School, whom I not seldom consulted with regards to his language.

As a child, Nínaistàku's father was called Naiístotstsòi (Charges-from-two-sides), and later Akétsikin (Woman-shoe), Iχ'tαtsíkiaupi (Sits-in-the-middle), Nínaistàku. Of his wives I only came to know Náipistsàke (Blanket-woman), who belonged to the Iχ'púχsimaiks (Fat-melters). She was the mother of the currently living Nínaistàku. His father's brother was U'nistaiíso (Calf-boss-ribs), who as a child was called

Itoχkítoχsinàmaχka (Takes-good-gun-on-top). Both brothers were chiefs among the Peigan.

Their father, the grandfather of the present Nínaistàku, was also a chief and was called Kipitáisuiekàksin (The-old-woman-stretched-a-leg). It is not known what his name was as a child.

The father of Kipitáisuiekàksin was called U`nistaiíso, the same as his son's name. This older U`nistaiíso was also a chief.

Nínaistàku could not tell any more stories about his family.

III Nínoχkyàio family

Nínoχkyàio (Bear-chief) was born in 1857 and he belongs to the clan of the Kαtáiimiks (Not-laughers). As a child he was called Itóminàmaχka (Takes-the-first-gun). Later he was called Nínoχkyàio, after the old Niókskatos (Three-suns), also called O'mαχsksisi, whose first name had been Nínoχkyàio.

Nínoχkyàio had been married to two women from the Ináksiks (Small-robes) family, called Paióta (Flying) and Mátsauauòtaniàke (Good-shield-woman), to a Blood Indian of unknown clan, called Itsúiinokå`χkumi (Elk-yells-in-the-water), and in the end with a woman of the Aápaitapìks (Blood-people) clan, first called Sépistàke (Owl-woman) and later Pαstséu. Only one of these women is still with Nínoχkyàio. He has had seven children, four boys and three girls.

Nínoχkyàio's father was first called Siékaii (Mink) and later A'paitsikina (Weasel-moccasin). In his tribe he was a distinguished chief. Of his three wives I mentioned Nínoχkyàio's mother, A'χsikimoi (Went-allright-to-the-upper-part-of-the-lodge), belonging to the I'naksikakoχpuyiks (Small-soft-grease-people), a granddaughter of chief Kipàái (False-pointing). Three sons from this marriage attained adulthood. Nínoχkyàio was the youngest; the older sons were Náipistsi (Blanket-robe), who died after his first war expedition, and Kétokipokàu

(Prairie-chicken-child), later called A'paitsikina. He was a famous leader and was killed in 1879 by the Sioux.

Nínoχkyàio's paternal grandfather was Mokákiepòk (Wise-child), later called A'paitsikina, a great warrior and chief. Of his four wives I know by name Nínoχkyàio's grandmother Nánainiki (Kill-the-chief). Nínoχkyàio did not know her clan.

Nínoχkyàio's paternal great-grandfather was called Itámiapì (The-only-old-man). His name as a child is not passed on. He was a great warrior of the Peigan. His oldest son was Mekyápi (Red-old-man), a chief who caused the emergence of the family name Kàmiχ'táiks (Buffalo-chips). Mokàkiepòk was a younger son.

Appendix B:
Social Organization of the Southern Peigans

by J.P.B. de Josselin de Jong
Conservator at the State Museum of Ethnography, Leiden. (Internationales Archiv für Ethnographie. Band XX. 1912:191–197).

In his paper entitled "Geslachts- en persoonsnamen der Peigans"[a] Prof. C.C. Uhlenbeck stated that – although the social organization of the Peigans appears to be widely different from that of many other tribes – we do not find any trace of original matriarchal totem-clans – yet one fact reminds us of those other organizations viz. the circumstance that these so-called "bands" of the Peigans are strictly exogamic.

As Prof. Uhlenbeck does not give any positive proofs for this statement and it seems to be assumed by some ethnologists[b] that the Blackfoot bands are *not* exogamic, I propose to show in this paper that his assertion was based upon a considerable number of solid facts from which one must needs arrive at the conclusion that the Peigan bands are genuine exogamic clans.

In the first place I call attention to the fact that my chief informant *Síkimiáχkitopi*[c] (Black-horse-rider), son of *Nínaistɑku* (Mountain-chief) expressed himself about sexual intercourse and marriage between persons belonging to the same band in the following strong terms: "it is considered a *mean, awful* thing."

Secondly I beg to remind the reader of Prof. Uhlenbeck's communication that the Fat-melters owe their reputation of being uncommonly shameless to the fact that they do not shrink from marrying within their own clan.

To the moral sense of my friend *Síkimiáχkitopi*, seducing one's own brother's wife and marrying a girl of one's own clan are similar proceedings: one is as horrible as the other. Anyone who had noticed the expression of his face, the sound of his voice and his short bashful laugh, as he told me these things, would be as thoroughly convinced of the truth of them, as I am. But since personal impressions are not to be taken as proofs, I shall communicate some facts, by which those impressions are fully confirmed. From the following list of names in connection with the respective clans it will appear that endogamic marriages occur rather frequently in the Fat-melters-clan only, which fact agrees perfectly with the independent statements of both our informants: *Síkimiáχkitopi* and Joseph Tatsey.

I. Husbands belonging to the *Fat-melters*-clan.

Akáinamαχka: Many-guns[d] (government's name: David Scabby-robe); married with *Enáksinopåχkumi*: Small-fox-howl-woman (same clan).

Ekotsésapopi: Red-plume; m.w. *Ékaistαpinnima*: Catches-before (Blood tribe, Canada).

Otαχkúisipistoyi: Yellow-owl; m.w. Margaret Spotted-bear (Black-doors).

Makúyisapopi: Wolf-plume; m.w. *Étomauayakeei*: First-strikes (All-chiefs).

O'mαχksístsepαnikim: Sparrow-hawk (g.n.: Mike Little-dog); m.w. *A'χsiksipistakei*: Indian-pillow-woman (same clan).

Penotúyomαχkani: Running-fisher; m.w. *Netásepiake*: Chase-after-enemy-alone-woman (same clan).

Manókini: New-Breast; m.w. *Innåske*: Long-face (same clan).

Enésikini: Buffalo-hide; m.w. *Kiχ'tsípimyake*: Spotted-woman (Black-doors).

A'pautsisapoyi: Looking-for-smoke; m.w. *Epetsístayake*: Dived-out-woman (Buffalo-chips).

E'tspyåχketopi: Middle-rider; m.w. *Kátaitåχkyayake*: Not-really-bear-woman (Black-doors).

Néokskaunistayi: Three-calf; m.w. *Námaimatake*: Takes-gun-woman (Blood tribe, Canada).

A'paisiksinαmmi: Black-weasel; m.w. *Påste: ?* or *Natóχkstse*: Medicine-shell (Bloods).

Sátapikstòkitayi: Split-ears; m.w. *Esináχsenikei*: Fine-killing (clan unknown).

Ísistsekoαni: Wolverine; m.w. *Páyotapoauαχkayi*: Walking-back-to (same clan).

Stάmiksesiksinαmmi: Black-bull; m.w. *Akénausei*: Makes-her-looks-like-woman (Blood tribe, Canada).

Nisámayokayi: Long-time-sleeping; m.w. *Páyotεniχ'kαtayi*: Calling-back (same clan).

O'ki: Root (g.n. Henry Hungry); m.w. *Neétαχtaitapiake*: River-people-woman (g.n.: Katie Smith, Cree tribe).

Sikskenayi: Black-face-man; m.w. *Sépisisoyàke*: Night-cuts-woman (same clan).

A'χsεnayi: Good-gun (g.n. Jim No-chief, nickname: Dandy Jim); m.w. *Ísksípyayi*: Brings-back (same clan).

I'mmoyésokasimi: Hairy-coat; m.w. *Kanókani*: Old-medicine-lodge (Bloods).

Sépanamαχka: Takes-gun-at-night (g.n.: John Night-gun); m.w. *Otχkúikaisi*: Yellow-squirrel (same clan).

Sákyautsisei: Still-smoking; m.w. *Istsitsáutåχpotàkei*: First-snowstorm-woman (same clan: daughter of Black-weasel's).

Sistsáuanayi: Bird-rattler; m.w. *Náipistsake*: Rag-woman (same clan).

Stάmiksesαχkùmapi: Bull-boy (g.n. Daniel Bull-Plume); m.w. *A'χsipiksakei*: Good-strikes-woman (Bloods).

Apinákuipeta: Morning-eagle; m.w. *Etåχkítauayakei*: Strikes-on-top-woman (Buffalo-chips).

Makúyistapistani: Strange-wolf; m.w. *Náyistotsinni*: Holds-on-both-sides (Blood tribe).

II. Husbands belonging to the *Bloods*-clan.

Nínaistαku: Chief-mountain (called Mountain-chief); m.w. *Ksístapinamayàke*: For-nothing-gun-woman (Blood tribe, Canada).

Síkimiåχkitopi: Black-horse-rider (g.n.: Walter Maintain-chief);

m.w. *Sesákunski*: Spotted-forehead (g.n. Annie Bull-plume, Blood tribe, Canada).

Íssokuyomαχkani: Heavy-runner; m.w. *Ksístapiniskimmɛ*: Nothing-buffalo-rock (All-chiefs).

Stάmiksonista: Bull-calf; m.w. *Náipistsake*: Rag-woman (different clan).

Nátχkotχkitopi: Double-rider; m.w. *Ksistúyetsima*: Was-astray (Northern Peigan tribe, Canada).

Námαχka: Takes-gun; m.w. *Akémi*: Woman-body (Fat-melters).

A'kaina: Old-chief; m.w. *Apinákake*: To-morrow-woman (different clan).

E'kasαχkumi: Shoots-ahead (g.n. John Old-chief); m.w. Emma Morning-gun (Fat-melters).

Páyotsinnautsei: Hold-each-other (g.n. John Kicking-woman, a wrong translation of *Kipitásoyekassin*, his father's name, which means: Old-woman-stretches-her-leg); m.w. *Matsòomótsta*: Fine-massacre (Buffalo-chips).

Síkάχkeka: Chew-black-bone; m.w. *Máni*, Indian pronunciation of Mary, (Not-laughers).

Sóatseiχ'pòtamiso: Tail-feather-coming-over-the-hill or (Indian nickname) *Akáunåyi*: Many-shots; (by the whites nicknamed "Brockie"); m.w. *Pikséksenɛtapyake*: Snake-Indian-woman (Fat-melters).

Sépistokosi: Owl-child; m.w. *Máni*: (Mary, Blood tribe, Canada).

A'yisuyisami: Medicine-boss-ribs; m.w. *Sikskyáke*: Black-face-woman (Bloods).

Sáukiχ'tsoyi: Stretch-out (g.n. John-Head-carrier); m.w. *Sepéinimake*: Night-catches-woman (Camp-in-a-bunch-people).

Páyotstso: Meet-together (g.n.: Barney Calf-ribs); m.w.

Matsésepii: Fine-chase-after (Fat-melters).

Sepistúikimani: Owl-top-feather; m.w. *Síksikekayàke*: Black-spot-on-back-woman (Not-laughers).

Íssoksínamayi: Heavy-gun; m.w. *A'χsotamake*: Fine-leader-woman and *Sékitsòake*: Black-good-looks-woman (both belong to the Bloods, they are full sisters).

Ksámαskinɛ: Hump-back; m.w. *Nåχkitsóake*: Good-looks-woman (Skunks).

Enéstauase: Buffalo-grown (called Buffalo-body); m.w. *A'uotanyake*: Shield-woman (Buffalo-chips).

Peksí: Chicken; m.w. *A'χsaipemi*: Came-inside-all-right (Black-patch-people).

Emåyénam: Hairy-looks (g.n. Oliver Sandoval, half-breed, father white); m.w. *Sekayáke*: Mink-woman (Bloods).

Éksisαkåyi: Meat-eater (g.n. Tom Kyaio, half-breed, father white); deceased wife: *Ayíkski*: Shady-face (Bloods).

Piyí: Pemmican (g.n. Peter Marceau, half-breed, father white); m.w. Maggie Rose (Lone-eaters or Lone-fighters[c]).

Ispíksise: Thick-ass (g.n. Peter Cadotte, half-breed, father white; m.w. *Matsóomótsta*: Fine-massacre (All-medicine men).

These four half-breeds were adopted and bred among the Blood-people but, as there does not exist any real family relation between them and this clan the marriages of two of them with Blood-girls are quite "comme il faut".

III. Husbands belonging to the *Lone-eaters-* (or *Lone-fighters-*)clan

Kátaisokàsimi: No-coat; m.w. *Máni* Mary (Not-laughers).

Soyá: Wades-in-water; m.w. *Sótoake*: Knife-case-woman (All-chiefs).

Kátaukyayo: No-bear (g.n. Henry No-bear); m.w. *Tápake* (Meaning unknown to S., same clan).

Mékaninnima: Painted-wing; m.w. *Étåχketauayake*: Strikes-on-top (Bloods).

Káka: (meaning unknown to S.; g.n. Eddy Running-crane); m.w. *Otsikóani*: Brown-calf (All-chiefs).

Makskeánikapi: Bad-looking-face-young-man; m.w. *Saχkáke*: Short-woman (Fat-melters).

Sépyoto: In-the-night-comes; m.w. *A'uatåχtsepiàke*: Chase-it-with-his-own-woman (Camp-in-a-bunch-people).

Séksipa: Bite; his deceased wife belonged to a different clan.

Nápiinna: Old-man-chief; m.w. *Nátχkosipistàke*: Double-owl-woman (Flat-head tribe).

IV. Husbands belonging to the *Black-patch-*clan

Imitáikoani: Little-dog; m.w. *Soyáuauαχkàye*: Walking-in[-water] (Bloods).

O'mαχkokuyàtose: Big-wolf-medicine; m.w. *Matsóomótsta*: Fine-massacre (Not-laughers).

O'mαχkaisto: Big-crow; m.w. *A'measeitsìtsko*: Bushes-up and *Apiksístsimake*: Glass-woman (both belong to the Lone-eaters).

A'ikαχtsei: Gambler; m.w. *Máni*: Mary (Not-laughers).

Stáχtapautsìmmi: Under-swims; (his wife belongs to the Bloods).

Pistspíta: Falls-inside (nickname); m.w. *Otsémi*: Guts-woman (Lone-eaters).

Stámiksèna: Bull-chief; m.w. *Aikáχpsiso*: Many-cuts-with (Fat-melters).

Manikápeinεmi: Young-man-chief; m.w. *A'uatåχtsìso*: Cuts-it-with-his-own (Blood tribe, Canada).

V. Husbands belonging to the *Buffalo-chips-*clan

Páχtsisimake: Stabs-by-mistake; m.w. *Ksestsikúmikamosàke*: Steals-in-the-daytime-woman (Bloods).

A'χkyapina: Home-gun; m.w. *Akayáχkuyinimake*: Many-pipes-woman (same-clan).

Neókskaina: Three-guns; m.w. *Siksístsiksena*: Black-snake (Not-laughers).

A'uakima: After-buffalo; m.w. *E'kaikχkane*: Nose-cut-already-off and *Aχkúyinimàke*: Pipe-woman (both belong to the same clan).

Pαχkápsαχkùmapi: Lazy-boy; m.w. *Otáki*: Shadow (clan?).

VI. Husbands belonging to the *Skunks-*clan

Sóatsis: Tail-feathers; m.w. *A'pekayàke*: Skunk-woman (Camp-in-a-bunch-people).

Nisámoχkotoki: Old-rock; m.w. *O'mαχkatayàke*: Big-bob-cat-woman (Camp-in-a-bunch-people).

Peyáni: Far-robe; m.w. *Nátχkotsikamosàke*: Double-steals-woman (Camp-in-a-bunch-people).

Páyotayàkχkumei: Aims-back; m.w. *Kayetså'χkumi*: Howls-on-top (Fat-melters).

Ekotsékakatosi: Red-star; m.w. *Nàχkàχksísake*: Has-nose-woman

(Bloods).

Pátα: Eating-grease; m.w. *Natóisεtsikumαχka*: Medicine-rattlers-running (Bloods).

Unistássαmme: Calf-looking; m.w. *Otáitapu*: Weasel-went-to (Bloods).

O'mαχkùnnikis: Big-teat; m.w. *Natoyínεmiskàke*: Medicine-pipe-woman (Not-laughers).

VII. Husbands belonging to the *Camp-in-a-bunch*-clan.

Mékskimyàuyi: Iron-eater; m.w. *Sikáipistsake*: Black-blanket-woman (Small-robes) and *Pistúske*: Night-hawk-face (Skunks).

Unisstáyi: Calf-robe; m.w. *E'tomauayàke*; Strikes-first-woman (Small-robes) and *Makáke*: Short-woman (Camp-in-a-bunch-people).

Kátsikomåχkitòpi: Day-rider; m.w. *Soyéniki*: Kills-in-the-water (Bloods).

Unistayákaupi: Calf-sitting; his deceased wife was *Matsóomótsta*: Fine-massacre (Bloods).

O'mαχksistòani: Big-knife; m.w. *Akáikiχ'tsìpimyàke*: Many-spots-woman (Bloods).

Otχtó: Heel; m.w. *Kayíχ'tsipiniki*: Spotted-kills (Bloods).

Mátsipáupi: Sit-up-again; m.w. *Natoómαχkiχ'kináake*: Medicine-sheep-woman (Buffalo-chips).

Mékskimmekìnni: Iron-necklace; m.w. *Etsípstsenìkyi*: Kills-inside (Not-laughers).

Ksináapi: Old-coyote; m.w. *Imαkséni*: Orphan (Not-laughers).

Apuyá: Light-coloured-face; m.w. *Nitsítake*: Lone-woman (Black-patch-people).

O'mαχkseksiskstαke: Big-beaver; m.w. *Sepyå'χkumi*: In-the-night-howls (Blood-tribe, Canada)

E'stskimautsisei: Flint-smoker (?); m.w. *Stáχtsiksiskstαki*: Under-beaver (Camp-in-a-bunch-people).

VIII. Husbands belonging to the *Not-laughers*-clan.

Nínåχkyayo: Bear-chief; m.w. *Etsóyinokåχkumi*: Howls-like-an-elk-in-the-water (Bloods).

Kyáyeputa: Bear-flying (?); his wife belongs to the All-medicine-men.

Tsáni: (John; g.n. John Big-lake); m.w. *Nátokesumyàke*: Two-times-waylay-woman (Buffalo-chips).

Akáinamαχka: Many-guns; m.w. *O'mαχkatayàke*: Big-bob-cat-woman (Black-patch-people).

O'mαχksikeisòmε: Big-moon; m.w. *Nisámunistαχsi*: Long-time-calf (Black-patch-people).

IX. Husbands belonging to the *Small-robes*-clan.

Nátsikαpαχpakùyesuyi: Double-blaze; m.w. *Natoyíksiskstαki*: Medicine-beaver (Camp-in-a-bunch-people).

Péta: Eagle; his wife belongs to the Blood tribe, Canada.

Apyómita: White-dog; m.w. *Soyéksini*: In water-hog (Northern Peigan tribe, Canada).

Mímmeksi: West-point-bank; m.w. *Káyåχkyòpi*: Her-head-towards-dry-meat (Bloods).

Nesótskinaa: Four-horns; m.w. *Ikakótsenàke*: Short-gros-ventre-woman (Bloods).

Pétautokàne: Eagle-head; m.w. *Etsímmake*: Needy-woman (Blood tribe, Canada).

Méksikàuaa: Red-feet; m.w. *Aní*: Annie (Black-patch-people).

X. Husbands belonging to the *All-chiefs*-clan.

Pétaikiχ'tsìpimi: Spotted-eagle; m.w. *Páyotåχkota*: Hands-it-to (Bloods).

Étskinàyi: Horn; m.w. *Mαtsóake*: Good-looking-woman (Fat-melters).

Stαmiksátose: Medicine-bull; m.w. *Etséke*: Sore-back (Buffalo-chips).

Etsúyåχkumi: Howls-in-the-water; m.w. *Myánistsìnamayàke*: All-different-gun-woman (Same clan).

Motúina: All-chief; m.w. *Enåksiniskìmmi*: Small-buffalo-rock (Camp-in-a-bunch-people).

Otsikôåχsoyis: Calf-tail; m.w. *Ayóχketsìnamayake*: Different-gun-woman (Bloods).

O'mαχksiniståmmi: Lodge-pole; m.w. *Sekí*: Greasy (Same clan).

Netå'χkina: Show-chief; m.w. *Tŏto* (nickname for "louse", Bloods).

Asenáikoαn: Cree; m.w. *A'kinis*: Agnes (Black-patch-people).

Ekotsésinopa: Red-fox; m.w. *Matsóomótsta*: Fine-massacre (Northern Peigan tribe, Canada).

Ekotsótokani: Red-head; m.w. *Nátokyauayàke*: Two-strike-woman (Camp-in-a-bunch-people).

Akáukαmαni: Many-begs-for; m.w. *Sapapístatsàke*: Spear-woman (Small-robes).

Asoyátsima: Side-bag; m.w. *Nátχkotsikamosàke*: Double-steals-woman (Bloods).

Anátsanαm: Pretty-face; m.w. *Koni*: Snow (Bloods).

Potάχkuyi: Make-fly; m.w. *Tsóni*: Julia (Black-patch-people).

Nátokesαpapistα`tsis: Two-spears; m.w. *Natoyíkana*: Medicine-light (same clan).

Enápitsi: Marrow-bone; m.w. *Potsínni*: Hold-each-other (same clan).

Manáisto: New-crow; m.w. *Otáikimàke*: Brass-woman (Camp-in-a-bunch-people).

Studying this list we find that out of twenty-six marriages of Fat-melters, here given, as many as eleven are endogamic (one uncertain).

In the Bloods-clan the proportion is entirely different: here we find twenty exogamic and five endogamic marriages. But among these five husbands there are two who do not count because they are half-breeds. If we also subtract the other two half-breeds from the whole number of exogamic marriages, the remainder amounts to eighteen exogamic against three endogamic ones.

Among the Lone-eaters we find eight exogamic marriages and one endogamic couple: reckoning with the fact that *Síkimiåχkitopi* considers the Lone-eaters and the Lone-fighters to be the same clan, one has to acknowledge that this last-mentioned couple too may be exogamic.

The nine Black-patch couples are all exogamic.

The Buffalo-chips, on the contrary, seem to show a tendency to tread in the steps of the Fat-melters (two exogamic three endogamic); however, the number of marriages noted is altogether too small to justify a conclusion in that line. If the Indians themselves looked at the Buffalo-chips in that way it would be a different matter, but, as it is, we may assume that a greater number of marriages of this clan would turn out a different proportion.

The eight marriages of Skunks are all exogamic.

Among the Camp-in-a-bunch-people we find two endogamic marriages out of fourteen altogether.

The Not-laughers' and the Small-robes' marriages (twelve altogether), are all exogamic.

Finally among the All-chiefs, the proportion is: four endogamic against fourteen exogamic marriages.

Leaving the Fat-melters out of account we find that out of eighty-three marriages only thirteen (possibly twelve) are endogamic. So the frequency of endogamic marriages among the Fat-melters in comparison with other clans is striking indeed. This fact, combined with the indisputable aversion the Indians themselves show with regard to endogamic marriages, proves undeniably that the Peigan "bands" are exogamic clans even at the present time, although it is not to be denied that the exogamic tendency has already lost some of its original strength.

Exogamy of the Peigans

by C.C. Uhlenbeck (Uhlenbeck 1912c, 254)

In his conclusive paper on the band-exogamy of the Peigans (Archiv XX, 191) Mr. de Josselin de Jong says, that I had characterized the so-called bands of that tribe as "strictly exogamic". The word "strictly" is here too much. I was very well aware, that endogamic marriages occasionally occur, not only among the Fat-melters. Therefore I stated in my paper on band-names and personal names, that "members of the same clan *usually* do not marry each other" ("leden van denzelfden clan trouwen *gewoonlijk* niet met elkander").

Appendix C:
Dances of the Peigan (De Dansen der Peigans)

by J.P.B. de Josselin de Jong

Published in: *Onze Eeuw. Maandschrift voor Staatkunde, Letteren, Wetenschap en Kunst* (*Our Century. Monthly Journal for Public Affairs, Literature, Science and Fine Arts*), 201–30 and 369–92. 12e Jaargang, derde deel. Haarlem – de Erven F. Bohn. 1912.

One of the three small peoples, who previously formed the mighty tribe of the Blackfeet (Síksika), are the Peigan (Pekáni), living in North West Montana and Southern Alberta. The two other peoples are known as Bloods (Káina) and the Blackfeet proper (Síksika) and, like the Northern Peigan, they live in Alberta.

The Blackfeet tribes are part of the largest Algonquin language family, which stretches from Labrador to the Saskatchewan River and from Churchill River to Alabama. So, among others, the Potawatomi, Sauk and Fox in Iowa and Kansas, the Ojibwe in Michigan, Wisconsin and Minnesota, and the Arapaho and Cheyenne in Oklahoma, South Dakota and Montana, can be considered their relatives. Of course they don't know about this relationship and a proud Peigan even feels insulted when you communicate that he is tightly related to the, according to him, despicable Cree, "who eat dog meat, yes, don't even hesitate to eat skunks." Still, a comparative study of the different dialects, aided by industrious ethnological research, gave the indubitable result long ago that all these tribes which are now known as Algonquin, indeed are members of one family. Where this family lived before its members spread out over a large part of Canada and the United States still cannot be stated with certainty, but their original homeland, their "*Urheimat.*" [homeland] is probably in the eastern part of Canada.

No wonder most Algonquin tribes have been alienated for a long time. There is no such thing as a communal "Algonquin culture"; just to give one example, the Blackfeet and the Ojibwe belong to very different cultural groups. The first are real prairie Indians, horse people, nomadically bent, born hunters even though these days there is not much to hunt for. Their material culture does not differ much from other, non-Algonquian prairie tribes. On the other hand, the Ojibwe are typical representatives of the so-called "forest-culture." They are not nomadic, only use the horse as a draught animal and are more inclined to agriculture and forestry. If one could only look at the material culture, the grouping of the several tribes would be much more difficult than is the case now. The study of language and "folklore" yields much more important data and from these data it is clear that, staying with the same example, the Blackfeet and the Ojibwe are closely related despite big differences in material culture.

The reason that I happen to mention the Blackfeet and Ojibwe is not just because they are a striking example of what I just stated, but it is also because I had the opportunity to get to know these tribes "in natura" and it is my intention to communicate in this essay something about the religious life of the first-mentioned people.

There is such a strong difference between the dancing of cultured people and that of the "savage," that it would be better to find a new name for the dancing of the "savages." Rhythmical body movements are something they have in common, but that is all. In general the dances of uncivilized tribes in North America can be defined as a religious ceremony, during which rhythmical movements guided by music takes place. I say in general, because there are dances, which have lost their religious character, because they are derived from foreign tribes or because changed circumstances resulted in the demise of a certain religious ceremony. This is so for different kinds of war dances, although the old times of war and buffalo hunting live on in the melancholic memories of the old people and youngsters enthuse over a pristine past that they only know from stories. But, actually the old as well as the young people have outgrown war and everything that goes with it to perform a heartfelt "scalp dance." This does not signify that the songs accompanying the dance, although they have lost the religious meaning of real prayer formulas, are not still being sung, yes, they are even appreciated more than songs of a more indifferent character. These and other circumstances make it very difficult to find out whether a certain dance at a certain moment still has religious meaning or not. One other question is whether for the real redskin dancing is so closely bound to religious sentiments that just through the physical movement he may easily progress into a more or less intense religious ecstasy. With "religious dances" we

only indicate dances, which basically have a certain religious thought of which the dancer is aware. One would tend to think that the religious or non-religious character of a dance would be sufficiently apparent from the conduct of the dancers. Nothing is further from the truth. A redskin can be inwardly completely serious, but at the same time he can hide his inner seriousness behind the utmost extreme outward gaiety, especially when stupidly laughing whites onlookers are around. That is how he protects himself against ridicule, that is how he hides his most sacred feelings from the brutish white man.

For the same reason one can not always rely on information from the redskins themselves, unless one has such a close relationship with one of them, that he does not mind speaking out about everything. I mention this to prepare the readers for a description of the different dances, but I will not be able to explain them with all the details. I will mainly relate what I have seen myself and to what redskins, whose information I deem trustworthy, have explained to me. I communicate several facts on the authority of Prof. Uhlenbeck, who spent more time than I did among the Peigan, who experienced more and in many aspects had a closer glimpse of their intimate lives.

Among the dances, now being performed by the Peigan, there are four, which qualify for discussion. In the first place, because in the eyes of the Blackfeet themselves, they are by far the most important, and secondly, because three are expressions of religious life and the fourth one, a dance in a more proper sense, is a typical Indian phenomenon.

This last one, in which the dancing itself is the main focus, originally did not belong to the Blackfeet. It is known as the "Grass dance," a seemingly meaningful name, which, in this case, does not mean anything, because any data connecting the name and the dance are lacking. The Indians can only say that they "got" the Grass dance from a foreign tribe – the Sioux – and dance it often because they like it, "just for fun." How the Sioux came into the possession of this dance, my "red" friend Black-Horse-Rider (Síkimiaχkitopi) told me the following story.[4]

Once upon a time a Sioux Indian lived by himself in a tipi. He used to hunt every day on the prairie. One day he went out, as usual. He stayed out the whole day, hunting on the prairie. At night he went back to his tent. Before he arrived at his tipi, it was dark. In front of his tipi was a range of high hills and when climbing this range, he heard the sound of a big drum. He stayed to listen to the sound and then he heard men singing and beating the drum and the jingling of bells. He stayed there for a while and it appeared very peculiar to him. At the same time he was afraid and longing to know the meaning of the sound. Finally he took courage and decided to go to his tipi to see what was happening there. Just before he arrived at the tipi, suddenly the noise stopped. He went on. Suddenly he saw many of a certain kind of birds leave his tipi. He understood very well that those birds had made the noise. He entered his tipi and went to bed. And once in bed he kept thinking about the drum and the bells he had heard and also about the song. It was a beautiful song and he longed to know what kind of a dance it was. He fell asleep. In his sleep he saw the birds which he had heard that same evening as a man. That man entered his tent while he slept and told him that he should not be angry that they came and disturbed him. Then the man said that he was going to give him the dance and teach him how to dance it. After he had said this, he told a few other men to come into the tipi. They all came in and sat around. They all had their faces painted different colours and all of them were beautifully dressed. Some wore buckskin clothes, a headdress made of feathers and porcupine quills, moccasins decorated with quills and they had tied bells around their legs. On the east side of the tipi he saw four men seated around a big drum and on the west side he saw several men wearing dance girdles decorated with feathers. Some had beautifully beaded rattles and small beaded axes. He also saw, on the east side, a man who had a whip and a sword and in the middle was a man with a beaded arrow and one other with a whistle, also beaded. While looking at all of this, the man whom he had seen first during his sleep said: "Look how well these young men

have painted their faces and how they are dressed and look at these other men with the dance girdles, they will act as leaders of the dance." Then he pointed out the man with the whip and told him that he was the man who would beat up everyone who didn't want to dance when the dancing was on. He stated the same thing about the man with the sword. Then he talked about the man with the whistle and the drummers. He urged him to watch well and to listen closely and then he ordered the drummers to continue their singing. Then all the drummers beat on the drum, shouted "how! how!" and started to sing. He heard wonderful songs. Then he saw all the young men dance around. After the dance had gone on for a while, the man told him, that now a song would be sung for the men wearing jingles. This happened and then the men with the jingles danced in a row around in the tipi four times. Then they stopped dancing. Then another song was sung. Now the man with the whip danced. Then there was a song for the man with the sword, then for the man with the whistle and finally also for the man with the arrow. That arrow was used as dog-meat fork. Then the man told him that he should memorize the dance very well in order to teach it to his people, especially to the young men.

When he woke up, he remembered everything precisely. He called up all the young man and they discussed it. They all liked the dance and wanted to dance it themselves. This was how this dance was first danced by the Sioux-Indians. Today it is called the "Grass dance."

One other story relates that the Grass dance was "discovered" by the Crow-Indians. They had watched a herd of antelope dance and became so enchanted by that dance, that they adopted it. The story does not mention whether this happened *with* or *without* consent from the antelopes, but the first option is most probable, because dances were "obtained," not "stolen." You can get a dance from people, from animals, yes, even from things, and also, "as a special favour from some 'spirit.'" In this last case it usually is accompanied by other good gifts, such as invulnerability, healing power, in short with one or more characteristic attributes of the "medicine-man." Here one can clearly see again that dance and religion are closely connected: a more in-depth study of Indian dances means at the same time to penetrate in the Indian mystic; as long as we are lacking the right insight, although so far most Indian dances have been described extensively, they have not yet been analysed with the help of all data, so we better stay off this tricky terrain.

I would rather communicate something about the dances themselves. The Grass dance takes place in the open air, within a fenced off circular space with a diameter of ten to twenty meters. Five or six men sit against the inside of the fence crouched around a big drum: they are the singers. They each have two drum sticks, (ordinary sticks with the ends of each wrapped in pieces of fabric or pieces of leather) with which they all at the same time beat the drum in pace with the rhythm of their singing. The singing is so peculiar, so unearthly, wild and erratic, that it is actually impossible to convey the image in words. When hearing this for the first time, you only hear a howling kind of cry, generally starting on a high note, then descending quickly, then rising up and falling down a few times in a strange way, to be cut off in a most unexpected way.

After having heard it a few times, you start to discover that it can surely be called singing and that the five or six singers know exactly what they are singing and that, indeed, they all sing the same songs. When you have come this far, you discover new things on every occasion. You notice that there is a difference between the various songs, and that each song has a rhythm of its own which the singers follow closely and that one person sings better than the other, that is, purer or more rhythmic. Of course all of this is no news, but it gives one a peculiar sense of satisfaction after having repeatedly listened carefully to finally start to hear what you had taken for granted. You could say – mutatis mutandis – the same about the dancing. The first impression is: a colourful rigged up group of painted redskins, whirling around without any order or regularity. You do see that they move their legs with the rhythm of the overpowering drum beat, but at the start you don't notice what kind of

movements they make, because of the variety of activity in the whole scene. After having watched for quite some time, you slowly start to see how their dance is organized and you start to admire their strength, their agility and the suppleness of their movements. You can only totally appreciate the dance by trying to do it yourself, then you finally sense how wooden and clumsy you appear among all these miraculously supple, effortless and rhythmically moving redskins, and you have to acknowledge that their dancing is an art with high demands. The movement itself is quite simple. One foot is lifted and stomped down firmly, but only with the heel touching the floor; immediately the rest of the foot follows. Then the whole foot is lifted again and firmly stomped down, but only with the ball of the foot resting on the ground, then also the other part follows immediately. Then the same movements are executed with the other foot. The knees are kept bent. All foot movements follow each other up quickly and in general the feet lift for a moment only and no higher then is necessary for the execution. As a result this short foot movement barely catches the eye and the whole impression is of a clip-clop crawl. You can make the steps as long or as short as you wish; one coming forward quicker then the other, but in general the shifting is normally slower than walking. Each dancer dances where he wants to. Some dance around the entire circle, others trace concentric circles within the big one, others cross the dance area in all directions. So all dancers mill past each other, there is never any jostling though and they never bump into each other. If many dancers are on the same small spot at the same time, so it is impossible to move, then they continue dancing on the same spot until a space frees up. They keep their distinguished calm; their movements stay quiet, supple and elegant. The upper body generally is kept slightly bent, with a straight back and the neck and head going aligned with the back, so the eyes are generally looking downward. Once in a while the head is flung abruptly backwards, especially at the start of the dance. The arms are nearly always kept at a rectangular angle, with the hands near the waist; sometimes a short distance from the body, sometimes resting on it.

With regard to the clothing, there is such a variety, that, in order not to omit anything, each individual should be described separately. This is because all kinds of old fashioned clothes and jewelry are gradually being replaced by modern products or, because the materials are so scarce and so difficult to obtain that they are forced to choose modern cloths and trinkets. The effort to look old fashioned and striking is dominating. Every redskin puts on what he can get and that is why fantastic plumage has replaced relative simplicity. An old fashioned buckskin outfit, decorated with beautiful beadwork and fringes and painted decorations are, of course, preferred. A redskin possessing such an outfit will not dress in tricot and velvet, not even when it is stiff with beadwork. With regard to the upper body clothing, most have to content themselves with a mostly beaded, black velvet vest or a similar broad band across the chest and back. Sometimes you see dancers whose only covering on the upper body consists of a thick layer of paint, preferably in bright yellow. The legs are thrust into thick, woollen, leggings of different colours and decorated in different fashions, or very thin woollen pants. In both cases the loins in the front and in the back are covered with two rectangular, customarily decorated pieces of cloth. Arm and leg bands with jingles are very common, and girdles, hung with bells as big as a fist, are no rarities. The coiffure is a very important item. Some have their hair in many thin braids down their back; others have it parted into flat strands, that, in order to keep their form, are smeared thickly with paint in several places. Others have their hair hang loosely down the back. Most wear headbands, which prevent their hair from flapping about and also serve to hold feathers or plumes. Everybody wears feathers and plumes. Eagle feathers are especially appreciated and the well-known big headdress, starting above the forehead and hanging down the back all the way to the heels, should be made out of eagle feathers. Today though, only a few can afford this costly show, because eagle feathers are rare and

so are extremely expensive. Fortunately there is one means of decorating left and that is affordable for everyone: paint, rather dye, because it is not paint according to our understanding, but a home-made chalky stuff which, when mixed with saliva, is fit to be used on the body. This beloved means of decoration is used widely. The most favourite colours are red, yellow and white, but also black, brown and green are much appreciated. The way of painting is in most cases dependent on a dancer's personal taste. Not much is left of the original meaning of certain decorations and colours, which undoubtedly they possessed in past times. Very seldom you find more than three different colours on one face, however fond they are of colourful adornment, because the redskin will not trespass certain aesthetic boundaries. Therefore it should be added that, even though they are no longer conscious of the meaning of certain color combinations, certain old rules are still observed.

So far men have only been discussed, but women also perform during the Grass dance, as they do in most dances. Her dance is also made up of specific and simple foot movements, which though they are less energetic, the whole movement comes across as a slow shuffling. They always move sideways and hold each other's hands, forming together a whole or a part of a circle. The foot movements are accompanied by a kind of hip swaying, however, the nature of it stays hidden from the onlookers, because the broad belt (mostly stiff with beadwork or short, copper nails) makes it impossible to closely observe the movement of this part of the body. Just like the men they are painted too, but usually less colourfully, and some are also decorated with feathers. Her costume though, consists of a long, shapeless dress of a bright, thick woollen fabric, with short, very wide sleeves. The colours are generally quite loud, especially on the lower part that is usually decorated with a few, wide, differently coloured horizontal edgings or stripes. Back and chest are hung with decorative bands of fringed beadwork with miniature bells or jingles and quills. Despite the loud colours, the whole lends an especially beautiful impression. The singing of the women differs a lot from that of the men;

it is *softer* in all respects. Men always sing from the chest; that is why the not so beautiful voices, which are not always the weakest, shine more than we think desirable. Women never do this, but always sing with a more or less muffled voice. The briskness, the unexpected stops that are proper to Indian singing is softened by the dragging kind of way that women sing. Especially with the lower tones of the women, their singing therefore sounds nostalgic, even sad, but often impressively beautiful.

In contrast to the men the women sing themselves when they dance. Only a very few times you will see a woman among the drummers, but this is not the custom. In general the women don't take much to dancing, and to the contrary, they are usually onlookers and this amuses them even more than the dancing. They often cheer on the slow men to enter the crowd and, judging from their gestures, they also don't refrain from criticism. They encircle the dance area, sit on colourful blankets, sometimes three or four double rows deep; open spaces, which become filled with babies, dogs and playing children. They form a gentle, easy to amuse, though mocking audience.

"The man with the whip," as mentioned in the story, also plays a role. The whip is a beautiful leather strap, decorated with beads and fringes with which he sometimes lashes out, walking around and yelling in the circle of worn-out men that are sitting down. His antics always cause lots of merriment; however, his encouragement is generally followed up.

Usually the dancing ends with a handing out of canned food that, differing from the custom of other dances, is not eaten on the dancing ground, but taken home by the various dancers.

From my description the reader will not have got the impression that we are dealing with a religious ceremony here. Nothing in the Grass dance, as it is performed today, gives such an impression. The circumstance that the dance is not bound to a certain time, but apparently takes place without an immediate reason or preparation, as long as there are sufficient partakers, indicates that the current Peigan only consider it a nice way of spending time, which can be explained very well because it does not originate with this tribe.

Before dealing with the real religious dances, it should be pointed out that a dance being religious in itself does not prove that it has belonged to a tribe since human memory began. Such dances are based on a certain religion with a certain religious imagery encountered generally not only in one, but also in many tribes. Sometimes it can be shown that they, one does not know how, surfaced in a certain area and spread from there as a powerful religious movement through a number of related and unrelated tribes. In all these tribes these dances surfaced in certain ritual performances and in all these tribes we find, as a result, a certain dance, with, apart from smaller or larger differences, a certain common element shining through. With the real religious dances it is true that it is difficult, if not impossible, to draw a line between indigenous and non-indigenous. That is why, while discussing religious dances, we will not touch this question, but, when we have an immediate reason, will only briefly point out the relationship of dances used by other tribes, which are grounded on the same religious ideas.

As mentioned previously, among the religious Peigan dances there are three, which especially deserve being discussed. These are the "*medicine-pipe*" or "*calumet*" dance, "the Sun dance" and the "Beaver dance." As the name indicates, the first is closely related to a whole complexity of religious images, which in ancient times and today are still being symbolized by the so-called "calumet." Originally the *calumet*, in a narrower sense (the reed-stem with related items dangling) and the pipe (stem with head) appear not to have had the same meaning. From older data, it appears that the functions of the *medicine pipe* in the religious and social life of the redskins (think of the "peace pipe") are based on those of the *calumet*, which is no longer in use. One cannot say with certainty which factors have led to this change, but it should be partly attributed to the ritual performances of smoking and the performance of certain acts with the calumet slowly combined into one ceremony, which could happen so much easier because at the calumet ceremonies, as with so many others, smoke or fire offerings would have taken place. In general the *calumet* or *medicine-pipe* dance has the character of a ritual ceremony the honor of the pipe, with the goal of placating the mystical, dangerous powers related to the pipe. For the Peigan, the pipe has a certain connection with thunder and lightning, but underneath are images of sickening or healing powers, which also can be attained through the pipe. The following is being told about the origin of the *medicine-pipe*.

A man was hit by lightning. He lay death the entire day, but then he came back to life again. Then he made a *medicine-pipe* and said that he got it from the thunder as he lay like dead after being hit by lightning. He also told his people that thunder is a man, who lives above us in another world. That is how the *medicine-pipe* was discovered.

According to the description (the author of this article has not been so fortunate as to see the sacred artifact himself) *the* pipe is described as follows: It has a round poplar wood stem, about one arm long and two centimeters thick, at the one end there is a square mouth piece about two centimeters long and one centimeter thick and at the other end it has a round piece the same size that is stuck in the lower part of the bowl (see below). Starting from the mouthpiece, three-ninths of the stem is covered in beads, the first and third part with white and the second with red beads. The rest of the stem is covered in yellow eagle feathers. Near the bowl hangs a decorative bundle consisting of twelve threads or strings of buckskin, covered in white eagle feathers, the shafts of which are covered in red, white and blue (porcupine) quills. The thread ends are connected to each other with a string of bells; under every thread (under the bells) hangs a lock of horsehair. Also hanging from the stem are three pairs of white beaded strings with yellow eagle plumes on the ends, one of these pairs hangs near the mouth piece and the other two are hanging one-third and two thirds respectively of the distance between the first pair and the twelve strings of buckskin mentioned above. The bowl consists of black (or painted black) stone and is made up of two parts, however,

the whole is always one piece, that is the actual bowl and the piece underneath. The bowl has a bulbous type earthenware shape with or without a short, wide neck. The lower part, which is always separated from the bowl by a short, round or square, narrower joint, may have different shapes, but is towards the stem end always longer than the diameter of the bowl. The height of the bowl with the lower part is about one-sixth of the stem length.

The pipe is the communal property of the whole tribe, but is always temporarily in the possession of a certain person whose role is to be the leader of the different *medicine-pipe* dances. When someone is sick, it might happen that he (or someone on his behalf) prays to the pipe with the silent vow that he will give a "feast" for the pipe if it chases out the disease. If the patient gets better, the "feast" actually takes place in the form of a dance in honor of the pipe. At the dance the recovered patient acts as leader as well as the new possessor of the pipe, who from that moment keeps possession until it is transferred to someone else in the same way. These thank you dances, which might take place at any time of the year – so several times per year the pipe might be in someone else's possession – should be distinguished from the real ritual *medicine-pipe* dance which is performed at specific times and, as I have already mentioned, is connected to thunder and lightning. "Black-horse-rider." who I mentioned previously, communicated the following about this dance.

In the fall or winter the *medicine-pipe* is taken from its wrapping and everyone is invited to look at it. The possessor of the pipe gives a blessing to all the people present in the tent and prays for them. Among the crowd are also the previous possessors of the pipe. After the sacred tobacco has been honoured by the possessor of the pipe, four of the previous possessors each get a drum. Then they beat the drum and sing medicine-pipe dance songs. One at a time the previous possessors rise and dance with the pipe and after a while the dance is ended. The possessor now puts the tobacco beside the pipe, then puts the pipe on the tobacco and finally blesses the pipe and stores it away. Then all present leave the tent. From then on nobody gets to see the pipe without its wrapping for the entire winter.

In spring when the first thunder is heard, everyone who wants to, without being invited, goes with gladness in his heart to the pipe's possessor. He gives a feast and has berry soup prepared for the thunder. This means that they will dance with the thunder and eat and smoke. The dance starts in the same way as in the fall or winter. When the dancing has ended, the possessor takes the tobacco, divides it into pieces and gives everyone present a piece, then they all smoke this in the pipe. Then they eat and drink the berry soup. When that is finished, they all pray to the thunder and say that they are glad to hear him again and to meet with him and eat and smoke with him. And everyone prays that he will not harm him or her during the summer. Then the dance is finished.

The use and the honouring of the calumet are not at all restricted to Algonquin tribes. Ritual acts in which the *medicine-pipe* plays a role has been found in over twenty-two tribes belonging to different language and cultural groups and so one may assume that all these acts can to be traced back to an ancient, perhaps even general Indian ritual. This appears even more probable when one observes the variety between in the religious images and expressions, such variety, that it is impossible to determine the actual ritual's core from the present chaos. My previous remarks regarding Indian dances in general can be noted: a summarizing study is still lacking, but one can already see that such a study very probably would not lead to undisputed results since the developmental history of the calumet ritual is too long for such a study.

Now a description of the third dance, the Sun dance, will be provided. It is of a different nature than the others. If the Grass dance was purely entertainment, one could say nearly a sport, and the *medicine-pipe* dance was one of the many ceremonies, which differentiated itself in the different tribes of the ancients, perhaps once a general Indian calumet ritual, the Sun dance, can not be compared to any of them. It belongs to the dances, which are transferred from tribe to tribe, with the religious images of which they are expressions, influencing the religious life of a whole group of tribes and blending in after a short or longer period. It is not a ceremony which one tribe "learned" from another tribe, but a powerful religious movement, which engulfed the prairie, picking up in one place the tribes' existing elements, elsewhere a bit changed by existing elements, but in the end intimately melting in with the religious conscience.

To convey the full religious meaning of this dance, to describe its relationship to the ancient ritual, thereby rendering a lively image of religious life born from this mutual impact, is impossible for me. Therefore a personal empathy, an intimate feeling, which I lack, is required. I only personally attended part of the Sun dance and not just the most important part. In Sun dance literature one can find many particularities, but the religious background remains veiled in a colourless dusk, the religious element covered by the rite. So what I will communicate about this dance is incomplete. Only after Prof. Uhlenbeck, who in 1911 for the second time spent a few months with the Peigan, has published his experiences and impressions, will it be possible to obtain a complete and particularly correct image of the Sun dance as a religious phenomenon.[5] At present the Sun dance, which was in ancient times in vogue with all prairie people, is performed by eight tribes, which are spread out over a large part of the prairie. These eight tribes represent three different language families, namely the Algonquin, Dakota or Sioux, and Shoshone. So at present it is still very spread out.

The original meaning of the dance has still not been determined. No one doubts that it is connected to the usual "Sun worship" in general and the data appear to indicate that we are generally dealing with an original summer solstice ceremony, but this is unverified and when the particularities of the dance in use at present with the different tribes is examined one encounters more puzzles. All these questions will not be mentioned here, but, before communicating anything further about the Blackfoot Sun dance, it would be desirable to briefly summarize what is learned about the essentials of the Sun dance in general from the existing descriptions.

Summer is the time indicated for the Sun dance, but it sometimes happens in the fall. Some tribes perform it annually and for others, especially the Algonquin, it is closely connected to the vow of a single individual, who is trying to prevent a disease or protect himself against some other dangerous power, especially lightning. This usage reminds us of the *medicine-pipe* dance, which with the Sun dance has another point of similarity. With the Arapaho (Algonquin tribe in Oklahoma) all those making vows, which precipitates the ceremony, function as priests (leaders) at the Sun dance. The other participants are making the minor vows and their participation is not *required*. Tribes where this is not the case, for example the Sioux, has the non-priest participants chosen by a specific priest-college that, if necessary, fills itself up. Usually the whole dance takes eight days to perform. During the first four days, preparing ceremonies take place in a "secret" *tipi* especially erected for that purpose. This is where the priests get together daily and spend time smoking, fasting, praying and "preparing" artifacts, which will be carried during the dance or used on the altar. The large *Medicine Lodge* is built on the last day of the secret rites. Choosing the site, gathering the poles and leafy branches and the erection itself is accompanied by all kinds of ceremonies. The *lodge* can be a round, roofless fenced in space with in a centre pole, or it can be a circular, partially covered structure made of poles with fork-shaped upper ends through which the roof poles run. The diameter is twenty to thirty meters. The entrance always faces the east. As soon as the *lodge* is finished, the priests leave the secret preparation tipi and go to the large *lodge*. That same evening the blessing of the lodge takes place and the following morning, the altar is erected on the west-side. With some tribes the altar is of a round or square piece of ground, cleared of grass and weeds, on which sometimes lie a pipe or a buffalo hide. Other tribes use a complicated design with coloured sand patterns and have sticks set in the ground decorated with rainbow symbols and shrubbery and saplings. When the altar is finished, the dancers who, apart from a loin cloth, are nude, are painted by the priests and given leafy wreaths to wear around their heads, necks, waists, wrists and ankles. Then the dance starts. It is of course performed differently by the different tribes. It appears that, in general, they whistle on flutes of bird bone, which was once understood to be symbolical of breathing. Another element that is found in all tribes is an offering, mainly to the sun. Self torture, which made the Sun dance into a most barbaric spectacle in some tribes such as the Cheyenne (Algonquin) and the Mandan (Sioux), is included among these offerings. Most often one hooked a rope, dangling from the fork of the centre pole, to a kind of meat peg stuck as a pin through the chest's skin to let oneself then be pulled up by it. Or the dancer dragged around the camp one of more buffalo skulls, connected to the skin of the back in the same manner. In some camps a dancer would cut off a piece of flesh from the arm or the shoulder and put this, together with tobacco, by way of offering, at the foot of the centre pole. A less offensive form of offering, which is still in use, is donating worn-out clothing as well as colourful rags and ribbons, which are hung on the centre pole.

After the Sun dance is finished the *lodge* and altar are not taken down; they are considered sacred and inviolable, the property of the sun.

According to G.A. Dorsey, who gave an extensive description of Sun dances of several tribes, the ritual is indeed based on a set of loosely connected, but still very different images. The centre pole was supposed to symbolize the Sun, but also the axis of heaven and earth, and, in some instances, the communal enemy of the tribe. Furthermore, the fork of the centre pole in the image appears to connect itself to the nest of the "thunderbird" which is based on the opinion that the Sun dance not only honours the Sun, but also other forces of nature. Dorsey describes the altar as a symbol of life and fertility and, according to him, the big, round *lodge* represents the entire earth. Like in so many other religious dances, honouring heaven's four areas plays a role in the Sun dances, which is clear from certain symbolic designs.

However, all of this is only a hypothesis and I mentioned it only as an introduction to my description of the Peigan Sun dance. But first I would mention one more fact, which sheds a peculiar light on the nature of the Sun dance and also explains the redskins' special tenacity for this dance.

Dorsey remarks that not only may the Sun dance be called the most important ceremony of the prairie tribes, but it also forms an integral part of their social organization. And indeed, in the wide circle of tipis encircling the big *lodge* during the Sun dance days, one sees more than an arbitrary group that for convenience sake camps in this way. What we see here, the entire tribe coming together, not just for the Sun dance, but for managing their mutual interests; to celebrate a feast together, to mourn together, in short, to be one for a short period of time. And, just as the centre of the camp circle is formed by the revered Sun *lodge*, so is the Sun dance also the spiritual kernel of all this social activity. It is the Sun dance that reminds them annually that they are one: one in religion, but also one in nationality and that is why the Sun dance is suited, more than anything else, to rescue them from soulless indifference whence they would certainly wander off due to the constant impact of civilization. When one keeps this in mind, one can easily understand that they would rather give up anything, except their Sun dance. For them it is the firm anchor of their national consciousness and indeed, as Dorsey states, an "existence condition." And now it also becomes clear why this dance continuously encountered such strong resistance from missionaries and government officials. It happened to be in both their best interests that the religious anchor of their nation's consciousness be weeded out as soon as possible. The missionary mainly fights the former, the government fights the latter and as both are indivisibly connected, both the government official as well as the missionary has declared holy war on the Sun dance. Perhaps the self-tortures previously mentioned

have contributed a lot. However, on the other hand, one can not deny that, though somewhat rough and anaesthetic in form, in principal they are no more unchristian than any other form of nature worship.

In order to return to the Blackfeet it first must be mentioned that the Sun dance, as witnessed by the Peigan and by me, clearly does not coincide with the general description given so far. On the one hand the ritual of the Peigan is less complicated than some of the other Algonquin prairie tribes, but on the other hand, has older and newer elements that one does not find with other tribes.

What is communicated here about the Peigan Sun dance was taken partly by witnessing it myself, but, as I have interviewed a redskin about it, to provide further information. I render his communication as literally as possible. The general account of the Sun dance by Sikimiaχkitopi is as follows:

All poles are lying on the ground and in the centre a deep hole has been dug. Beside it lies a big, heavy pole or trunk with a fork at the upper end. As an offering to the Sun some birch branches, clothes and cotton rags are tied to the fork. In the evening all inhabitants of the camp get together and are divided into four groups; one group for each of the four winds. In each group a few men carry a side pole and the others each hold onto the roof pole that is connected to the side pole. They all stand beside each other, in a circle around the hole and sing and cheer. The women in each group stand behind their husbands and sing along with them. This is the honor song that is sung before the erection of the big pole lying in the centre. The man and the woman, who are the "makers" of the *Medicine Lodge*, stand, in the centre, on the pole. They do this in order to be seen by the sun and to make the sun aware that they are the people who "made" the *lodge*. The man wears a blanket as his only piece of clothing and his body is painted entirely black. His wife wears an elk dress and a medicine head dress. After having prayed, they dismount the pole: everyone is now cheering. Finally some men raise the big pole and stick the lower end in the hole. Then the other men, carrying the poles, raise them all at the same time and place the ends (of the roof poles) in the fork. This all happens very quickly. Now the big pole is put upright, the roof poles pushed up and the side poles put into the ground. Now the *lodge* is built. The sides are covered with leafy branches as a cover against the sun. In the meantime the Sun goes down. Everyone goes to his tent for supper. Afterward they go together again to the *medicine-lodge*. In the west part of the lodge is a separate canopy, covered with leafy branches, about ten square feet, in which one man is seated: this man has to dance through the day and night. Beside this separate part five or six men sit around a big drum. They beat the drum and sing the Sun dance songs. As soon as they start to sing, the man who is sitting alone rises and dances, blowing continuously on a whistle, without leaving his place, until the song is over. For four days and four nights he does not eat anything, he just sits there and most of the time he dances. In the meantime a big chief is chosen to relate the story of his war deeds and horse stealing during the first night in the *Medicine Lodge*. He also tells other stories from his life and about the many dangers he escaped. And he shows how he acted in old times. He does not do that to be seen and heard by everyone: he gives away a lot, guns and horses. Those in the lodge get them as presents. He stops telling his stories at dawn and then another chief is chosen. This one then takes his turn and tells about his life; how he used to kill his enemies, get their scalps and their guns and how he stole horses from the enemy camp at night. He too parts with many horses and other possessions and finishes his story at dusk. Then again another chief performs and this goes on for four days and four nights. All inhabitants of the camp are allowed to be at the dances day and night. When the Sun dance has ended, the camp is broken up and the different families go in all directions to hunt and to pile up winter stocks.

Partly as an addition and as a comment, in a certain sense an account that Prof. Uhlenbeck heard from another redskin is useful. The main gist of it follows here.[g] By the time the Sun dance will take place,

the men go out to catch buffalo; the women pick berries and gather willow branches for the sweat lodges. When these preparations are finished, they sing for the couple that will "make" the *lodge*. The following morning they go together to the place where the *lodge* will be erected and start to work: some cut the centre pole, others the side and the roof poles. The women make soup and drag on little trees. Before they start the actual erecting, the Sun is being honoured with a buffalo tongue by wise women; then they give the buffalo tongue to their spouses and to relatives. At night, when the *lodge* is erected, all the societies enter the lodge and a dance takes place. The following morning the Sun dance starts. The drum is being beaten on split hides by old men and their daughters. When the elders are old and foolish, they tell all kind of untrue heroic facts and think that the people will praise them and that they will get one more wife; these are bad, old men. Then the soup and the meat are brought in. The Sun dancer gets a pipe and the offerings are given to him. He then paints the faces of the people.

From what is communicated here, you can see how things go in general, but a few facts still require some explanation. A big part of the preparations, such as the catching of buffalo, cutting wood etc. is done by the various "warrior societies" which, apart from the function indicated by their name, also have to perform other social and religious duties. It appears that the "Crazy-dogs" society, which had the reputation of being a warrior group of unparalleled courage, in peace time formed a kind of police corps charged with maintaining order and discipline in the camp. Because maintaining order is necessary when a large number of people camp together, it is understandable that the performance of such a corps is one of the social elements, inseparably connected to the formation of the camp circle, only then the entire social organization can and is due to develop freely.

The couple called by Sikimiaχkitopi the "makers of the *lodge*" apparently performs the same role as the person called "the lodge maker" by the Arapahoes and the Cheyenne. This is the person who made a vow to sponsor; meaning to pay the expenses of a Sun dance after a certain vow was fulfilled.

It is more difficult to determine who the "Sun dancer" was, mentioned in the second story. I can only provide the following details, derived from Prof. Uhlenbeck's notes, about the man who performed this role during the Sun dance of 1911.

He sat in a separate part of the lodge. Around his head he was wearing a wreath, and he was wrapped in a thin, long white robe with broad, yellow trim, that hung open in the front. His upper body and legs were naked and painted yellow; his face was painted in several patterns. In his right hand he held a feather, from which three tassels dangled, and in his left hand a little green branch. Time and again he spread his arms wide and then crossed them again over his breast. Between his teeth he held a wooden whistle. From the booth he came to the front and danced there time and again on the same spot. Time and again people approached him; in deep reverence they passed in front of the canopy. From one married couple, the man gave him a pipe and the woman brought a piece of cloth stretched on a stick with some green leaves around it. First they stood praying. Then the Sun dancer danced for a long time in front of them; then they entered the booth and prayed there for quite some time.

Apparently this person performs one or another priest-like role, but from the few data it can not be determined whether he is considered to be a representative of the sun and as such, accepts the offerings to this deity, or if he simply acts as leader of the entire offering ceremony.

It is peculiar that, at the Peigan, he dances alone. In this regard the Peigan ceremony differs from all the others and it makes one suspect, (of course there is no proof) that it will have been different with this tribe too. The performance of the chiefs telling their life histories and mentioning their heroic acts is easier to explain. It is, at a glance, quite a childlike performance. It reminds one strongly of "playing Indian" done by white children, but in reality it is not that senseless. There is an ancient, very widely used way that Indians count heroic war deeds.

This counting occurs in accordance with certain rules; some facts can be counted, others cannot. The hero, giving his account of his heroic deeds for a large audience, will touch or beat one or another item at every countable fact. Originally they count the number of times they touched an enemy – who would have been close to him tough – and then also other acts which one could perform only in the immediate proximity of the enemy. This custom is called "*counting coup*" and when they tell about an old chief who, for example "*counted coup*" ten times it means that he performed ten memorable warrior deeds. It included not only touching (or wounding, killing) of an enemy during a struggle, but also several other acts such as stealing of horse and women and also other deeds which, according to our concepts are not courageous, such as assassination (of course just of enemies, meaning any redskin not belonging to a friendly tribe).

"Counting coup" may take place at all solemn ceremonies and with the Peigan it is still in use during the Sun dance. That currently this has slowly degenerated into childlike bragging, from the scornful remark of a redskin it apparently does not escape the Indians themselves either, is not incomprehensible. At present there is no opportunity for any new "*coups*" so "*counting*" has lost its actual character somewhat. "Counting coup" on the occasion of the Sun dance also used to be done at the Dakota (Sioux), who now no longer do the Sun dance. It still occurs among the Cheyenne, however, not *in* the *lodge* but, (before the lodge is erected) at the spot where the centre pole will stand. As Prof. Uhlenbeck told me, at the Peigan it also happens *outside* the lo*dge*.

A summary of what presently is known about the Peigan Sun dance, can be recapped as follows: The core of the entire ceremony of the offering to the Sun is where a temporary priest acts as a mediator or representative of the deity. Dancing is only done by the priest. "*Counting coup*" adds to the glory of the ceremony. Undoubtedly the Sun dance for the

Peigan is connected to a vow that was made, just as was the case with other tribes. The person or the persons (always a couple) who made the vow, are the "*lodge-makers*." The female partner, – this does not become clear from what is said previously – is the main person; she is the *medicine woman*. During the Sun dance and even long before that, the attention of the entire tribe is focussed on her. Only a woman whose behavior is impeccable – in the first place she is required to be chaste – duly can fulfil this high duty, which rests on her during these days. She not only acts as the main character of the Sun dance ceremony, but also as the confessor for the women of her tribe; before the dance starts, she receives them. In case disasters or accidents occurs, they tend to blame the *medicine-woman*; if nothing happens and everything goes smoothly, it is convincing proof that the *medicine-woman* was conscious of her high vocation. In the summer of 1911 when Prof. Uhlenbeck attended the Sun dance, in more than one aspect the Peigan faced bad luck: public opinion judged that the *medicine-woman* certainly had not been chaste.

The significant moment of the dance itself is raising the centre pole. During the ceremony if ever there is talk of religious ecstasy, it is at this moment. For the audience, – I did not attend it – it must be an extraordinary spectacle and – as Prof. Uhlenbeck told me – for the redskins themselves the act of raising is the most solemn moment of the entire dance.

With the aforementioned I discussed the highlights of the Blackfoot Sun dance; I mentioned previously that I don't dare to speak out about the deeper religious meaning of it and I did not even touch on the various details. Especially with regard to many details, a comparative study of similar ceremonies from other tribes will reveal much.

Part II

The last dance to be discussed, the "Beaver dance" and what I describe now, is of a very different nature. In general the Beaver dance ritual is more transparent than that of the Sun dance, but parallels with other tribes are lacking or are hidden in other non-researched or barely researched ceremonies. In contrast, in the folklore of the three Blackfoot speaking tribes one finds several stories that deal directly with the origin of the Beaver dance or are indirectly connected to it and they contribute much towards the right concept of this ceremony. Síkimiaχkitopi told me the following with regard to the origin of the Beaver dance.

In ancient times the Indians had a certain dance that was only danced by women. As they danced, they were dressed in the same manner as their lover and the dance was called the "love dance." One day the women were dancing this dance. Among them was a poor young woman. She was married to a middle-aged man, who had several other wives apart from her. In general she was only half dressed and she was never clean. Now she was dressed in the same way as "Scabby-round-robe," so everyone in the camp understood that she was in love with him. S.r.r. was a poor boy, who wandered from one tent to the other. When he heard that this young woman dressed like him, he left, without telling his relatives where he went. Before he left camp, the young woman said during the dance: "I will marry my lover when the river water is warm," meaning: in springtime.

S.r.r. left and encountered a beaver colony. The head of the beavers invited him to spend the winter in his home. So he stayed in the beaver lodge for the winter. He noticed that the beaver had one hundred sticks and that he set aside one stick every day. Once the hundred sticks were all in the pile, seven winter months had passed by. He had often observed the old beaver and his wife and children and noticed that the youngest child, who always looked dirty and had a large stomach, was always ordered to sit at the entrance. He always felt pity for the young beaver. Once the seven months had gone by, the old beaver went out once in a while. Once, when he was out again, the oldest beaver boy said to S.r.r.: "Friend, I will help you. Before you return home, my father will ask you what you want from me as a present. I want to give you two things: ask for my youngest brother, who always sits at the entrance and ask for the gnawing stick. He will refuse four times and say that you must ask for other things than the boy and the gnawing stick. Don't give up though, but four times do everything you can to get them. Perhaps he will give you both, but he is very fond of him and I am not sure that he wants to part with him." S.r.r. answered that he would try his best. When the old beaver returned he said to S.r.r.: "Do you see this green leaf?" S.r.r. answered that he saw it. Then the beaver said: "It is spring and it is getting time for you to go home my boy. Here are seven things. Pick two of them." Then S.r.r. said to the old beaver: "My dear father, take pity on me. I have told you that I ran away from my family for shame that young woman was dressed like me. I have done my best to stay here. Think about my tenacity in having stayed here for seven months without ever seeing land. If you only knew how I longed for my family, you would pity me and help me as much as you can. I will tell you what I would like to have: I want the gnawing stick and your youngest son." Then the old beaver said: "No! I will not give him to you, he is young and I love him dearly. He is not sacred and the stick is not sacred either. You have no use for it, it is only an ordinary stick." S.r.r. insisted, though, four times. Then the old beaver finally said: "Well yes, I will give them to you. You are wise to want to have just these two things, but now listen well to what I will tell you and don't forget it. That stick is very sacred and for the rest of your life will be very useful to you." Then he told him about the young beaver, that he, too, was very sacred and would always help him with his great power. Then S.r.r. left. He held the stick in his hand and had the young beaver tied to his girdle. After a while he came across a river with steep banks. He wondered how he could cross the river. After having given it some thought, he suddenly heard the little beaver say: "Father I will help you cross the river, but you have to be very careful. I will build a dam, straight across, but you have to lay down flat on the ground and keep your eyes shut. Whatever you hear, don't look up." So he lay down flat and closed his eyes. Suddenly he heard a lot of noise like beavers building a dam. By magic the young beaver had called to life a lot of beavers and now they were busy building a dam. S.r.r. was dying to see what was going on, but restrained himself and did not look up. Finally, when the beavers had nearly reached the other bank, he did look up. He saw nothing. The young beaver was very angry and said: "Father I will give it another try, but don't look, it won't help you." S.r.r. promised not to look this time and again he lay down flat with his eyes closed. Again he heard the sounds of beavers building a dam. This time he held out longer; the beavers were closer to the other bank than the previous time when he looked again. Again he saw nothing. The young beaver gave him the same admonishment and this time he promised that he would not look for sure. Again he heard the same noises and tried to suppress his curiosity, but when the beavers were even closer by the other bank than the last time, he still looked again. Then the young beaver said that he would try only one more time, this was his last chance. He lay down flat again and intended not to look for any reason. And when he heard the same noise again, he managed to refrain himself and lay quietly down with closed eyes, even though he still longed to look. This time the dam reached the other bank. Then the young beaver said, "Now you can rise, our dam is ready and now we will cross." Once they had crossed the dam, the young beaver sang a few beaver songs and said to S.r.r. that later he could have these songs and that he would get an entire Beaver dance outfit and would be leader of the dance and that, by magic, he would know all these songs by heart. Once they had gone across and S.r.r. took his first step on the bank, he saw the beaver dam behind him break down, float down the river and disappear. They continued on their journey. Camping in one place after the other, they finally reached his tribe's camp. It was early in the morning when they first saw the tents. Then S.r.r. saw a young man who had gone out to the prairie to catch horses. He approached him, warned him, when he came close, not to come any closer and said to him: "Go back to the camp and tell my friends to prepare four sweat lodges for me as soon as possible.

Then I will come to the camp." The young man went to the camp, did what he was told to do and spread the news around. Now everyone had heard that S.r.r. was back. His friends made him four sweat lodges and told him that they had finished. Then he came. He cleansed himself in the sweat lodges and when he was done he told everyone that he had lived with the beaver the whole winter and that this beaver had treated him very kindly. He also told them that he had got the Beaver dance and that he would fix the outfit later. Then he said to his young friend, "We will go to war without anyone knowing where we will go."

They did just that. Along the road he told his friend about the beaver with whom he had lived the whole winter and who had suggested going to war seven times and each time he had to kill one person. When they saw their enemies, he said: "I will be the first man to kill the enemy. Stay here and wait for me. I will approach the enemy alone." So he approached his enemy by himself. He met with the chief and told him that he would kill him. The chief then tried to pierce him with his spear. S.r.r. sang his magical Beaver dance song and warded off the spear with his beaver stick. The chief pierced the stick instead of S.r.r.'s heart. Then S.r.r. raised his stick and beat him to death. He picked up the chief's spear, scalped him, and also took his bow and arrows with him. With all this he went back to his friend. They divided up the arrows. As they were returning and were close to the camp, they sang an honor song. Everyone in the camp heard them and said: "There is S.r.r. returning from his outing." S.r.r.'s girl friend was busy picking berries so a few people went to her and told her that her lover was coming and that she should come along. When she heard that, she dropped all the berries, she had picked, on the ground and ran towards her lover. S.r.r. gave her the bow and the spear and half of the scalp and told her to give them to her husband. Once she did this, he ordered her to change into a clean outfit, to wash herself and to prepare a meal for him. She washed, changed her clothes and got ready a few things for S.r.r. Then S.r.r. was invited to have a meal in the tent and his host told him that

he could make his girlfriend as his wife. He did that because S.r.r. gave him the spear, the bow and half of the scalp as a present. That is how S.r.r. got his lover as his wife. Not long later he called up his tribesmen and his friend and told them that he and his friend again were going on the war path. This time many tribesmen went with them. After a while they saw the Crow Indians across a river. Then S.r.r. said to his friend, so no one could overhear it: "I will swim across the river to the Crows and kill their chief. Once I have killed him I will turn to the East and dive into the water. Then our men will walk towards the East, thinking that I will come ashore east from here. However, I will come ashore on this point and then both of us will be alone." Once he had made this appointment with his friend he said loudly to his men: "I will swim across and kill their chief." They were all very upset and begged him not to do that. After all, they all had encountered their enemy so it was much better to go home and sing an honor song because they had seen their enemies. But S.r.r. said that he would never do that again. In the future he would kill the enemy. So he took his beaver stick and swam across the river. From the other bank the Crow chief waded towards him. When S.r.r. saw this, he also started to wade and they approached each other. While wading forward, S.r.r. sang his Beaver dance song. He sang these words, "Man, help me, do your best and save my live." Then the Crow chief tried to spear him through the heart, but S.r.r. held his beaver stick in front of him and the Crow chief only touched the stick. Then S.r.r. grabbed his spear and beat him to death with his stick. The followers of the Crow chief, very upset, fled and S.r.r.'s friends cheered him. Then S.r.r. dived to the east in the river with the Crow's body. His friends then all ran to the east because they thought he would come ashore on that side, but under water, S.r.r. changed direction and swam straight to the spot where his friend stood. They scalped the Crow and divided the scalp and S.r.r. also kept the spear. Once they were done, their friends suddenly noticed that S.r.r. had gone to his friend with the body of the Crow. So they all came to him and he said to them: "In the future we have to kill our enemy." Then they returned to the camp. On their way they sang honor songs. S.r.r.'s wife was again picking berries, when she heard people calling that he husband was on his way, again she dropped all her berries on the ground and walked toward her husband and kissed him. This time S.r.r. gave half of the scalp and the spear to the former husband of his wife. In exchange he got his second wife. So now S.r.r. had two wives. Some time later he again went on the warpath just with his friend. Again he gained a scalp and a spear and in exchange for the booty he again got a wife. The same man had now given him three of his four wives. Finally he went on the warpath for the fourth time, this time heading for the Snake Indians. He met up with them, there was heavy fighting and he killed and scalped several of them. He also seized bows, arrows and spears and also shared them with his friend. When his tribesmen heard them sing honor songs this time, they all walked towards them, honoured them and made S.r.r. chief of the tribe and his friend deputy chief. And they held a council and agreed that in the future they should have good chiefs such as S.r.r., courageous, honest men. Since then the Peigan had honest, courageous chiefs who fought in many fights. S.r.r. never lied to anyone of his own tribe and was never quarrelsome. He was always friendly. For half of his last war booty S.r.r. got his fourth wife. As well, the man donated his tent and all his possessions to him. And S.r.r. also got the Beaver dance outfit he possessed. The same man served S.r.r. for the rest of his live as a servant. S.r.r. then told his tribesmen that the beaver with which he had spent the winter gave him many songs and all the animal skins that belong to the Beaver dance and that he had to tie these skins in one bundle and keep them as something sacred. He told them that he had learned the dance. He also told them that the beaver had made him powerful and that he would not only be a chief, but also a medicine man. Everything turned out as the beaver had told him.

So S.r.r. killed many different animals, skinned them and prayed to the skins. After he had prayed to the skins, he packed them all together and put them in one bundle with four beaver sticks, four other sacred sticks to pick up ash with and a bag with rattles. Then he performed the dance as the beaver had taught him. And his tribesmen saw the dance and knew that S.r.r. was the first man to dance the Beaver dance and everyone revered the dance. S.r.r. lived for a long time in his big tent with his four wives and his servant who always served the altar during the dance.

Several points in this story require further explanation, which I will give further on. First I will relate a very peculiar version drawn up by Prof. Uhlenbeck, especially because several obscure points in the first story are cleared up by this version.

In the first story the version starts to mention the peculiar dance of the women, dressed as "lovers," but added on is the statement that a man was always very pleased when his wife (one of his wives) had a lover and that he encouraged her to have one, "so the women were not afraid." The following information about the dance outfit of the young women is related: She had dirt on her cheeks and a narrow strip of buffalo hide as a hat. The corners of her dress were cut round and the dress itself looked scabby. When the young man saw her, he said to his friend: "Tell me later what she says," and left. The woman says: "When the river water is warm, I will prove that my lover is a war hero." When the young man learned this from his friend, he said: "I shall go someplace else, because I feel ashamed." He then arrived at the beavers, assisted magically by the young beaver. After telling the old beaver his story, the beaver said: "Look at my possessions, take whatever you want from them." He answers though: "I will not take anything, but I love my younger brother very much so I will take him and nothing else." After considerable discussion the old beaver finally promises to give him the beaver on the condition that he will stay the whole winter in the beaver lodge. But first he is allowed to tell his friend that he has found a good home. So, he gets together with his friend, who tells him that the tribesmen will go to war in spring, so by that time he should be back.

Then at the beaver lodge he learns the beaver songs. He gets seven sticks and every month he has to take one, point it toward the moon, and put it down. After all seven are put down, his time is up. When he finally leaves he has also acquired *supernatural power over water*. The young beaver is *changed into a beaver skin*, which he carries around his neck.

The tribe goes to war. He and his friend separate from the others. After arriving at the river and seeing the enemy on the other bank, S.r.r. dives into the water and appears right in front of the enemy after having swum across the river underwater. The chief approaches him and shoots an arrow at him but hits the beaver skin, which is now *changed into a stick*. S.R.R. kills the chief and swims back with his scalp. His friend gets half of it. Upon returning to the camp the young woman learns this from her husband and then throws the berries she just picked on the ground. S.r.r. gives her the booty *for her husband*. In exchange he gets the woman, the tent and the yellow dog.

After the second war expedition he obtains the man's second wife in a similar fashion. After the third he gets the last woman and the man himself who then stays with him as a servant. He himself becomes the head-chief.

From these two versions it becomes clear what we should consider to be the kernel of the Beaver dance story. In order to elucidate this even more, I will provide one more story, which though it deals with the same theme, for the rest deviates so much from the first one that it can't actually be called a variant thereof.

A man camps, alone with his wives, near St. Mary's lake. His youngest wife, who went out to haul water, meets a young man at the lake who says that he has come to meet her and take her away. They intentionally let her husband conceive the plan to camp there, in order to take her away when he is occupying himself with his snares. He persuades her to come with him. She has to close her eyes and then he takes her along to the lake, under water. When after a while she is allowed to open her eyes she is in a large tent. They marry. Her former husband and her older sister (his other wife) don't understand what could have happened to her. They move away and then return the following summer to the old camping place. The beaver now says to the woman that she should go to her former husband, but should return right away. She already has a child, a young beaver. She goes to her first husband and tells him what happened. He is not angry, but respects her sacredness. When she returns to the beaver, he asks whether the man was angry with the child. She answers: "He felt great pity, but he was not angry at it." The beaver then says: "Because your husband pitied my son, you will go back to him." He gives her his "Beaver bundle" for her husband.

She goes back, the man gets the Beaver bundle and, during his sleep, the beaver teaches him how to sing the Beaver dance. "That is how he got water." Then he says to the Sun, the moon and the morning star: "Teach me twice seven songs." That happens. Then the son says: "When the moon is up, then sing these songs." That is how beaver-*medicine* comes into the possession of those who *have water* (meaning those who have the Beaver bundle).

Despite the great difference in the details, the three stories correspond completely on two points: a man spends some time under water with beavers (I) and returns to his fellow human beings with a certain supernatural power (II). I don't separate these two elements because of the previously related stories, but because in other stories, from other tribes as well, both elements occur separately.

"Beaver-*medicine*," also called "supernatural power over water" or, briefly "water" apparently is not transferred along the path of a mystical connection between beavers and the person they want to favor, but through the transfer of certain artifacts. The possessor of these artifacts derived his magical power from them, indirectly he derives it from the magical power of the beaver itself (for example the skin) or things connected to it (for example the stick). That actually this image forms the basis of the Beaver dance story is clear from a close comparison of the three versions. In the first story S.R.R. obtains the young beaver alive and the beaver stick. The little beaver shows signs of his magical power by helping him across the river as described, but then disappears forever from the story. In contrast the stick is mentioned later again; an unfailing defence and a formidable weapon. In the second story, apparently before being taken away, the young beaver turns into a beaver skin which later, when circumstances require such, turns into a stick. When we take into account that the young beaver is tied to the girdle in the first story (in the second around the neck) and that, whenever there is talk about beavers in a ritual, beaver skins are meant, then likely in the first story we should not think of a beaver, but of its skin. In the third story there is only talk of a Beaver bundle and here it is expressly stated that "having water" (= "the possession of supernatural power over water") has the same meaning as "the possession of the Beaver bundle." The "supernatural power over water" in the first place is apparently meant to have the ability to stay under water for a long time. In the folklore of several tribes it is clear that magical power is attributed to the beaver property and so it is not hard to imagine why primitive people, for whom any likeness meant a relationship, came to consider this property, the few times it was encountered by people, as a magical gift from the beavers.

When now we look at the secondary elements in the three stories, first of all we notice the peculiar women's dance. It is said that the women then "dress like their lovers" and that their husbands look upon this conduct cheerfully and encourage them to do it. Then it is related that S.r.r., when he learns from his friend what happened, leaves in shame. In order to understand this, firstly we have to take into account the position of the married woman and as well the way in which they used to obtain a wife.

In general a man had several wives. The oldest and the first wife held a position reminiscent of married women in cultured people, but the other, younger women were sometimes no more than slaving concubines. So this circumstance explains something: namely, that a man under certain circumstances was ready to give away one of his younger wives. Courting the hand of a woman went as follows. When a young man had chosen a certain girl, he went on the warpath, seized scalps and other booty and upon his return offered this to the father of the girl. It goes without saying that he knew what this meant and would give the warrior his daughter in exchange. According to our story a man could also obtain someone else's wife in this way. It seems that, in general, men were very fond of such gifts (it was a great honor to get something like that), so many spouses gracefully parted with one of his wives for a gift. From there it is only one step further, for the husband to encourage his wives to co-operate. Seen in this light, the peculiar behavior of the women is explainable. A young woman, already having a lover, – it is not important whether she already had a certain love connection with him – apparently indicated in the manner described that she expected to become his legal wife within a certain time period and so would ask him to substantiate her expectations. It will now be clear why S.r.r. felt ashamed. The fact that a young woman openly announced that she wanted him as her husband, was in itself no reason to feel ashamed. But it probably bothered him that he, poor gentleman that he was, saw no chance to live up to her invitation, meaning to buy her from her husband. So he did what a redskin in such case must do; he left for the wide world, despondent, but still not with a sparkle of hope that "something would turn up."

There is not much to say about the stay with the beavers. The time counting method in the first story is peculiar. It is not clear with which units one counted. From the other version it is clear that the length of the stay was for seven moon months, so maybe the figure of one hundred does originally not belong in the story. Why the young beaver has a large stomach and always looks dirty is not explained either. Perhaps this story is connected to the usual fairy tale element of the performance of an especially beautiful, rich or magical and very strong being in the shape of one or another kind of unseemly animal, but this is merely a hypothesis.

It is fun to see the dallying of the old beaver in his attempts to persuade S.r.r. to denounce the gifts he had asked for. Why in the end, does he give in? It seems that the old beaver doesn't control of the situation completely, meaning magically controls it: the young beaver seems to be in a magical state too and by repeating his request *four times*, S.r.r. charms along. – According to the first story – both of them are too powerful for the old beaver and so he must give in.

In the way in which the magical beaver dam came about, we recognize a fairy tale motive that is known throughout the world: the breaking of a temporary ("spell") by not adhering strictly to a prescribed conduct. Sometimes the results are a failure and in other cases, like here, the attempt is repeated several times, in the end with a good result. The number of times in our story is four. One may recall that we come across the number four quite often in these stories and in Indian folklore it is often repeated. For each separate case it can't always be explained and it can mean a number of things, but usually it has to do with the four winds. If Peigan are still aware of the meaning is another question. I don't believe they are, but this is not for certain.

So far the main points of the story with regard to the origin of the Beaver dance have been discussed. A few points requiring further explanation will be discussed when dealing with the ritual itself. As the Beaver dance is so peculiar and a brief description is not sufficient, the following detailed description, given to my by Síkimiaχkitopi is presented in its entirety.

I attended a dance several times, but never saw the entire performance and did not take notes, which is reason enough to give the floor entirely to Sikimiaχkitopi. As for the Sun dance, I will just add to his comments some statements from Prof. Uhlenbeck, who in 1911 attended a whole Beaver dance, yes, even participated.

The leader of the Beaver dance sits near his Beaver bundle. He is praying. Everyone sings. He prays to the sun, the moon and the morning star because the sun, the moon and the morning star are entitled to be part of the Beaver dance. On the other side of the Beaver bundle sits his wife. After praying he picks a young man from the audience to serve at the altar. Then the painting follows. The leader first paints himself, the men who will sing with him and then the boys. This is done so that they will be happy and free of disease. During the painting he is continually praying and singing. His wife paints the women and the girls. Then everything is prepared for dancing and singing. Therefore he calls the young man in charge of this and gives him his medicine stick and a bundle of pieces of buffalo hide. And he says to him, "sit right in front of the entrance and hold these pieces of buffalo hide with your left hand and hold the medicine stick in your right hand directly in front of your chest, and when I sing, pay attention to when I say: 'the old man who walks in this direction now enters the sacred road'; then put the buffalo hide in the ashes and push it in deeper with the medicine stick. Then go to the entrance and make defensive gestures as if someone is trying to hurt you. Then take some charcoal from the fire and put it on the altar." When all of this is done as the leader ordered it, the young man returns the *medicine* stick to him. Now the leader takes some *sweet grass [savastana odorata]* and puts it on the charcoal so the *sweet grass* starts to smoke. This means that the Beaver bundle and everyone present are going to be blessed. Now the regular singing and dancing starts. The leader first sings many songs about the Sun and the moon and also very many about the morning star. Then he sings a few songs about the deer, elk and a few other animals that live in the mountains. Then he takes a square piece of buffalo hide from the bundle, on it are drawings of lizards, and he starts to pray to the lizards. After the praying to the lizards is ended, he takes one of the rattles from the bundle, blesses it and sings a song about the crows and other birds. He then takes out all the other rattles and hands them out. Now when he worships the crows and sings about their habits, the others are ready to beat with their rattles on the buffalo hides, which lay in front of them. The leader repeats in his song the words: "I like my rattles." After he has pronounced these words four times, he beats on the *medicine* skin with his rattle and all the others imitate him, and sing along with him, while continuing to beat on the skins with the rattles. And these are the songs that take about a half-day to sing. Next the leader starts to pray and sing to about four or five beaver skins and he orders a few women, his own wife and three or four others, to kneel down in front of him. When they have finished worshipping the beaver skins, he gives one of them to his wife and the other skins to the other four women. Then he starts to sing the beaver songs again and the women start dancing. They move their knees and imitate the movements of a live beaver with the skins. For a while they make diving movements with them and then they stand up and start a round dance, each with a beaver skin on their shoulder. The leader of the women holds her beaver skin in her hands. They dance around four times and then sit down. Now the leader of the dance is tired of singing and rests for a while. The young man who serves at the altar fills up the medicine-pipe and gives it to the leader. He first holds it toward the sun and prays for a quite a while, then he holds it toward the moon, which he calls "the old woman." Next he points it downward and prays to the ground and to the trees growing in it and all the animals and mountains and the grass too. Then he lights the pipe and let it go around from right to left, but only the men smoke. The women have their own pipe and smoke it just as the men do. After smoking for a while, the young man, who serves at the altar, gets the stick again and picks up some charcoal with it. He puts the charcoal on the altar. The leader takes a braid from the *sweet grass*, tears a piece off, puts it on the charcoal so it starts to smoke. Then he worships his Beaver bundle. Next, the dancing with the skunk-skins follows. The women do this in the same manner as with the beaver skins. Then the summer- and winter-weasel follow, which are being honoured by the women as well, but with this dance the women stay standing or go down

on their knees. Each animal has a separate song and the men as well as the women know all these songs. Next it is the mink's turn, though it is honoured by only one man, who is indicated for this by the leader. The leader starts to sing, the others present join in and then that one man indicated by the leader dances around in the lodge four times with the skin of the mink. Then the stick, representing the beaver works, follows. The leader puts the four sticks in front of him and starts to sing. His wife and three other women now kneel in front of the sticks and start dancing on their knees. They sit like beavers building a dam. Then they each pick up a stick and put it between their front teeth, just like a beaver holding a stick and dance four times around the *lodge*. After this is finished, they all sit down again. Then the leader starts to worship the *mountain lion*. He holds the medicine stick raised in his left hand and with the right hand he picks up a mountain lion tail. But this time there is no rattling, just singing. He makes the tail flip up and down as if it were alive. He does that four times and then puts it with the other artifacts. The mice, whose turn is next, are being put aside and are only honoured by the singing of their songs. Then the *prairie-chicken* follows and not the entire skins, but only the tail feathers are used. The leader puts them in front of him and then the four women kneel again while imitating the movements of the *prairie chicken* by their knee-dance, it is not honoured in any other way. The seagull follows after the *prairie chicken* and is sung to, but there is no dancing with it. Then the swan follows and he is only honoured by the leader. The leader holds the swan-skin and dances with it around the *lodge* four times while the others sing. Once this is done, about twelve hours have passed since the beginning of the dance.

Then the leader puts a few buffalo hooves tied together in front of him. He kneels down and his wife kneels down at the other side. Then they pray to the hooves and perform a knee-dance. Then they drop their heads down like a male and female buffalo about to butt heads, and they roar like mad buffaloes. After doing this for a while, they get up and dance around the *lodge*. Sometimes the man stands still during the dance and looks around like a very angry buffalo would, and then he and his wife butt their heads together. They dance four times around the *lodge* and then the woman sits down. The leader keeps dancing alone and looks to see if he can spot among the audience a friend who has his wife with him. If he finds one, he goes to that woman, puts the buffalo hooves in front of her and sits down himself. Now everyone laughs and shouts at the woman that she should rise and dance around the *lodge*. So she stands up and dances around the *lodge*, imitating a buffalo cow. Then she holds the hooves in her hand. Then she takes a turn by looking for a friend who is there with her husband and throws the hooves down in front of him. Everyone then shouts at the man that he should get up and dance around. The woman stands in front of him and acts like an angry buffalo cow. The man stands up and then they dance together around the tent. This is repeated by several men and women. Finally the hooves are laid down again with the contents of the Beaver bundle. Then a dog skin is being honoured: the leader of the women dances around the lodge with it four times. Then the leader puts away all the sacred artifacts. The young man who serves the altar gets the *medicine-stick*, picks up some charcoal and puts that on the altar. The leader tears off a piece of his *sweet-grass* braid and puts it on the charcoal. The sacred artifacts are being honoured with the smoke.

There is berry soup and boiled meat. The young man who serves at the altar now hands this out to the persons present. When everyone has soup and meat, the leader takes one berry from his soup and holds it up with his right hand. All the others do this too. First he prays to the sun, and all the others with him, then to the moon, then to the morning star. Then the leader holds his berry against the ground, all the others do the same and they all pray to the ground, the rivers, creeks, lakes, animals, rocks, trees and the grass. Then everyone buries the berry with which they prayed in the ground and they cheerfully start eating their meat and drinking their soup. This feast meal means that they eat with the

sacred artifacts of the Beaver dance. And they invite the sun, the moon, the morning star and all water, rocks, trees and animals to partake.

This ends Síkimiaχkitopi's story.

Prof. Uhlenbeck noticed at the Beaver dance all kinds of things, which deviated from Síkimiaχkitopi's narrative, but because the details are of minor importance, I don't want to elaborate on them. However, it should be mentioned that the otter and the bear, which Síkimiaχkitopi does not mention, play a big role in the ritual and that all or nearly all animals which are represented in the Beaver bundle during the dance are being symbolized dramatically. In the summer of 1911 it happened to Prof. Uhlenbeck that the dancing women, who imitated the gestures and the sounds of the bear, encouraged him repeatedly to rise and, by dancing opposite to them, try to do the same, but he only acted partly upon this encouragement.

I will now go through S.' description and explain and complete this where necessary.

The dance takes place in a regular, large tipi (conical tent) which normally at the east side (where the entrance is) extends into a shelter from the sun and is specifically erected for the onlookers outside the tipi. Opposite the entrance, on the west side lies the Beaver bundle (more about it later). To the north side of the Beaver bundle the leader of the ceremony is seated, so the Beaver bundle is on his right side. Beside him, along the tent wall, ten or twelve men, "whom help him," are seated. These are the men who are being painted and who, from the beginning on, actively perform during the ceremony. In front of these men, three of four buffalo hides are spread out. The rest of the northern tent wall is occupied with male onlookers, who also, as related in the description of S. perform during the dance. Also among them is the young altar boy. He has a plank lying in front of him. The wife of the leader sits to the south of the Beaver bundle; she too has a few women helpers beside her. Next to them the female onlookers are seated, so the male and female onlookers are seated opposite each other. The altar is in front (to the east) of the

Beaver bundle. It is a square, shallow hole. The "hearth" in the centre of the tipi is a circle of big stones in which a fire is burning. To the east of it the food is ready: pots with soup and big chunks of meat. The space around the fire that is kept clear is called the "dance circle."

The Beaver bundle consists of all the sacred artifacts used during the ritual. To mention them all is impossible because one Beaver bundle may differ from another, not just because certain artifacts are lacking, but also because new ones can be added. In general the following things can be found among the Beaver dance paraphernalia: 1. a few rattles (a pear-shaped bag of buffalo hide in which are little pebbles with a stick stuck in the tapered end); 2. five or six beaver skins; 3. five or six beaver rat skins; 4. three or four tail feathers from a *prairie chicken*; 5. two *medicine*-pipes; 6. six or seven different kinds of duck skins; 7. three or four different kinds of goose skins; 8. two or three swan heads with necks; 9. two or three squirrel skins; 10. two or three crow feathers; 11. two or three mountain squirrel skins; 12. two or three mice skins; 13. one or two rat skins; 14. one or two vison skins (a kind of weasel); 15. two or three eagle tail feathers; 16. three or four summer weasel skins; 17. three or four winter weasel skins ; 18: one dog tail; 19. one piece of buffalo hide with hair on it; 20. four or five beaver sticks; 21. three or four bone whistles (made of bird bones); 22. three or four small bags with dye; 23. five or six *medicine*-sticks; 24. ten or twelve braids of grass (*sweet grass*); 25. a small bag of pine tree needles; 26. two bundles of buffalo hooves; 27. one bundle of elk hoofs; 28. an iron whistle; 29. three or four Indian tobacco plants. To this should be added: one otter skin and something representing the bear.

There is probably a story connected to each of these artifacts, which explains the relationship of each animal to the Beaver dance. The following peculiar history is told about the elk hooves and the crow feather:

The "wife" of an elk ran away with a "young man" (a young male elk). Her husband went looking for her. He met a caribou and asked him to go along with him. Together they continued on. Then they saw a crow, which was also invited to come along. They went to the Porcupine Hills. The crow kept flying ahead and time and again when it saw elk, it came back and informed the others. They then would go to meet the elk, find nothing and continue with their journey. Once they had arrived at the Porcupine Hills, the crow saw her and told the elk. They stopped near a big cotton wood tree and the elk said: "If this heavy tree is the one who ran off with my wife, I will treat it like this" and he violently threw himself against the tree with his horns. It just shook a bit, nothing more. Then the moss deer did what it could, but had as much luck. His legs pounded to the ground while he ran toward the tree. He kicked it and his hoof went through the trunk (not felling the tree). Then they went to the elk. The elk said to the one who stole his wife: "I am here looking for my wife." "Yes," the other one said, "let's gamble for our (!) wife; by using this big pine tree; we shall gamble for her." Then the first husband ran toward the tree, attacking it with his horns, but couldn't move it. The other one felled it. Then he said to the three: "when you stir up trouble, this is how you will fare too." Then they became afraid and left. On the road the crow said: "I could have beaten him." "But how?" "I would have sat on his horns and picked out one of his eyes and then his other eye too." Then the moss deer said: "Let's go back, we will pay him for the woman, I with my hooves, the deer with his horns and the crow with a few of his feathers." They did accordingly. They went back and the elk got his wife back.

During his wanderings the other elk came upon a man who lived alone and who possessed the Beaver bundle. The man welcomed him and gave him something to eat. After they had eaten, the elk gave him the feathers, the hooves and the pieces of horn and said to him: "You have treated me well and I believe that these things are very valuable for you, so store them in your Beaver bundle." Then the elk left. After he had gone the man's wife was considering that they did not know the songs for these things and sent her husband after the elk to bring him back. That happened and he taught them the songs. And so even today, those having a Beaver bundle still dance with these three things.

In case such traditions are connected with all the other Beaver dance paraphernalia, which, as I already indicated, is very probable, it casts some light on the genesis of the entire ritual. As the dance is done now, it appears to be more of a general worshipping of all nature's hidden life and lifeless magical powers than a worshipping of a special water-cult (water beings respectively). Because of the circumstance that honouring beavers today is still the main element and that for the redskins in the first place the Beaver dance in its entirety connects with the beaver story, it seems clear that water and beaver worship should really be considered as the essence. The development of the Beaver dance ritual could be explained in different manners, but no single explanation would be preferred above another if the tradition narrated here did not indicate the direction in which we must look for the solution.

It is said that a certain magical power is hidden in certain in certain body parts of animals. It is not stated how this magical power expresses itself, but none of the involved people (animals respectively) doubt its existence. These magical artifacts are given by the possessor to someone as a present and by the recipient added to his Beaver dance paraphernalia. So we see – as is common with all kinds of tribes – magical artifacts with their belonging songs being incorporated into an existing ritual as a new part of it. This is also the case when, as far as can be determined, there is no relationship whatsoever between existing ritual and what is added to it. With regard to the Beaver dance, this is only partly true. Here specifically several *animals* are being honoured and for the "savage" redskins, *all* animals belong to one big family, just as men do, rather, as redskins do (for the whites hold a particular position in the cosmos). That very different types of animals are being honoured together is therefore quite very comprehensible. However, another question is: why *certain* animals enjoy the honor of being honored, why are always *certain* animals in the folklore in the foreground. Síkimiaχkitopi does say that all creatures are

honoured in the Beaver dance, but it is remarkable that only certain animals are mentioned and also only the animals, which are represented in the Beaver bundle. It appears that certain animals are honoured, but in order not to make the others jealous, the rest of the cosmos, along with the other animals, are included. We can not figure out how to explain this phenomena with the data presently at our disposal, but a good guess could be *totemic* animal worship. The animals honoured then could be considered the *totems* of the several exogamic groups ("clans"). As not even one trace of *totemic* clans is discovered with the Peigan, this guess is for the time being, up in the air. We will no longer elaborate on this point, but rather follow the proceedings of the ceremony and consider a few more important points.

After the preparations are finished and the man and woman "assisting" are being painted red on the forehead and chin, the leader gives the necessary instructions to the altar boy. It is strange that the leader doesn't have to be a medicine man. Anyone, who has the required "outfit" can lead the dance as such. Here it can be clearly seen again that the magical power is with the *artifacts*, any person in possession of and handling these artifacts derives from them a certain priest-like ordination that qualify him to perform sacred acts with good results. The altar boy is only a servant. Still, he also performs very important acts. At a certain moment it is his responsibility to drive away from the entrance evil spirits, which of course are lurking. He has to do this when the leader, during the song, pronounces the following words: "the old man that walks in this direction, now comes onto the sacred road," meaning, "the sun, who strides in this direction, now enters the *lodge*." The meaning of these words is probably that from now on the sun participates in the dance, that at this moment during the sacred acts the mystical connection between the sun and the dancers has been established.

After the Sun has been welcomed with a smoke offering, the actual activities commence. First the sun, the moon and the morning star are honoured with songs and then it is the turn for all kinds of animals.

When the leader beats his rattles, he beats on a piece of buffalo hide with lizards depicted on it. Lizards are considered to be especially good-natured animals, yes, as the only ones who would suffer such treatment (*mis*treatment) unpunished. If nothing had been depicted on it, the original bearer of the hide, the buffalo, would think that *he* was being beaten – and when he gets angry he is not at all easy to deal with.

As for the sequence of the different parts, we can divide the dance into three units. Honouring the crows and the beavers takes place first. This part ends with a break during which the pipe goes around. After the break the dance is picked up again with a smoke offering. Now a large number of animals are honoured. After they have all had their turn, again a smoke offering takes place and with that the official part ends. The paraphernalia are stored away and a joyous feast meal of meat and berry soup ends the long, solemn gathering.

While the crows are being honoured, at the same time a kind of initiation of the rattles takes pace. After the leader has beaten four times with his rattle on the buffalo hide, he pronounces these words: "I like my rattles." Perhaps the purpose of this formula is also to please the rattles; just as the hide has to be placated to let themselves be beaten on by the rattles, these rattles also have to be placated with their less pleasant function. So they are being flattered by saying: "How beautiful though these rattles are."

Then the peculiar beaver worship starts, which is actually separated into two parts: before the break the beaver is present in general, in his quality as a beaver; after the break he is remembered specifically for his peculiar activities.

In the last part especially there are peculiar sacred acts in which the heavenly bodies, the earth and everything on it are being invited to the meal. The solemn funeral of a berry that first symbolically is offered to the celestial bodies and to the earth as a symbol of the feast meal, does not likely mean that one berry is being offered to the earth, but it may mean that the sacred act of invitation has ended so that they can now celebrate with the thought that the entire cosmos participates. If the berry would be a genuine offering, that does explain why just the earth is treated so generously while the celestial bodies don't get anything because it is hard to consider just the showing of the berry as an offering. That would be even too mystical to a redskin as it is clearly apparent from his manner of offering in general.

After the feast everyone goes home and in general this will be about dusk because most dances preferably are not performed at night.

With this I have related everything that I wanted to communicate in this paper. I hope that the reader is given an impression of what is called "Indian culture" through this very superficial acquaintance with the four dances, Strange and erratic as this culture comes across at first sight, anyone who is willing to judge honestly and fairly, will come to the conclusion, that among all the incomprehensible and erratic aspects, there is not much that is really strange to us, that we have undeniably outgrown. And while reflecting upon this, one can also imagine that any attempt to transform this people in a few decennia into a "civilized nation." which means to model their mentality after ours, is doomed hopelessly to fail. Moreover, the people charged with this task are unable to cope with their duty, partly through ignorant fanaticism and partly because of egotism or indifference.

I don't want to go deeper into this subject, because I don't mean to write about redskins in general. I only want to add that firstly, the Indians are to be considered an oppressed, mistreated people and that they are entitled to as much sympathy as any other oppressed nation. If the really "civilized" people outside America would acknowledge this and speak out about it (as is presently done in international politics), then perhaps we would succeed in convincing America, so backwards in regard to civilization, of this truth and this would benefit the redskins immensely.

Literature

Hall Robert L.A., *Archaeology of the Soul*, University of Illinois Press, 1997.

Footnotes

a Verslagen en Mededeelingen der Koninklijke Akademie van Wetenschappen, Afdeeling *Letterkunde*, 4e Reeks, Deel XI pag. 4 sqq.

b Cf. f.i. C. Wissler, *Social life of the Blackfoot Indians*, New-York 1911, pag. 18 sqq; for more literature see Uhlenbeck loc. cit. pag. 25–26.

c My system of spelling is, in the main, the same as Prof. Uhlenbeck's. Later on, when the whole of my linguistic materials will be treated critically, I shall account for the differences. Here it is only desirable to state that I often write *e* where Prof. Uhlenbeck writes *i*. This difference will be readily understood by consulting the "Explanation of the graphical system" given in Prof. Uhlenbeck's "Original Blackfoot texts."

d As a rule I have kept the translations as they were given by *Síkimiáχkitopi*. I am well aware that in many cases they might be improved, especially embellished, by moulding the components into a grammatical construction, but as it is not my intention to review these names critically just now, I prefer to leave them, for the present, unchanged. In a few cases only I have judged it necessary to make some alteration in order to prevent misunderstanding. On the whole, the components of these names will be clear to anybody who has studied Prof. Uhlenbeck's Blackfoot-texts; but in several cases the interpretation of the whole composition will be found to offer some difficulty.

e *Síkimiáχkitopi* told me that Lone-eaters and Lone-fighters are different names for the same clan; it is, however, quite evident that he is wrong (cf. aforementioned works).

f Probably the ending is wrong: Prof. Uhlenbeck is sure of having heard more than once: *Manikápinau*.

g Uhlenbeck attended the entire ceremony and could monitor these communications; of course they are not at all complete, but, as one will see, Prof. Uhlenbeck has them, where necessary, supplemented for me.

NOTES

Notes to Preface and Introductions

1 This diary is in the Mrs. W. Uhlenbeck fonds. M 8116. Glenbow Archives, Calgary, Alberta.

2 "Naw peu ooch eta cots" refers to an area currently known as Napi's Playground.

3 The word "Blackfoot" is used to refer to the language and culture of the Blackfoot people. The name "Blackfeet" refers to their southern (i.e., U.S.) division, living on the Blackfeet Reservation, where these texts were collected. The name of the northern (i.e., Canadian) division, however, is "Blackfoot."

4 During a telephone conversation in December 1999 with E.M. Uhlenbeck, a grand-nephew of C. C. Uhlenbeck, he referred to Mrs. Uhlenbeck as "Aunt Willy."

5 A fictionalized account of a battle between attacking Assiniboines and Piegans camped by Fort Mackenzie, painted by Bodmer who witnessed it, is given in *Prairie-Flower*, a dime-novel version of French author Gustave Aimard's *Balle-Franche* (Eggermont-Molenaar 2001).

6 See the diary entry of July 23, 1911.

7 This biographical introduction is partly based on the obituary written in Dutch by J.P.B. de Josselin de Jong for the *Jaarboek van de Koninklijke Nederlandse Akademie van Wetenschappen* (1951–52). We refer to the English translation (De Josselin de Jong 1952).

8 Letters by C. C. Uhlenbeck to "Dick" in the years 1936 and 1937 are signed "Kees." In: Nationaal Archief in The Hague.

9 In 1916 C. C. Uhlenbeck published *Die Uhlenbecks: Eine alte Velberter Familie*, in which he describes the glorious past of his ancestors and the two buildings of the Eulenbeck estate.

10 Uhlenbeck to J. W. Muller, January 9, 1899, University Library Leiden, Dousakamer. Uhlenbeck must have referred to the summer of 1898.

11 In C. C. Uhlenbeck's letter, signed "Kees," to his nephew Dick (Lugano, March 24, 1937), he wrote, in Dutch, that he received "Many letters, especially from the Spengler children and grandchildren."

12 Officially Uhlenbeck was appointed to lecture in Gothic, Anglo-Saxon, Middle High German, and the old languages and literature of the Germanic people. In 1913 Comparative Linguistics of the Indo-Germanic languages would be added.

13 Jacob Grimm (1785–1863). German author, famous for his collection of folksongs and folktales.

14 Haan, S.W.M.A. den, *Inventaris van het archief van het Heilige Geest- of Arme Wees- en Kinderhuis te Leiden, 1334–1979*. Leidse Inventarissen, Leiden 1990.

15 The historian Pieter Geyl qualified a number of colleagues in less pleasing terms; he called Uhlenbeck a "neuroticus." His biographer, L. J. Rogier in his memoriam added, "Substantially all these characteristics were adhered to by other authorities such as P.J. van Winter, F.K.H. Kossman and especially J.S. Bartstra..." (Rogiers "Herdenking van [In memoriam] P. Geyl, 1967). Also, letter of L.J. Rogier to E.M. Uhlenbeck, January 12, 1968, stating that Bartstra had said that Uhlenbeck was "even more than that" (Katholiek Documentatie Centrum, Archief Rogier, nr. 1331).

16 Dr. Pierre Daniël Chantepie de la Saussaye, was Professor of Religious History in Amsterdam, and later, from 1899 to 1916, in Leiden. Hofstee 1991, 130, about Dr.

Chantepie: "For Chantepie, however, the interest in the relation between christianity and other religions had become the most challenging issue. He had gathered many data from all kinds of sources, such as ethnographic reports and letters from missionaries etc." Dr. Chantepie de la Saussaye was also the biographer of the famous Dutch poet Nicolaas Beets.

17 This stay at the Red Lake Reservation, U.S.A., resulted in De Josselin de Jong's "*Original Odzibwe-Texts,*" published in the *Baessler-Archiv* in 1913. In this year (1913) De Josselin de Jong was Curator at the State Museum of Ethnography, Leiden, the Netherlands.

18 According to the autobiographical notes of Robert H. van Gulik, cited in Barkman (1993).

19 Uhlenbeck to C. H. de Goeje, October 27, 1913. University Library Leiden, Dousakamer. Five years later, Uhlenbeck complained about his health in a letter to Franz Boas (May 18, 1918): "As soon as my health will permit it, I shall write a paper for the Journal [i.e., *The International Journal of American Linguistics* of which Boas was the editor-in-chief], but I think I shall have to wait a long time. I suffer from neurasthenia and insomnia so that I shall have to take rest during the whole summer."

20 De Josselin de Jong did not continue to study Amerindian languages after defending his thesis. He got interested in the Caribbean region and Indonesia and in 1922 was appointed as professor of anthropology at the University of Leiden. He is considered to be the founding father of anthropology in the Netherlands.

21 Like De Josselin de Jong, Geers too left the field of Indian linguistics not long after defending his thesis. Ultimately, in 1947 he was appointed lecturer (and later professor) in Spanish at the University of Groningen. More about his career (in Dutch) and his bibliography (in English) at http://www.leidenuniv.nl/host/mnl/mnl/levens/67-68/geers.htm.

22 Letter (May 22, 1918) C. C. Uhlenbeck to the "College of Curatoren" of the University of Leiden, wherein he requests sick leave from "the end of this week until the start of the new Academic year" [which was September] (trans. Mary Eggermont-Molenaar). University Library of Leiden. Dousakamer.

23 Details about the development of this thinking are to be found in the contribution of Inge Genee in this volume.

24 Archives of Leiden University, Correspondence "College van Curatoren," University Library of Leiden. Dousakamer.

25 Dr. Jan Brabers kindly searched the University of Nijmegen archives for us but was unable to find any reference to this affair. No wonder, as it appeared that at the time Van Gulik was still a high school student. However, neither was anything found in the Municipal Archives in Nijmegen, where the archives of the Stedelijk Gymnasium (grammar school) are kept.

26 De Josselin de Jong referred to "undergraduates" (in the Dutch text: "studenten"), whereas Van Gulik – and his friend Schnitger – were in 1926 strictly speaking still high school students (in Dutch: "middelbare scholieren").

27 From 1899 on, when Uhlenbeck went to Leiden, Nicolaas van Wijk, later professor in Balto-Slavic languages, for a while visited Uhlenbeck on Saturday afternoons to read Sanskrit with him. (Kindly communicated to us by Jan Paul Hinrichs, Leiden, biographer of Nicolaas van Wijk.)

28 It was Dr. Wilt Idema (Harvard), who pointed out that it was Van Gulik who was referred to as one of Uhlenbeck's "undergraduate students" and who provided us with copies of Van Gulik's – unpublished – autobiographical notes. More of these notes were handed to us by Dr. Willem van Gulik (Leiden). C. D. Barkman used and paraphrased these notes in his biography of Van Gulik (Barkman 1993, 25).

29 R. H. van Gulik, pp. 9–10 (pages in editor's possession).

30 Uhlenbeck to De Goeje, September 4, 1948. Dousakamer, University Library Leiden.

31 Information kindly provided to us by Prof. E. M. Uhlenbeck (Voorhout, The Netherlands).

32 Cf. Wied zum Neuwied (reprinted in 1906, 149): "The enemy gradually retreated, and concentrated themselves in several detachments on the brow of the hill, and this gave us an opportunity to open the gate, with due precaution, and view the destroyed tents and the bodies of the slain. The Indian who was killed near the fort especially interested me, because I wished to obtain his skull." Wied zum Neuwied's editor added in a footnote (n. 122): "See description of the battle as given by Culbertson in M. R. Audubon, *Audubon and his Journals* (New York, 1897), ii, pp. 133–136; also in Montana Historical Society *Contributions*, iii, pp. 207–209. The Prince here omits reference to his own participation, and to the fact that he was possibly the slayer of the Assiniboin. – Ed."

33 Case file #M8116 (90/79). Glenbow Archives, Calgary.

34 Mrs. Cramer was a 'Friend of the Maxwell Museum,' in Albuquerque, New Mexico. She and Elsa Heman know each other through *Servas*, according to its website, "an international, non-profit, non-governmental organization, based on understanding, tolerance and world peace, an organization of hosts and travelers, based on volunteer work, founded in 1949." In a letter of January 2003, Elsa Heman-Ortt wrote that Mrs. Cramer urged her to send the diary to a museum. And that is what happened.

35 H. Samek-Norton is author of *The Blackfoot Confederacy, 1880–1920: A comparative study of Canadian and U.S. Indian policy.* Albuquerque: University of New Mexico Press, 1987.

36 As we will see later, that period of contact must have been in the years 1930–32, the first two years of the Uhlenbecks' period in the city of Amersfoort, the Netherlands.

37 In 1905 Felix Ortt began a 'free' marriage with Tine Hinlopen. Their life together ended in 1932, in which year he married Maria Theresia Zeijlemaker.

38 A quite detailed biography and photograph of Felix Louis Ortt can be found in Dutch at: www.iisg.nl/bwsa/bios/ortt.html.

39 One of Ortt's most remarkable works is *Christelijk Anarchisme*, a brochure on the tenets of the Doukhobors, published in 1898. The cost of the brochure was 15 cents,

and the profits were to support the "vervolgde Duchoboren in Rusland" ("persecuted Doukhobors in Russia").

40 During World War II, Elsa Ortt's brother played a role in the so-called England Spiel. "22 Mei [1942]: Ernst Willem de Jonge en Felix Ortt, uitgezonden door Mi-6, worden met behulp van Van de Waals gearresteerd." Source: http://home.hetnet.nl/~bkolster/ Englandspiel/Geschiedenis.htm. While most of his fellow agents perished in Mauthausen, Felix Ortt and some others must have perished in Rawics or during their transport to Mauthausen. Rep (1977, 332–33). Elsa Heman in her letter of January 18, 2003: "My brother was not missing. We got official notice of the Red Cross that he 'died of exhaustion in a concentration camp'." Elsa Heman-Ortt now (2003), at the age of about 90, is active in a peace movement.

41 Throughout the diary we will see that the Blackfeet call the mid-day meal "supper" and the evening meal "dinner" and Willy followed this practise.

42 See Appendix A of this volume for an English translation of this lecture.

43 Paragraphs like this make one wonder whether ethnographers ever reflected on their own "civilization" or whether that is possible.

44 The translation is mine since, at time of writing (2004), the official translation was not yet available.

45 Biesheuvel, J.M.A. (1983) "Een Geleerde onder de Indianen" (*A Scholar among the Indians*) in: *De Steen der Wijzen* (*The Philosophers' Stone*), Amsterdam: Meulenhoff.

46 The subtitle of this book, *A Professor and his Wife among the Blackfeet*, is derived from the title of this short story.

47 This short story of 1983 is found in Biesheuvel's *De Steen der Wijzen* (1983, 188–94). Aert Hendrik Kuipers is author of *The Shuswap Language: Grammar, Texts, Dictionary* (1974) and *A Classified English-Shuswap Word-list* (1975).

48 Soer, the Dutch Jesuit, whom we will encounter in Willy's diary, wrote about his visit to an Indian household: "there were obtrusive evidences of paganism around them: sweet incense burning in honor of the sun, a medicine bag, and a fish-rod, which latter had apparently some reference to the name of the old pagan proprietor of the shack – Running Fisher." Soer went on to erect an altar and was, "happy in the midst of depressing idolatry to see the young Christian couple adore the Saviour of mankind and receive the Bread of Life (1910, 18)."

49 "In addition, children were forbidden to speak the Blackfeet language in the schools (U.S. Comm. Ind. Affairs 1893:174). Several informants, who attended either agency or mission schools during the first decades of the twentieth century, recall being punished for 'speaking Indian' in the schools or dormitories" (McFee 1972, 52).

Notes to Part I

1 Browning is seat of the tribal government of the Blackfeet Reservation, 2,400 square miles, at present 8,500 inhabitants, in Montana. The area for this reservation was assigned in 1851 at the Fort Laramie Treaty and established in 1874. The town of Browning started to grow around Kipp's trading post about 1900 (Farr 1984, 40–42). Dempsey (2002, 212): "but in 1889 [Kipp, a former whiskey trader] became a licensed trader and was permitted to move onto the reservation with his Piegan wife … he ran [the former trading post] as a store and a stopping place … he died in Browning in 1913."

2 Joseph Tatsey, ½ Blood, ¼ Piegan, 46 years (DeMarce 1980, 250), was Uhlenbeck's "teacher" in 1910 too, when Uhlenbeck researched Blackfoot language with his former student De Josselin de Jong.

3 Joseph Kipp, 61 years, ¼ Mandan (DeMarce 1980, 143), was the "mixed blood" son of the trader Kipp, who had established in the 1830s the first American trading post, Fort McKenzie, later Fort Benton, on the Piegan hunting grounds. The Kipp settlement is recorded for the first time in the *Ancient Indian Chronology* of an old Blood Indian Chief whose name was "Bad Head" (Pakapotokon) by the time of his death. The incidents Bad Head related were depicted as pictographs on rawhide and start in 1810. For the year 1831, the *Ancient Indian Chronology* states: "Kipp otsisitapipi etotoartay" – A white man "Kipp" establishes a post at the confluence of Bear River and the Missouri (Middleton 1952, 173). For more on Kipp's establishment, see Bradley (1966[1917], VIII: 244–50).

4 The Mandans used to live on the banks of the Missouri. They were visited in 1738 (and described) by the French Canadian explorer Pierre Gaultier Varenne de la Verendrye. Grinnell (1892, 287) about them "In the year 1845, the Blackfeet were decimated by the small-pox. This disease appears to have travelled up the Missouri River; and in the early years, between 1840 and 1850, it swept away hosts of Mandans."

5 Alcohol was not allowed because of the 1834 prohibition against selling alcohol to Indians by the American government. However, illegal whiskey traders, bootleggers, made alcohol widely available.

6 Willy Kennedy, 11 years, was the son of John Kennedy, ½ Piegan, and Mary Pablo, ¾ Piegan. Mary was previously married to Jerry Potts (DeMarce 1980, 140). Charlie Potts, 21 years, 7/8 Blood, was the son of Mary Pablo and Jerry Potts, ½ breed (DeMarce 1980, 140).

7 J. H. Sherburne was a former employer, later a friend of Robert Scriver, collector and author of *The Blackfeet: Artists of the Northern Plains* (1990). Sherburne, as Willy noticed, also collected Native artifacts. At present these are part of the J. H. Sherburne Collection, Mansfield Library, University of Montana, Missoula. Willy was right: according to Rosier (2001, 47, 59), Sherburne was "perhaps the most wealthiest and powerful white resident of Browning.… The Sherburne Mercantile Company acquired 40,000 acres of Indian land partly through the manipulation of debts incurred by Indians at its general store."

8 Eagle Calf or White Man, 69 years, ½ Piegan, was the brother of Tatsey's mother (DeMarce 1980, 276, and Kehoe 1960, 431). Eagle Calf is called Pietaunesta in Blackfoot. Willy spells his name in Blackfoot in several ways. According to Blackfeet Tribal Business Council and DeMarce (1998, 412), "Good Strike Woman had an adopted son named Eagle Calf. He was a white man, a napiquon, and was also called 'Whiteman.'"

9 Charlie's mother, Mrs. Nixon, was also Mary Ann Camp, 31 years, ½ Piegan. She was the wife of Frank Camp, who in 1908 was jailed. Mary Ann lived on and off with Fred Hicks and married him in 1909 (DeMarce 1980, 62). Shortly later she must have married Nixon.

10 Charlie's youngest sister is not listed in DeMarce (1980), only a younger brother Edward, 6 years.

11 The "agent" at that time was George Steel who "required a total of 54 agency-personnel, including Indian police … and thirteen full-time teachers." This agency was located at Willow Creek, near Kipp's trading post in 1895. "Those entering the reservation were required to register at the agency office within 12 hours" (Farr 1984, 40). Little Dog, 57 years, full Piegan, was "as his father, one of the more noted Piegan warriors. During the 1880 period, his band served to police a portion of the reservation and in 1882, massacred a band of Crees in Dead Indian Coulee on the south side of the Marias River. A few days later, Cree scalps, 'not yet dry" were being bartered for whiskey in the saloons of Fort Benton. The Crees had encroached on the Blackfeet Reserve to steal horses." Little Dog was the spokesman for the Blackfeet during the negotiations for the 1896 treaty when the western border of the Reservation was re-defined (Diettert 1992, 67–73). Little Dog was married to Walking In the Water, 27 years, full Piegan, and had 6 children, 4 of whom died in infancy (DeMarce 1980, 152).

12 "I have come at last.…" According to Vera Crowshoe of Peigan Nation, Alberta, Canada, "there is no 'I am sorry' in our culture. It is what you call Indian time. You accept someone being late. And if you don't accept it, you can get back at him. When you made a serious mistake, you say that it was an accident and give the hurt person something you really care about" (personal communication, June 2002).

13 The Holy Family Mission school opened in 1890 (with the help of a $14,000 gift of the Philadelphia family, Drexel) and was closed because of lack of funds in 1940 (Harrod 1971, 94). Anthony Joseph Drexel (1826–1893) and Francis Martin Drexel (1792–1863) were Philadelphia-based bankers and philanthropists. Francis Martin was also a painter. His daughter Katherine (1858–1955) established a new religious order, the Sisters of the Blessed Sacrament for Indians and Colored People, and financed many schools and educational institutions, the Holy Family Mission on the Blackfeet Reservation being one of them (Garraty 1999, 6:914–17).Subscription by William E. Farr (1984, 24) under a ca 1898 picture of the Holy Family Mission school kids where most children spent the entire year: "The purpose of the students' isolation, of course, was for the school to break down the old habits, to convert them to 'civilization,' by eradicating traditional languages, values, and daily practices." Several informants who attended either agency or mission schools during the first decades of the twentieth century recall being punished for "speaking Indian" in the schools or dormitories (McFee 1972, 52).

14 Tatsey's wife was Annie Tatsey, 41 years, ½ Piegan. Hattie was born July 4, 1892 (and married to Charley Guardipee). Tatsey's old mother was Susan Tatsey; she was allotted land under the name of Susan Campbell, ½ Piegan (DeMarce 1980, 250).

15 Wilma Adams is Hattie's daughter born in 1922.

16 Tatsey's children were Josephine, born in 1890; Hattie, 1892; John, 1894; Joseph, 1896; Elisabeth, 1899; David, 1901; Irving, 1904; Mary, 1906; and George, 1908 (DeMarce 1980, 250).

17 Young Bear Chief was 53 years, full Piegan. First wife: Fine Shield Woman, full Piegan, children: Eddie Bear Chief, 30 years, Medicine Pipe Woman, Sebastian Bearchief, Joseph Bear Chief. Second wife: Elk Yells In The Water, 44 years, ½ Blood, ½ Piegan; children: Lizzie Bear Chief, 11 years, and Cecilia Bear Chief, 4 years. Young Bear Chief was once married to Medicine Shell. Child from that marriage is Petrified Rock, wife of Joseph Still Smoking (DeMarce 1980, 287).

18 Father (Superior) Bougis, "in addition to his heavy administrative duties, composed a grammar of the Blackfoot language, wrote numerous questions for confession, and authored an introduction to Blackfoot grammar for missionaries and teachers" (Harrod 1971, 86). Father Bougis composed this introduction and grammar in 1894. "In October, 1893, Father Bougis complained to Agent Cooke about one runaway boy and suggested that the boy be disciplined. In January of the following year, Bougis again contacted the agent concerning boys who had left the mission" (Harrod 1971, 89). "The famous Louis Riel, leader of the Cree Rebellion against the British in Canada in 1885, taught at St. Peter's until that year. He was succeeded by a Jesuit Scholastic, Peter Bougis, who inherited a class of 'seventeen Indian boys and eighteen half-breed boys'" (Black 1960, 27, note 3 (Schoenberg 1959)). In the fall of 1891 Father Bougis went to the Holy Family Mission. (Personal conversation with Sister Dolores Brinkel).

19 Aloysius Soer was born in 1853 in Oldenzaal, the Netherlands and died in Missoula, Montana, in 1931. From 1882 on, he was a Jesuit missionary in America, from 1886–1931 employed in "The Rocky Mountains," i.e., the Holy Family Mission. "Father Soer was also busy translating liturgical and Biblical texts into the Blackfoot tongue" (Harrod, 1971, 86). Harrod mentions Soer's sermon "to the Indians, Heart Butte, Instructions for the First Sunday in Lent 1904" (97). Harrod also states that Soer made regular trips to Heart Butte and that under his leadership the little church, St. Peter Claver, was completed in 1911 (191). "St. Peter Claver was born in 1580 in Catalonia, became a priest in Cartagena, Colombia and was declared a saint in 1888. In Colombia St. Peter's day is declared 'human rights day'" (Maes, n.d., 9).

20 "Lewe Kasoos" was Louis Lavarro, 12 years, son of Tackler Mountain Chief, first wife of Joseph Lavarro (Joe Casuse), 37 years, ½ Piegan (DeMarce 1980, 148). Peter Bear Leggings, 13 years, was the son of Charging Home, 30 years, ¼ Piegan, the second wife of Nelson Henault, 30 years, ¼ Piegan (DeMarce 1980, 127). James Red Fox, 13 years, was a son of Red Fox, 37, full Piegan, and Good Victory, 33 years, full Piegan (DeMarce 1980, 213). James Vielle, 13 years, was the son of Frank Vielle, 44 years, ½ Piegan, and Susan The Hoofs Vielle, 46 years, full Piegan (DeMarce 1980, 264).

21 Willy's father, John Kennedy, 34 years, ½ Piegan, was married to Mary Pablo, who died in May 1906. William had two younger sisters, Esther and Lizzie (DeMarce 1980, 140).

22 Sebastian, 17 years, and Eddie Bear Chief, 30 years, were the sons of Young Bear Chief and his first wife, Fine Shield Woman, full Piegan, deceased (DeMarce 1980, 287).

23 Elk Yells in the Water, 44 years, ½ Blood, ½ Piegan, was Bear Chief's second wife (DeMarce 1980, 287).

24 Translation is something like "Little writing Indians." Most likely, they wrote to Uhlenbeck.

25 Cf. McClintock (1910, 24): "We attended a meeting held by a white missionary in our valley. I led the singing and sat in the front row with Bear Chief and Eagle Child, who were prominent Indians. They listened gravely and attentively but understood not a single word. They were broad-minded chiefs and came as an example to other Indians; to show they approved of the missionary and of his religious ceremony."

26 The Sandhills is an area in south Saskatchewan where "all their ancestors are invisible to men, but pursuing about the same career they did in life. Their ghosts sometimes visit the living and talk to them in a whistling sound which they hear in the sighing of the wind, the creaking of lodge poles and the rustling of leaves" (Bradley 1876, IX: 266). McClintock (1923, 115) on the Sandhills: "We call it the Sand Hills, a white alkali country – far east on the plains. It is surrounded by quicksand that the living may not enter. The ghost people chase ghost buffalo and antelope."

27 Brother Galdes, a Jesuit lay-brother, was "a good man, exceedingly capable and diligent. In 1909 he started his 25 years at the Mission with utmost devotion" (Black 1960, 55).

28 Plains Indians used to put their dead on scaffolds in trees, cf. Grinnell (1961, 96–97). This custom might have been outlawed when in 1883 Congress authorized the Court of Indian Offences. Later a Code of Indian Offences was drawn up and scaffolding the deceased might have been prohibited under "prohibited Indian Practices." Cf. "It was only upon the insistence of the Catholic Church and an Indian agent in 1905 that interment came to be the norm" (Farnell 1955, 192). Farnell writes about the Assiniboin Fort Belknap Reservation. This might have been the course of affairs on the Blackfeet Reservation too.

29 "Hopjes" is a typically Dutch kind of dark brown coffee candy.

30 Bear Chief is one of the delegates of the Piegan council members who traveled to Washington, D.C., in 1903, "to provide information on the Blackfeet independent of the local agent" (Farr 1984, 64). At that occasion he might have traveled to New York too.

31 Montana, as well as the Canadian province of Alberta, is known for its many discoveries of dinosaurs.

32 *Natos* is Blackfoot for "sun." In combinations with other words it is also used for "medicine" (McClean n.d.). "Natoi-, -ataoi- holy, cf. natoyï (in.), natósiu (an.) is holy (has medicine power)" (Uhlenbeck 1938, 79). Cf. Duvall's notes about Nato-as in the Duvall Papers (1904–11, 2:577), "the word Na-to-as as I make it means sacred turnip. [T]his turnip represents the turnip the women who was taken up and was fordiden

[sic] interpret explain meaning clear interpretation translation forbidden natop^wa natoyup^wa."

33 Cathy was the youngest of the Tatsey children, not yet listed in DeMarce (1980).

34 John Guardipee, 15 years, was the son of Alex Guardipee, ½ Piegan, ¼ Cree, and his second wife, Grass Snake, full Piegan (DeMarce 1980, 116). Charlie Guardipee was Hattie Tatsey's husband.

35 Walter's father was "old" or Frank Mountain Chief or Big Brave, no age listed, full Piegan (DeMarce 1980, 30). Mountain Chief was one of the signers of the 1855 Lame Bull treaty (Jackson. 2000, 176ff.); (cf. Harrod 1971, 45–46). Dempsey (1994, 42) mentions that Mountain Chief in his later years became a prominent chief. Actually Mountain Chief was the tribal leader from 1860 to 1875 (Foley n.d., 405). Dempsey (2002, 205) on Big Brave: "Big Brave, son of the great leader Mountain Chief ... was falsely charged, put in jail and got out."

36 Painted Wing (also known as Morning Eagle), no age listed, had eight wives: Kills In The Middle; Old Woman Snake, deceased; Medicine Spring; Under Rat, deceased; Crow Eyed Woman, deceased; Good Otter, deceased; Hits on Top; and Bird Wing, deceased (DeMarce 1980, 151). Tail Feathers, 63 years, full Piegan, was the husband of Petrified Rock, deceased, and later of Mary Calf Robe (DeMarce 1980, 249).

37 It is more likely that the fellow sang about berries instead of cherries.

38 In 1898, after a severe winter and a shortage of feed, the irrigation engineer for the Blackfeet agency recommended extension of the irrigation canals in order to increase hay production. This project was started around 1908 and "provided an additional source of labor and income for many Indians" (McFee 1972, 51ff.). "The United States Bureau of Reclamation had hired the Indians to build a large irrigation ditch between the St. Mary and Milk Rivers ... the workmen felt their compensation was too low. Grinnell spoke with the Indian leaders, and wrested a promise of higher pay from bureau engineer Cyrus Babb" (Diettert 1992, 87).

39 Brocky or Tail Feathers Coming over the Hill, 68 years, full Piegan, was the husband of Many Killing, deceased, Both Go In (or Both Going), living with Chewing Black Bones (the son of her sister Double Catches), Snake Woman, 48 years, and Falling Off The Bank, deceased (DeMarce 1980, 44, 258). In De Josselin de Jong (1914, 120), the name Black Bones is spelled as Chew-black-bone (Síkå keka). Diettert (1992, 98) on Brocky: "The Grinnells launched their first 'Glacier' experience at the Blackfeet Medicine Lodge on the Fourth of July [1911]. Blackfeet friend and storyteller Brocky, blind and gap-toothed gave Elisabeth his walking stick."

40 William Russell, 57 years, ½ Blackfeet, was the husband of Mary Russell (Strikes At One Another). According to DeMarce (1980, 224), his father, John T. Russell, was a white man and his mother, Glittering In Front, 51 years, full Piegan.

41 Walter Mountain Chief was the son of Big Brave (Frank Mountain Chief) and his fourth wife, Hates To Stay Alone, full Piegan (DeMarce 1980, 30). The other son of Big Brave and Hates To Stay Alone was Antoine Mountain Chief, 31 years, married (DeMarce 1980, 183). In 1910 Walter was the main informant of Jan de Josselin de Jong, who refers to him as Síkimiå kitopi (Black-horse-rider) (1914, 120).

42 Jan de Jong is Jan de Josselin de Jong.

43 Walter's mother, Hates To Stay Alone, deceased, was old Mountain Chief's fourth wife. His wife in 1911 was Gun Woman For Nothing, 54 years, full Piegan. Her children with old Mountain Chief were Tackler (or "the oldest sister" – Kasoos), 30 years, and Emma, 16 years (DeMarce 1980, 30). In DeMarce (1980, 148), the name of the fifth wife is registered as Not A Real Gun.

44 Jack Big Moon (no age listed), ¾ Piegan, married to Long Time Calf, 48 years (DeMarce 1980, 32).

45 One of Uhlenbeck's work methods was to read Blackfoot texts and hope for correction from his audience.

46 Irene Shoots was probably the daughter of Bill Shoots One Another, 47 years, full Piegan, and Bird Tail Woman, 50 years, full Piegan. Their twelve-year-old daughter (Irene?) is listed as Hollering This Way (DeMarce 1980, 235).

47 Big Nose, a little boy (see DeMarce 1980, 214), was probably a son of Charley Reevis. Cf. De Josselin de Jong (1917, 116) a son of Charles Reevis was Louis, called Big-nose.

48 According to De Josselin de Jong I(14, 116) the main chief of the Fat-melters, (Three-sun) was called Big-nose by the whites. Nyókskatosi had adopted Charles Reevis, and Reevis adopted David, whose government name was Scabby -robe.

49 Helena is now the capital of the State of Montana.

50 Nelson Henault, 30 years, ¼ Piegan, divorced Hester Trombley in 1908 and married Charging Home, the widow of Bear Leggings, in 1908 (DeMarce 1980, 127).

51 The fact that the skin is spread out means that the bundle was already opened when the Uhlenbecks entered the *tipi*.

52 McClintock (n.d.) states that during "many years of close association with the Blackfoot tribe, from 1896 to 1912, I knew of three beaver bundles and was present during the performance of the rituals pertaining to them. Their three owners or guardians were Chief Mad Wolf, my foster-father, Wolf Plume and Tom Kyio, all of the Blackfoot Reservation in Montana." Kehoe (1995a, xxv) notes that Tom Kiyo (*kiááyo* = bear) in 1911 opened the Head Carrier's Beaver Bundle "so Duvall could take notes" and that Kiyo was listed in the 1890 census as being twenty-eight years old and married to the nineteen-year-old Good Medicine.

53 Rose, 32 years, was the daughter of Mountain Chief and his third wife, Fine Stealing Woman, full Piegan, deceased (DeMarce 1980, 30).

54 Rosy's husband was Louis Marcereau (Marceau), 45 years, ¾ Piegan (DeMarce 1980, 167).

55 This is the so-called war cry meant to encourage men going on the warpath.

56 Before sunset one is supposed to wipe off the face paint and bury the tissue with the paint in the earth (personal communication with North Peigan participants after a bundle opening in the 1990s at Peigan Nation, Canada).

57 Painted Wing (also called Morning Eagle) figures in a number of books: Lancaster (1966, 112) refers to Morning Eagle, who said that he was not a medicine man, but "cured the son of Flat Tail by singing hand game songs." Morning Eagle also figures in the story *The Battle at Six Persons* (ibid., 201). McClintock (n.d.) mentions Morning Eagle ("a famous warrior") together with Lame Bull, Tearing Lodge, No Bear, Little Owl, Many Guns, Black Bull, and Rattler, the medicine-man and doctor, as "the part-owners of the Beaver bundle." In McClintock (1923, 300), Morning Eagle participates in a Brave Dog Society ceremony.

58 These two brothers were John Henault (Eagle Ribs), 29 years, ½ Piegan, mother Good Victory, living with Henry Head Carrier, and Steven Henault, 33 years, 3/8 Piegan, 1/8 Cree, mother Maggie Henault whose father was Aleck Guardipee (DeMarce 1980, 127). Maggie was also Nelson Henault's mother.

59 The text of Red Wing can be found at http://home.kc.rr.com/cwha/redwing_original_lyrics.htm.

60 New Breast, 45 years, full Piegan, was the husband of Long Face New Breast, 61 years, full Piegan. They divorced in 1907. New Breast then married Caught Alone, 30 years (DeMarce 1980). The son was apparently not John New Breast, 21 years, as "the little Indian played delightful." New Breast and Caught Alone might have had a baby after the registration in 1907–08 .

61 This girl must have been born after the registration too.

62 Peter Bear Leggings' stepfather is Nelson Henault, 30 years.

63 His mother is Charging Home, 50 years (DeMarce 1980, 127). In the 1908 registration (DeMarce 1980), Nelson is listed as 27 years, his wife, 47 years. Charging Home was previously married to Bear Leggings, children were Peter, New Woman, 10 years, Lucie, wife of Peter Cadotte and Rachel, wife of Mike Big Leg. She had no children with Takes Gun On Both Sides.

64 End of Notebook I.

65 At the "feasts" in July the Sun dance and the Beaver dance will take place.

66 George Day Rider was the son of Lone Horn, who was a half-brother of Louise Big Plume, the mother of David Duvall (DeMarce 1980, 84 and 192). Also, Crawls Away, 43 years, full Piegan, wife of Peter Day Rider, had a first husband, George Lone Horn, full Piegan, deceased. With him she had one child, George Lone Horn.

67 Charly Guardipee was the son of Eli Guardipee. According to Wilma Adams, Browning, the Guardipees were Shoshones/Sioux (personal communication, September, 2002).

68 Anna Hesseling was the wife of Dr. D. C. Hesseling, author of *Het Afrikaans* (1899) and several other linguistic books and one of Uhlenbeck's colleagues at the University of Leiden (http://www.afrikaans.com/indeks1.html). "Jan" is Jan de Josselin de Jong.

69 Cf. Geers (1917, 118): "Sokapi – *good, fine, well.* 1° as an independent verb: *sokápsiu* (an.), *sokápiu* (in.an.) *is good, is fine.* 2° as a verbal prefix *well*: *sokápiìa saie that he may skin it well* obt. 32.10." Cf. Uhlenbeck (1938, III), *sokap-* good, well, as an adjective-verb *sokápsiu* (an.), *sokápiu* (in.), *is good*.

70 Mary Bear Leggings, 10 years, daughter of Nelson Henault and Charging Home, is listed as New Woman Girl, 10 years (DeMarce 1980, 127).

71 It would be tempting to translate "het avondmaal" as "the Last Supper." As the Uhlenbecks were not religious, it would amaze me that she would hand out a picture of the Last Supper.

72 Sam Scabby Robe, 25 years, was the son of Scabby Robe, a brother of Charley Reevis, 35 years, ½ Piegan (DeMarce 1980, 214), and he was the husband of Yelling Kit Fox, sister of Jim Blood's wife, Owl Handsome Woman (DeMarce 1980, 42). Sam and David Scabby Robe were also stepsons of Charles Reevis(De Josselin de Jong 1914, 116).

73 "Jimmy" Shoots was George Shoots Close At Night, 15 years, son of Shoots Close At Night, 44 years, full Piegan, and Chipping Too Deep, 37 years (DeMarce 1980, 234).

74 Oliver Day Rider, 14 years, was the son of Mike Day Rider, 41 years, full Piegan, and Helen Day Rider, 33 years, full Piegan (DeMarce 1980, 83). "Joe" or Jack Day Rider, same parents as Oliver, was 11 years old (DeMarce 1980, 83).

75 As an Executive Order in 1873 further reduced Blackfeet land, in 1875 the agency was moved up north to Badger Creek. So the Old Agency was actually a new agency. It was the place where from the 1880s on government rations were issued (Farr 1984, 13). In 1895 a new agency was built at Willow Creek.

76 "… and in 1872 a Black named David Green was living with the Peigan" (Dempsey 1994, 93). Nicodemus Green, 35 years, ½ Piegan, father Dave Green, Negro, mother Two Strikes, full Piegan. Nicodemus had no children with his first two wives. He had a son with his third wife, Long Time Hawk Woman, Joe Green, 10 years. The other children might have been those of Long Time Hawk's half-brother Night Gun, who died and left three children (DeMarce 1980, 113).

77 Willy underlined the word "seems." Uhlenbeck (1912a, viii) bemoans the fact that one "could not spend so many hours with me, as I should have liked and needed." Willy had three sisters: Cornelia, Guda, and Margaritha.

78 *The Brothers Karamazov*: a novel in four parts and an epilogue by Fyodor Dostoyevsky, 1821–1881.

79 This compilation of Arabic stories from the ninth and the fourteenth century is also known as Arabian Nights. Cf: http://en2.wikipedia.org/wiki/Arabian_Nights.

80 Nelson's previous wife was Hester Trombley, now (in 1908) wife of Joe Trombley (DeMarce 1980, 127).

81 The old way of burying, on a scaffold or in a tree, was outlawed. Lancaster (1966, 94) noted that between July 1883 and July 1884 five or six hundred people died of starvation, that there were so many that "they just left the rough boxes (rough coffins) on top of the ridge right out in the open."

82 The idea is that the spirit of these artifacts would accompany the spirit of the deceased (personal communication, in 1992, with Harvey Crowchild, member of the Tsuu T'ina tribe near Calgary). Cf. Macleans (1986, 67).

83 De Josselin de Jong (1912, 395) pondered over the meaning of this gesture. At several bundle openings that I attended, people told me that putting a piece of food on the floor (rubbing a berry in the ground) is meant to give something back to Mother Earth, "One takes and one gives. It is a way of staying in balance."

84 Henry Hungry, 31 years, full Piegan, was the son of Three Buttes and Taking Gun First (DeMarce 1980, 133).

85 "Davy" Rutherford is Dewey Rutherford, 13 years old, son of Richard, ½ Piegan, and Eliza Rutherford, ½ Piegan (DeMarce 1980, 224).

86 Mrs. "Saintgodard" is Philomene St. Goddard, 39 years, ½ Piegan. She was the wife of Osa St. Goddard, a white man (DeMarce 1980, 226).

87 "Steward" J. Hazelett, 27 years, 1/8 Piegan, single, father white, mother ¼ Piegan (DeMarce 1980, 122). According to Rosier (2001, 59) Stuart Hazelett was a "mixed blood lease clerc."

88 Frank Racine, 33 years, ½ Piegan, was married to Nettie Schildt, 27 years, ½ Piegan (DeMarce 1980, 211). Frank was a half-brother of Annie Tatsey (DeMarce 1980, 211).

89 Jim Four Horns, 57 years old, had no children with his first two wives. Helen Paul was a daughter of Jim and Kills At The Edge Of The Water, his third wife. Benjamin Four Horns was a son of Jim and Gros Ventre Short Woman, his fourth wife (DeMarce 1980, 103). Willy Owl Child, 12 years, was the son of Owl Child, 56, full Piegan, and Mollie Owl Child, 45 years, full Piegan (DeMarce 1980, 200).

90 "Father" Owl Child, 56 years, was son of old Mountain Chief (DeMarce 1980, 30).

91 "Stephan Henault's girl" was Marion Henault, born in 1902 (DeMarce 1980, 127).

92 Caroline Henault, 29 years, 1/8 Piegan, was the daughter of Joseph Stuart, white, and Mary Stuart, ¼ Piegan, daughter of Isaac and Isabelle Trombley (DeMarce 1980, 127).

93 Mabel Fox, 11 years, was the daughter of Alexander Fox, ¼ Piegan, and Annie Fox, who in 1911 lived with Pete Cobell, ½ Cree (DeMarce 1980, 103).

94 Lise Bussemaker, or Elisabeth Hendrika Herman Vervoort, was the spouse of Dr. C.H.T. Bussemaker, Professor of History at the University of Leiden from 1905 to 1914 (Biografisch Woordenboek van Nederland, 1:104).

95 Eksisakayi or Meat Eater, whose government name was Tom Kyaio, Blood band, half-breed, father white, was married to Ayíkski (Shady-face), Blood (deceases)(De Josselin de Jong 1914, 121). According to DeMarce (1980, 228), Tom's government name was Thomas Sanderville, 51 years, ¾ Piegan. Father Isador Sanderville, Mother Maggie Marcereau. First wife, Shady-face, deceased, had 2 children, now dead, no issue. With his second wife, Little Glittering, 33 years, full Piegan, he had five children: William Sanderville, 15 years, Nellie Sanderville, 10 years, Irene Sanderville, 8 years, and Oliver Sanderville II, born June 1, 1909 (DeMarce 1980, 228). Little Glittering is mentioned as full sister of Oliver Sanderville, wife of Thomas Sanderville, "died, leaving son" (DeMarce 1980, 226).

96 Indeed, Tom Kjeijo (or "Kiyo," as he is called in the Duvall papers) narrated the origin of the beaver bundle to Duvall on February 15, 1911 (cf. David C. Duvall Papers, 1904–11, 1:82–89, handwritten copy, Glenbow Archives).

97 Albert Spearson was the son of Frank Spearson and Yellow Beaver (deceased) (DeMarce 1980, 94).

98 Willy's sister Guda lived with her husband, Adriaan Frederik Kerrebijn, in Haarlem, the Netherlands.

99 Owl Child had two older sons, Joseph, 21, and Louis, 19 years old (DeMarce 1980, 200).

100 Jim Black Bone might be "Síkå keka" (Chew-back-bone), married to Máni (Indian pronunciation of Mary), "Not Laughers" (De Josselin de Jong 1914, 120). "Other 'heads of families' of the Not-Laughers [we heard about] were: Nínnå kyayo, (Bear Chief), ... , Tsáni (John), g.n. John Big-Lake, ... , Akáinam ka (Many Guns), ... , and Óm ksikeisòma Big Moon" (De Josselin de Jong 1914, 125).

101 Edward Camps was 6 years old (DeMarce 1980, 62).

102 Dr. George Bird Grinnell, author of *Blackfoot Lodge Tales* and *When the Buffalo Ran*. He was also a conservationist, founder of the Audubon Society and editor of the journal *The Forest and Stream*. While Ewers (1952, 316) calls Grinnell "one of the Blackfoot Indians' staunchest friends," Lancaster (1962, 87) relates how "Agent Steel, ... that so-called 'friend of the Indians,' George Bird Grinnell ... and other Whites had become convinced that the eastern portion of the Continental Divide in northern Montana contained gold in large quantities." So, they wanted to purchase the "westernmost portion of what remained of Blackfoot territory in the United States." Mrs. Grinnell, formerly Elizabeth Curtis Williams, was in 1901, "a twenty-four year-old widow who was interested in photography," and had been attracted to Grinnell, "since September 1892, when, at the age of fourteen, she read an article he wrote for Scribner's Magazine, called 'The Last of the Buffalo.'" In 1902 they married (Diettert 1992, 67, 80).

103 "Jan" is Jan de Josselin de Jong.

104 Maggie, daughter of Aleck Guardipee and No Charge, mother of Stephen, Nelson and Theresa Henault, lived at Badger Creek (DeMarce 1980, 128).

105 A Crow dance is generally held "on Sundays and at the time of the new moon. Everybody may look in, but only members [of the Crow-Water Society] can come inside of the tipi or ceremonial circle" (Wissler 1913, 437, citing Iron, the founder of this society).

106 According to Bradley (1876 [1923]: IX, 271), "Cut noses were very common among the women in 1833.... Since then the custom has gradually died out and seems now to be wholly discontinued." Willy's observation contradicts Bradley's statement.

107 Patrick was the son of Peter Marceau and Tackler Mountain Chief. He was adopted by Rosy and her husband, Louis Marceau (DeMarce 1980, 167).

108 Mrs. Maude Martin, 33 years, white, was the wife of Charles Martin, 43 years, full Piegan. Five daughters are listed: Rose (Rosa), 16 years; Rena, 12 years; Leslie, 8 years; Nina and Ada, 6 years (DeMarce 1980, 168).

109 Lien was Elizabeth Paulina van den Hoek. Jan married her on June 2, 1911.

110 Cor and Daatje were Willy's sisters, Cornelia and Guda.

111 The Crazy Dog Society (Knut-some-taix) or Mad Dog Society is founded by the Gros Ventre chiefs, Big Road and Wolf-Skin-Around-His-Neck (McClintock 1923, 452). According to Bradley (1896 [1966]: II, 219), citing Little Face, the Crows once lived near Arkansas and separated during a time of scarcity. One group went on to live near the Mandans and "are now known as the Minnetarees or Gros Ventres. The other camp became the Crows of the present time."

112 The mission boy must have been George White Dog, 10 years. The older brother was Henry, 16 years. Both were sons of White Dog, 59 years, full Piegan, and Medicine Pipe Woman, deceased, full Piegan (DeMarce 1980, 274). A five- or six-year-old sister of George and Henry, Dirt Snake, was given to Peter Eagle. "This girl died. Her mother [Medicine Pipe Woman] died on the ditch in the fall of 1908" (DeMarce 1980, 94).

113 The name of Margaret Wetzel's (Joseph Kipp's third wife, deceased) father was Simons (DeMarce 1980, 143). Mrs. "Symons" might have the mother or the sister of his third wife

114 Cf. the sham fight described by McClintock (1910, 321): "Bear Chief kept firing his rifle into the air, over the heads of the crowd; and after every shot an acting warrior fell dead."

115 End of Notebook II.

116 Mrs. Chantepie de la Saussaye is Regina Marie Martin, daughter of an Amsterdam banker. Dr. A. Beets was in 1903 chairman of the Board of Trustees of the Leiden orphanage, editor of the *Dictionary of the Dutch Language*, and related to the famous Dutch poet Nicolaas Beets (Chantepie de la Saussaye 1904, vi).

117 Thomas Dawson, 49 years, ½ Gros Ventre, was married to Isabelle Dawson, ½ Piegan, 47 years. Isabelle was the granddaughter of Malcolm Clarke "and was present in 1869 when Peter Owl Child's band raided the ranch on Little Prickly Pear Creek and murdered her father and wounded brother Horace. (R.J.E.)" (DeMarce 1980, 83). According to Little Bear (1996, 106), Clark, known to the Piegans as Four Bears, was "a man of violent temper who had beaten Owl Child and seduced his wife." R.J.E. is Robert Ege, who, according to Darrel Kipp (personal communication, April, 2002), started the project that resulted in the publication of DeMarce (1980).

118 From 1903 to 1912 Willy was a Trustee of the "Stichting Heilige Geest- of Arme Wees-en Kinderhuis," a Protestant orphanage in Leiden. In 1912 she resigned because of the poor health of her husband. Mother and Father Bouwman were caretakers (acted as "parents") of the orphans (Haan 1990).

119 Professor A.E.J. Holwerda (1843–1923) was professor of classical archaeology at the University of Leiden.

120 Father John B. Carroll, S.J., "was responsible for St. Michael's Church, built as a mission station on Willow Creek from 1904–1916…. After the location of St. Michael's was settled, Father Caroll turned his attention to driving out the demons of Indian superstition and confronting the evils of Indian culture." Furthermore, Carroll was "one of the priests who made the harshest recommendations for coercion by the government" (Harrod 1971, 98).

121 Hermine Hartevelt was Willy's fellow trustee (1905–10) of the Leiden orphanage.

122 David C. Duvall (Pretty Face or Ta-Nat-Ski), 33 years, ½ Piegan, was the son of Charles Duvall and Yellow Bird (Louise Big Plume). In 1900 he had married Gretchen Duvall (half-sister of White Dog and of Margaret Eagle Head, wife of Hart Schulz [the son of author James Williard Schulz] and sister of the Marceau's) and in January 1911 he married Cecile Trombley. In 1903 Duvall was engaged as an interpreter by Clark Wissler. Later he collected narratives and statements to send them as written accounts to Wissler. Kehoe (1995, xii) about Duvall: "Wissler prepared the wealth of data recorded by Duvall in the Anthropological Papers of the American Museum of Natural History, under the titles *Material Culture of the Blackfoot Indian* (1910), *Social Life of the Blackfoot Indians* (1911), *Ceremonial Bundles of the Blackfoot Indians* (1912) and *Societies and Dance Associations of the Blackfoot Indians* (1913). Only the first volume, the 1908 publication on mythology, lists Duvall as co-author, but it is clear from the 1912 correspondence between Wissler and James Eagle Child that Duvall alone had the intelligence and diplomacy to elicit from the elder men and women the data on nineteenth-century Blackfoot culture that Wissler would publish."

123 Willy spelled the name as Marcaut. Aleck Marceau's sister, Cecile Trombley, Duvall's 1911 wife, was earlier, in 1908, married to Alfred Trombley (DeMarce 1980, 166).

124 Bennet Nobel, 12 years, was the son of Lillie Bennet, 30 years. Lillie was a sister of David Duvall. When Lillie was three years old she was kidnapped by a friend of her deceased father. She married George Bennet, white, in 1898. In 1907 she came back to live on the Reservation, where she passed away (DeMarce 1980, 28).

125 Mrs. Powell, 40 years, half-breed, was the second wife of Hunter Powell, 52 years, ½ Shoshone. Daughter Ellen Elizabeth was 11 years (DeMarce 1980, 210).

126 Racine's children, Henri, Movina, Eugene, and Albert, were 9, 7, 5, and 3 years (DeMarce 1980, 211).

127 The "Schildtboy" was Carroll Stillman Schildt, 12 years, son of Harry Schildt, white, and Nellie McMullen Schildt, full Piegan, deceased (DeMarce 1980, 211, 229).

128 The "Zijlvests" was the Kerrebijn family of Willy's sister Guda. Their address was Zijlvest 167, Haarlem.

129 Annie Langley, Tatsey's wife, 40 years, ½ Piegan, was the daughter of Pete, a Frenchman, raised by Louis Langley and Always Singing, full Piegan. Josephine was born in 1890 (DeMarce 1980, 250).

130 Mad Plume, 61 years, full Piegan, married to Kills at Night, 50 years, had 7 children ranging in age from 37 to 2 years (DeMarce 1980, 162).

131 Mabel (listed as Marion) Henault's parents married on December 20, 1899 at Dupuyer (DeMarce 1980, 127).

132 It was not so much lack of diligence that caused the Blackfeet (still) not to eat fish. According to Vera Crowshoe (personal communication, June 2002), the Blackfeet or Blackfoot did not eat fish because "they come from the water, from something unknown. They have another spirit." "The Upper-world spirits – sun, moon, eagles, birds etc. – were considered sacred. The Earth spirits were considered good and bad and the Under-world spirits as bad and evil" (personal communication, Hugh Dempsey, June, 2002). Dempsey added: "One band on the Blood reserve started to eat fish to avoid starvation. That was so peculiar, that they were called The Fisheaters." De Josselin de Jong (1914, 127) mentions a band, The Fish-eaters (Mamyáyeks), under the heading: "Some clans of the Bloods, Canada." Cf. Appendix B to this volume.

133 Mad Plume's oldest son, Albert, had two children, Mary, 9 years, and Jack, 3 or 4 years (DeMarce 1980, 162).

134 James Blood, 51 years, full Piegan, was a half-brother of old Mountain Chief. Jim was married to Owl Handsome Woman, 32 years, and was the father of Mary Walking Under, 8 years, Lizzie Red Calf, 6 years, and a baby boy, born January 1, 1908, not yet named (DeMarce 1980, 42).

135 In one of the travel accounts in Jackson (2003, 40), it appears that "Clot of Blood" is also a place name: "By early June they were back at the height of land near Camas Creek in a place [north of Salt Lake] that they knew as Kut-o-yis (clot of blood)."

136 Richard Mad Plume, 26 years, son of Mad Plume and Kills At Night, 51 year, full Piegan.

137 Both New Breast, 42 years old, and his first wife, Long Face New Breast, 58 years, were both full Piegan. The couple separated in September, 1907. New Breast's second wife was Caught Alone, 30 years, full Piegan. They married in September, 1907 (DeMarce 1980, 190).

138 The oldest Guardipee, Eli, was 54 years, 3/8 Snake (DeMarce 1980, 116).

139 Henri Frank Racine, son of Julia and Frank Racine, was, according to DeMarce (1980, 211), 9 years, so about 6 in 1908.

140 DeMarce (1980, 228) lists Harry A. Schildt, white, as 57 years in 1907–08. So he was about 60–61 in 1911.

141 *Adam Bede* by George Eliot (pseudonym of Mary Ann Evans), written in 1859, is a story about a carpenter's love for a woman who is pregnant by another man.

142 White Quiver, 48 years, full Piegan, married, lost his first wife and three children. He then married Wing, lost again three children, but had one daughter with her, Josephine, 15 years (DeMarce 1980, 277). White Quiver's Christian burial, in the 1930s, is described by Gold (1963, 204–10) and compared with an imaginary "pagan" burial.

143 Seville, Babb, and Heart Butte were irrigation districts on the Blackfeet Reservation and are now hamlets.

143a De Josselin de Jong would later express a contrary opinion: "Before finishing this Introduction I wish to express my gratitude to those who have in any way assisted me during my stay in Montana. To my friend Black-horse-rider [Ed:This is Walter Mountain-Chief] I owe a great debt of gratitude for the zeal and willingness with which he acquitted himself of his twofold task as a narrator-interpreter. We were working together for many weeks, day after day, often from morning till night. I writing and asking, he narrating and explaining—surely not an easy thing for a healthy, strong, young Indian whose abhorence of a chair is only equalled by his innate fondness of a running horse (De Josselin de Jong 1914, 4)."

144 Joe Tatsey was born in June 1896, so 15 years (DeMarce 1980, 250).

145 The Indian way of teaching is not to lecture but to have people, children, learn by experience (numerous personal discussions with North Peigan and Tsuu T'ina friends).

146 "Jan" and Lien de Josselin de Jong spent that same summer, 1911, at the Red Lake Reservation, "located in the northern Minnesota counties of Beltrami and Clearwater, approximately 27 miles north of Bemidji. Tribal headquarters are in Red Lake, Minnesota" (website of Red Lake Reservation).

147 Mrs. De Jong might be De Josselin de Jong's mother. In 1893 the name "De Jong" was changed by Royal Decree into "De Josselin de Jong."

148 Tatsey had his ranch there. "Ranch is on Birch Creek. About 1 square mile under fence. Is on outside of government fence" (DeMarce 1980, 251).

149 On behalf of the K.A.W. (Royal Academy of Sciences) Johannes Müller, Amsterdam, had already printed Uhlenbeck's *Original Blackfoot Texts* (1911a).

150 Maggie Shoots First (Irene's cousin), 12 years, daughter of Red Calf, 48 years and her fourth husband, Shoots First, 39 years, ½ Piegan, ½ Crow (DeMarce 1980, 235).

151 Mrs. Olson was an aunt of Samuel B. Dunbar, 50 years, white, who was married to Mary L. Arnoux, 37 years, ¼ Piegan (DeMarce 1980, 92).

152 End of Notebook III.

153 Apparently July 25 was too hot and too busy for writing in the diary. There is no diary entry for that day.

154 Eagle Calf (White Man) had no children with his first wife. With his second wife, Jessie Pepion, he had Prairie Chicken Shoe, son, died, leaving Mary Prairie Chicken Shoe, 15 years, and Louis Prairie Chicken Shoe, 13 years, who were adopted by Four Horns. The mother of Mary and Louis was Medicine Standard, a full Piegan. With Home Victory, his third wife, he had John Whiteman. With Many Buffalo Rocks, his fourth wife, he had Duck Head, married, and Adam and Peter White Man, both married. With his fifth wife, Many Victoria, 48 years, full Piegan, he had Paul White Man, born in December 1907. James and Richard White Man, 10 and 4 years, were the children he had with Pine Needles Woman, his sixth wife. Both his fifth and sixth wives had Chief Eagle as father and Catches At The Shore as mother (DeMarce 1980, 275).

155 Weasel Head's wife was Mary Weasel Head, 68 years, full Piegan. Weasel Head was Mary's third husband (DeMarce 1980, 270).

156 Duck Head, 45 years, ¾ Piegan, is the son of White Man (i.e., Eagle Calf) and his fourth wife (Many Buffalo Rocks). Duck Head's first two wives died. Duck Head was the second husband of his present wife, Assiniboine Sneeze, 49 years, full Piegan (DeMarce 1980, 92).

157 James and Richard (Jim and Dick) were children of White Man and Pine Needles Woman (Sweet Grass Woman), 46 years (DeMarce 1980, 275). Mary Duck Head, 15 years, was the daughter of Duck Head and his third wife, Assiniboine Sneeze (DeMarce 1980, 92).

158 Owl Child, 53 years, was a half-brother of Walter's father (DeMarce 1980, 200).

159 Peter "Step by Mistake," 17 years, was the son of Thomas Stabs by Mistake, 41 years, full Piegan, and Steals in the Daytime, 38 years, full Piegan, daughter of old Mountain Chief and his second wife, Bird Sailing this Way (DeMarce 1980, 242).

160 "Sister Margaret" or Margaritha was probably Willy's sister. Her first sister Margaritha was born in 1867 and died that same year. Her next sister was born in 1868 and was also called Margaritha.

161 Mike Big Lake, 30 years, full Piegan, was married to Rachel Big Leg (DeMarce 1980, 31).

162 The healthy three-year-old son was August Big Leg (DeMarce 1980, 31).

163 The "even younger daughter" was Millie Big Leg, born April 1909 (DeMarce 1980, 31).

164 After all, it is Sunday, so the Crow Medicine dance is being held again.

165 Cf. Wissler (1916, 447): "In 1909 Big-spring bought the stick game dance bundle from a Gros Ventre." Gros Ventres split in the late 1600s from the Arapaho, were in the late 1700s allied with the Blackfeet, and were decimated in the 1800s by small-pox. By the Lame Bull Treaty of 1855, they got one area of land together with the Piegan. In 1861 they became hostile with the Blackfeet, and in 1878 they settled on the Fort Belknap Reservation in Montana.

166 A shade is a construction made of canvas or leafy branches that provides shade for people seated on the ground.

167 Willy notes: "not sisters." This remark implies that she knew about polygamy customs of men marrying sisters. Bradley (1923[1966b]: IX, 273) on this matter: "Polygamy is extensively practiced among the Blackfeet and the number of wives a man may have is only limited by his ability to procure and support them. If the eldest daughter of a family is first married, it is tacitly understood that younger sisters are bound to her husband likewise, and as fast as they arrive at the proper age they are sent to him without ceremony."

168 Jim War Bonnet was the son of Wary Go In With, the sister of Good Looking Down, the second wife of Eagle Flag, 83 years, full Piegan (DeMarce 1980, 95).

169 Willy Sanderville, 12 years, was the son of Thomas Sanderville, 48 years, ½ Piegan, and his second wife Mary Sanderville (Little Glittering), full Piegan (DeMarce 1980, 228). Wied (1906, 132n9) notes about Thomas' father, "Isidore Sandoval was long

employed on the upper Missouri by the American Fur Company. In 1832 he was one of the men sent with Kipp to begin the Blackfoot trade.... He was a valued interpreter and clerk.... Finally he quarreled with Alexander Harvey, who shot and killed him in the store at Fort Union." The name Sandoval was anglicized to Sanderville. According to Uhlenbeck (1938, 123) the proper spelling of "Kjaijoes" is *kyáio* – meaning "bear."

170 War Bonnet's wife was Kills In Front, who was previously married to Alex Guardipee (DeMarce 1980, 116).

171 "Katojes" is how Willy spelled "Kutoyis," the Blackfoot name for Clot-of-Blood, the main character of the story told on July 16.

172 George Speck is not listed among the grandchildren of Eagle Calf.

173 James White Man, 13 years, was the son of White Man (Eagle Calf) and his sixth wife, Pine Needles Women (Sweet Grass Woman), 46 years.

174 Many Guns, 49 years, full Piegan, was first married to Steals In The Daytime, now wife of Stabs By Mistake. He then married Bird Widow, who died. His third wife was Josephine Many Guns (DeMarce 1980, 164). John Red Fox, 16 years, was the oldest son of Red Fox, 37 years, full Piegan, and Good Victory, 33 years, full Piegan (DeMarce 1980, 231).

175 One more story of Bear Chief's life is to be found in Dempsey (2002, 20): "A Peigan woman, the wife of Split Ears, recalled another time when Bear Chief and his family went to Fort Benton. 'The whites there began shooting at them,' she said, 'and they fled up to the Island. The whites killed all but one old woman.'"

176 Little Bull is not listed in DeMarce (1980), but is mentioned by Harrod (1971, 47): "Between September, 1883, and March, 1884, nearly six hundred Blackfeet starved to death.... For instance, six out of fourteen died in Running Crane's family and six out of nine in Little Bull's family." The "small boy Many Guns" that Willy refers to was George Many Guns, 13 years, son of Many Guns, 49 years, full Piegan, and his third wife, Josephine Many Guns, 31 years (DeMarce 1980, 164).

177 James Oldman Chief, 18 years, was the son of Old Man Chief, 45 years, full Piegan, and Rose Old Man Chief, 41 years, full Piegan (DeMarce 1980, 197).

178 Running Wolf? It might have been George White Dog, 10 years, as his grandfather's name was Running Wolf (DeMarce 1980, 274). That same evening, George's brother, Henry White Dog, is also around. One Running Wolf figures in the story "Loss and Capture of the Thunder Pipe" (Crowshoe and Manneschmidt 2002, 64). He is the Running Wolf who told McClintock (1910, 400) how his people changed his name from Running Wolf to Natosin Nepe-e (or Brings-down-the-Sun), after he told them his dream. Running Wolf (Brings-down-the-Sun) died on April 2, 1910 (Eggermont and Callens 2005 (in press)).

179 Henry White Dog, 16 years, lived with his 10 year-old brother George at his father's place, in 1908, no wife at present (DeMarce 1980, 274).

180 The policeman Horn was possibly George Horn, 45 years, Gros Ventre (DeMarce 1980, 130).

181 Dick Sanderville, 45 years, ¾ Piegan, was the son of Isadore, ½ Piegan, and Margaret Sanderville, full Piegan. He was married to Eloise Tear Lodge, now wife of John Eagle Ribs. Second wife was Nancy Sheppard, 39 years, 3/8 Piegan, children Bridget, 11 years, and Martha, born on January 23, 1911 (DeMarce 1980, 227).

Peter White Man, 30 years, ¾ Piegan, married to Annie White Man, 23 years, full Piegan, was a son of Eagle Calf (DeMarce 1980, 276).

182 "Pietanesta" is Eagle Calf's name in Blackfoot (Lancaster 1966, 176): "Ah-po-nés-ta – White Calf." (Uhlenbeck 1938, 126): "Pitau – *Eagle*."

183 George Lone Eater, 32 years, full Piegan, was married to Maggie Lone Eater, 21 years. He had two small children of nearly 5 and just 4 years old (DeMarce 1980, 156). James Spotted Eagle, 39 years, ¾ Piegan, was the son of Spotted Eagle and Beaver Woman, as was Thomas Spotted Eagle, also 39, same parents (DeMarce 1980, 241). Running Crane was either Edward, 37 years, or John, 27 years, both full Piegan. John was a reservation policeman (DeMarce 1980, 20).

184 Crow Eyes, 49 years, was the son of Many Crow and Straight Up Head (DeMarce 1980, 79).

185 Jack Day Rider, son of Mike and Helen Paul Day Rider, is listed as 8 years old in 1908 (DeMarce 1980, 83), so must have been around 11 years in 1911.

186 George Duck Head, 10 years, was the son of Duck Head and his first wife, Cream Horse Rider, deceased (DeMarce 1980, 92). Duck Head's first name, Andy, is not listed in DeMarce (1980).

187 Harry Horn, 31 years, was the brother of Thomas Horn. He was married to Agnes Horn, 23 years, 7/8 Piegan, daughter of Richard and Louise Sanderville (DeMarce 1980, 130). Henri No Bear, 44 years, full Piegan, was married to Sure Woman (Real Woman), 39 years, full Piegan (DeMarce 1980, 192).

188 As said, bear = *kyáio*. Cf. *–kyai-*. Uhlenbeck (1938, 123) goes on with: "Taboo-substitutes for bear are paksíkoyi (sticky-mouth), óma kitsìsi (big bob-tail)."

189 "Jim" or James Fine Bull, 63 years, full Piegan, children of his first wife all dead, no children with his second wife. James, married to Scatter Woman, 55 years, 2 children (DeMarce 1980, 99).

190 Scriver (1990, 290) mentions a Charley Gannon: "There was also an honest-to-God Texas gunman by the name of Charley Gannon. He gunned down a railroad detective and then shot himself at the Rim Ranch 40 miles northeast of Browning." Scriver adds that he was in grade 5 or 6 at that time, so must have been about 11 years old, so Gannon shot himself around 1925. Did Willy spell the name wrong?

191 Black Bird is the Gros Ventre. The "older Indian" is Bad Old Man, 81, full Piegan. With his third wife, Double Strike, he had a son, Mike Bad Old Man. His fourth wife, Strikes by Mistake, was the mother of Adam White Man's wife (DeMarce 1980, 24). Sign language: "Some research with reference to the origin and wide dissemination of Indian sign language in North America" is to be found in Tomkins (1926, 89–91). Examples of its use can be found in Wissler (1966, 206), Grinnell (1962, 6)

Tatsey (1971, 68–69), and in *Bear-chief's life-story*, see the Collage (this volume), June 17.

192 "*Mìstapak! mìstapak!*" Uhlenbeck (1920, 69, 74*)*: *Mist-ap-, -ist-ap – awat*, cf. the independent verb *áiistapò* goes away, is gone away, *mìstapot* (*mìstaput*) go away (see *mist – away* and *ap-* about).

193 Wiebke Johanna Wijn was the wife of Eduard Melchior, Willy's younger brother by three years.

194 Owl Top Feathers, 48 years, full Piegan, was married to Black Striped Back Woman, 59 years (DeMarce 1980, 201).

195 Tom No Bear, listed as 13 years in Demarce in 1908, was a son of Henry No Bear and Sure or Real Woman (Ta-Pa-Kee) (DeMarce 1980, 192).

196 John Head Carrier, 29 years, full Piegan, was the son of Head Carrier and Caught and husband of Susie Iron Eater (DeMarce 1980, 123).

197 Peter Running Crane, 12 years in 1908, was one of the six children of Edward Running Crane, 37 years, full Piegan, and Nellie Running Crane, 32 years, ¾ Piegan (DeMarce 1980, 220).

198 John Horn? Many Different Gun Woman, 37 years, ¾ Piegan, wife of Thomas Horn, had a son named John, 18 years, by her first husband, William Gallagher, a white man. With Thomas she had a son George Horn, 11 years (DeMarce 1980, 131).

199 Uhlenbeck and Van Gulik (1934, 254) on "*nistamoe*": "*nist mó* (*nist móa*) an. my brother-in-law, obv. *nistαmói*, pl. *nist móiaiks*; *ost mói* his (her) brother-in-law, pl. *ost móiks*, *ust móiks*."

200 Gros Ventre Jim is George Horn, 45 years, Gros Ventre, son of George Horn, deceased, and Otter Woman, full Gros Ventre (DeMarce 1980, 130).

201 We cannot say for sure who this Mr. Evans was, but he may have been John Morgan Evans, mayor of Missoula at that time. See http://bioguide.congress.gov/scripts/biodisplay.pl?index=E000247 and Rosier (2001, 27).

202 End of Notebook IV.

203 The son of Big Crow? Big Crow or (Hairy Face), first wife Blanket Woman, second wife Blue Bead Crockery Woman, no children listed (DeMarce 1980, 31). Paul Running Crane, 13 years, was the son of Edward and Nellie Running Crane (DeMarce 1980, 220).

204 Jim Blood's wife was Owl Handsome Woman, 32 years, full Piegan. Three of their children died in infancy; the remaining were Mary Walking Under, 8 years, Lizzie Red Calf, 6 years, and a baby boy, born January 1, 1908, yet unnamed (DeMarce 1980, 42).

205 John Sanderville, 23 years, son of Oliver and Mary Sanderville (DeMarce 1980, 226).

206 Three brothers Calf Robe listed: Albert, 31 years, mother Bad Woman, she lives with her son-in-law Tail Feathers; Frank, 40 years, mother Strikes First, she lives with Richard Calf Robe; and Joseph Calf Robe, 40 years, also son of Bad Woman. All three brothers have Calf Robe as father (DeMarce 1980, 58–59).

207 David "Salloway" might be a son of Eli Guardipee's sister Josephine and Gabriel Salway (DeMarce 1980, 116).

208 George Champagne, 19 years, was the son of the second wife of George Horn's wife, Susie, and her former, deceased husband, Peter Champagne (DeMarce 1980, 130).

209 Jack Vielle, 15 years, is the son of Frank Vielle, 43 years, ½ Piegan, and Susan The Hoofs Vielle, 46 years, full Piegan (DeMarce 1980, 264). Cousin Peter is one of the five children of John and Mary Vielle (DeMarce 1980, 265).

210 Tatsey's sister was Louise, the wife of Robert Tingley. Louise's father was John Campbell, the first husband of Tatsey's mother, Susan Tatsey (DeMarce 1980, 250).

211 John "Horn"? Thomas Horn's wife, Many Different Gun Woman, 37 years, ¾ Piegan, did have a son John, 15 years, by her first husband, William Gallagher, a white man (DeMarce 1980, 131).

212 James Gambler, 35 years, full Piegan, was the husband of Annie Gambler, ½ Piegan, ½ Gros Ventre (DeMarce 1980, 107).

213 Elmer Rattler, 35 years, was the son of Mad Plume and Kills At Night. Elmer was the husband of Minnie Casuse (DeMarce 1980, 162). According to DeMarce (1980, 162), the oldest son of Mad Plume was Albert, 37 years.

214 The Crow Medicine dance is described in Wissler (1916, 436–40). Iron, founder of this dance, was also Wissler's informant on this dance. Iron was a brother of Singing Under, Jim Blood's mother. There was another brother, also named Iron, deceased, who left a son, Makes Cold Weather (DeMarce 1980, 42).

215 The wife of John (listed as James) Eagle Head, 26 years, full Piegan, was Mary Head Carrier, 19 years. Her father, "Sa-aukje," was Henry Head Carrier (Moves Out) (DeMarce 1980, 95). Good Victory, the mother of John Henault, was – in 1908 – living with Henry Head Carrier (DeMarce 1980, 126) .

216 Curly Bear's first wife, Good Persuade, deceased. They had one child, Cream Horse Hides, wife of Duck Head, who died, leaving 4 children. Curley Bear's second wife was Driving Away At Night, deceased, no children. His third wife was Cutting With Goods, deceased. They had one son, Charley, 28, single, lives in St. Louis, Missouri. Left reserve in 1899. His fourth wife was Surrendering, living, full Piegan, six children: Annie Curley Bear, 11 years, Fine Muskrat, girl, 6 years, baby boy (in 1907–08), unnamed, 5 years, three had died. His fifth wife was Extravagant Woman, full Piegan, living, 48 years, died in spring of 1908. Six children, 5 dead, 1 living, Small Mouth Woman, 15 years (DeMarce 1980, 80). So Willy met with Surrendering, 46 years, full Piegan.

217 Maggie Champagne, 12 years, daughter of Louis Champagne and Assiniboine Sneeze, now wife of Duck Head (DeMarce 1980, 62). Dora Vielle, 10 years, is the daughter of Thomas Vielle, 36 years, and Josephine Hardwicke Vielle, 38 years, both ½ Piegan (DeMarce 1980, 265).

218 *"Sakoo-Akè"* is how Willy spelled *"Sakóàke,"* the name given to her. Uhlenbeck and Van Gulik (1934, 329): *Sakóàke (-àkeua)* an. *Last-woman*, a certain white woman's Indian name, obv. *-àke* (i). Geers (1917, 110): "Sako – last. 1° as an element of nominal forms: Sakóàke *Last-woman* (name given to Mrs. Uhlenbeck)." Uhlenbeck (1938, 65): "Sakóàke *Last-woman* (a woman's name) (: *àké woman*)." Letter from Elsa Heman-Ortt (November 29, 2002): "Uhlenbeck called his wife with the Blackfoot name for 'wise woman' – of course I forgot the name. But it certainly was so – she was the wise and not he."

219 First One Russell, 42 years, full Piegan, was married to Isabelle, 32 years, ½ Piegan, ½ Blood (DeMarce 1980, 223).

220 Chippeways are a group of Native North Americans, whose name is also spelled as Ojibway and Chippewa. Their own name is Anishnaabe.

221 Cf. Rosier (2001, 16). During a hearing of the Joint Commission of Congress in 1914, someone testified that, "Trachoma and tuberculosis, combined with insufficient rations, were killing both young and old full-bloods, particularly in the Heart Butte and Old Agency districts, where most of the tribe's full-bloods lived in cramped, poorly ventilated quarters; most mixed-bloods and whites lived east of Browning or in the town itself."

222 "When you know about someone who died, you just go there. These days we notify people outside the reserve" (personal communication, Vera Crowshoe, April 2002).

223 Adam White Man, 37 years, ¾ Piegan, was a son of Eagle Calf and a grandson of Charles Marcereau. He was married to Hannah White Man, 41 years, ½ Piegan. His adopted child was Clarence Austin, 10 years, ½ Piegan (DeMarce 1980, 275).

224 John Gobert, 39 years, ½ Piegan, father Rock Gobert, mother Mary Gobert, full Piegan, deceased, wife Susan Gobert, lived on Two Medicine Creek, 1 and ½ miles above the Mission (DeMarce 1980, 108).

225 Susie Horn, Eagle Calf's married daughter, 42 years, ¾ Piegan, was first married to Peter Champagne. Her daughter Maggie was 17 years (DeMarce 1980, 130).

226 Gamblers mentioned are Gambler #1, 55 years, full Piegan, married to Annie Gambler, 60 years, ½ Piegan (DeMarce 1980, 106).

227 Louise, wife of Robert Tingley, half-sister, same mother, daughter of John Campbell (DeMarce 1980, 250).

228 The story, by Charles Perrault, in which this line occurs is *La Barbe Bleue, in Contes de ma mère l'Oye, ou Histoires ou contes du temps passé avec des moralités* (*Mother Goose Tales*), 1st ed., Barbin, 1697.

229 Oosterbeek is a small town in the province of Gelderland, the Netherlands.

230 George Mad Plume, 22 years, still had two younger brothers: Mike, 14 years, John, 13 years. An even younger sister, Last Gun Woman, died. The youngest sister, Ella Mad Plume, was born October 1, 1909 (DeMarce 1980, 162).

231 Bear chief's daughters, Lizzie, 11 [8 years old in 1908] years and Cecilia, listed as 1 year old in 1908 (DeMarce 1980, 287).

232 End of Notebook V.

233 Wagner, 34 years, ¾ Piegan, son of William Russell and married to Mary Wagner, 39 years, full Blood (DeMarce 1980, 267) (or it was Jack Wagner, half-brother; see DeMarce 1980, 72?).

234 Peter Weasel Head, 22 years (in 1908 in jail), son of Weasel Head and his third wife Mary Weasel Head, 68 years (DeMarce 1980, 270).

235 It looks as if Willy uses a form of *po sapo tsi* (*po apsaksi-*) *to come out this way* (Uhlenbeck and Van Gulik 1934, 318). There is a sentence in Stocken (1976, 5) that reads: "Children come with me and I will teach you" (*"Kanaipokaks poksapok kitakast-sinimatsohpoau"*).

236 *"Sokapiy"* is another "spelling" of the Blackfoot word for *"good."*

237 Apparently Dick is playing a sham fight.

238 *"Kot tam"* will be another spelling for *"goddamn"* and *"Ko ahat"* for *"go ahead."*

239 The two Gobert boys were John's sons. Apart from two older daughters he had three sons: Irving (1901), William (1904), and Edward (1906) (DeMarce 1980, 109).

240 John Big Lake was a half-brother, same mother, of Mike Big Lake (DeMarce 1980, 31).

241 Dennis Boy Chief was the son of Boy Chief and his third wife, Being A Fox, deceased (DeMarce 1980, 40). The many boys "Saingodard" might have been the brothers of Osa St. Goddard, 46 years, white. They were Pierre, Joe, Nels, John, Phillip, Charley, and Barney (DeMarce 1980, 226).

242 "Percy" or Perry Spotted Bear is a half-brother of Pete Spotted Bear, 30 years (DeMarce 1980, 240).

243 "Young" or John Running Crane, 27 years, full Piegan, was the son of Wolf Coming Up Hill and Front Strike and married Isabelle, the daughter of Pete After Buffalo, now (1908) the wife of John Wren. John was a reservation policeman (DeMarce 1980, 220).

244 Anna Boerlage was the wife of J. G. Boerlage, a Leiden botanist.

245 Joe First One, 11 years, was the son of First One Russell and Isabelle (DeMarce 1980, 223).

246 At the time Nieuwe Rijn 69 was the Uhlenbecks' address in Leiden.

247 Freddie might have listened to one of Father Soer's sermons according to whom the devil "is the bad spirit, God's enemy. God made the devil. He made him before He made the first man, about 6000 years ago" (Harrod 1971, 193). Darwin's theory that creation – the devil included – would be older than 6,000 years was at the time suppressed by the Vatican and today still is by numerous American churches.

248 Painted Wing is the same person as Morning Eagle, the old Indian we encountered before. DeMarce (1980, 39) states that Strikes on Top, wife of Morning Eagle, was a paternal aunt of Black Bull, 35 years, full Piegan. According to DeMarce (1980, 117), Strikes On Top, wife of Painted Wing, was the grandmother of Mary Guardipee. To

top it off, DeMarce (1980, 151) states that Little Blaze, 32 years, full Piegan, was mar-
-ried, no children, and was the son of Painted Wing's third wife, Medicine Spring.

249 Minnie, 8 years, was the oldest daughter of Adam and Hannah White Man. Clarence
Austin, 10 years, ½ Piegan, was their adopted child (DeMarce 1980, 275).

250 These two "housewives" of Eagle Calf were Many Victoria, 48 years, full Piegan, and
Pine Needles Woman (Sweet Grass Woman), 46 years (DeMarce 1980, 275).

251 As said, Blackfoot or Blackfeet don't say thanks. What I understand from different
sources is that it has to do with the concept of having an equal spirit. People would
rather say: "I have a really good use for this."

252 Duck Head's first wife was Cream Horse Rider, deceased, full Piegan. Children:
Josephine, 24 years, wife of Albert Fast Buffalo Horse; Mary Duck Head, 15 years;
and George Duck Head, 10 years. With his second wife (no name), deceased, he had
no children. His present wife was Assiniboine Sneeze, was previously married to Louis
Champagne. She had children with Champagne, Mary Champagne, 12 years, living
with Duck Head, George Champagne, age unknown, living with Louis Champagne.
Second husband, Duck Head, no children. Lives in coulee near Old Agency, Running
Crane's place (DeMarce 1980, 92).

253 The oldest Wagner boy is Jack Wagner, 11 years, son of John (Jack) and Mary Wagner.
John (Jack) Wagner, 34 years, ¾ Piegan, is the son of William Russell, living, and of
Pipe Woman, living, wife of Frank Harrison, full Blood Indian. John's wife is Mary
Wagner, 39 years, full Blood, daughter of Red Crow and Water Bird, both deceased.
Their other children are Lilly Wagner, 15 years, Joseph, 9 years, and Chester, 5 years
(DeMarce 1980, 266, 267).

254 Apparently the ladies left without saying goodbye, and this was not the first or the last
time that Willy had to endure sudden take-offs. Vera Crowshoe told me in this regard
about the Indian notion that life is a circle; saying "goodbye" is seen as a break in that
circle. One rather says: "See you Wednesday or whenever."

255 "Jupur" should be Dupuyer, one of the oldest towns along the Rocky Mountain front
named after Dupuyer Creek, which came from the French word "depouilles," which
was used by the trappers to describe the back fat of the buffalo. It was considered a
delicacy by both the white men and the Indians. This town was a supply point for
ranches and the freight route between Fort Benton and Fort Browning. The first
post office was established in 1882 with Julian Byrd as postmaster. Access to Boone
and Crockett's Theodore Roosevelt Ranch is southwest of town (http://visitmt.com/
Pictures/Cities/Dupuyer_road.jpg).

256 The pictures "Mr. Cole" took couldn't be found. This Dr. Cole was not the famous
archeologist Dr. Fay-Cooper Cole. "Our princess" at the time was the Dutch Princess
Juliana, then six years of age.

257 "Beigaben" are items, whose spirits are to accompany the spirit of the deceased.

258 Such loghouse was a compromise – at the time the Blackfeet didn't want to bury their
dead in the earth.

259 Frank Guardipee, 40 years, ½ Cree, ½ Piegan, was (in 1908) married to Mary
Guardipee, 33 years, ½ Piegan. Mary's mother was Strikes on Top, wife of Painted
Wing (or Morning Eagle) (DeMarce 1980, 117).

260 The widow Duvall-Marceau was a sister of Louis Marceau (Tatsey's brother-in-law),
the wife of John Pepion, later of Alfred Trombley and from January 1911–July 10, 1911
the wife of Duvall (DeMarce 1980, 93).

261 Green Grass Bull, 50 years, full Piegan, was married to Medicine Crooked Stick, deceased; Different Kill, 51 years. Eight children with his third wife, 3 living (DeMarce
1980, 114).

262 Jimmy Fine Bull's mother is Scatter Woman, 55 years, full Piegan (DeMarce 1980,
99).

263 Walter might have been busy, not only with his "ditch-work." That he was much more
than a "water-boy" is apparent from the *Glacier Chief* report on his death on February
6, 1942: "Mountain Chief, 94, and last hereditary chief of the Blackfeet Indians, who
died at his house on the reservation Monday, was buried Wednesday in the cemetery
here following funeral service at the Church of the Little Flower. Mountain Chief,
blind and confined to his home for some years, but otherwise in good health, died
suddenly after complaining of having difficulty in breathing. He had been about his
yard shortly before and succumbed quietly while lying on his bed. Mountain Chief
was born on Old Man River in Canada in 1848 and remembered the Treaty of 1855 of
which his father was a signer. He was present at the time it was signed. By this treaty
all the land south of the Missouri River claimed by the Blackfeet in Montana was
given to the United States. He was known as a great warrior and, according to Dick
Sanderville, took part in a great many Indian fights during his lifetime. He met also
many of the Presidents, including Theodore Roosevelt, McKinley, Wilson, Taft, and
Queen Marie of Rumania. He participated in the sale of land, which is now Glacier
Park to the government. Mountain Chief was a friend of General Hugh L. Scott. In
1930 he had his last visit with the general at the International Peace Conference of the
Indian tribes at Browning, when the universal sign language was recorded on movie
film under the direction of Scott. He is survived by his son Walter; daughter Rosie
Mad Wolf; and four grandsons: Peter Stabs by Mistake, Patrick Marceau and Joe
Mountain Chief, all living near Heart Butte, and Aloysious Red Fox, who is in the
army in Alaska. There are 14 great grandchildren."

264 Young Man Chief is listed (DeMarce 1980, 234) as the father of Shoots First, 36
years, ½ Piegan, ½ Blood. However, he is listed as deceased. According to Robert
Gilham (see acknowledgments), Young Man Chief died in 1909, so who walked into
the Uhlenbeck tent in 1911? No Coat, 50 years, full Piegan, no children with first
two wives. Third wife is Killed For Nothing. Daughter is Annie No Coat, 15 years
(DeMarce 1980, 193).

265 Eli Guardipee's younger brother was William Guardipee, born March 30, 1903
(DeMarce 1980, 116).

266 John Tatsey would write and not just to the Uhlenbecks. The editor of Tatsey's collected writings wrote in the Preface (Tatsey 1971, 3): "For seven of his 18 years as a
tribal policeman on the Blackfeet Indian Reservation, John Tatsey (Weasel Necklace)

wrote a weekly newspaper column for the Glacier Reporter at Browning, Montana.... Many of these Indians, born in the 1880's and 1890's are unable or unwilling to talk about the transition to the white man's way of life. Few can recall the stories of Indian life told them by their tepee-living forebears and few can relate the red man's version of events which played such important roles in their way of life. John Tatsey is an exception to the rule." John Tatsey started his career as a policeman in the early 1950s. His newspaper columns and other recorded stories were published in 1971.

Notes to Part II

1 I would like to thank the following persons and institutions: the Document Delivery Service department of the University of Lethbridge for tracking many hard-to-get items in the bibliography; the American Philosophical Society, the Dousa library of the University of Leiden, and the Museum of Civilization in Hull, Quebec, for providing me with copies of correspondence from and to C. C. Uhlenbeck; Jan Brabers of the Catholic University Nijmegen for sending us items from the KDC (Catholic Documentation Centre); Peter Bakker for numerous references, for extensive comments on several versions of this paper, and for his generous support and encouragement throughout my work on Uhlenbeck; Heike Bödeker, Jacqueline Borsje, Mary Eggermont-Molenaar, Jan van Eijk, Don Frantz, Piet Genee, Spike Gildea, Victor Golla, Kees Hengeveld, Darrell Kipp, E. F. K. Koerner, John Koontz, Winfred P. Lehmann, Jan Noordegraaf, Dan O'Donnell, Hein van der Voort, and Lourens de Vries for comments and/or references. The research for this chapter was supported in part by a research start-up grant and a travel grant from the Faculty of Arts and Science of the University of Lethbridge. Translations of citations from Uhlenbeck's work are mine.

2 Information about the activities and publications of the Piegan Institute can be found on its website at http://www.pieganinstitute.org.

3 It is not possible in the context of this section to cover Uhlenbeck's whole career as a linguist. I focus on aspects of his work with North American languages that are relevant for a better understanding of what happened in the summers of 1910 and 1911. For a full account of Uhlenbeck's contribution to linguistics, his work on Indo-European languages, which is virtually ignored here, and his work on non-Indo-European languages other than Algonquian, which is only mentioned very briefly, would have to be taken into consideration.

4 See Swiggers (1988, 225) for a very brief overview of Uhlenbeck's most important Indo-European work.

5 His most important works on Basque are Uhlenbeck (1892, 1903, 1905, 1907, 1923, 1932, 1942, 1946). See also Swiggers (1988, 225–26) and the *in memoriam* in Bouda (1951).

6 Toward the end of Uhlenbeck's career the search for genetic relatives of Basque was still not over and he stated optimistically: "The future of Basque studies lies in the comparison with the languages of the Caucasus" (1946, 23).

7 On Eskimo-Uralic, e.g., Uhlenbeck (1905, 1907); on Eskimo-Indo-European, e.g., Uhlenbeck (1905, 1935a,b, 1936, 1941). See Thalbitzer (1944) for an evaluation of Uhlenbeck's work on Eskimo-Indo-European. On Eskimo-Algonquian, e.g., Uhlenbeck (1948, 224). For a recent reevaluation of the complex linguistic and archaeological situation in the Arctic, see Fortescue (1998).

8 For Van Gulik, see Barkman and De Vries-Van der Hoeven (1993) and Chih-Mai (1968); for Geers, see Oostendorp (1968); for De Josselin de Jong, see Effert (1992) and Locher (1965); for Van Ginneken, see Noordegraaf (2002). An incomplete list of others who wrote their doctoral dissertations under Uhlenbeck's supervision also includes Arend Odé (doctorate 1924).

9 In his early publications (1911a, 1912a, 1913a,b), there seems to be no awareness of a distinction between phonetic and phonemic transcription. In the preface to the second set of texts (1912a, vii) he reacts with irritation to the criticism of his treatment of the Blackfoot sound system in the 1911 text collection in a review in the *American Anthropologist*. He does address variant pronunciations (1911a, vii; 1938, 5–6). By the time he writes the *Grammar*, Uhlenbeck is clearly aware of the theoretical issues but unable to apply them to his own material, and he never provides a phonemic analysis of Blackfoot. He addresses the problem of how to distinguish between phonemic and phonetic distinctions in the phonology section of the *Grammar* (1938, 1). While he indicates that some of the phonetic symbols used are perhaps not necessary in a broad transcription, he does not dispense with them or improve in any way upon his earlier analysis; as a result, the *Grammar* still uses 11 vowel symbols (10 in the 1911 text collection, 9 in a paper on nominal flexion (1913b, 4–5), most of which can be either long or short, thus in effect doubling the number of vowels to around 20. Frantz (1991, 1–2) distinguishes 3; because vowel length is distinctive there are 6 vowel phonemes (exclusive of diphthongs). Uhlenbeck was also inconsistent in writing glottal stops, geminates (long vowels and consonants), and pitch accent, and he often confused vowel length with secondary stress. For instance, he writes *nókós* for *nóko's(a)* 'my son, child,' missing the glottal stop; *ísk(a)* for *íssk(a)* 'pail,' missing the length of *-ss-*; *maistó* for *mai'stóó(wa)* 'crow,' missing both the glottal stop and the long vowel *-oo-* (all examples from Uhlenbeck 1938, 11). The word meaning "woman" is written *àké* (ibid., 12) for *aakíí(wa)*, with a grave accent on the first syllable; this is an example of Uhlenbeck hearing vowel length as "secondary accent." (I owe these observations and examples to Don Frantz.) Compare also Sapir's criticism of Uhlenbeck's failing to recognize fairly straightforward phonetic processes (Sapir 1917b, 79–80), which is, incidentally, completely ignored by Uhlenbeck in the *Grammar* (1938, 49).

10 "M. E. kan es nicht zweifelhaft sein, dass der indogermanische Sprachbau, wie wir ihn aus der Vergleichung der verschiedenen Sprachen rekonstruieren können, sich aus einen polysynthetischen, suffigierenden und infigierenden Sprachtypus entwickelt hat.... Darauf deutet die Wurzelvariation mit ihrer unendlichen Mannigfaltigkeit, welche sich nur durch die Zusammenwirkung der verschiedenartigsten Faktoren erklären lässt; ... darauf das Mediopassivum, das uns an die Verba mit inkorporierten Dativ und Objektskasus des Baskischen und der Amerikanischen Sprachen erinnert. Auch in unserem Falle können wir uns auf schlagende Parallellen in stammfremden polysynthetischen Sprachen berufen. Um von den Sprachen der Ureinwohner Amerikas zu geschweigen, obwohl sich z. B. das Grönlandische und das Dakota heranziehen liessen, so ist es doch allgemein bekannt, dass die Basken nur den

Underschied von Agente und Patiente, nicht aber den von Nominativ und Akkusativ kennen" (1901, 171).

11 Early treatments of animacy in Algonquian in, e.g., 1909, 28–33; 1913a, 174–77; 1913b, 6–8; 1914, 5–7; for a late synthesis see the *Grammar* (1938, 18–21).

12 Uhlenbeck's most explicit treatment of possession in North American languages is in Uhlenbeck (1916b), with a highly critical review in Sapir (1917b); see also the *Grammar* (1938, 49–58, 70–77).

13 Lehmann (1993, 213–15) groups four of these five characteristics (animacy in nouns, inclusive vs. exclusive first person plural pronouns, two types of possession, centripetal vs. centrifugal verb flexion) together in his complex of traits characteristic of active languages, which he argues Pre-Indo-European (early Indo-European) to have been; he cites Uhlenbeck on the Indo-European case system (208, 223–24). Schmidt's (1979) list includes, among others, animacy, rudimentary nominal inflection and number, Subject-Object-Verb basic word order, polysynthetic morphology, and two types of possession; he discusses Uhlenbeck as the first of four important proponents of the theory that early Indo-European was an ergative and/or active language. See also Orr (2001).

14 The term "ergativity" was not generally applied to this phenomenon until at least 1928 (Dixon 1994, 3). Uhlenbeck could perhaps have known about it then, but I have not seen him use the term in his later publications either.

15 Dixon (1994, 90–91) analyzes the Algonquian centripetal/centrifugal or direct/inverse markings as a split-S system with the split caused by the semantics of the NP in terms of its place on the nominal hierarchy. Mithun (1999, 222) notes that the Algonquian system is often seen as prototypical and points out differences with real passives (ibid., 225).

16 Or 'split subject' (Dixon 1994, 73).

17 Sapir's analysis was met with jealous admiration by the famous Americanist A. L. Kroeber in a personal letter (1917, cited in Golla 1984, 259–60). De Josselin de Jong's (1952, 151–52) representation of Uhlenbeck's work on the *casus energeticus* and *casus inertiae* presents a misleadingly positive picture. First of all, it is clear from Sapir's review that the facts concerning the "passivity" of the transitive verb in many languages constituted a well-known and much-discussed issue at the time. It goes back at least to Schuchardt (1895). It is therefore not correct to refer to "his *discovery* of the passive character of the verbum transitivum" (De Josselin de Jong 1952, 251; emphasis added) – this incorrectly suggests that Uhlenbeck was a pioneer in this area. Second, the presentation leaves the impression that Uhlenbeck's work on the *casus energeticus* and *casus inertiae* became accepted wisdom, while, as we have just seen, it was already under criticism in its own time and has no real representation in modern linguistic thinking.

18 Uhlenbeck himself had suggested that "yourself [Boas] or another American scholar will review my papers" (to Franz Boas, letter of January 11, 1917), to which Boas responded that "[i]f it is agreeable to you, I will ask Dr. Sapir to send me reviews of your articles" (Franz Boas to Uhlenbeck, letter of February 6, 1917; both from the Dousa

library at the University of Leiden). Sapir read Dutch, which he had taken as an undergraduate at Columbia (Darnell 1990, 7).

19 Good recent general discussions of these issues are given in Thomason and Kaufman (1988) and Thomason (2001).

20 In a similar vein Uhlenbeck discusses similarities between Basque on the one hand and Caucasian and what was then called Hamitic on the other (1942, 330); between Eskimo on the one hand and Indo-European and Uralic on the other (1935a; see Thalbitzer [1944] for a critique); between Algonquian on the one hand and Ritwan (Wiyot and Yurok) on the other (1927c; 1939; see Swiggers [1988, 230–32] for a critique; also Goddard [1975]); and even between Wiyot and Yurok themselves (1939, 2–3).

21 Similarly, in 1946 he seems to have been of the opinion that a distant genetic affiliation of Basque and Caucasian was now definitively established (1946, 15), while it remains to be seen whether the relationship between Basque and Hamitic is the result of genetic affiliation or of ancient borrowing.

22 In the same article he compares Algonquian morphophonology with Hungarian (1909, 22), Algonquian noun morphology with Eskimo and Indo-European (24–25), noun incorporation in Ojibwe with Eskimo (34), negative verb conjugation in Ojibwe with Turkish and Old Norse (35), and obviation in Ojibwe with the difference between Latin *eius* and *suus* (27), without in fact suggesting anything in particular about an explanation for these similarities.

23 For instance, when comparing the verbal morphology of North American Indian languages with that of Basque, he refers to "an inner, psychological affinity" (1907, 21), and later in the same article, when discussing similarities between Basque and Finno-Ugric, he sees languages as "organisms" that have a certain "linguistic consciousness" or "linguistic intuition" (*taalgevoel*) which can be quite specific, as is clear when he mentions a Basque "case intuition" (*casusgevoel*) (36). In later work we find references to "intimate psychological agreement" (1923, 106), "inner being" (1923, 30), and so on.

24 The language can not have been a barrier for Bloomfield, who read Dutch and even taught it to prospective spies during the Second World War. He also published a course on "Colloquial Dutch." Rather than ignoring Uhlenbeck, Bloomfield may have been ignoring Blackfoot, which is too much of a marginal language in the Algonquian family and therefore could not play a central role in a general overview of the Algonquian family (see Goddard [1994]; I am grateful to Peter Bakker for suggesting this explanation to me). Perhaps also the breakdown of regular communications during the war may have had a role to play in this "oversight" on Bloomfield's part: he may have had the reference but no access to the actual book. Uhlenbeck himself in an article on Basque published just after the war complains about the difficulty in acquiring scholarly publications from other countries (1946, 14). Much earlier he attributes the neglect of his work on Basque by scholars of Basque to the fact that his colleagues do not read Dutch: "Recently I read the sentence 'Rossica non leguntur.' One could also say: 'Batava non leguntur'" (1923, 117n).

25 The reader wonders how a man who says, "I do not have a good education of the whiteman language, I cannot speak it fluently" comes to use words such as "falter" and "compassionate." In his preface, Bullchild thanks his "dear friend randy Croce of Mennieapoli" (see Croce 1983).

26 *Loci classici* for these challenges are Clifford and Marcus (1986) and Asad (1973).

27 In 1911, David Duvall asked Wissler for a "talking machine" to record songs. Wissler replied, "One trouble is that owing to the delicacy of the mechanism, considerable experience is necessary to operate it" (quoted in Kehoe 1995a, viii). The "delicacy of the mechanism" would certainly have been affected by the jouncing wagon trip Willy Uhlenbeck describes.

28 See Kehoe (1992) for an analysis of "Clot-of-Blood" that points out its classical aesthetics.

29 Blackfoot also saw the Seven Stars as a ladle, i.e., the Big Dipper. That image is obvious. Seeing the constellation as a bear is not.

30 This migration story has several other versions (e.g., Wilson 1886–90, 184, 243; Morice 1893, 12; Chittenden and Richardson 1905, 3:949; Wissler 1995, 22n3; Grinnell 1962, 12; Lupson 1999, 16), indicating that the story has Sarcee origins.

31 Uhlenbeck in obt p. 94 in Addenda et corrigenda: "The name *Mekyápi* has been translated (pp. 1 sq.70) by "Red-man," as that ancient chief is often called in English, but the literal translation is "Red-old-man," -*api* being the form which *nápi* takes, when used as second member of a compound.

32 Uhlenbeck also discussed "clan" names in the lecture "Geslachts- en Persoonsnamen der Peigans" (Patronymics and Proper Names of the Peigans), which he presented at the Royal Academy of Sciences in Amsterdam in 1911. This lecture, translated into English, is published here as Appendix A.

33 Uhlenbeck refers to "The elk and his wife. First version." In this volume under July 20.

34 Uhlenbeck published *A Concise Blackfoot Grammar* in 1938.

35 For the Grass dance and the origin of the Beaver dance (as well as the Medicine pipe and the Sun dance), see De Josselin de Jong in Appendix C (this volume).

36 It seems that Uhlenbeck figures in this story ("white man," "teaching").

37 The text in Blackfoot that accompanies the following story is left out.

38 This text in *International Archives d'Ethnographie* is accompanied by the text in Blackfoot, which is left out here. For the songs that Uhlenbeck mentions, see the Collage (this volume), June 12 and August 1, *Bear Chief's Life-story*.

39 Uhlenbeck in nsbt, p. 248 in Addenda et corrigenda: "I use this opportunity to correct a less accurate statement in Bear-chief's life-story (*Original Blackfoot Texts*, 87). The meaning of the word *natósiu*, mentioned there, is 'has (or: having) supernatural power,' when speaking about a person or an animate thing in general. The inanimate equivalent is *natoyíu*. The supernatural power itself, the *orenda* of the Iroquois, is expressed by a verbal abstract noun (*otátosini* 'his supernatural power' occurs in this new series of texts, 164). *Natósi(ua)* as an animate noun means 'anybody who (or: any-thing which) has supernatural power,' and is used especially for the sun, the moon, a medicine-man."

40 *Bear Chief's Cosmogony* can be found in the Collage (this volume), June 11.

41 For Motúina, see Appendix B, "X All-chiefs clan" of this volume, where Eagle Calf/Motúina is listed under his clan or band affiliation with his fourth wife, Many-buffalo-rock. Also in De Josselin de Jong (1914, 126).

Notes to Appendices

1 Translation from Dutch by Mary Eggermont-Molenaar. In "Social Organization of the Southern Peigans," *Internationales Archiv für Ethnographie*, Band XX, 1912: pp. 191–97), Dr. J.P.B. de Josselin de Jong comments on this lecture and provides a list of "clans." Though Uhlenbeck writes in his lecture about clans, in a short reply by Uhlenbeck on De Josselin de Jong's paper, "Exogamy of the Peigans" (*Internationales Archiv für Ethnographie*, Band XX, 1912), Uhlenbeck refers to this same lecture, "Geslachts- en Persoonsnamen der Peigans," as *Band-names and Personal names*. Since several members of (North) Peigan Nation told me that the notion of bands or clans was not a Blackfoot notion, and because Uhlenbeck also uses the word "Geslachtsnamen" in this lecture, I would have chosen for a literal translation of "Geslachtsnamen" = "Family Names." However, as in the Uhlenbeck eulogy by De Josselin de Jong (1952), the title is translated as "Patronymics and Proper Names of the Peigans," I use his translation.

2 Josselin de Jong (1912, 191–97) comments on Uhlenbeck's lecture and provides a list of clans. That Uhlenbeck himself treated these terms as interchangeable is confirmed in the following statement: "Therefore I stated in my paper on *band*-names and personal names, that 'members of the same *clan* usually do not marry each other'" (Uhlenbeck 1912, 254, emphasis added). Cf. the end of the second paragraph of De Josselin de Jong (1912, 191), where these terms are used interchangeably as well.

3 The word "geuzen" was used for the first time on April 5, 1566. On that day in Brussels about 300 "lower" noblemen and citizens offered a petition to Margareta of Parma, Governess of the Netherlands: they petitioned for absolution of anti-protestants law and congregation of the Staten-Generaal. During this public audience Charles, Comte de Berlaymont, saw that Margareta got nervous. He said to her, in French, "Have no fear, they are only gueux [beggars]." Since the people who opposed (whatever) in the Netherlands took over this label, Gueux, or Geuzen. After Belgium was separated from the Netherlands in 1830, freethinkers adopted this label. It is also the motto of the Free University of Brussels that was established in 1835 (personal communication, Hugo de Schepper, 2003).

4 Black-Horse-Rider is also known as Walter Mountain Chief.

5 "Peigan" should here be read as "Southern Piegan."